Contents

DIAGRAMS – The Higher Organization of the Wehrmacht

Contents

PART V – SETTING SUN
November 1942–Summer 1944

PART VI – THE DEATH-THROES
Summer 1944 – May 1945

APPENDICES

NOTES

Contents

Contents

v

Published in the United States of America by
Presidio Press, 31 Pamaron Way, Novato, CA 94949

Distributed in Great Britain by
Greenhill Books
Park House, 1 Russell Gardens
London NW11 9NN

First published in Germany under the title
Im Hauptquartier der deutschen Wehrmacht 1939-1945

Library of Congress Cataloging-in-Publication Data

Warlimont, Walter, 1894-
    [Im Hauptquartier der deutschen Wehrmacht 1939-1945. English]
  Inside Hitler's headquarters, 1939-45 / Walter Warlimont;
translated from the German by R.H. Barry.
      p. cm.
  Translation of: Im Hauptquartier der deutschen Wehrmacht 1939-1945.
  Includes bibliographical references.
  ISBN 0-89141-395-2
    1. Germany—Armed forces—History—World War, 1939-1945.
  2. Germany—Armed Forces—Headquarters. 3. Strategy. I. Title.
  D757.W2613   1964
  940.54' 1343—dc20
                                      90-33812
                                        CIP

Printed in the United States of America

INSIDE HITLER'S
HEADQUARTERS
1939−45.

WALTER WARLIMONT

Translated from the German by R. H. Barry

★
PRESIDIO

INSIDE HITLER'S HEADQUARTERS

Foreword

THE FORTUNES OF German Supreme Headquarters (the 'Führer's Headquarters') in the Second World War were closely bound up with those of the man whose name it bore. At times it was looked upon as the fount of brilliant plans of campaign and the repository of all the highest qualities of military leadership; for many it remained, even long after the course of the war had turned against Germany, a sanctuary of security in which implicit confidence could be reposed; in the end everyone, whether a member of the Wehrmacht or not, heaped upon it their curses at the defeat of their country. Even today, when so much of the dust thrown up by the collapse of Germany has settled, no one who lived in that time will thank you for awakening memories of 'the Führer's Headquarters'.

In large measure of course these currents of German public opinion were, and still are, directed at Hitler personally in his capacity as 'Supreme Commander of the Wehrmacht'. But in company with Hitler, although only as a junior partner, any officer who occupied a senior staff appointment in that headquarters must carry his share of the burden – not so much because other people have charged him with it, but because his whole career has been one of conscious acceptance of a high degree of responsibility. True, the regulations in force at the time laid down otherwise and expressly eliminated the so-called 'joint responsibility' of senior staff officers which Ludendorff had regarded as a golden rule; it is also true that only on rare occasions during the war did any question of right or wrong have a bearing on the course of events in German Supreme Headquarters; finally the Allied War Crimes Tribunals eventually came to completely self-contradictory decisions on this subject. Yet a residue of responsibility remains with which the conscience of each individual must continue to wrestle. Even making allowance for the normal human error and failure all who worked in that headquarters must feel that the fateful goddesses of the ancients

ix

cast over them their shadow and their spell: Choros who dazzled with success, Hybris who threatened the victims with loss of moral and intellectual equilibrium, and finally the Atae who made those under the spell believe that they could achieve the impossible.[1]

Although, in spite of all this, I have undertaken to write this account, I do so determined, indeed compelled, to follow the dictates of unbiased historical research. Moreover I hope thereby to fulfil a personal obligation towards those who at one time worked with me. For the picture so far presented of the nature and functioning of German Supreme Headquarters and therefore of the Defence Staff of the German Armed Forces had been one-sided – perhaps not surprising since so many of the senior officers who would have been best qualified to shed light on the question came to a violent end.

I need hardly add, however, that the fact that this book is angled in this particular direction has not been allowed to influence the over-riding determination to arrive at the truth. I have been guided throughout solely by the endeavour to shed further light upon events and reach a fuller understanding of them. Weaknesses and failures are not here presented as the case for the prosecution, nor achievements and successes as that for the defence. Nevertheless this book will show more clearly than have other post-war accounts that, when dealing with a man like Hitler, the possibilities of individual decision and independent action diminished in direct proportion to the closeness of the relationship between him and the officer concerned. This was in large measure true of Keitel and Jodl, the two generals at the head of O K W, and of their subordinate staff officers of whom I was one; but many have borne witness to the fact that hardly one of the great theatre commanders, when summoned to make a presentation or report at the headquarters, was proof against the overpowering influence of the presence of Hitler. To this extent the 'case for the defence' of the senior officers of O K W is no more than an aspect of the truth. What the conclusions to be drawn from this are must be left to the judgment of history.

Naturally I have in many instances drawn upon my personal experiences as source material. If any reader doubts me I can only reply that these memories can, in the majority of cases, be cross-checked by a large number of officers of the former Wehrmacht, some of whom are still in important military appointments today. In addition the picture is completed and supported by quotations from orders and other documents hitherto only partially published, by extracts from memoirs and other post-war publications recognized as reliable evidence and finally by the shorthand records of Hitler's Headquarters Conferences. I spent several years collecting and sifting the material before starting to draft the text in the summer of 1960. I have avoided any argument about the 'legends' or the authenticity of the numerous 'factual reports' which have sprung up around German Supreme Headquarters. I have also left out of account connected events not within or directly concerning the military sphere.

In accordance with German military terminology the word 'headquarters' is used in this book to denote both the function of operational command at the highest level and the location of the High Command.

My warmest thanks are due to the publisher Dr Wolfgang Metzner, to Dr Hans-Adolf Jacobsen and above all to my erstwhile colleague, Colonel (retd) Otto Wien of the Air Staff. They have all contributed in many different ways to the publication of this book; in particular Colonel Wien took immense pains in checking the manuscript.

This book is dedicated to all those who lived and worked with me in German Supreme Headquarters.

WALTER WARLIMONT

ROTTACH-EGERN AM TEGERNSEE
FEBRUARY 1962

PART 1

THE BACKGROUND

WHEN THE Second World War broke out no established headquarters existed capable of undertaking the overall direction of the German war effort. On 1 September 1939 the lone will of one man at the head of the German Reich, riding roughshod over all opposition and all last-minute hopes of peace, loosed war upon the world. That same evening a gaily-dressed assemblage of officers and 'responsible civilian authorities' was collected on the spur of the moment in the Winter Garden of the Old Reich Chancellery to hear the daily situation report. As Colonel of the OKW Operations Staff* I was summoned to present the report; the scene was so reminiscent of a stage-set of the camp of Wallenstein that it almost took my breath away. I did not get very far with the report. Hitler was interested primarily only in how many miles the army had advanced across the Polish frontiers, information which was at once provided in parade-ground voices by busy little aides. Göring considered that, as a result of the reports of 'his' Air Force, he was far better informed than anyone else; in any case he looked down on all staff work and poured scorn upon *Directive No. 1 for the Conduct of the War*[1] which had just been issued by OKW. Although it was signed by Hitler this document drew from him the memorable comment: 'What am I supposed to

* The term 'Operations Staff' is used here and throughout this book to denote the branch within the Supreme Command of the Wehrmacht (Oberkommando der Wehrmacht – OKW) which emerged from the reorganization of 7 February 1938. This grouped together the National Defence (Landesverteidigung) Section (Section L — the Operations Section) and the Signals Section. It was initially (up to 8 August 1940) entitled 'Armed Forces Operations Office'. In the spring of 1939 the Press and Propaganda Sections were added to it. The Chief of the Operations Staff was immediately subordinate to the Chief of OKW and was in charge of the sections referred to above. For a short period after its creation the post of Chief of OKW Operations Staff was held by a General Officer (Major-General von Viebahn) with one General Staff Officer as Personal Assistant. From the spring of 1938 to 23 August 1939 the officer in charge of Section L (Colonel Jodl up to November 1938 and myself thereafter) 'double-banked' this appointment with his own (see diagram, p. 4).

3

The Background

Diagram I

THE HIGHER ORGANIZATION OF
THE WEHRMACHT

Situation at the Outbreak of War – Organization by Services

```
The Supreme Command
Oberkommando der Wehrmacht (OKW)
```

The Führer and Supreme Commander of the Wehrmacht
Chief of Staff of OKW (Chief OKW) – Keitel
Chief of the Wehrmacht Operations Office (or Staff) – Chief
OKW Ops Staff: Jodl
Chief of National Defence Section (Chief L Section): Warlimont

Army	Navy	Air Force
Oberkommando des Heeres (OKH)* (Army High Command)	*Oberkommando der Kriegsmarine* (OKM)* (Navy High Command)	*Oberkommando der Luftwaffe* (OKL)* (Air Force High Command) (Official title only introduced in 1944)
C.-in-C. Army: von Brauchitsch. Chief of Staff Army: Halder.	C.-in-C. Navy and Chief of Naval Operations: Raeder. Chief of Staff Navy: Schniewind.	Reich Minister for Aviation and C.-in-C. Air: Göring. Chief of Staff Air: Jeschonnek.

Army Groups
Armies
Corps
Divisions

Naval Group Commands
Admiral Commanding Fleet
Naval District Commanders
Regional Coastal Defence
Commanders
Senior Officers:
  U Boats
  Destroyers
  Torpedo Boats
  Minesweepers
  Coastal Forces

Air Fleets
Air Divisions
Units:
  Reconnaissance
  Bomber
  Fighter
  Interceptor
  Dive Bomber
  Ground Attack
Air districts (Luftgaue)
  commanding Fighter and
  A.A. units.

Also included in OKW were the Amt Ausland/Abwehr (Secret Service – Canaris), the Wirtschafts- und Rustungsamt (Economics and Armaments – Thomas), the Allgemeine Wehrmachtsamt (General Armed Forces Office – Reinecke) together with the Legal and Administrative Sections

* Oberkommando des Heeres (Kriegsmarine, Luftwaffe) – OKH, OKM, OKL = High Command of the Army (Navy, Air Force). It is a generic term used to describe the overall staff of the Army (Navy, Air Force) including its C.-in-C. These abbreviations will be used throughout this book.

4

do with this bumf? I've known all this for ages'. Visitors and order-
lies were coming and going. I slipped out unnoticed and thoroughly
disillusioned by the contrast between such goings-on and the gravity
of the moment.

I had been Keitel's senior operations staff officer since the autumn
of 1938. He called me in next day and told me that Hitler proposed to
follow the campaign on the Polish frontiers from his train, the so-
called 'Führer Special'; there was, however, only one place available
for a senior officer of OKW; this raised the question whether I
should go or whether the seat should be given to Major General
Jodl, who had come back on mobilization as Chief of the OKW
Operations Staff.[2] I had not a moment's hesitation in advising that
Jodl should go; I had meanwhile become very depressed by certain
additional indications of Hitler's methods of conducting military
operations and in any case Jodl had a prior claim to the seat. So on
3 September the 'Führer Special' set off in a vague easterly direction
with no definite destination; it was peopled primarily by the so-
called 'personal entourage' in which the military were far out-
numbered by civilians. During the Polish campaign this train
arrogated to itself the title 'Führer's Headquarters'. In fact this was
a complete misnomer, for the great 'brains' on the train had not
even the most elementary facilities for exercising command. The real
operations staff remained behind in Berlin.[3]

All this raises the question how such a disorderly state of affairs
could have arisen and what the reasons for it were. To answer this
question I must deal briefly with the problems which had for some
time been connected with the so-called 'higher organization' of the
Wehrmacht, problems which were destined subsequently to have an
increasing, and indeed decisive, influence upon the nature and
functioning of German Supreme Headquarters right up to the end
of the war.

CHAPTER 1

The Higher Organization of the Wehrmacht

THE COMMANDER-IN-CHIEF AND HIS STAFF

When General (later Field-Marshal) von Blomberg was appointed Reich Defence Minister in 1933, he was at the same time nominated 'Commander-in-Chief of the Wehrmacht'.[1] Although, under the Weimar Republic, successive Ministers of Defence had had similar prerogatives and powers of command, Blomberg was different in that he felt it was his mission to follow the pattern of centralized government and therefore decided that his overriding task was to create a powerful 'High Command'. When it was announced in March 1935 that Germany had 'regained her liberty of action' in defence matters, Blomberg became 'Reich Minister for War and Commander-in-Chief of the Wehrmacht' and he was determined that his new command organization should have substance and authority. He had authority over the Army, the Navy and the Air Force and he set himself the task of creating an organization for unified command of all branches of the Wehrmacht on the pattern of the Reich's centralized system of government. He maintained that he should be responsible for the co-ordinated direction, not only of military operations, but also of the other weapons of 'total war'[2] such as war propaganda and economic warfare, and even of civil defence throughout the public services.[3]

This rigid pattern of a military command organization, followed through right to the top with unimpeachable logic, led the Germany of those days to adopt a system which none of the other great military powers had attempted and – be it added at once – in which none of them followed the German example. Even more indicative was the fact that no one, even in the purely military sphere, considered the new command organization acceptable or even a necessary evil. General Beck considered the French higher organization of 1940 a model of efficiency.[4] The solution to the problem of unified direction

6

adopted by the Anglo-Saxon powers was to place the Commanders-in-Chief of the Army, Navy and Air Force on an equal footing under the chairmanship of one who was *primus inter pares*.

From 1918 up to this time the President of the Reich had been the titular Head of the Armed Forces, as in most other democratic constitutions; in general however he had exercised his prerogatives only in a limited field, primarily that of personnel and protocol. The new Commander-in-Chief of the Wehrmacht with his all-embracing power of command had therefore first to carve out his niche between the Head of State on the one hand and the Commanders-in-Chief of the three Services on the other. In the nature of things this could only mean that the Commanders-in-Chief of the Army, the Navy and the Air Force, who had hitherto wielded independent authority in their own spheres, in particular in that of operations, had to renounce a substantial part of their prerogatives in favour of the superior commander now to be interposed between them and the Head of the State. A further consequence was that the Commanders-in-Chief of the Services found themselves pushed a whole level down in the military hierarchy, and this before it had been possible fully to examine the practicability of such a division of authority and therefore of responsibility.

The changed situation became crystal clear to the Services when, from 1934 on, the Commander-in-Chief of the Wehrmacht began, albeit somewhat tentatively, to increase the senior posts in his Ministry, This had hitherto been entitled the 'Office of the Minister'[5] and as such dealt primarily only with administrative matters; now however it began to expand to include an embryo staff for the unified operational direction of the Wehrmacht. It was clearly the intention that *vis-à-vis* the operations staffs of the three Services, this inter-service staff should perform a superior co-ordinating function. In the light of the situation in Germany at the time however this type of organization could hardly be expected to be acceptable to any of the three Services: first and foremost not to the Army General Staff, the Army being by far the largest and most important of the Services: nor to the Naval Staff since it was accustomed to exercise independent authority in naval operational matters: nor finally to the newly established Air Staff with its growing ambitions. Even in the days when King or Kaiser had overall power of command there had never been a superior operational staff exercising authority over the Army and Navy; in those days the 'Great General Staff' of the Army, later, during the First World War, entitled 'Supreme Command of the Army', had in effect taken the main decisions on the overall direction of the war.[6]

THE UNITY OF THE WEHRMACHT, INTERNAL AND EXTERNAL

It was therefore OKH* and the Army General Staff which offered the most bitter and stubborn resistance to Blomberg and his 'Operational Defence Staff'. The Commander-in-Chief of the Army, Colonel-General** Freiherr von Fritsch, was convinced that, Germany being a continental power, the Army must continue to be the decisive arm of the Wehrmacht of the future, notwithstanding the newly developed theories of air warfare. He therefore demanded that in war the Army should have the deciding voice in operational matters concerning the Wehrmacht as a whole. 'The Commander-in-Chief of the Army must be in the lead in war' was a sentence in one of the memoranda which passed between the Army Staff and OKW in the mid nineteen-thirties. 'He must therefore be the principal adviser of the Head of State in all matters concerning the conduct of war, including naval and air matters, and must be his sole adviser on questions of warfare on land.'[7] Fritsch felt all the more justified in taking up this attitude since all important posts in the new superior co-ordinating defence staff were occupied by Army generals and staff officers, who naturally gave priority to Army matters. These particular pre-occupations did not affect the other two Services; but their Commanders-in-Chief and Staffs found other grounds on which to defend their independence against OKW; Grand Admiral Raeder, Commander-in-Chief of the Navy, based his case on a fact of geography, that the continental position of the Reich implied that the Navy would be little affected by a unified High Command; Göring who was both Reich Minister for Aviation and Commander-in-Chief of the Luftwaffe, relied upon his superior position both in the State and the Party and upon his close personal relationship with Hitler. Blomberg's memoirs, written in 1943, say that: 'Göring definitely found it difficult to accept that he was not the senior officer of the Wehrmacht but was on the second level with two others equal to him.'

* See footnote to Diagram 1 (p. 4).
** Colonel-General (Generaloberst) is a rank which has no parallel in the British or US Armies. It is above full General but below Field Marshal or General of the Army.

8

Under these circumstances there was bound to be bitter resistance to Blomberg and still more his Operations Staff. In the course of normal business there were ever-increasing differences of opinion in high places in the Wehrmacht; but in addition OKW's war games, study periods and skeleton exercises and the only 'Wehrmacht manœuvres' held (in 1937), all of which were designed to try out and practise the new command organization, led to fresh criticism from below and to well-nigh open rebellion – a most unmilitary state of affairs.

In spite of this the Commander-in-Chief of the Wehrmacht continued to follow his self-appointed line, apparently entirely unruffled. From 1935 onwards he received blind, almost passionate, support from the Chief of his Operations Staff,[8] Colonel Jodl, who threw himself so wholeheartedly into his job that he even refused the appointment of Chief of Staff of the Luftwaffe.[9] The long-term object was the creation of a 'Wehrmacht Ministry' and an all-embracing Wehrmacht General Staff which would include the Luftwaffe, still at the time part of Göring's Ministry of Aviation. In addition, as early as 1937 the question of 'Wehrmacht Territorial Commanders' subordinate to OKW came up for decision. The proposal was that these commanders should replace the Army Territorial (Wehrkreis) Commanders and should be responsible for all questions affecting the Wehrmacht as a whole, including local military authority, internal security, intelligence, administration and supply. Jodl notes in his diary (27 January) that when this plan was first mooted the Commander-in-Chief of the Army handed in his resignation, also that on 15 July Hitler turned down the proposal.

The strained official relations which resulted from these disagreements even affected personal relationships. As a result moreover there appeared an unprecedented division in the ranks of the senior officers of the Army; they carried their immediate subordinates along with them and the result was little short of a split on political lines throughout the body of senior officers – revolutionary Nazi upstarts on one side and the Army traditionalists on the other. This later became a significant factor in developments within Supreme Headquarters.

In spite of all this it must be admitted that Blomberg's military intuition could, when all said and done, have saved the higher organization of the Wehrmacht from degenerating into chaos, from which it was not far removed. More important still, he could have used his co-ordinating role and his military authority to exert a decisive and generally restraining influence upon military policy, or at any rate on Hitler's military planning. Certain significant developments, indicative of Blomberg's views at the time, lend weight to this supposition. For instance, when, on 5 November 1937, Hitler revealed[10] to a restricted circle his warlike intentions based on the *Lebensraum* theory, the Commanders-in-Chief of the Wehrmacht and of the Army were in complete accord in raising objection to them. Blomberg's report of 13 December 1937 on the military preparations against Czechoslovakia which Hitler had demanded, laid special emphasis on the total inadequacy of the Wehrmacht's war potential, particularly as regards ammunition supply;[11] his real reason for stressing this factor was undoubtedly opposition to this dangerous type of policy. It is moreover not generally known that a year earlier he had been so vigorous in his opposition to increased involvement of the Army in the Spanish Civil War, that it was hardly necessary for the Commander-in-Chief of the Army to intervene.[12] Last but not least be it remembered that well on into the war Hitler was apt to give vent to his recurring dislike of generals, the General Staff and its training, and the mental outlook of the Army as a whole in these words: 'all that goes back to the time when Blomberg's broad shoulders came between me and the Wehrmacht'.[13]

HITLER'S SEIZURE OF MILITARY POWER

On 4 February 1938 Hitler was presented with an opportunity, unhappily only too suitable, to get rid of this 'obstacle' and he took over *de facto* command of the Wehrmacht as 'Supreme Commander'. The circumstances are well known and need not be repeated here. There was henceforth no intermediate level between him and the Commanders-in-Chief of the Army, Navy and Air Force except in so far as this was provided by Blomberg's staff which Hitler took over intact with Keitel as 'Chief of OKW'.

The resulting order was drafted by Hitler with his usual tendency to flamboyant expression; it first appeared in the basic decree on the overall command of the Wehrmacht dated 4 February 1938 (*Reichsgesetzblatt* [*Official Gazette*] of 5 February 1938, Part 1). It was this, together with the fact that the drafting by OKW and the Reich Chancellery was unclear and ambiguous which gave rise to the notion, still held by some, that OKW was an independent military authority under command of Keitel. That is not true. In fact Keitel fulfilled the function of a high level Chief of Staff to the Supreme Commander of the Wehrmacht, Hitler, who alone had overall power of command. Wherever therefore OKW appears as a superior Headquarters with powers of command, Hitler must be considered to have been involved. In exactly the same way OKH in the full sense of the term included the Commander-in-Chief of the Army and only exercised authority over the Army in his name. (See also p. 20 of this book.)

Hitler's assumption of command led to a spate of written and oral representations from the Army and Navy reopening the conflict about a superior co-ordinating Defence Staff and in particular its most important part, the Operations Staff. At this point Göring sided with Keitel, but all later experience goes to show that this was out of no sudden affection for OKW. The deciding factor with him, apart from the fact that he never wavered in his implicit 'disciple relationship' to Hitler, was almost certainly his personal ambition to take over command of a unified Wehrmacht. Although initially he found that the immediate succession to Blomberg was denied him,[14] he probably counted upon Hitler nominating him to the High Command of the Wehrmacht at the very least as permanent Deputy. It was no doubt reasons such as these, rather than his position as Commander-in-Chief of the Luftwaffe, which led him to support the Chief of OKW and the Commander-in-Chief of the Navy in offering the most vigorous resistance to the demands of the new Commander-in-Chief of the Army, Colonel-General von Brauchitsch, who had immediately resurrected those of his predecessor. Now that Hitler had himself taken over Supreme Command of the Wehrmacht, the demands of the Army were specifically aimed at ensuring that his senior adviser on all matters of military strategy should be, not some more or less specially designed OKW Staff, but the Commander-in-Chief of the Army with his own Chief of Staff; the Operations Staff of OKW should, it was proposed, be incorporated into the General Staff of the Army.[15]

It is a remarkable fact that the grounds on which General Beck, the Army Chief of Staff, put forward to Keitel in February 1938 the renewed claims of the Army were word for word the same as the views expressed by Hitler in one of his first discussions with the Chief of OKW. Jodl's notes record both as arguing: 'in Germany the Army is the deciding factor'. Although Beck once more drew from this the conclusion that 'it must therefore be the directing element in war', Hitler was sufficiently perspicacious not to go further than to say, 'the other services play only auxiliary and complementary roles'.[16] His argument was just as logical as that of Beck, but as a politician he took care not to let his future leadership of the Wehrmacht become too closely tied to OKH or the Army General Staff, of whose views he was only too well aware. Beck's claim was aimed at something far more than the achievement of the only sound higher organization of the Wehrmacht of that time; his object in trying to get the overall direction of the Wehrmacht into the hands of the Army was not to 'conduct' the war but to avoid it. This emerged clearly, later events notwithstanding, when he wrote: 'Policy is governed by the capacity of the Army. The Army is the most powerful and decisive instrument of policy and the capacity of the Army determines the limits within which the aims of policy must be confined.' It was these unpublicized but decisive differences of opinion, unrecognized at the time and in many ways still unrecognized today, which showed that after February 1938 the Army was still as far, if not further, from obtaining the solution it wanted than it had been before. In the spring of 1938 Hitler finally and publicly re-confirmed the existing organization, thereby putting an end to the battle of giants which had carried the disagreements outside the sphere of organization and had begun to affect appointments to the senior posts in the Army.[17] This decision set the seal on the victory of Keitel and Jodl who had been staff officers to Blomberg for many years and were the principal supporters of the system founded by him. All too soon it proved to be a fatal error. Keitel and Jodl saw in it no more than the institution of a direct link between the highest level staff of the Wehrmacht and the all-embracing authority of the Dictator; they therefore looked forward to an end to all the difficulties over the unified command of the Wehrmacht. What they obviously failed to realize was that, with Hitler's assumption of command over the Wehrmacht, the staff of OKW had lost the purely military character which it had hitherto preserved. In other words the Supreme Command of the Wehrmacht, which under Blomberg had been 'a military authority capable of defending its professional interests against the political leaders *and capable of acting on its own responsibility* vis-à-vis *the Government*', became henceforth the 'working staff' or to put it even more clearly, the 'military bureau' of Hitler, the politician.[18] It was no more than a few weeks before the new

Supreme Commander began to misuse the Armed Forces to further his aims in the game of power politics and this time without meeting any opposition at the highest level.

General Keitel had basically neither the ability nor the character to be military Chief of Staff to a man like Hitler and he allowed himself to be degraded immediately and unresistingly to the position of *Chef de Bureau*. He did not realize that it had never been intended that he should be anything else. Certain remarks by Blomberg in the spring of 1945 when he was under arrest in Nuremberg, are relevant here. When I expressed astonishment that Keitel had been appointed Head of OKW, Blomberg replied that at the end of January 1938 he had been both unable and unwilling to put forward to Hitler the name of any officer whom he thought fit to be in charge of the OKW Staff under Hitler. When Hitler asked 'What's the name of that general who's been in your office up to now?' Blomberg replied, 'Oh, Keitel; there's no question of him; he's nothing but the man who runs my office.' Seizing on this straight away Hitler said at once: 'That's exactly the man I'm looking for.'

For a long time Keitel maintained his confidence in the high-sounding phrases which Hitler had used when investing him with the office of Chief of OKW:[19] 'You are my confidant and sole adviser in all questions concerning the Wehrmacht.' He was honestly convinced that his appointment required him to identify himself unquestioningly with the wishes and instructions of his Supreme Commander, even though he might not personally agree with them, and to represent them faithfully to all those involved. Based on these words of Hitler this conviction became more and more his rule of life. He worked conscientiously to this end and apparently to no other; he was a tireless worker but had no very firm personal convictions and was therefore inclined always to seek a compromise; in his position these characteristics were fatal.[20]

Jodl too, though for other reasons and with other intentions, brought to his job a determination to suppress any criticism of the 'Führer's genius' which he or others might feel. The most striking illustration is the entry in his diary for 10 August 1938: 'I was summoned to the Berghof with senior officers of the Army. After dinner the Führer talked for nearly three hours explaining his line of thought on political questions. Thereafter certain of the generals tried to point out to the Führer that we were by no means ready. This was to say the least unfortunate. There are a number of reasons for this pusillanimous attitude which is unhappily fairly widespread in the Army General Staff. To begin with the General Staff is obsessed with memories of the past and instead of doing what it is told and getting on with its military job, thinks it is responsible for political decisions. It does get on with its job with all its old devotion but its heart is not in it because in the last analysis it does not believe in the genius of the Führer. It is all very well to compare him to Charles XII. As sure as fate the result of all this belly-aching will be not only enormous political damage – for all the world knows about the differences of opinion between the generals and the Führer – but also some danger to the morale of the troops. However no doubt the Führer will find some unexpected means of raising the morale both of the troops and of the nation when the time arrives.'

The boundless confidence which Keitel and Jodl had in Hitler and their feeling that unified command of the Wehrmacht on the pattern they desired was now assured, led these two men into being instrumental in deepening the disagreements between the Supreme Command and the General Staff of the Army, although both were Army officers by profession. The basic unity of the Wehrmacht was therefore affected by disagreement over what was in any case a highly questionable form of organization; and this situation was aggravated by the fact that several senior officers of OKW considered it to be their duty to appear second to none in their enthusiasm for improving relations with 'the Party'.

On the other hand as a result of the confusion into which Hitler's European policy continually threw the Wehrmacht from the spring of 1938 on, no more thought was given nor practical steps taken further to build up a system of unified military command. Hitler by nature worked in a disorderly manner and was averse to anything institutionalized. Although therefore he called the OKW his personal staff, he disregarded the organizational implications of this title. He did indeed give Keitel on 18 February a renewed assurance that he 'would never take a decision affecting the Wehrmacht without first hearing the views of his Chief of Staff'.[21] Yet only a few weeks later, when preparations for the Austrian Anschluss were begun, he created complete confusion, instead of allowing time and opportunity for orderly military planning, although such planning was intended solely to further his own political adventures.

The first move occurred during the night 9–10 March when the news arrived of Schuschnigg's ordinance for a plebiscite. The

Supreme Commander summoned urgently Göring, Reichenau (from Cairo) and two other generals whom he knew personally to discuss with them the military measures required to threaten and exert pressure on Austria. Keitel was apparently only informed of what had happened early on 10 March by Hitler's personal staff and, writes Jodl, 'set off for the Reich Chancellery at 10 a.m. I hurried after him to give him the old draft' (of a staff study). Later the Chief of Staff of the Army was summoned and he reported to Hitler that the Army was in no way prepared to undertake such a task. Nevertheless within five hours improvised orders had to be got out to make the units detailed capable of movement. With this background a 'directive' was issued by OKW on 11 March which among other things announced that Hitler would himself take command of the operation. The Navy, acting on its own responsibility and without any participation on the part of OKW, took precautionary measures against possible wider repercussions and ordered 'all ships to make for home ports'. Keitel's own description of the part he played is typical:[22]

> The next night (10–11 March) was hell for me. There was telephone call after telephone call from the Army General Staff, from Brauchitsch and finally about 4 a.m. from the then Chief of the OKW Operations Staff, General von Viebahn, all imploring me to work on the Führer to give up the move into Austria. I had not the smallest intention even of putting the question to the Führer. I *promised* to do so and shortly afterwards *without having done it* rang back to say that he had refused. The Führer never knew anything about all this; if he had, his opinion of the Army Chiefs would have been shattering and I wanted to save both sides that experience. (Author's italics.)

In the same year certain events connected with the 'Green Plan' (preparations for a surprise attack on Czechoslovakia in the wings of the Sudeten crisis) led to the most serious upheavals in the relationship between the Supreme Commander and his staff on the one hand and OKH on the other. I was at that time commanding a regiment in Düsseldorf, and I got my first impression of the situation when, in the late spring of 1938, I was summoned to Berlin for the co-ordinating conference on the staff study dealing with the Green Plan to be conducted by General Beck, the Chief of Staff of the Army. Not a single member of OKW, neither Keitel, nor Jodl nor any of their staff officers were among the large number of people present. When I enquired in some astonishment about this, Colonel Hossbach, Head of the General Staff Personnel Section, gave the equally astounding reply, 'what we are dealing with here is Army business and nothing to do with OKW'. Beck's conference which followed turned out to be little more than an attack on the plans and orders drawn up by Hitler and the Staff of OKW; Colonel-General von Brauchitsch, Commander-in-Chief of the Army gave only half-hearted support to Beck's views. It is no secret, however, that Beck attempted to counter Hitler's intentions in a number of other ways and this eventually led to his dismissal in the summer of 1938.

Certain other events provide typical examples of the differences of opinion which continued under Halder, Beck's successor as Chief of Staff of the Army. During the night of 9–10 September 1938 at the Party Rally in Nuremberg an argument took place which went on till 4 am; in the face of stubborn opposition from the Army chiefs Hitler demanded an alteration in the carefully worked-out plans for the advance and subsequent operations. Keitel was only an onlooker but on his return to Berlin he lamented to Jodl 'that the Commander-in-Chief of the Army, von Brauchitsch, in whose appointment he had played so large a part, had proved a great disappointment to him, that he had not been able to stop the argument which had led to the discomfiture of the Army Commander-in-Chief and of General Halder'. The Chief of OKW took the opportunity 'in the light of his unhappy experiences in Nuremberg to give a most energetic address' to the officers on the staff of OKW, emphasizing that 'he would not tolerate any officer in OKW giving voice to criticism, doubts or complaints'. Colonel Jodl supported Keitel to the full and expressed the hope that as a result of Hitler's 'great day of reckoning with Czechoslovakia' announced in his speech of 12 September 'many in the country and in the officer corps will blush with shame at their pusillanimity and smugness'. The entry in his diary ends with the following significant sentences:

> Moreover the Führer is aware that the Commander-in-Chief of the Army asked his Commanders to support him in his attempt to make the Führer see sense on the subject of the adventure into which he seems determined to plunge. The Commander-in-Chief himself, so he said, unfortunately had no influence with the Führer. The atmosphere in Nüremberg was consequently cool and

frosty. It is tragic that the Führer should have the whole nation behind him with the single exception of the Army generals.

In my opinion it is only by action that they can now atone for their faults of lack of character and discipline. It is the same problem as in 1914. There is only one undisciplined element in the Army – the generals, and in the last analysis this comes from the fact that they are arrogant. They have neither confidence nor discipline because they cannot recognize the Führer's genius. This is no doubt to some extent due to the fact that they still look on him as the Corporal of the First World War instead of the greatest statesman since Bismarck.[23]

These early events were enough to demonstrate the dangers which were bound to arise from the combination of Hitler's fatal policies with his pretensions to military leadership. The Dictator had been agile enough to nip in the bud the efforts of the new Commander-in-Chief of the Army to emulate his predecessor in his conception of the duties of his office and of the 'highest responsibility to the nation as a whole'.[24] which it carried with it. What was more, those at the head of the Führer's 'working staff', OKW, openly expressed their displeasure that Brauchitsch, supported by Halder, should try to put over his point of view even in matters of purely military policy. They once more made it clear that their conception of their over-riding duty was to carry out Hitler's wishes and where required smooth the path for him in the military sphere. This was clearly a very different objective from that which Blomberg had set himself. The development of the staff which he had set up had been prematurely interrupted, the Operations Staff being still restricted to about six to eight officers; it now found itself confined to an ill-defined sphere of activity, floating between the intuitive political initiatives of the Dictator and their military consequences – on the one it was totally without influence, on the other its possibility of action depended upon the degree of recognition accorded it by the High Commands of the three Services. In these circumstances it was hardly surprising that OKW found it even more difficult than before to carve out a position for itself in the traditionally hidebound structure of the Wehrmacht and that it had no authority other than that which Hitler was occasionally willing to lend it.[25]

At the height of the Sudeten crisis I was appointed to succeed Jodl on the OKW Operations Staff; my own experiences during the take-over period will show even more clearly the position of OKW at the time. Jodl began with a short survey of the situation, giving the new-comer clearly to understand that the object of the military prepara-tions then in train was not merely the incorporation of the Sudeten-land in the Reich but the complete extinction of Czechoslovakia as an independent state. He then turned to the tensions within the Wehrmacht. General Beck, the Chief of Staff of the Army, had been dismissed, he said, because of his resistance to Hitler's plans and Halder had been nominated as his successor; no publicity was, how-ever, to be given to this for the moment and even the wider circles within the Wehrmacht were to be kept in ignorance. In spite of this change of personalities however a strong current of resistance to Hitler's intentions and plans persisted within the Army General Staff. It was therefore all the more incumbent upon every member of OKW to make his own position quite clear and adjust his per-sonal relationships with the Army General Staff accordingly.

I was utterly dismayed by both parts of Jodl's dissertation and had no inclination to go into them further. Instead I made an effort to get some idea of the world-wide tasks which I supposed would fall to the lot of the highest level staff of the Wehrmacht in this excep-tionally strained situation. I imagined that the prospects of England and France as potential enemies and of Italy and Japan as allies must have led to wide-ranging strategic studies. Jodl however gave me no answer but merely referred me to the map on which were plotted all the details of the advance against Czechoslovakia; he also indicated that there was some intention of occupying the Siegfried Line as a precautionary measure. Taken as a whole all this could not but produce the extraordinary impression that the principal, if not the only, preoccupation of the OKW Operations Staff was to give patronizing acceptance to the plans which the Army General Staff had made for Army operations against Czechoslovakia and themselves take over command of those operations. In comparison any question of unified command of the Wehrmacht as a whole in the strategic sense was pushed completely into the background but this was however probably unavoidable since the machinery for carrying out such a task was non-existent.

NEW DRIVE AND NEW ORGANIZATION

The nine months from November 1938 to August 1939 during which, as Jodl's successor, I was Chief of the National Defence Section (Sec-

tion L) and Chief of the OKW
bring about any fundamental c
in which we should move was
that OKW could only impro
ness if it ceased trying to be
Wehrmacht and established
Wehrmacht itself; it woul
Hitler but primarily fro
effort I did actually m
Jodl (he had bee
previous pos*
should b
the Arr
march
back into the pos

Staff were not enough to
situation. The direction
o me, for I had realized
on of patent ineffective-
etween Hitler and the
d a central part, of the
seek support not from
Staff. As part of this
*at Major General
— to his

The occupation of the 'remaining Czech lands' in March 1939 and the seizure of Memel at the end of that month produced no particular lessons concerning co-operation at the highest level within the Wehrmacht. On the other hand no sooner had the preparatory period for the Polish campaign begun than the complete absence of any external or internal discipline in the highest military quarters became terrifyingly obvious.

At the end of March, without having called for any form of official advice from the Wehrmacht, Hitler dropped an almost casual hint to the Commander-in-Chief of the Army that he would use force to compel Poland to accept his demands, if by late summer no agreement had been reached through diplomatic channels. Only a few days later did the Chief of OKW learn of this 'expression of intent'; he thereupon ordered the Operations Staff to bring up to date by an addendum the so-called *Directive for the Co-ordination of the Preparation of the Wehrmacht for War*; this was issued annually at the beginning of the 'mobilization year' and had gone out in the autumn of 1938. In accordance with generally accepted peace-time staff procedure this directive was intended only to lay down the broad lines on which preparation for operations, training and organization should proceed; now however, just as in the year before in the case of Czechoslovakia, a new discordant element was introduced. It was no longer a question of dealing with one of the tasks with which, depending on the world situation, the Wehrmacht *might* be confronted during the course of the year; the problem now was to prepare for an act of war, linked from the outset to defined political conditions and, most important of all, based upon a pre-planned time-table.

In view of the far-reaching importance of this document and in the light of my views on the relationship which should exist between OKW and the General Staff of the Army, I felt it right to go over the draft of the key section of the addendum word by word with the Deputy Chief of Staff of the Army (OQI), General Heinrich von Stülpnagel; he obtained the agreement of his Chief of Staff. I hoped in this way to ensure that no unnecessary limitations were placed on the Army and to seize on every opportunity of leaving the Commander-in-Chief of the Army a free hand both in general and in detail. The Navy and Air Force, through their representatives in OKW, kept an eye on the tasks allotted to them and drafted the relevant paragraphs themselves. The resulting draft was then, in accordance with standing orders, produced in 'Führer type', ie very large lettering which Hitler could read without glasses, and taken personally to the Reich Chancellery by Keitel. The document was returned to OKW a few days later with an introductory political paragraph in Hitler's own handwriting. It was distributed by the OKW Operations Staff to the Army, Navy and Air Force Commands and to certain other key organizations under a dateline of 3 April.[27]

During the next few months the situation which I had observed at the time of the Sudeten crisis was repeated; it proved that, faced with Hitler's method of working, there was no function for a high-level inter-service operations staff other than to serve as a military 'registry' for acts of Government policy. Once again there was a complete lack of strategical direction on matters outside the scope of the Polish campaign and the defence of the western frontier of Germany. All OKW could do therefore was to assemble the plans already worked out by the Army, the Navy, and the Air Force, primarily of course those of the Army General Staff.

As far as the High Commands of the three Services were concerned, they arrived at the necessary agreements during their preparations through liaison officers; they could see no necessity for participation by the OKW Operations Staff and had no occasion to call for a referee. In fact the Commanders-in-Chief and their staffs, freed from the obstacle of a superior intermediary which the Commander-in-Chief of the Wehrmacht had represented, found all the more reason to cultivate a direct relationship with Hitler. They discovered that the aides, who formed part of Hitler's personal staff, provided an easy method of jumping or by-passing the hated OKW as often as they wished. Even the Chief of OKW was thus pushed more and more into the background. Instead of the 'sole adviser in Wehrmacht matters', his role *vis-à-vis* the Services degenerated into that of a go-between, if not of a whipping boy who had thrust upon him as germane to his appointment all those jobs which were considered to be hot potatoes and which no one else, therefore, wished to handle. I have many memories of instances of this sort of thing from the time when I was in this office but am not very clear on the details since the questions were primarily internal matters such as relations with the Labour Service and the SS. A good example however is to be found in Jodl's diary of the period of the Sudeten crisis in 1938:

28 September. The day of greatest crisis. Increasing reports of precautionary measures by England and France, amounting to partial mobilization.

The Commander-in-Chief, Army (von Brauchitsch) brought great pressure on the Chief of OKW pointing out that it was his responsibility to try to dissuade Hitler from any action outside the Sudeten area.

Keitel had already burnt his fingers over this sort of thing before and it has already been shown how he normally reacted to such representations. The following is a further illustration concerning a question even more directly his responsibility:

Hitler had had a 'bombardment of Prague' included in the plans for the offensive against Czechoslovakia.[28] The Foreign Ministry liaison officer to OKW registered a plea that the Hradzin area should be spared as far as possible. The Chief of OKW's answer was:[29]

General Keitel has already raised this question with the Führer. The latter consulted Marshal Göring and concluded that he would reserve to himself the decision regarding this attack. General Keitel can do no other than abide by this decision. If there is to be any question of changing it the Minister (Ribbentrop) must himself approach Marshal Göring or the Führer.

The forces struggling for power at the summit of the Wehrmacht had therefore in a mere year from Hitler's 'assumption of command' quietly achieved that which had hitherto been denied them in spite of so many proposals, memoranda and oral representations; they had more or less eliminated from the chain of command of the Wehrmacht the Operations Staff of OKW and that staff found itself barred even from direct access to Hitler to whom in theory it was responsible. The Army General Staff was so carried away by this apparent success that, in spite of all my attempts to meet them halfway, they did not continue their previous close co-operation with Section L. This was unfortunate since the section would thus have been linked closely to the Army Staff, in the long run undoubtedly the correct solution and the course which the Army Staff had hitherto intended to follow.

The only beneficiary of this development was Hitler; it accorded well with his system of 'division of the power of command and dispersal of authority',[30] and he was thus enabled to play off one against the other. The resulting ineffectiveness of the high level staffs of the Wehrmacht, with all the fateful consequences which that entailed, stemmed therefore not only from faulty organization in OKW but in large measure from the attitude of the Services who looked down on Hitler's 'working staff' instead of making common cause with it against Hitler.

THE ROAD TO WAR

A further striking indication of the position and prestige of the OKW Operations Staff emerged on 23 May 1939 on the occasion of the 'presentation' (to use the terminology of the Nuremberg War Crimes Tribunal), given by senior Army Staff officers in the Reich Chancellery, when they submitted to Hitler the plans for the advance and operations against Poland. OKW had not been informed of the plans beforehand nor was it represented at the conference other than by its Chief, although the Commanders-in-Chief of the other two Services were present; Keitel did not even react when Hitler, disregarding completely the existence of his own Operations Staff, demanded that, among other measures designed to prepare for the forthcoming offensive in Europe, 'a small study group be formed within OKW'. This group was to include representatives of the three Services and was to be charged with 'the paper preparations for operations at the highest level (this presumably meant at the highest strategical level) and those preparations in the technical and organizational fields which necessarily stem therefrom'.[31] The task which Hitler was thus attempting to describe in somewhat unmilitary terms was precisely that which in any properly organized system must have fallen to the OKW Operations Staff; this was indeed the task for which the staff had originally been intended – as the organ rightly responsible for the defence of the Reich and its people – not as a staff for preparing a 'plan of attack'. In any case after the conference no more was ever heard either of the much-heralded strategic guide-lines or of the 'study group'.

The 23 May conference provided a further and significant indication of Hitler's complete lack of method and consistency in his relationships with senior officers of the Wehrmacht. Only the day before, on 22 May, the 'Pact of Steel' had been concluded after prolonged negotiations with Italy and had been signed in Berlin at a solemn ceremony attended by all senior military personalities. There was a secret additional protocol to this treaty which was quite clearly a military alliance and which laid down accordingly far-reaching obligations for the Wehrmacht. No military authority had taken part in the preparation or conclusion of the Pact; moreover on the single occasion when the German and Italian staffs under Generals Keitel and Pariani were allowed to meet (in Innsbruck at the end of March to early April 1939) Hitler expressly forbade discussion of questions of strategy; similarly on 23 May he told his audience nothing of the important military clauses of the treaty. Of all that he must have said on the subject only the following sentences were passed on by the Senior Military Aide, Lieutenant-Colonel Schmundt: 'Secrecy (meaning secrecy of the plans for Poland) is an overriding prerequisite for success. Our objectives must be kept secret from Italy and Japan. The break through the Maginot Line remains a problem for Italy and that must be examined.'[32]

Although I was the senior officer of the OKW Operations Staff I could discover no more about what had gone on at this conference than Keitel had seen fit to tell me. This meant nothing, except for matters directly connected with the Polish campaign. What I did learn however, allied to simultaneous developments on the political front, left me in no doubt that Hitler's intentions, hitherto confined to 'walk-over' wars, were now something much more serious. In the spring of 1939 we in the Operations Staff, in which Jodl's long-established senior staff officer, the then Lieutenant-Colonel Zeitzler, had been succeeded by Lieutenant-Colonel von Lossberg, had no relish for the role of Hitler's 'working staff' for objects such as this. We were fully aware of the distressing weakness of our own position and from this time on we concentrated our energies on trying to counter by such means and on such opportunities as were available to us Hitler's drive against Poland and consequent headlong career towards another world war.

The first attempt was based upon knowledge of the Supreme Commander's predilection for quantitative arguments – irrespective of whether they had any direct bearing on his war plans; the object was to convince him, even though he refused to reckon upon their intervention, that the armament of the West European powers was vastly superior to the German war potential. This plan was put to the Chief of OKW and its true purpose frankly explained to him; it collapsed because, after rapid consideration of it, Keitel turned it down on the grounds that Hitler would immediately perceive that its intention was to influence his decisions and would as a result lose confidence in his staff. The next proposal was that, as in previous years, a major Wehrmacht war game should be laid on by OKW in the summer of 1939, that it should be based more or less on the existing world situation and that it should be proposed to Hitler that he should direct it himself. It was emphasized to the Chief of OKW that this proposal might well have better prospects of success if he would point out emphatically to Hitler the considerable publicity possibilities, both internal and external, which this would offer him as Supreme Commander of the Wehrmacht. This plan would in the course of the war game have brought Hitler face to face with the fateful consequences of his adventures but it too failed to get past Keitel. He declared that it was asking the impossible to load the Führer and Chancellor of the Reich with the burden of running a war game. The counter-argument that Hitler proposed in any case to direct the Wehrmacht in war met with no success.[33]

As a result of these experiences and in view of the personality of Keitel it all too soon became obvious that there was little the Operations Staff could do by methods such as these to influence the course of events more effectively. Meanwhile however nothing further emerged from Hitler or his entourage tending to increase the danger of war; on the other side the staffs of the Services continued to refuse to associate Section L with their further preparations. So in these last weeks before the greatest war in history the officers of the highest level staff of the Wehrmacht found themselves in a peculiar, uneasy vacuum. The only task of any importance they had was the drawing up of a timetable, on the lines of those used for the 'walk-over wars', for actions to be taken should the conflict with Poland have to be settled by force. This was based upon reports from the Army, Navy and Air Force; it listed the most important preparatory measures and laid down the latest dates by which Hitler must take final decisions on the issue of the necessary orders. In addition to instructions for camouflage against enemy reconnaissance, it set out the time limit up to which, in the last resort, the decision to go over from the approach march to the attack could be held pending or postponed.[34] This time-table was a typical example of the 'registry-type' work which the staff had to do; it clearly had nothing to do with the decision for peace or war.[35]

From the middle of August, by which time Hitler had long been established in the Berghof, he began to give signs of increased activity in military matters; this consisted almost exclusively of the issue of a stream of new demands and requirements concerning the Army's plans for the move forward. In so far as the Chief of OKW knew what was going on at all through Hitler's aides, he confined himself to making verbal representations to the Chief of Staff of the Army on the lines of Hitler's wishes. His object in using this procedure was to avoid unduly arousing the Army's opposition or giving cause for new dissensions such as had been produced in the previous year by Hitler's personal interventions and the OKW written directives. It must be admitted that considerable improvements in the plans for the move forward of the Army were the result.

On 22 August, in the great reception hall of the Berghof, Hitler gave an address lasting several hours to all senior officers of the Wehrmacht who would be in command on land, sea or in the air in the event of operations against Poland. He left little doubt that recourse to force would be necessary.[36] The real object of this speech however was once and for all to convince the generals and admirals of the correctness of his policy and in particular of his certainty that the Western powers would not intervene. Only the previous day it had become known that Stalin was ready to conclude a non-aggression pact with the Reich and this of course lent very considerable weight to his theory. During the afternoon the commanders gave detailed presentations of their operational plans down to Army level. Hitler showed himself extremely well-informed on all details and did not hesitate to produce further suggestions of his own, without any reference to the Chief of OKW or the Head of Section L, both of whom were present.

The procedure was therefore that of a propaganda speech followed by presentations by the individual commanders who, with certain significant exceptions, took the opportunity of stressing their military confidence in Hitler. This set a pattern which, as political leader and Supreme Commander, Hitler turned into a habit; it was destined to be repeated before all the great campaigns or other important developments right through to the Ardennes offensive at the end of 1944. It could however be no substitute for the well-tried and convincing method of a war game.

On 23 August, without even waiting for the latest possible date laid down in the 'time-table', Hitler in his impatience ordered the Wehrmacht to launch the attack on Poland on 26 August; this brought tension almost to breaking point. The task of the OKW Operations Staff at this juncture was, among other things, to inform all the highest authorities in the Reich and the Party, so that they could set in motion all the measures designed to support the Wehrmacht, protect the population and regulate the public life of the country in the event of war. Here again Hitler's complete disregard of any orderly military procedure became glaringly obvious. Under the direction of OKW, working with practically every Ministry and with the 'Chancellery' of the Party, minute preparations for war had been worked out over a number of years and, following normal military practice, had been incorporated in a 'mobilization book for civilian authorities'. At the last minute these preparations were now brushed aside and thrown into confusion on two counts. In Hitler's view the Polish campaign did not count as a war but only as a 'special employment' of the Wehrmacht; he therefore demanded that until further orders no steps should be taken leading to lasting disturbance of the life of the country. Considerable portions of the Wehrmacht had to be mobilized between 26 and 31 August but the armaments industry and with it the greater part of the manufacturing industry of the country was not to follow suit before 3 September.[37] This caused all kinds of difficulties. Initially the principal sufferer was industry, for this mobilization by stages, cutting across the plans carefully worked out over the years, meant that men liable for service had to be released even if classified as essential workers; this later rebounded on the Wehrmacht which had to undertake the detailed and laborious task of weeding out these specialists. The final blow against this crumbling organization took place when, on the very day that war broke out, Göring persuaded Hitler to remove from OKW its co-ordinating function even in these matters. The duties which had hitherto been carried out by the 'secretariat' of the OKW Operations Staff were transferred to the Reich Chancellery; the Reich Defence Committee which had been presided over by OKW was dissolved and replaced by a 'Ministerial Council for the Defence of the Reich' in which the Party wielded decisive influence. The provisions of the *Law for the Defence of the Reich*, the second draft of which had already considerably curtailed the authority of the military, was set aside and so the Wehrmacht was finally pushed out of any position of responsibility for the 'leadership of the nation in war'. The Chief of OKW was not even given a hearing; yet he raised no objection.

Late in the afternoon of 25 August Hitler cancelled the orders for the attack on Poland for political reasons which are a matter of history. Since the cut-off date laid down in the time-table was practically upon us, the decision was immediately telephoned to all concerned. Shortly thereafter I received an urgent summons to follow Keitel to the Reich Chancellery. All that was required was one sentence from Section L, Hitler's military 'bureau', confirming the order in writing. On the way to the Chancellery I had felt much relieved since I imagined that once again peace had been preserved but even before I had had time to draft the order that feeling had given way to one of deep disillusionment, for as I entered, Schmundt greeted me with the words historically so significant that they deserve to be quoted: 'Don't start celebrating too soon; it's only a question of a few days' postponement!'

The picture of confusion presented by the Reich Chancellery at that moment was, for a trained staff officer, both repugnant and horrifying to a degree. I kept asking myself whether, if war was really only round the corner, the Supreme Commander intended his headquarters to continue in this atmosphere of feverish activity and disorder. The question was all the more relevant in that by this time, apart from OKW, only the Naval Staff remained in its peacetime headquarters in Berlin. The Army and Air Force Staffs had already gone over to their mobilization organization and manning and were in process of moving to the working and living quarters prepared in advance for use in war; OKH was in a camp consisting partly of hutted, partly of protected accommodation on the edge of the Zossen training area, some twenty-five to thirty miles south of Berlin; the Air Staff was in the Wildpark Air Force Cadet College near Potsdam. But no move was planned for OKW during the period leading up to

1 September; it would in any case have been too late; there could be no question in the circumstances of using the alternative accommodation organized under Blomberg in a series of villas in the suburb of Berlin–Dahlem, although this was protected and provided with the necessary signals facilities – and no other arrangements had been made.

It is not possible to say with certainty what reasons had led Hitler to turn down all proposals for the organization of an OKW War Headquarters. When the Chief of OKW had put forward a semicomplete plan to house it in a newly completed barracks in the Potsdam area, Hitler had stated that, as Supreme Commander, he could not move out of Berlin westwards when the Wehrmacht was marching east; to the public that would look like running away from danger! On the face of it this was no more than a pretext for avoiding taking a decision but in fact it is more likely that he felt that in times of stress he could only exert the necessary influence from the seat of government, Berlin, and that he must therefore remain in the capital.[38] The fact that Berlin lay midway between east and west may well have reinforced his determination, since, by remaining there, he would give proof of his pretended confidence that the Western powers would not intervene. The fact that in spite of this he took the surprising decision to leave Berlin on 3 September was probably no more than another indication of the man's instability of character – he preferred improvisation to considered action; alternatively it may have been due simply to an emotional urge to be near the troops; finally it is almost certain that the desire to extract the greatest possible propaganda value from the role of great military leader which he had arrogated to himself, had something to do with the decision.

Even Hitler can hardly have expected to be able to direct operations in a proper, orderly military manner from his train, however well provided with signals facilities it might be. He can hardly have failed to realize that something much more akin to a properly organized staff would be necessary than merely Keitel and Jodl, his own and their aides and the Army and Air Force liaison officers who had been hurriedly summoned to the train (another entirely unforeseen move designed to squeeze out OKW). But it was of much more importance to him that he should not be deprived of his usual entourage from the Party and the Press, his photographers and his doctors, his security guards and even his trusted female following who formed the audience for conversation and music in the evenings. In any case this was the way he had gone around during the 'walk-over wars', the way he had gone to Austria, through the Sudetenland and to Prague. After all the Polish campaign was nothing more than a 'special employment' of the Wehrmacht.[39]

CHAPTER 2

Lessons of the Polish Campaign

THE FIRST INSTRUCTIONS implementing this unified command of the Wehrmacht were 'Directives' Nos. 1 and 2, issued in Berlin on 31 August, and 3 September 1939 respectively; both titles included the additional words 'for the conduct of the war'. They have already been referred to in another context. Starting from the issue of these directives, OKW instructions became analogous both in form and content to operation orders, in the sense of those words generally accepted by the Prussian–German General Staff. Operation orders were addressed to a commander's direct subordinates and designedly avoided giving any indication of his intentions beyond that which was clearly *essential and concerned with the foreseeable future*. True directives on the other hand were supposed to remain valid for the longest possible time. In accordance with the higher organization of the Wehrmacht established in 1939, the OKW Directives were in the first instance addressed merely to the staffs of the Army, Navy and Air Force. Later were added an increasing number of organizations directly subordinate to OKW and the character of the directives changed more and more.[1] There was moreover a gradual deterioration in the quality of the orders issued on the German side. As against this the directive for the invasion of Europe issued on 12 February 1944 by the Combined Chiefs of Staff to General Eisenhower is a real classic; it is short and couched in general terms. Its key section (Paragraph 2 – Task) read as follows:

> You will enter the continent of Europe and, in conjunction with the other United Nations, undertake operations aimed at the heart of Germany and the destruction of her Armed Forces. The date of entering the continent is the month of May 1944. After adequate Channel ports have been secured, exploitation will be directed to securing an area that will facilitate both ground and air operations against the enemy.

30

Directive no. 1 took on at the point where the last preparatory measures laid down in the 'time-table' left off. The issue of a code word was all that was required to set in motion the plans of the three Services approved by Hitler for 'solution of the problem by force'. This code word was issued by the office of the Reich Chancellery at 00.30 hours on 31 August, ie fourteen hours before the time-table cut-off time. The directive merely said 'the attack on Poland will be carried out in accordance with the preparations made for Case White (Poland)'. The proposals of the three Services also formed the basis for the instructions to 'those elements of the Wehrmacht operating in the West'. In the event of the opening of hostilities by England and France these forces, which were very weak, were ordered to 'ensure that the conditions for a successful conclusion of the operations against Poland were maintained, while at the same time economizing their forces to the utmost'. Although the contents of this instruction were common knowledge, Jodl laid great stress on its issue; he was undoubtedly primarily concerned with its documentary importance as a factor in establishing unified command of the Wehrmacht.

It was much the same with Directive no. 2 which followed immediately on the declarations of war by England and France. Only a limited number of practical measures against the Western powers were ordered or 'permitted', such as the laying of minefields and the opening of the attack on merchant shipping but even these were no 'brainchild' of OKW. In this case they issued from the Naval Staff and had already been put to Hitler by the Commander-in-Chief of the Navy and approved by him. The directive did no more than give them the stamp of a Supreme Headquarters order.

Hitler had now landed us unintentionally and against all good counsel in a war on two fronts and both these directives show clearly what a large number of tasks for a unified Defence Staff in reality existed in such a situation. But Hitler's policy towards Poland had been governed by impatience and rage; as a result the man who was both Head of the State and Supreme Commander had never given the highest-level military staff of the country the opportunity to check the contents of these directives against a sober, factual appreciation of the overall political and military situation; this would at once have shown up the possibility of a second World War. There had been no follow-up to Hitler's 'closing address' of 23 May 1939; Section L did not even know what he had said. Once its proposal for a wide-ranging strategic war game in the spring of 1939 had been turned down, the Staff had no material on which to base any preparatory studies of its own. It was organized merely as the Supreme Commander's personal staff, not as a General Staff of the Wehrmacht; it would therefore have had to have the fullest co-operation from the staffs of the Army, Navy and Air Force in order to establish the basis for the opening situation of such a war game, and this co-operation would only have been forthcoming if ordered by Hitler personally.[2] Now that, contrary to all assurances from the highest political quarters, the Western powers had intervened on the side of Poland, the Supreme Commander gave neither his own staff nor those of the Services any indication of intentions such as would have allowed them at least to examine likely further developments. This showed a lack of foresight of which this was the first instance but which was destined to rub like a scarlet thread through Hitler's exercise of command throughout the war.

The sudden departure for the front, the fact that he was divorcing himself from his own staff and from the Commanders-in-Chief of the Services, the inadequate operating facilities in the 'Führer Special' – all this was merely another example of Hitler's predilection for working in an atmosphere of disorder and snap decisions. Keitel's notes at Nuremberg contain the following:

> The Führer Special was stationed in the training area of Gross-Born (Pomerania); from this area we went off every other day on tours of the front lasting from early morning to late at night, visiting Army and Corps Headquarters. At each place the Führer had the situation presented to him; occasionally he happened to meet the Commander-in-Chief of the Army. Hitler very seldom intervened in the conduct of operations; I can myself only think of two instances. Otherwise he did no more than give his point of view, discuss with the Commander-in-Chief of the Army and make suggestions. He never committed himself so far as to give an order.

More than any other one man the higher direction of operations was in the hands of the Chief of Staff of the Army. Yet throughout the entire campaign he never even once spoke on the telephone either to Hitler or to Keitel or to Jodl or even to Colonel von Vormann, the Army liaison officer on the train.[3]

The first month of the war saw the rapid and overwhelming success of operations against Poland and the 'miracle' (to use this hackneyed word yet again) of the French strategy of static defence in the West.

This provided no test of the capacity of the improvised headquarters to undertake greater things. All that was required were the 'situation reports' which were carried on in the same disorderly fashion as in the early days of September in the Reich Chancellery. They were based on information passed twice daily by the Army, Navy and Air Force to Section L, the rump of OKW remaining in Berlin; they were followed by endless discussions in Hitler's office-carriage, conducted more for his own benefit than for that of his audience. The daily 'Wehrmacht communiqué' was prepared in draft by the Public Relations Section, put in final draft form on the train by Jodl (this became the standard procedure) and finally approved by Hitler, usually after making certain alterations of his own. The only evidence of any thought being given during this period to wider subjects was the issue of Directives nos. 3 and 4 on 9 and 25 September respectively. These dealt primarily with the transfer to the Western Front of such Army and Air forces as could be spared and with additional precautionary measures against England and France.[4] The broad lines were worked out in the train; they were then sent 'in draft' to Section L, whose job it was to check through them with the Operations Sections of the Services. Once the draft had been thus worked over and confirmed it was sent back to Jodl who, via Keitel, got Hitler's signature and was responsible for distribution.

The officers of Section L in Berlin hardly had enough to do; they made it their job however to keep in the closest possible touch with the staffs of the Services. Section L also undertook by means of a daily presentation of the situation to keep in the picture the other sections of OKW, all of which were still in their peace-time offices. The following were normally present at these meetings – Heads of Sections, the War Diary officer, and liaison officers from the Intelligence and Counter-espionage bureau, the Economics and Arms Industry office, the Public Relations Section, Signal Service, Transport Division and the Foreign Ministry. After the reports from the field, information from abroad and other important occurrences had been presented, I normally, as Chief of Section L, held an internal conference with my immediate staff at which I passed on to them any considerations or intentions of higher authority of which I might have heard and gave instructions for any special jobs. As Chief of the Section it was also my responsibility to put the 'Führer's Deputy', Rudolf Hess, in the picture from time to time regarding the war situation. This took place in his office in the Wilhelmstrasse. The only lasting memory I have of these meetings is that after my short *exposé* of the situation, not a further word would be spoken.

In addition I made considerable efforts to maintain personal touch with my superiors as far as this was possible. The first flight I made for this purpose, about 10 September, took me to Ilnau in Upper Silesia whither the train had moved from Pomerania. Once more I got the impression of a camp living in a state of feverish activity, quite foreign to the normal picture of a Supreme Headquarters. In spite of the good progress of operations in Poland and the continued lull in the West a visitor to the Headquarters soon got an unmistakable impression that people were uneasy; this showed itself particularly in the strenuous efforts being made to achieve a more rapid build up of Army reserves. For this purpose Hitler turned first to the increased manpower which mobilization had placed at the disposal of Himmler and Dalüge and organized a 'Police Division'. The reason may have been the one officially given, that there was a large reserve of trained manpower in the police. The Party and political implications of this measure however disquieted even Keitel; Jodl cleverly contrived to avoid taking any position in this first ticklish case of this type. This did not alter the fact however that the necessary orders had to be issued through Section L of Jodl's staff, a fact which, in the eyes of the Army, linked OKW even more closely with the Party.

The move of the Red Army into Poland gave me another even more striking proof of the fact that basically there was no headquarters organization capable of functioning itself or of issuing instructions to others. About midnight on 16–17 September I received a telephone call in Berlin from our Military Attaché in Moscow, General Köstring; he informed me of the imminent entry of Russian formations into Eastern Poland. Köstring was clearly, as he later admitted, completely ignorant of the set-up at the head of affairs; at the other end of the line, I, as Chief of the OKW Operations Section, found his information almost unintelligible since I was completely without knowledge of any agreements on the subject or of any possibility that this might happen. All I could do was to assure him that I would pass the information on at once. Even Keitel and Jodl knew nothing about it. One of them, on first hearing the news that the Russians were on the move, replied with the horrified question 'who against?' Precious hours were wasted before the resulting essential orders could be got out. Serious and bloody encounters between German and Russian troops were only too likely since they were now advancing towards each other with merely the remnants of the Polish forces between them, and in places our armies were already 125 miles beyond the demarcation line agreed by Ribbentrop with the Russians but of which the Wehrmacht had never been informed.[5]

On the afternoon of 17 September the Russian Military Attaché Berlin, accompanied by Admiral Canaris, appeared in Section L's offices in the Bendlerstrasse to get from me information regarding the objectives attained and moves carried out by German troops in Poland. He was a Colonel, dressed in a brown battledress blouse, and he listened to my information poker-faced and without a word. There was a significant sequel to this. The next morning Jodl told me over the telephone that the night before Stalin himself had rung Ribbentrop from Moscow and reproached him bitterly because, according to information from his Military Attaché, German forces intended to hold on to the oil area of Drohobycz in South Poland. This, he said, was a violation of the demarcation line laid down in the secret annexe to the 23 August Treaty.[6] Knowing our shortage of oil but not knowing about the treaty, I had particularly stressed to the Military Attaché our claim to this area, so I saw myself as the first sacrificial lamb to be offered on the altar of this questionable Russo-German friendship. Then however I heard from Jodl that when Ribbentrop had protested against the military meddling in and upsetting his political plans, Hitler had turned on his Foreign Minister and dismissed him with the words 'when diplomats make mistakes in war, it's always supposed to be the fault of the soldiers'. The affair was closed and there were no further consequences. As was so often to happen later however, no one drew the obvious conclusion from this of the necessity for real co-operation between the Foreign Ministry and the High Command, in spite of the facts that both headed up to Hitler and the Foreign Minister was continually beside him. Ribbentrop, Himmler and Lammers, the Head of the Reich Chancellery, were in permanent attendance on Hitler and counted as part of the 'Führer's Headquarters'; they had their own train with the code-name 'Heinrich'.

The clearest indication of the true position within the highest level German command organization is however provided by something which was by far the most important development of this period, and a development in the purely military sphere – Hitler's decision to extend the war by an early attack in the West. The rapid victory which followed in the spring of 1940 seemed for a time to prove Hitler right; this and the eventual catastrophe make it almost impossible to give any true picture of the impression made on nearly everyone in the high-level staffs when Hitler's intention became known. The declaration of war by the Western powers on 3 September had had a shattering effect upon senior officers who remembered the first World War and were aware of the unpreparedness of the German armed forces of 1939. But now the two sides had lain opposite each other for several weeks, occupying the fortifications on either side of the Franco-German frontier and almost completely inactive. It is hardly to be wondered at that this fact, combined with the rapid elimination of Poland as a political and military factor, should have raised high hopes, particularly within the Wehrmacht, that the war could somehow be brought to an end by political means before the centre of Western Europe went down for the second time in a quarter of a century in ruins and ashes amid fearful losses in blood and treasure. In the last resort, people thought, a firm defensive attitude could be adopted in the West, backed shortly by the mass of the German forces; industrial and agricultural goods could be freely imported from the east and eventually the West would be ready to conclude peace. The Army Staff had already issued initial instructions for the bulk of the Army to go over to the defensive.[7]

No one can say on what day the Supreme Commander reached the decision to take the offensive in the West or what influenced him to do so. One thing is clear; the Commander-in-Chief of the Army was the man most intimately involved; yet when Brauchitsch appeared on the train on 9 and again on 12 September, on the first occasion spending no less than two hours alone with Hitler, the latter breathed not a word to him of his intentions. After this conference Brauchitsch asked Vormann whether Hitler had any ideas of attacking in the West. When Vormann replied in the negative Brauchitsch added: 'You know we cannot do that; we cannot attack the Maginot Line. You must let me know at once if ideas of this sort come up even in the course of conversation.' It is also clear that no other senior officer was consulted before the decision was made, in spite of the fact that it was tantamount to no less than a decision to embark on a second World War. I myself learnt of it when I visited the headquarters for the second time on 20 September (the offices had then been transferred from the train to the Casino Hotel in Zoppot). Keitel, who appeared thunderstruck, told me of it with the most serious warning not to let out a word about it and with the caution that Hitler's intention must be treated as Top Secret. Even he, the Chief of OKW and the 'sole adviser in Wehrmacht matters', had not been told by Hitler but had learnt of it through one of the aides! Keitel considered that there was therefore no possibility open to him of making representations against it. As far as I was concerned, I decided at once to take up the cudgels against this decision of Hitler's and to do so not via the Chief of OKW nor via Jodl who had shut up again like a clam, but in collaboration with the Army General Staff. There could be no duty more important than that of saving the people and the country from a second World War. The only channel open at the moment seemed to be that of the Army General Staff; the lead-in was also obvious because I knew from my regular contacts with the Deputy Chief of Staff (I) that General von Stülpnagel had been instructed by the Commander-in-Chief to work up an appreciation of his (the Commander-in-Chief's) concept of the war in the West – an entirely defensive war continued if necessary for years; General von Stülpnagel was looking for all possible arguments to support this thesis. The Zossen channel did not however produce the results I had hoped for.[8] Up to 27 September the Army Staff appear to have taken no notice of my information. At any rate about this time they asked General von Vormann again whether Hitler had any plans for an offensive and appeared quite satisfied when he replied with a categorical negative.

On 27 September, the day after his return to Berlin, Hitler assembled the Commanders-in-Chief of the Army, Navy and Air Force, with Keitel and myself, in the new Reich Chancellery and informed them of his intentions. All, including even Göring, were clearly entirely taken aback. None of them had apparently read or at any rate grasped the full import of the sentence in OKW Directive no. 4 just issued, 'the capacity to implement at any time an offensive strategy in the West must be maintained'. Hitler had a slip of paper on which he had written a few key words to remind him of the background of his decision and the broad directives for operations which he wished to give. As soon as he had finished speaking he tossed it into the fire in his study; no one had spoken a word in protest.

Although it obviously had its serious implications, there was a comic-opera side to the proceedings which one or two scenes I witnessed during my stay in Zoppot will illustrate. Early in the morning twenty to thirty cars were assembled two abreast in the hotel drive to go to the area of operations north of Gdingen. It was the job of General Rommel,* the Headquarters Commandant, to get this cortège moving, with Hitler at its head. When I asked in astonishment why they drove two abreast, Rommel replied that, after many unhappy experiences, he had laid on this 'order of march' because it offered the best hope of satisfying the precedence and protocol requirements of the large number of non-military visitors who had meanwhile flowed into the headquarters. In this way at least six or eight of them, two car-loads, could be level with each other and at the same distance from Hitler, and for them that was more important than anything. In spite of this Rommel had another unhappy experience that day; the cortège went down a narrow track where the two-abreast formation was no longer possible and the majority of the cars were held up at a barrier while Hitler and the leaders drove on. The word was immediately passed round to those left behind that the tour had been temporarily interrupted so that Hitler might pay a short visit to a field hospital near by; nevertheless, although they were almost on the battlefield, Martin Bormann, the Head of the Party Chancellery made a fearful scene and cursed General Rommel in outrageous language because of the supposed slight inflicted on him. There was nothing Rommel could do in answer to such insolence. When I straightway gave vent to my indignation at Bormann's behaviour, Rommel merely asked me to tell Schmundt, the senior military aide, equally forcibly what I thought about it.

* The General of later Western Desert fame (see Part 1 Introduction Note 3).

PART II

THE BUILD-UP OF THE HEADQUARTERS

September 1939 – May 1940

CHAPTER 1

The Setting

IT SEEMS THAT early in September 1939 the opinion had already begun to form within the 'Führer Special' that the fluid, cramped, *ad hoc* organization of the mobile headquarters would not measure up to greater command responsibilities in the future. A new, more solid organization was required if the Supreme Commander was to command in the full military sense of that word, ie if he was himself to direct, not merely war planning, but *actual operations*.

It is unlikely that Hitler was the moving spirit behind this change. As far as he was concerned he seemed entirely satisfied with the part he had played in the Polish campaign. In any case he had no comprehension of the machinery necessary for command in the field and so is unlikely to have drawn the necessary conclusions. On the other hand it seems certain that Jodl must have found conditions in the 'Führer Special' unsatisfactory, particularly in the light of his own ambitious picture of a rigid unified command organization for the Wehrmacht; it is therefore inherently probable that it was he who pressed for a better organization of the headquarters in the future. The first essentials were a close knit and efficient staff, which in Jodl's view could be provided by the OKW Operations Staff, and an adequate signals network.

These conditions were most likely to be met if Hitler had decided, as he subsequently did, to follow the example of all his allies and enemies, Mussolini, Churchill, Roosevelt and, so far as we know, Stalin, and remain at the seat of government in Berlin. It appears however that, initially at any rate, this was supposed to be only a temporary solution. In any case, when I first visited the 'Führer Special' on 10 September, I was instructed by Jodl to reconnoitre for a Field Headquarters for OKW in west central Germany, from which the later phases of the war could be conducted. I remember vividly that among the instructions was one probably

41

emanating from Hitler himself, to keep out of range of long-range artillery but subject to this to get as near as possible to the Western Front. There had also to be accommodation for the Army and Air Force staffs in the immediate vicinity.

The most suitable location for the first headquarters in the field was found by a Staff officer of Section L. It was situated in the eastern foothills of the Taunus in the area Giessen-Nauheim but it was only at the turn of the year 1944–5, after more than five years of war, that the headquarters ultimately came to rest there. All requirements appeared to be met by the old family estate of Ziegenberg which included a country house and extensive farm buildings. The owner was apparently ready to sell, so the alterations and installation began at once under the direction of Todt, the General Inspector for Construction Work. The preparations could not however be completed in time for the offensive in the West which Hitler had set for late autumn 1939. In October therefore temporary accommodation was arranged for Section L in a special train which was to follow the 'Führer Special' as necessary. To begin with it was a modest affair of three coaches, two sleeping cars and a third half-office, half-restaurant, but in the course of the war it gradually grew into two full-size special trains, permanently available for the office accommodation and movement of the essential elements of the Operations Staff.

In the event the opening of the offensive in the West was continuously postponed because of weather conditions. Meanwhile however Hitler's military aides, as was indeed their job, became more and more intimately involved in the question of the Field Headquarters. It soon emerged that the location chosen by Section L did not meet Hitler's personal wishes in many respects. He did not want to live in a country house, it appeared, and he did not want to have cowsheds, horses and farm noises all round him. The aides started looking round on their own and immediately began to consider an entirely different lay-out. Something suitable was soon found in the rear area of the Siegfried Line. Three similar groups of forts were selected, one in the north near Münstereifel, one in the centre near Landstuhl in Pfalz and one in the south in the Black Forest not far from the Kniebis. In the middle of February it became clear that the signals installations at Ziegenberg could not be ready before June. Hitler thereupon finally decided that 'when operations opened' he would go not to Ziegenberg but to Felsennest (Crag's

Nest), the code name which had meanwhile been given to the location near Münstereifel. He had already ordered that OKH should be located in the same area and he took occasion now to insist upon this, personally selecting a neighbouring hunting lodge as the headquarters for the Army Commander-in-Chief and Chief of Staff with a working staff which was to be kept to a minimum. The Air Force was left to choose their headquarters as they saw fit. The special train known as 'Heinrich', housing Ribbentrop, Lammers and Himmler, was banished to the right bank of the Rhine.

The order that OKH should be located immediately alongside the Führer's Headquarters obviously had deeper implications. This is clear from the fact that Keitel decided to pass on the order in person, hoping to get Hitler's requirements accepted by high sounding phrases. Unexpectedly he encountered no opposition. Hitler's intention was obviously to ride the Army on a tight rein but Halder probably thought that this physical proximity offered the Army the best chance of ensuring that it had a decisive influence on the course of operations and the conduct of the war as a whole while at the same time freeing it from the tutelage of OKW. How differently it all turned out!

The question of the construction of a Field Headquarters was finally settled when Jodl gave instructions to the Chief Signals Officer that the group of forts nicknamed Felsennest and (for the Army) the neighbouring 'Forsterei' must be ready for occupation by 11 March 1940.[1]

CHAPTER 2

The Picture Within

ON HIS RETURN from the eastern frontier Hitler went back as before to the Reich Chancellery in Berlin, leaving it only for an occasional stay in Berchtesgaden and a Christmas visit to certain Waffen-SS* units on the Western Front. During his journeys the military personnel accompanying him were his aides; on the 'Führer Special' however he had got into the habit of working closely with the two senior officers of OKW and this pattern continued in Berlin. On his instructions two offices on the first floor of the Old Reich Chancellery were made available for Keitel and Jodl; they were immediately adjoining the Parliament Chamber which was used as map- and briefing-room. This meant that, although they themselves may hardly have realized it, the two generals had now become part of Hitler's *maison militaire* and so of his so-called 'immediate entourage'. General Jodl at any rate normally went to lunch in the mess where the numerous 'Great Ones' of the Third Reich were to be found.

At first sight this 'New Order' may appear of little consequence but in fact it undoubtedly stemmed from Hitler's unerring instinct for the division of authority and to a very large extent it set the stage for the whole subsequent headquarters 'system' with all its tensions and discords. Most important, from the Army point of view it opened the door to those 'irresponsible backstairs influences' which General Beck, during the earlier arguments on organization, had stated 'had no place in the organization for command and leadership in war'.[1] The daily situation reports, which Hitler continued as in the Polish campaign, were an important factor. In the nature of things the vast majority of the questions dealt with concerned the Army, yet there was no representative of the Army General Staff present; the only people who took part were the members of the

* The Waffen-SS was the armed section of the Schutz-Staffel (SS), the protective guard of the Nazi Party. The Waffen-SS was wholly militarized and consisted of long-term volunteers recruited, trained, supplied and administered by the SS.

maison militaire, Keitel, Jodl and the aides, and usually Göring's 'personal liaison officer', General Bodenschatz. The Army liaison officer had meanwhile, at Jodl's instigation, been excluded from the circle as being unnecessary. The Head of Section L and his officers were normally *not* included even when they had just returned from some special assignment at the front or elsewhere.[2] It was not long before General Jodl pushed his way into the position of principal reporting officer. He was well fitted both by character and training to be an assistant to a superior commander and by this means he put himself on the same level as his superior, the Chief of OKW, and frequently by-passed him. Keitel seemed to be resigned to saying nothing at all except to give emphatic support to Hitler's ideas. Jodl delegated parts of the report dealing with the events of the day to the two staff officers who had been detailed as assistants to him. From now on Hitler's aides were in general reduced to the role of spectators – this too on Jodl's instructions.

These presentations were for the most part based upon the reports and intelligence which Section L was responsible for collecting from the Services. Naturally these dealt primarily only with occurrences and changes on the day in question and did not go into more far-reaching problems of the type which proper personal contact with the troops brings to the notice of a Commander at any level. This did not however disconcert either Hitler or the OKW Generals who were always buzzing round him. They went calmly on working out their arguments and decisions on a totally inadequate basis and continually facing the Commander-in-Chief of the Army with preconceived ideas, sometimes even with *faits accomplis*.

There was another equally serious danger stemming from these arrangements. The Chief of OKW and the Chief of the Operations Staff fell completely under the spell of Hitler and at the same time became more and more divorced from the thinking of the Wehrmacht in general and that of their own Service, the Army, in particular. These were the men who, when Blomberg departed, had worried and fought for a unified command of the Wehrmacht; yet now their actions were a major factor in destroying its solidarity.

TENSIONS AND FAILURES WITHIN THE OKW OPERATIONS STAFF

The root of the dissensions lay within Jodl's own staff. As soon as he returned to Berlin I had asked for another posting. Although we knew each other no better than before, I had gained an increasing impression during the Polish campaign that we were mutually incompatible. There were, however, a number of other good reasons why I wished to get away. In the first place, at the moment when the majority of senior officers were getting more responsible positions, I could see myself being restricted to a more junior post than ever. This would not of itself have been a good enough reason in war but my experience hitherto had made it clear to me that, seeing how Jodl regarded and used my post, there was no real job alongside him for a Colonel of the General Staff. I therefore submitted that another posting for me would probably be in the general interest; I could point out that at the end of September I had allowed the majority of the officers who had been posted to my Section on mobilization to move on.

General Jodl, as was his habit, gave me no definite answer and meanwhile my distaste for the whole atmosphere of Supreme Headquarters grew, the more it became clear what the set-up in fact was. Back in 1938 Jodl had characterized the relationship of OKW to Hitler by calling it the 'working staff'. Now that he had become a member of the immediate entourage he applied this term to those parts of Section L which he used to assist him in his day-to-day staff work. The result was that the Section, which on a mobile footing consisted only of twelve to fifteen officers, was further split up when the move to the Field Headquarters took place. Compare with this the fact that just before the outbreak of war the peace establishment of the Army General Staff alone included twelve sections under five Deputy Chiefs of Staff. The war establishment was about one thousand officers.[3]

There was however a far more important hidden meaning in this use of the term 'working staff' by Jodl, something which became a governing factor in all later developments of the methods of work at Supreme Headquarters. Contrary to all Army General Staff tradition but following Hitler's example, Jodl regarded the officers of his staff not as colleagues who had the right to think for themselves, to make suggestions and to advise, but as a machine for the elaboration and issue of orders. von Lossberg says in his book:

Jodl was taciturn by nature and did not hold with long discussions. He seldom accepted anyone else's advice. He would give his staff under Warlimont clearly defined jobs; even Warlimont was in his

46

eyes merely a subordinate who had no authority to act on his own, as officers of a high level staff would normally expect.

But this method of work was not merely a personal quirk of Jodl's; it was entirely in line with his conception of a new type of General Staff such as Göring had tried to introduce into the Luftwaffe in the spring of 1939; in both cases the concept undoubtedly sprang from the National-Socialist principle 'implicit obedience upwards and un-questioned authority downwards'.[4] This was nothing less than the injection by Jodl of Hitler's method of work into the sphere of General Staff procedure; instead of the German Army's well-tried system of 'allotment of tasks', a new type of command organization was spring-ing up, one which was determined to impose its will by means of orders dealing with everything in the most minute detail.

Jodl's natural tendencies were reinforced by the distances which, contrary to all normal practice, he put between himself and his staff. The physical distance might be measured in minutes in a car, for instance, initially the Bendlerstrasse to the Reich Chancellery in Berlin, or later in the majority of the Field Headquarters from 'Area 1' to 'Area 2'; or it might be measured in hours in an aeroplane, as happened in 1940–1 when Jodl spent weeks at a time at Hitler's retreat in Berchtesgaden. The actual distance was of little consequence. What did matter was that as a result of this physical separation and because it suited him, Jodl dropped more and more into the habit of drafting Hitler's directives himself and using Sec-tion L merely to get any necessary agreement to his draft from the Army, Navy and Air Force, or more often merely as a secretariat and registry.[5] For the same reason a 'normal channel' for oral communi-cations to and from the High Commands of the Services grew up; this by-passed Section L which got only scrappy information, generally too late; it began and ended solely with Jodl since he was the only reliable source of information on Hitler's thoughts and in-tentions.

A further consequence of this physical separation was that for the junior members of his staff it became almost as difficult to see General Jodl as to see Hitler himself. From the personal point of view many of the more senior officers, myself among them, fully appreciated the priceless advantage of being relieved of dancing attendance upon Hit-ler and of being able to work in the healthier atmosphere of a purely military staff. From the official point of view however we were isolated

47

and frequently excluded from the march of events, a fact which militated considerably against the formation of the unified Operations Staff so much desired by Jodl.

These aspects of the work of the staff were deplorable but in the field of policy and the conduct of the war in general there were far deeper disagreements between the Chief of the OKW Operations Staff and myself as his senior staff officer. Jodl's blind faith in Hitler, expressed in most unmilitary terms in the panegyrics in his diary, came ultimately to govern his whole outlook and his every action, though he never said a word on the subject. On 15 October 1939 when the argument with the Army about the offensive in the West was in full swing, his diary reads: 'Even though we may act one hundred per cent contrary to the doctrine of the General Staff, we shall win this war because we have better troops, better armament, stronger nerves and decisive leadership which knows where it is going.' I was never able to harbour such illusions. Between the two senior officers of the Operations Staff there was not therefore that basis of mutual confidence which would have enabled us to discuss frankly and so to eliminate our differences of opinion on questions of peace and war or on the general lines on which the war was being waged, let alone the far more delicate subject of National-Socialist policy both from the sociological aspect within Germany and from the general point of view in the occupied territories.[6] In the autumn of 1939 I made two further attempts to influence the course of events myself but the time factor and the limited freedom of movement accorded the Chief of a Section in OKW doomed both to failure. I tried by every means, official and private, to make use of the other escape route, that of being posted away from OKW and back to troops. This was once more refused me on the grounds that there was a great shortage of senior General Staff officers; finally in the autumn of 1943 Hitler laid down in writing that there were to be no more changes of personnel in certain key posts in the headquarters. Some twenty officers in OKW, OKH and OKL, mostly of General Officer rank, were affected; they were given to understand that they must be content with the fact that they had served with troops in the first World War.[7] Hitler's real reason for issuing this order was probably not merely his increasing 'dislike of new faces' but his fear of an attempt on his life. It was not until after 20 July 1944 that these officers had any hope of moving to other employment, always provided that a move did not take them to hospital, a court martial or the gallows. The well-known reproach that many staff officers in the higher echelons had become 'red tabs' had something in it, but could hardly be applied justifiably to those I refer to here.

During the build-up period between the campaigns in Poland and in France no progress was made in eliminating the ambiguities over the position of the Supreme Commander's staff and its responsibilities within the structure of the Wehrmacht; these remained just as far from a solution as in the years before the war. No doubt General Jodl felt that his concept of OKW as Hitler's military 'working staff' was fully justified in that, since the beginning of the war, the Dictator had devoted the greater part of his time to military matters, as demonstrated by the fact that he now generally appeared in some form of uniform; moreover it was plain for all to see that the senior officers of OKW had now been brought into the closest physical proximity to him. On the other hand this concept of a 'working staff' merely reinforced Hitler's tendency to use the staff, even in war, as his military bureau, as a kind of speaking tube, as the machine, in fact, which drafted and supervised the execution of the orders which he considered he had the right to give in the military sphere as in all others. Perhaps the most striking illustration of this peculiar relationship is the fact that in Jodl's diary of this period there is hardly ever an entry for those days on which for some reason Hitler did not appear at the daily briefing.[8]

In these circumstances the remaining officers of the OKW Operations Staff, who were not so directly under the spell of the Supreme Commander and of whom I as the Chief of Section L was the most senior, should have realized that their immediate and most pressing task was to strengthen the organization and improve the standing of the staff so that it could meet the increasing demands of the war. This did not occur and it must be admitted that this failure cannot be laid at the door either of the dissensions and discords within the staff or of the continued resistance offered by the High Commands of the Services. Looking back some excuse may be found in the fact that all *later* proposals for improving the existing unsatisfactory situation invariably came to nought as a result of the totally negative attitude of Jodl.

So during this period of the build-up of Supreme Headquarters no thought was given at all to the organization plans current in the mid-thirties which had visualized the creation of a real, effective

General Staff of the Wehrmacht. Instead the responsibilities of the highest-level Wehrmacht staff in its existing ill-defined field developed *ad hoc* without any clear rule or direction.

An outstanding illustration of the situation was the fact, already referred to, that it was Hitler personally, alone and unaided, who took the decision to launch an attack in the West and laid down the general lines on which the operation was to be conducted. Moreover the procedure followed in this case was *not* that of 'normal military staff work'. Jodl went into this aspect of the question in some detail in his evidence before the International Military Tribunal, saying that: 'the Commander-in-Chief, in this case Hitler in person, received data for the decisions to be made, maps, strength returns of both our own and enemy forces and information about the enemy'.[9] In fact Hitler's procedure was the exact opposite. His order for an attack in the West was based primarily on his own intuitive appreciation of the enemy and entirely disregarded the fact that, once the war had spread beyond Poland, his freedom of decision in politico-military questions was limited. In the case of other subsequent decisions, in particular his attack on Russia, his declaration of war on the United States, and last but not least his pressure on Italy to enter the war, he was literally mesmerized by his own concept of the political situation and did not take the military implications adequately into account. This was a perverted application of the classic principle that diplomacy governs strategy. He had access to exhaustive statistical information on the armaments of foreign powers, their fortifications and the strength of their naval and air forces; in general he was well aware of the facts of military geography. But all these factors added up in his mind to an exercise in wishful thinking and when he later asked for concrete military facts and information he only took account of them to the extent that they supported the opinions he had already formed. Anything else was as a rule rejected out of hand and ascribed to 'General Staff defeatism'.

On 9 October 1939 Hitler issued a comprehensive *aide-memoire*, entirely his own production, seeking to justify his plans and instructions for an offensive in the West, to which he knew that the Army was strongly opposed.[10] Jodl stated at Nuremberg: 'It was dictated word for word by the Führer himself and was completed in two nights.'[11] At this stage it was the job of the OKW Operations Staff to dress up Hitler's plans and desires in the form of a directive and this went out the same day as no. 6. There were eight short paragraphs, the last of which read: 'I request Commanders-in-Chief to submit to me (Hitler) their detailed plans based on this directive at the earliest moment and to keep me constantly informed of progress through OKW.'[12]

This formula became the rule for subsequent similar directives. Those not versed in military matters can however hardly be expected to see that this concealed an important fact; it was the Army General Staff which had to work out the real plan for distribution of forces and the first phase of the operations – the operation order in fact; at the same time the other two Services, particularly the Air Force, had to work out the main lines of their own detailed plans. The OKW Operations Staff was incapable of 'laying on operations'; prior to the autumn of 1944 there is not a single instance of it having done so, though oddly enough General Jodl in evidence before the Nuremberg Tribunal claimed that it had; he presumably had his eye on the war historians.[13] The preparatory stages of the Western campaign can be studied in detail on the basis of ample documentary evidence; they show quite clearly that the general lines of an 'operation' only began to emerge when the Army operation order was issued and that the OKW directive did no more than give general indications. The proof of this can be seen in the facts given below.

On 21 October Keitel presented to Hitler the 'Army Intentions for Operation Yellow' (the West). This had been forwarded two days before by the Army Staff to OKW through Section L in the form of a draft operation order. (In this case the Commander-in-Chief of the Army left it to the Chief of OKW to present what was 'Army business', something which he had never done before and never did again. This was his way of showing his disagreement with the basic directive already issued by Hitler.)

Jodl himself prepared a sketch map, showing the distribution of forces, including those of the Air Force; but this had been agreed between the Army and Air Staffs without any participation by OKW. Hitler commented on these plans and added certain additional requirements.[14] Keitel and Jodl went out together next day to Zossen to inform Halder of Hitler's observations and additional requirements.[15]

After considerable further discussion between Hitler and the senior officers of OKW on one side and the Army Commander-in-Chief and Chief of Staff on the other, the Army issued a revised operation order on 29 October.

This was authenticated as an order for the Wehrmacht by *Directive no. 8 for the Conduct of the War* issued by OKW on 20 November 1939. It contained certain additional provisions demanded by Hitler.[16]

A similar procedure produced Army Operation Order no. 3 dated 30 January 1940 and finally no. 4 dated 24 February 1940 on which the offensive in May was eventually carried out.[17] It is worth noting that Hitler played a considerable part in the transformation of his own original plan into that on which the successful campaign in France was eventually fought, the so-called *Manstein Plan*[18] Jodl however opposed it up to the very last moment. OKW's only contribution therefore to the development of the plan for operations in the West lay in the discussions which took place almost daily between Hitler, Keitel and Jodl. The outcome of these was passed on to the Services where necessary, sometimes orally, sometimes in writing, either by the two generals themselves or by Section L officers on their instructions. This process applied also to the orders for the so-called 'special operations' to which Hitler's own ever-active brain gave birth in large numbers and various forms; there were to be *coups* by load-carrying gliders, assault pioneers and small parachute units to capture important bridges and frontier fortifications at the outset of the attack in the West and so ensure that the main movements could proceed rapidly and smoothly. The OKW Operations Staff was also the 'official channel' for the thirteen orders which were issued, starting on 7 November 1939 and following each other over a period of two months at two- to seven-day intervals, laying down and then postponing the date for the attack.[19] Finally there were certain instructions which were to some extent more the original work of OKW; examples are the *General Instructions for Enemy Deception* intended to mislead the enemy regarding our intentions; and the 'time-table', dated 22 February 1940, which, as before, listed the decisions to be taken by Hitler in accordance with the intentions and plans he had already approved, in each case laying down the last-possible date depending on the time factor, the subject and the deception possibilities.

A number of high-level, primarily organizational, tasks also fell to the lot of OKW. These consisted principally of tapping all the human and material resources of the Reich in order to plug the numerous gaps in equipment and assemble the necessary stocks for supply in the field.[20] It was also necessary to work out with the com-

petent Reich authorities and to codify basic principles for the administration of occupied territory.[21] The above were in the first instance
the job of the 'Organization' and 'Administration' Working Groups
of Section L. At the same time Jodl was using the other two sections
of the staff for numerous tasks, such as setting up a signals network
for Supreme Headquarters and preparations for propaganda during
the offensive.

In addition to matters specifically connected with the offensive in
the West, OKW also issued directives on the war against merchant
shipping at sea; these were based entirely on the plans and proposals
of the Navy and Air Force. The efforts of OKW were aimed
primarily at an effective concentration of the limited resources of
both services against the most important targets; they did not however in general get their way against any particular requirement of
the Air Force and its Commander-in-Chief, Göring.[22]

During this period of the build-up of the headquarters all the
energies of the Operations Staff were absorbed in giving form and
expression to Hitler's wishes regarding the forthcoming offensive in
the West. As a result it failed to look into the politico-military and
strategic future or study possible future developments of the war and
so work out the basis even for a *post hoc* 'war plan'. This is proved
and underlined by the fact that the Mediterranean theatre was
almost totally neglected and that when the Western campaign was
brought to a successful conclusion after barely six weeks, Supreme
Headquarters had no plans for and had done no preliminary work on
any further operations. Seeing the way the war had developed and
had there been adequate direction from the Chief of the Operations
Staff, there would have been an excellent opportunity here to get the
highest level staff of the Wehrmacht back to the original purpose for
which it was intended. This would have allowed the staff to achieve
something and its standing would have been correspondingly improved; from the military point of view it would have constituted a
highly desirable counter-weight to its continued misuse as the
Supreme Commander's *bureau* and it might even have allowed it to
have some influence upon his arbitrary decisions; the position of the
staff *vis-à-vis* the High Commands of the Services would also have
been stronger. What actually happened was that it continued to for-
feit all respect as a result of Hitler's continual interference with the
preparations and later with the actual conduct of operations. Finally

if the staff had been so used, General Jodl would necessarily have been brought into close contact with the Chiefs of Staff of the Services,, something which throughout the war was either totally neglected or at any rate never became established custom.

On the other side were directing organizations which fully proved their worth, the Chiefs of Staff Committee in England, the Joint Chiefs of Staff in the United States and the combination of the two, the Combined Chiefs of Staff. The Chiefs of Staff in England and the Commanders-in-Chief of the Services in the United States met more or less daily and laid down the broad lines of strategy in all its aspects. Churchill was just as much his own Supreme Commander as was Hitler, yet the views and decisions of the Chiefs of Staff generally prevailed when there were differences of opinion. In fact the advice of the British Chiefs of Staff and the US Joint Chiefs was a deciding factor in Allied strategy.[23] At the comparable level in Germany there was nothing but a disastrous vacuum.

Looking back on all this, such lack of foresight seems almost incomprehensible. As things were of course the Operations Staff was in no better position than before to undertake more important work unless Hitler had agreed to it and ordered it; in the first place the manpower and resources at the disposal of Section L were still strictly limited and it could do little more than express opinions; secondly, because there was such a general aversion to OKW, voluntary co-operation from the staffs of the Services would not have been forthcoming. In fact Hitler did nothing to set planning in motion. What is more, a number of hints from him, which might at least have been used as starting points, were disregarded and in many cases did not even come to the ears of the Chief of Section L or his officers. Examples of this are some of Hitler's observations in his *aide-memoire* of 9 October 1939; in this he pointed out that victory over France would open up considerable stretches of the Atlantic coastline, as a result of which the war could be brought to an end by 'all-out employment of the Luftwaffe against the heart of British resistance'. This idea was elaborated in certain OKW directives issued during the winter 1939–40 dealing with preparatory measures for the 'siege of England'; there was however no thorough-going examination of the likelihood of this strategy succeeding, a particularly pertinent question in view of our complete inexperience in 'strategic air warfare' and shortage of submarines.

Furthermore during these months no thought was given in Supreme Headquarters to the possibility of an invasion of the British Isles. Jodl took no action on this subject although the entries in his diary show that, as early as November 1939, he – though not his staff – knew that the Naval Staff was examining the problem and at the beginning of December that the Army Staff was doing likewise. Even when, in May and again in June 1940 (to anticipate for a moment) the Commander-in-Chief of the Navy presented the results of his staff study to Hitler,[24] Jodl did nothing, probably because at that time Hitler showed no interest. The criticism was often made that senior officers, including Hitler himself, were prisoners of their memories of the first World War and therefore did not reckon on such a resounding success of the offensive in the West.[25] This may have been true in the autumn of 1939 but it clearly was not early in 1940.

As regards Italy, the Supreme Commander gave much thought in the spring of 1940 to getting his ally in the much-vaunted 'Pact of Steel' to send twenty to thirty divisions to attack the Maginot Line from German territory in the direction of the Plateau de Langres. This idea was the subject of detailed staff studies by the Army.[26] On the other hand, as already pointed out, no consideration was given to the larger strategic problems stemming from the alliance – for instance the problems and prospects of a Mediterranean strategy conducted either in concert with Italy or single-handed. It is true that for a time the military strategists busied themselves with precautionary measures against the threat which Weygand's French Army in Syria was rightly thought to pose to the Salonika area and the Rumanian oilfields. That no more was done as regards the Mediterranean area was undoubtedly due to the fact that Hitler had already decided to leave it entirely to the Italians;[27] Mussolini moreover was of the same mind and the General Staff in Rome even more insistent.

Last but not least the Eastern Front ought to have been a matter for strategic study at the latest by the spring of 1940. During a conversation in the Reich Chancellery on 27 March 1940 Hitler mentioned that 'he was keeping the situation in the East under the closest observation'. Both Jodl and the Chief of Staff of the Army were present; the fact that this did not alert either to the great strategic problems involved is more excusable in the case of Halder than in that of Jodl. There were nevertheless a number of indications of potential trouble such as the Russian attitude on the demarcation line in Poland and Hitler's hesitancy in making the deliveries of war material to Soviet Russia agreed in the treaty. These should have been enough to cause any clear-thinking military command at least to set in motion studies of the problem, if not to issue the most emphatic *warnings*.[28]

To sum up it must be admitted that the staff of OKW made very little use of the time available for the build-up of a high-level head-quarters (ie up to the spring of 1940) to prepare the Wehrmacht for the greater demands which the subsequent conduct of the war was to make upon it. This was all the more serious in that there was now no von Moltke or von Schlieffen and therefore no peace-time General Staff studies looking beyond the immediate objective of the defence of the country. Instead the OKW Operations Staff was occupied primarily with Hitler's 'special operations'; it had a tendency to take over responsibility for the operational plans and measures of the Army General Staff or even, as will be seen in the case of Norway and Denmark, to cut the Army out altogether and take over the Army's job. This meant that it was diverted from its true responsibilities and that it totally failed to consider the wider implications.

RELATIONSHIPS WITH THE SERVICES

Since late autumn 1938 there had been hardly any outward signs of difficulties in the relations between OKW and the Services or – the heart of the problem – between OKW and OKH. These flared up again at once, however, on 27 September 1939 when Hitler ordered the offensive in the West. For the Army the problem was not merely to counter OKW's 'meddling in operational matters', which they so much resented and of which Jodl's previous activities had furnished so many examples. Hitler had now taken a decision completely over the head of the Army and, as shown above, had included in his decision his own general directions for the conduct of the operations; he was laying down not only 'when' but 'how'.[29] Fundamentally this could mean nothing less than that the Supreme Commander now intended to take over command of the Army himself. If this was in fact his intention he ought at the same time to have taken over OKH or the General Staff of the Army, as being by far the most effective command organization in the Wehrmacht, and have cut OKW out of these questions; this would at least have been an original method of solving the problem of higher organization; it would have provided the best possible core for the Supreme Headquarters which was in process of forming and it would have given the Army General Staff the position which it merited. The procedure adopted by Hitler in encroaching on the preserves of the Army was exactly the opposite. All he was interested in was to reinforce his position in the military field, as in all others, as the man having sole power of command; he did not want expert, responsible advice since, from the Army at any rate, that might sometimes imply opposition and warnings, as had happened in the past and was to happen again in the future. Instead he was determined to have 'unquestioned authority downwards'. He had decided that during the forthcoming campaign the Commander-in-Chief of the Army should be tied to the same location as Supreme Headquarters and accompanied only by his Chief of Staff and a reduced staff; his real reason was to achieve more rapidly and more surely his object of concentrating power in his own hands, to reduce the General Staff of the Army to the level of an executive mechanism for his decisions and orders comparable to the OKW Operations Staff, but at the same time, from the material point of view, to make maximum use of its command network, which he knew he could not replace and the efficiency of which he recognized. So in the autumn of 1939, the Army saw itself faced with just that situation against which Colonel-General Freiherr von Fritsch had warned during the earlier arguments about higher organization. 'No one can expect a Commander-in-Chief to win battles,' he had said, 'if he is working on a concept with which he does not agree.'[30] In the end the rule for the relationship between the Supreme Commander and the General Staff was that which Hitler so often described by quoting the example of the NCO and his section of eight men.

Generals Keitel and Jodl had had no part in the Supreme Commander's decision to take the offensive in the West. In this case also however, they ranged themselves solidly behind him and so found themselves in the same state of conflict with the Army as at the time of the Sudeten crisis. The same applied, though less acutely, to their staff. Keitel himself was not without certain misgivings over Hitler's actions and intentions but as things were he did his best to mediate, in a one-sided fashion of course, and to reconcile the Army leaders to the requirements of the Dictator by fair words and a stream of assurances.[31] Jodl on the other hand clearly looked upon this development as a considerable step forward in the process of cutting the Army staff down to size, as he had always wanted to do. He did not waste time in trying to get any further delimitation of responsibilities laid down but he had not a moment's hesitation in making full use of the springboard Hitler had now offered him and seizing every opportunity to push himself into the chain of command of the Army. The door was now wide open to those 'irresponsible backstairs influences' against which Beck had warned.

The Commander-in-Chief of the Army and his Chief of Staff did not of course give way to the demands of the Supreme Command without a struggle. They could see before them the parting of the ways, roads leading in two totally opposing directions; one ideology with its roots in the dictatorial authority of the National-Socialist movement believed that it could bend the German people, indeed the entire world, to its will; the other, with its roots in the heritage of the Prussian-German military tradition of duty would not shrink even from a *coup d'état* if that would save the nation from disaster. But at the height of the autumn 1938 crisis Brauchitsch had done no more than point out 'with oaths' to the Chief of OKW where his responsibility lay; so now, in spite of all the strong words used beforehand, he could not bring himself personally to oppose Hitler's decision to attack in the West. This naturally further weakened the Army's claim to a decisive voice in war planning and it also carried with it the immediate implication that the Army must draft its plans for the operation in accordance with Hitler's concept and against its own convictions.

In these circumstances the Army confined itself to 'passive resistance' but this, together with renewed representations by Halder demanding in Jodl's words to be 'given a free hand',[32] merely reinforced Hitler's determination. Finally, on 5 November 1939, the first key date for the issue of orders in final form, the Commander-in-Chief of the Army, with the unanimous support of the senior commanders on the Western Front, came out openly against taking the offensive and therefore against the war plan in general. But by then things had gone so far that all Hitler did was to bring the meeting to an end in short order and in the most peremptory manner.[33] There was next a somewhat similar dramatic scene on 23 November when Hitler summoned all the Army Generals and, in the presence of equally high-ranking representatives of the other two Services, upbraided them for being beset by fears and held them up as doubters who were always tugging at his coat-sleeves. Brauchitsch immediately offered his resignation but this made no impression.[34] From the turn of the year onwards nevertheless, the Army seemed to be increasingly prepared to accept Hitler's intentions and the tension accordingly eased for a time. The real reason for this undoubtedly lay in the greater prospects of success now that the opening of the offensive had been postponed to the spring of 1940. But this did not alter the fact that the balance of power between Hitler and OKW on the one hand and the Army on the other had swung heavily against the Army; there was to be disastrous proof of this later.

The acute differences of opinion between OKW and OKH which flared up again during the build-up period of Supreme Headquarters stemmed from differing points of view regarding Hitler and his strategy. It should here be re-emphasized that, contrary to the widespread belief both in Germany and among the Allies during the war, it would be incorrect and unjust to assume that all officers of OKW and the Army were involved. As already shown, there was a split right through OKW and no fewer than two Chiefs of Sections, Admiral Canaris and General Thomas, together with the vast majority of their officers were on the side of the Army. Against this certain of Halder's successors as Chief of Staff of the Army were apparently, at any rate for a time, determined not to be out-done in their devotion to Hitler and his leadership. In 1942 and 1944 Generals Zeitzler and Guderian called on the General Staff of the Army to give proof of their belief in National-Socialist doctrine,[35] something which even Jodl never did to his staff.

In this connection Colonel-General von Reichenau, who has been much misjudged, was an outstanding example of one who retained his intellectual independence. There had been no doubt that originally he was fully prepared to come to terms with National-Socialism and in the crisis of January–February 1938 Hitler had exerted great pressure to have him nominated as successor to Colonel-General von Fritsch. Even Keitel and Jodl however had resisted this, thinking that it would be unacceptable to the majority of senior officers.[36] Even before the start of the Polish campaign Reichenau had manifested serious doubts regarding Hitler's military policy and finally in the autumn of 1939 he came out openly against the idea of opening up the war by offensive action in the West.[37] The position was exactly reversed two years later when, in December 1941, Hitler turned him down as successor to Brauchitsch saying 'that man's too politically-minded for me and if the cat's away the mice will play'.[38]

During these months the Navy and Air Force made no claim to a deciding voice in strategy at any rate as far as the Western Front was concerned. The Chief of Staff of the Luftwaffe did make a proposal on 1 February 1940, and again in more detail on 6 February[39] that Holland and Norway should be occupied as bases for air action against England, the only method of bringing the war decisively to an end, that 'Belgian neutrality should be guaranteed for the duration of the war' and that the Siegfried Line should be occupied defensively against France. This proposal was not seriously considered at the time and was never pursued further. Questions concerning preparations for and command of operations were in general entirely Army business, but in any case the Naval and Air Commanders-in-Chief knew from their pre-war experience how to evade Hitler's influence and pressure or, if differences of opinion did occur, how to get their own way. Hitler had considerable respect for Göring and Raeder and this meant that even Jodl, who was naturally no expert in naval or air matters, treated them with marked circumspection. In contrast to the Army both Services were able to preserve a considerable degree of independence as a result of the specialized nature of their business and the personalities of their Commanders-in-Chief; in the case of the Navy, apart from certain isolated instances, this persisted throughout the war. For the Air Force difficulties began only when the continuous drain on its strength and the ineffectiveness of Göring later necessitated personal intervention by Hitler.

Up to a late stage in the war correspondence between the Navy and Air Force on the one hand and Hitler or OKW on the other was carried on with every mark of consideration for their Commanders-in-Chief, both in regard to the form in which communications were drafted and the procedure employed. Only occasionally did they have to make oral presentations on matters concerning their Services and they contrived to preserve their independence further by keeping aloof from the mob of military personalities in Hitler's entourage who invariably crowded round the Army leaders whenever they appeared in the Chancellery. Raeder has left a record of his conversations with Hitler,[40] at which usually only one or two, sometimes none, of his staff were present. All the doors were invariably shut when Göring went in and in any case he could come and go as he liked at Hitler's normal briefings. It was only on a few occasions that he exerted any clear and definite influence on strategy but there are plenty of indications to show that this private relationship between the Big Two of the Third Reich led to a number of disastrous consequences. When it suited him, Göring would by-pass Jodl and send his Chief of Staff direct to Hitler. The procedures adopted by the Commanders-in-Chief of the Navy and Air Force had the further disadvantage that on numerous occasions even Jodl was left in ignorance of the decisions reached by Hitler.[41]

As regards the Army however even the forms of words used by Hitler and his team of Generals seemed designed to indicate disregard of the Army Commander-in-Chief's prerogatives; the fact that the Army was the decisive factor in overall strategy cannot be the only explanation of this attitude.

The Commander-in-Chief and Chief of Staff of the Army as a rule only appeared for a personal discussion with Hitler when they were summoned to do so, and in these months of build-up the occasions on which this happened could be counted on the fingers of both hands. Up to the beginning of December 1939 no Army representative was present even at the meteorological conferences at which Hitler decided on the date for or the postponement of the offensive.[42] This reserve on the part of the Army had been clear from Halder's attitude during the Polish campaign; it is hardly surprising in view of the complete antithesis between Hitler's methods and the 'Zossen frame of mind'.[43] Brauchitsch had always in his other high military appointments given proof of outstanding ability and a presence commanding respect, but a meeting with Hitler seemed actually to have some physical effect on him, indeed he often appeared practically paralysed. Halder was completely at one with his Commander-in-Chief but he was clearly less susceptible to atmosphere and had the confidence born of the fact that in any argument he was head and shoulders above Hitler's normal advisers and that thanks to his complete mastery of his subject and his unfailing clarity of expression, he could always overcome any objections. When however, as mentioned above, it was left to Keitel to present to Hitler the first Army operation order for the attack in the West, it became clear that passive resistance was not enough to protect the interests of the Army.

Another result of the latent tension between OKW and the Army was that, when doing business verbally with OKH, Keitel and Jodl did not deal on their own level; Keitel dealt with Halder and Jodl with the Chief of the Operations Section, at that time Colonel von Greiffenberg. It was von Greiffenberg or his senior Staff Officer, Lieutenant-Colonel Heusinger, who were normally called to the Chancellery by Jodl when new 'thoughts' from Hitler had to be passed on to, or rather put over on, OKH;[44] this was the case even when the 'thoughts' were of far-reaching importance. Jodl always treated Halder outwardly with all military courtesy, yet his diary shows that only once during these eight or nine months did he have any prolonged discussion with him. Equally, there was only one meeting between Jodl and Halder's principal subordinate, General von Stülpnagel and this only took place after an agreement on improved co-operation had been reached between Keitel and Halder.[45]

Those who should really have been doing so therefore did not meet anything like often enough. On the other hand, just as in the days before the invasion of Austria in the spring of 1938, the Chancellery took to going over the head of OKH and dealing with individual generals, who for some reason happened to be in favour at the time. For instance Hitler discussed with General Busch, at the time Commander of the Sixteenth Army, his initial plan for organizing a special offensive formation for the break-through in the Ardennes; similarly Keitel called on General Guderian for detailed advice on the same subject.[46] In this connection it is of interest that it was only on 17 February 1940 that General von Manstein gave Hitler 'after lunch his ideas on Army Group A's operations'.[47] In other words this was the occasion when the first real step was taken leading to the new plan for the offensive in the West which was so successfully carried out in May 1940. General von Manstein was not in particular favour with Hitler, though there is no truth in the tale that he only got an audience through machinations on the part of Hitler's aides. He was one of those newly promoted Corps commanders for whom there was a standing order that, when in Berlin, they should report to Hitler.

A few months later Jodl even went so far as to think himself entitled to propose actual names for appointments of senior commanders in the Army[48] – but this of course took place during the period of preparation for the occupation of Denmark and Norway when, as will be seen, interference by OKW with the Army's responsibilities had become the rule.

As time went on the most important written communications issued during this period and subsequently by Supreme Headquarters, the so-called *OKW Directives*, fell more or less clearly into two categories. In the first were those primarily of a strategical nature, such as *Directive no. 6*, in which Hitler made known his decisions in broad terms as guide lines for future strategy. In the second category were those like *Directive no. 8* dealing with the initial operations of a campaign or the later stages of an operation after the intermediate objectives had been attained; these clearly trespassed upon the prerogatives of the Army General Staff and in effect transferred command to OKW. In each case Jodl either drafted the text himself in accordance with Hitler's detailed instructions or, as usually happened, gave Section L a basis to work on in note form.

The same procedure was adopted for the OKW *Special Instructions* dealing with matters connected with individual campaigns. Their preparation led to particular difficulties; their political content was laid down by Hitler himself; there were however a large number of other provisions, such as closing of frontiers, cutting of communications, currency rates, etc., which had to be agreed with the civil authorities but which for security reasons could not be dealt with ahead of time.

It became increasingly difficult to deal with the mass of paperwork which grew as the scope of the war widened, owing to the fact that, unless the name and authority of Hitler could be used in each individual case, OKW carried just as little weight as before.[49]

RELATIONS WITH ALLIES

From the military point of view Germany stood alone during the months between the Polish and French campaigns. Italy, the only ally worth consideration, had revoked when war broke out and persisted in the equivocal position of 'non-belligerent'. Hitler was bitterly disappointed but apparently failed to realize that it was partially his own fault. In January 1940 the Dictator temporarily came round to the view expressed in a Section L study asked for by Jodl that Germany could not expect much advantage from Italian participation in the war, particularly in view of her expected large-scale demands for war material.[50] At about this time Hitler told the assembled commanders-in-chief to 'spread false information' and apparently indicated General Marras, the Italian Military Attaché in Berlin, as one of the intended recipients. All this did not offer OKW much encouragement to look ahead and lay the groundwork of an organization for an allied strategy with Italy, nor did it provide a basis on which to work. The situation changed considerably on 19 March when Hitler 'returned beaming and extremely satisfied from a meeting with the Duce, who now seemed prepared for an early entry into the war'.[51] The only basis however on which the proposed co-operation could start was the *Disposition of Forces Map* which Hitler had had with him for his first meeting with Mussolini and which, as was invariably the case later, gave much exaggerated figures with the object of deceiving both our Allies and the enemy.[52] There were at the time 157½ divisions capable of taking the field but the map showed 200 German Army formations, a figure achieved principally by including the 100,000 men in the Replacement Army. On the German side therefore the initial enthusiasm not unnaturally soon gave way to disillusionment, and it was with considerable misgivings that the staff got to work on the basic objectives of a combined strategy intended as a basis for a strategic discussion when the two staffs met for a more intimate *prise de contact*.[53] This state of mind is strikingly illustrated by an entry in Jodl's diary a few days later:

> Told the Führer how we proposed to handle the forthcoming discussions with the Italian General Staff. First put the question through Military Attaché Rome how they think they can help us. Then proceed to the possibility of an operation across the Upper Rhine. No staff talks before we have shown our hand.[54]

It soon became clear that the Italian military leaders were still totally opposed to their country entering the war and consequently even less inclined than we were to embark on any closer co-operation. On 4 April 1940 a memorandum by Marshal Badoglio, then Chief of the Comando Supremo, includes this: 'there must be no binding relationship with the German General Staff; they are grasping and overbearing by nature and will tend to subordinate Italian intentions and wishes to their own'. On 11 April 1940 General Graziani, then Chief of Staff of the Army, wrote: 'contacts with Berlin should be limited to general exchanges of view'.[55] It is therefore perhaps hardly surprising that no further thought was given to preparations for setting up the type of staff which might have been charged by both partners with working out the strategy of a common war effort.

This situation continued throughout the period during which the Axis Powers pursued a common strategy. It stemmed primarily from Hitler's – not unjustified – mistrust of those around Mussolini and his refusal therefore to let them know of his plans beforehand. On their side the Italians started on the basis of 'parallel strategy' but gradually found themselves forced more or less to tag along with that of Germany. Hitler refused to exert any greater pressure in order to avoid 'offending the Duce and so damaging the most valuable connecting link in the Axis, the mutual confidence between the two Heads of State'.[56] Subsequent events make it more likely that his true reason for this attitude was to safeguard Mussolini's prestige, since he was the real protagonist of the 'Axis policy' in Italy and had to carry with him the people, the armed forces and not least the royal family.

The Military Commissions set up in January 1942 under the Three-Power Pact between Italy, Japan and Germany, which might have made some pretence of being an allied directing organization on the lines of the Combined Chiefs of Staff, were never allowed to do the work for which they were designed, at any rate as far as Hitler was concerned. The German members were so selected that they had no detailed knowledge of our plans and they were expressly forbidden to deal with any strategic problems which had to be kept secret from the enemy. As a result the Commissions had no real *raison d'être*.

Instead of organizing a combined staff working on forward planning in an orderly manner, Hitler therefore concentrated all allied work primarily in his own hands. There were occasional meetings with leading statesmen and desultory exchanges of correspondence which will be referred to later. These were his main methods of conducting allied strategy throughout the war. The Military, Naval and Air Attachés in the allied capitals were raised to the status of 'high-level liaison officers' but they were given only sufficient information to enable them, where necessary, to pour oil on troubled waters. As far as Italy was concerned, the 'German General accredited to Italian Supreme Headquarters', General von Rintelen, was located alongside that headquarters in Rome and was authorized to attend the daily briefings;[57] he at least appeared more frequently than his Italian opposite number, whom one seldom met either in Berlin or in Hitler's headquarters in the field.

CHAPTER 3

Denmark and Norway — a Special Case

THE GERMAN INVASION of Denmark and Norway[1] in the spring of 1940 took place while the headquarters was still unready and still scattered in and around Berlin. From the point of view of the organization for strategic direction which is the theme of this book, it was in many respects an exceptional situation. Briefly the salient features were as follows:

1 The idea was originally put to Hitler by the Commander-in-Chief of the Navy primarily on defensive grounds; initially Hitler regarded it with some hesitation but later took it over as his own idea and followed it up pertinaciously; as a result the original purely military and strategic reasons for the operation became subordinated to his own world-wide expansionist aims.

2 The chain of responsibility for the preparation and command of the Army formations detailed for this campaign by-passed the Commander-in-Chief of the Army, his Chief of Staff and Operations Section. Instead these tasks, which should have been those of OKH, were taken over by Hitler himself, assisted merely by the OKW Operations Staff and certain other organizations specially set up for the purpose.

3 The employment of a command system such as this, running counter to all previous usage, completely upset the organization of the headquarters before it was fully formed.

4 Last but not least, the crisis associated with this campaign brought out into the open all Hitler's deficiencies of character and military knowledge of which his leadership in the later stages of the war gave striking and disastrous proof.

To go into detail – on 12 December 1939 when the Russo-Finnish Winter War had just broken out, Grand Admiral Raeder warned Hitler of the danger for German strategy and war economy of a British

66

occupation of Norway (see point 1 above); it is clear that in this he was not merely exercising his undoubted right but was doing no more than his duty as Commander-in-Chief of the Navy.[2] Although he did not know it at the time, he and Winston Churchill had exactly the same idea; at precisely the same time the latter, who was First Lord of the Admiralty, was pressing for the occupation of the more important Norwegian ports, including Narvik and Bergen, with the object of ensuring that England was in command of the Norwegian coast line.[3] It would in fact been a serious dereliction of duty on Raeder's part if he had not made known his point of view, for it rested on sound grounds. It is the responsibility of the statesman to draw the conclusions from representations such as this; such at least is the generally recognized relationship between policy and strategy.

Hitler chose to solve the problem by military methods. The same day he discussed the question with Keitel and Jodl in the Reich Chancellery. From this emerged certain questions and certain studies to be undertaken by the OKW Operations Staff; they are thus described by Jodl in his diary: 'two alternative possibilities: what happens if we are called in; what do we do if we have to go in by force? OKW to undertake the necessary studies'.[4]

It might appear from this that Hitler felt that he had done all that was necessary as Supreme Commander when he directed the military organizations concerned to study the alternative bases of an operation presenting problems quite new for German strategy. The following additional note by Jodl, however, somewhat alters the picture: 'the ex-Minister for War to be associated with these studies'. This referred to Quisling who had appeared in Berlin without the authority of the legitimate Norwegian Government and in fact as in opposition to it. These sentences from Jodl's notes moreover carried a double meaning of considerable importance but perceptible only to those immediately involved. Hitler clearly thought of Quisling as the man by whom 'we might be called in' or as a valuable go-between in the case in which 'we have to go in by force'. It is of interest here to compare the following passage in Churchill's memorandum in support of his proposal for a British occupation of Norway: 'acting in the name of the Covenant and as virtual mandatories of the League and all it stands for, we have a right, and indeed are bound in duty, to abrogate for a space some of the conventions of the very laws we seek to consolidate and reaffirm'.[5]

Hitler was now irrevocably set upon this adventure. The original military reasons for the operation had lost their urgency with the rapid conclusion of the Russo-Finnish Winter War on 12 March 1940; it was now based solely upon a political viewpoint and the political will of the Dictator. The *Altmark* incident provided a further spur and his principal concern now became to find some obviously adequate pretext for the occupation of Norway. When the first news of the Russo-Finnish agreement arrived on 10 March 1940 Jodl wrote: 'the military situation is disquieting for if peace is concluded rapidly it will be difficult to find a good reason for undertaking this operation'. He put it even more clearly two days later: 'now that peace has been concluded between Finland and Russia, England has no political reason to go into Norway – but neither have we'.[6]

These events led me once again to quite different conclusions. Independently of the discussions in the Reich Chancellery and in fact without adequate information about them, I had prepared an 'appreciation of the situation' which I put to Jodl; in this I emphasized my opinion that occupation of Scandinavia was now no longer necessary. I based this upon the – to my mind convincing – reasoning that the forthcoming German offensive in the West would tie down all available British and French forces and that there was therefore no need to worry about British attempts on Norway in the foreseeable future.[7] Jodl's reasoning was exactly the opposite; his opinion was that the British would probably 'lay hands on Narvik at once' if Germany violated the neutrality of the Low Countries when the campaign in the West opened. He looked at the situation from a totally different basis of reasoning as is shown by the entry in his diary for 13 March: 'the Führer has not yet ordered Exercise Weser [the code name for the Norway operation]. He is still looking for a reason for it.'[8]

Hitler's own subsequent words and actions make quite clear what were the main reasons which decided him to adhere to the plans for the occupation of Denmark and Norway, the directive for which had meanwhile been issued on 1 March. The words were put into his mouth by Reichsleiter Rosenberg on the evening of 9 April, the first day of the operation: 'just as Bismarck's Reich was born in 1866, so will the Great German Reich be born from what is going on to-day'.[9] Such generalized expressions covered the possibility of gaining further elbow room for the prosecution of the naval and air war against England[10] and, looking further into the future, freeing German sea power from the narrow confines of the German Bight.

68

The Commander-in-Chief of the Navy had shown that he had sufficient influence within the headquarters to put across his pre-occupation over the possibility of British seizure of Scandinavia; later he tried, but without success, to counter the consequences of what he had done by stressing the advantages of keeping Norway neutral.[11] Similarly General von Falkenhorst tried to gain time for further 'diplomatic action' before military measures were taken, hoping in this way to avoid the use of force altogether. This was peremptorily refused by Hitler. In the same way Jodl snubbed officers occupying important lower grade posts just as he had snubbed me previously. The entry in his diary for 28 March reads: 'certain naval officers seem to be lukewarm about Exercise Weser and want a shot in the arm. Even von Falkenhorst's three immediate subordin-ates keep on bringing up points which are none of their business.'[12]

These words were redolent of Hitler's outlook and determination; they were characteristic of the 'spirit of the Reich Chancellery' which looked upon any weighing of pros and cons as pusillanimity and recognized only 'boldness'. Here was another example of that permanent fundamental failure of the headquarters – it thought it could command and exercise leadership down to the smallest details without keeping its finger on the pulse of the troops or their com-manders.

As everybody knows, the Allies also stuck to their decision to occupy Norway and on 7 April – again almost simultaneously with the German move forward – began to embark troops for the occupa-tion of Norwegian ports. It is not so generally recognized that the defensive and economic reasons which had originally been behind the German move, were rapidly overtaken by other considerations. On 24 May 1940 the British War Cabinet was forced by the over-whelming pressure of the German offensive in the West to recall the Allied troops from the Narvik area, the last but also the most impor-tant area of Norwegian soil they still held. The evacuation was com-pleted on 10 June 1940; yet although they were never attacked, Ger-man forces remained in full strength in Denmark and Norway right up to the Armistice of May 1945.

The second point of interest regarding the Norwegian campaign was the command organization. It was specially designed for the purpose and ran counter to all rules and all normal practice.

It seemed likely that this would be a combined operation requiring close co-operation by considerable forces of all three Services. At first sight this would seem to demand a unified Wehrmacht command and so at last provide some justification for the existence of the OKW Operations Staff. When he looked at the position more closely, however, General Jodl must have remembered that the weakness of his own staff during the Wehrmacht manœuvres in the autumn of 1937 had compelled OKW to confine itself to giving general directives and leave the laying on of the exercises both in general and in detail to the Army General Staff. The OKW staff had got no bigger meanwhile and, faced with a problem of real war, Jodl had to look round for a way out similar to that which he had used hardly two years before during the preparation of the manœuvres. With this in view and apparently convinced that the main burden of operations against Norway would fall on the Luftwaffe, his first inclination was to hand over the preparation and command of the Norwegian operation to the Air Staff, working on general directives from OKW. On 13 December Hitler had issued an order that 'a very small staff should examine methods of occupying Norway'; against all established practice Jodl passed this to the Senior Air Staff Officer in Section L, Captain Freiherr Speck von Sternburg. A few days later he discussed the 'Norwegian situation' with the Chief of Staff of the Luftwaffe, General Jeschonnek, the main subject of his discussion being 'how should the Norwegian question be handled in future'. It appears that when Jodl reported this conversation Hitler intervened at once and ordered that 'the Norwegian operation should be kept under our own hand'. The job therefore came back to the OKW Operations Staff.[13]

By the end of December a first project had been worked out in Section L and submitted to Hitler. This was passed somewhat later to the High Commands of the Services but apparently only unofficially. With only minor alterations this project repeated the previous proposal that a high-level staff for the further preparation of the operation should be set up under the Commander-in-Chief of the Luftwaffe. Hitler, always on the lookout for new organizations which would satisfy his thirst for power, seized upon this and agreed that there must be a special staff for the occupation of Norway, but rejected the idea that it should be subordinated to the Luftwaffe, demanding instead that the special staff should be incorporated in OKW itself.[14] Jodl had clearly intended to put the Luftwaffe in the lead but eventually Hitler refused it even this last crumb of comfort;

he refused to put a Luftwaffe officer at the head of the special staff and gave orders that the staff should be organized on a basis of equality between the three Services and consist of one qualified operations staff officer from each of them under command of the Chief of OKW. Göring apparently immediately protested but without success.[15]

The reasons behind Hitler's attitude emerged clearly from the initial sentences of the order of 27 January which read that the study of operations in the north will be carried out 'under my immediate and personal influence and in close co-ordination with the general conduct of the war'. As subsequent events proved, he meant by this nothing less than that he considered himself best qualified to command an unusual and particularly difficult operation of the type of Exercise Weser. In addition he obviously considered this the simplest method of nipping in the bud the aspirations of the Luftwaffe which Jodl had prematurely aroused. On this and other similar occasions he gave it as his opinion that the General Staff of the Luftwaffe and probably also its Commander-in-Chief, Göring himself, had insufficient training to prepare large-scale combined operations. Lastly he probably realized quicker than did Jodl that the main burden of Exercise Weser would fall not on the Luftwaffe but on the Navy. The naval staff was however organized purely for naval operations and could not have been given the task of the overall direction of a combined operation.

The first sign of Göring's rage and disappointment at the way in which 'his' Luftwaffe had been treated was the fact that, as Jodl laconically remarks, the 'Luftwaffe representative' did not appear on 5 February when the 'special staff' was assembled and briefed by Keitel.[16] So for the next few days there were only two officers, one from the Navy and one from the Army, who started work on this project. They worked in close contact with Section L and had offices next door. Apart, however, from the general considerations contained in the 'Study of Operations in the North' they had no basis on which to work. Scandinavia had never been studied by the German General Staff in the past. Even maps were unobtainable. Moreover it soon became clear that the 'special staff' formed no better basis or framework for an effective command organization than did the OKW Operations Staff itself.

The *Altmark* incident was a further incentive and Hitler, who had hesitated for so long, now began to lay great stress upon 'the preparation of the operation known as Exercise Weser'. As a result on 19 February Jodl reached the conclusion that rapid results could only be achieved by a properly organized headquarters provided with all the necessary resources for exercising command. The same day Hitler gave approval to Jodl's proposal that 'a fresh Commanding General, complete with staff, should be designated by the Army and charged with the further preparation and subsequently the command of the entire enterprise under the general direction of OKW'.[17]

As a result of this proposal of Jodl's a proper nucleus of the command organization for Exercise Weser was eventually set up. But there were still more extraordinary developments to come. At last after all this vacillation, the Army had once more become the central factor in this undertaking. OKW did not however turn to the Commander-in-Chief of the Army who, in view of the special nature of the operation, would undoubtedly have detailed at least an Army Group or Army headquarters for the job; instead they acted entirely on their own and detailed a Corps Headquarters, ie the lowest level command organization which could possibly have been considered. They can hardly have thought that the Army would have been unwilling to make a higher level headquarters available because of the forthcoming campaign in the West. It seems much more likely that Jodl and the Head of the Personnel Section saw in this an opportunity to present themselves as new-style officers on the Hitler model as opposed to the ordinary run of Army officers by proposing the *man* who in their view was most suitable for the job irrespective of his *rank*. OKH was merely told that 'the Führer wishes to speak to General von Falkenhorst since he is an expert on Finland'.[18] This form of words was used to conceal Hitler's real intentions. The facts are that Falkenhorst, who was Commander of XXI Corps, had been a Staff Officer during operations in the Baltic-Finnish area during the first World War.

Falkenhorst was summoned by Hitler the very next day and briefed. He and XXI Corps Headquarters, into which was incorporated the previous Special Staff, then set to work, still in close co-operation with Section L; this produced the extraordinary picture that the Supreme Commander relied for all matters concerning the participation of the Army in the Norwegian operation not upon the Army General Staff, but upon a Corps Headquarters and the latter under OKW was responsible for overall command of the operation! At the same time Keitel and Jodl went over the head of OKH and, working direct with the Commander of the Replacement Army, set to work to select the divisions which they considered best suited for Exercise Weser. This was the first occasion on which the Army Chief of Staff had learnt anything in detail about the plans for the occupation of Denmark and Norway; his notes on the subject end with the resigned comment: 'not a single word has passed between the Führer and the Commander-in-Chief of the Army on this subject. Get that on the record for the war historians'.[19]

The following was all that the Army received as justification for Hitler's unprecedented disregard of OKH: 'Headquarters XXI Corps is to be placed under OKW in order to avoid difficulties with the Luftwaffe'.[20] This was not very convincing and a few days later Göring's intervention showed that it meant nothing whatsoever; in fact it was only another method of expressing Hitler's determination to exert 'his direct and personal influence' on the forthcoming combined campaign and to earn the laurels of a victorious commander in the field which he so earnestly desired. The other simpler explanation, that Hitler did not wish to overload OKH with the Norwegian operation in view of the simultaneous preparations for the campaign in the West, does not hold water; it was only the Operations Section and the higher levels of OKH which were cut out of the chain of command; full use was made of the remaining Army Staff Sections, for instance Intelligence, Transport and Supply; the work load thrown on the latter was all the greater because they were now responsible to two masters. The command organization as set up for the Norwegian campaign may have appeared as an improvisation but it was the prototype for the so-called 'OKW Theatres of War' which were set up from time to time all through the later years of the war.

It is interesting to compare the disorder in the military sphere created by authoritarian leadership with the exemplary simplicity of the command organization adopted by the democracies for the great Anglo-Saxon landing operations in North Africa in November 1942 and in Normandy in June 1944. The salient features of this were as follows:

1 Agreement was reached between the Heads of State upon the nationality of the Supreme Commander and on the selection of the man best suited for the post (General Eisenhower); he was then given the highest military rank.

73

2 The Combined Chiefs of Staffs issued a short directive to the Supreme Commander.

3 All headquarters and formations detailed for the operation were subordinated to the Supreme Commander irrespective of nationality and Service. The Supreme Commander and his staff had sole responsibility for the preparation and conduct of the operation and for subsequent military government.[21]

The final point of interest in this campaign was the determination of Hitler and his staff to be directly responsible for command. Their capabilities were put to a severe test shortly after the issue of the basic 'Directive for Exercise Weser'. Falkenhorst and his Corps Headquarters had worked quickly and efficiently. Their plan was presented to Hitler verbally and agreed by him; Jodl thereupon drafted 'the directive' which Section L merely had to 'put in final form'. Jodl had clearly become so used to regarding the Norwegian operation as Hitler's personal business that he even omitted the usual procedure of gaining contact with the High Commands of the Services; he included in his directive details of the number and type of forces which the Army and Luftwaffe were to contribute and in addition laid down that the Luftwaffe units working with the Army should be for practical purposes under General von Falkenhorst.[22]

This broke all the rules. The following notes by those most intimately involved give the clearest picture of the consequences of this and of its related effects upon the relationship between Hitler and the Wehrmacht leaders.

1 March

HALDER: They did not keep their promise to get in touch with us before drawing up their requirements.

JODL: Violent protest from Commander-in-Chief Army over formations to be detached.

Discussion between myself and Jeschonnek. Reduction of requirements.

2 March

HALDER: Keitel wants good troops. von Brauchitsch points out that twenty per cent of our general reserve will be tied up in this operation.

JODL: Agreement with the Army. Göring is furious and gave the Chief of OKW a dressing down. Went to see the Führer at

74

1 pm. New requirements issued during the afternoon. Somewhat reduced after conversation with Army and Luftwaffe.

3 March

JODL: The Führer was very insistent on the necessity of rapid and violent action in Norway. Commander-in-Chief of the Luftwaffe protests against any subordination of Luftwaffe units to Headquarters XXI Corps.

4 March

JODL: All Luftwaffe units will be under XX Air Corps. This will get its orders from the Commander-in-Chief of the Luftwaffe in accordance with the requirements of XXI Corps. General Bodenschatz complains that the Field-Marshal [Göring] was not kept in the picture regarding Exercise Weser. No Luftwaffe officer was consulted beforehand. Subordination to XXI Corps is unacceptable. He is furious with General Keitel. I put him right.

5 March

JODL: High-level conference on Exercise Weser with the three Commanders-in-Chief. The Field-Marshal is furious at not being consulted earlier. He demands the floor and maintains that all preparatory work undertaken to date is useless. Result:

(a) Stronger forces to be employed in the Narvik area.

(b) The Navy to station warships in the ports.

(c) ...

(d) Six divisions detailed for Norway.

6 March

JODL: Preparatory measures seem now to be firm. The Führer has signed the directive which includes all alterations stemming from the 5 March conference. No further alterations will be accepted.

The following are the most striking points which emerge from the above; they may be taken as typical of the state of affairs in German Headquarters at the time:

1 The orders issued by OKW proved so inadequate that one of their directives was objected to by the recipients and had to be altered even though it had already been issued and signed by Hitler; this is of course contrary to all normal military practice, let alone to the rules of a 'Führer State'.

2 As a result of the special command organization adopted the Commander-in-Chief of the Army was pushed completely out

into the cold; for instance, he was not even summoned to attend Hitler's final conference on 2 April with the Commanders-in-Chief and General von Falkenhorst about Exercise Weser. Yet he raised no objections.[23] The Commander-in-Chief of the Luftwaffe on the other hand refused to give up command of any of the Air Force formations detailed to support the Army and refused to subordinate them even temporarily to an Army Corps Headquarters.[24] He contrived to get away with this.

3 The Luftwaffe was left a free hand regarding the size of the air forces to be detailed. On the other hand, in spite of numerous objections from OKH, the army forces employed were increased by a complete division and numerous individual units.[25]

4 The Navy made no pretence of trying to be in the lead; yet when Hitler demanded that warships should be stationed in Norwegian ports after the landing had been completed and the Navy objected, Hitler let this requirement drop.[26]

5 At several conferences at which a large number of people were present, Hitler hesitated to go against either Göring or Raeder. Later however, within his own restricted circle, he was apt to use strong terms and appear to insist upon his requirements being met.

These incidents during the preparatory period throw some doubt upon Hitler's qualities as a military commander. His deficiencies were however illustrated much more clearly during the campaign itself. On the evening of the first day he started with a lofty vision of the 'Great German Reich' but he entirely failed to realize that in any major operation there will be periods of crisis and these duly arrived. They produced a spectacle of pitiable weakness lasting more than a week. Jodl on the other hand rose to the occasion and was to a large extent responsible for the successful outcome of the campaign. The entries in his diary may be regarded as completely reliable evidence and, together with certain extracts from Halder's notes, give an intimate picture of what went on and a fair basis for forming a judgment.

14 April

JODL: Dietl is not being attacked but has become separated from the Northern Group.* Hitler became terribly agitated. Every detail must be ordered from here.

* General Dietl was in command of the Narvik group. This consisted primarily of one Mountain Infantry Regiment of 3 Mountain Division. What Jodl means here by 'Northern Group' is not clear.

HALDER: General von Brauchitsch returns from a meeting with the Führer. Result: it is not thought possible to hold Narvik. 'We have had bad luck' (Hitler's words).

15–16 April

JODL: The Navy is being criticized because the battle fleet has not been engaged[27] and because it has not been able to get the transports moving sooner. There is no justification for this – I (Jodl) opposed this energetically.

HALDER: Commander-in-Chief hears from Keitel that Narvik is to be evacuated. We cannot allow this – conversation with Jodl[28] – Jodl's reply: Narvik cannot be held. The Mountain units must be withdrawn to the mountains. It has not yet been decided whether we shall have to give up the whole Narvik area.

17 April

JODL: The Führer is again agitated and considers that the Dietl group must move south or be evacuated. I (Jodl) point out to him most emphatically that:

(a) A move south is impossible.

(b) We can only evacuate a limited proportion of the group, we shall lose a large number of aircraft and badly affect the morale of the Dietl group.

The group can hold out for a long time on the Swedish frontier. One must not give a situation up for lost until it is in fact lost.

15.30 hours. Further argument regarding the orders to be given to the Narvik group. Every unfavourable piece of information makes the Führer fear the worst. The Chief of L Section and the Army member of the Section produce an appreciation of the situation with which I am in full agreement.[29]

I show the appreciation to the Führer. It proves that we have nothing like enough long-range aircraft to be able to evacuate troops from Narvik. An instruction is issued on the lines that we (Jodl, Chief of L Section and Army member) wish. Concentrate, hold on and do not give up.

On Hitler's orders a professor who knows Norway is brought over from Innsbruck to give advice as to whether mountain troops can get from Narvik to Sauske. From my knowledge of climbing I am sure this cannot be done.

In the evening the Führer signs an order to Dietl 'to hold on as long as possible'.

18 April

JODL: The Führer is calm again. There is even a possibility that yesterday evening's order will be altered to lay more emphasis on holding and concentrating. A calmer day. A good thing for overwrought nerves.

HALDER: (a) Jodl calls: the Commander-in-Chief must speak to the Führer about Narvik.[30] Effects on the morale of the Army.

(b) The Führer's reply: 'Narvik cannot be held in the long run.' Yesterday the Führer wanted to evacuate troops from Narvik, though initially he had given up this idea.

19 April

JODL: New crisis.

Political action has failed. The Führer considers that force must now be used. Gauleiter Terboven must be sent in. Göring is working in the same direction. He is critical of the facts that insufficiently energetic action has been taken against the civilian population and that the Navy has not landed sufficient troops. The Air Force cannot do everything. The Chief of OKW stumps out of the room. We are once more facing complete chaos in the command system. Hitler insists on giving orders on every detail, any co-ordinated work by the existing military command set-up is impossible. Terboven arrives in the evening. The Führer briefs him alone after dinner. It is questionable whether we shall be able to restrict him to the activities of a civil Commissar as Section L proposes. Must speak to him personally.

20 April

JODL: The Führer's birthday. All excitements are over. Air Force reports have clearly put into the Führer's head the idea that the Norwegians will undertake large-scale partisan warfare and sabotage. I had already resisted this idea on 19 April. We must do nothing to cause the Norwegians to offer passive still less active resistance. That would simply be to play the game of the English.

21 April

JODL: On evening 20 April Keitel had a prolonged argument with Hitler in order to ensure that the directive to Terboven was so drafted that it took account of military requirements. The Führer wants to run a large ship (the *Bremen*) with personnel and material into Trondhjem. Commander-in-Chief Navy considers this completely impossible.

22 April

JODL: The Führer is increasingly agitated about the English landings at Andalsnes (Namsos). I point out to him the difficult position in which the English are; they have no serviceable port or airfield.

23 April

JODL: Agitation increasing. The forces in Narvik must be re-organized at once to make 3 Mountain Division battleworthy once more.

24 April

JODL: Situation seems better.

25 April

JODL: Optimism continues.

30 April

JODL: At 13.55 hours I was able to tell the Führer that communications had been established over land between Oslo and Trondhjem.[31] The Führer is beside himself with joy. I had to sit next to him at lunch.

As a result of the above any unbiased observer must admit that the success of the Norwegian campaign owed nothing to Hitler but had been won in spite of his amateurish interventions by the combined efforts of highly trained commanders and troops. In particular it should be noted that, if Hitler had had his way, Narvik, the real key point of the entire operation, would have been needlessly evacuated only a few days after it had been occupied and after the Navy had lost almost half its strength in heavy destroyers.

This had been the first attempt on the part of the Dictator to subordinate the organization for command and leadership of an operation in war to his own personal ambition and thirst for political prestige. The end result had been satisfactory thanks to intelligent co-operation at all levels within the Wehrmacht but this could not eradicate the impression of truly terrifying weakness of character on the part of the man who was at the head of the Reich. Jodl's diary is enough to produce a striking picture of agitation and lack of balance but I can add a personal impression from these critical days. It so happened that I had to see Jodl in the Reich Chancellery and there was Hitler hunched on a chair in a corner, unnoticed and staring in front of him, a picture of brooding gloom. He appeared to be waiting for some new piece of news which would save the situation and in order not to lose a moment intended to take it on the same telephone line as the Chief of his Operations Staff. I turned away in order not to have to look at so undignified a picture. I could not however help making a mental comparison with the great commanders of German history; they must have felt themselves destined to be leaders on the basis of their character, self-discipline and experience. The 'astonishment evoked by Moltke's imperturbable calm and self-assurance on the battlefields of Bohemia and France' is still a household word. The great historian who wrote these words ascribed Moltke's outlook and bearing more to 'complete clarity of mind than to an effort of will power'; in his view the real fundamental basis of Moltke's calm lay 'in the depths of his character in which a high degree of intelligence was blended with unshakable moral conviction'.[32]

What lay in the 'depths of Hitler's character' was something very different, as the Norwegian campaign had proved, if indeed any further proof were necessary. Some of the confusion of those days in the Reich Chancellery must of course be put down to the lack of organization of the headquarters, if anything consisting of so many scattered parts can be called a headquarters. At the height of the crisis General Jodl frequently intervened with considerable 'moral courage'; it must not be forgotten however that it was he who had earlier done his utmost to overcome all objections to Hitler's determination to take over the command himself and that he had had a decisive influence in the exclusion of OKH from the chain of command. It should therefore have been no surprise at least to Jodl that Hitler's ambition now burst all bounds and that he started to meddle even in tactical details – a warning of what his leadership was to be like in the future. In matters of detail the fact that the senior officers of OKW were located in the Reich Chancellery was another important factor; this made it only too easy for Hitler merely to go from one room to another and pester them continually with new questions and new requirements; they on the other hand persisted in their refusal to take their immediate subordinates in Section L into their confidence. The latter who were physically separate and therefore able to keep themselves entirely free from the pressures associated with the presence of Hitler, were able to make some contribution greater perhaps than at any later stage, by stiffening the resistance offered to Hitler by the Chief of the Operations Staff.

All these experiences led to no change either in the external or internal organization of the Field Headquarters which was now shortly to be constituted. As far as the organization and exercise of command at the highest level were concerned, the Norwegian campaign had been little short of a perilous enterprise but as a result of its successful outcome everyone was now ready to forget its disadvantages and dissensions and apparently, as was soon to become clear, to consider this system to be the normal rule. The most dangerous result was the effect on the position of Jodl; henceforth he 'had' to sit next to Hitler at meals and was to do so for more than two years to come; moreover he had given proof of character and thereby confirmed the confidence of the Supreme Commander in his military judgment; this was a position which laid on him great responsibilities and, to say the least, it was questionable whether this was right.

PART III

THE PERIOD OF OVERWHELMING MILITARY SUCCESS

May 1940 – December 1941

CHAPTER 1

The Curtain Rises

AT THE BEGINNING of May came the 'news of victory in Norway',[1] giving the green light for the opening of the offensive in the West. Jodl had proposed that the two operations should be 'interdependent both in timing and forces employed';[2] Hitler, however, decided that the new campaign should open 'after an interval of a few days' and of the two his views proved to be the sounder for a considerable proportion of the Air Force was still tied down in Norway into the early part of May.

The days immediately preceding the opening of the Western offensive were uneasy ones; meteorological reports, orders and counter-orders once more followed each other with ever-increasing rapidity. It was the staff of the Commander-in-Chief Air which 'made up' the weather and his air forces and parachute formations were more dependent on good weather than were other branches of the Wehrmacht; he was therefore primarily responsible for the continual postponements. There was still no Army representative present at the discussions on the subject in the Reich Chancellery, and the opinion of the Army was not even asked for. The Army 'merely' had to keep two million men continuously ready to move at twenty-four hours' notice. By 7 May Hitler had become 'very agitated at this continual postponement because of the danger of a leak'; the next day he stated that he was still 'very agitated' and was not prepared to wait longer. All the same he allowed Göring to extract one more final postponement from him 'against his better judgment – but not a day longer', to use his own words. This meant that Hitler had in fact finally given the order to go without waiting for the essential prerequisite of favourable weather, the cause of all these months of postponement; the Chief of OKW of course backed him up in his usual dutiful manner. But luck was with him. At 9 pm on 9 May, ie half an hour before the moment which the time-table

85

laid down as 'the final cut-off time for confirmation by the Führer of the order to attack', the Chief of Staff of the Luftwaffe was able to report that 'weather on 10 May will be good'.[3] This earned the Head of the Luftwaffe's Meteorological Service a gold watch.

Early on the morning of 10 May the different groups which were subsequently to constitute German Supreme Headquarters in the field, arrived in the Euskirchen area from various directions and at various times, some by rail and some by air. The 'Führer Special' with Hitler and the usual entourage had started the afternoon before from a small station near Berlin, proceeding north; it was to turn west only after dark. I and the key officers of Section L left about midnight from an airfield near Spandau in an aircraft of the OKW 'Communications' Squadron. The remaining officers, with the clerks, typists, draughtsmen and signals personnel followed in the section's special train. At the same time the Commander-in-Chief Army, with his Chief of Staff, moved from Zossen to the 'hunting lodge' near Hitler's headquarters; he had with him only a very reduced staff consisting of the Operations Section and Intelligence Section – Foreign Armies West, neither at full strength; the remaining sections of OKH were located in Giessen and Bad Godesberg.

By 6 am the 'field echelon' of Section L was assembled in a large farmhouse in the village of Rodert just above the town of Münstereifel; only a few hundred yards away the Army could be seen streaming west on every road and track; the early morning sky was black with our aircraft. Some simple but extremely practical alterations, hardly visible from outside, had been made to the farmhouse during the preceding weeks, and as a result it provided most adequate working and living accommodation for our fifteen officers and clerks, together with the thirty or forty ancillary personnel. To everybody's disgust, however, it was found that parts of the building were occupied by members of Hitler's personal entourage, including his bodyguard, who, as we soon discovered, adopted a camp regime which resulted in a permanent hubbub day and night. Spirits were probably all the higher there since rations were charged against Hitler's household and so were unlimited; this applied also to all officers included in HQ Area 1. By contrast the field echelon of Section L was rationed on the same scale as any other Army unit. There was no contact at any level between Section L and its neighbours in the farmhouse. They were never under the same roof again in any other Headquarters location. During the afternoon of this first day in 'Felsennest' Hitler and his following appeared in Section L offices. He spoke a word or two to the officers he happened more or less to know, but as far as the majority of the members of his 'working staff' were concerned, both officers and other ranks, he was just as distant as he always was later. Throughout all the subsequent years of war he never again entered HQ Area 2.

A path, which lost itself in low scrub one or two hundred yards further on, led up from the farmhouse through a high barbed-wire fence to Hitler's quarters, HQ Area 1. Here he lived with the usual entourage of generals and aides from the Chancellery in Berlin. The concrete fortifications which served as working and living accommodation covered a wide area. Even the mess was in a pill-box. The central point, however, was a small wooden hut, no more than 9–12 feet square, up on a hill, which was the map- and briefing-room and in which all the more important conferences took place. Here there was a fine view over the mountains and woods of the Eifel, a peaceful spring scene made all the more attractive by the close quarters and unaccustomed surroundings in which we were living.

After the war Jodl told the International Military Tribunal:

> The Führer's Headquarters was a cross between a cloister and a concentration camp. . . . Apart from many exalting moments our life in the Führer's Headquarters was in the long run a martyrdom for us soldiers; for it was not a military headquarters at all, it was a civilian one and we soldiers were guests there. It is not easy to be a guest anywhere for five and a half years.[4]

Although in May 1940 any such thoughts were far from Jodl's mind, he was to a large extent responsible for this situation since he had let himself drift into the 'working-staff' relationship with Hitler. His description is of course primarily applicable only to Hitler's immediate entourage; the officers of HQ Area 2, where only soldiers were to be seen, led a completely military existence. Jodl's words however give a strikingly apt description of the life and atmosphere of the entire headquarters. It was characteristic that in the inner circle the non-military were in the majority; it was also characteristic that most of them had decked themselves out in some sort of field-grey uniform, often with badges of rank of their own choosing. At this period the trouble was not so much an influx of leaders of the Party intent on maintaining a proper balance against the military in Hitler's immediate circle; they were still comparatively few in number. No, in the last analysis it was Hitler himself who dominated the headquarters and was responsible for its mental outlook, its outward appearance and its atmosphere.

Hitler made great play of his experience as a soldier in the first World War; he had exerted a considerable influence on the build-up of the new Wehrmacht; since the outbreak of war he had devoted almost all his thoughts and energies to military affairs. But none of this could compensate for the fact that he failed to arouse that team spirit which is the hallmark of a soldier's existence in all countries and which demands from every member of the Service, on pain of being blackballed from the military community, single-mindedness of thought and action, confidence and loyalty, frankness and self-sacrifice. Hitler made no effort to win the confidence of the officers around him. Mercilessly he eyed their strong points and their weaknesses and he was ever ready to fulfil the threat contained in his speech to senior commanders on 23 November 1939: 'I will stop at nothing and I shall crush anyone who opposes me'. He never spoke frankly and straightforwardly; he was continually trying to deceive, to put on an act, to achieve some prestige or propaganda purpose. The following is another characteristic passage from Jodl's evidence at Nüremberg, though it gives only a partial picture: 'he would speak in one way to the politicians or to the Party and in quite another to the Wehrmacht, in one way to the SS and in quite another to the Wehrmacht or the politicians'. This was the way he acted even in the highest Wehrmacht circles; he had only one object – to guard against any threat to his régime and to enhance his personal reputation and that of the Party.

It was all this, so foreign to the normal military way of life, to which Jodl was referring when he spoke of a 'civilian Headquarters'. This was what made the Army officers in HQ Area 2 look longingly at OKH nearby; although they were directly responsible to Hitler over these, they did not have to be in direct contact with him and were 'among their own sort'. There was a good indication of what most people thought and felt soon afterwards when the senior military aide had the idea of occasionally inviting an officer from Section L to meals at Hitler's table in the Area 1 pillbox. At first the more junior officers were enthusiastic about this but later a 'detail list' had to be made out for no one would go voluntarily. They much preferred to be with their own colleagues when off duty rather than listen to Hitler's 'table talk'.

The day's programme in Felsennest, and later in other places, was very like that in Berlin. At stated times during the day and night the Army, Navy and Air Force would report; at least twice in each twenty-four hours Section L had to collect these reports, sift them, add situation maps and send them by orderly to the Chief of the Operations Staff. General Jodl then prepared the 'briefing' which took place in the briefing-room with Hitler in the chair and at which, as before, only the members of the *maison militaire* were present. Separate reports on events of particular importance were either made to Hitler direct over the telephone by the Commanders-in-Chief of the Services or arrived with Section L and were immediately passed on to Jodl. These sometimes led to special meetings of the inner circle which took place in the briefing-room amidst constant comings and goings.

An example of the extraordinary way in which business was conducted was the procedure for reporting and discussing events at the front. Between the campaigns in Poland and Norway the habit had grown up of trying to run the battle in detail from the headquarters and the system had been tried out on a small scale in Norway. This dangerous game now continued, in spite of all Halder's warnings and in spite of the facts that we were now faced with a formidable enemy and were dealing with a rapidly changing situation. Diffuse discussion led to opinions, opinions to decisions and decisions to written directives or even direct intervention in dispositions already ordered by some military headquarters; although OKH was within a stone's throw, this was generally done without any previous reference to them. The best the Army leaders could expect was occasionally to be summoned to a briefing for some special reason but, just as in the preparatory period, they then found themselves faced with preconceived ideas which only tiresome and time-wasting argument could alter. Keitel's description of this period is as follows:[5]

I was on the road literally every other day, mostly in the area of von Rundstedt's Army Group. His Chief of Staff, General von Sodenstern, was an old friend of mine and I could talk to him quite openly about everything, even the Führer's special requirements. I did not have to wonder whether he would report to OKH

(Halder) about 'interference' by Supreme Headquarters, which would have made me unpopular all over again.

There was therefore very soon an atmosphere of tension between these two neighbouring high-level headquarters. But on the side of OKW stood Hitler, dominating everything, impatient and suspicious; he had no idea of time and space and refused to wait and let things develop; at the decisive moment, as in the case of Narvik, he would take fright at the boldness of his own decisions and then abdicate his authority and allow the situation to develop uncontrolled. Close at his side stood Keitel who, as always considered his sole duty to be to support Hitler, at the same time doing all he could to smooth things down in all directions and where possible eliminate any obstacles to Hitler's wishes. Jodl's influence was even greater. He had apparently forgotten all the lessons of the Norwegian campaign and he now seemed determined to ensure that the 'Führer's genius' should win the day against the 'indiscipline of the generals'; he did not appear to realize that the 'pusillanimity' which he had previously ascribed to the General Staff had now become Hitler's sole prerogative. The bitterness of the disagreements stands out clearly from the entries in his diary.[6] Lastly the busy little aides came to the fore once more, acting as liaison officers to the higher level operational headquarters and merely passing on Hitler's views and decisions without the smallest regard for the wider issues.

Turning now to OKH, the Commander-in-Chief, Colonel-General von Brauchitsch, was on the move by air or road almost every day, doing his utmost to maintain personal contact with the troops; they after all are the most decisive and important factor for any military commander, whether in a headquarters or at unit level – far more important than all plans and orders. His personal touch with events did not however seem to give him the assurance necessary to get his point of view across in face of Hitler, nor did he seem able to assert his undoubted right that the advice listened to should be his rather than that of OKW. Even Halder did not put up a fight about this. He was complete master of his job as Chief of Staff and he had around him a host of staff officers all trained in the same mould, thinking on the same lines and knit together by bonds of mutual confidence; he must have felt that, if he waited long enough, the built-in superiority of this command organization would ultimately prove itself. In fact he excelled himself on numerous occasions during this campaign when Hitler's nerve failed. His diary testifies to his own achievements and those of his staff and is a worthy memorial of this great campaign which will outlast our times.

In the background was Göring, always on the watch. His liaison officer had general's rank and kept him continuously up to date with the changing currents of opinion in the headquarters. As Commander-in-Chief Air and Crown Prince of National-Socialism he was determined to keep a check on any military glory which the 'reactionary' Army might gain in the eyes of the people. His train was stationed not far away and invariably at the critical moment his voice was to be heard on the telephone or his formidable person seen entering the Headquarters. As before there were generally no witnesses at his meetings with Hitler. Their outcome, however, left no doubt that he remained 'the Führer's most trusted follower', at any rate in so far as relations with OKH were concerned.[7] In fairness, however, it should be recorded that Göring was very conscious of his position as a military man, and later on in the war frequently intervened successfully on behalf of individual Army officers whom Hitler had condemned to death or ignominious punishment for some trivial reason.

This interplay and manœuvring between the 'Great' left Section L officers little freedom of action. They did not attend Hitler's briefings; even more frequently than the Army leaders therefore they found themselves faced with ready-made decisions; in general there was little they could do to exert any significant influence upon these decisions, except when, as in the case of Dunkirk, indignation rose so high that it broke all bounds. In other less pressing situations there were still on occasions limited possibilities of 'interpretation', designed either to tone down the contents and form of an order issuing from the headquarters, or to adapt it more closely to the actual situation.

The mainspring and basis for this unobtrusive activity on the part of myself and the Army officers of Section L was the fact that on our level we maintained personal contact with the Army Staff and were on terms of confidence with them;[8] we also visited the front whenever possible. Even on these occasions, however, we had little freedom of action for except when the aides were used, Hitler's orders and wishes were passed on by no less a person than the Chief of OKW.

The officers of Section L generally had no specific task when they travelled; all they could do therefore was to look up their friends or visit units without being able to act as 'contact men' for the Headquarters. Moreover Jodl showed remarkably little interest in any impressions brought back from these trips. For instance on the day Paris was captured, thinking back to the first World War, and overwhelmed by the historical significance of the event, I suddenly decided to take off in a *Storch* with another officer in a second one and landed in the Place de la Concorde, where not a soul was to be seen; I then watched a whole division march into the city. Yet when I got back to the Headquarters, not one of my superior officers took the smallest interest in what I had seen. Neither Hitler nor Jodl looked with favour on senior officers of OKW maintaining contact with the Army staff or visiting the front; they apparently feared that each side might exert some evil influence on the other – a point of view which would never even enter the head of any normally-thinking soldier. This and many other similar side lights only became known after the war.

In view of all this it will hardly be surprising if the picture of life in Supreme Headquarters, as it will be presented in the following chapters, seems to be dominated by disagreements and tensions between the senior officers of OKW and OKH. There were deep-rooted antagonisms which even in the 'period of overwhelming military success' proved more compelling than any sense of solidarity to which these successes may temporarily have given rise. Often enough the successes themselves led to fresh tensions because, whether looked at from the military or political point of view, under Hitler's leadership they were nothing but 'lost victories'.

CHAPTER 2

The Campaign in the West

As EARLY AS 14 May, only four days after the start of the campaign, Hitler issued *Directive no. 11* giving his initial general instructions for the subsequent phases of operations. Its contents were already partly known and had been partly overtaken by events; it referred, for instance, to the Dutch Army 'the resistance of which must be rapidly broken'; in fact, the Dutch capitulated that very day. To judge from this, the true purpose of the directive was to make it crystal clear to OKH that the Supreme Commander did not intend to act as he had in Poland but was now determined to direct operations himself. There is a pertinent entry in Jodl's diary which shows what was the true intention behind this initial instruction; in fact, Supreme Headquarters now proposed to trespass upon the responsibility of the Army to the extent of giving actual *orders*. Thanks however to the twist which Section L was able to give the directive at the drafting stage, on the surface it followed the general lines of its predecessors and consisted of an 'indication of objectives'. Jodl's diary of 14 May contains merely the short terse sentence: 'issue of Directive no. 11 ordering the concentration of all armoured and motorized formations under Fourth Army'; in its final form as drafted by Section L, the directive gives the pre-requisite for success as 'a thrust in all possible strength north of the Aisne and in a north-westerly direction'; this illustrates clearly the difference between an order and a directive.

The Chief of Staff of the Army attached so little importance to this directive that he gave it only a passing reference in his notes. The first comparatively minor upheavals in the headquarters however took place when it became clear that considerable time would be required for the resulting lateral movements; these involved the transfer of a number of armoured and motorized formations from Belgium to the left flank which was to carry out the attack. I myself saw Hitler on the end of a field telephone, struggling to make himself understood and hauling the Commander-in-Chief of Sixth Army, General von Reichenau, over the coals because he was supposed to have been dilatory in releasing one of the armoured corps. Jodl notes on 16 May: 'the Führer is pressing hard for the transfer of all armoured and motorized formations from Army Group B to Army Group A'. Keitel flew straightaway to the headquarters of Army Group B to drum home Hitler's orders but the time required and the difficulties involved in these movements were considerable; Halder's notes of the same date will make this clear even to the non-military reader; he wrote: 'what we now have to do is to concentrate forces on either flank of the breakthrough; this means creating a corridor through Sixth Army area to the right flank and through Sixteenth Army area to the left flank'. A few hours later he added that the Armoured Corps detailed by Hitler should have been left to fight in its previous area in order fully to exploit the success already gained.

The next day there was an incident of another sort. Probably as a result of a long conversation with Göring the previous evening, Hitler suddenly cancelled all previously prepared orders for the institution of military government in the Netherlands. He disregarded completely the fact that this area was nothing like pacified and was still practically in the operations zone and, for purely Party and political purposes, ordered the installation of civil government on the lines of that in Poland and Norway. Section L immediately protested to the Chief of OKW against this disregard of military requirements but without success. The final sentences in Halder's diary of 17 May on hearing of this are no mere record of his impressions of this particular incident; he said: 'their behaviour in this question of military government in Holland is further proof of the complete insincerity of Supreme Headquarters in its dealings with OKH'.

This was the atmosphere when the first *serious* collision between the two occurred. The occasion was nothing less than the central feature of the entire operation, the most rapid possible breakthrough to the coast. The main body of the German armoured formations had crossed the Meuse and was pressing on westwards uninterruptedly and faster than anybody had expected; at this juncture the points of view of Supreme Headquarters and OKH diverged completely. On 16 May Halder had hardly been able to conceal his pride when he wrote: 'the breakthrough is developing on almost classical lines.... Counter-attacks by enemy armour have been smashed. The distances covered by the infantry are outstanding.' He was working on reliable information and was quite clear in his mind that the French forces moving up from the south were 'too weak at present to attack'; his only thought therefore was to continue the rapid armoured advance as vigorously as possible. In his view the formations following in echelon could provide completely adequate security for the southern flank. The next morning, after considering the situation again, he concluded that 'we can secure this front later, using the follow-up forces'. Hitler thought quite differently. Although he had played a considerable part in the bold conception of the armoured operation, he now became obsessed with the protection of the flank. He clung to the idea of a 'pearl necklace' of infantry divisions which, although they had to march and had horse transport, he insisted must be in position before the armoured attack could proceed. At mid-day on 17 May he told the Commander-in-Chief of the Army that 'he considered the principal danger to be from the south' (Halder merely notes in his diary: 'I can see no danger whatsoever at the moment') and hurried off himself that same afternoon by road to Bastogne to emphasize his preoccupations to the Commander-in-Chief of Army Group A, Field-Marshal von Rundstedt. There he said that under no circumstances must there be any form of setback at this moment since that would be a dangerous morale-raiser for the enemy. At the moment decision depended not so much on a rapid thrust to the Channel as on the ability to secure as quickly as possible an absolutely sound *defence* on the Aisne and later on the Somme, even if it involved temporary delay of the advance to the west.[1]

By the evening of 17 May, therefore, Halder had become worried; he writes: 'A most unfortunate day. The Führer is terribly nervous. He is frightened by his own success, is unwilling to take any risks and is trying to hold us back.' Once more Halder examined the situation afresh the following morning and once more came to the conclusion that there was only one solution – to carry on the operation 'without the smallest delay; every hour is precious'. A little later, at the unusually early hour (for HQ Area 1) of 10 am, he found himself involved with Brauchitsch in a 'most unpleasant argument' with Hitler. Jodl notes: 'it has been a high-tension day. OKH has not carried out the instruction to build up the southern flank as rapidly as possible. The Army Commander-in-Chief and General Halder were summoned at once and given the most explicit orders to take the necessary measures'. Without even waiting for OKH to issue the orders, Keitel once more hurried off by air to Rundstedt's head-quarters to impress upon his Chief of Staff the necessity of carrying out Hitler's instructions at once. Jodl, clearly unwilling to be left out of things, took it upon himself to issue a supplementary order, instructing '1 Mountain Division and the rear elements of Fourth Army to turn south' – an unpardonable but typical interference in army business.[2] Halder returned to the hunting lodge furious; still in the heat of the moment, he wrote:

> they have a completely different conception in the Führer's head-quarters; the Führer is full of an incomprehensible fear about the southern flank. He rages and shouts that we are going about it the right way to ruin the entire operation and are running the risk of defeat. He entirely refuses to carry on with the operation west-wards.[3]

By late afternoon, however, all this had once more been overtaken by events. In addition to the new *Directive no. 12*, an 'official record' setting out the results of the morning's discussion was sent to OKH, further to underline the determination of the Supreme Commander – a most unusual procedure which had never been employed before. Yet at 6 pm the same day Hitler was talked round by Halder and now gave permission for the advance to continue. The Army Chief of Staff acknowledged this result with the words 'so the right thing is going to happen after all', but he added that it was happening 'amid general irritation and in a form which would make it look as if it was the work of OKW'.[3] Events had moved so fast that we in Section L only heard of the incident after it was all over.

Hitler's complete lack of balance is well illustrated by Jodl's diary of the next few days; he was determined to retain the power he had arrogated to himself but, having no depth of knowledge or experience, his moods and emotions swayed him from one extreme to the other and the diary registers them like a thermometer. For instance, on 19 May there was 'great concern' in OKW about Franco-British armoured attacks from the north, although Halder considered that they fitted in exactly with his concept of the operations and he 'welcomed them'; the result was that these two high-level headquarters passed on completely contradictory demands for air support. On the evening of 20 May, by which time, only ten days after the opening of the campaign, the mouth of the Somme had been reached at Abbe-ville and several enemy armies to the north were facing encirclement, there was a scene of rejoicing in 'Felsennest' unusual for a military headquarters. Jodl describes it as follows: 'the Führer is beside himself with joy. He pays high tribute to the German Army and its leaders.' On the evening of 21 May, Hitler is again 'somewhat uneasy because the infantry divisions are not pushing forward fast enough'. Jodl himself observed that 'he remained in the map-room up to 1.30 am'.[4]

The next day saw the beginning of the events which led to the drama of Dunkirk. Daily, even hourly, Hitler was interfering in the conduct of operations, thus giving the lie to his solemn 'tribute' and showing that he had no confidence in the leadership of the army. The influence he exerted at this moment was decisive for the outcome of the campaign, perhaps even for that of the entire war and it was not to the benefit of Germany. The course of events is well known and already belongs to history but one or two sidelights from my personal experiences in the headquarters may round off the picture.

Once more there were the usual contestants in the struggle: on one side Hitler, with Keitel and Jodl and above all Göring; on the other, Brauchitsch and Halder fully supported by the army officers of Section L. Once more Hitler and his supporters thought that they were the fount of all knowledge and went ruthlessly into action to impose their point of view and their will upon OKH. On 25 May, after numerous 'unpleasant discussions', Halder was finally forced to recognize that the decision was unalterable, saying: 'the mobile forces on the left flank who have no enemy in front of them, are to be halted on the express wish of the Führer'. The next day he summed up the whole miserable situation in the following bitter, sarcastic sentences: 'on the orders of Supreme Headquarters, the armoured and motorized formations are now rooted to the spot on high ground between Bethune and St Omer and are not allowed to attack although they are in a position to take the enemy in rear'. Meanwhile, Army Group B, which consisted entirely of infantry divisions, was 'moving up through Belgium so that it can run up against an enemy who has withdrawn with caution and is still full of fight; it will therefore be permitted to make some slow and costly progress'.[5] Meanwhile, the enemy had made rapid preparations to evacuate the forces we had surrounded and get them across the Channel during the next few days.

Just like Halder and those around him, the army officers of Section L were flabbergasted by Hitler's orders when they heard of them – which they did, curiously enough, only through OKH. They seemed entirely incomprehensible. Without a moment's hesitation, I and Lossberg set off on the path 'up there' in order, as a first step, to get some idea of the situation. Jodl obviously did not want to see us and did not appear entirely convinced himself; he explained that he, Keitel and Hitler had all learned enough about the marshy plain of Flanders in the first World War to know that armour could not be employed there. Tanks would be confined to the narrow roads and shot up one after the other, and therefore in view of the losses they had sustained already, would not be available for the second phase of the offensive in France. What had still to be done in Flanders could confidently be left to the Luftwaffe. Göring had given Hitler an assurance that his air forces were perfectly capable of completing the encirclement of the enemy on the seaward side. Apparently what had happened was this: late in the afternoon of 23 May, Göring was sitting at a heavy oak table beside his train with his Chief of Staff (General Jeschonnek) and his Chief Signals Officer, when the news arrived that the enemy in Flanders was almost surrounded. Göring reacted in a flash. Banging his great fist on the table, he shouted: 'this is a wonderful opportunity for the Luftwaffe. I must speak to the Führer at once. Get me on.' In the telephone conversation which followed, he used every sort of language to persuade Hitler that this was a unique opportunity for his air force. If the Führer would give the order that this was an operation to be left to the Luftwaffe alone, he would give an unconditional assurance that he would annihilate the remnants of the enemy; all he wanted he said was a free run; in other words, the tanks must be withdrawn sufficiently far from the western side of the pocket to ensure that they were not in danger from our own bombing. Hitler was as quick as Göring to approve this plan without further consideration. Jeschonnek and Jodl rapidly fixed the details, including the withdrawal of certain armoured units and the exact timing for the start of the air attack.[6]

This being the state of affairs, it soon became clear that it was entirely useless for me to emphasize that I had spent many holidays on the Belgian coast in the years before the war and therefore had personal knowledge of the fact that the terrain in Flanders had altered considerably since 1918. I expressed doubts as to the effectiveness of the Luftwaffe at night or in bad weather but this produced no reaction either. The memory of this conversation still rankles but in the light of the results of subsequent research, two points from it stand out as remarkable: Jodl made not a single reference to the belief current in many quarters that Field-Marshal von Rundstedt was in agreement with Hitler's orders; yet he must have known that in view of the enormous respect in which Rundstedt was held by all staff officers at the time, there could have been no better argument to overcome the opposition of his subordinates; equally he never even hinted at political motives which might lead Hitler to wish to let the British Expeditionary Force go.[7] As far as Rundstedt's views are concerned, there is nothing on the subject in Halder's diary; on the contrary, on the 26 May he notes: 'Rundstedt too is clearly not hanging on any longer and has gone forward to Hoth and Kleist in order to get things clear for the further advance of the mobile formations.' This makes it clear that although in some respects the views held and orders given by Field-Marshal von Rundstedt and his staff – to say nothing of OKH – happened to coincide with those of Hitler, their objects were entirely different. Instead, everything points to the fact that Rundstedt had merely temporarily halted the armoured formations to let them close up and reorganize. OKH would certainly have raised no objection to this but Hitler seized on it as an excuse to interrupt the course of operations at the decisive moment. In fact, Field-Marshal von Rundstedt stated after the war that the armour was held back 'solely and exclusively on an explicit order from Hitler who feared that it would not be in sufficient strength for the second phase of the campaign; that his (Rundstedt's) headquarters objected, pointing out that it was more important to bring the first phase of the campaign to a successful conclusion; finally, that when he visited the headquarters later, Hitler stated that he had hoped to come to some rapid agreement with England if he let the British Expeditionary Force escape.[8]

The armour was eventually allowed to go again early in the afternoon of 26 May but, as is well-known, this was too late to prevent the evacuation of the bulk of the British and French forces. The action of the Luftwaffe merely made this operation somewhat more difficult.

To complete the picture of this period, there follow one or two impressions of subsequent phases of the western campaign; they are typical of the atmosphere and methods of the headquarters.

There was no consistency in Hitler's attitude to his Italian allies but it was probably on military grounds alone that, shortly after the mouth of the Somme had been reached on 20 May, he abandoned the extraordinary plan for the employment of a number of Italian divisions north of the Alps.[9] On the other hand, when a note from Mussolini, dated 30 May, arrived, announcing that Italy proposed to enter the war on 5 June, to the fury of the Italian dictator Hitler replied that it would be better to wait for a few days – an attitude hardly compatible with the political aims of the Axis. The reason given was that Italy's entry might have an adverse effect upon the second phase of German operations in Central France, scheduled to begin about the same time.[10] This looked a bit thin anyway and must in fact be regarded as highly suspect, for at about this time Halder notes in his diary that the Commander-in-Chief of the Army had been informed that Italy would only enter the war *some time in the next few weeks.*[11] At the same time, Mussolini once more urged that there should be German-Italian staff talks, but Hitler replied evasively. It almost begins to look from all this as if he was carried away by the unexpectedly sweeping victory gained by the Wehrmacht and now did not want to be bothered with an ally or to have to share with him the fruits of victory and peace. OKW was able to find out sometimes more, sometimes less, about Hitler's ostensible or secret intentions; one fact emerged however, even more clearly than before from all this – there could no longer be any question of preparing a combined war plan or even an operation requiring co-operation by the two allies.

When Italy entered the war, therefore, on 10 June, 'parallel strategy' was the order of the day; there was no combined command or organization; there was not even the outline of an agreement on plans and objectives.[12]

The second phase of operations in France opened on 5 June. It had hardly begun before a new fundamental difference of opinion arose between Hitler and the Army chiefs. Halder followed the well-tried principles of the General staff and described the immediate objectives as follows: 'the object of our operations must be the destruction of the *remaining enemy forces*'. The next day, however, the Commander-in-Chief of the Army, on his return from a meeting with Hitler, summed up the latter's point of view as follows: 'he wants first to secure *the Lorraine iron ore basin* so as to deprive France of her armaments industry'.[13] As it turned out, our victory was so complete that both Halder's and Hitler's objects were attained simultaneously;

but Hitler could never subsequently be convinced that 'the achievement and – most important of all – the retention of a territorial
objective presupposes the defeat of the enemy's armed forces' and
that 'so long as this military issue is undecided ... the attainment of
territorial aims in the form of economically valuable areas remains
problematical and their long-term retention a sheer impossibility'.[14]
Once again the Commander-in-Chief of the Army, his Chief of Staff
and senior commanders received no support from any quarter during
this argument; Jodl said nothing, Keitel and Göring agreed with
Hitler, the latter probably because he was technical Director of the
Four Year Plan.

The headquarters' stay in 'Felsennest' ended on 3 June. Before
leaving Hitler ordered that the entire area should be preserved as a
'national monument'; every room was to be kept unchanged, every
name-plate was to remain upon its door. I and my companions had
certain qualms about this move to turn the first location of the headquarters into a national memorial. Could we be all that sure that the
part played by Hitler and his military staff in the great victory in
France merited it? The operation had in fact been the brain-child of
General von Manstein, but as no more than a Corps Commander he
had, as he himself said, 'in effect been fated to be little more than an
onlooker for most of the first phase of the campaign in the West'.[15]
Hitler's preservation order did not cover the O K H 'hunting lodge',
although they had in fact been the architects of the victory.

An army of OT workers* was busy on the new headquarters' site
in the small village of Bruly de Pêche in southern Belgium. When the
main body of Section L officers arrived by air, the last touches were
still being put to the bunker constructed for Hitler himself; the
garden was being laid out and gravel paths put down; the 'holy of
holies' even included a little fountain. The village had been cleared
of its inhabitants and when Hitler arrived two hours later it was like a
morgue. The Third Reich was fond of 'up to the minute programmes' and here, in war-time, a considerable task, for which only
eight days were available, had been completed on the dot. The map-
room was in the local school, Section L offices were in wooden huts
but living accommodation was in a country house nearby, since the

---

* OT stands for 'Todt Organization' so named after its first director, Dr Todt.
This was a semi-official organization of the Hitler period charged with major construction work such as the Autobahn, the Siegfried Line, etc. It was similarly employed during the war.

village itself was occupied by Hitler's immediate entourage. OKH was located some miles away in the neighbourhood of Chimay.

At some time during the few days before the campaign ended, I myself witnessed a remarkable conversation between Hitler and Göring which took place in the open in the village square. They were discussing the British air attacks on the residential areas of certain German cities, which had just begun to have some effect. Göring was talking big on the lines of his previous warnings to the enemy against such adventures; he was not prepared to tolerate this any longer and wanted to 'give them back ten bombs for every one of theirs'. Without hesitating for a second, Hitler expressly forbade anything of the sort. He said he thought it quite possible that the British Government was so shaken by Dunkirk that it had temporarily lost its head, alternatively that the reason for the attacks on the civil population was that the British bombers had inaccurate bomb sights and were flown by untrained crews. In any case he thought we should wait for a time before taking counter measures. This was the sort of attitude which the Reich had adopted in the international negotiations during the thirties and which governed the orders issued before the beginning of the great air offensive against England. As always in matters concerning the Air Force, OKW was merely a spectator of this encounter between Hitler and Göring and took no part in the argument.

In the middle of June, the staff found itself suddenly faced with a task for which it was totally unprepared, the drafting of the Armistice Agreement with France. On 17 June, as soon as it was known that the French had asked for an armistice, Hitler set off for Munich for a meeting with Mussolini, leaving no instructions behind him. We were assailed with suggestions from all sides but came to the conclusion that we could find no better basis than the terms laid down by the Allies at Compiègne in November 1918. The picture changed when Hitler returned on 19 June; he laid down as a principle that the utmost caution should be used; he had already impressed this on the Italians in Munich. Nothing must be included which would jeopardize the cessation of hostilities and therefore no demands should be made other than those essential to ensure that France could not resume hostilities. He let it quietly be known that as a result his demands in the final peace treaty would be that much higher. As a result of this policy and because of the haste in which the agreement was prepared, there was an omission which was later to prove disastrous and which ran counter to Italian wishes – adequate security precautions were not included in regard to French North Africa.

After the great day of 21 June[16] at Compiègne where the French negotiators showed much dignity, the headquarters was scattered to the winds. Hitler went off to visit first World War battlefields in France with two old comrades from his company of that time. Early in the morning of one of these splendid summer days, without telling anybody, he got an expert to take him on a tour of the great buildings and other architectural beauties of Paris. On the other hand, although the plans for it were well advanced, he gave up the idea of holding a large-scale parade to symbolize the fact that the French capital was now to be occupied for the remainder of the war; Göring would not take responsibility for defence against air attack, a piece of writing on the wall of which those who thought at all in those intoxicating days of victory took due note. Some of the officers of Section L availed themselves of the first opportunity to visit the ruins and wrecks in the Dunkirk area.

OKH was now allowed by Hitler to go where it liked and it moved to Fontainebleau. From 25 June onwards the scattered groups of Supreme Headquarters gradually collected together again in the northern Black Forest area in one of the groups of fortifications prepared before the outbreak of war and named 'Tannenberg'. Hitler had decided on a short stay here before going back to Berlin, primarily so that he could visit the great forts of the French Maginot line. The members of Section L lived and worked in a near-by hotel on the Black Forest highway. All visitors had of course previously been barred from the hotel and we received a special instruction from Hitler's household to compensate the proprietor for the loss thus inflicted on him by making the fullest possible use of his cellar. This we did.

CHAPTER 3

Transition from West to East

PAST DEAD CENTRE

The bustle of the Armistice negotiations with France was soon over and the OKW Operations Staff officers found themselves once more in a vacuum which, as the days went by, seemed to them less and less reconcilable with their ideas of what work in a forward planning staff should be. We knew of course, that the 'siege' of the British Isles was in progress; in the middle of June we had ourselves drafted orders reducing the strength of the Army to 120 divisions in order that the forces and resources thus released might be made available to the other two Services for the struggle against England, now the one remaining enemy.[1]

This question of the reduction of the Army merits a short digression. The order included a note to the effect that the paragraphs dealing with the armoured and motorized divisions of the Army did not apply to Waffen-SS formations. This was a development to which General Jodl had already drawn attention in his diary on 25 May 1940, as follows: 'the plan for an unlimited expansion of the SS is disturbing'. When I happened to see Halder alone about the middle of June he remarked sarcastically that I had better start looking round for another job since the Army would be abolished any minute. During the winter 1939–40, Hitler had let fall a chance, but undoubtedly intentional, remark to the effect that he only intended to make use of the Waffen-SS as an 'Armed State Police'; I included this in an official instruction but was immediately summoned by Keitel and told to withdraw it. In October 1940, the 'Reichsführer SS [Himmler] once more pressed for a considerable increase in the strength of the 'Leibstandarte Adolf Hitler'. Section L thereupon made a detailed proposal to Jodl with the object of clarifying the relationship between the Wehrmacht and the Waffen-SS and preventing the build-up of a military organization not under

command of OKW. The salient points of our memorandum were
as follows:

1 Confirmation of the basic order which Hitler himself had given
  that the Waffen-SS was a political organization of the National-
  Socialist Party intended for internal tasks of a police nature.
2 Confirmation of the fact already laid down by law that personnel replacement and equipment were the prerogatives solely
  of OKW.
3 Waffen-SS units temporarily incorporated in the Army to retain
  their military status only so long as they were so incorporated.
4 Those parts of the SS organization which did not belong to the
  Waffen-SS to have no military powers of command and not to
  have the right to wear military badges of rank or field-grey
  uniform.

This memorandum which had a suitable covering letter addressed to
the 'Reichsführer SS' was never heard of again.[2]

To return to the main theme. We were doubtful whether measures
such as these would of themselves bring us early victory and peace, in
view of the weakness of the Navy and the still limited striking power
of the Luftwaffe which Dunkirk had just proved. It seemed to us
therefore, that here was perhaps the unique opportunity for the
OKW Operations Staff to emerge from its subordinate position as a
'working staff', to cease simply hanging upon Hitler's every word
and wish, and instead to come out strongly with some original thinking on future strategy. In this situation when the end seemed almost
in sight, we could not believe that it was right to leave the Army, the
most effective and well-tried weapon at the disposal of the Wehrmacht, lying completely idle.

But where to turn, where to strike in order to reach a decision?
Apart from the isolated outpost of Gibraltar there was no enemy on
the continent of Europe. North Africa was considered to belong to
the Mediterranean littoral and therefore to be the preserve of our
Italian ally; in any case the general view was that now that the
French and British armies had been completely defeated, there was
nothing to do there which could not be done by the Italians. The
objective which offered the greatest possibilities, the real solution,
lay much closer home; a landing in England! The question had been
raised some weeks before, during the Dunkirk period, in a discussion
between Section L officers round the fireplace in the farmhouse at

Rodert. We had discussed whether it would not be better to drive straight across the Channel on the heels of the English and leave the rest of France to look after itself for the moment. The idea had merely been raised in the enthusiasm of the moment and dropped just as quickly. Now, however, it raised its head once more and this time it could not be pushed aside; with it came the thought that it was perhaps a serious omission not to have examined the problem long before this.[3]

Armed with one or two half-prepared plans, I took the first opportunity of walking the few hundred yards from our Black Forest hotel to HQ Area 1 group of forts. There I got a most lukewarm reception from Jodl. He never liked being bothered by suggestions from his staff if they diverged in any way from the set course of his strategy, but in this case he appeared to be very much in two minds. It seems probable that he himself thought on the same lines as we did, but did not want to let out the fact that Grand Admiral Raeder had brought up this subject only shortly before, that Hitler had shown little interest in it and in fact had pushed it aside without further consideration.[4] Jodl's unenthusiastic attitude seemed so incomprehensible to me that on the way back I went to see the Foreign Ministry Representative to the Headquarters, thinking there might be some political reason behind it. There I was given some information in most guarded terms about diplomatic soundings of the attitude of London which might perhaps make any military action against England unnecessary. This information however produced no satisfactory military reason for the German Supreme Command apparently to be stuck at dead centre. Other thoughts crowded in upon me spontaneously, ideas such as those of the Italian Foreign Minister Count Ciano, who wrote after the meeting in Munich: 'Hitler is now the gambler who has made a big scoop and would like to get up from the table risking nothing more.'[5]

Nevertheless, we did not give up in Section L. We checked that once again we had the agreement of OKH[6] and in addition we felt sure that we could count upon OKM. The first result of our efforts, though only a moderately important one, was the signature on 28 June of an OKW instruction to the effect that in order to mislead the enemy 'all available information media' should spread the word that we were preparing a landing in Ireland to draw the net round England tighter and reinforce the 'siege'.

Meanwhile Jodl also was anxious to get future intentions clarified.

On the day after Hitler arrived at 'Tannenberg' he submitted to him his own appreciation of the situation. He was obviously keeping his eye on Hitler's unenthusiastic attitude to Raeder's proposals and also on the current diplomatic soundings. He therefore presented the invasion of England merely as the 'last resort'. Jodl's reasoning went as follows: Germany's victory over England was now only a question of time; as a result we could and should follow a policy in future of minimizing the risks and economizing our forces. The first step must be to use the Luftwaffe's superiority to eliminate the Royal Air Force and its maintenance organization. There should next be co-ordinated sea and air attacks against the import routes and stocks of vital supplies for the British Isles; these should be combined with occasional terror attacks against centres of population. Invasion by land should be the *coup de grâce* and should only take place when the English people's will to resist had thus been broken and the Government was on the verge of capitulation. Preparations should begin at once and the object could be expected to be achieved by the end of August or early September. In addition the possibilities of a strategy aimed at the periphery of the British Empire should not be forgotten and should be examined; approaches should be made to those countries likely to be affected by the break-up of the British Empire, Italy in the first place, but also Spain, Russia and Japan.[7]

Jodl's staff knew nothing of the contents or even of the existence of this memorandum, nor of the considerable differences between the views of the Chief of the Operations Staff and their own. They were doing their utmost to concentrate all possible resources for the landing in England, known as 'Operation Sea Lion', since they held this to be the most effective form of attack and the best method of rounding off and concluding the German war plan; in Jodl's concept however, the landing was only the last and least important link in a chain of other measures primarily the responsibility of the Luftwaffe.

Hitler finally approved Jodl's plan and it formed the basis for the OKW orders of 2 and 16 July; the first of these set in motion the general long-term preparations for a landing; the second, only fourteen days later, laid down more detailed instructions. Yet a third order, this time an OKW directive (no. 17), was issued on 1 August 1940, headed *Conduct of Air and Sea Warfare against England*; among other things this laid down the targets which the German Air Force was to put out of action as soon as possible 'in order to establish the necessary conditions for the final conquest of England'.[8]

The Period of Overwhelming Military Success

As a sidelight on relations with Italy it is of interest that on 10 July, ie between the issue of the two orders referred to above, Hitler wrote to Mussolini saying among other things that 'the programme for the attack on England has been pursued and studied in the greatest detail for months past'.[9]

All these orders which were drafted by Section L officers on Jodl's instructions, left these 'young Turks'[10] with the impression that their ideas had won the day. Reading them it seemed that the preliminary battle for air superiority, later called the 'Blitz' by the English, was no more than the first phase of the landing operation which itself would be the culminating point of the entire undertaking – but it was still of course a prerequisite that the Luftwaffe did its job.

Assuming that this was the intention, Section L officers thereupon devoted their entire mental and physical energies to overcoming the various obstacles to the landing project which seemed to arise almost daily.[11] Never before or since had there been such an opportunity for them to use their own initiative in the preparation of an operation – but never had their superiors, Hitler included, been so flabby and lukewarm in their support. There were many instances, but it was particularly remarkable that, even taking into account the usual consideration with which Hitler always treated Göring and the Luftwaffe, he accepted almost without comment the great delay in the opening of the air offensive against England. In the end this did not begin until 13 August, ie nearly two months after the Armistice with France.[12] I simply could not understand the situation; shortly after the middle of September, during a tour of the front, I visited the headquarters of 2 Air Fleet at Cap Gris Nez and there learnt that discussions on the support of the Channel crossing and the landing operations had only just begun and that no definite conclusions had yet been reached. On the other hand, both from the air and from visiting some of the docks, I had seen transports and landing craft piled up in all the Channel coast ports.[13]

When I reported to him on my trip, and in spite of the fact that I was his senior Operations Staff Officer, Jodl left me entirely in the dark regarding his own proposals and Hitler's intentions to make the air the decisive factor in the operations against England and to leave the landing to follow on afterwards as a sort of appendage. Section L officers and so far as one could judge their opposite numbers in OKH and OKM, continued to work on the assumption that the achievement of air superiority over the British Isles was merely the prerequisite for a successful landing and that it was the landing itself which would be the decisive phase of the operation. These were two totally different conceptions; they differed not only in their aims but in their methods, timings and objectives. Since the war the results of a number of high level studies conducted by the Luftwaffe towards the end of the thirties have been published; all led to the conclusion that in all probability the Luftwaffe, even with the support of the Navy, would not be able to bring about the capitulation of Great Britain and that this could only be achieved by an *occupation* of the British Isles[14] – add all this up and it is clear that we officers in the higher levels of OKW were being misled and deceived. Hitler at least must have been fully briefed by Göring on the limitations to the capabilities of the Luftwaffe.

The other idea which Jodl had put forward in his memorandum of the end of June – to attack the British Empire from the periphery – was for the moment not followed up. About a month later, however, entirely independently but almost simultaneously, both Section L and OKH made certain moves in this direction, although on a limited scale. The seed was sown by a verbal report from the German Military Attaché in Rome, General von Rintelen, to the effect that not much was to be expected from the Italian advance on Egypt for which we had been waiting in vain for weeks. Since at the same time we had growing doubts whether Hitler really intended to proceed with the landing in England, Section L included in an 'Appreciation of the Overall Situation' submitted to Jodl on 30 July 1940, the proposal 'to offer the Italians some armoured forces for their attack on the Suez Canal'. Jodl linked this proposal with a verbal suggestion to the same effect which the Commander-in-Chief of the Army had made to Hitler.[15] As a result he managed, although with some difficulty, to get the Supreme Commander to agree that he should write to OKH and OKM asking them to examine in more detail the possibilities of providing our ally with assistance on these lines. The introductory sentences of this memorandum (dated 12 August) as finally approved by Hitler once more showed clearly the morass of uncertainty in which German strategy was labouring during this period. The memorandum ran:

On the assumption that:

(a) Operation Sea Lion is not carried out this year,

(b) the Italian offensive against the Suez Canal is either unsuccessful or postponed until the autumn,
there is a *possibility* that the Führer *might consider* the detachment of certain armoured forces to the Italians to assist in this attack or in its resumption.[16]

Probably as a result of what he had learned from this incident and in response to renewed representations from OKH pressing for some indication of intentions, Jodl submitted a fresh 'Appreciation of the Situation' to Hitler the next day, 13 August. Once more he gave entirely his own point of view saying: 'under no circumstances must the landing operation fail. The political consequences of a fiasco might be much more far reaching than the military.' In the same vein he added that in his view unless all the necessary conditions were fulfilled, including those concerning the naval situation, 'the landing must be considered a desperate venture, something which might have to be undertaken in a desperate situation but on which we have no necessity to embark at the moment'. Jodl continued: 'England can be brought to her knees by other methods' and then proceeded to propose certain other possibilities for a real common war effort with Italy against the British Empire instead of the present unprofitable 'war in parallel'; for instance Italian Air Forces and submarines might be brought round in the greatest possible strength to tighten the investment of the British Isles: in addition to the advance against Egypt, preparations might be made in agreement with Spain and Italy for the capture of Gibraltar.[17]

In so far as they appeared to lend support to a landing in England, Jodl's staff did their best to take over these ideas and push them forward. Hitler however, received all these proposals with equal lack of enthusiasm and in cases where they had anything to do with the Mediterranean, only considered them after considerable delay and then let them drift into the background just as he was doing with the landing in England. At the beginning of September 1940 he gave instructions that the occupation of the larger groups of islands in the Eastern Atlantic should be examined – Madeira, the Canaries, the Azores and Cape Verde – and that the 'possible occupation of Portugal' should be considered; this looked more like tactics designed to turn everyone's attention away from Operation Sea Lion than serious intentions. Some plans were produced by OKM and given a first critical examination by the OKW Operations Staff; Jodl offered no objection and in fact issued certain additional instructions on the subject, with the result that this useless and fruitless activity remained on the agenda for months.[18]

Meanwhile a development had occurred which more than any other single factor was destined to put paid to the plans for a landing in England: Hitler's thoughts turned suddenly against Soviet Russia! The rapidity with which this frightful decision was taken was equalled only by the immensity of its consequences, some of which are still with us today.

The headquarters had spent a short period in Berlin and after Hitler's speech to the Reichstag of 19 July, in which he held out little hope of a peaceful agreement with England, had bit by bit collected together again in the area of Berchtesgaden; Section L was in its special train *Atlas* in Bad Reichenhall Station. During the sitting of the Reichstag, a number of military honours had been conferred, among them the promotion of Jodl to full General straight from Major-General. We were all surprised therefore when, on 29 July, he indicated that he wished to speak to the senior officers of Section L. We all imagined that, although we had not done very much, this unusual visitation must be concerned with some special recognition following our victory in the West.[19] Four of us were present[20] sitting at individual tables in the restaurant-car. Instead of what we expected, Jodl went round ensuring that all doors and windows were closed and then, without any preamble, disclosed to us that Hitler had decided to rid the world 'once and for all' of the danger of Bolshevism by a surprise attack on Soviet Russia to be carried out at the earliest possible moment, ie in May 1941.

The effect of Jodl's words was electric. Our consternation was, if possible, even greater when we realized from his answers to our initial questions that the struggle against England was not necessarily to be concluded first but that on the contrary, victory over Russia, the last 'force on the continent', was supposed to be the best method of forcing England to make peace if this had not proved possible by other means. There was almost a chorus of objections – did not this mean that by our decision we were bringing upon ourselves the war on two fronts which up to now we had been fortunate enough to avoid? And if the bulk of the army was to be let loose eastwards what was to be done about the air war which was already having increasingly serious effects upon our cities? In any case why this sudden change when only a year earlier the 'pact of friendship and non-aggression' had been concluded with Moscow and celebrated with such enthusiasm and when, so far as anybody knew, the provisions in the agreement for the delivery of Russian war material to Germany had been carried out punctually and fully? Jodl countered every question and had an answer to everything although he convinced none of us. Two of his answers stand out in my memory: first, when he repeated Hitler's view and probably his own also, that the collision with Bolshevism was bound to come and that it was better therefore to have this campaign now, when we were at the height of our military power, than to have to call the German people to arms once more in the years to come; secondly, when he said that at the latest by the autumn of 1941 the full strength of the Luftwaffe, brought to a new pitch of efficiency by further victories in the east, would once more be available for employment against England. At the end of an hour of bitter argument it became clear what we had to do – produce a draft of a preparatory order for the immediate transport, movement and accommodation of the bulk of the Army and Air Force to the occupied areas of western Poland (where communications incidentally were poor). Under the heading 'build-up in the east' this order was included in the records of the prosecution at Nüremberg as the first document dealing with 'aggression' against Soviet Russia.[21]

What was the background to this sudden reversal of all our planning? Shortly after Jodl's disclosure, we happened to discover that Hitler had originally been determined to launch the attack in the late summer of 1940. The most urgent representations from Keitel and Jodl, set out in a memorandum which I have myself seen, had been necessary to convince the Supreme Commander that the time and space factors alone, together with the weather conditions, rendered this plan totally impracticable. The service which the senior officers of OKW thus rendered should not be under-estimated, although there is every reason to suppose that they were thinking of no more than a temporary postponement. Nevertheless, it did offer other and more potent political and military voices the opportunity of using the time thus gained to range themselves against this ghastly development. As far as anybody knows, however, nothing of the sort occurred.

To complete the picture, it is worth mentioning certain other important developments of this period (in the order of their occurrence), of which I only became aware after the war. As already mentioned, Hitler had already hinted at this possibility to his immediate circle as early as the spring of 1940. In a conversation with Field-Marshal von Rundstedt on 2 June 1940 recorded by the late General von Sodenstern who was present, Hitler said that now that he imagined England was ready for peace, he would begin to settle the account with Bolshevism.[22]

Halder's diary of this period illustrates Hitler's double talk:

22 May 1940. Commander-in-Chief had a discussion with the Führer and raised the question of the attitude of Russia. The Führer thinks that if he insists Russia will limit her demands to Bessarabia. *26 June 1940*. The attitude of Russia is in the foreground of foreign policy questions. The general opinion seems to be that the Bessarabian question can be solved without war.

At the beginning of July 1940 Sir Stafford Cripps, the British Ambassador in Moscow, handed Stalin a memorandum from Winston Churchill, the contents of which were passed by the Soviet Government to the German Embassy in Moscow a few days later; it urged Russia to change sides and act against Germany.

Further entries in Halder's diary:

3 July 1940. (Recording a conversation with the head of his Operations Section.) The most pressing problems at the moment are England and ... the East. As regards the latter, the main question is how to deal Russia a military blow which will force her to recognize Germany's preponderant role in Europe. *13 July 1940*. (After a conversation with Hitler.) The question in the forefront of the Führer's mind is why England is still unwilling to make peace; like us, he thinks that the answer is that England still has some hope of action on the part of Russia. *22 July 1940*. (Recording a conversation with the Commander-in-Chief of the Army.) The latter appears to have summed up his impressions of a discussion he had had with Hitler the previous day by the following instruction: 'The problem of Russia must be dealt with. We must begin thinking about this.'[23] *30 July 1940*. (An extract from an appreciation of the situation worked out with the Commander-in-Chief of the Army.) If we cannot reach a decision against England, the danger remains that England will ally herself with Russia; the question then is whether we should carry on a war on two fronts, one of which would be Russia. Answer: Better remain friends with Russia.[24]

Finally – 31 July 1940 some of Hitler's statements in the Berghof:

> Russia is the factor by which England sets the greatest store. ... If Russia is beaten, England's last hope is gone. Germany is then master of Europe and the Balkans. ... Decision: As a result of this argument, Russia must be dealt with. Spring 1941.*

These few extracts show unmistakably that Hitler's determination to turn against Russia was from the outset an unconditional and 'unalterable' decision – to use his own oft-repeated phrase. It is also clear that the decisive period during which he was forming this decision was approximately the middle of July 1940, ie about the same time at which the military managed to get him to agree the orders for the landing in England. The real background to his decision undoubtedly lay in his permanent, deep-rooted and deadly hatred of Bolshevism.

The relative importance of the two decisions is now crystal clear. It was already unmistakable to all those involved by the summer of 1940. Thus the dead centre in German strategy was passed; we were not nearing the end of the war; we were starting a new phase.

DISSENSIONS NEW AND OLD

Once more some of the few who were in the know, whether members of Section L or not, found themselves faced with the overpowering question of how to counter Hitler's fresh intentions, how to avoid this new and apparently limitless extension of the war both in time and space. There was no need to study the problem further; no one could doubt for an instant that 'it was better to keep friends with Russia' or that an attack on Russia carried with it a fearful threat for our nation and our country. What we needed at this moment was a soldier at the head of the Wehrmacht, someone who would have given us confidence, who would have shown some understanding, to whom we could have gone with military arguments and who could then have used his personal authority and that given him by the solid backing of the Wehrmacht to oppose the Dictator and counter

* All underlinings in original.

this decision which he had taken upon political and ideological grounds; but there was no one. Now we began really to see why Hitler had been so determined to eliminate any such possibility, why he had himself taken over the position of Supreme Commander of the Wehrmacht and at the same time, supported by the senior officers of OKW, turned that organization merely into his own 'working staff'.

Section L could not work other than through the Chief of the Operations Staff. But there was not the slightest possibility of getting him to change his mind, particularly on a question of such wide political and strategic significance; there was even less hope with Keitel who was beginning to show himself more and more dependent upon Jodl. Nevertheless, at the beginning of August, the Senior Naval Officer in Section L set off for Berchtesgaden to point out to Jodl what were the likely long-term effects upon the position of Germany if the Wehrmacht now turned east, leaving England's sea power still unconquered. This step seemed all the more necessary, since the Commander-in-Chief Navy had not yet even been told of Hitler's plans[25] and was not yet intended to know. The meeting, however, merely confirmed what we already knew: Jodl used this opportunity to stress that Hitler rated British sea power very high and did not consider that we were yet strong enough to strike decisively at the British Isles; for this very reason, therefore, we must 'go round' via Russia.[26]

This was no more convincing than had been Jodl's previous statements. As a result, we in Section L came gradually to the conclusion that we must do all we could to keep the way open for Operation Sea Lion. This seemed now to be the only possibility of avoiding the Russian adventure. It hardly seemed possible that Hitler had allowed all the far-reaching preparations for a crossing of the Channel to proceed merely as a threat and as bluff. In a number of remarks he continued to give the impression that he would still be ready to agree to the plan for a landing if only it could first be shown that we had gained adequate air superiority; this would at least have secured him against any further danger from British naval and air forces. I myself heard him say that he was prepared to see German soldiers die fighting for Germany but that he would not be responsible for sending them in thousands to the bottom of the sea without firing a shot. This seemed to lend support to the theory that he had not altogether given up the idea.

There is no doubt that as things developed, Hitler's interest in the landing operation waned the more he became occupied with the Russian problem and the less likely it became that, due to the unfavourable weather, the results of the air war would come up to expectations. During the latter part of the summer he did in fact allow the preparations for the landing to proceed but presumably only as a bluff and a threat; finally on 12 October 1940 the weather conditions forced him to inform the leaders of the Wehrmacht officially that the operation must be abandoned – supposedly only temporarily. In passing, it should be noted that he did revive Operation Sea Lion for a short time in the spring of 1941 for deception purposes. At that time the Information Service was ordered to broadcast the story that the move towards Russia was only being undertaken to divert attention from the forthcoming landing in England.

The Navy and Air Force were not sorry to see the landing called off; the former had never been keen on it and the latter had not been able to provide the essential prerequisite of undisputed air superiority over the Channel. Neither OKH nor Section L had wavered in maintaining that air superiority was absolutely necessary; they had hoped however that, as the tactics and equipment of the Luftwaffe improved, it would be able to obtain an adequate degree of superiority. Although they had worked separately, both had continued to make every effort to keep the operation alive somehow. The story of the production of *Directive no. 18*, dated 12 November 1940, shows how hard Section L was still striving in this direction, and at the same time how limited its opportunities for exerting any effective influence were. The directive laid down the broad lines of future German strategy; in the first draft, I put Operation Sea Lion at the beginning and gave it as the primary objective for the spring of 1941. The next day Jodl pointed out to me that this order of things might well accord with the ideas of OKH but not with those of Hitler. Once more I objected, going so far as to say that the question whether the landing was abandoned or not might well be decisive for the whole outcome of the war. Jodl agreed with me but nevertheless moved the section dealing with Operation Sea Lion from the beginning to the end of the directive – obviously knowing better than I did what Hitler wanted. At the same time he toned down the wording of the relevant paragraphs from Section L's original draft.[27] Hitler's attitude to the operation is summarized in the following extract from a letter to Mussolini dated 20 January 1941:

An attack on the British Isles remains the ultimate aim. In this case however, Germany is like someone who has only one shot in his gun; if he misses, the situation will be worse than before. We could never attempt a second landing since failure would mean the loss of so much equipment. England would then not have to bother further about a landing and could employ the bulk of her forces where she wanted on the periphery. So long as the attack has not taken place however, the British must always take into account the possibility of it.[28]

Operation Sea Lion was thus itself the victim of the *coup de grâce* which it was supposed to administer to the British Isles.

As the prospects of early large-scale operations gradually receded, the headquarters had once more split up into scattered groups. On 29 August, just after the first British air attacks on Berlin, Hitler had returned to the capital and taken up residence as before in the Reich Chancellery with his immediate entourage. In order to retain its mobility, the field echelon of Section L remained for the moment in its special train in a siding at the Grunewald Station. As time went on and winter approached, we began to look for permanent staff quarters which could provide both working and living accommodation. By the middle of November we were installed in the barracks of the Cavalry School at Krampnitz near Potsdam, completed just before the outbreak of war; as a result, we were about an hour by road from the Reich Chancellery. Section L remained there during the early months of the new year, while Jodl and Keitel stayed with Hitler in Berchtesgaden. OKH had remained in Fontainebleau until the decision on Operation Sea Lion had been made and had then returned to its huts in Zossen. OKM remained as before in its peacetime location on the Tirpitz Embankment in Berlin; OKL had returned to its group of forts in Wildpark near Potsdam.

In general, therefore, the conditions in the autumn of 1940, were the same as before the beginning of the campaign in France. Communications between the scattered groups of the headquarters and the headquarters of the Services were maintained by couriers, specially selected officers or officials. As before, Section L collected reports from the Services on which were based Jodl's daily briefings in the Reich Chancellery or in the Berghof. The Commanders-in-Chief of the Army, the Navy and the Air Force were summoned only at considerable intervals to make verbal reports or to receive instruction and information from Hitler; during these meetings he frequently discussed the fluid political situation. There were only occasional written directives from OKW to ensure that strategy was co-ordinated.

The headquarters had now taken definite shape and may well have given the impression to the outside observer that at the head of the Wehrmacht there was now a smooth-running machine; to anyone who looked more closely, however, it was clear that Supreme Headquarters still lacked any organization or method. In the first place in spite of the fact that we were no longer dealing with individual campaigns and that the theatre of war covered considerable portions of the entire globe, there was still no committee bringing together the Chiefs of Staff of the Army, Navy and Air Force, and the Chief of the OKW Operations Staff; none of them had even suggested such a thing. In the same way the three Commanders-in-Chief of the Services never met except on special occasions and then only in the dominating presence of Hitler, which ruled out any real discussion. Still worse however – while the Navy and Air Force ground on with the siege of England with inadequate resources, the Army was occupied in staff studies and war games from which gradually emerged the operational outlines of the campaign in Russia which was to despatch the German Wehrmacht to perdition – and all this without the smallest participation on the part of the Chief of the OKW Operations Staff. A third, though obviously less important point – until well into 1941 the Chief of the OKW Operations Staff was separated from Section L, his strategical section, by the distances between Berlin-Krampnitz and Berchtesgaden; contact was maintained only by telephone and occasional air trips by the heads of Sections.

The much heralded 'unity of strategic direction of the Wehrmacht' in the real and proper sense of the term therefore existed, as before, on paper only. During the preparatory period for the landing in England general staff work at the higher level had lacked co-ordination and unity of direction; so now a multiplicity of different points of view and opinions began to emerge.

Certain remarks by Hitler about this time concerning the importance of OKW give some idea of how equivocal the title itself was (whether or not it be taken to include Hitler himself) and at the same time give a picture of how Hitler regarded and employed his position as military leader. The occasion was the problem of the equipment and employment of the Fleet Air Arm which had led to many arguments between the Navy and the Air Force. Although the Operations Staff had examined and set out exhaustively the pros and cons, Hitler made no firm decision; instead he gave vent to a long-winded speech, extracts from which are as follows:

> Differences of opinions such as this between Services prove once more the necessity for a strong OKW. If there were no superior co-ordinating authority responsible for taking a decision there would, for instance, be a danger in this case, that research into the use of torpedoes from aircraft would not be further pursued and might even be stopped altogether. From the point of view of the war as a whole it is completely immaterial whether airborne torpedoes are used by the Air Force or the Navy; the important point is that air torpedoes should be used by the Service that can make the best use of them.
>
> Another lesson of arguments such as these is that Supreme Headquarters must keep a firm hold on things in order to ensure that the capabilities of all three Services are used to the best advantage. It is the job of OKW to do this. This is all the more true today since the Führer's authority means that in the last analysis a decision can always be made.
>
> Looking into the future increasing authority for OKW is desirable. The Führer's place might one day be taken by a man who might be the best possible politician but who may not have so much military knowledge and ability. He would have to have a very strong OKW, otherwise there would be considerable danger of the forces of the three Services being wasted in various directions instead of being concentrated on one single objective. In that case the Wehrmacht would never be able to give of its best and that would be a position for which no one would wish to be responsible in war when the existence of the Reich is at stake.[29]

Up to December 1940 I and the officers of Section L, just like Jodl. had little to do with preparations for the Eastern campaign, far less in fact than in the case of the earlier great campaigns. In any case we in Section L were still doing all we could to further those plans which it seemed might keep the Wehrmacht concentrated in the West. OKW *Directive no. 18* has already been referred to; the first drafts were completed in July and August 1940 and when it was finally issued on 12 November it seemed that our plans were somewhat nearer fruition. In the forefront was the plan for an attack on Gibraltar on which Hitler continued to lay great stress once the landing in England had been called off, in spite of his somewhat unpromising meeting with General Franco on 23 October. The original intention had been to destroy the harbour from the air and so force the British Fleet to evacuate it; Section L however, now proposed that the object of the operation should be the capture of the Rock from the landward side. There is an interesting sidelight here in Jodl's diary of 1 November 1940 on the unity of direction of the Wehrmacht: 'Head of Section L reports that the Luftwaffe does not wish to become involved in reconnaissance over Gibraltar and that Göring intends to speak to the Führer on the subject.'[30]

At the same time we in Section L continued to pursue, though with less energy, the second plan visualizing the despatch of an Air Corps and an Armoured Corps to assist the hesitant Italian advance on the Suez Canal. It seemed to us that this two-pronged attack against the main British bases might enable us ultimately to 'destroy the British position in the Mediterranean' and so turn the course of the war in another direction. For a time Hitler appeared to agree but later refused to give any further support to the Italians. As his primary reason he cited the Italian reluctance to accept any assistance for their attack on Greece. His attitude was also no doubt affected by the continued refusal of Mussolini and his Comando Supremo to accept German help – they could not after all be compelled to do so.[31] Hitler was probably not sorry to have to give up the idea of an expedition to North Africa because he was thinking on lines quite different to the supporters of this plan and did not wish to prejudice his designs on Russia by the detachment of forces elsewhere. For the same reason he stipulated that the attack on Gibraltar must take place no later than the beginning of February.

During this period Section L's 'natural ally' proved to be OKM; they had meanwhile learned of Hitler's plans for an attack on the Soviet Union and considered them to be both irrelevant and disastrous. The Senior Naval Officer in Section L went quietly but determinedly to work to cement this community of outlook and as a result a third proposal designed to divert attention from the East was produced; this visualized 'combined German/Italian worldwide naval strategy'. This idea too was in the first instance agreed by Hitler but it ultimately came to nothing because he was not prepared to agree to its first prerequisite – that the Mediterranean area must be cleared of the enemy.[32]

I was impressed by the possibilities of these developments and on 1 November 1940 during a discussion of 'Intentions for the Conduct of the War during the Winter' tried a new approach to General Jodl stating that these plans were 'not by themselves adequate'. If we did not send German troops to Libya the Italian offensive against Egypt was unlikely to achieve any decisive results; the Mediterranean area would not therefore be cleared of the enemy. The Italian Fleet would therefore still be confined to the Mediterranean and there would be no question of its employment in the Atlantic in co-operation with the German heavy naval forces. I do not know whether Jodl was convinced or not; in any case he maintained that we should achieve adequate superiority in the Mediterranean area as a result of the capture of Gibraltar and the despatch of German air formations to Sicily which had meanwhile been decided upon.[33] This was all that was included in *Directive no. 18*.

Finally, well to the fore in the instruction was a plan on which I had worked especially hard: military co-operation with France. The connotation which subsequent wartime events have given to the word 'collaboration' has resulted in it being officially considered by both sides as a disreputable activity; for the officers involved at the time, however, it implied no more than an attempt to use all their resources and such methods as were open to them to reach a genuine agreement with their European neighbour. In the circumstances this could only mean that we were trying to persuade France to change sides and fight against England or, in the words of the directive, to begin with combined security measures and from them to develop 'full participation of France in the war against England'. Further justification for this attempt lay in the fact that no other undertakings seemed to offer greater possibilities of preventing the dreaded extension of the war eastwards and of influencing the United States in our favour.

This is not the place to go into the chequered history of Franco-German military relations which were continuously upset by Hitler's game of political deceit. The initial steps are, however, worth describing for they were closely linked to the British attacks in July 1940 on French naval units in the harbours of Mers-el-Kebir and Dakar. A number of feelers were put out by high French quarters in Wiesbaden and later in Vichy. Then when the attempt at a landing at Dakar took place on 23 September 1940, the staff made further representations to Jodl who finally declared that: 'he had taken every opportunity, in concert with the Chief of Section L, to persuade the Führer of the far-reaching possibilities offered by the employment of combined German and French resources in the all-important struggle against England'. He then made a passing reference to a 'change in the Führer's views' which had apparently already taken place and continued to follow my own line completely: 'we must be quite clear that this implies a complete change in our fundamental ideas on the future conduct and objectives of the war'. Finally Jodl surprised us all by announcing Hitler's intention to meet Marshal Petain, which in fact he did a month later, on 24 October.[34]

In our earlier discussions Jodl had asked me for a more detailed examination of the 'forms of co-operation with France'. I proposed as a first principle that 'it must be demonstrated to the French that they will be serving *their own* national interests by siding with us'. This would from the outset exclude anything other than *passive* co-operation in the war against the *British Isles*; on the other hand in my view the security and maintenance of the French *Colonial Empire* was in the interests of both sides. The Armistice Agreement should be so interpreted that it served this end and we should not allow ourselves to be overinfluenced by consideration for the Italians to whom special proposals had simultaneously been made.[35] These were the military aims, but in the succeeding weeks, both before and after Hitler's meeting with Marshal Petain, the 'thorny political problems'[36] raised by this policy were brought up from all sides and came ever more to the forefront. From time to time the Italians would assure us that they had no objection but in fact they felt that any Franco-German reconciliation would endanger their own war aims and therefore opposed us; they were supported by Ribbentrop.[37] In this connection Marshal Petain is supposed to have said, though we did not know this at the time: 'it will take six months to discuss and another six months to forget it'. Keitel felt himself to be the guardian of the Armistice Agreement which bore his name; he was therefore an energetic supporter of Hitler's theory that: 'if there is to be any agreement with France it must carry with it additional conditions beyond those laid down in the Armistice Agreement'.[38] The hopeful wording of *Directive no. 18* had therefore lost much of its weight before the directive even appeared.

I had meanwhile been selected to assist Ambassador Abetz in the negotiations with the French in Paris.[39] (It later became clear that I was selected not so much for my experience abroad and knowledge of French as because my rank and position would make it easier for either side to disown me.) On a number of occasions I urged on Jodl the desirability of a 'generous settlement'; I also stressed that our guiding principle should be: 'this is no time for half measures'. Keitel had meanwhile stiffened Hitler in his determination 'to negotiate with the French only step by step'. I pointed out that:

> This would not help German strategic interests; it would put off to the Greek kalends the time when bases in Africa would be available for the war against England; we could not expect the French to agree the German requirements for the re-establishment of peace and order in their African colonies, still less really co-operate in the struggle against England in the foreseeable future.

In spite of all the representations to the contrary Hitler's final instructions to his military representative were merely an order to 'adopt a receptive attitude'.[40]

The first meeting with the French took place in the German Embassy in Paris on 29 November; the atmosphere was free and easy and we negotiated on a footing of complete equality – a remarkable fact seeing that the two sides had been at war less than six months before. The French were represented by the Commanders-in-Chief of the Army and Navy, General Huntsiger and Admiral Darlan, together with an Air Force staff officer who appeared in ceremonial uniform. Indicative of the atmosphere was the fact that at a later meeting General Huntsiger, with typical French wit and sense of the historical, pointed out that during the war of 1870 a French general with a German name, General Wimpffen, and a German general with a French name, General Verdy du Vernois, had met and that history was now repeating itself. To my considerable surprise I found that in addition to these personalities the Deputy Prime Minister, Pierre Laval, was present. It soon became clear that he and Darlan were the driving force. Huntziger was obviously designedly cautious and proposed to consider only long-range problems concerning far-off Central African areas; I, however, went against my instructions and raised the question of increased protective measures for French North-west and West Africa, which from the military point of view seemed to me to be the most immediate and urgent objective of any military co-operation with France. From the strategic point of view these areas guarded Europe's weak southern flank; they were also an area of considerable economic importance outside the British blockade. Laval and Darlan grasped the point fully and appeared perfectly ready to discuss.

A second meeting took place on 10 December in the same place and with the same participants. The French produced answers to the questions I had raised and they seemed to offer considerable possibilities. My previous conviction was reinforced that in general terms it was only the French themselves who could successfully defend their overseas possessions. I therefore considered that the main object of future meetings must be to make them capable of doing so, but this would involve generous military concessions going far outside the provisions of the Armistice Agreement, combined with the necessary political and military 'integration'.

However, this was not the only, nor indeed the last, occasion on which an officer of German Supreme Headquarters found that, from the moment at which he was despatched on a mission, he could never be sure whether the object of his mission would remain the same or whether he would be supported by those who had despatched him; the threads of delicate negotiations were all too often dropped or torn to ribbons as a result of the mood of the moment at Supreme Headquarters. After the first meeting with the French Hitler had, contrary to his usual practice, actually listened to my report, though with marked lack of enthusiasm. While I was in Paris the second time, however, detailed reports reached him regarding the unreliability of General Weygand, the French Commander-in-Chief in North Africa, who was already under suspicion; he at once had an OKW Directive issued laying down that should French North Africa break with Vichy, the whole of France was to be occupied and the French Fleet taken into custody. This being the case, therefore, when my written report of the second meeting with the French reached him in Berchtesgaden he considered it hardly worth the paper it was written on, although Jodl's diary had said: 'we must strike while the iron is hot; if our allies have any further setbacks (meaning the Italians in Libya) the result may all too easily be a stiffening of the French attitude'. On 13 December Petain suddenly dismissed, and temporarily arrested, his deputy Laval, who had been the architect of co-operation on the French side; Hitler promptly abandoned all pretence at diplomacy and once more adopted towards France the attitude of the victor.[41] It is of interest that according to General

Weygand's *Memoirs*, Churchill had tried to persuade Marshal Petain in November 1940 to go to French North Africa promising him if he did so considerable British forces to 'protect' French North African possessions.[42]

It was not until almost six months later, in the second half of May 1941, that the combined efforts of Admiral Darlan, who had succeeded Laval at the head of Petain's government, and Ambassador Abetz succeeded in persuading Hitler to resume the military conversations.[43] As a result of negotiations lasting more than ten days, once more conducted between Huntziger and myself, firm agreements were concluded and drawn up in proper protocol form. Unfortunately they never led to the political or strategic results for which their German supporters had hoped since we were now on the threshold of the Russian campaign. The agreements included provisions for French support in the struggle for the Nile valley and the Middle East and guarantees for French North and West Africa against England; in the situation created by the Russian venture these were of even greater importance than before, since they provided security in our rear. Hitler, however, never availed himself of the considerable possibilities thus offered. His suspicious attitude meant that any real military agreement was impossible. Politically he regarded himself as the unfettered overlord of Europe and had no intention of tying his hands in the way demanded by the French as a *quid pro quo*.[44] It must be admitted moreover that Marshal Petain showed no inclination to ratify the military agreements of the Paris protocol and therefore kept pitching his political demands higher and higher, apparently as a result of pressure from General Weygand and the United States Ambassador in Vichy, Admiral Leahy.[45]

When I returned from Paris towards the end of May, it soon became clear to me which way things were going. To begin with, the attitude adopted by Keitel and Jodl towards my report was frosty and uninterested; this was even clearer when they took the unprecedented step of allowing me to go alone to the Berghof to present the report to Hitler. Next, whilst we were standing at the conference table in the great window of the Berghof, Ribbentrop appeared, somewhat late and giving the impression of someone carrying more than his fair share of the burden and having too much to do. I managed to keep Hitler's attention at least for the period during which I was making my report; when, however, I began to point out the advantages on the one side and the dangers on the other which the attitude of France in North and West Africa might mean for us, Ribbentrop interrupted me with the memorable comment: 'you don't have to worry about all this, my Führer! If anything happens in Africa, General Rommel has only to turn his armour round to bring that scum to heel. We don't need the French for that.' He took his hand out of his pocket for a moment and waved it across the map of the Mediterranean spread out in front of Hitler, indicating the whole area from the Egyptian-Libyan frontier across Tunis, Algeria and Morocco right down to Dakar! I was fortunately spared the necessity of having to answer this myself for Hitler asked me 'just to tell the Foreign Minister' what sort of distances we were dealing with in Africa, what communications were available in these areas for the proposed movements of armoured formations and what other obstacles there might be. Hitler at least showed that he had a somewhat better grasp of military matters than his Foreign Minister, but that was as far as he went.

During the next few months great events took place; the French lost Syria which they could never have held even with German support, and on the German side came the great initial successes in Russia; all this threatened to push the agreements totally into limbo. It was not until August–September 1941, during a temporary lull in operations in the East, that Section L was able to get a new instruction issued to the Armistice Commission in Wiesbaden to re-start the negotiations on the fulfilment of the protocols. Little progress was made, for our negotiators were continually looking over their shoulders towards Italy and were forbidden to make any real concessions such as would have enabled the French to undertake the tasks proposed for them. The German Ambassador in Paris did contrive to organize one final meeting in Berlin at the end of December 1941; France was represented by the new Commander-in-Chief in North Africa, Marshal Juin, and on our side Göring was supposed to conduct the negotiations. The meeting was however, entirely overshadowed by the serious German crisis in Russia and the entry of the United States into the war. The distinguished French visitors were kept waiting more than an hour while Göring was persuaded to let himself be hurriedly briefed by me on the military aspect of the negotiations; during the conversation with the French which followed he kept apparently going to sleep. This was no doubt intended to demonstrate Hitler's lack of interest in the whole business; he always said that if things were going well, there was no need to negotiate and that if things were going badly, as they then were, he did not wish to. Hitler's real attitude to the negotiations with France emerges from certain confidential conversations recorded in Goebbels' diary as follows:

22 January 1942. The French could render us some service in North Africa but it isn't sufficiently important for us to meet their wishes. *7 March 1942.* The Vichy Frenchmen would be ready under certain circumstances not only to give up their neutrality, but also to take an active hand in the war. That is however something the Führer does not want to do.... We must definitely eliminate France's military and political power from any future armed conflict in Europe. Here the Führer is following a very subtle national – political instinct. *26 April 1942.* Talk about collaboration is intended only for the moment.

Under these circumstances, it is not surprising that negotiations came rapidly to an end without result.

THE MEDITERRANEAN, THE BALKANS AND THE MIDDLE EAST

But we have anticipated and must now go back to the end of 1940. Since the issue of *Directive no. 18* all the other proposals visualizing a solution through action on the periphery had temporarily come to nought. This situation was characteristic of the first months of 1941. The real reason for it undoubtedly lay in the fact that the overall direction of the war on the German side must have seemed to the outside world even more woolly, aimless and paralytic than in fact it was. It must bear some of the responsibility for the severe reverses suffered by our Italian ally at sea, in Greece and in North Africa. Similarly General Franco refused to give his agreement to the attack on Gibraltar, not, as Hitler opined, as a result of these Italian reverses but because there was still no German landing in England; at least this was the reason he gave to Admiral Canaris who had been sent to Madrid to complete the agreement. As a result a proposal to send Jodl to Madrid to present to Franco a plan for the attack never came off.[46] It looks therefore as if Jodl's August 1940 appreciation that 'England could be brought to her knees by other means' would probably have proved false even if Hitler had given his full support to all the other plans for action against England.

In the middle of November 1940, Keitel and Jodl were due to meet for the first time the head of the Italian Comando Supremo, Marshal Badoglio. Section L had to carry out much of the preparatory work, including the typing of a speech prepared by Jodl. In the light of the many warning and danger signs facing Axis strategy at the end of 1940, we did not find the speech very convincing to say the least of it. It showed every sign of wishful thinking, including for instance: 'the war has been won, it can no longer be lost, it has now merely to be brought to an end. All that is necessary is to force England to realize that she has lost the war.'[47] Grand Admiral Raeder was much nearer the truth when he told Hitler at the end of 1940:

The naval staff regards the British fleet as the decisive factor for the outcome of the war; it is now no longer possible to drive it from the Mediterranean as we have so often proposed. Instead a situation is now developing in Africa which is most dangerous both for Germany and Europe.[48]

The first German action to assist Italy took place in mid-December 1940 when X Air Corps was transferred to Southern Italy;[49] shortly after the turn of the year events in Libya and Greece forced us to despatch Rommel's Expeditionary Corps to North Africa and to detach considerable German forces for the campaign in the Balkans. As far as the two Dictators were concerned this assistance was unwillingly given and unwillingly accepted. There had been months of discussion between Hitler and Mussolini on the one hand and between Hitler and the army and air leaders on the other before these decisions finally emerged.[50] In all this the OKW Operations Staff was entirely restricted to its role of a working staff; in other words, its primary job was half-military half-political, co-ordinating the views of our friends and allies – particularly necessary in the Balkans. In addition we had to draft the orders giving effect to Hitler's decisions which themselves were entirely based on the proposals of OKH and we had to supervise the preparations for the various operations. I myself was detailed to carry on negotiations with the Bulgarian General Staff and the directions given me by Hitler are a good illustration of his method of working with allies.[51] They ran:

I propose to keep the overall direction of this campaign in my own hands, including the allotment of objectives for the Italian and Hungarian forces within the framework of the operation as a whole. Our requirements must be presented in a form which takes account of the susceptibilities of our allies and leaves open to the Italian and Hungarian Heads of State the possibility of presenting themselves to their peoples and their armed forces as independent military leaders. C.-in-C. Army and C.-in-C. Air are to send to me our requirements to ensure the co-ordination of operations and I will then transmit these by personal letter to the Duce and The Regent, Horthy, in the form of proposals and desires.

Even before the short campaign in the Balkans opened on 6 April and while it was in progress, Hitler and his immediate entourage still could not keep themselves from interfering in army operations.[52] Their reasons were always the same. The following extracts from Halder's diary of 1941 are illustrative:

5 April. (Referring to Hitler's regard for Hungarian and Italian susceptibilities.) So once again the operational command has to hang on to the political coat-tails and this time it is only a question of momentary political problems. We are losing any clear consistent concept of the operation and are in danger of getting lost in a mass of unco-ordinated individual undertakings. Always the same picture. One has to have strong nerves to stand up to it.

7 April. Call from Jeschonnek saying that Göring has been complaining to the Führer of the unsatisfactory progress of XVIII Corps. So the blasted squabbling goes on.

11 April. I told them forcibly how disgusted I was with this continual interference in operations. Their timidity, their desire to avoid all risks but to gather in victories nevertheless, may be a good idea politically but militarily it is intolerable.

The German reaction in North Africa and in the Balkans was directed essentially against England; from the outset however, it was completely overshadowed by the forthcoming Russian campaign and basically therefore the campaigns were entirely defensive. Their success was such that by the middle of April 1941 an unexpectedly favourable strategic situation had developed which might perhaps have offered an opportunity to change the whole course of the war. X Air Corps was extremely successful but most important of all was the impetuous advance of Rommel's comparatively small forces, right up to the Libyan-Egyptian frontier, exceeding anybody's expectations; at the same time, both commanders and troops were doing outstandingly well in the Balkans. The British had always regarded the Mediterranean as a bridge and not as a dividing line and they had therefore always expected that the full weight of the Luftwaffe would reach out beyond Crete to exert a real threat against the fleet in Alexandria and British bases in the central and eastern Mediterranean. The views of the US Navy were even more extreme; they visualized that with the occupation of Crete, the British fleet would be driven from the Mediterranean and even considered an end to the war to be possible.[53] Meanwhile however, all German Supreme Headquarters was worrying about was not to be tied down in the Balkans a day longer than necessary in order not to have further to postpone the opening of the Russian campaign.[54]

There was an opportunity here for centralized strategic direction of operations on both shores of the Mediterranean; in fact the original OKW order of 10 December 1940 authorizing the despatch of X Air Corps gave as its area of operations the whole of the eastern Mediterranean including the Ionian and Aegean seas, as proposed by OKL.[55] The situation was however just the same as in the spring of 1940 when we had reached the Channel with such unexpected rapidity; strategy, except in cases where it was to be purely defensive, was entirely subordinated to the plans already made and forward planning dealt only with the period and circumstances following the successful conclusion of the campaign in the East. Moreover it must be admitted that it would at this stage have been extremely difficult suddenly to alter the strategy; the Wehrmacht was now spread so wide that the problems of supply, both by land and sea, the facts of geography and a number of other factors which could not easily be altered, would have made this impossible. There is eloquent proof in the fact that our attempts in May and June–July 1941 to assist the rising in Iraq and the French in Syria, came to nothing.[56] Nevertheless it seems clear that had we had a flexible High Command which had taken timely steps to prepare for all eventualities, this was an occasion when a fresh examination of future strategy should have been made; but the man we had at the head of our forces was simply the standard bearer of the anti-Bolshevik crusade.

Instead of forward planning therefore all that the Operations Staff had to do were tasks of minor importance. For instance, on 22 April, Jodl was despatched by Hitler to the Epirus to conclude a second armistice agreement with the Greeks, the first, concluded by

Field Marshal List, the Commander-in-Chief of the victorious German Twelfth Army and agreed by Hitler, having been found not to satisfy Mussolini's requirements – a procedure unprecedented in the entire history of war.[57] In addition, while the Balkan campaign was in progress, Section L had to produce an appreciation to show whether it was more important for future strategy in the Mediterranean to occupy Crete or Malta. All officers of the section, whether from the Army, Navy or Air Force, together with myself, voted unanimously for the capture of Malta since this seemed to be the only way to secure permanently the sea-route to North Africa. Our views were, however, overtaken by events even before they reached Jodl. Hitler was determined that Crete should not remain in the hands of the British because of the danger of air attacks on the Rumanian oil-fields and he had further agreed with the Luftwaffe that from a base in Crete there were far-reaching possibilities for offensive action in the eastern Mediterranean.[58] A curious incident occurred in this connection; shortly afterwards Hitler's senior aide, Colonel Schmundt, appeared in our offices and demanded that no mention should be made in Section L's war diary of these differences of opinion within Supreme Headquarters or of any similar cases which might occur in the future.[59]

During the Balkan campaign the field headquarters was housed in two special trains at the entrances to two tunnels on a closed stretch of line in Steiermark. When it returned to its offices in and around Berlin, the OKW Operations Staff was faced with a new and entirely unexpected task – to see how and with what we could carry out Hitler's order 'to give rapid support by all possible means to Iraq's struggle against the British'. It soon became clear that rapid assistance could only be furnished by using the light weapons still maintained in French Army depots in Syria under the provisions of the Armistice Agreement. All available forces of the Luftwaffe were occupied in the forthcoming landing operation in Crete; in any case, air action in Iraq would have required the construction of bases for which we should have to have had not only the agreement of the French administration in Syria but tacit acceptance on the part of the Turks. A few Air Force officers, including one of Field Marshal von Blomberg's sons, reached Iraq and were killed there, but by the end of May the Iraqi revolution had petered out in the face of strong British pressure.[60]

The OKW Operations Staff was faced with a similar situation

when, on 8 June, British and Gaullist forces moved into Syria from Palestine; the problem was how to assist the French in accordance with agreements recently arrived at in Paris. Hitler eventually, but far too late, agreed to an odd plan whereby a number of French battalions were to be transported by rail from France through southern Germany and the occupied Balkan areas to Salonika and simultaneously certain mobile units of the French Navy and Air Force were to be moved through the Mediterranean to bases in Greece. But after all the previous delays and haggling, this did not mean much. These forces could not get to Syria through the defensive ring which the British Fleet had thrown round Cyprus, and the German X Air Corps, which had to fight at the limit of its range, could not act effectively against the British cruiser squadron off Beirut. In fact, the French in Syria collapsed on 12 July 1941 after little more than a month of fighting.[61]

This failure showed clearly that long-term preparations were necessary for military operations in these far distant areas; nevertheless, just at this time, in June 1941, the draft of *Directive no. 32* appeared in the German headquarters, a document of considerable importance in the history of the war. It opened with an appreciation of the situation on the continent of Europe which 'once the Russian armed forces had been smashed' would be ruled entirely by the Axis Powers; the draft then laid down that the objective should be to assault 'the British position in the Mediterranean and western Asia by a two-pronged attack from Libya through Egypt, from Bulgaria through Turkey and if necessary also from Trans-Caucasia through Iran'. In the West the plan once more included the capture of Gibraltar.[62]

This was indeed the most ambitious German strategic concept 'of all time' and it stemmed from Hitler; in February 1941 he had even ordered Section L to study a move against India through Afghanistan.[63] Early in April 1941, on the assumption that the campaign in the East would be over in a few months, he had contemplated a 'large-scale offensive in North Africa' in the autumn[64] and in a conversation with Count Ciano at the conclusion of the Balkan campaign, he had touched on the possibility of a move through Turkey and Syria.[65] Finally the idea of capturing Gibraltar and then occupying French Morocco had been frequently considered and as frequently put off, though each time supposedly only temporarily. In view of all these possibilities, OKH began to agitate for 'early information on forthcoming operations after the conclusion of the Russian campaign';[66] in light of their experiences during the first two years of war, this was no more than a wise precaution. A good indication of the broad lines on which the Army was thinking is given by the headings in Halder's diary of 7 April 1941 'general requirements for future organization' and 'table of requirements'; this gives a detailed list by numbers of units and arms of the service of 'operational groupings' divided into Spanish Morocco, North Africa/Egypt, Anatolia and Afghanistan. By the beginning of June therefore it is clear that the Army Staff thought that the time had come for OKW to issue a new directive on these subjects. Meanwhile OKM sent in an appreciation of the situation, concluding that the primary objective should be the attainment of complete superiority in the eastern Mediterranean.[67] A few days later on 19 June, the OKW Operations Staff sent a first draft of the directive to the Services High Commands.

There is no need to go further into the prospects of this ambitious strategy since it was entirely dependent on the outcome of the Russian campaign. In so far as my subject is concerned, all I wish to prove is that it was not simply megalomania on the part of German Supreme Headquarters or the headquarters of the Services which was responsible for these ideas. Even on the enemy side for instance, Churchill and the British Chiefs of Staff were seriously concerned with the possibilities of German plans of this nature as soon as the attack on Russia took place.[68] I have laid particular emphasis on these long-range plans because many historians have either refused to recognise their existence or simply did not know about them. They have therefore labelled OKW as an organization which 'ran in continental blinkers' and have tried to present the Army members of OKW as those primarily responsible.

There were a number of subsequent developments of importance as disproving both these accusations, that of megalomania, and that of having an exclusively continental outlook. For instance, my initial instructions to my staff as a result of the OKH request for an indication of future intentions show that I was primarily concerned to avoid further geographical extension of the war and did not intend our thinking to be inhibited by considerations of purely land strategy. I laid down:

1 Clear up the Mediterranean by the capture of Gibraltar, Malta, Cyprus and the Suez Canal;

2 Build up a strong position in Europe and West Africa against the British/American alliance;

3 Invade England as the *coup de grâce*.[69]

My purpose here was clearly to swing the centre of gravity of German military power back to the West. The second draft of *Directive no. 32*, however, laid down that the primary objective of future operations should be the Middle East; this point of view was supported by Hitler but was also that of OKH and OKM; it seemed to be the natural sequel to our large-scale initial successes in Russia. No mention was made of Malta. The protection of the coast of North and West Africa was to be the job of the French with German air support; Hitler appeared for the time being to be willing to allow them the necessary reinforcements.

The ultimate objective of all these plans in the draft directive was England. As soon as the campaign in the East was over, the 'siege' was to be resumed in full force; the lifeline of the Empire through the Mediterranean was to be cut and as soon as a 'collapse' of the British Isles appeared imminent, an end was to be brought about 'through a landing, in England'.

CHAPTER 4

The Eastern Campaign –
the Preparatory Period

OKH IN THE LEAD

One of the more remarkable facts in the history of German Supreme Headquarters is that from the end of June to the beginning of
December 1940 the highest-level staff of the Wehrmacht and its
Supreme Commander played only a very small part in the preparations for the greatest campaign of the Second World War. There
was no carefully thought-out plan as a basis for action against
Russia such as would have been made in the old days by the Prussian-German General Staff; moreover as opposed to his procedure
during the period prior to the western campaign, Hitler's views on
the conduct of operations were confined merely to a few passing
remarks. Halder's diary of 31 July 1940 merely says:

Destruction of the power of Russia. To be achieved by:
1 A thrust towards Kiev with flank on the Dnieper.
2 Thrust through the Baltic States in direction Moscow.
Finally, pincer operation from north and south. Later a separate
operation against the Baku oil fields. We can then see the extent
to which Finland and Turkey are involved.

The working out of the entire plan of campaign together with
the move forward and initial objectives was left completely in the
hands of OKH; they included the Luftwaffe and Navy in their
planning at the appropriate time. The Operations Staff of Supreme
Headquarters was entirely on the touchline. General Jodl was never
once invited either as a visitor or an observer to the large-scale war
games which the Army Staff held in the autumn of 1940, nor, as far
as one knows, did he make any attempt to play any important part in
the planning, as he should have done in view of his job and position.

The only exception of any significance was the fact that in the summer of 1940 he ordered Section L to work out on their own the basic factors governing an operation against Soviet Russia, but this was, as he admitted, merely to familiarize him with the geographical and other military conditions before the Army leaders presented their proposals to Hitler.[1] At the beginning of September Section L was ordered by Jodl to inform the office of Admiral Canaris that the 'eastern area' would be much more heavily occupied in the next few weeks and give the Admiral certain instructions for concealment.[2] In addition in the Autumn of 1940 the Operations Staff had something to do with the despatch of Army and Air Force 'military missions' to Rumania which, as everybody knew, were connected with the preparations for the Eastern campaign. This took Rome completely by surprise and was described by Mussolini as a German 'occupation' of Rumania. He used it as the final excuse for his attack on Greece. Ciano's diary of 12 October 1940 records him as saying: 'this time I am going to pay him (Hitler) back in his own coin; he will find out from the papers that I have occupied Greece'. These words are only quoted as a further illustration of the degree of mutual confidence existing between the two allies. The Russians naturally did not look upon the despatch of German troops to Rumania with any favour. On 13 November Molotov asked Hitler whether he would like it if Russia despatched a military mission to Bulgaria; Hitler could nevertheless justifiably point out that 'the Rumanian Government had expressly asked Germany to send a military mission'.[3]

On 12 November 1940, the day before Molotov's arrival in Berlin, the famous OKW *Directive no. 18* dealing with 'Strategy in the Immediate Future' was issued; this confirms the state of affairs I have just described in regard to the preparations for the eastern campaign. It merely says:

> Political discussions for the purpose of clarifying the attitude of Russia in the immediate future have already begun. Regardless of the outcome of these conversations all preparations for the East for which verbal orders have already been given will be continued. Further directives will follow on the subject as soon as the basic operational plan of the Army has been submitted to me and approved.[4]

General Jodl was therefore to a certain extent right when, during cross-examination in Nuremberg in 1946, he stated:

I was not the first who made preparations for an attack on the Soviet Union. To my surprise I discovered here, through the witness Paulus, that long before we concerned ourselves with any orders of this kind, plans of attack were already worked out in the General Staff of the Army.[5]

It matters little that at another point in the same testimony Jodl claimed that his main task was 'to carry out the staff work necessary to put Hitler's decisions into the proper military form for them to be used by the entire Wehrmacht machine.' The fact remains that these events show yet again that at the culminating point of the war the set-up of Supreme Headquarters of the Wehrmacht in no way measured up to the requirements of real strategic direction.

INTERFERENCE BY HITLER

It might be thought that after all its previous experiences OKW had designedly avoided becoming involved in working out the plan of operations for the Eastern campaign; but this is completely disproved by subsequent events. When the Army leaders presented the results of their detailed studies in broad terms to Hitler on 5 December, he initially gave their plan his unconditional approval, although he made certain comments which gave some indication of the lines on which he was later to interfere. He gave instructions that: 'preparations were to proceed at full swing on the basis of the planning so far carried out.' This was the moment chosen by Jodl to order Section L to turn what was purely Army business into a directive from OKW following the usual procedure, ie working in collaboration with the Operations Sections of the Services. In doing so Jodl stressed that:

> The Führer is determined to carry through this operation in the east since the Army will never again be as strong as it is at this moment and Soviet Russia has recently given one more proof that she will always, whenever possible, stand in Germany's path.[6]

The first draft of the directive was prepared while I was away in Paris; it had certain gaps in it and on 16 December I presented a second draft to Jodl. In doing so I emphasized that: 'Section L was engaged upon an appreciation of the situation in a war on two fronts and that it showed that the question of fuel consumption merited particular consideration.' All that happened was that the Chief of

OKW issued orders severely restricting the consumption of fuel prior to the start of major operations[7] War planning had gone far too far to be influenced by considerations of this sort.

During the next few days it became clear that Hitler's thinking was limited to the manner and method in which the forthcoming operations should be initiated and conducted. Accordingly when Jodl presented the draft of the directive to him on 17 December he ordered 'a considerable alteration'. OKH had from the outset considered that the crucial factor for success of the entire campaign was that the main weight of the attack should be directed towards Moscow because in all probability this was the best method of ensuring that the main enemy forces were brought to battle and defeated. Hitler however, now gave orders that, as soon as the Soviet Armies in White Russia had been broken, Army Group Centre was to divert a considerable proportion of its mobile forces northwards 'in order, in co-operation with Army Group North, to annihilate enemy forces in the Baltic area'; the advance towards Moscow was to be continued only when Leningrad and Kronstadt had been captured.[8] The reasons which led him to this decision are typical; as so often before and even more later, he disregarded the invariable first principle of all strategy, the destruction of the enemy forces, and instead went chasing after less important objectives. He had his eye on 'rapidly cutting the Russians off from the Baltic Sea area in order to keep it clear for imports of value to the war effort' and because it provided the shortest line of communication to Finland; a month later he was still saying that this was the 'most important task'.[9]

So with a stroke of the pen a new concept of the main lines of the campaign against Russia was substituted for that which the OKH had worked out as a result of months of painstaking examination and cross-checking from all angles by the best military brains available. Any idea that the study carried out in Section L had anything to do with this momentous decision is wide of the mark for the very good reason that, as always, our study had been agreed beforehand with the Operations Section of OKH. The idea is further disproved by the fact that when, as will be shown later, similar differences of opinion arose in the summer of 1941, Section L wrote two appreciations emphatically supporting the Army point of view. There is moreover nothing to show that Jodl had any influence in bringing Hitler to this decision. It does seem probable however that, contrary

138

to his practice during the preparatory period for the Western campaign, he did not give OKH a second opportunity of putting their point of view. Instead he seems to have thought himself entitled to re-draft this vital paragraph in the directive which now received the well known title 'Barbarossa' instead of its previous code names 'Otto' and 'Fritz'.[10] Thus was produced the patched-up document which set the Wehrmacht off on the fateful road to the east. It was consecrated next day by Hitler's signature.

In this case Jodl had completely slipped back into his role as merely head of a working staff and had raised no objections; the Army likewise, suddenly faced with this major alteration in its plans, accepted the situation in silence.[11] It later became known that their reasoning was that in time the course of the campaign would compel even Hitler to go back to the original Army concept. This was to a certain extent taking the easy way out and it proved to be no more than self-deception.

For a time after the issue of the 'Barbarossa' directive the main role in further preparations for the Eastern campaign was once more left to the Army. This was particularly evident during the three great conferences held between January and the middle of March, the first two in Berchtesgaden and the last in Berlin; during these Hitler took his decisions regarding the move forward and the initial objectives for the operations and they were based upon the proposals of the Army leaders.[12] This did not however mean that OKH was any more in accord with Hitler's plans for action against Soviet Russia than it had been when these plans were first produced towards the end of July 1940. After a conversation with the Commander-in-Chief of the Army on 28 January 1941 Halder notes in his diary:

> Barbarossa ... does not affect England. It does not noticeably strengthen our economy. We must not underestimate the risks we are running in the West. It is even possible that Italy will collapse after the loss of her colonies and then we shall have a southern front through Spain, Italy and Greece. If we are then tied down in Russia that will make the situation even more difficult.

In so far as the Operation Staff of Supreme Headquarters was concerned in these events General Jodl continued to act as Hitler's permanent adviser, working independently and after his own manner, just as he normally did at the daily briefings in the restricted circle of the *maison militaire*. Whatever suggestions he may have made in regard to the eastern campaign and in whatever special desires of Hitler he may have taken some hand, he cannot in any single instance have based his views on any detailed studies made by his staff. His normal method of working was to rely upon himself alone and the further and longer he was divorced from Section L the more marked this tendency became. He did not appear to realize that the undoubted authority which he now had stemmed almost entirely from the fact that he was now a permanent member of Hitler's entourage and not from his position as Chief of the OKW Operations Staff; in theory he supported the organization but in practise allowed it to wither.

During January and February the forthcoming Russian campaign gradually absorbed the efforts of the entire Wehrmacht; yet in the peculiar existence which I and the officers of Section L led in our offices in Krampnitz near Berlin, we were hardly touched by it all. During this period the division of the high-level staffs into those concerned with the East and those concerned with the other theatres of war began to make its appearance, an arrangement which was later to have such unfortunate consequences; during this period also, the disadvantages for the staff inherent in its permanent separation from its Chief became particularly evident. The information which we could get from General Jodl, who was always a man of few words, or from some hurried note by one of the aides,[13] was so inadequate that, for instance, on 18 January during one of my weekly visits to Berchtesgaden I had to ask Jodl 'whether the Führer was still firm in his intention to carry out Operation Barbarossa'. I think it was on this occasion, after Jodl had replied that Hitler was still determined to carry out the eastern operation that he indicated his aversion to what he regarded as questioning and worrying with the unforgettable words: 'the Russian colossus will be proved to be a pig's bladder; prick it and it will burst'.[14] Jodl exaggerated here even more than Hitler who is supposed to have said at a conference on 9 January: 'the Russian Armed Forces are like a headless colossus with feet of clay but we cannot with certainty forsee what they might become in the future. The Russians must not be underestimated. All available resources must therefore be used in the German attack'.[15]

I and the officers of Section L were not necessarily in agreement with these views in 'high quarters'. As before we took it upon ourselves in dealing with the few jobs that came to us in connection with the eastern campaign to work in the closest possible collaboration with the staffs of the Services. But both the subjects and the objects of our activities were comparatively low-level stuff and had little to do with what should have been the real job of the highest-level strategic staff. For instance I attended an OKH conference with the heads of the Organization and Supply Branches, at that time Colonels Munch and von Tippelskirch; this gave rise to much detailed work in a number of fields in order to try to meet the very large requirements of the eastern campaign in load-carrying vehicles, tyres, spare parts and fuel. We also had to collect from the Services orders, maps and other basic material, from which among other things we could draw up a 'time-table' for the orders which Hitler had to issue. During these months Section L's only job in connection with the Russian campaign bearing any relation to the work of a true strategic staff was to ensure that instructions for the further conduct of the war against England and the protection of the occupied territories in Western Europe were in consonance with the new situation. Closely related to this was the job already referred to, to make use of all possible information media to mislead the enemy by presenting the 'movement against Russia as the greatest deception operation in military history' designed to 'divert attention from the final preparations for the invasion of England'.[16]

From the beginning of March the eastern campaign had first call on the activity of all sections of German Headquarters. About the middle of the month however, when movement was already in full swing, Hitler once more interfered in the basic operational plan of the Army; he simply ordered that Twelfth Army on the southern flank of the entire front should not attack from Moldavia. He considered that the considerable obstacle of the Dniestr would best be tackled from the rear and therefore ordered that Sixth Army on the northern flank of Army Group South should be reinforced in the area of Lublin by all available mobile formations. It is not known whether Jodl had any hand in this new arbitrary decision apart from discussing it at the daily briefing, as was always done with such 'suggestions' by the Supreme Commander. It seems that Hitler made known this decision during a five-and-a-half-hour conference with the Army leaders and their staff officer Colonel Heusinger and apparently they raised no objection. This and other interventions by Hitler in operational matters had an increasingly disturbing effect upon the whole basis of the operational plan for the East and Halder's diary shows clearly with what grumbling and distaste they were received.[17] The effects of the Supreme Commander's determination to play the role of great war leader can be seen by the very great difficulties encountered in the advance of Army Group South during the first weeks of the campaign.

A further most important decision was taken at this juncture, one that primarily concerned the command organization at the highest Wehrmacht levels but this time, be it noted, it was a decision not by Hitler but by the Commander-in-Chief of the Army. In OKH there was still smouldering resentment at their exclusion from the Norwegian campaign and in Jodl's view it was this which caused Field Marshal von Brauchitsch at this point to declare that 'he was leaving it to OKW to issue all orders' concerning the proposed advance from Norway and Finland against the Russian White Sea area.[18]

As a result of this a second 'OKW theatre of war' was set up in Finland. The Norwegian campaign had in many respects been a special case but now the Commander-in-Chief of the Army of his own accord surrendered to OKW, in other words to Hitler, his responsibility for and his powers of command over a considerable number of Army formations in a purely land theatre of war. Shortly before the opening of the Eastern campaign OKW had proposed to the Finnish Supreme Commander, Field Marshal Mannerheim, that he should take command of all forces, including German forces, operating from Finland; he had however refused. The result was that as far as northern Finland was concerned, the Chief of the OKW Operations Staff had to take over the job of Chief of Staff of the Army and Section L that of the Army Operations Section. Neither however had anything even remotely resembling the competence and machinery for this job such as the comparable Army organizations possessed and neither was capable of undertaking the direction of operations except in the narrowest sense of that word; everything else such as organization, replacements, supply and rationing had to be done by OKH, as in Norway.

To try to assess the results of this peculiar command organization would be waste of time and lead to interminable argument. One thing is certain – the solution adopted was certainly not the best and was not even a good one; it is also certain that had there been a stronger personality at the head of the Army, he would have done all he could to bring the Army formations in Norway under his command once more rather than doing exactly the reverse. It would seem that the Chief of Staff of the Army did not agree either with his Commander-in-Chief's action or with the objectives allotted to the troops in Norway which originated with Hitler. On 14 May 1941 he noted in his diary: 'the whole undertaking is merely an expedition; it is not an operation of war. It is a pity to squander forces by using them in this area.'

THE ALLIES

Because of the campaign in the Balkans the attack on Russia had to be postponed from the middle of May to 22 June. Before the attack began one of the special tasks reserved to OKW was to get in touch with our friends and allies to persuade them to make common cause with us in the attack in the East. In this case also however, the possibilities of independent initiative on the part of the staff were very limited.

In the first place Hitler would only allow even to be considered as participants those countries which were either neighbours of Russia and therefore in a position to assist the German advance, or had some account of their own to settle with the Soviets. The initial choice was therefore limited to Rumania and Finland. He considered that at a later stage it might perhaps be possible to include Hungary and Slovakia. Sweden also came into the picture early on as being capable of furnishing indirect support, for instance by allowing troop transports to cross her territory towards Finland. As far as the principal ally, Italy, was concerned, the order was that our intentions must be kept secret. The strictest instructions were laid down regarding the timing and form of approaches to all other states; the Eastern campaign was regarded as a preventive war to be opened by a surprise attack; in any case the principles upon which Hitler conducted any military coalition are well known.[19]

The Finns were considered particularly reliable in spite of the fact that they were not really allies of Germany but were in the somewhat equivocal position of 'comrades in arms'; it was only with them that short 'General Staff discussions' were held at the beginning of June. In accordance with the special command organization applicable to Finnish territory these discussions were primarily the business of the OKW Operations Staff. On this occasion also General Jodl could not help opening the discussions by the phrase that the war was already won and now had only to be brought to an end. When the OKW discussions were concluded, OKH and the Finnish delegation dealt with the questions which would arise when the German and Finnish forces gained contact in the area of Lake Ladoga.[20] Hitler himself dealt with Marshal Antonescu, the Rumanian leader.[21] For all further discussions the OKW Operations Staff was directed to work through the senior Military Attaché accredited to the government concerned or through a senior officer specially despatched for the purpose[22] who, on the lines of the similar appointment in Italy, was later generally entitled 'German General accredited to the headquarters of the ... Armed Forces'. There was however no case in which the natural and obvious solution was adopted, the establishment of a permanent staff authorized by two or more partners to work out a common strategy. The following extracts from Halder's diary of 29 June (one week after the opening of the attack) illustrate the results achieved; they show some of the initial fruits of our contacts with allied and friendly states or the offers made by them on their own account:

> Hungary reports that the 'Carpathian Corps' will be ready to move on 2 July.
>
> Italy put forward her proposals for the organization of the Corps she proposes to send to Russia; it will be 40,000 strong.
>
> Slovakia is contributing two divisions and a motorized brigade.
>
> Spain wants to send a 'Legion'; 15,000 men.
>
> Finland submits a new plan of attack which is in accordance with our wishes.

As far as the substance of the negotiations with the allies was concerned the Operations Staff was in general similarly restricted as in the case of OKW Directives for our own operations; in other words all it could do was to put forward views and proposals which had been worked out by OKH in the framework of their movement and operational plans and subsequently approved by Hitler. In view of the weakness of Italy there was no question of broad strategic measures such as would necessarily have fallen within the province of the highest-level staff of the Wehrmacht; the only occasion for these would have been an agreement with Japan based on the 'Three-Power Pact' of 27 September 1940, whereby she would have moved against Soviet Russia in the Far East. Such a possibility however, did not enter into the calculations of either side. That this was so on the Japanese side was made very clear when, in the middle of April 1941, the Japanese Foreign Minister took the opportunity of his return journey from a prolonged stay in Berlin to sign a treaty of neutrality with the Soviet Union in Moscow. This was entirely unexpected but on the German side people consoled themselves with the thought that, having thus secured herself in the rear, Japan would be able to act all the more vigorously against the British in the Far East. This meant that the two allies could continue to agree that victory over England remained the final and most important objective. Even after the opening of the campaign against Russia little thought was given to the possibility of direct Japanese assistance as proved by the fact that, after a period of disillusionment, the old confidence in an imminent collapse of the Soviets revived in the autumn of 1941. The overweening self-assurance in German headquarters was illustrated by the phrase coined when Japan was thought to have made an offer of assistance: 'we don't need anyone just to strip the corpses'![23]

Just as the political side had previously prevented the Wehrmacht exercising any influence on relations with Italy, so it was now excluded from anything to do with the development of the Japanese alliance; as far as is known however, no representations against this were made. The highest military circles – and this applies not merely to the senior officers of the Wehrmacht – apparently shared Hitler's view that the campaign against Russia would probably go quickly. This does not alter that fact that in basic strategic questions such as these the Operations Staff was in no position to express any differing views since it had come to consider itself merely as the military working staff of Hitler. In all questions concerning military co-operation with Japan the Navy was the Service most intimately concerned, but throughout this period any ideas on the subject which emerged either from OKW or OKM dealt exclusively with the support of Japan in her forthcoming struggle against England and possibly also against the United States. That part of OKW *Directive no. 24* of 5 March 1941 dealing with this subject was based upon a memorandum from OKM and an attached study by Section L; it laid down basic instructions the last sentence of which read: 'no mention whatever of Operation Barbarossa will be made to the Japanese'.[24]

FINAL INSTRUCTIONS

There were a number of other tasks which, under Jodl's direction, fell to the lot of Section L during the final preparatory period for the Russian campaign; we had to collect the results of reconnaissance by the Army, Navy and Air Force for the usual daily briefings; we had to put over to OKH repeated 'desires' by Hitler for major or minor alterations in the plans for the move forward or in the initial object- ives; finally we had to run the 'OKW theatre of war' in Finland through the Corps Headquarters Norway which had been placed in command in that area. All Hitler's initiatives were the product of his own ceaselessly working brain and as far as anybody knows they were immediately and without further consideration transformed into orders both by his immediate entourage (ie primarily by Jodl) and also by the headquarters to which they were addressed. The following are examples:

On 8 March General Jodl handed to me 'new instructions from the Führer' laying down:

> The operation against Petsamo in Finland to be extended to include the capture of Murmansk.
>
> To this end Dietl's Mountain Corps to be reinforced by a mobile group including heavy tanks.
>
> The harbours of Murmansk and Archangel to be mined.
>
> The approaches to the Pripet Marshes in Central Russia to be mined.
>
> Anti-aircraft defence of the Rumanian oilfields to be reinforced.

Hitler's instructions on 16 June:

> Owing to the very great width of the front the date of the attack in the East not to be dependent on weather conditions.
>
> The division on the northernmost flank of Army Group North not to attack but to remain on the defensive; the centre and left flank of Ninth Army (Army Group Centre) to be reinforced from the reserves to guard against Russian flank attacks.
>
> 72 Infantry Division in Rumania to be made 'mobile' (ie motor- ized) to guard against possible landings on the Black Sea coast.[25]

Hitler was therefore breaking all the rules governing the activity either of the Head of a State or of a Supreme Commander. The culminating point of this procedure was the 'Great Conference' in the Reich Chancellery in Berlin on 14 June 1941. All commanders of Army Groups, Armies, Armoured Groups and the comparable Naval and Air Force commanders were assembled and in the presence of the senior officers of the High Commands of the three Services and of OKW, together with their immediate subordinates, made to give Hitler in complete detail their tasks and intentions. This involved the arrival of a very large number of senior officers and for concealment purposes Hitler's personal office issued detailed instructions laying down which of the various entrances to the Old and New Reich Chancelleries were to be used and the times at which everybody should arrive. The presentations took place in the Parliament Chamber of the Old Reich Chancellery; those taking part were divided by sectors of the front into individual groups, were summoned by name to appear at stated intervals and were greeted by Hitler in a casual manner. The conference broke off at 2.0 pm for lunch to which all were invited; at the end of the meal Hitler made a 'wide-ranging political speech' in which he explained once more the reasons for the attack on Russia and stated yet again that the collapse of Russia would lead to England giving up the struggle. As far as any outside observer could judge all those present were in confident mood.[26]

Among other preparatory measures for which OKW was responsible mention must be made of the 'time-table'. This was the last and most comprehensive document of the series; it was based upon information and requirements from the three Services and its compilation led to numerous problems owing to its comprehensive nature and the inter-dependence of the measures dealing with the East, the West and the North. The whole time-table had to be worked over a second time when the attack was postponed, owing to the campaign in the Balkans.[27] In addition a number of questions had to be discussed with the office of Admiral Canaris such as the closing of frontiers and communications in the areas bordering on Russia; governing factors were the necessity to achieve surprise and the desire to allow Russian trains carrying valuable war material to enter Germany up to the last moment; as far as I remember the intention was that the last goods train from Russia should be allowed across the German frontier at midnight 21–22 June.[28]

Finally Section L had one peculiar task; it was instructed to assemble information on all frontier violations and similar probings by the Russian Army and Air Force during recent months in the form of notes to the Foreign Ministry, some of which were to be back-dated. According to their importance from the point of view of international law these reports were to be signed by me in the case of minor incidents, by General Jodl in the case of moderately serious incidents and by the Chief of OKW in the case of incidents of major importance. It was not difficult to guess the purpose behind this; it was made crystal clear on 19 June when the Foreign Ministry liaison officer to OKW told me that: 'yesterday evening the Führer instructed the Foreign Minister to address to him, on the basis of the OKW reports of Russian frontier violations received to date, a final appeal on the lines that the menace of Russian movements makes any further delay dangerous'.[29] As far as I remember these 'special reports' were based on actual happenings of which there were plenty.[30]

The conclusions which Hitler now proceeded to draw from this 'game in which everybody had his part to play' were far byond anything justified by the facts. Although there was little else to be expected, those of us who were intimately involved were seized with a feeling of discomfort and disquiet. All these preliminaries seemed to raise the spectre of 'an unjust war' – something which had never entered into the calculations of an officer whose whole career was founded upon the concept of 'the justice of his cause'. Admittedly it was later established that the Soviets were at a much higher state of military preparedness than anyone had thought, as proved by the vast numbers of prisoners captured during the battles on the frontiers and the newly constructed airfields in the frontier zone which were found to be fully occupied; this could not however altogether erase the persistent impression of injustice. We could only comfort ourselves with the thought that, although we had to admit that they were not very obvious, there were probably 'reasons of State' which of course were a law unto themselves and which were perhaps in some degree justified by previous Soviet armed incursions into Finland and Rumania.

THE 'CRIMINAL ORDER'

Even these standards could not be applied to Hitler's requirements as regards the so-called 'special matters'. I refer here to those orders which were later labelled 'criminal' and with which the Operations Staff and Section L necessarily had something to do. It seems to me to be necessary at this point to go into some detail regarding the circumstances surrounding the production of these orders, all the more so since the descriptions so far published are based primarily upon the judgments of the Nuremberg Tribunals and, like those Tribunals, have taken little account of the evidence of anyone like myself directly concerned. I propose to follow the production of these orders step by step, producing full documentary and other proof. Before starting on this process however, both the survivors of those days and the present generation should pause for a moment and get two facts into the forefront of their minds:

1 The Dictator was now at the height of his power and his authority was unfettered; he was supported almost unanimously by the German people; he was as firmly obsessed by a 'crusading ideal' as were some of his later opponents;[31] as a result he was open to no counter-argument; his intentions could only be countered with any prospect of success by working under cover.

2 The limited possibilities open to an officer of making representations and the conflict of duty with which he was faced. His innate background was one of discipline, law and honour, based on the historical example of the leaders of the Prussian and German States; now in the midst of a life and death war (and this is no attempt to minimize the well-known criminal acts and propensities of the Hitler regime, though, be it noted, it was internationally recognized), he found himself suddenly in revolt against orders given by the Head of his State and his Government because those orders were incompatible with his code of military ethics.

There is a further extraneous consideration: in the case of an advance into Russia it was more difficult than anywhere else for the Commander-in-Chief of the Army to give up his so-called 'right of unlimited authority'; it was not conceivable that in the 'operational area' or the connected 'rear areas' there should be any other German organization exercising powers for which they were not responsible to the Army independently of C.-in-C. Army and the higher headquarters to whom he had delegated authority. This meant that the Commander-in-Chief of the Army was forced to come to the necessary agreements with those superior authorities to whom were responsible the Special Detachments of 'SD'* and police which Hitler forced upon the Army; but they did not belong to the Wehrmacht and the Commander-in-Chief had no idea what were the real tasks of these 'Special Employment' organizations.

With the knowledge we possess today the starting point of the chain of events, from the point of view of both substance and time, seems to be the comments made by General Jodl on 3 March 1941 on the draft of *Instructions on Special Matters attached to Directive no. 21 (Operation Barbarossa)*; this had been sent to him by Section L as a piece of routine staff work which normally preceded any campaign; it was usually headed *Special Instructions*. He made a few introductory remarks to the effect that he had 'shown the Führer the draft' which he had in fact previously somewhat altered himself. He then summarized Hitler's 'directions' for the 'final version' as follows:[32]

The forthcoming campaign is more than a mere armed conflict; it is a collision between two different ideologies. In view of the size of the area involved, this war will not be ended merely by the defeat of the enemy armed forces. The entire area must be split up into different states each with their own government with which we can then conclude peace.

The formation of these governments requires great political ability and must rest upon well-thought-out principles.

Any large-scale revolution gives rise to events which cannot subsequently be expunged. The socialist ideal can no longer be wiped out in the Russia of today. From the internal point of view the formation of new states and governments must inevitably be based on this principle. The Bolshevist-Jewish intelligentsia must be eliminated as having been the 'oppressor' of the people up to now. The old bourgeois and aristocratic intelligentsia, in so far as it still exists among the émigrés, does not come into the picture either. It would be rejected by the Russian people and is basically anti-German. This applies particularly to the ex-Baltic States.

Furthermore we must under all circumstances avoid allowing a nationalist Russia to appear in place of Bolshevist Russia, for history shows that this will also once more become anti-German.

* SD – Sicherheitsdienst – Security Service.

Our object is to construct as soon as possible and using the minimum of military force, socialist states which will be dependent upon us.

This is a task so difficult that it cannot be entrusted to the Army.

Jodl then continued:[33] 'in accordance with these instructions from the Führer the Directive must be re-drafted as follows':

1 The Army must have an operational area. This must however be no deeper than is necessary. No military government should be set up in rear of this area. Instead Reich Commissars should be appointed for defined regions of considerable size, the boundaries of which should follow ethnographical lines. It will be the task of the commissars rapidly to build up the political machinery of the new states. Alongside the commissars, there should be 'Wehrmacht Territorial Commanders'; they will be responsible to the Commander-in-Chief of the Army only for purely military questions directly connected with the conduct of operations; for all other matters they will be responsible to OKW. Their staffs will include organizations to deal with matters which are clearly the province of the Wehrmacht (war economy, signals, internal security, etc.). The bulk of the police forces will be responsible to the Reich Commissars.

2 Frontiers will only be closed where they abut on the zone of operations. If it proves necessary *to employ organizations responsible to the Reichsführer SS* in this area as well as the Secret Field Security police* the approval of the Reichsführer SS must be obtained. *This may be necessary since all Bolshevist leaders or commissars must be liquidated forthwith.* There is no question of courts martial having anything to do with these matters; they should not deal with any legal matters other than those internal to the armed forces.

3 In Section III of the draft instructions (for Rumania, Slovakia, Hungary and Finland) there should merely be an indication that, if the Commander-in-Chief of the Army finds it necessary to ask for any special powers in these countries, a request to that effect should be forwarded to OKW which will then get in touch with the Foreign Ministry. There can be no question of the Army making 'direct application' to German representatives in these countries for such powers.

* Himmler.

'The draft should be finalized as soon as possible and re-typed in double spacing to allow the Führer to make further alterations. You are authorized to get in touch with OKH. There is no need for the moment to discuss with Secretary of State Dr Stuckart (the Reich Ministry for Interior) or Backe (Reich Ministry for Food).[34] The *Instructions on Special Matters* were thereupon re-drafted by Section L and signed by the Chief of OKW on 13 March 1941; they are given textually below. They may serve as an example of the so called *OKW Special Instructions* normally issued at the beginning of a campaign but in this case they covered a considerably broader field in accordance with Hitler's instructions and had also had to be altered fundamentally, primarily in so far as concerned the reduction in the area of the operations zone. It should also be noted that even in its final form there is no mention of the 'Bolshevist-Jewish intelligentsia' or of the 'Bolshevist leaders and commissars' particularly referred to by Hitler.

Oberkommando der Wehrmacht
WF St/Abt L (IV/Qu)
44125/41 g. K. Chefs

Top Secret	HQ in the Field
By Hand of Officer only	13 March 1941

Ref: WF St/Abt L(1) No. 33408/40
g. K. Chefs dated 18 December 1940   Copy No. 4 of 5

Instructions on Special Matters (Annexe to Directive No. 21) (Operation Barbarossa).

I. *The Operations Zone and Plenary Powers*

1. At latest four weeks before the beginning of operations OKW will issue instructions bringing into force for the areas of East Prussia and Poland the powers of command and regulations for supply appropriate to an operational zone. These will be valid within the Wehrmacht only. OKH will put forward their requirements in good time in agreement with Commander-in-Chief Air.

It is not proposed to issue a declaration constituting East Prussia and Poland an operations zone. Commander-in-Chief Army is however authorized by virtue of the Führer's decrees of 19 and 21 October 1939 (which have not been published) to take such measures as are necessary to ensure the fulfilment of his military task and to safeguard his forces. This authority may be delegated to Commanders-in-Chief of Army Groups and Armies. These instructions will have precedence over any other obligations and instructions of civilian authorities.

2. Russian territory occupied in the course of operations will, as soon as the progress of operations allows, be split up into states each with their own government in accordance with Special Instructions. As a result:

(a) As the Army advances across the frontiers of the Reich and of neighbouring states the depth of the resulting Army operations zone should be kept to the minimum. In this zone Commander-in-Chief Army is authorized to exercise plenary powers and is further authorized to delegate these to Commanders-in-Chief of Army Groups and Armies.

(b) In order to prepare the political and administrative organization the Reichsführer SS has been given by the Führer certain special tasks within the operations zone of the Army; these stem from the necessity finally to settle the conflict between two opposing political systems. Within the framework of these tasks the Reichsführer SS will act independently and on his own responsibility. This is however without prejudice to the overriding plenary power hereby accorded to Commander-in-Chief Army and the authorities to whom it may be delegated by him. The Reichsführer SS is responsible that military operations are not affected by any measures necessary to carry out his task. Details will be settled direct between OKH and the Reichführer SS.

(c) As soon as the operations zone has reached a sufficient depth a rear boundary will be laid down. The occupied area in rear of the operations zone will have its own political administration. It will be divided ethnographically and follow the Army Group boundaries. It will initially consist of North (Baltic), Centre (White Russia), South (Ukraine). In these areas the political administration will be transferred to Reich Commissars who will receive their instructions from the Führer.

3. In order to deal with military problems in the administered areas in rear of the operations zone Wehrmacht commanders will be appointed who will be responsible to the Chief of OKW.

The Wehrmacht Territorial Commander will be the senior representative of the Wehrmacht in the area concerned and will have all military powers of command. He will be charged with the duties of a Territorial Commander and will have the prerogatives of an Army or Corps Commander.

In this capacity he will be responsible for the following:

(a) Close co-operation with the Reich Commissar in order to support him in his political role.

(b) Exploitation of the country and protection of economic assets of value to the German economy (see para. 4 below).

(c) Exploitation of the country for supply of the forces in accordance with the requirements of OKH.

(d) Military security throughout the area against insurrection, sabotage and enemy parachute attacks; airfields, supply routes and supply installations are of particular importance.

(e) Road traffic regulations.

(f) Regulations for the accommodation of the Wehrmacht, police and prisoners-of-war organizations in so far as these are located in the area.

As far as the civilian authorities are concerned the Wehrmacht commander is authorized to take such measures as are necessary to carry out his military tasks. In this case his instructions will take precedence over all others including those of the Reich Commissar.

Subsequent instructions will be issued on procedures, appointments and allocations of the necessary forces.

The moment at which the Wehrmacht commander will take over command will be laid down as soon as the military position allows a change in the command organization to be made without adverse effect on operations. Up to this point the authorities installed by OKH will remain operative on the same basis as laid down for the Wehrmacht commanders.

4. The Führer has charged the Reichsmarschall* with the co-ordination of the economic administration both in the operations zone and the administrative zone; the latter has delegated this task to the head of the Armaments Office. Special Instructions will be issued by OKW (Armaments Office).

5. The bulk of the police forces will be responsible to the Reich Commissars. Requirements for the detachment of police forces to the operations zone will be forwarded in good time by OKH to OKW Operations Staff – Section L.

* Göring.

6. Special orders and instructions will be issued regarding the attitude of the troops to the civilian population and the responsibility of Courts Martial.

II. *Movement of Persons and Goods, Signal Traffic*

7. Special instructions will be issued by the OKW Operations Staff before the beginning of operations laying down the measures necessary to restrict the movement of persons and goods into Russia and the use of communications.

8. When operations begin C.in-C. Army will close the German/Russian frontier and later the rear boundary of the operations zone to the movement of all non-military persons and goods and to all communications with the exception of those belonging to police units under the Reichsführer SS employed in accordance with the Führer's instructions. Accommodation and rationing of these units will be the responsibility of OKH (Q Branch) which is authorized to ask, where necessary, for Liaison Officers from the Reichsführer SS.

The closing of the frontier is applicable also to senior personalities and representatives of the Central Reich Authorities and of the headquarters of the Party. The Central Reich Authorities and headquarters of the Party will be informed accordingly by the OKW Operations Staff. Exceptions will be authorized only by C.-in-C. Army and headquarters to whom he has delegated authority.

Requests for authority to enter will be addressed exclusively to C.-in-C. Army except for the police organizations subordinate to the Reichsführer SS for which special regulations will be made.

III. *Instructions for Rumania, Slovakia, Hungary and Finland*

9. Special agreements with these States will be made by OKW in collaboration with the Foreign Ministry in accordance with the requirements of the High Commands of the Services. In the event of special powers proving necessary during the subsequent course of operations application will be made to OKW.

10. Special police measures designed for the immediate protection of the troops may be taken even if special powers have not been granted.

Further instructions on the subject will be issued later.

11. Special instructions applicable to the territory of these States will be issued on the following:

> Rationing, forage, accommodation and equipment
> Local purchase and import of goods
> Currency and payments for services
> Pay of the troops
> Claims for damages
> Postal and telegraph traffic
> Traffic regulations
> Legal matters.

The Services and other sections of OKW should submit to the OKW Operations Staff – Section L by 27 March 1941 any requirements on these subjects to be put to the Government of the countries concerned.

IV. *Instructions for Sweden*

12. Since Sweden can be no more than a transit area no special powers are visualized for the commanders of German troops. They have however, both the right and duty to take any measures necessary for the immediate protection of rail transports against acts of sabotage and other attacks.

der Chef des Oberkommandos der Wehrmacht
Keitel

Distribution

Commander-in-Chief Army	Copy no. 1
Commander-in-Chief Navy	Copy no. 2
Minister for Aviation and Commander-in-Chief Air	Copy no. 3
Operations Staff	Copy no. 4
Section L	Copy no. 5

The wording of the instructions regarding the 'special tasks' (Section I para. 2(b)) leaves little doubt that Hitler himself inserted them in the 'double spacing' of the second draft: they constitute his instructions to the Reichsführer SS and only he, as opposed to any Wehrmacht authority, could authorize the 'Chief of the German Police' to act independently and on his own authority. The following points were of particular importance for the subsequent chain of events and should be emphasized for the benefit of those who may not be so well acquainted with the circumstances of the time;

1 The 'general instructions' of 3 March left open the question whether the Reichsführer SS was authorized to operate in the

Army operations zone. This had now however become an established fact and the final draft of the instructions did not give either OKW or OKH any opportunity to exert their influence upon the action of the SS.

2 No further indication is given regarding the nature or scope of these 'special tasks'. It is merely indicated that the employment of a political police force is visualized. The Wehrmacht had, however, no more authority or capacity to influence them or their methods than it had in the Reich itself. In view of conditions within the Soviet Union there could be no question that it was both necessary and wise to take energetic police measures to secure the rear areas of the battle zone. But the last sentence of para. 2(b) does not imply that the tasks of the Reichsführer SS had to be agreed in detail with OKH. This provision merely indicates that the two authorities had to reach mutual agreements regarding the entry into the Army operational zone of organizations subordinate to the Reichsführer SS, on any limitations to their freedom of movement in relation to the battle front and on their accommodation, rationing and supply.

The *Instructions* having been thus provisionally decided, we in Section L were critical of them, primarily because they appeared to represent a further interference with the prerogatives of Commander-in-Chief Army in the operations zone, about which there had been so much argument, also because we feared that they would lead to new difficulties with OKH. Contrary to our expectations, however, the Army apparently rapidly accommodated itself to the instructions laid down by Hitler. On 13 March Halder notes: 'meeting Wagner-Heydrich: police questions' and next day acknowledges receipt of the OKW instruction with the words: 'Special Instruction Barbarossa' without special comment.[35] Apparently also, there were no appreciable reactions outside OKH to the exaggerated phrases regarding his intentions in the 'rear areas' in the East which Hitler used a few days later during his closing address to Commander-in-Chief Army and his senior staff officers at the large-scale briefing already mentioned.[36] Judging however from one's knowledge of the personalities involved, they must have become all the more determined to set a definite limit to the activities of the Reichsführer SS and his minions and keep them as far away as possible. In view of their special powers in the operations zone they had plenty of opportunity of doing this; for instance they could forbid movement on roads and restrict the issue of fuel.

This was no doubt the spirit in which General Wagner, who had always been more insistent than anybody on the necessity for preserving the integrity of the Commander-in-Chief's power of command within the operational zone, conducted the necessary discussions with Heydrich:[37] on his side the latter undoubtedly took good care not to let out a word about the true character of the 'special tasks'. The resulting order was made available in draft by OKH to the OKW Operations Staff; it is clear from the text, which is reproduced below, that there was nothing questionable or objectionable in it.

26 March 1941

Secret

ARMY HIGH COMMAND
ARMY GENERAL STAFF/QMG

In order to carry out certain special Security Police tasks which are not within the province of the Army it will be necessary to employ certain Special Detachments (Sonderkommandos) of the Security Service (SD) in the operations zone.

With the agreement of the Chief of the Security Police and of the SD, the employment of the Security Police (SP) and of the SD in the zone of operations will be governed by the following rules:

1. *Tasks*
(a) In the Army Rear Area:

Prior to the opening of operations, listing of certain concrete objects (material, archives, card indexes of anti-German or anti-government organizations, associations, groups, etc.) and certain important individuals (leading émigrés, saboteurs, terrorists, etc.).

The Commander-in-Chief of an Army is authorized to forbid the employment of these special detachments in those parts of the Army area in which their employment might have adverse effects upon operations.

(b) In the communications zone:

To discover and stamp out anti-German and anti-government movements in so far as these do not form part of the enemy's armed forces, provision of general information to the commander of the communications zone regarding the political situation.

Co-operation with Field Security officers or Field Security units will be governed by the 'principles for co-operation between the Secret State Police and the Field Security organization of the Wehrmacht' agreed with the Security Branch of the Reich War Ministry on 1 January 1937.

2. Co-operation between the Special Detachments and the military authorities in the rear army area (see 1 (a) above). The Special Detachments of the Security Police (SD) will carry out their tasks on their own responsibility. They will be under the orders of Armies for movement, rations and accommodation. This does not affect the authority of the Chief of the SP and SD in matters of discipline and jurisprudence. They will receive their technical instructions from the Chief of the SP and SD but where necessary their activity will be restricted by orders from Army headquarters (see para. 1(a) above).

A representative of the Chief of the SP and the SD will be installed in each Army area for the central direction of these detachments. It will be his duty to inform the Commander-in-Chief of the Army concerned in good time of the instructions he receives from the Chief of the SP and the SD. The military commander is authorized to give this representative such instructions as may be necessary to avoid any interference with military operations; such instructions will have precedence over all others.

These representatives are at all times to work in close co-operation with the Intelligence Section of headquarters; the military authorities may demand the appointment of a liaison official to the Intelligence Section; it is the duty of the Intelligence Section to co-ordinate the work of the Special Detachments with that of the military Security Service and of the Secret Field Security Police and with the requirements of operations.

The Special Detachments are authorized, within the framework of their task and on their own responsibility, to take executive measures affecting the civilian population. In this connection it is their duty to work in the closest co-operation with the Field Security Service. Any measures which may have an effect on operations must be agreed by the Commander-in-Chief of the Army concerned.

3. Co-operation between groups or detachments of the Security Police (or SD) and the commander in the communications zone (see para. 1(b) above).

[Text as in para. 2 above merely substituting the appropriate headquarters and organizations.]

4. Division of responsibility between Special Detachments (Sonderkommandos), Field Detachments (Einsatzkommandos) and Field Sections (Einsatzgruppen) on one side and the Secret Field Security police on the other.

Questions of political security within the Army and the immediate protection of the troops remain the task of the Secret Field Security Police alone. Any problems of this nature are to be transferred forthwith by the Special Detachments, Field Detachments or Field Sections to the Secret Field Security Police; similarly the latter are to transfer to the Special Detachments, Field Detachments or Field Sections without delay any problems falling within their province. On all other questions the agreement of 1 January 1937 will apply (see para. 1 above).

Signed...............

None of those officers who took part in the discussions or in the drafting of these orders had the smallest inkling that under cover of these agreements and by virtue of a secret instruction from Hitler to Himmler the 'Field Sections of the SD' would proceed, immediately the campaign had begun, to the systematic mass murder of Jews in the rear areas of the Eastern front.

The first occasion on which Hitler openly demanded unlawful action from the Wehrmacht was on 30 March 1941. On that date he made a speech lasting almost two and a half hours to some 200 to 250 senior officers, consisting of the Commanders-in-Chief of the three Services and the senior Army, Navy and Air Force commanders selected for the Eastern campaign together with their senior staff officers.[38] The meeting took place in a large conference room at the Ebertstrasse end of the Great Hall of the New Reich Chancellery; the hall was entirely full and those present were seated in long rows of chairs according to rank and seniority. The object was clearly the same as that of Hitler's similar 'appeals' on 22 August and 23 November 1939 prior to the Polish and Western campaigns ie to indoctrinate the higher-level commanders and their senior staff o fficers with his views on the probable course of the forthcoming campaign. But in this case he also intended to indicate to the assembled company the special requirements which in his view would arise from the Eastern campaign as a result of its character as a 'struggle between two opposing ideologies'. He spoke in forceful terms. He was undoubtedly aware that ideologically there was still a great gulf between him and this assembly of the cream of the German officer corps. They sat there before him in stubborn silence, a silence broken only twice – when the assembly rose first as he entered through a door in the rear and went up to the rostrum, and later when he departed the same way. Otherwise not a hand moved and not a word was spoken but by him.

It was this speech by Hitler which gave birth to the *Commissar Order* and to the decree concerning the use of court-martial procedure in the 'Barbarossa' area, known for short as the *Barbarossa Order*. As far as the *Commissar Order* was concerned the Supreme Commander of the Wehrmacht laid it down in his speech that Soviet commissars and officials were to be treated as criminals whether they belonged to the armed forces or to the civilian administration. They were not therefore to be regarded as soldiers nor to be treated as prisoners of war. When captured they were to be handed over to the Field Sections of the SD or if this was not possible, shot on the spot by the troops. As regards the *Barbarossa Order*, Hitler had already laid it down on 3 March that courts martial were to deal only with the troops; he now developed this theme further and enunciated two principles: first, that in his dealings with 'hostile inhabitants' the German soldier need not be bound by the letter of the laws of war or of disciplinary instructions but that on the contrary 'any type of attack by the inhabitants against the Wehrmacht' should be dealt with with the utmost severity, including summary execution without court martial procedure. He justified these instructions primarily by his conviction that Bolshevism was as he put it 'a sociological crime'; as regards the commissars and officials he pointed out the inhuman cruelties of which they had been guilty when the Red Army had moved into Poland, the Baltic States, Finland and Rumania. Starting from this point he used every turn of phrase to convince his audience that, when fighting the Soviets, there was no place for soldierly chivalry or 'out-of-date notions' of military comradeship. This was a struggle in which not only must the Red Army be beaten in the field but communism must be exterminated for all time.

The Period of Overwhelming Military Success

Many have subsequently expressed the view that Hitler's fulminations should have led some of those present to give vent to some protest or adverse reaction after he had departed. There is nothing to show that anything of the sort happened; I was myself present and none of the contemporary accounts so far published make any mention of such a thing. Halder, for instance, made full notes of what went on and he ends merely by giving the sense of Hitler's final words: 'one of the sacrifices which commanders have to make is to overcome any scruples they may have'; in the margin he has written, obviously to remind himself: 'order by C.-in-C.' Immediately thereafter follows the entry: 'mid-day: everybody present at lunch – afternoon: conference with the Führer'. Subsequent entries make it clear that both the lunch and the conference took place with a restricted circle of 'Army Group commanders and some of their subordinates'; the only name appearing is that of Guderian abbreviated 'Gud'. As regards the conference Halder merely notes: 'nothing new'. It may therefore be taken as certain that none of those present availed themselves of the opportunity even to mention the demands made by Hitler during the morning. It was generally realized of course, that, as had frequently been proved before, open opposition generally did more harm than good. The real reasons however for this lack of reaction on the part of the most senior officers of the Army were probably that the majority of them had not followed Hitler's long diatribe in detail, that others had not grasped the full meaning of his proposals and that others thought it better first to look into these questions more deeply or to follow normal military practice and await the reaction of their superiors. Even the late Field Marshal von Bock, who later emerged as an opponent of the *Commissar Order* and whose observations in his diary are usually particularly outspoken, makes no special comment on the meeting or the restricted conference which followed. I personally was present only for Hitler's speech in the morning.

In his evidence before the International Military Tribunal Field Marshal Keitel simply stated: 'at any rate they did not do so [address the Führer] after that discussion'.[39] He may, of course, merely have meant that he had no knowledge of any reactions or objections to Hitler's plan. His words can however, equally well be taken to mean that as Chief of OKW, whose job it would have been to translate Hitler's requirements into orders and thereby elaborate and confirm them, he took no action. This interpretation does not however fit in with the picture presented by the Chief of OKW either during or subsequent to the war and it does not therefore seem that it can be regarded as in any way valid. This was a particularly agitated period – the Balkan campaign was in progress, Crete had just been captured, negotiations with France had just been started, events were on the move in North Africa and the Middle East, Hess had flown to England and the *Bismarck* had been sunk; there seems little doubt therefore that all these upheavals contributed to Hitler's intentions being forgotten in a conspiracy of silence. It is moreover an incontestable fact that in this case neither Keitel nor Jodl gave me any instructions to prepare drafts of the resulting orders – quite contrary to their normal practice of hanging upon Hitler's every nod and wish. As far as I was concerned I took good care never to refer to the demands made by Hitler even in casual conversation.[40]

The conspiracy of silence had lasted more than five weeks and seemed to be fulfilling its object when a memorandum from OKH dated 6 May set things going again. This appeared to emanate from 'the Commander-in-Chief of the Army' and was headed 'General Officer specially employed by C.-in-C. Army (Legal Section)'; it was addressed 'to Chief OKW – Section L – personal for General Warlimont'. It consisted of the draft of an order entitled *General Instructions for dealing with political leaders and for the co-ordinated execution of the task allotted on 31 March 1941.*[41] Section 1, entitled 'the Army area', contained a general description of what commissars were, following the lines of Hitler's remarks in his speech of 30 March. It then continued:

Political authorities and leaders (commissars) constitute a special menace to the security of the troops and the pacification of conquered territory.

If such persons are captured by the troops or otherwise apprehended they will be brought before an officer who has disciplinary powers of punishment. The latter will summon two military witnesses (officer or NCO rank) and establish that the person captured or apprehended is a political personality or leader (Commissar). If adequate proof of his political position is forthcoming, the officer will forthwith order his execution and ensure that it is carried out.

The political leaders (commissars) in Russian units belong to the category of political officials. It is of particular importance that they should be immediately detected and segregated since they will be the ones primarily responsible for continuing propaganda if sent back to Germany as prisoners of war. They should be liquidated if possible at prisoners-of-war collecting points or at the latest on passage through the transit camps. The same applies to commissars in the civil administration and the Party and other political personalities with whom the troops may come in contact. Political leaders in economic and technical organizations need only be apprehended in those individual cases in which they take some action against the Wehrmacht.

Political leaders and commissars who are captured will not be sent to the rear.'

The 'General Officer specially employed' was subordinate not to the Chief of Staff of the Army but direct to the Commander-in-Chief. Halder's diary however, makes it clear that, because of its special importance, he had seen the draft of this order. The relevant entry for 6 May states:

'Conference with General Müller (specially employed) and the Judge Advocate General:

(a) Issue of an order on the lines of the Führer's last speech to General officers. The troops must be aware that the Eastern campaign is an ideological struggle.

(b) Questions of the competence of courts martial.

As the recipient of this memorandum in OKW my reaction was one of pained surprise. Up to now Hitler's verbal instructions had been known only to a restricted circle of senior officers, most of whom had undoubtedly forgotten about them long ago. Now here was the Commander-in-Chief of the Army apparently thinking it necessary to put these instructions in writing and issue them as a definite order to the troops together with 'detailed instructions for their execution'. The original of the Army memorandum exists and my immediate reaction stands out clearly from the note thereon in my own handwriting which was in cautious terms and reads: 'it remains to be seen whether a written instruction of this sort is necessary. Must be shown to and discussed with Chief OKW. Issue instructions of our own?'[42]

I handed this comment on as a basis for consideration to the Working Group in Section L most immediately concerned – 'Administration'. At the same time I took the Army draft out of the 'normal channel' in spite of the fact that in accordance with the general 'office instructions' it should have been my job to check the text to ensure that it was in agreement with Hitler's verbal instructions and submit the document to the addressee (Keitel) with any necessary comments. I did not even tell Keitel or Jodl that the Army draft had arrived and used the time thus gained to work with certain members of the Administration Group who thought as I did, trying to find ways and means which would make it possible to avoid the issue of a written order of this sort. With this in mind I took the following action:

1 The army draft was handed for further action to the Legal Section of OKW. The reason for this was that the Legal Section of OKH had clearly had a great deal to do with the drafting of the text; I also felt that legal arguments were more likely to convince the Chief of OKW than any protestations of mine.

   Result: Telephone call from the Chief of the Legal Section, the late Dr Lehmann, to the effect that Keitel had forbidden him to have anything to do with the subject. The Army draft was returned to Section L on 9 May.[43]

2 I had a confidential conversation with General Wagner, the QMG of the Army, who was of the same seniority as myself and a personal friend, in order to see whether there was any possibility of getting the Army draft order withdrawn. It was General Wagner who shortly before had been detailed by C.-in-C. Army to carry out the negotiations with Heydrich.

   Result: Wagner refused categorically. He gave as his reason that, as a result of his impressions of his talk with Heydrich, he was convinced that it was necessary to submit a draft order on this subject to Hitler. If this was not done, there was a danger that Hitler would send the SD right up into the forward areas so that it could be used to carry out his wishes.[44] Wagner added however, that OKH was determined that there should be no excesses and for this very reason had prepared an order for the maintenance of discipline. It would be distributed down to the smallest units in the army. Finally he advised me most emphatically 'to keep my nose out of this business'.[45] This meant that the idea of suppressing the order had to be abandoned.

3 I next decided to try to make use of a document which had just come to the knowledge of Section L – *Memorandum no. 3* from 'Reichsleiter' Rosenberg to Hitler. In this Rosenberg who was 'Minister for the East' – designate, explained that he would be unable to build up a civil administration in the occupied areas if he could not make use of the civil commissars and officials. His proposal was that only 'senior and very senior' officials should be liquidated in accordance with Hitler's instructions.

OKW in general and Section L in particular had nothing to do with the institution of civil government in the East. Having now however been reassured by what I had heard from Wagner concerning the forward Army areas, I felt that the Wehrmacht might be able, by supporting Rosenberg's ideas, to introduce some better procedure than the simple persecution of commissars and officials who did not happen to belong to the Red Army.

These investigations took approximately a week. It was only after they were completed and when, as far as one could judge, they offered considerable possibilities of preventing the *Commissar Order* being carried out, that I drafted an 'office minute' dated 12 May. This began as follows:

I. OKH has submitted a draft instruction attached as Annexe 1.

I then summarized the salient points of the Army draft and concluded with the following comments by Section L:

II. As against this, *Memorandum no. 3* by Reichsleiter Rosenberg visualizes that only the senior and most senior officials should be liquidated since officials working in the administration of provinces, communes and economic enterprises are essential for the administration of occupied territory.

III. It will therefore be necessary for the Führer to decide what the governing principles should be.'

As regards para. II above Section L proposes that:

(1) officials who take action against the troops should be liquidated as being guerillas.

(2) officials who are guilty of no hostile action should initially be left undisturbed. Only as we penetrate further into the country will it be possible to decide whether the remaining

officials should be left where they are or handed over to the Special Detachments (of the SD) in so far as the latter are not in a position to take them over themselves.

(3) Political officials in units should be handled *in accordance with the proposals of OKH*. They should not be recognized as prisoners of war and should be liquidated at latest at the transit camp stage. In no case should they be sent to the rear.[46]

This minute I purposely sent not to Keitel who was the addressee of the Army draft but to Jodl from whom I thought that in this case I would get more understanding and support. In order to get this note in perspective – or before too hasty a criticism of it is made – it should be emphasized that a 'minute' was not a draft of an order but was merely intended to summarize a problem and where possible influence the views of the superior officer. It should also be noted that in the circumstances there was nothing to be gained by individual officers coming out in open opposition and so offering themselves up as martyrs; the only effective procedure in the case of an order of this nature from Hitler was to do all one could to sabotage it by manipulating the content and drafting of the resulting orders. I need hardly add that this sort of game of verbal hide-and-seek was anything but an enjoyable process, even when successful. In this case I was in a position similar to that of the commanders in the field who later found that there was only one way out of this situation; they worked out a complicated procedure whereby, after careful consideration of the total number of prisoners taken, they from time to time reported that a certain number of commissars had been shot; in fact they had been neither counted nor segregated, still less shot.[47] Not all officers were so unfortunate; but those who found themselves unprepared and against their will faced with this situation can at least claim this: they did not act as they have often been reproached for doing 'in order to save face' but in obedience to the rules of justice and humanity which their conscience dictated to them.

As regards the contents of the minute the following points should be noted: the reference to Rosenberg, who was a highly placed member of the Party, was primarily made in the hope that it would have some effect upon Hitler; I had never had any other connections either with Rosenberg or his office. My own proposal went considerably further than that of Rosenberg; I proposed that no differentiation of rank should be made between officials and that they should only be subject to the recognized laws of war against guerillas if they had actually taken hostile action against German troops. Finally I remember perfectly clearly that I myself added the last paragraph (III 3); I thought that by emphasizing this point I would assist the Army to keep out the SD and would leave it a freer hand; in addition I thought that it would make it easier to gain acceptance for the other counter-proposals I had made.

Once this minute had been sent to Jodl, Section L for the moment had nothing to do with the further handling of the case. As far as I remember it was only in Nuremberg after the war that I saw Jodl's manuscript comments on the minute– 'must be put to the Führer again (13 May)' and 'we must assume that they will take reprisals against German airmen; best to present the whole thing as a matter of reprisals'. In his evidence before the International Tribunal[48] General Jodl stated:

> Now in this case, by my notation, I wanted to indicate to Field Marshal Keitel a new way by which one might possibly still circumvent this order which had been demanded.... I was of the opinion that first of all we should wait and see whether the commissars would actually act as the Führer expected them to act and if his suspicions were confirmed, then make use of reprisals.

Nothing is known to this day of the discussions either in the Reich Chancellery or in the Berghof which presumably took place as a result.

The next time I became involved in this business was when I returned at the end of May from the prolonged negotiations in Paris. On my table in the special train *Atlas*, which was in its usual siding in Salzburg station, I found the final version of the *Commissar Order* as approved by Hitler. The first glance showed that my own proposals based on those of Rosenberg had been included almost word for word in place of the corresponding paragraphs in the Army draft.[49] I was extremely gratified and I also noted that the order carried no signature, which meant that there was no necessity for the addressees to 'report compliance' to Hitler or OKW. I therefore decided myself to sign a covering memorandum addressed to OKH and OKL. My main thought here was to avoid the significant omissions (no signature, no requirement for reports from the Army) being noticed subsequently and made good. Furthermore, this enabled me to add a sentence limiting distribution of the written order 'to Commanders-in-Chief of Armies or Air Fleets'.[50] My view was that as a result all those who thought the same way as I did would be given a further handle to get round the order. As far as my own immediate superiors were concerned, Keitel and Jodl, not a word on the entire subject passed between us either before or since.

This is the unvarnished and, so far as one can see today, complete account of the production of the *Commissar Order*. It will be seen that the only part played in its drafting either by me as Chief of Section L or by any of my officers was to contribute to a considerable watering down.[51] This account both of the chain of events and of the attitude of those involved is a good example of the sort of thing which happened on a number of other occasions in connection with orders of a similar nature when given by Hitler. Just as happened however to a certain extent in this case, his instructions regarding the powers of courts martial in the East were prepared by other sections of OKW in Berlin without any participation by Section L; even Jodl could only exert his personal influence through occasional conversations with Keitel. As far as the military staffs in Supreme Headquarters were concerned, apart perhaps from Hitler's immediate entourage, when further important instances of this type of thing occurred, they were either left in complete ignorance or came to know of them only when they received the final version of the order already signed by Hitler.[52]

The same is true of the further course of events concerning the *Commissar Order*; as far as I know this was dealt with subsequently only by the inmost circles and by them only on two occasions.[53] On 26 September 1941, ie after the campaign had been in progress some three months, a memorandum arrived from OKH dated 23 September, again signed by General Müller, which stated that the experience of the campaign showed that 'the previous instructions for the handling of commissars should be re-examined'.[54] Jodl sent this back with the manuscript comment: 'the Führer is averse to any alteration in the orders already issued for dealing with political commissars'. Then on 6 May 1942, ie a year to the day after the production of the first Army draft of the order, the official diary of the Historical Section of OKW carries the entry:

the Führer gives instructions that in order to increase the readiness to desert or to capitulate of Soviet Russian troops who have been surrounded, authorization is given temporarily and as an experiment for a guarantee to be given in such cases that the lives of commanders, commissars and *politruks** will be spared.[55]

As far as I remember this instruction of Hitler's was the result of personal representations by Field Marshal von Kluge. In effect it meant that the *Commissar Order* had been formally cancelled.[56] Meanwhile it must be assumed that in spite of all efforts to the contrary the order was carried out in certain areas during the first weeks of the Eastern campaign, although not a single report on the subject was ever submitted to Supreme Headquarters. On the other hand there is no doubt that in fact the order had lost all practical significance at the latest by the beginning of the serious winter crisis of early December 1941.

But even during the early period of the Russian campaign it is clear that in the areas in which the Wehrmacht was fighting or in occupation this order was only carried out to a very limited degree. There can be no more convincing proof of this than the fact that in the height of the summer of 1941 vast numbers of commissars of every grade and category were to be found in the prisoner-of-war camps; I did not know of this at the time, nor how Hitler found out about it; I did not know either of his *Instruction for the handling of Soviet Prisoners of War* which was clearly the sequel to his discovery.[57]

As far as one can see this fresh order was primarily intended to make up for that which had not been done in the forward areas by 'segregating' commissars and officials in the prisoner-of-war camps. In the post-war period it has been held in certain quarters to be an integral part of the original *Commissar Order*. That is incorrect. In fact, there was only one man, Hitler, who was both officially and personally involved in the authorship and drafting of both orders; his unhappy Chief of OKW was also involved but only as a recipient. The addressees in the two cases were completely different; the first order was addressed to the Field Headquarters, the second to the Wehrmacht Prisoner-of-War Service. Probably as a result of his experiences with the fighting troops, Hitler cut this Service also out of the chain of command and in the second order merely instructed it to open the gates of the camps to Himmler's minions. As far as the fighting troops were concerned the result was quite different; it was realized that the unlawful treatment meted out to commissars

---

* *Politruks* were the lowest level political commissars in units. The word 'commanders' appears to be an error for 'officials'.

in the prisoner-of-war camps would soon become known to the enemy and that he would then draw the conclusion that his troops must fight to the last round. It was probably this which led to the June 1942 order regarding prisoner-of-war camps being considerably watered down, though it was never cancelled.

One point must be made in conclusion of this murky chapter in my memories: even in military circles the observation is often made that in North Africa and Italy the German Army 'fought like gentlemen', an observation which implies that the Army in the East did the opposite. This is a completely unjustified disparagement of the bulk of the German Army. Quite apart from the fact that there were many transfers of divisions between East and West, it is nearer the truth to say that the German soldier of the second World War contrived to maintain his traditional dignity in the East as elsewhere in spite of the unparallelled strain to which he was subjected by the actions, not merely of the enemy, but of his own 'Supreme Commander'.

CHAPTER 5

The Eastern Campaign – From the Start of the Campaign to the Winter Crisis

THE NEW FIELD HEADQUARTERS

The Army moved across the frontier at first light on 22 June. This time Hitler did not adopt the procedure he had followed in the West in 1940, but waited some thirty-six hours to see the course of events before ordering the move of the headquarters to East Prussia. It was not until midday the following day, the first day of mobilization in the Soviet Union, that the various echelons of Supreme Headquarters got on the move eastwards by air and rail. The field echelon of Section L, the strength and organization of which was unchanged, left at 1445 hours from Berlin-Grünewald for an unknown destination; the following morning at 0345 hours it reached its appointed place in the Forest of Görlitz, a few miles east of Rastenburg.

The detraining point was a halt on a local line and only a few hundred yards away we found the new HQ Area 2. It was entirely surrounded by high barbed-wire fencing and was hardly visible from the road; the majority of the offices were in wooden huts around a simple country inn, in normal times a visiting spot for the people of Rastenburg. It looked as if the regulations governing the Berlin Ministries had been followed as regards size of rooms, numbers of windows and furnishing. Even more remarkable was a semi-underground construction looking like a long railway sleeping car with a row of doors side by side; this proved to contain additional offices and sleeping accommodation for the officers; I even had a double room. The concrete walls were covered with wooden panelling painted in cheerful colours; there were built-in cupboards, glazed basins and baths with water laid on, central heating and every type of electrical gadget – hardly compatible with one's normal picture of a 'field' headquarters. I was the first, a few nights later, to get out of this catacomb; initially I installed myself in the special train which was still in the station nearby; later I moved into the old inn where to begin with the proprietor was still living, and where we established a simple type of officers' mess. The other members of Section L soon followed my example and moved into the office huts.

In addition to the field echelon of the staff, parts of the so-called 'Führer Guard Battalion' of the Army were also accommodated in HQ Area 2; this provided the sentries and its commander did duty as Headquarters Commandant. We saw and had little to do with each other; nevertheless in this part of the headquarters we were completely among our own sort and there were no non-military types about.

On the other side of the road and about half a mile to the east was HQ Area 1 where were to be found Hitler and his entourage from 'State, Party and Wehrmacht'; on the military side this meant Keitel, Jodl and the aides, as before, and in addition the newly appointed 'historian', Colonel Scherff. Here there were also some wooden huts which served as conference room, mess and administrative offices. In general the inhabitants lived and worked in concrete bunkers which were above ground and contained two or more small rooms. Newly constructed roads and tracks criss-crossed the entire area which was sheltered by thick trees. Hitler's hut and bunker lay at the extreme northern end, all windows as usual facing north, since he disliked the sun. He was also responsible for the name 'Wolfschanze' (Wolf's Lair), still used by the Poles when showing people round the camp which has now become one of the local sights.

OKH was about an hour away by road, in the woods near Angerburg; Göring and his staff also were not far off. It is indicative of relationships at the highest levels that in more than three years I never once visited OKL, whereas I was continually in touch with OKH both officially and off duty. This reminds me of another typical difference between the two of a somewhat different sort: when the Army leaders visited 'Wolfschanze' they came in a small, grey, extremely antiquated railway carriage which was no doubt still fit for service on this local line. When Göring came, however, it was in a snorting Diesel train of at least three or four of the most modern coaches, brightly painted and blazing with light, with white-coated attendants and every modern comfort; it occupied a hundred yards or more of the single track line. OKM remained in Berlin, but during one of the early months of the campaign an Admiral appeared as its permanent representative; he was accommodated in HQ Area 1.

Although, when the advance started, 'Wolfschanze' was unusually close to the front, the loneliness of the place was hardly conducive to that sense of being in close touch with great military events which we had had at the comparable period of the western campaign. The whole area was so vast that, even in those early days, when one got on the road 'to the front' only the odd unit was to be seen. I had hoped to follow my procedure of the western campaign and keep in touch with events at the front but that soon became impossible even by using a light aircraft (*Storch*). There was then nothing to do but change to a normal communications aircraft which meant that, in the few hours available, it was generally impossible to land at the place I intended and make the contacts I required. These flights invariably left me with two impressions: first the unmistakable differences in the countryside on either side of the frontier, showing up far more clearly from the air than they could on any map; on the one side was the ancient civilized country of East Prussia with its well-tended farms, well-managed forests, weedless fields and heathlands, tree-shaded roads and tracks and finally its well-ordered pattern of rivers and lakes – all so strikingly different from the general aspect of the country on the eastern side: secondly, and of far greater military significance, the desolation of the apparently limitless plain stretching eastwards, in which the men and horses of the marching infantry divisions seemed almost to become lost.

With the armoured and motorized formations in the lead the front moved rapidly eastwards and the more it did so the lonelier it became in the woods near Rastenburg. Because of the vast distances involved the possibilities of flights to the front became fewer and fewer; one visit for instance took me to Dietl's Corps near the North Cape. This meant that a visit might well involve several days and nights and there was probably nowhere to stay on arrival; naturally for an absence of this length special authorization was necessary and, as before, this was only unwillingly accorded by Jodl. I therefore looked for, and found, other less warlike methods of avoiding suffocation in our prison of concrete and wood. For instance, once or twice a week I would go over early in the morning with the well-known show rider Colonel Momm, who was at the time a staff assistant, to the stud at Rastenburg, where there were excellent horses, and come back a new man after an hour's riding. Once one had got through the barbed wire and the minefields there were good walks in the neighbourhood of the camp, through the lakes and woods of the old well-tended East Prussian countryside and I frequently availed myself of this possibility of recreation during the early hours of the afternoon which were generally quiet. Soon one or two of us would be invited to a simple evening meal, for which we were more than grateful, in one of the country houses in the neighbourhood; I remember particular the Dohnas and Donhoffs who later came to a frightful end, some after 20 July 1944 and some when the Russians moved in. In this connection I must relate one incident as being illustrative of the atmosphere within the headquarters. I received one of these invitations through the Foreign Ministry representative to the headquarters who had been given a high rank in the SS. The invitation was called off at the last moment because, as I discovered later, he had just learnt that Himmler had forbidden members of the SS to have anything to do with me when off duty, giving as his reason that I had on several occasions adopted an attitude hostile to the SS.

Such diversions did not affect the daily programme of work in the office during these first months, which were months of victory. As usual a considerable part of the work of the field echelon of Section L consisted of collecting each morning and evening the reports from the Army, Navy and Air Force, sifting them and despatching them by courier to the Chief of the Operations Staff, together with their attached 'situation maps' brought up to date by the staff's draughts-men. The reports now came from East, West, North Africa, the Bal-kans, the remaining area of the Mediterranean and, in much greater detail of course, from the 'OKW theatres of war'. Thereafter we held our own conference and 'over there' Hitler's briefing took place; Area 1 also held a briefing in the evenings. As before, no officer of the Operations Staff except Jodl was present at these con-ferences. I also had another routine job which normally took place each evening, the briefing of the War Diary Officer on the most important events of the day; this often led to a very frank ex-change of views on the opinions of others and the prospects of the campaign.

At this point the Army Sub-section of Section L introduced an innovation which I welcomed with enthusiasm; they took it upon themselves to attach from time to time to the morning report a so-called 'brief appreciation' of the situation. This procedure had two objects: first to bring to the notice of the Chief of the Operations Staff prior to Hitler's midday briefing, the views and intentions of OKH, which after all was the headquarters really responsible for directing operations; secondly, to get Jodl perhaps at last to work with his own staff in a normal general staff manner. Neither of these objects was achieved. After a week or two Jodl told me that he could well do without these appreciations; he would much prefer it if people took trouble to ensure that there were no errors in the situation maps. As I pointed out to him, this reply was little short of insulting; basically however it showed that the 'Supreme Command', as represented merely by Hitler and Jodl, was still determined to exercise unrestricted authority even over the widespread battle in the East and still thought that it was the fount of all knowledge and therefore had no need of advice. As far as the atmosphere within the staff and upon its methods of work was concerned, the result of this was that whole days often went by without my speaking to or even meeting General Jodl, let alone having anything to do with him when off duty; conversely as far as he was concerned HQ Area 2 long remained some unknown enclosure which he had hardly ever entered but where his 'working staff' was to be found.

Section L's work on matters outside its true operational scope had increased considerably meanwhile as a result of the extension of the theatre of war; this primarily affected the Sections remaining in Berlin – Organization, Replacements and Equipment, Co-operation with the civil authorities. Correspondence was despatched by courier, one in each direction by air daily at midday, and one in each direction by night by express between Rastenburg and Berlin. Liaison officers from the most important branches and sections of OKW (Secret Service, Equipment, Propaganda) were attached to the field echelon of Section L and they maintained contact with their head offices by similar methods. The heads of branches and sections themselves visited 'Wolfschanze' from time to time[1]; in the intervals the liaison officers were responsible, by keeping in touch with Section L, for ensuring that their Sections in Berlin were working in accordance with the views of Supreme Headquarters. Jodl showed little interest in matters of this nature. A special channel had therefore developed some time previously which by-passed him and ran direct from me to the Chief of OKW. This procedure did not however apply to those problems within the province of the Operations Staff which either emanated from Hitler or had to be decided by him. This should be particularly emphasized in the light of Jodl's subsequent statements at Nuremberg where he said:

> beginning with the year 1941 it became the practice for me and my operational branch (!) to report to the Führer direct on all matters concerning strategics while Field Marshal Keitel, using my quartermaster department as a sort of personal working staff, took over all other tasks.'[2]

The communications system had to carry all the military head-quarters traffic including the daily Wehrmacht reports, and also that of the State, Party and Press authorities attached to the head-quarters. It therefore rapidly became so overloaded that it made one wonder whether a German Supreme Headquarters in the Field did not present more disadvantages than advantages. The fact that the courier trains between Berlin and Rastenburg were nightly shuffling back and forth an ever-increasing number of officers, officials and party functionaries, made the location of the headquarters appear more and more extraordinary the longer the Russian campaign lasted. The final and most significant point however is that in East Prussia Hitler was, so to speak, in a little corner sheltered from the blast; neither he nor his immediate entourage got any direct impression either of the severity of the struggle on the main front on the one hand or of the blazing effects of the air war on German cities on the other.

Looking back, there can be very little doubt that in this situation a field headquarters had not only lost all purpose but was in all probability a distorting factor, not without influence in prolonging the war. Hitler was determined to keep all political and military power in Germany in his own hands; he was the overlord of large portions of Europe which were either occupied or the territories of his allies. By the onset of the winter crisis in December 1941, at the latest, he and his headquarters should have followed the example of all the other states engaged in the war and been located in his capital or in its immediate vicinity. This might moreover have removed from him and his advisers, before it was too late, the temptation to try to command each individual division on the Eastern Front and it would have forced them so much the more to deal with the realities of the overall situation. But instead, over the course of three years 'Wolfschanze' was turned into a 'fortress'; the barbed-wire fences and the minefields became thicker and the concrete blocks stuck up like superstructures of old-style cruisers; in addition underground rooms and passages of an unknown extent were constructed beneath the Berghof, whither Hitler still went for sometimes shorter, sometimes longer periods. Other spacious headquarters were constructed at incredible cost at Vinnitsa in the Ukraine, at Soissons in France, on the Ziegenberg estate in the area of Nauhein-Giessen and finally, near Breslau; apart from that at Vinnitsa none was occupied except for the shortest periods; some were never used at all. When Hitler finally came to rest in Berlin in January 1945 any possibility of real leadership or direction had long since disappeared.

CROSS-CURRENTS IN SUPREME HEADQUARTERS AS THE
PENDULUM BEGINS TO SWING

When the headquarters set itself up in East Prussia almost a year had gone by since Hitler had developed his concept that England could be forced to make peace by going round through the back door via the 'overthrow' of Soviet Russia. In July 1940 he had developed this as follows: 'if England's hope of assistance from Russia disappears she has no hope of America either'. This idea was rounded off by his subsequent instructions for 'preparations for the period subsequent to Barbarossa'[3] and this set the stage for the political and strategic activity of Supreme Headquarters during the summer of 1941.

Objectives such as this offered ample opportunities for true strategic direction of the Wehrmacht but the resulting far-reaching tasks were in the end only partially dealt with by Supreme Headquarters. For Hitler and also for his Chief of the Operations Staff the day-to-day events of the Eastern campaign overshadowed everything. Instead of being content to keep an eye on developments to ensure that they were on the right strategic lines and where necessary guiding them by new general instructions, the customary interference in the Army's responsibilities started again only a few weeks later. Hand in hand with this the exercise of command as practised by the headquarters became increasingly and disastrously distorted by the strategic principle which soon came to dominate everything, the stubborn struggle for 'every inch' of Russian territory.

The Russian campaign brought ever more clearly to the fore the true reason for these aberrations – Hitler's limitless suspicion and overriding determination to exercise his authority, the glaring inadequacies of his self-taught generalship and his incapacity to subordinate to well-tried military principles his own wishful thinking, based on politics, economics, and prestige desiderata. His permanent entourage in HQ Area 1, believing as they did that he had second-sight and could not go wrong, egged him on rather than restraining him; moreover he was actually confirmed in his determination to play the part of supreme military leader by the fact that in Norway and Northern Finland he was in direct command; the buffer of OKH did not exist there and he could run affairs as he pleased. Meanwhile, the 'OKW theatres of war' placed upon the OKW Operaions Staff an ever-increasing burden which, merely from the organizational point of view, it was in no position to carry, and which increasingly diverted it from its true purpose – that of providing a high level Wehrmacht staff. A number of other increasingly serious difficulties arose as a result of the progressive disintegration of the Army command organization but neither these nor the realization of the effects upon OKW were enough to stop Hitler going his own way in this matter as in all others.

THE FIRST PHASE

The first phase of the eastern campaign may be taken as covering approximately two to three weeks, ie up to early July 1941. It was marked by an unusual measure of accord between OKW and OKH. The great victories in the frontier battles and the rapid gains of territory, at any rate in the centre and north, made even the most persistent sceptics think alike and gave rise to hopes such as those voiced by Halder in his diary of 3 July:

> Looked at overall we can already say that we have carried out our job of smashing the bulk of the Russian Army this side of the Duna and Dnieper. I believe that a certain captured Russian general was right when he said that east of the Duna and Dnieper we have only got to deal with scattered forces which will not of themselves be strong enough to offer any serious resistance to German operations. I am therefore not exaggerating when I say that the campaign against Russia was won in fourteen days. Of course it is not at an end yet. Owing to the extent of the territory and the stubborn resistance of the enemy, who is using everything he has got, that will take us many weeks yet.[4]

With the hind-sight of today such comments by Halder may appear astounding to many people; they should however be set alongside a passage from Winston Churchill's speech in a secret session of the House of Commons on 25 June 1941; he then said: 'in a few months, or even less, we may be exposed to the most frightful invasion the world has ever seen'.[5] This shows that the Head of the British Government was clearly reckoning upon an early victory for Germany in the East and that, like Hitler, he also looked upon the German advance into Russia as a way round via the back-door to the *coup de grâce* against England.

Hitler himself stated to his immediate entourage on 4 July: 'to all intents and purposes the Russians have lost the war' and congratulated himself on what a good thing it was 'that we smashed the Russian armour and air forces right at the beginning'. The Russians' he went on 'can never replace them'.[6] His appreciation of the situation therefore agreed generally with that of the Army. Accordingly during these early weeks he did not meddle with the conduct of operations in the East apart from certain pressure and nagging at OKH to get them to close the great 'pocket' more rapidly and securely, and later, just as in the West, being beset by 'fear' for the flanks of the armoured thrusts which had driven far ahead.[7] Similarly Hitler left the Luftwaffe alone, particularly since once its initial 'operational' activities against airfields and other targets deep into Russia had been completed, it was in general used only for 'tactical' tasks in close co-operation with OKH and Headquarters of Army Groups.

The campaign seemed to be going quickly and successfully and so in this case also there was little opportunity for the Supreme Commander or his staff to do any real job of overall direction. Meanwhile, just as in the West, Hitler was already drawing far-reaching, premature conclusions and busying himself with the resulting follow-up action. As early as the beginning of July, after discussions with the Commander-in-Chief of the Army, he gave the Chief of OKW detailed instructions for 'the distribution of personnel and equipment' and in particular for the Army's 'tank programme'. Two orders were issued which may be summarized as follows: the Army to be 'considerably' reduced numerically with the exception of the armoured and motorized divisions which should be increased to thirty-six and eighteen respectively by 1 May 1942 – in both cases including the SS divisions. The building programme for the Navy to be restricted to that 'immediately necessary for the conduct of the war against England and, if she should enter the war, against America'; large-scale increase of the Luftwaffe.

There were certain additional instructions which bore witness to his complete confidence in the outcome of the Russian campaign; their salient points were: the Eastern Front must make do with the armoured forces it already had and apart from two armoured divisions still in Germany, any further reinforcement of the armour in the East must be approved by Hitler. The manufacture of new weapons, ammunition and equipment for the Army must 'forthwith' be geared to its future reduced strength; any orders to industry over and above this should be cancelled. This did not apply to tanks, anti-tank guns and tropical equipment (the latter for 4 Armoured Division). At the same time the 'explosives' programme should concentrate upon the requirements of the Luftwaffe (bombs and anti-aircraft ammunition) at the expense of the requirements of the Army.

All too soon it was destined to become clear that from the strategic point of view these orders far anticipated the course of events; furthermore they had a serious and prejudicial effect on the subsequent course of the Eastern campaign.[8]

THE SECOND PHASE

Hitler's instructions for equipment requirements for the continuation of the war against the British Commonwealth were put into final form by Section L after various exchanges of view, both verbally and on paper, with the relevant branches of the High Commands of the Services. Meanwhile at the daily briefings in HQ Area 1 people were already occupied with the second phase of the eastern campaign. The discussions were carried on principally by Hitler and Jodl; the central problem around which they revolved was that which had been left unsolved in December of the previous year: Hitler still wanted to 'divert considerable mobile forces northwards' to capture Leningrad and Kronstadt and so completely clear the Baltic area of the enemy; the Army plan however was to concentrate the entire strength of the Wehrmacht on the capture of Moscow as being the focal point of Russian resistance. The directive on Barbarossa had referred to the possibility of 'the simultaneous pursuit of both objectives' but had stated that 'this could only be done in the event of a surprisingly rapid collapse of Russian resistance'; remarkably enough this idea was never mentioned in spite of the extremely favourable view generally taken of the situation. On the contrary, in view of the fact that south of the Pripet marshes the front was hanging far back, an idea was resurrected which had previously only been discussed in the innermost circle, that of diverting forces from the centre southwards.'[9]

As was his habit General Jodl asked for no advice or support from his staff, in spite of the fact that on 4 July he stated that 'the forthcoming decision will probably be the most difficult of the whole war'; moreover there were several indications that he had not made up his own mind. He realized however that the views of the Army were entirely at variance with those of Hitler and was apparently not prepared this time to carry the responsibility of being Hitler's sole adviser. Contrary to his normal practice therefore he acted entirely correctly in this case, in that he tried to bring OKH back into the discussions in good time. On 5 July he commented: 'the moment is approaching when the decision must be taken on the future conduct of operations, in particular on the further employment of the armoured forces. Since this decision may be decisive for the whole war – is perhaps the only decisive decision in this war – General Jodl considered it essential that Commander-in-Chief Army should discuss his views and intentions with the Führer before laying down further objectives.'[10]

In OKH they apparently saw no reason to raise this question again at this time; even more than in December 1940 they now hoped that it would automatically be solved by the future march of events. Halder for instance, when Hitler called on him on his birthday on 30 June, noted that by bringing up armoured formations from Army Group Centre it might perhaps be possible to 'clear up the whole situation in the north' before the bulk of the infantry divisions were concentrated in the Smolensk area for the decisive attack on Moscow. After a discussion with Hitler on 8 July Halder did not exclude a temporary diversion southwards; a few days later he explained to Brauchitsch:

> I am not all that wedded to the idea of the two armoured groups in Army Group Centre pressing on eastwards. I can well visualize the necessity of diverting considerable portions of Hoth's forces (Armoured Group 3) to the north and Guderian's (Armoured

Group 2) to the south – perhaps to drive down even as far as Kiev. In both cases however the prerequisite is that Hoth and Guderian should first break through eastwards and so get the necessary freedom of manœuvre.[11]

For a time therefore it seemed that there were possibilities of finding a compromise between the opposing points of view without OKH having to give up, even temporarily, its real objective, Moscow; but as the enemy resistance gradually stiffened the total divergence between the two points of view became ever clearer. Hand in hand with this went an almost classic instance of the basic fault in Hitler's leadership, the desire to command in detail without having studied the background adequately. As early as 14 July we find Halder writing: 'this perpetual interference by the Führer in matters the circumstances of which he does not understand, is becoming a scourge which will eventually be intolerable'. Starting in the second ten days of July this situation got worse and worse until it eventually reached the proportions of a quarrel increasingly affecting the entire headquarters; only at the end of August, when Hitler issued orders, was it settled and then only so far as the outside world was concerned.

The first OKW directive of the Eastern campaign (no. 33) was issued on 19 July and appeared to be more or less in consonance with the proposals which the Army leaders had made verbally to Hitler a few days previously. Before the resulting movements had begun however, the Supreme Commander, without further consultation with OKH, issued a 'supplement to *Directive no. 33*' dated 23 July, intended to ensure finally that his wishes were executed. The objectives in the south were now to be, not only Kiev, but Kharkov and the lower Don, Caucasia and the Crimea; as soon as Army Group North had reached its objectives, which it was expected to do soon, OKH was to order it to send 'considerable forces, including Armoured Group 3 back to Germany'! Similarly as soon as action in the Smolensk area was completed, the Luftwaffe was ordered to send a number of dive bomber groups to Finland to assist Dietl's corps in the area of the North Cape. This flight of strategic fancy continued: 'this will also reduce the temptation for England to intervene in the fighting along the Arctic coast'. The Directive also ordered air attacks on Moscow; these had nothing to do with the objectives of the campaign but were regarded as reprisals for

Russian bombing of Bucharest and Helsinki. Neither at this time nor later did the Luftwaffe achieve anything of operational importance either against Moscow or against Leningrad, though according to OKW *Directive no. 35* of 6 September there was to be 'a large-scale attack' on the latter.[12]

Jodl having apparently done what he could to stop this dispersal of forces, it was unlikely that the verbal representations made by the Army immediately thereafter would have any effect. Halder noted:

> He (Hitler) has decided on his objectives and sticks to them without considering what the enemy may do or taking account of any other points of view. This means that von Bock will have to give up his armoured groups and advance on Moscow with infantry alone. In any case the Führer takes no interest in Moscow at the moment, only in Leningrad'.

When Brauchitsch returned from a tour of the front all he did was to call up Keitel and protest that Hitler's instruction could not be carried out in the immediate future since 'the necessary prior conditions had not been fulfilled'. This obviously achieved even less than Halder's protests.

Even Hitler however had to change his mind in the next few days as a result of the increasing resistance of the Red Army along almost the entire front and the urgent necessity for a period of rest and recuperation for the armoured and motorized forces. This only took place after 'long-winded and sometimes violent arguments with the Army leaders over missed opportunities for encirclement'. Moreover Hitler now began increasingly to take the command of operations into his own hands. He declared: 'the Russians will not be beaten by large-scale victories because they simply do not recognize that they have been beaten. They must therefore be smashed piecemeal by small tactical operations.' Halder was prepared to agree that there might be something in Hitler's views but nevertheless he wrote: 'this line of thought looks to me like the death knell of the mobile operations we have conducted so far'; he even thought he could see the spectre of static warfare raising its head. It was on this occasion that Halder found that Hitler 'simply rejected his arguments regarding the importance of Moscow without producing any real reasons against them'.[13]

As always Jodl was the only representative of the OKW Operations Staff present during these discussions with the Army; either while they were in progress or during his subsequent talks alone with Hitler he apparently found a soft spot and took the next opportunity to put in his oar on the side of the attack on Moscow. He did not base his argument on the importance of capturing the enemy capital but on his conviction that it was only here that considerable enemy forces could be found and defeated. Hitler once more countered this argument with an economic one – that it was essential as soon as possible to 'lay hands' on the industrial area and coalfields of the Donetz Basin and on the Caucasian oilfields. Then on the very next day, probably as a result of unfavourable situation reports from centre and north, he suddenly appeared ready to give up his large-scale operations in the south.

So, on the evening of 28 July Halder was once more inveighing to his Commander-in-Chief against 'the absurdity of the operations now ordered, which will result in a dispersal of our forces and bring the decisive operation against Moscow to a standstill'. Meanwhile however we in the OKW Operations Staff felt happier and went to work straightaway confirming Hitler's change of mind by a new directive – no. 34. The introduction to this read:

> The development of the situation in the last few days, the appearance of stronger enemy forces on the front and to the flanks of Army Group Centre, the supply position and the need to give 2nd and 3rd Armoured Groups about ten days to rehabilitate their units make it necessary to postpone for the moment further tasks and objectives.

The more detailed paragraphs of the instruction laid down that both Army Groups North and South must now make do with their own forces, whereas Army Group Centre should retain all its armoured formations but temporarily adopt a defensive attitude. Halder thereupon wrote:

> This solution means that all thinking soldiers are now freed from the frightful spectre of the last few days during which it looked as if the entire eastern operation would be bogged down as a result of the Führer's stubbornness. At last a little light on the horizon once more![14]

In fairness it must be admitted that this victory over Hitler's recklessness must primarily be ascribed to the situation and the other circumstances mentioned in *Directive no. 34*. Nevertheless it still gives

me some satisfaction to recall that for once Jodl made common
cause with OKH, and that in the end it was his feel for the psychological moment that carried the day in bringing Hitler round to
a more sensible point of view. For the moment however we had
done no more than set the stage for a resumption of the offensive on
Moscow. For a time there was calm but new doubts soon began to
appear as to how firm these decisions were. During the next few
days Hitler made a series of visits to the headquarters of Army
Groups, and on several occasions started propaganding his own plans
and ideas – entirely in character and undoubtedly with the intention
of undermining from below the point of view of OKH. On 21 July
when visiting Field Marshal von Leeb in Army Group North he
characterized Moscow as 'merely a geographical idea' and adduced
the 'Slav national character' as a new factor leading him to count
upon an early collapse of the Soviets. On 4 August at Headquarters
Army Group Centre he put the attack on Moscow third in order of
importance in his plans. He stated that it was much more important
to deprive the Russians of 'their vital areas': first Leningrad and the
Baltic coast with its highly developed industry, supposed to include
the only factory capable of producing heavy tanks: secondly the
Donetz basin with Kharkov, the 'essential basis of the Russian
economy', the loss of which would result in the 'certain collapse of
the entire enemy economy'. He let fall an admission at this point,
obviously intended as a criticism of the military intelligence service,
that 'the decision to attack Russia would have been considerably
more difficult' if he had been informed beforehand of the large
numbers of tanks and aircraft which the enemy possessed. He expressed similar views on 6 August when visiting Field Marshal von
Rundstedt at Headquarters Army Group South. Yet certain remarks
he let fall in Supreme Headquarters during the period between these
two visits convinced the Commander-in-Chief of the Army that
Hitler was now fully aware of the importance of Moscow![15]

Halder was at the centre of all these cross-currents. On 7 August
he had a personal discussion alone with Jodl – something which had
not happened for as long as anybody could remember. Halder no
doubt hoped thereby to broaden the newly developed understanding
between the two. He started with the basic question: 'do we want to
beat the enemy or go after economic objectives?' To this Jodl replied
that 'the Führer thinks we can do both at the same time'. Halder
thereupon developed his idea that nothing should be detached for

Leningrad which could be used for Moscow. On the other hand in 'the question of Moscow *or* Ukraine as opposed to Moscow *and* Ukraine we must come down on the side of 'and' because 'if we do not, we shall not be able to wear the enemy down before the autumn'. To do this however, he said, there was no need for additional forces in the south; instead we should concentrate everything on 'operations aiming at more distant and decisive objectives' – by which he meant principally Moscow. When Halder left he was convinced that he had stiffened Jodl in his support for the views of the Army.[16]

Subsequent developments seemed initially to support this. The first move was on 10 August, when Jodl submitted to Hitler an appreciation of the situation prepared by Section L in full agreement with the Operations Section of OKH. This began by proving, as usual with the support of maps and strength tables, that the enemy was strongest opposite the centre of the front and that therefore the most important objective was the annihilation of this enemy grouping, followed by the capture of Moscow. Operations from the centre into the areas of Army Groups North and South were attractive but must be subordinated to the Moscow operation or postponed to a later date. The attack on Moscow would begin at the end of August with the infantry divisions in the centre and the armoured groups on the flanks.

By this means we were in fact successful in getting Hitler to issue on 12 August a *Supplement to Directive no. 34* which at last gave agreement to the attack on Moscow, although on numerous conditions some of which were difficult to fulfil. For instance Army Group Centre was only to move forward when 'the threat to the flanks had been entirely overcome' and when completion of the operations against Leningrad was in sight; the object here was, however, now restricted to the encirclement of the city. A more accurate appreciation of the value of the Soviet capital, hitherto 'merely a geographical idea', then followed: 'the object must then be to deprive the enemy, before the coming of winter, of his governmental, armament and traffic centre around Moscow, and thus prevent the re-building of his defeated forces and the orderly working of government control'. As Halder wanted, the directive also stated that after its victory at Uman, Army Group South should be able to reach its ultimate objectives – the Crimea, the Donetz basin and even Batum – with the forces it already had.[17]

The OKW Operations Staff had hardly had time to get used to the idea that it had really done something, when a few days later there were some local setbacks in Army Group North. Although Halder and Army Group Headquarters considered them unimportant, they led to 'great agitation on the part of the Supreme Commander' and as a result to fresh direct interventions by Hitler. His instructions to OKH laid down that, since no other reserves were available, a number of individual armoured divisions from Army Group Centre should forthwith be despatched to the north to deal with the enemy breakthrough in the area of Staraia Russa. Once more there was complete lack of consideration of the 'prerequisites' to which reference has so often been made. Field Marshal von Bock called Hitler's order an 'impossible demand', since the armoured divisions concerned were in some cases engaged on maintenance and therefore incapable of movement, and in others were essential for the defence of Army Group Centre.

Halder thereupon put all possible pressure upon his Commander-in-Chief; but the latter was evidently weary of struggling and was unwilling to 'go against the decisions of higher authority'. He finally contented himself with saying: 'let someone talk to Jodl about it'.[18]

In view of this continual vacillation at the top the Operations Section of OKH under Heusinger adopted an unusual procedure – undoubtedly with Halder's knowledge. They prepared an *aide-mémoire* on the future conduct of operations addressed initially to the Commander-in-Chief of the Army; on the same day, 18 August, Section L under my direction submitted to Jodl a new appreciation of the situation.[19] Both these documents expressed the views of the middle range of general staff officers, the 'young Turks'. They produced once more every argument for keeping Moscow as the objective, based in the case of the Army *aide-mémoire* on the situation in the East and in that of Section L on the overall situation; they also stressed again that Army Groups North and South already had adequate forces to carry out the other tasks allotted to them.

I cannot now remember whether or how Jodl made use of this submission from his staff. The Commander-in-Chief of the Army sent his Operations Section's *aide mémoire* on to Hitler and allowed its author to discuss it with Jodl in Wolfschanze. Heusinger's book of memoirs is characterized by a certain 'poetic licence' but there are some passages in his account of this interview on 20 August which are of importance not so much for their bearing on the immediate subject as for the picture they give of the atmosphere of the head-quarters. For instance, after having gone over the well known factual pros and cons, he records Jodl as saying:

Moreover he (Hitler) has an instinctive aversion to treading the same path as Napoleon. Moscow gives him a sinister feeling. He fears that there might there be a life and death struggle with Bolshevism.

To which Heusinger replies.

And that is exactly why Moscow is the direction we must take. We must defeat the enemy forces. That must be the object and then everything else will fall into our lap.

And Jodl replies:

That's what you say. Now I will tell you what the Führer's answer will be: There is at the moment a much better possibility of beating the Russian forces. Their main grouping is now east of Kiev.

Heusinger thereupon raised the question of the winter, the onset of which would occur shortly in the northern and central sectors but only somewhat later in the south; asking Jodl to support the *aide-mémoire* he finally got him to agree that:

I will do what I can. But you must admit that the Führer's reasons are well thought out and cannot be pushed aside just like that. We must not try to compel him to do something which goes against his inner convictions. His intuition has generally been right. You can't deny that!

Heusinger concluded:

Unfortunately he's not been right all the time! I remember Dunkirk. And we are afraid that once again we are going to miss a decisive opportunity.[20]

It seems highly probable that by 21 August Hitler had already rejected the Army *aide-mémoire* after discussion with Keitel and Jodl; at any rate on that day the two OKW generals adopted the old procedure which had not been used for some time and appeared together in Halder's office in the Angerburg camp, in order to win him over to Hitler's point of view or at least to damp down opposition. It appears that, when finally driven into a corner during this meeting, Jodl fell back upon the view he had expressed to Heusinger – that he could produce no concrete objections to the Army point of view 'but the Führer had a sixth sense'. That was merely another way of expressing the boundless faith in the 'Führer's genius' of which he had so often given proof before and to which any rational thinking was entirely subordinated. Halder merely comments drily that in face of such an attitude 'any logical arguments were useless'.[21]

Jodl was compelled that same evening to put Hitler's new and now final orders in the form of a written instruction to OKH. This memorandum opened as follows: 'the Army proposal of 18 August for future strategy in the East is not in accord with my views'. It then repeated the view that Moscow was not the most important objective but that it was more important, before the onset of winter, to reach the Crimea and the Donetz basin in the south and 'cut off Russian oil supplies from the Caucasus area'; in the north to invest Leningrad closely and effect a junction with the Finns. There was then a new requirement: 'forthwith to make use of the exceptionally favourable operational situation to carry out a concentric operation from the inner flanks of Army Groups South and Centre, against the Soviet Fifth Army in the area of Kiev'.

Bock's Army Group (Centre), which OKH had proposed should be maintained at full strength and made primarily responsible for the attack on Moscow, was to remain on the defensive with such forces as were left to it, until, as the last paragraph of the instruction expressly laid down, all the conditions for a further advance on Moscow as in the *Supplement to Directive no. 34* had been fulfilled. The 'attractive possibilities of operations from the centre' had therefore won the day over the central strategy around which the whole eastern campaign had been planned.[22]

When this 'Führer's instruction' reached the camp at Angerburg next day Halder's immediate reaction was: 'this instruction is decisive for the outcome of this entire campaign'. The effect on the Commander-in-Chief of the Army and his Chief of Staff of this answer to their *aide mémoire* was therefore pretty depressing, but on the very same day Hitler rubbed salt into the wound by sending them a 'study' which he had himself drafted. Although we had now been at war for a full two years he proceeded to read the Army leaders a lesson on the handling of 'mobile formations' which he said should be used as 'an operational weapon in the hand of the

Supreme Commander' just like the Luftwaffe. Then with considerable asperity he made a totally unjustified comparison with the Luftwaffe saying that Göring had acted on this principle 'with logic and energy', whereas the Army was apparently not capable of 'generally grasping these ideas and acting upon them without further ado'. He even reproached Brauchitsch with 'not getting the necessary grip'; by this he meant that the Commander-in-Chief allowed his senior subordinate commanders to have too great an influence on strategy; I myself often heard him say this later. Once more Halder's entry in his diary for this day, 22 August, is forceful and clear:

> In my view the situation resulting from the Führer's interference is intolerable for the Army. These individual instructions by the Führer produce a situation of order, counter-order and disorder and no one can be held responsible but he himself personally; OKH as now constituted is engaged on its fourth victorious campaign and its reputation should not be sullied by the instructions now received. In addition the way the Commander-in-Chief has been treated is a scandal. I have accordingly suggested to the Commander-in-Chief that he should ask to be relieved of his office and propose that I should also be relieved at the same time.

He had however to add immediately thereafter:

> Commander-in-Chief refuses because he considers that in practice he would not be relieved and there would therefore be no change.

As a result of efforts by Halder a last attempt was made, via General Guderian, to see whether Hitler could possibly be made to change his mind. There are various accounts of the meeting which took place on 23 August in the headquarters at Wolfschanze. They all agree however that Guderian, who was considered by OKH as the most likely to be successful, was the sole representative of the Army and found himself faced by Hitler and his entire entourage. Whatever the course of the discussion may have been[23] it did nothing to change Hitler's determination. During the next few weeks the Battle of Kiev resulted in the well-known large-scale victory – but it was a tactical success only. As a result a private meeting took place on 30 August between Hitler and the Commander-in-Chief of the Army during which there was a 'reconciliation'. Brauchitsch maintained that this cancelled Hitler's insulting 'study'. For those who know the background however there can be little doubt that, although for the moment he pretended to imitate it, Hitler took Brauchitsch's chivalrous attitude merely as a sign of weakness and lack of character and considered the outcome of this encounter simply as another victory over his opponents in the Army.[24]

Thus for the moment the quarrels regarding future strategy in the eastern campaign came to an end. Once more the OKW Operations Staff had been compelled to act far more than was its right on matters which were the responsibility of the Army. The time had now arrived however when plans and prospects of German strategy in the widest sense had to be re-examined. *Directive no. 33* dated 19 July had contained an instruction of a type to which in those days we had become unaccustomed: 'in the West and North the possibility of British attacks on the Channel Islands and the Norwegian coast must be borne in mind'. All the ambitious offensive plans drawn up a few months before for the 'post-Barbarossa phase' had to be adjusted to the development of the situation in the East. In this connection at the end of July OKH had put forward proposals for limiting the scope of operations; these were to postpone the date for the two-pronged attack on Egypt from Syria and Cyrenaica to the spring of 1942 but to keep to the capture of Gibraltar in the autumn of 1941;[25] even these had now been overtaken by events.

In the light of these facts and probably (though not certainly) on instructions from Jodl resulting from his daily talks with Hitler, Section L produced at the end of August an 'OKW memorandum approved by the Führer' on the strategic situation in the late summer of 1941. This study was something of a strategic mile-stone; it re-iterated the principle that, even though it might take longer than had been forseen, the collapse of Russia must first be brought about 'by the use of all forces which can be spared from other fronts' before proceeding to the final objective which remained unchanged 'to overthrow England and force her to make peace'. It continued that even in the most favourable circumstances 'it was hardly likely that army and air forces would be available for decisive operations in the Mediterranean, the Atlantic or on the Spanish mainland before the spring of 1942'. As a result of this situation a stiffer attitude on the part of the neutrals was anticipated; for instance a move through Turkey without her permission, which had previously been considered, was no longer possible; moreover we had to reckon that England would take the initiative with increasing energy. It was already becoming clear that England's main object was to disrupt Germany's position on the European continent by striking from the Mediterranean area, if possible in collaboration with the United States; there were a number of indications, such as the establishment of British troops in southern Iran, which had just been reported, and the continued build-up of the British key position either side of the Suez Canal. In any case the position of the Axis Powers in North Africa had for some time been getting steadily more difficult because of the dangerously increasing losses of sea transports, the principal cause of the continued postponement of the capture of Tobruk. Since the bulk of German military forces were likely to remain tied down in the East for some time to come, the memorandum concluded that the threatening situation in the Mediterranean area necessitated more energetic political action, even if this involved some damage to Italian interests.[26]

These warnings did, for the immediate future, produce certain, though inadequate, improvements in the Mediterranean area. On the debit side, this was the last occasion on which the elimination of Soviet Russia was depicted as a preliminary step to the ultimate battle against the British Commonwealth; it was soon to become the all-exclusive task of the German Wehrmacht pursued by Hitler with a fury which made him blind to all other considerations.

THE THIRD PHASE

The 'Battle of Kiev' towards the end of August, looked at from German headquarters, marks the beginning of the third phase of the eastern campaign of 1941. Great new victories were won on all the battlefields of Russia and during these few months there was complete agreement on the necessity of trying to reach Moscow before the onset of winter. There was therefore no occasion for further interference of any importance by Hitler. The introduction to the only OKW instruction dealing with the eastern campaign issued during this period (*no. 35* dated 6 September) emphasizes that it is in agreement with the proposals of the Commander-in-Chief of the Army.[27]

OKH was however still worried lest the right moment for the decisive thrust on Moscow should be allowed to pass.[28] Neither in that headquarters nor in HQ Area 2 of Supreme Headquarters did people feel inclined to join in the paeans of victory with which Hitler announced after the 'twin battle of Viasma-Briansk' that 'the military victory in the East has been won and Russia is finished'.[29] After the 'mud glue-pot period' shortly after the middle of November, Army Group Centre moved on Moscow again, making some encouraging progress, and people generally began to get optimistic once more, though all were worried about the enormous exertions called for from the troops. I remember particularly one unforgettable indication of optimism from those days: the Deputy Chief of Staff I from OKH, at that time Lieutentant-General Paulus, appeared in Section L's hut in order to talk over in detail with me and Colonel von Lossberg instructions for the period following the capture of Moscow. Objectives far beyond the Russian capital were considered. (Halder's diary mentions such places as Jaroslav, Rybinsk and even Vologda).[30] Only the minimum essential forces were to winter in the 'forward area'; an Army Group headquarters was to take over command of the entire front and a large proportion of the Army, together with the other higher headquarters, was to be withdrawn.

This optimism both within the Wehrmacht and among the general public received a rude shock when, on 29 November, a Russian attack compelled Army Group South to evacuate Rostov which it had captured a week earlier and when the widely respected Commander-in-Chief of the Army Group, Field Marshal von Rundstedt, was thereupon summarily dismissed. He had sent a telegram to Hitler asking him either to rescind his order that the troops must re-occupy positions forward of the defensive line of the Mius valley or 'charge someone else with the command of the Army Group'. Two hours later, in the middle of the night, Heusinger asked Jodl whether the order had now been withdrawn; Jodl replied: 'by no means; the Führer has not changed the order. Rundstedt has been relieved of his command and Reichenau has been given command of the Army Group.' When Heusinger exclaimed: 'Not possible! But that's not possible!', Jodl put down the receiver. The Commander-in-Chief of the Army had not even been asked. Nevertheless on the very next afternoon Hitler was compelled to concede to Reichenau that which he had denied to Rundstedt.[31]

We were soon to see further and more serious consequences of Hitler's disorderly, 'improvised' method of command.

As already mentioned, one of the special tasks of the OKW Operations Staff, in addition to its normal duties, was to do the job of the

Chief of Staff of the Army and the Army Operations Section in the 'OKW theatres of war'. During the summer of 1941 the most important of these areas was Northern Finland, where were two German and one Finnish Army Corps.[32] From time to time OKW strategy directives were issued to the Commander-in-Chief, Colonel-General von Falkenhorst, similar to those normally issued to the High Commands of the Services. Naturally this meant that Falkenhorst had greater opportunities for individual initiative than the Army Commanders directly under OKH. On the other hand the very limited results achieved were soon of themselves enough to show that the attempt to exercise operational and even tactical command through OKW was an even greater failure when OKH was cut out of the chain. As a result of these experiences, an attempt was made to bolster up the directives to the Commander-in-Chief in Northern Finland by detailed instructions for their execution but it soon became clear that this too was no substitute for the action of OKH; it remained the real father and mother and the true command organization for all units of the army. Examples of the type of OKW orders issued are as follows:

1 Order of 13 August, as a result of a visit by myself to Falkenhorst and Dietl beginning with the words: 'as a result of the presentation by the Chief of Section L of an appreciation of the situation by Corps Headquarters Norway the Führer has decided to resume the attack with objective Murmansk'.

2 OKW *Directive no. 36* of 22 September instructed that the attack on Louhi and on Murmansk should be halted and that on Kandalaksha should be resumed, in order 'to capture at least the western part of the Fisherman's Peninsula before the onset of winter'.

3 OKW *Directive no. 37* dated 10 October 1941 states: 'after the defeat or destruction of the main Russian forces in the principal theatre of operations, there will be no compelling reason to tie down Russian forces in Finland'; this was followed by the instruction: 'to make all preparations, beginning while it is still winter, for the final capture of Murmansk, the Fisherman's Peninsula and the Murmansk railway next year'.

4 The scope and diversity of the problems dealt with in the 'special instructions' dated 5 October 1941 show particularly clearly with how many matters outside its real province the

OKW Operation Staff had to deal; for instance these instructions were concerned with: timely supply of food, forage and fuel and construction of depots; allocation of huts and heating equipment for winter quarters and camps; use of return-space in sea transports for iron ore; authorization for local purchase of load-carrying vehicles in Sweden; material for construction of field railways; winter clothing.

In passing it should be noted here that Halder's diary shows clearly that OKH had taken preliminary steps for the supply of winter clothing to the entire army as early as the late summer of 1941.[33]

Norway was however the OKW theatre of war Number One, even during the Russian campaign; it remained so throughout the rest of the war. In Hitler's eyes there was always a danger of landings and Norway therefore had to be reinforced continuously by every conceivable means. This involved an expenditure of time on the part of the staff, effort on the part of the troops and work of almost every other sort which was in no way justified by any enemy plans.

From the early summer of 1941 Hitler began more and more to use the OKW Operations Staff as his command organization for all theatres of war other than the East, corresponding direct with the local army commanders in the areas concerned. He was entirely unmoved by the obvious disadvantages of this peculiar command organization and apparently encountered no objection from any quarter. In the Balkans and the widespread neighbouring area from the Aegean and Crete up to Dalmatia there was a 'Commander-in-Chief of the Armed Forces South-East'. It was via the OKW Operations Staff that he received his orders for the pacification of the country in face of the widespread risings which soon broke out and later for the defence of the coasts and islands; conversely it was via the OKW Operations Staff that he had to submit for approval in full detail his plans for dealing with the risings.[34] In this connection I had a great deal to do with the Bulgars. Their only active participation in the war consisted of the provision of a number of occupation divisions in Macedonia and Thrace; people in Sofia were however always concerned with the dangers which threatened the periphery of the European theatre of war and therefore continuously looked to the OKW Operations Staff for support and assistance, not only for their appreciation of the situation but for reinforcement of the defensive potential of their country. A great deal of business also went on between German Supreme Headquarters and Zagreb; there the 'German General Officer Plenipotentiary', the Austrian Glaise von Horstenau, left no stone unturned to assist in pacifying the country which was badly governed and divided against itself; he also did all he could to get some contribution to the German war effort from the Croats, whose military qualities had been proved in the days of the Danubian monarchy. We were in somewhat less close touch with the Slovaks, the Hungarians and the Rumanians who had all furnished contingents of greater or lesser strength for the eastern campaign and therefore dealt principally with OKH; there was however no clear division of responsibility.

From the autumn of 1941, the Mediterranean area became an additional OKW theatre of war of a special type. Nominally the supreme command belonged to the Italians, but Rommel's dominating role in North Africa and the vulnerability of the sea communications in his rear meant that Hitler was continually trying to exert more influence on developments. For this purpose he soon came to make use of the OKW Operations Staff, though no order was ever issued transferring responsibility from OKH to OKW.

The memorandum of the end of August had laid stress upon the dangers which the situation in the Mediterranean area presented for the Axis powers and it was here that these dangers first became apparent. Hitler was in full agreement with Jodl that all available army and air forces must be kept concentrated against Soviet Russia. Similarly, the Navy was unwilling to divert submarines from the main traffic routes in the North Atlantic, and Hitler was also hampered by Italian susceptibilities. In the end therefore it was only the daily reports of the serious losses of ships and cargoes which forced him to take further protective measures. It was not until 13 September that he could bring himself to order OKM – now however 'with all speed' – to transfer six U-boats to the Mediterranean; not long after a further fifteen followed. Shortly afterwards he instructed the Luftwaffe that the primary task of X Air Corps, the main body of which was still in Crete, should now be the protection of our own transports to North Africa instead of the attack 'on enemy shipping and British supplies in Egypt' which had hitherto been its main objectives. As often happened, however, in the case of orders which he had not himself given, Göring made subsequent representations to Hitler and managed to get this instruction restricted to 'the provision of an air umbrella' for the Italian escort 'for particularly important transports moving from Italy to Tripoli'. In addition he gave express orders that 'there was no question' of moving X Air Corps to Sicily in order to attack Malta which was the principal base for the British sea and air attacks.[35]

It was not until after the supposedly final victory over Soviet Russia at Viasma and Briansk that I managed to get anything done. Sea traffic across the Mediterranean had meanwhile practically been brought to a standstill. Halder's diary of 9 November 1941 notes: 'convoy no. 51 torpedoed. Every ship carrying German equipment for the Armoured Group in Africa sunk by English surface forces.' Jodl was still unwilling to act. I therefore bypassed him and finally, via Keitel, got Hitler to issue preparatory orders at the end of October and final orders at the beginning of December for the transfer to the Mediterranean of the Headquarters of an Air Fleet under Kesselring and another strong Air Corps (no. XI). This meant that considerable air forces were withdrawn from the eastern front only a few days before the collapse of our offensive on Moscow.[36] The further delay was due primarily to Hitler's concern for Mussolini's prestige. In letters exchanged between the two on 29 October and 6 November 1941, German assistance is only indirectly hinted at but even so is only unwillingly accepted. The entry in Ciano's diary of 9 November 1941 is however significant; 'under the circumstances (ie in view of the serious shipping losses) we have no right to complain if Hitler sends Kesselring as commander in the south'.

Hitler's attitude to the situation in the West was quite the opposite of that towards the Mediterranean and North Africa. Warnings had already been issued in July, and on 20 October 1941 on his own initiative he issued an OKW order for 'build up and defence of the English Channel Islands'. This instruction opened by stating that 'large-scale English operations against the Western occupied areas remain unlikely'; nevertheless it continued that 'account must be taken of the possibility that the English may at any time carry out isolated attacks as the result of pressure from their Eastern allies and for political and propaganda reasons; in particular they may attempt to recapture the Channel Islands which are of considerable importance for our escort traffic.'

With this order Hitler in fact transferred responsibility for the Western occupied areas from OKH to OKW, although no special pronouncement was ever made on the subject. Furthermore the orders for the fortification of the Channel Islands went into immense detail, going so far as to lay down, for instance, the number and type of coastal batteries, details of reinforced concrete works and the thickness of their walls in millimetres; monthly reports had to be rendered on the progress of construction. In the course of the year therefore, just as happened later for the whole Atlantic Wall, Hitler amassed a collection of very large-scale maps which he kept locked up in his own desk and which from time to time he examined himself. He even ordered disciplinary punishment one day for the officer responsible for keeping these maps up to date because one anti-aircraft battery too many or too few had been shown in the Channel Islands.

These tasks led to an immense mass of detailed work without any corresponding additional manpower becoming available for the 'Army Sub-Section' of Section L. At the same time the OKW Operations Staff was given another job more within its true province. In December 1941, that is before the turn of the tide in the East, Hitler decided, entirely on his own, that an order should be prepared for 'the construction of a "new West Wall" to assure the protection of the Arctic, North Sea and Atlantic Coasts'. The strategic object was laid down as being 'to assure protection against any landing operation even of very considerable strength with the employment of the smallest possible number of static forces'. In order of urgency of construction Norway was once more Number One. Next came the coasts of Belgium and France which, by agreement between Section L and the High Commands of the Services, were divided into the following sectors: in the first category the area between the mouths of the Scheldt and Seine, the area south of Brest and the area from Quiberon to the Gironde; in the second category the Normandy and Brittany peninsulas; third place was allotted to the coasts of Holland and the western and northern coasts of Jutland; last came the German Bight. Fortifications on the coasts of the Baltic were to be dismantled and only the approaches through the Kattegat were to remain blocked.[37]

This was the first appearance in broad terms of Hitler's subsequent 'Fortress Europe'. The first outline plan prepared at this time however was clearly based upon the assumption, proved by the provisions for the Baltic area, that Russia would be dealt with in the foreseeable future, a prerequisite which was never even remotely achieved. The idea also probably sprang primarily from the desire to ensure that by fortification of the coast a secure base, not requiring large land forces, should be available for the future air and submarine war against England. This order showed at once that there had been a change of view regarding the future course of the war and its probable duration; subsequently the fortification of the coasts of the occupied areas in the west was to take on a quite different far wider and deeper significance. In the light of subsequent developments and looked at overall, this order, whether intentionally or not, marks the beginning of the period when, strategically, Germany was forced on to the defensive.

PART IV

THE TURN OF THE TIDE

December 1941 – November 1942

CHAPTER 1

General Survey

EARLY IN December 1941, following up its success at Rostov, the Red Army, almost overnight, snatched the initiative all along the front and thus administered to German Supreme Headquarters a series of shocks such as it had never known before. By a remarkable coincidence the retreat in North Africa occurred simultaneously, bringing Rommel's Army back to its March 1941 starting point on the edge of the Gulf of Syrtes; but such was the commotion that this was hardly noticed. Initially Hitler attempted to shut his eyes to what was really happening but finally by the middle of December the menace of catastrophe in the East in all its seriousness brooked no further self-deception. Hitler played the ostrich just long enough, however, to declare war on the United States of America on 11 December following the Japanese attack on Pearl Harbour.

This was another entirely independent decision on which no advice from the Wehrmacht had either been asked or given; as a result we were now faced with a war on two fronts in the most serious conceivable form. Hitler's war plan had hitherto aimed at the rapid elimination of Russia as 'a factor of military importance' in order subsequently to use the concentrated power of the Wehrmacht to bring the war in the West to an end. Now the best that could be hoped for was to escape being crushed between two enemies in east and west whose combined war potential was vastly superior to our own. Naturally the first consideration was to overcome the serious crisis on the Eastern front, but it was no less important and urgent to adapt the overall war plan to the new circumstances. Instead we had merely 'improvised' decisions by Hitler, leading in November 1942 to the encirclement of the Sixth Army at Stalingrad and, again almost simultaneously, to the ruin of Rommel's Army in North Africa – a just and almost inevitable reward.

It was not merely in the strategical and operational field that

Hitler's leadership left its unmistakable mark during this year. The clearer the portents became that the overall war situation had now swung against us, the more he seemed to become determined, in so far as internal affairs were concerned, further to tamper with the high-level command organization of the Wehrmacht and by changing both its form and the personalities who manned it, to make it a completely pliable tool of his will. The fragments which remained after this process of disintegration he collected together in his own hands, in order further to increase his already almost limitless power and, after his own manner, spread chaos in this field as in all others.

CHAPTER 2

The Winter Crisis 1941–42

A SUDDEN TURN OF EVENTS

On 2 December 1941 the Supreme Commander of the Wehrmacht set off on a rapid flight to the First Panzer Army in the southern sector of the eastern front, witch-hunting after the supposed failures on the part of commanders which had led to the withdrawal from Rostov. He completely bypassed OKH and apparently had not the smallest conception that he personally might have had any responsibility for what had happened.[1] It was on this day that OKH began to receive reports of a completely unprecedented nature; Army Groups Centre and North reported simultaneously that the troops were at the end of their tether; Army Group Centre added that nowhere would they be able to withstand a concentrated counter-attack such as had occurred during the attack on Moscow; temperatures of minus 30–35°C were paralysing the troops and making weapons unusable. The possible consequences of this imminent 'danger of a severe defeat' were described as limitless; there was even talk of a 'most serious crisis of confidence' – and that in the crack divisions of Guderian's Panzer Army. Field Marshal von Bock reported 'disagreements with his Army commanders' necessitating the intervention of the Commander-in-Chief of the Army.[2]

The majority of these reports from Commanders-in-Chief and their staffs reached OKH by telephone; they were probably not transmitted to Supreme Headquarters word for word.[3] There is however no doubt that Field Marshal von Brauchitsch and his Chief of Staff did all they could to give Hitler an unvarnished picture of the situation. Nevertheless after a 'conference with the Führer' on 6 December Halder notes: 'he (Hitler) refuses to take any account of comparative figures of strengths' and insists that 'our superiority is proved by the number of prisoners taken etc.'. Other entries in Halder's diary of this date dealing with different subjects show that

Hitler entirely refused to recognize the facts. He did admit that the troops must have time for rest and recuperation but at the same time insisted that everywhere his own particular objectives should be pursued – for example, in the south the occupation of the Donetz Basin and preparations for the capture of the oil area of Maikop, in the north the junction with the Finns. The following day almost in desperation Halder explodes in his diary:

> The experiences of today have been shattering and humiliating. The C.-in-C. is little more than a post box. The Führer is dealing over his head with Commanders-in-Chief of Army Groups. The most frightful aspect however is that the Supreme Command has no conception of the state of the troops and goes on trying to patch things up like a village cobbler when only big decisions can do any good.

By 8 December however a more realistic view prevailed in Hitler's headquarters and the initial conclusions from the new situation were drawn in OKW *Directive no. 39*. This ordered the army to abandon completely 'all major offensive operations and to go over to the defensive'; the reasons given were 'the severe winter weather which has come surprisingly early and the consequent difficulties in bringing up supplies' but in fact the order did no more than recognize a situation which the enemy had forced upon us a few days earlier. It was nevertheless of considerable importance that Hitler now left it to OKH to issue the subsequent instructions laying down the defensive positions which they considered best calculated to economize our forces. Nonetheless he limited the Army's freedom of action by the additional instruction that areas of operational or economic importance must be retained and that, unless forced to do so by the enemy, other withdrawals were only to be authorized once defensive positions had been constructed in the rear; further, that the necessary conditions for a resumption of major offensive operations in 1942 must be maintained. The objectives which had not been reached were listed in the directive as 'special tasks' for the immediate future and to them was now added an order for the capture of Sebastopol. The main piece of advice given to the Army in order to make good their losses was to comb out their rearward services. The only provision for any further strength increases was an exchange of divisions with the occupied areas in the West; the latter were told that they must accept 'a weakening of our forces' during the winter. No other reserves were available.[4] Halder's diary of 30 November 1941 notes:

> 'total losses on the eastern front (not counting sick) 743,112, ie 23·12 per cent of the average total strength of 3.2 million.... On the Eastern Front the Army is short of 340,000 men, ie 50 per cent of the fighting strength of the infantry. Companies have a fighting strength of 50–60 men. At home there are only 33,000 men available. Only at most 50 per cent of load-carrying vehicles are runners.

From the strategic point of view these new instructions represented nothing less than an admission of the bankruptcy of Hitler's war plan of July 1940 – to say nothing of the studies and projects of the summer of 1941. In view of this and considering that the recent paeans of triumph regarding the supposed final victory over Soviet Russia were still echoing round, it will probably be agreed that by this directive Jodl and his staff had achieved as much as could be expected for the moment. Without a murmur OKH issued an operation order on these lines the same day, introducing it with the assertion that objectives allotted at the opening of the campaign had been achieved. All too soon however it became apparent that in his 'fanatical' determination to hold on to what had been won and to restrict any initiative, Hitler proposed to contravene the principles which he himself had just laid down. In any case this instruction did little to help the front line troops for the immediate future; the cold was intense and they suddenly found themselves without their usual superiority. Too much had already been asked of them during the offensive; now they faced a period during which they must call upon their last reserves of energy to make good past and present mistakes and retrieve the situation created by the far too ambitious objectives set by their leaders – the blame cannot be laid at the door of Hitler and OKW alone.

ENTRY INTO THE WAR OF JAPAN AND THE UNITED STATES

Just at this time an event took place which, perhaps more than any other single factor, enabled German Supreme Headquarters to pass over the change in the situation in the East without more serious upheaval – the Japanese entry into the war and her initial success against the United States. The entire headquarters, even including

HQ Area 2, seemed to be caught up in an ecstasy of rejoicing; the few who, even at this moment, felt they could see further, became ever lonelier. The sudden entry of our Far Eastern ally however, gave rise to no official instructions. We did not even know why, immediately afterwards, Hitler and his entourage, including Generals Keitel and Jodl, took the train for Berlin. The reason was soon clear. During the afternoon of 11 December he appeared before the Reichstag and, in the full glare of publicity, declared war on the United States of America. This produced the following memorable telephone conversation:

> Jodl, calling me from Berlin (I was just finishing lunch and discussing this latest development with certain officers of the staff): 'You have heard that the Führer has just declared war on America?'
> Myself: 'Yes and we couldn't be more surprised.'
> Jodl: 'The staff must now examine where the United States is most likely to employ the bulk of her forces initially, the Far East or Europe. We cannot take further decisions until that has been clarified.'
> Myself: 'Agreed; this examination is obviously necessary, but so far we have never even considered a war against the United States and so have no data on which to base this examination; we can therefore hardly undertake this job just like that.'
> Jodl: 'See what you can do. When we get back tomorrow we will talk about this in more detail.'

This and no more was the beginning for our headquarters of German strategy against America which was to reach its end on the banks of the Elbe in May 1945.

The *Directive on Co-operation with Japan* dated 5 March 1941 has already been mentioned; it laid down that 'the common aim of strategy must be represented as the swift conquest of England in order to keep America out of the war'. By the same instruction the Commander-in-Chief of the Navy had been charged with 'the co-ordination of operational plans' (which dealt only with the war at sea) and Hitler had never failed to stress to him even after Roosevelt's 'order to shoot', the importance of avoiding anything which might give cause to the United States to enter the war.[5] Any Chief of the OKW Operations Staff worthy of the name would certainly have told his staff in good time to get busy with the questions thrown up by this co-operation but Jodl still apparently thought that his primary job was to act as a second Chief of Staff of the Army. Had this not been so the data collected, combined with Hitler's own inclinations, might perhaps have enabled him to exert enough influence on decisions so as at least to postpone participation by the United States in the war in Europe.

As things were Hitler's declaration of war on the United States was little more than an empty gesture (apart from the submarine war which was rapidly extended to the east coast of America where it found many worthwhile targets).[6] The same was true of the *German-Japanese Agreement on Combined War Strategy* which Hitler authorized his Foreign Minister to sign on the day of his Reichstag speech. Moreover the ideas which he put forward shortly after, on 3 January 1942, to the Japanese Ambassador, General Oshima, were based on little more than wishful thinking. He started from the premise that 'never before in history have two such mighty military powers so far separated from each other – Japan and Germany – stood together in war'; from this he drew the conclusion that:

> provided we co-ordinate our military operations in detail, this offers our strategy the possibility of exerting a leverage which will have powerful effects on the enemy, since he will thereby be forced continually to change the focal point of his operations and thus disperse his forces without prospect of achieving decisive results.

He considered further that: 'the United States would not dare to carry out offensive operations in the Eastern Asian area'. It was however Ribbentrop who put his finger on the immediate possibilities in the East when he said that 'Japan may perhaps be in a position to attack Russia in May'. Oshima also considered it a natural sequel that once the 'New Order in East Asia' had been established 'Japan must one day defeat Russia'. Hitler however still maintained that 'for Germany the most important point was that Japan should not go under in face of the Anglo-Saxon powers. England remains our main enemy. We shall certainly not go under in face of the Russians'.[7]

Although we had no very sure grounds for saying so, we in the OKW Operations Staff, in agreement with the office of Admiral Canaris, rapidly came to the conclusion that the Americans' primary object would be to defeat Germany. Pending further information, however, we did not think that the time had yet arrived when major US forces were likely to appear in the European or African theatres. Japan was the better prepared for war, we argued, and this fact would initially weigh in favour of the Axis powers, particularly if, as seemed likely, the Japanese were prepared to contain considerable Russian forces in the Far East in spite of their non-aggression pact with Moscow.

On 18 January 1942 the Chief of OKW and the plenipotentiaries of the comparable Italian and Japanese Chiefs of Staff signed in Berlin *Military Agreements between Germany, Italy and Japan* stemming from the December political agreement. This was headed *Secret Official Document*, an expression not employed in military circles; this shows clearly that it was compiled under the direction of the Foreign Ministry and most probably by the Military Commission of the Three-Power Pact. As already pointed out, this Axis organization had never been informed of German strategic intentions; the only concrete results therefore that emerged from these agreements were the definition of certain chop-lines for the war against merchant shipping at sea and the enunciation of principles for co-operation in general military subjects such as signals, supply, technical and equipment problems. Any disclosure of strategic objectives was avoided by broad-brush enumeration of all possible theatres of war round the globe. England and the United States were the only enemies considered; no mention was made of Russia.[8]

Vis-à-vis Japan this document was characterized by the same degree of deception and insincerity as had become the rule for relations with Italy. The OKW Operations Staff had no part in its drafting and did not even see it. Subsequent German-Japanese military contacts were limited to occasional visits by Japanese officers to German Supreme Headquarters when Hitler himself received the Ambassador, General Oshima, while Keitel and Jodl occupied themselves with his subordinates. No Japanese officer ever entered HQ Area 2 where the real military work of the headquarters went on.

Fifteen months later, even Hitler had changed his views regarding relations with Japan. At his briefing on 5 April 1943 the following conversation took place:

JODL: The Japanese are convinced that during 1943 the European Theatre will remain the focal point.

HITLER: That doesn't please us so much.

JODL: The evacuation of Guadalcanal (by the Japanese) has been successful.

HITLER: You mustn't believe what the Japanese say. I don't believe a word of it.

JODL: One can't believe them simply because they are the only people who tell you something in apparent good faith and looking as if they were telling the truth.

HITLER: They lie to beat the band; everything they say has always got some background motive of deception. What have the Japanese done recently? Look at it! It's ludicrous that Japan can't raise more than thirty infantry divisions. Japan has more inhabitants than Germany. She could raise 120 divisions. Anyway we don't know how many she has really. The only thing I can't make out is the tank problem. Have they modern tanks or not?

ONE OF THE AIDES: They've told us just as little about their tanks as they have of their aircraft.

HITLER: They said nothing about their ships and suddenly there they were with the heaviest capital ships in the world. They said nothing about aircraft carriers and all of a sudden here they are with the largest number of aircraft carriers. They haven't said a word, I tell you not a word. If they've really got plans for something we shall never hear about them, and if they tell us that they have got plans for an operation in the south I shall be inclined to conclude that they are going to do something in the north rather than that anything is going to happen in the south.[9]

This conversation hardly does justice to the considerable services to the common war effort rendered by the Japanese. For instance, the situation in the Mediterranean theatre was eased by the withdrawal of considerable British naval and air forces to the Far East and this, with our own submarine and air reinforcements, enabled Rommel to drive the English back to the western approaches of Tobruk at the end of January 1942. In addition German 'blockade runners' were loaded in Japanese ports with raw materials, particularly rubber, and given considerable assistance on their voyage – an important, if not indispensable, contribution to the continuance of the war in Europe. On the other hand, in spite of numerous attempts through diplomatic channels, we did not succeed in getting any form of Japanese support in the struggle against the Soviet Union.[10] As everybody knows however, this fidelity to their treaty received only a scurvy reward from the Russians who, in the final stages of the war in 1945, took part from Manchuria in the converging attack on Japan.

CHANGES OF ORGANIZATION AND PERSONNEL AT THE HEAD OF THE WEHRMACHT

When Hitler returned from Berlin the crisis on the Eastern Front had reached a height best illustrated by the entry in Halder's diary on the evening of 15 December 1941: 'first serious discussion with the Commander-in-Chief regarding the situation; he is most depressed and sees no way out for the army from its present difficult position'. Field Marshal von Brauchitsch's attitude was probably considerably influenced by his poor state of health; ten days before this he had in fact decided to ask to be relieved.[11] Supreme Headquarters as a whole however now became greatly alarmed. One of the first consequences was a series of changes of personnel and organization which included by far and away the most important, the assumption by Hitler on 19 December of the post of Commander-in-Chief of the Army – and this was no temporary emergency measure; he was to hold on to it right up to the end.

Field Marshal von Brauchitsch had been at the head of the Army for almost four years; yet on 19 December Hitler let him go without any decoration or any other form of recognition on his retirement. Goebbels leaves no doubt what was behind this procedure, unusual in the case of the retirement of a senior officer; on 20 March 1942, after one of his rare visits to the Headquarters, he cleverly distorts the facts in his diary:

> Brauchitsch bears a great deal of responsibility for this. The Führer spoke of him only in terms of contempt. A vain, cowardly wretch who could not even appraise the situation, much less master it. By his constant interference and consistent disobedience he completely spoiled the entire plan for the eastern campaign as it was designed with crystal clarity by the Führer. The Führer had a plan that was bound to lead to victory. Had Brauchitsch done what was asked of him and what he really should have done, our

position in the East today would be entirely different. The Führer had no intention whatever of going to Moscow. He wanted to cut off the Caucasus and thereby strike the Soviet system at its most vulnerable point. But Brauchitsch and his general staff knew better. Brauchitsch always urged going to Moscow. He wanted prestige successes instead of factual successes. The Führer described him as a coward and a nincompoop. He also had tried to weaken the plan of campaign for the West. But here the Führer was able to intervene in time.

This description had of course a propaganda object; Goebbels had for some time been uneasy over the 'apprehension among the people' and the lowering of morale which followed the dismissal of Brauchitsch.[12] The object was to strike another blow at the traditionally high regard in which the Army and its senior officers were held by the German people, thereby, it was thought, assisting and gaining credit for the 'Party'; to this end use was made of the totally unjustified accusation that it was the fault of the Commander-in-Chief of the Army that winter clothing did not reach the front in good time;[13] the desperate situation from which the army in the East had only barely been extracted was also blamed on him. This perversion of the truth may also have been intended to prevent a more widespread realization of the fact that the repeated warnings which 'the generals' had given year in and year out against Hitler's reckless war policy were, in spite of all passing victories, at last beginning to prove themselves only too true.

The fact that Goebbels was trying to do more than merely justify the dismissal of von Brauchitsch is shown by further entries in his diary for 20 and 21 March 1942 where he says:

There are now quite different views about the senior officers of the German Wehrmacht than there were after the French campaign. The senior officers who have risen from the General Staff are incapable of withstanding severe strain and major tests of character. That is something they have not learned. They have not been adequately schooled on the Prussian model. The initial victories in this war made them all too prone to believe that everything would succeed at the first go and that hardly any real difficulties would be encountered anywhere.[14]

After a conversation with Göring, Goebbels adds in his diary:

We are in complete agreement about the Wehrmacht. Göring has the most abysmal contempt for the cowardly generals. Field Marshal Keitel, he said, was not tough enough. He was probably responsible for the fact that the plan of campaign in the East did not function properly. He carried the Führer's commands to OKH with shaking knees. Brauchitsch was not the only one at fault.

Finally Goebbels attributes the following to General Schmundt, Hitler's senior military aide and a purblind idealist:

Schmundt complained bitterly about the indolence (sic) of a number of senior officers who either do not want, or in some cases are unable, to understand the Führer. They are thereby robbing themselves, as General Schmundt put it, of the greatest happiness any of our contemporaries can experience – that of serving a genius.

In the most important field, that of responsibility for command, Hitler's decision in December 1941 to take over the command of the Army himself did little more than set the seal upon a situation which already existed. The official announcement was therefore probably made merely to eliminate the possibility of any other potential candidates being proposed; the object may have been to forestall a possible claim by Göring or even Himmler to take over command of the army.[15] There is however a famous utterance by Hitler in this connection of historical significance and later recorded by Halder in his memoirs as follows:

Anyone can do the little job of directing operations in war. The task of the Commander-in-Chief is to educate the Army to be National-Socialist. I do not know any Army general who can do this as I want it done. I have therefore decided to take over command of the Army myself.

The parallel between these events and those of 4 February 1938 when Hitler took over *de facto* supreme command of the Wehrmacht should not be overlooked. He had an unfailing instinct for opportunities of increasing his own power and destroying that of others and so once again took advantage of the breach which opened before him. His self-conceit was limitless; it later led him to try to command at practically every level in the army, down to battalion and company; he therefore certainly had not the smallest doubt that he would be a better Commander-in-Chief than anybody else. He could be sure that he would be acclaimed by his immediate entourage; for instance when Guderian urged upon Jodl in November 1943 that Hitler should give up command of the Army, the latter is supposed to have replied 'icily': 'do you know of a better Supreme Commander than Adolf Hitler?'[16] There is an even more important comparison with 1938; the Army was now in the position in which the Wehrmacht as a whole had been at the beginning of 1938 when Hitler took over supreme command; it had lost its unquestioned leader who, with his expert knowledge and experience, was responsible for representing its views against those of the political authority.   Thus a process of disintegration began at the top and spread throughout the Army. General Heusinger describes the resulting situation at the end of December 1941 as follows and from my own experience I can vouch for his accuracy:

> Hitler is apparently interested only in two things, the actual directions of operations and the personnel department. Thus all important matters are concentrated in his hand. No one is at the moment responsible for training, organization, replacements, administration, the work of the inspectorates of each arm of the Service, or for education. Keitel is supposed to undertake the greater part of these difficult jobs, to some extent as Hitler's deputy. Soon he won't know whether he is Chief of OKW or Deputy Commander-in-Chief of the Army. Everything else will have to be left to the Chief of the Staff of the Army. This division of responsibility finally breaks up the command organization. The chaos at the head of affairs is becoming greater every moment.[17]

There was in fact never any clear definition of what jobs previously the province of the Commander-in-Chief of the Army were to be taken over by Field Marshal Keitel. From the middle of January 1942 General Buhle, who up to that date had been Chief of the Organization Section in OKH was placed under him. His designation 'Chief of the Army Staff attached to the Chief of OKW' is enough in itself to demonstrate the growing confusion.[18]

As if this were not enough, Hitler now followed the pattern which had begun to take shape during the preceding months and restricted the operational responsibility of OKH finally and solely to the Eastern Front. What had hitherto, apart from Norway and Finland, been regarded as an exception to the rule, now that he was Commander-in-Chief of the Army became the normal system, although no instructions on the subject were ever issued. As a result, from the operational point of view, any unified command of the Army ceased to exist; apart from Hitler, no one had authority over all the forces of the Army and therefore over the reserves, and no one else could order movements of forces from one theatre of war to another. A further result was that the OKW Operations Staff had less and less time to spare for its true job, that of overall strategy. Heusinger was right when he wrote later that the staff had 'been debased from the level of a command organization responsible for overall direction to that of the individual Services'.[19]

In a critical situation such as this there was another much more obvious solution: to merge the operational staffs of OKW and OKH, both of which were now directly responsible to Hitler; but at this point the idea was not even considered. Jodl did indeed indicate to me at the time that Hitler had toyed with the idea of nominating him (Jodl) Chief of Staff of the Army in place of Halder and that he considered himself lucky to have escaped being ordered into the job. Combination of these two offices in the hand of one man would however have been entirely opposed to Hitler's innermost convictions, for he always followed the principle of division of authority. Still less therefore would he have been likely, now that he had himself become Commander-in-Chief of the Army, to take over the General Staff of the Army; it had never given up its old plan of making itself the core of the Wehrmacht General Staff and that would have given it a voice in matters of major strategy and a position superior to the Navy and Luftwaffe. Heusinger and many others thought that this was 'a more favourable opportunity than ever before' but they were considering the purely military aspect only. Hitler did not want unity; he preferred diversity, such unity as there was being concentrated in his person alone. In contrast to some of his previous remarks he was now not even prepared to recognize the value of the *technical* contribution made by the Army general staff; for instance when he took over the office of Commander-in-Chief, he commented ill-humouredly and unjustly: 'the Army works too rigidly. Compare with the Luftwaffe. Quite differently trained by Göring.'[20] He also remarked to one of his aides: 'General Staff officers do too much thinking for me. They make everything too complicated. That goes even for Halder. It is a good thing that I have done away with the joint responsibility of the General Staff.'[21] He had an even greater dislike of the spirit of which the Army General Staff was a personification – that of sober responsible work. Finally it was remarkable that just as before, and just as was always to be, this man who was so ruthless in other directions was apparently afraid of any suspicion that he was in any way subordinating either the 'Reichsmarschall' or the Commander-in-Chief Navy to the Army.

On 1 January 1942 a reorganization within the OKW Operations Staff came into force independently of these developments; this did nothing to alter either the standing or method of work of the staff but must be mentioned at this point because of the new official designations to which it gave rise. The 'National Defence Section' (Section L) ceased to exist as such; its Chief (myself) was then designated 'Deputy Chief of the OKW Operations Staff'. The heads of the three working groups dealing with operations within Section L were designated 'Senior general staff officers Army (or Air)' and 'Senior naval staff officer in the OKW Operations Staff'; their posts and those of the heads of the organization and administrative groups were raised to the level of 'sections'.

Those who know what goes on in a military staff will label these changes as a further example of that universal process for which the Americans have coined the phrase 'empire building'; I must myself admit to being the author of them. In my defence however, I must say that I was not merely serving my own interests but was just as much concerned to get my immediate subordinates, almost all of whom were colonels of the general staff, posts which corresponded to their rank. A disadvantage of the change was that there was henceforth no collective title for the most important group within the operations staff which had hitherto been known as Section L. Instead the title 'Central Operations Staff' was used or 'Jodl's staff', the latter principally by Jodl himself. From my point of view a much more serious disadvantage was that after the war my new title saddled me in the eyes of other nationals with a much greater load of responsibility than that of Chief of a Section.

When Hitler was informed by Jodl of these changes the only interest he apparently took in them was to demand that Colonel von Lossberg should be replaced by another officer in the post of 'Senior General Staff Officer (Army) in the OKW Operations Staff.' The reason for this surprising requirement apparently was that he had never forgotten Lossberg's critical attitude during his own pitiful manifestations of weakness at the time of the Norwegian campaign. Hitler knew nothing about the other achievements of this outstanding staff officer who had subsequently given proof of his worth, particularly in difficult situations; but this is not surprising since he knew nothing of what went on in his 'military working staff'. None of the senior officers whose duty it should have been, made any move to have Lossberg retained. It was not merely that

Diagram 2

HIGHER ORGANIZATION OF THE WEHRMACHT

SITUATION AT THE TURN OF THE YEAR 1941–42

Organization by Theatres of War, splitting up command of the Army

The Supreme Command
Oberkommando der Wehrmacht
(OKW)

The Führer and Supreme Commander of the Wehrmacht
Chief of the OKW Staff (Chief of OKW): Keitel
Chief of the OKW Operations Staff (Chief of the Operations Staff): Jodl
Deputy Chief of the Operations Staff: Warlimont
Overall strategy; theatres of war directly under OKW and
the Army formations employed therein
Norway (C.-in-C. Norway: von Falkenhorst) – from April 1940
North Finland (XX Mountain Corps: von Falkenhorst, Dietl and others) –
from June 1941.
Balkans (C.-in-C. South-east: List, Löhr and others)
North Africa (German – Italian Panzer Army: Rommel)
West (C.-in-C. West: von Witzleben, von Rundstedt and others)

C.-in-C. Army von Brauchitsch From 19 December 1941: Hitler Chief of Staff, Army: Halder	Navy As Diagram 1 Chief of Staff, Navy from June 1941 Fricke	Luftwaffe As Diagram 1
Eastern Theatre of War only		

we were working in a 'civilian headquarters'; we were becoming increasingly divorced from people of our own sort and by much more than merely the barbed wire surrounding the headquarters area. Lossberg's successor as a result of this change, which took place in the middle of January 1942, was Colonel Freiherr Treusch von Buttlar-Brandenfels who had up to that time been senior staff officer in Corps Headquarters Norway. He worked with me for more than three years and proved an excellent officer and companion.

A LOOK AT HITLER'S BRIEFING CONFERENCES

The fact that Hitler had now taken over the direct command of the Army considerably changed the character of the daily briefing conferences; the pressure of the raging crisis at the front also had its effect. On 19 December Halder notes in his diary: 'new methods of work: daily conference with Director of Transport, Director of Signals and Quartermaster General'; though not specifically mentioned, the Chief of the Operations Section General Heusinger was also present (Hitler had promoted him Major General on 23 December on Halder's recommendation). This arrangement was a more or less natural consequence of Hitler's new position. Moreover my personal impression was that Halder was at the time making a fresh attempt to overcome personal dislikes and other obstacles and as far as possible to cultivate and use his new direct official relationship with Hitler in the interests of the Army as a whole. It soon became clear however that more than this was necessary to overcome their inherent differences.

The first obstacle to Halder's attempt to meet Hitler half way was the manner in which these conferences were conducted. Whether designedly or not, Hitler and his immediate entourage continued to follow the previous routine. As before the Army staff had to send their situation report early in the morning and in writing to HQ Area 2. As before, these reports were then combined with those from the other theatres of war and used by Jodl as the basis of his briefing of Hitler. As far as the east was concerned Jodl followed his previous practice and merely dealt with the situation in broad terms using a 1:1 million scale map. During this process it was inevitable – and he undoubtedly intended that it should be so – that critical and wide ranging discussions took place on matters intimately concerned with the Army's responsibilities in the eastern theatre; the same was the case with the regular discussions which he held alone with Hitler in the evenings or during the night. It was only when this initial portion of the midday briefing conference was concluded that Halder would appear with his staff. He would then deal with the situation in the East in detail using a 1:300,000 scale map or even larger in special cases. Just as had happened before, however, during the special conferences with the Army leaders, he almost invariably found himself faced with minds already made up and decisions already taken. He had a much more detailed knowledge of the situation and everything to do with it but naturally his task was immeasurably more difficult as a result.

During the nine months for which Halder was to remain as Chief of Staff of the Army he managed to accommodate himself to these arrangements. He even accepted that Hitler's orders for the summer offensive of 1942, although dealing entirely with the Eastern Front, should be drafted and issued by the OKW Operations Staff. As will be shown later, it was not until he had been succeeded by Zeitzler at the end of September 1942 that any change was made in Jodl's activity either at the briefing conferences or as regards the issue of orders to the Eastern Front. Zeitzler however, with Hitler's agreement, fell into the opposite trap, that of totally excluding the OKW Operations Staff from anything to do with operations in the East, even including their effects upon the other theatres of war. Jodl appeared hardly to realize what was happening, although his staff made frequent protests to him. This seems to be proved by the fact that the account of these events which he gave the International Military Tribunal in Nuremberg[22] was accurate neither as regards his own personal activities nor the general course of events He said:

> This condition changed completely when, in the beginning of 1942, the Führer himself assumed supreme command of the Army. . . . It stands to reason that the Führer, as Supreme Commander of the Armed Forces, could not issue orders through Jodl to himself in his capacity of C.-in-C. of the Army and then have them carried out through Generaloberst Zeitzler. Consequently a separation came about.

The one fact that emerges from all the inaccuracies in this statement is the total confusion existing in the higher organization.

To return to the question of Halder and the briefing conferences. His position was aggravated by the fact that he had to appear as a visitor in a headquarters to which he did not belong. When he took the floor he was the personification of the highest traditions of the German General Staff, both in knowledge and judgement, in style and approach; yet Hitler's attitude to him gradually became that of the magistrate in a police court. The staff officers accompanying Halder were never very numerous and, in accordance with normal military practice, kept themselves in the background, ready as necessary to give more detailed information on the subjects with which they were particularly concerned. Hitler on the other hand appeared surrounded by an ever-increasing number of the members of his *maison militaire,* who now included a representative of the Waffen-SS; they had all now lived together for years and had more or less forgotten what 'military behaviour' was. Keitel was one of them; he could hardly wait for some catchword or pause in Hitler's flow of speech to indicate by some word or gesture that, without further ado, he was in agreement.[23] Jodl was another; he always had at least one hand in his trouser pocket and usually thought it better to keep his mouth shut when ticklish questions were under discussion, although occasionally he supported Halder's point of view. The worst were the other personalities 'also present'; for the most part they had no responsibility; yet as if they were at some public meeting, they would help Hitler with comments and interjections, which they could be sure would be enthusiastically received.

Hitler's flow of speech however must have been the worst, well-nigh physically intolerable, burden which Halder – and not only Halder – had to bear. The urgent concrete questions and proposals under discussion would be drowned in this ceaseless repetitive torrent of words in which matters old and new, important and unimportant were jumbled up together. There would also frequently be long-winded telephone conversations with senior commanders at the front; sometimes the latter used their knowledge of the time at which the briefing conferences took place to try to get urgent decisions out of Hitler;[24] alternatively he would call them up in the vague hope that they would be able to provide him with more pleasant information than that produced by Halder. Ministers, Secretaries of State and other non-military experts, usually from the Traffic Control Authorities, were also frequently summoned from Berlin at short notice to attend the briefing conferences, there to be questioned, lectured or threatened. No doubt Hitler's idea was to demonstrate that there was complete unity of direction. Hours and hours were spent every day in this fashion – a vast waste both of time and energy for those involved who had other responsibilities. [25]

However, the heaviest burden which Halder had to carry was undoubtedly the fact that he was forced to co-operate in the methods of command which Hitler, throwing off all restraint, now began to use. From the middle of December he laid down for the entire eastern theatre of war the same single and overriding principle which he had imposed on Army Group South after the evacuation of Rostov: that the front was to remain where it had come to rest – not a single step backwards. It was even more graphically expressed in the slogan: 'every man will defend himself where he stands'. [26]

It could not then, nor can it now, be denied that in the existing situation [27] an order of this nature was both correct and indeed essential if issued as a *general operational directive*; it contrasted with Brauchitsch's remark that he could see no way out of the situation. It is also true that the fact that the order was issued in Hitler's name ensured that it got down to the individual soldier and in most cases caused them to pull out their last reserves of energy, whether as a result of fear or of enthusiasm. As against this however there can be no doubt that exaggerated insistence on this principle, to which Hitler clung against all good sense, led to immense losses which could never be made good. Almost daily the Army Chief of Staff argued stubbornly against the rigidity of this order, so incompatible with the exercise of high command; gradually however, as he himself said, he sank to the position of being merely 'the representative of Hitler's military bureau for the eastern theatre of war'. [28] He was therefore finally forced to follow the same path which General Jodl and his 'working staff' had taken of their own free will – to the contempt of the Army. Hitler's method of command moreover, deprived the experienced generals at the front of that latitude in the application of operational principles essential in every tactical situation. Time and again Hitler would say during his briefing conferences about this time: 'generals must obey orders just like any private soldier. I am in command and everybody must obey me without question. I carry the responsibility! I and no one else! Any idea other than this I shall eradicate root and branch.' [29]

Parallel with this Hitler instituted a new policy for appointments patently directed against OKH. On 18 December 'for health reasons' Field Marshal von Bock was relieved as Commander-in-

Chief of Army Group Centre by Field Marshal von Kluge. A few days later, on 22 December, after a discussion with Hitler during which he had tried to explain the consequences of his rigid defence order, even Guderian was relieved of his command, to which he was never restored throughout the war. Subsequent actions in this field were little short of unbridled tyranny and accompanied by every form of ignominy; for instance Colonel-General Hoeppner, the commander of Fourth Panzer Army was dismissed from the Wehrmacht for 'insubordination and cowardice'; General Förster was summarily 'demoted' from command of VI Army Corps; he had previously been Inspector of Engineers and Fortifications and had been out of favour with Hitler ever since the arguments about the construction of the Siegfried Line in 1938. On 29 December Halder comments in his diary on the extraordinary manner in which Förster was dismissed: 'dramatic discussions on the telephone between the Führer's headquarters and Richthofen who, though he is an Air Force general, is temporarily to take over command of the Corps after the dismissal of Förster'. On 15 January 1942 Halder's diary contains the stony comment: 'von Leeb has asked to be relieved. Strauss is at the end of his tether. von Reichenau has had a stroke'.[30]

Leeb and Guderian were not the only generals who, instead of being regularly visited in their headquarters by von Brauchitsch, now had to make frequent flights to the distant headquarters in East Prussia and there spend whole days arguing with Hitler as to how his principle of rigid defence could be made to accord with the actual state of affairs at the front.[31] Their efforts however remained fruitless, all the more so because from the end of January 1942 the front began to solidify again on its own. This appeared to prove Hitler's theory right; he unfortunately drew from it the disastrous conclusion that his principle of rigid defence must always and in all circumstances be correct and he applied it throughout the rest of the war. The propaganda line now became Goebbels' phrase: 'the Führer alone saved the Eastern Front this winter'.[32] Ciano notes in his diary on 29 April 1942: 'Ribbentrop particularly plays his usual record ... that the ice of Russia has been conquered by the genius of Hitler. That is the strong dish that is served up to me'.

From the end of December 1941 I was ordered by Jodl to attend the midday briefing conferences regularly. According to an instruction from Jodl the purpose of my presence was supposed to be to allow me to follow up immediately on questions or decisions which emerged, in so far as they concerned the OKW Operations Staff, thereby relieving him of work. Jodl subsequently stated that: 'these briefing conferences were in fact orders. On the basis of the presentation the Führer decided forthwith what the orders for the next few days should be.'[33] In fact, as will become clear, it was almost impossible to get Hitler to take even the most urgent decisions 'forthwith' and never 'for the next few days'; his decisions were all too often overtaken by events.[34]

Shortly thereafter I was able to persuade Jodl to allow me to take on part of the presentation of the situation, primarily by pointing out that one of my subordinates, the Senior Naval Staff Officer, invariably presented the naval situation. To me and to any observant participant it was particularly striking that if my report led to any questions or discussion Hitler invariably turned to Jodl and that Jodl was the only one whom he addressed by name.

This new arrangement kept me, as Deputy Chief of the OKW Operations Staff, extraordinarily busy each morning. Each day started with the compilation of the written morning reports together with the despatch of other urgent business. I then held my conference with my own immediate staff which I had brought forward to 11 am and at which problems of every sort and description were invariably raised. When this was finished I went over by car to HQ Area 1 to give Jodl the latest reports hurriedly and in summary form. I then took part in Hitler's briefing conference which at this time often lasted two to three hours or longer; on getting back to my own area I gave my own staff instructions on the most urgent matters, usually in the form of short notes which during the course of the day frequently had to be turned into telegrams to other headquarters or drafts of orders and cover notes to the Chief of the OKW Operations Staff. The second half of the day was quieter; I would have a late lunch and then, whenever possible, a walk through the woods nearby accompanied by one or other of my friends on the staff. After the nervous tension of the morning I would frequently let myself go without mincing words, for every day I would get back shaken to the core by what had occurred during the hours I was in Hitler's presence, shaken not only by the man himself but by his method of command. As a perhaps unimportant sidelight it may be added that Hitler knew no foreign language and therefore mispronounced foreign names and titles in a way which made one writhe; for instance 'United Press' (with accent upon the

'U') 'Tschemberlein' instead of Chamberlain, 'Eisenh-o-wer' (to rhyme with 'hoer'). His permanent entourage were 'faithful' and imitated him.

Late afternoon and evening were chock full of normal staff work. Such was the pattern of the day and – a point worth mentioning because it was not without its effects – it became a regular sequence completely at variance with that followed in HQ Area 1. Over there, apart from Field Marshal Keitel who was always at work, people had taken on Hitler's habits – in other words they slept late into the morning and then worked far into the night.

CHAPTER 3

A New Start

THE BASIC STRATEGY

While every effort was being devoted to warding off the Russian counter-attack, German Supreme Headquarters never lost either its confidence or its determination to regain the initiative in the East as soon as the winter was over and never to give it up again. Even so it was already thought necessary for the Party to keep an eye on 'morale' in the higher staffs of the Wehrmacht. Goebbels, for instance, notes in his diary on 21 January 1942 that he had instructed the OKW Liaison Officer to the Ministry of Propaganda to give him a written report to be passed on to Hitler on 'officers in OKW and OKH who are guilty of fostering defeatism' – meaning the members of the OKW and Army offices in Berlin. Three days later he notes that he had had 'a talk with General Schmundt concerning conditions in OKW. The Führer had sent him (Schmundt) to Berlin expressly to remedy the situation.' On 25 January there is the entry: 'I had a long talk with Admiral Canaris concerning the reprehensible attitude of a number of OKW and OKH officers.'

Hitler was of course the main protagonist and propagandist for the spirit of confidence and determination. In a conversation with the Japanese Ambassador on 3 January 1942 he had for once revealed his true intentions, saying:

> the object is to resume the offensive towards the Caucasus as soon as the weather allows. This is the most important direction for an offensive; we must reach the oil fields there and also in Iran and Iraq. Once we have got there we hope that we can assist the rise of the freedom movement in the Arab world. Naturally we shall also do all we can to obliterate Moscow and Leningrad.

Hitler also gave the Japanese Ambassador to understand that there would soon be an improvement in the situation in North Africa and in that of Rommel's army, which according to the plans for action in the Middle East was to form the southern arm of the pincer.[1] In his speech in Berlin on Memorial Day in the middle of March he rang down the curtain on the crisis; he expressed himself even more forcibly and once more showed evidence of wishful thinking when he said: 'during the coming summer the Soviets will be completely destroyed. There is no longer any escape for them. So this summer will be the decisive phase of this war. The Bolshevists will be thrown back so far that they will never again touch the cultured soil of Europe.'[2]

These extravagant expressions of determination were repeated at ever greater length and ever more frequent intervals during the briefing conferences. They testify to a fanaticism which alone can explain why no other objectives for future strategy were either ever considered by Hitler or even suggested. Looking back on those days Heusinger says – this time definitely describing what actually occurred without any 'poetic licence':

> for a long time Halder examined the idea whether we should not definitely go over to the defensive in the East, since further offensive operations seemed to be beyond our strength. *But it is impossible even to mention this to Hitler.* What then? If we let the Russians get their second wind and the menace of America increases, then we have surrendered the initiative to the enemy and shall never get it back again. We can therefore only do one thing – try once more, in spite of all drawbacks.[3]

This shows clearly that both OKH and the OKW Operations Staff were true to the well-established rules of strategy and considered that the object of the overall war plan for 1942 must be somehow to eliminate one enemy before the other could deploy his full strength. Under the pressure of events therefore the military view to this extent coincided with the hotch-potch of political, ideological and economic ideas on which Hitler's strategy was based. As will be seen however, the two did not agree either on methods or objectives.

This was another situation in which there would have been a really important job for a true Wehrmacht Operations Staff, had there been one which did not regard itself merely as Hitler's military working staff and which did not preen itself on doing double duty as the High Command of the Army. At the very least it should have examined the possibilities of other solutions. There is no point in getting lost in speculation; suffice it to recall the prospects still offered by a broad agreement with France. This was now clearly of particular significance since Germany was now faced by the two strongest maritime powers in the world. If a really annihilating blow could have been struck against their sea traffic and merchant shipping by a continuously increasing number of U-boats and a concentrated force of Luftwaffe formations working from bases on French territory, it might have been possible to delay Allied landings in Europe and North Africa and also place considerable obstacles in the way of the deployment of superior Allied air power over the continent of Europe. Moreover the Red Army in the east was to a great extent dependent upon sea-borne supplies from the Western powers, it would therefore probably have been unable to undertake major operations for some time had we transferred our main effort to the maritime and air war in the Atlantic. This would have been all the more effective had we succeeded in getting the Japanese to adopt a common war strategy for this purpose if for nothing else.

None of this, however, happened nor was it even suggested. Within his military circle Hitler dominated even the processes of thought; his influence was almost tangible even though privately people might reject his ideas; the longer each individual was forced to spend with him, the closer he was and the more he was ground into the daily routine of the headquarters, the stronger that influence became. Moreover the Commanders-in-Chief of the Navy and Air Force made no move, although as before they still bypassed the Operations Staff and had direct access to Hitler; it may have been that they had at last reached some understanding between themselves or that their senior staff officers had found some way of having detailed discussions with Jodl. In any case under the pressure of the crisis, Raeder and Göring accepted without demur an order from Hitler dated 10 January 1942 which had been prepared by the Organization Section of the OKW Operations Staff in collaboration with the Economics and Armaments Office of OKW, giving directions for the equipment of the Wehrmacht. This swung the armaments programme in favour of the Army 'as a result of the changed situation' and restricted the programmes for the Navy and Air Force to that which could be provided from such raw materials as might remain.[4] It is of interest that this order also laid down that there could be no question of raising new Waffen-SS formations if they required additional German equipment. Hitler completely disregarded this instruction, although he himself had issued it. This no doubt set the example for all other interested parties who did all they could to evade the other provisions of the order – to the considerable disadvantage of the Army.

Göring's views at this time, as reported by Goebbels in his diary, are of interest. On 31 March 1942 he notes that: 'the Reichsmarschall is particularly cautious in making any forecasts'. Shortly afterwards, after a conversation with the Chief of Staff of the Navy on 12 June 1942, Halder's diary contains an explosion of anger about the Navy and its plans:

> The picture of the general situation which the Navy has made for itself is completely at variance with our sober appreciations. Those people are dreaming in terms of continents. Based on their experience of Army operations hitherto, they simply assume that according to our whim of the moment we can decide whether and when we will move overland from the Caucasus to the Persian Gulf or drive from Cyrenaica through Egypt to the Suez Canal. They talk of land operations via Italian Africa to the East African coast and South Africa. They talk arrogantly about the problems of the Atlantic and irresponsibly about the Black Sea. One is wasting one's breath talking to them.'[5]

This being the situation there was that much less opposition to Hitler's will.

METHODS AND OBJECTIVES IN THE EAST

The overall war plan was therefore laid down autocratically by Hitler, but in addition in his new capacity as Commander-in-Chief of the Army he now took complete and immediate charge of the direction of *operations*. During the preparatory periods for the earlier great campaigns he had restricted himself to general instructions, criticism and other contributions of greater or lesser importance; now however binding instructions and orders were issued laying down everything in detail far greater than anything to which the German Army was accustomed.

It is clear that by 12 February 1942 the higher levels of the Wehrmacht were already aware of the main lines of Hitler's plans. At about that time written instructions were issued both by OKW and

OKH, though initially with the object of misleading the enemy; subsequently OKM issued an order for preparations in the Black Sea Area.[6] On 20 March Goebbels noted in his diary: 'the Führer again has a perfectly clear plan for the coming spring and summer. ... His aims are the Caucasus. Leningrad and Moscow. . . . Limited offensives will be carried out with devastating impact.'

On the afternoon of 28 March a special conference was held in Supreme Headquarters; for reasons of secrecy Hitler's personal office invited only a very limited number of people from the highest-level staffs of the Wehrmacht, the Army and the Luftwaffe. Initially I was not invited and was only able to take part after emphatic representations to Jodl pointing out that this would affect the standing of his own staff. At this conference the Chief of Staff of the Army presented in detail the plans for the move forward for the summer campaign on the lines on which they had already been explained verbally.[7] All that is necessary to say about them here is that Hitler, undeterred by recent reverses, had gone back to his basic concept of December 1940 and summer 1941; once more he proposed that the decisive areas should be the outermost flanks of this widespread front. There was only one difference; he had grasped the fact that the Army was no longer at full strength and that losses could not be made good; he had therefore been compelled to go for his two objectives successively rather than simultaneously, beginning in the south with the Caucasus. For the present (and contrary to Goebbels' comment in his diary) Moscow did not figure as an objective at all.

No objections were raised from any quarter. Halder had already on many occasions protested against this extraordinary echelon arrangement for the opening of the offensive, against the widely diverging directions in which subsequent attacks were to take place and above all against the excessive width and depth planned for the offensives. Now, as we stood in that room, his discomfort could be felt almost physically.[8] This was perhaps another reason why Hitler's chief aide appeared next day in Halder's office in the Angerburg Camp to complain once more about 'apparent lack of confidence in the Führer'. Schmundt seems to have said that Army staff officers must be brought to have far more conviction in the greatness of Hitler and must be unmistakably ready to follow and accede to his train of thought. Halder countered by observing that no one could arouse confidence in others if he was not prepared to give it himself; Hitler's mistrust had long been apparent to the General Staff right down to its lowest levels. A few weeks later Halder notes in his diary: 'once more there is a great hate on in OKW (obviously meaning in Hitler's immediate entourage) against the General Staff'.[9]

Jodl must have had a great deal to do with the working out of Hitler's operational plans. Yet a few weeks later even he, talking to Colonel Scherff, Hitler's 'war historian'[10] who was a complete disciple, stated that: 'in view of the reduced strengths in Army Groups Centre and North, Operation Blue-Brunswick (this was its code name at the time)[11] involved very great risk should the Russians make a determined attack towards Smolensk'. He added however that: 'it seemed questionable to him whether the Russians had either the courage or the forces to do this. The Führer was in agreement with him that as a result of German operations in the south Russian forces would automatically (sic) be drawn off in that direction.'[12]

As usual Jodl never discussed the matter in detail either with me as his deputy or with his staff; he never made any observations; he merely instructed us to get out the normal form of OKW directive summarizing the Army's proposals as they had been presented and approved by Hitler on 28 March. Things being as they were the Staff made a special effort to limit the contents of the directive to 'tasks' and eliminate any unnecessary restrictions on OKH. The result was the exact opposite of that intended. Hitler seized upon the opportunity of showing how he interpreted his role as Commander-in-Chief of the Army. When Jodl submitted the 'draft' to him on 4 April he said that he would 'work over this directive himself'. The next day his 'historian' commented with unconcealed pride: 'the Führer has drastically amended the draft of *Directive no. 41* and included important passages drafted by himself. In particular the section dealing with the main operation has been entirely redrafted by the Führer.'[13] As a result of this labour a document emerged on 5 April;[14] it was long and repetitive; it jumbled up operational instructions and universally known strategic principles; in general it was unclear and in detail it was complicated; its terms and expressions were such that even to non-military eyes the difference between it and the normal form of German General Staff document, the product of years of instruction and experience, must have been only too obvious.

The directive laid down that: 'all available forces' of the European allies should be employed and in the preceding weeks Keitel had visited the various capitals on Hitler's instructions. He had succeeded in getting the Italians and Hungarians each to provide a full-strength Army and the Rumanians to provide two further Armies in addition to their formations already on the Eastern Front.[15] The OKW Operations Staff had nothing to do with these journeys of Keitel's nor with the preparations for them; similarly, apart from certain administrative questions, the resulting important additional agreements were dealt with by OKH. In this case there was no exchange of personal letters between Hitler and Heads of State or Heads of Government; he merely laid down subsequently that the allied contingents were to be kept concentrated in their own army area under their own commanders. The Hungarians and Rumanians, although both allies of Germany, were sworn enemies; when therefore the sectors of the front to be held by the allies were laid down (directive dated 5 April) provision was made, although in veiled terms, to keep the two widely separated by slipping the Italians in between them. In general the allies were allotted only defensive tasks and they were reinforced by German counter-attack reserves and most important of all, by German anti-tank units. This was the first occasion on which the allies had been required to co-operate on a continuous front; Hitler produced the guiding principle during one of his briefing conferences at the time: 'the secret of getting our allies to stick to it is to give proof of fanatical loyalty to the alliance.'[16]

The next two months were occupied by the victorious campaign in the Crimea culminating in the capture of Sebastopol, the recovery of the Kharkov area and final preparations for Operations Blue-Brunswick. From the point of view of the OKW Operations Staff we were back in the position which we had known before; in other words apart from the collection of the daily situation reports, we were hardly affected by these great strategic events. An exception to this rule was, of course, General Jodl; he made as little distinction as did Hitler between matters concerning the Wehrmacht as a whole and those which concerned the Army. As a result, apparently without even realizing it, he became increasingly divorced from his own staff. Instead he and the other officers in HQ Area 1 came to form a group of their own, knit together by the fact that they were always in each other's company, on duty, at meals, at the occasional 'mess evenings' and last but not least by the presence of the *genius loci*. In addition to Scherff, General Buhle the 'Chief of Army Staff attached to the Chief of OKW' soon became one of them; he rapidly contrived to bypass Keitel and establish a direct relationship with

Hitler. From 13 April 1942 another member was the 'permanent representative of the Commander-in-Chief Navy to Supreme Headquarters in the Field', at this time Vice Admiral Krancke. All these officers together with their personal assistants and aides were members of HQ Area 1.

This division into 'main' and 'secondary' headquarters continued when a new headquarters location was established about this time at Vinnitsa in the Ukraine. The only officer from HQ Area 2 whom Hitler's aides included was Colonel Momm, who once more did his job excellently, showing consideration for everybody from General Officer down to private soldier.

THE OKW THEATRES OF WAR

In the view of the OKW Operations Staff one of the most urgent tasks was to reorganize the command set-up in the so-called OKW theatres of war, the object being to get each under a single commander-in-chief. This was the obvious form of organization for the direction of inter-Service operations; in addition, by 1942, the war had assumed such world-wide proportions that it was neither possible nor right for Supreme Headquarters to try to direct other than 'on a loose rein', that is by the issue of broad operational directives. In any case the OKW Operations Staff was so small that it seemed essential to delegate the greatest possible plenary power to theatre commanders and at the same time try to get some order into the almost impenetrable jungle of authorities and chains of command which were a feature of the temporarily 'inactive' theatres of war. Both the Navy and Air Force maintained their own headquarters in these theatres in addition to and on the same level as those of the Army; all were independent of each other and there was no unified command even for the defence of the area concerned. There were other authorities each of which had their own chain of command; to mention only the most important: the Chief of the Army Staff attached to OKW for equipment questions; the Army Quartermaster General for administration in the rear area; the 'Reichsführer SS' for the numerous special interests of the Waffen-SS.

There was no point in even considering a reorganization in Norway since the command organization there was based upon Hitler's own instructions of 1940 and he thought that they were the best possible; moreover the personalities occupying the senior posts (including 'Reichskommissar' Terboven) meant that the prospects of any reorganization were hopeless. There was no question of Northern Finland either since this was regarded primarily as a land theatre of war. In North Africa Rommel's prestige was so great that it would have been a work of supererogation to upset his relationship with the Italians, who were in theory in command there, by making changes in our own organization.

In the remaining theatres of war or occupied territories we never, either at this time or later, succeeded in establishing a truly unified high command. This is true of the whole western theatre from the northern tip of Holland to the Pyrenees and of the vast complex of south-east Europe and the Balkans down to the Aegean and Crete. For instance in the Mediterranean area Kesselring was nominated 'Commander-in-Chief South' but for a long time his powers were in fact restricted to command of Second Air Fleet. Hitler was fond of such high sounding titles for headquarters, and of others such as 'assault divisions' for new formations which had never been tested in battle or 'brigades' for reinforced battalions etc. As far as plenary powers were concerned however he preferred to keep them himself – and went on collecting them. Similarly in the West there appeared 'Commander-in-Chief West' – from the beginning of March he was Field Marshal von Rundstedt who had been recalled to service; in the Balkans there was already 'Wehrmacht Commander-in-Chief South-east'; but neither of the high-level Army headquarters so nominated, Army Group D in Paris and Army Group E in Salonica, were given any real powers of command beyond those they already had over the army formations in their area. Hitler was still shy of doing anything to displease either Grand Admiral Raeder or Göring, but probably in the last analysis it was his revolutionary background which made him unwilling to allow any substantial bodies of the Wehrmacht in the individual theatres of war to be subordinated to one man, now that he had himself destroyed the authority over all theatres previously concentrated in the hands of OKH.

Jodl presumably knew that this deep-rooted aversion existed and it was therefore probably mainly for this reason that he rejected all his staff's arguments on the military necessity of a more stream-lined command organization. He was quite prepared to accept that he and his staff would have to call on Hitler for assistance in the various jobs which now came their way from the OKW theatres of war; this was necessary on several occasions in May 1942. Scherff records the following instances: 'the Führer commands that all information and assistance necessary for the overall direction of the Wehrmacht be furnished to his military staff, OKW, when requested and without reservation,' and a little later: 'High Commands of the Services are hereby notified that they are not empowered to issue orders to forces under headquarters tactically subordinate to OKW except with the Führer's agreement.'[17]

These instructions are a striking proof of how weak the position of the OKW Operations Staff still was. As the enemy surged in to the attack of 'Fortress Europe' from west, south and south-east, fresh interventions by Hitler and more and more confused command relationships were to make it even worse.

The overall command organization was therefore highly unsatisfactory. The same was true of the command organization in coastal areas laid down in an OKW directive (no. 40 dated 23 March 1942). The intention of the OKW Operations Staff was to achieve unified command for defence against hostile landings by laying down certain principles about which there had been much argument. A few days later Commander-in-Chief Navy issued certain 'addenda' which considerably altered the directive and twisted it so as to give superior authority to the Navy. This arrangement was accepted by Hitler and put into force in spite of all protests from the Operations Staff and the (so-called) Commanders-in-Chief of the OKW theatres of war, particularly those in the West and in Norway. On Hitler's instructions the Chief of OKW had finally to sign a supplementary order on 5 December 1942 which laid down that in the immediate coastal area there should be divided command as requested by the Navy: seaward defence and all preparations for it to be under sole command of 'coastal commodores' ie naval officers who would receive their orders only from naval headquarters; defence on land to be under command of the Army.[18] This instruction produced a dividing line which, from the point of view both of time and space, was totally impracticable. The inadequacy of our coastal defences is practical proof that this was one more typical monstrosity in the chaos of the German command organization.

At this period the only OKW theatre of war in which land operations of any importance were in progress was North Africa. At the beginning of 1942 Supreme Headquarters had no influence on these whatsoever; Rommel's sudden new break-through eastward came as just as much of a surprise to Hitler in East Prussia as it did to Mussolini in Rome. Rommel later found it necessary to call for German help for the later stages of his offensive, by-passing the Italian authorities who had other views; at the same time Kesselring reported that, after months of bombing, he considered that he had almost completed his task of 'eliminating' the installations of the British base on Malta and that the island was cut off from all reinforcement by sea. Only when all this had happened did Hitler and Mussolini with their immediate advisers meet in Berchtesgaden at the end of April in order to decide upon a timetable and objectives for future strategy in the Mediterranean area in the summer of 1942.

Once again we felt the lack of careful preparatory work by an inter-allied staff. Only a few days and only a few hours each day were available for the discussions; in any case they came too late, as always both sides played their cards close to their chest and Jodl was the only member of the OKW Operations Staff present. In this case the whole basis for the discussions was particularly difficult and results more than usually problematical; the Italians put the capture of Malta ahead of any other objective but they could not undertake the operation with their own forces alone and could not even give a date by which they would be ready to participate. On the German side we were not even at one among ourselves; Rommel did not know the state of affairs regarding Malta and therefore pressed for the resumption of his offensive towards the Suez Canal saying that otherwise he might be forestalled by an English attack; Kesselring considered that we could, and indeed should, take Malta by *coup de main* as an immediate follow-up to the air bombardment; finally Hitler, as before, did not believe that a landing in Malta would be successful and therefore was more inclined towards the attack on Egypt. He may temporarily have weakened in his purpose or more likely he was simply putting on an act but in any case he finally agreed to a compromise proposal; this envisaged Rommel's Army going no further than the Libyan-Egyptian frontier in order that by the middle of July or at the latest by the middle of August, in either case at full moon, all might be ready for the landing on Malta.

A bare ten days later, shortly after 10 May, Kesselring reported completion of the destruction of the installations on Malta. Yet this was the moment chosen by Hitler to authorize Göring, who was also opposed to the attack on Malta, to transfer parts of Second Air

Fleet to the Eastern Front; simultaneously he stated that if there was the smallest sign of danger in the West or in Norway the possibility of further withdrawals of air forces from the Mediterranean must be reckoned with.[19] These decisions and a number of 'most sceptical' comments on his own decision about Malta, coming only three weeks after the discussions with the Italians, made the OKW Operations Staff feel that final clarification was urgently necessary – all the more so because in the meanwhile selected German assault troops together with the necessary transports and equipment had been concentrated in Sicily. As so frequently happened when he was undecided, the only decision Hitler made was to summon the responsible commander to the headquarters in East Prussia to make a verbal report; in this case it was the renowned expert in parachute operations, General Student. His presentation was given on 21 May and he made it clear that he was confident of success; he was fully supported by the Chief of Staff of the Luftwaffe, Jeschonnek, though both must have been aware that Göring was opposed to the operation; support also came from the Navy and from the German and Italian authorities in Rome where a special inter-allied Malta staff had meanwhile been formed and had got to work – the first instance of such a thing during the war.

All this however meant nothing to Hitler; he flew into a rage and in the presence of Student brushed aside without further consideration all plans and proposals, saying that they ran counter to his ideas. Up to this point Jodl had kept himself very much in the background; it was now therefore too late for him to get his staff to weigh up the pros and cons once more and the whole thing was over before the Italians had even heard of, still less been given any information about, this most important decision concerning their theatre of war in the Mediterranean. Without having looked at the question in any detail Hitler produced a series of new arguments: that once Rommel had reached the Libyan-Egyptian frontier again supplies for North Africa could be routed past Malta to Tobruk: that we had no need of Malta and should therefore merely prepare for the landing operation 'in theory' so as to throw dust in the eyes of the Italians. Although, therefore, preparations went ahead temporarily in order to deceive the Italians, in fact the key section of the OKW order on future strategy in the Mediterranean resulting from the 4 May agreement in Berchtesgaden fell to the ground.[20]

In the spring of 1942 therefore prospects for a long-range offensive strategy in North Africa and the Eastern Mediterranean (whether including Malta or not) were just as unclear as they had been in the previous summer. As far as the other OKW theatres of war were concerned, the OKW Operations Staff was ordered to re-examine in detail all previous plans and orders in the light of the latest developments in the world situation. On the one side was the fact that the main body of the Wehrmacht was still committed on the Eastern Front; on the other was the continually increasing offensive capacity of the Western powers; of only slightly less importance was the increasingly reserved attitude of Spain and Hitler's continued refusal to reach an understanding with France. On 25 April there had been a discussion at the briefing conference of the possibilities of landings by the English and Americans in French and Spanish Morocco and on the Iberian peninsula, but in spite of these apprehensions the OKW directive which resulted from our re-examination (no. 42 dated 29 May 1942) could do no other, as far as the Western Mediterranean area was concerned, than lay down dates for possible operations far later than had previously been intended. The capture of Gibraltar was no longer a possibility; in the event therefore of an Allied attack on North Africa the only possible counter-measure was the occupation of unoccupied France; even this however could only be done in an improvised form dependent on the forces available to Commander-in-Chief West when the moment arrived and provided the Italians would participate by occupying the French Mediterranean coast and Corsica. In the event of a landing in Spain or Portugal it was considered that Commander-in-Chief West should be able to occupy the southern foothills of the Pyrenees and subsequently the harbours on the northern Spanish coast, though in practice this would hardly have been possible unless some prior agreement had been reached with Spain.[21]

As far as the reinforcement of our defensive capability in the West was concerned, I myself examined the situation on the spot; as a result the OKW Operations Staff considered that the only action necessary was to include the Dutch coast, which had hitherto been neglected, in the overall defensive system under Commander-in-Chief West.[22] About the middle of June, Hitler began to manifest 'great uneasiness at the possibility of attempts at landings' on the Atlantic coast; in his usual way he became daily more excited about it, stating that he visualized the possibility of 'massive employment of parachute troops'. Initially these preoccupations led him to do no more than give general directions that adequate Army and Air forces must be retained in the West and that a 'reserve of U-boats' must be maintained. On 26 June however arrived a report that 'small vessels were being concentrated along the south coast of England.' This was enough to cause him to order up immediate reinforcements and even to consider, immediately before the opening of the offensive in the East, the transfer to the west of his own 'SS Leibstandarte' and an additional SS armoured division.[23]

Throughout the winter Hitler had never ceased pressing for reinforcements for Norway and had thus deprived the Eastern Front of tens of thousands of men. 3 Mountain Division was brought up to full strength, twenty fortress battalions and numerous coastal batteries were formed and kept at full strength. Finally the Balkans – in view of the shortage of forces and the increasingly uncertain attitude of Turkey there was no longer any question of using this area as a starting point for an offensive towards the Middle East, and there now began a never ending series of 'anti-partisan operations' designed to re-establish order in the interior; the defence of the coasts was due to supplant them in importance later. At the end of April and early May I made a trip through some of the disturbed areas; this gave the OKW Operations Staff a more detailed picture of the situation and so provided the necessary basis for further orders which, as already mentioned, Hitler regarded as exclusively his responsibility even in 'anti-partisan' warfare.[24]

On 6 June a comprehensive paper on *War Potential 1942* was sent out over my signature.[25] This was a revealing and in many ways conclusive document; it is a good example of the type of work done by the OKW Operations Staff during this period of 'the new start'. Apart from the fields in which some progress had been made it set out clearly those gaps and shortages in the manpower and equipment of the Wehrmacht which could not be made good. Coming shortly before the end of the third year of war, it should have been of decisive importance for any thinking, responsible leader. Notable extracts are as follows:

ARMY:

Personnel shortage on the Eastern Front on 1 May 625,000 men; the winter losses cannot be entirely made good.

Armoured divisions in Army Groups Centre and North will have only one tank battalion each (approximately 40 to 50 tanks).

Ammunition difficulties must be reckoned with in August 1942; they may be sufficient to affect operations; replacement from stocks of C.-in-C. West.

Mobility is considerably affected by shortage of load-carrying vehicles and horses which cannot be made good. A measure of demotorization is unavoidable.

At present there are no further reserves available in Germany.

NAVY:

Situation generally favourable (not entirely agreed to by C.-in-C. Navy).

LUFTWAFFE:

From 1 May 1941 figures for aircraft serviceable have fallen to an average of 50–60 per cent of establishment.

The establishment of anti-aircraft artillery has been raised considerably but manpower is short.

RECRUITING:

The call up of the 1923 class in April 1941 means that we are anticipating by 18 months.

ARMAMENT:

During this year oil supply will be one of the weakest points of our economy; it may well influence the operational capabilities of all three Services, the armaments industry and deliveries to our allies (particularly Italy).

Serious shortage of raw material for tanks, aircraft, U-boats, lorries and signal equipment.

SUMMARY:

Our war potential is lower than it was in spring 1941. It must be compensated by the infliction of increased losses on the enemy, superior leadership and increased efforts on the part of the troops, quality of weapons and increased emphasis on anti-tank defence. By these means we can ensure superiority at those decisive points where we decide to concentrate.

It is doubtful whether the Supreme Commander even saw this comprehensive analysis; Jodl took little interest in this aspect of command activity and Keitel would hardly have dared to send it on. In any case all Hitler's subsequent behaviour shows that he was quite prepared to try to bend far more concrete facts than these to his 'fanatical' determination.

CHAPTER 4

Greater Crisis on the Horizon

THE SEEDS

The summer offensive in the East started in earnest in the second half of June 1942. Prior to this a number of events had taken place which were only too well calculated in Hitler's eyes to justify his forecast of the course of events for the year. The Crimea had been almost completely occupied; the area Kharkov-Izyum had been captured, providing a valuable jumping-off area for the new offensive and inflicting severe losses on the enemy in the process; Rommel had captured Tobruk and scored a resounding victory over the British Eighth Army.

As far as North Africa was concerned, Hitler had long since quietly come to the decision that the landing on Malta should not take place and it was now easy for him to press this view upon Mussolini. There was an exchange of letters between the two – even in so urgent a situation this remained the main means of communication; to justify his decision Hitler merely referred to 'this historic hour' and invoked 'the goddess of fortune on the battlefield' who, if not seized by victorious commanders at the moment of victory, 'frequently never smiles again'. There was still a chorus of warning voices, in this case primarily from the Comando Supremo in Rome and from Kesselring but in this moment of exaltation they remained unheeded. Armed with a memorandum from his staff giving 'all the arguments pro and con', Jodl did make one more attempt to revive the plans for the capture of Malta which had been worked out with the Italians only two months before; but a few words from Hitler were enough to satisfy him. Meanwhile Rommel, who had been promoted Field Marshal after the capture of Tobruk, had wasted no time waiting for orders but on his own initiative was already in pursuit of the beaten enemy towards Cairo and the Suez Canal. He and German Supreme Headquarters – though not the Italians – were therefore taken completely by surprise when in the early days of July on the heights of El Alamein the first signs appeared of that crisis which was to end in the loss of the whole of North Africa.[1]

In the East the great victories in the Crimea and at Kharkov-Izyum led Hitler to the premature conclusion that Russian resistance was considerably weaker than in the previous year. He therefore decided that the summer offensive would reach its objectives 'more easily and more rapidly' and proposed in the first instance not to employ all the armoured formations allotted. He immediately started considering further plans among which the 'subsequent operation against Moscow' once more raised its head.[2] In the staffs of OKW and OKH there was naturally general satisfaction that, after so severe a winter, German offensive capacity should be found to be unimpaired; nevertheless the general opinion was less confident than that of Hitler. As the end of June approached and the summer offensive had still not started we began to ask ourselves whether we should ever be ready to act in the West, whether Hitler was sufficiently clear on the strategic interdependence between East and West and whether the war against Bolshevism was not increasingly threatening to become an end in itself. Certain of Hitler's remarks at the briefing conferences were ominously reminiscent of Goebbels' comments in March 1942; describing his conversations in Supreme Headquarters he had listed the objectives as 'the Caucasus, Leningrad and Moscow' and continued:

> If these aims are attained, he (Hitler) is determined, whatever the circumstances, to end the campaign at the beginning of next October and to go into winter quarters early. He intends possibly to construct a gigantic line of defence and to let the eastern campaign rest there. . . . This may mean a 'Hundred Years War' in the east ... like that of England in India.[3]

This was a Utopia which seemed to us unattainable from all points of view – political, economic and military. In any case we in the General Staff had no liking for these plans because, when all was said and done, they perpetuated the war on two fronts which we had brought upon ourselves. Similarly we could not bring ourselves to agree with Hitler's direction of operations which seemed to us risky in the extreme. But, as before, there was no safety valve, no possibility of real discussion of such doubts and discontents with either of the two generals at the head of the OKW Operations Staff. Jodl in particular followed the example of Hitler's immediate entourage and gave an impression of unbounded confidence. There was therefore little his subordinates could do but wait for subsequent developments either to prove Hitler right or force him to make the necessary adjustments and set reasonable limits to his plans. No one imagined however that we were on the way to an even greater crisis than in the previous winter. No one could have foreseen how Hitler was to exercise his power of supreme command; in fact he proved more overbearing and less open to advice than ever before and it was this which was the decisive factor in bringing about the awful crisis of the second Russian winter 1942–43.

SUMMER 1942

When the great new summer offensive began on 28 June 1942 Hitler found himself faced for the first time with the full import of the new responsibilities which he had arrogated to himself as Commander-in-Chief of the Army – that of directing great army formations in an extremely perilous offensive operation. The somewhat superficial judgment of contemporary historians had attributed to him 'an eye for operational opportunities' and 'an instinct in strategic matters' singling him out from the 'experts' who surrounded him. These qualities may have given the Wehrmacht that extra drive on a number of occasions but they were now not enough. Now he really had to prove whether he had those qualities which many a non-military man in fact has; now he really had to get on top of the job which hitherto he had been able to leave to the 'experts'; now he had to ensure that his airy-fairy thoughts fitted the hard facts of life – primarily the relative strengths of the two sides and the factors of time and space.

It seems doubtful whether Hitler ever even realized that these problems existed. In any case he never considered taking the obvious course – hitherto the rule before all major operations – of testing his ambitious plans and working them out in greater detail by means of war games and paper exercises. He apparently thought that it was enough to have a short discussion of his main ideas with Army Group South, which he did on 1 June – without taking the Chief of

Staff of the Army with him. Outwardly the procedure remained unchanged; it was simply the normal system and routine – reports were rendered as usual, briefing conferences were held, orders were issued in normal form. Though he was now directly responsible for the fortunes or misfortunes of the Army in the East, he seemed to find this compatible with spending weeks and months in the Berghof, during which time the Chief of Staff of the Army with the entire OKH remained behind in East Prussia and was seen by Hitler perhaps once a week. As against this, there were more and more frequent verbal discussions with generals commanding on the Eastern Front, who almost invariably had to come to Supreme Headquarters for the purpose, generally at moments of crisis.

All this is not to say that Hitler purposely neglected his job of commanding the Army – the time and attention he gave to it are enough to show that. Nevertheless it was only too obvious what a difference there was between him and a *military* commander who throughout his career had prepared himself for this great responsibility and had no other object in life. A man like Hitler could not be expected to grasp the full import of the job which he had taken over; quite apart from the fact that in many respects he was ignorant of the basic principles of the exercise of command, he was overloaded with other responsibilities, and finally it was not in his nature. As regards enemy intelligence he only accepted what suited him and often refused even to listen to unpalatable information. As before, time and space were for him only vague ideas which should not be allowed to affect the determination of a man who knew where he was going. As a soldier of the first World War, he felt himself better qualified than any of his advisers to judge the capacity of the troops, and this was the subject of interminable and repetitive dissertations. In the end, however, it was generally pushed into the background and forgotten. He had already shown that strategically he did not understand the principle of concentrating forces at the decisive point; now he proved incapable of applying it tactically also, so nervous was he of exposing himself to attack anywhere. For years he had kept the whole world on tenterhooks by sudden adventurous decisions but now, when unexpected situations presented themselves, he proved incapable of taking even the most urgent decisions in good time. He became less and less prepared to give senior commanders long-term directives and so allow them to act on their own initiative within a broad framework. Even more than within his own headquarters he now showed that he lacked the most important quality of a military leader, knowledge of men and the understanding and *mutual confidence* which spring therefrom.[4]

These were the manifestations and hallmarks of Hitler's method of command of the Army. Their consequences became ever clearer. Directions were given which were not primarily based on military requirements but designed in at least equal degree to satisfy political, prestige and economic purposes; the conquest and occupation of territory was therefore placed first in importance. The resources necessary to reach the objectives laid down were frequently not available. Pursuit of these objectives was stubbornly continued 'to the last man and last round' even when the troops had long since been overtaxed, reserves had been used up and ultimate catastrophe threatened. Decisions were almost invariably late and therefore disastrously overtaken by events with the result that the initiative passed increasingly to the enemy and one position after another was lost. Orders were issued in a form which stifled all independent initiative; they were those of a self-satisfied know-all, shuffling battalions and divisions hither and thither and losing entire armies in the process. His pattern of personal behaviour was characterized by complete absence of self-criticism; instead there was suspicion, nagging and raging against everybody, as a result of which the best brains in the Army gradually disappeared and proven generals were passed on to history as cowards and traitors.

In these circumstances tension and uneasiness set in only a few days after the opening of the offensive. Hitler had just paid a renewed visit to Army Group South, where was the decisive point for the breakthrough on which all subsequent moves depended. The confused situation around Voronezh soon led to the first serious dissensions. On 6 July Halder writes: 'there was another fearful scene about the command of the Army Group at the Führer's conference'. He follows this up later with this comment:

A number of telephone calls during the day with von Bock (these were most uncomfortable), with the Führer, with Keitel (OKW) and with von Sodenstern, Chief of Staff of Army Group South. Always on the same subject. This cross-telephoning on subjects which ought to be quietly thought over and on which clear orders

245

should then be issued, is agonizing. Keitel's senseless chatter is insufferable.

A week later things had gone so far that Field Marshal von Bock, the Commander-in-Chief on the attacking front, was dismissed a second time with 'expressions of the utmost indignation'; his Chief of Staff was only saved from the same fate by the intervention of Halder. Hitler justified his decision by quoting a previous 'unfortunate proposal' by the Army Group which, however, had never been carried out; he never failed subsequently to ascribe the failure of the entire offensive to Bock's dilatoriness at Voronezh.[5]

By the middle of July the offensive had advanced so far that OKW and OKH moved on the 16th into the new headquarters at Vinnitsa in the Ukraine. OKH was accommodated on the edge of the town; Hitler and the staff of OKW occupied a camp in the woods a few miles north-east of Vinnitsa, christened by Hitler himself with the code name 'Werwolf' (Werewolf). HQ Areas 1 and 2 were only a few hundred yards from each other in the open woodland, the former in huts, the latter in log cabins. Security precautions seemed to be hardly stricter than in East Prussia. The civil population was still there both in town and countryside and in general appeared friendly. We used to walk unescorted through the woods and swim in the River Bug nearby (only of course the members of HQ Area 2 during their off-duty periods) and there were never any incidents. The summer sky was cloudless, the heat was stifling, and Hitler, one was given to understand, was particularly affected by it. This probably contributed to the disagreements and explosions which reached an unprecedented height in the weeks and months which followed.

In North Africa, Rommel had just had to give up all his ambitious plans and go on to the defensive before the heights of El Alamein. His situation was so serious that he was inclined to withdraw forthwith to the Libyan frontier position but Hitler considered that the forty miles between the impassable Qattara depression and the Mediterranean coast was far and away the best defensive position in the whole of North Africa. At the end of July, on my own initiative and with no particular mission, I made a trip to Rommel's forward headquarters in order to get a picture of the situation. By the time I arrived Rommel was once more thinking of taking the offensive, thereby achieving the rare feat of being in agreement with both the German and Italian Supreme Headquarters at the same time. On the return journey I had talks with our own and allied authorities in Bucharest, Salonika and Athens, and then with the Italian High Command in Rome; this gave me a good overall picture of the situation in the Mediterranean area and when I got back to the Ukraine I was able to give my impressions at the next briefing conference in HQ Area 1. Based on what I had seen I gave a general picture of the difficult position in which Rommel was, pointing out that the German-Italian Army was in the open desert and facing an enemy who, from the point of view of both equipment and ammunition supply, had become considerably superior on land, on sea and in the air. Rommel was at the time always treated leniently and Hitler took this quietly. There was only one explosion of impatience, this time from Göring. Hitler called out to him: 'do you hear that, Göring, carpet-bombing in the desert!' This apparently annoyed him and he turned on me, spitting out invective and saying that 'amateurs' should not be allowed to make reports or pass judgment upon the air situation.

Hitler's estimate of the scale of the initial victories in the eastern offensive became ever greater; the more it did so however the more he considered that we must reckon on landing attempts by the Allies in the West in order to relieve the Russians. On 6 July Halder registered both disappointment and apprehension, commenting in his diary that 'as announced a few days earlier, the Führer refuses for this reason to release the SS Leibstandarte Adolf Hitler which would be of considerable value for First Panzer Army's attack'. Three days later Hitler's apprehensions had as usual so far increased that he gave categorical orders for this division and certain other considerable reinforcements to be moved to the West, disregarding the fact that the SS division was fully battle-worthy and one of the few reserves behind the decisive flank of the main offensive front. The culminating point was reached on 23 July when Hitler broke all the rules governing the right of a Supreme Commander to order dispositions of forces in detail, rode roughshod over the vigorous opposition of Halder and in this case of Jodl also, and ordered the Panzer Grenadier Division Grossdeutschland, one of the élite formations of the army, to halt in the midst of its attack and prepare to move to the West.[6]

One or two points are worthy of note in this connection: the order for the move of the SS Division mentioned Normandy as well as the Straits and the area Dieppe-le Havre as among the areas of the coast probably most threatened: on 19 August 1942 the twenty-four hour surprise raid by British and Canadian forces on Dieppe took place; the forces already available in the West prior to 9 July were however perfectly adequate to deal with it: the orders for the Grossdeutschland Division were later changed and it was employed for defensive tasks on the Eastern Front in Army Group Centre.

There were now to be further instances of interference with operations by Hitler. While the move down the Don from Voronezh was actually in progress, 9 and 11 Armoured Divisions were detached to Army Group Centre. OKW *Directive no. 43* dated 11 July 1942 had laid down that after clearing the Crimea the main body of Eleventh Army was to advance across the road from Kertsch and move forward on either side of the lower Caucasus, a direction which offered considerable prospects of success. Entirely on his own Hitler now decided to postpone the Caucasus operation, use only a small portion of Eleventh Army for it and to switch the main body northwards for the attack on Leningrad.[7]

These and similar occurrences give a picture of the profound differences of opinion regarding the situation in the earlier phase of the offensive on the Eastern Front; they overshadowed all thoughts and actions within the headquarters. By 24 July the attack from Voronezh had reached the middle and lower Don from west of Stalingrad down to Rostov; Hitler considered that this enormous gain of territory indicated that the success of the offensive was more or less assured and that subsequent operations would be in the nature of a pursuit.[8] In OKH however, and in the OKW Operations Staff we were still waiting for a real great victory; it seemed to us that the enemy had still nowhere been brought to battle, as the small number of prisoners and the small amount of captured equipment proved.

The background was therefore one of deep disagreements on essential matters. As a rule they were only hinted at but they found expression in increasingly numerous and serious dissensions on matters of tactical detail. On 18 July for instance Halder writes:

Yesterday I made a suggestion which was peremptorily turned down in favour of a senseless concentration on the northern bank of the Don against Rostov. Today at the Führer's conference my suggestion was suddenly accepted and an order issued by the

All Highest that the Don should be crossed on a wide front and the Battle of Stalingrad begun.

On the same subject he says in his diary of 23 July:

> Führer's conference: on 17 July, against my advice, he ordered a concentration of armoured formations against Rostov. It must now be clear even to the amateur that there is a senseless concentration of mobile formations in the Rostov area and that the vital outer flank is going short. I gave emphatic warnings that both of these things would happen. Those on the spot, where victory is within their grasp, are furious with the High Command and reproach it bitterly.

Finally Halder turns from details to the overall picture and, only a bare month after the opening of the offensive, writes:

> This continual underestimation of the enemy is gradually becoming both ludicrous and dangerous. It is becoming more and more intolerable. It is impossible to do serious work. The hallmark of this so-called 'leadership' is a pathological reaction to the impressions of the moment and complete misconception of the mechanism of command and its limitations.

On 29 July Halder reverts again to the 'concentration' at Rostov on which Hitler had as usual insisted – by no means the last time he was to do so. He says: 'fearful excitement. Intolerable language used about other people's mistakes when they are merely carrying out orders which he (Hitler) himself has issued.'

Thus the stage was set for the stormy briefing conference of the following day; though no one realized it at the time, it was the opening scene of a disastrous chain of events leading to the catastrophe of Stalingrad. Once again it is Halder who puts his finger on the point; with a bitter dig at the characteristic attitude of Jodl he writes:

> At the Führer's conference General Jodl took the floor. In solemn tones he stated that the fate of the Caucasus would be decided at Stalingrad. Forces must therefore be diverted from Army Group A to Army Group B (Army Group South had meanwhile been divided into A and B); so the idea which I put to the Führer six days ago but which was then understood by none of the great brains of OKW has now been served up afresh and accepted.

It is clear from this that everybody agreed upon the importance of the Stalingrad area. This was in fact to a certain extent a new conception; in his initial plans Hitler had considered the city as of importance only as an 'industrial and communications centre' and laid down that it must be secured in order to guard the flank of the main operation into the Caucasus.[9] As operations developed however the conviction grew that adequate security for further operations could only be guaranteed by the complete conquest of the Stalingrad area, and this had been set out as an order in OKW *Directive no. 45* dated 23 July on the 'continuation of Operation Blue-Brunswick'. Many people think that it was as a result of *Directive no. 45* that our forces were dispersed and, as it were, lost in the vast areas between the Black Sea and the Caspian. I do not agree. The real cause of this development lay rather in the objectives laid down in and the wording of Hitler's original plans for this highly questionable operation; the directive merely highlighted the diverging directions in which further advances were to take place.[10] If further proof of this is needed it is provided by Halder's diary of 16 July, that is a week before the issue of OKW *Directive no. 45.* He says:

> Discussion with Gehlen (Chief of the Intelligence Section – Foreign Armies East) and Heusinger; basic ideas for the forthcoming battle at Stalingrad. We must carry on the battle of Rostov both north and south of the Don but at the same time we must get ready for the battle of Stalingrad and perhaps even initiate it.

Although therefore all concerned were apparently agreed on the importance of Stalingrad as the hinge on which the entire future campaign depended, there were plenty of other causes of controversy. Hitler was still set on reaching more or less in one movement all his other objectives: the entire northern and eastern shores of the Black Sea, the cutting of the Grozny and Osetia roads over the Caucasus 'if possible at the top of the passes', the western shore of the Caspian Sea with Baku and the lower Volga from Astrakhan to Stalingrad – to mention no more than the list given in *Directive no. 45.* The arguments became ever fiercer, particularly from the middle of August when the momentum of the offensive began to wane as a result of shortage of forces and transport. Instead of recognizing the factual limitations however, Hitler now began to exert pressure in all directions.[11] Army Groups and Armies proved unable to reach his objectives, so he now began to try to force decisions by shuffling individual divisions about himself.

A number of things contributed to the explosive atmosphere of the headquarters: the heat of the Ukranian summer was stifling; on the middle Don the forces of our allies proved to be only moderately battle-worthy; above all Russian counter-attacks against Army Group Centre in the area of Rzhev began to look menacing. Field Marshal von Kluge, Commander-in-Chief Centre, appeared in Werwolf on 8 August and made a pressing plea to be allowed to clear up this situation by using the two armoured divisions (9 and 11) which had been moved to his command from the area of the offensive. Hitler however mulishly insisted that the two divisions must be used offensively to iron out the Ssuchinitschi salient which was a leftover from the winter crisis, maintaining that this would provide a jumping off point for the subsequent drive on Moscow. Kluge remained quite unmoved by all his arguments and finally marched out with the unforgettable words: 'you, my Führer, therefore assume responsibility for this'. I had previously served under Kluge and had the greatest respect for him; this answer and his general bearing seemed to me exemplary. They did not prevent him from being summoned to headquarters once more two weeks later and accused of being responsible for the failure of the operation 'because of his dispositions'.[12]

Ssuchinitschi was therefore a further festering point of controversy. Meanwhile however the situation at Rzhev had become untenable; its sequel was of historic significance. Two days later on 24 August at the midday conference Halder again urged that Ninth Army, which was fighting at Rzhev, should be allowed the necessary freedom of manœuvre and authorized to withdraw to a shorter line which could be held by its dwindling forces. This led to a collision which, only nine months after the departure of its Commander-in-Chief, was to deprive the German Army of its Chief of the General Staff who had been the real brain behind its victorious campaigns. The proposal ran counter to Hitler's cardinal principle of command and obviously annoyed him. 'You always come here with the same proposal' he threw back at Halder, 'that of withdrawal', and then in the same breath proceeded to make a series of highly disparaging remarks in which in this case he even included the fighting troops. He ended his tirade with the words: 'I expect commanders to be as tough as the fighting troops.' There was an atmosphere of extreme tension; Halder was now furious and he raised his voice as he replied: 'I am tough enough, my Führer. But out there brave men and young officers are falling in thousands simply because their commanders are not allowed to make the only reasonable decision and have their hands tied behind their backs.' Hitler recoiled, fixed Halder with a long malevolent stare and ground out hoarsely: 'Colonel-General Halder, how dare you use language like that to me! Do you think you can teach me what the man at the front is thinking? What do you know about what goes on at the front? Where were you in the First World War? And you try to pretend to me that I don't understand what it's like at the front. I won't stand that! It's outrageous!'

Those present at the conference dispersed, shattered. At Rzhev the bloody battle for a piece of ground which had long since become worthless went on as before. But it was now clear that the final breach between these two men, who were as different as chalk from cheese, could not be far off.[13]

STORM SIGNALS

Starting late August–early September a series of widely differing events took place covering the whole sweep from the most distant areas of the front to the Supreme Headquarters in Ukraine. Both individually and collectively they could only be described as storm signals.

The *air war* over Germany had entered a new phase with the first heavy attack on Cologne at the end of May 1942. The large numbers of enemy bombers employed and the superiority of their equipment gave rise to the most serious apprehensions for the future. It led to the first serious conflict between Hitler and OKL, the subject being their 'Reports of Victory' which appeared regularly in the daily Wehrmacht summary. Hitler commented: 'I never shrink from the truth however unpalatable it may be but I must know it if I am to draw the correct conclusions.'[14]

In *North Africa* Rommel's offensive, which he had planned and then postponed for so long, began on the evening of 30 August. But on 1 September he was forced to break it off, owing primarily to the enemy's great air superiority and two days later he was back in his starting positions in front of El Alamein. Although this return to the defensive did not necessarily mean that all the old distant ob-

jectives had finally been given up, we in German Supreme Headquarters were clearer than they were in Rome that the British under
their new commander, General Montgomery, would now be champ-
ing at the bit. There seemed no doubt that Rommel would be able
to repulse the attack which was obviously coming; Hitler was convinced that there was no better defensive position than that in front of
El Alamein.

There was now no question of the capture of *Malta* which had
risen from its ashes and presented a greater threat than ever to sea
traffic. In Italian Supreme Headquarters they were making preparations for an occupation of Tunisia to protect their North African
colonial empire; Hitler, however, was still obsessed by the idea
that this would drive French North Africa into the arms of de Gaulle
and issued the most urgent warnings against premature action. As
far as *the South* was concerned, he was far more worried about Crete,
particularly now that Rommel was back on the defensive; one of the
best of the Army's infantry divisions (no. 22) had to be transferred
there. He was also concerned about the disturbed areas on the
northern shore of the Eastern Mediterranean since, as always, he
regarded these primarily as the first line of defence for the Rumanian
oil fields.[15]

Hitler's preoccupation with *the West* was in no way set at rest by
the successful defence of Dieppe – which in any case had been much
exaggerated for propaganda purposes. He now began to worry about
the coast south of the mouth of the Loire and moved additional
formations into France. The only forces available however were the
recruiting divisions of the Replacement Army; there were no other
reserves. This was the start of a procedure which had adverse effects
upon equipment, mobility and battle experience, and its results were
felt during the defence against the invasion of June 1944. It is of
some interest that these latest instructions once again mentioned
Normandy as a likely landing area.[16]

Against *Norway* there was no threat; yet as always it absorbed a
high proportion of our shrinking forces and resources.

In *Finland* the orders still were for a combined German–Finnish
attack to cut the Murmansk railway and thereby block at least this
route for the supply of Western war material to Russia which was
reaching ever greater proportions. But by the autumn of 1942 the
prospects of doing this were shrinking visibly. The most important
prerequisite, the capture of Leningrad, had figured in Hitler's plans

for the 1942 offensive as taking place 'in September at the latest'; wiser counsels now prevailed and this was recognized to be impossible; a number of divisions of Manstein's Army had been sent from the Crimea to the extreme north but by the end of August the enemy had seized the initiative there and the divisions were frittered away one after the other on defensive tasks. At the headquarters in Vinnitsa Hitler had given his orders on 23 August to the Commander-in-Chief North, Field Marshal von Küchler, and the next day to Manstein; they were: stage 1, 'make a junction with the Finns (via the Karelian Peninsula); stage 2, occupy Leningrad and raze it to the ground' (!). The fact that all this went wrong was ascribed by Hitler primarily to 'half-hearted leadership'. General Jodl knew no more about what was going on in the Leningrad area than did Hitler, but he agreed with this condemnation of the commanders. He even supported Hitler when the latter referred to the entire body of 'senior commanders' as being 'intellectually conceited and incapable of learning or of seeing the wood for the trees'.

von Küchler's presence and his calm factual way of presenting a case had initially appeared to inspire confidence in Hitler. Now, however, he cut von Küchler out of the chain of command and charged Manstein with sole command in the decisive sector, thereby involving himself directly in the command of operations in the Leningrad area. The only resources to hand were a solitary Mountain division which was really intended for Finland and a force of four (!) Tiger tanks, the first to appear at the front. Hitler expected great things from these 'new weapons' which he was convinced would be decisive. Section L's war diary comment a few days later: 'one Tiger is already out of action', shows what we in the staff thought of such paltry numbers, quite apart from the fact that it soon emerged that these tanks were too heavy for the bridges in the area of operations. The Operations Staff was made to prepare a directive (no. 47) for the capture of Leningrad but when the draft was submitted to Hitler on 3 September he put it in his pending tray. There it stayed. The second phase of the summer offensive was therefore abandoned before it had ever begun.[17]

Meanwhile heavy pressure continued against *Army Group Centre*. In addition partisan activities in the rear areas became so serious that the Operations Staff issued a special directive signed by Hitler (no. 46 dated 18 August 1942)[18] in a renewed attempt to stamp out the movement. At this time I used to prepare a report on the 'partisan war' approximately every two weeks. It must have been shortly after this that, while I was giving this report at the briefing conference, I was interrupted by frantic signals from Keitel and Jodl. After this the report was no longer presented at the briefing conferences, apparently in order not to worry Hitler.

For Supreme Headquarters however, by far the most serious shocks came from the southern sector of the Eastern Front. At the midday conference on 16 August Halder had produced an old Russian map which had been captured somewhere and had pointed out the similarities between the present situation and that of the Red Army in 1920. It was commanded by Stalin at the time and had made a surprise attack across the lower Don between Stalingrad and Rostov, inflicting a decisive defeat on Wrangels' 'White Guard'. Hitler's interest was immediately aroused. The only result however was an order for the urgent move of one German armoured division (no. 22) to support the threatened sector which was defended by the Italian Eighth Army. A little later he ordered up two infantry divisions, one of them from the flank where the attack was in progress. The best defence however against any Russian initiative of this sort he considered to be the rapid capture of Stalingrad and the resulting release of forces – and in this he was quite right.[19]

Stalingrad was still the focal point of the battle but, apart from the advance to the Volga north of the city, there had now for some time been little but local progress there. Hitler's impatience increased and on 28 August fuel was added to the fire by Göring, whose contacts always kept him fully informed of the atmosphere in Supreme Headquarters. With his usual pomp and circumstance he appeared at the briefing conference and read out a report from the Commander of the Close Support Aircraft at Stalingrad, General Freiherr von Richthofen, to the effect that 'there was no question of major enemy forces being in the area. During reconnaissance northwards the Luftwaffe had had difficulty in finding any enemy forces at all, although the country was completely without cover.' Even Hitler did not seem to be prepared to believe this report altogether, but he showed clearly enough where his suspicions lay by issuing an order that the higher Headquarters in Army Group B should be moved closer to the front. This 'enfilade fire' from Göring however left certain effects behind it. It was enough in any case further to increase the general feeling of tension.[20]

At this time it was the fact that progress in the Caucasus was falling short of his expectations which caused Hitler far greater vexation. On 21 August Halder notes: 'the Führer is very agitated'; this was followed by the comment, repeated daily, that the 'situation was more or less unchanged'. On 30 August the Operations Staff War Diary notes: 'the Führer is very dissatisfied with the situation in Army Group A'.

The next day Field Marshal List, Commander-in-Chief of Army Group A, was ordered to Vinnitsa to report in person. He gave a calm, balanced picture of the situation which seemed to put an end to all apprehensions. While he was there Hitler did no more than enumerate the large number of objectives set for the offensive; the immediate objectives included three important passes over the western Caucasus giving access to the Black Sea coast; more distant objectives were the oil area of Grosny and the mouth of the Volga at Astrakhan. 'Only' the capture of Baku was he ready 'if necessary to postpone to next year'. Field Marshal List with a few others was invited by Hitler to lunch in his log cabin, where apparently he played host with unwonted geniality. Thus, loaded up with new objectives but without having been promised any worthwhile reinforcements in forces or resources, Field Marshal List took his aircraft back to Stalino.

During the next few days some progress was made, including the capture of the harbour of Novorossisk around which a prolonged battle had raged. Hitler's impatience however had now reached such a pitch that on 7 September he despatched Jodl, whom normally he would hardly allow to leave his side, to Army Group A to press once more for the advance to be speeded up. Jodl returned the same evening; the report he made to Hitler produced a crisis which shook Supreme Headquarters to its foundations, the like of which was not to be seen until the last months of the war. Jodl reported that, contrary to Hitler's forebodings, Field Marshal List was adhering strictly to the instructions he had received and that he (Jodl) agreed with the views of the Army Group regarding what could be done in the future. For the first time Hitler flew into a rage with Jodl, accusing him not only of being a partisan of the Army Group but of having been talked round by List when he had merely been despatched to transmit orders. Jodl's hackles rose and he argued back.[21]

I was not present when this occurred. Jodl told me about it the next day, also outlining the resulting orders from Hitler and from then on I was involved in subsequent developments. The entire existence and work of the headquarters seemed paralysed. Hitler shut himself up in his sunless blockhouse and apparently only left it after dark, taking care not to be seen. The map room, which during the preceding days and weeks had daily been the scene of prolonged discussions and furious arguments, lay deserted. The briefing conferences now took place in Hitler's own hut; they were limited to the smallest possible number of essential reporting officers and the procedure – or lack of it – was quite different. Not a word more than necessary was spoken; the atmosphere was glacial. Ever since the French campaign Hitler had gone twice a day to the mess to take meals with the members of HQ Area 1; he no longer appeared. The briefing conferences were eventually resumed in their old form but Hitler never appeared in the mess again. His chair in the dining room stood empty for some time and was then taken over by Bormann. Forty-eight hours later ten to twelve shorthand typists from the Reichstag appeared in the headquarters, were put into uniform, took the oath of allegiance to Hitler himself and subsequently, two at a time, were invariably present at all military discussions.

On 9 September Hitler informed Field Marshal List via Keitel and Halder that he was relieved of his command. Hitler himself took over command of Army Group A that same evening! At the same time Keitel had to tell Halder that he also would shortly be relieved. The word also went round that Keitel was to be relieved by Kesselring and Jodl by Paulus, Commander of Sixth Army, the latter however only after the capture of Stalingrad. This caused both the OKW generals, contrary to their normal habit, to confide in me. Keitel had shown himself an unquestioning 'disciple' of Hitler and had had nothing whatsoever to do with what had happened; nevertheless he was treated in the same despicable way as Jodl. When I saw him privately he asked me whether I thought he could continue in his job and still retain his self respect, a question which, as I told him, only he could answer. Jodl for his part admitted that he had been wrong; one should never, he said, try to point out to a dictator where he has gone wrong since this will shake his self-confidence, the main pillar upon which his personality and his actions are based. Having thus acknowledged what was evidently still his opinion of Hitler, he said: 'I only trust he will try to find a successor for me among the Army generals! But he will never again have such

257

staunch National-Socialists as me and Scherff' (the 'historian'). Finally he said to me: 'keep yourself out of the briefing conferences from now on; it's too depressing having to go through that'.[22]

As a result of all this I did not see Hitler for several weeks. Being now able to stand back and look at things from a distance, what had occurred seemed to me to be of ever greater significance from the overall point of view. But it was only when some time later I was once more ordered to attend the briefing conferences that the full import of what had happened really seemed to strike me. Instead of greeting me when I entered the log cabin, Hitler fixed me with a long malevolent stare and suddenly I thought: the man's confidence has gone; he has realized that his deadly game is moving to its appointed end, that Soviet Russia is not going to be overthrown at the second attempt and that now the war on two fronts, which he has unleashed by his wanton arbitrary actions, will grind the Reich to powder. My thoughts ran on: that is why he can no longer bear to have around him the generals who have too often been witnesses of his faults, his errors, his illusions and his day dreams; that is why he wishes to get away from them, why he wishes to see people around him who he feels have unlimited and unshakable confidence in him.

In the event the only one of the proposed personnel changes which took place was that of the Chief of Staff of the Army; this was due primarily to the pressure of the continuously deteriorating situation which meant that neither Kesselring nor Paulus could be spared from their posts in the Mediterranean and at Stalingrad. Colonel-General Halder was dismissed on 24 September without further promotion or any other form of recognition. His diary is a striking example of the great traditions of the Prussian-German General Staff triumphing over all unpleasantness; commenting on his last meeting with Hitler he remarks: 'my nervous energy is used up and his is not as good as it was. We must part'. Hitler now prepared to follow quite different principles in his command of the Army. They cannot be better illustrated than by his further remark which Halder notes tersely: 'necessity to educate the General Staff in fanatical belief in an ideal. He is determined to make his will prevail throughout the Army.' Elsewhere he reports Hitler as saying: 'in view of the tasks now facing the Army, rather than relying upon technical competence, it must be inspired by the fervour of belief in National-Socialism'.[23]

With this new background Hitler chose for the job of Army

Chief of Staff General Zeitzler – to everybody's considerable surprise. The story of Zeitzler's nomination is of interest since it illustrates not only the differences between Zeitzler and Halder and their
respective positions but also how it came about that, after eighteen
months in the job, Zeitzler too became totally estranged from Hitler
and was finally dismissed in June 1944.[24]

It has already been mentioned that in the spring of 1939 Zeitzler
had for some time been senior Army Staff Officer in Section L of
OKW; there, as a subordinate of Jodl, he had been one of the most
energetic supporters of the unified command of the Wehrmacht.
Thereafter as Chief of Staff in the higher headquarters of armoured
formations he had gained exceptional experience and shown much
merit in all the great campaigns of the war. He was a close friend of
Schmundt, Hitler's chief military aide, and it was probably due to
this fact that Hitler, who generally took little notice of staff officers,
even those in senior posts, knew Zeitzler personally and had even,
contrary to all rules, sometimes received him for personal discussions
without whoever might be his commander at the time.[25] In the
middle of April 1942 Zeitzler had been nominated Chief of Staff to
Commander-in-Chief West – again as a result of a proposal by
Schmundt and a personal choice by Hitler. In this post he had
expressly been given the special job of shaking up the Army in
the West so as to fit it for the defence of the coasts of 'Fortress
Europe'. He went about this job circumspectly but assiduously,
keeping Supreme Headquarters continually informed by copies of
orders both on 'principle' and 'detail'. The culmination of this
peculiar procedure came with the raid on Dieppe on 19 August 1942;
primarily as a result of Zeitzler's reports this affair was greatly
exaggerated in Supreme Headquarters reports; on his side he made
remarkably good use of it to further the cause of coastal defence.
There therefore seems no reason to doubt the following report by an
eye witness: 'a few days after Dieppe and after his major collision
with Halder Hitler expressed the wish to have at his side in future as
Chief of Staff of the Army "someone like this chap Zeitzler", a
staff officer whom he had always found to be optimistic and ready
for anything, who wouldn't mind asking for a helping hand in
difficult situations and who would not be prone to Halder's "eternal
second thoughts".' This would probably have been enough to ensure
Zeitzler's nomination but at this moment Göring was suddenly
announced. As invariably happened his 'contact man' in Supreme

Headquarters had kept him informed and at the last moment passed him urgent information as to what was afoot; so, as the Reichsmarschall entered the map room, he said: 'my Führer, I have had sleepless nights over your eternal difficulties with this fellow Halder. You must get rid of him, and I know a successor who will cause you no worry at all: Zeitzler, he is the right man for you.'[26]

In his take-over address to the officers of OKH the new Chief of Staff confirmed all that had been expected as a result of his nomination. He said among other things:

> I require the following from every Staff Officer: he must believe in the Führer and in his method of command. He must on every occasion radiate this confidence to his subordinates and those around him. I have no use for anybody on the General Staff who cannot meet these requirements.[27]

As far as I remember Zeitzler issued a similar order to staff officers of the Higher Headquarters in the field. It created a considerable and lasting sensation. Zeitzler was promoted to full general when he took over. Initially he had to devote all his time to dealing with the continuing bitter battles in the East, particularly since Hitler, accompanied by his immediate entourage, thought this a good moment to leave the headquarters and spend approximately a week in Berlin. The daily business of rendering reports to the Reich Chancellery via HQ Area 2's lines from the Ukraine went on more or less unchanged and the 'change of scene' was thought to be good for Hitler after all the shocks of the previous weeks, since it got him away from the atmosphere of worry. Nevertheless this absence hardly seemed to accord with the duties he had arrogated to himself as Commander-in-Chief of the Army and in addition as Commander-in-Chief of Army Group A in the far-off Caucasus.

When he returned, the normal routine of the day recommenced in Supreme Headquarters but at the briefing conferences there were now and were for a long time to be, 'sheep and goats'. Zeitzler was looked at and spoken to with the utmost friendliness and as usually happened in the inner circle of the 'great ones', Göring and the rest of the 'court' followed suit. Jodl meanwhile gradually managed to work his way out of the dungeon of 'disfavour'. Here was at last an opportunity for Jodl to organize a sort of 'Chiefs of Staff Committee' and so at least on this level give the Higher Command of the Wehrmacht some definite organization – for the new Chief of Staff of the

Army was junior to him. Apparently however he never even realized that the opportunity existed, or at any rate made no use of it. Probably he realized only too well that, even if Zeitzler had agreed, neither Hitler nor the Commanders-in-Chief Navy and Air would have tolerated this type of 'shadow cabinet'.

As against this it was hardly surprising that Zeitzler should try to make use of the universal favour in which he obviously stood and perhaps also of the weakness in Jodl's position, to do away with the overlapping of command responsibilities in the East and recover some of the authority which OKH had lost. Put bluntly this implied the elimination of the continual assumption of authority by Jodl and OKW over matters which were traditionally the province of OKH both in the East and in the OKW theatres of war. It might thus have been possible without too much upheaval to clean up the higher organization of the Wehrmacht and free the OKW Operations Staff to put all their brains and energy into the job of working out overall strategy.

Having been with Jodl in Section L over a period of years, Zeitzler was only too well aware of the problems of 'higher organization'. There is nothing to show however that when he met Jodl this subject was discussed. To judge from the way he worked he was likely to have found it much more urgent to take some immediate practical steps to clear the decks regarding the part to be played by Jodl in the direction of operations in the East. He probably had no need of advice from any so called 'neutral' member of Supreme Headquarters; he merely adopted the simplest method of getting what he wanted – by arranging that in future he should be the first to speak at the midday conferences; whenever possible he also appeared at the 'evening conference'. He also got agreement to another innovation – that plans and intentions for the East should be dealt with in special meetings between him and Hitler alone (with only the stenographers present). These developments did not of course take place overnight but they apparently encountered no resistance. Their effect was to make Jodl's regular *exposé* of the situation in the East superfluous and thus to remove the opportunity for interference with the command of the Army which had been the rule ever since the Sudeten crisis of 1938.[28]

The natural sequel was that Zeitzler attempted to do away with the 'OKW theatres of war' and re-establish the prerogatives of the Army in these areas also. It is not known whether he even raised this question with Hitler but in any case he did not get the latter's agreement. As might be expected, the result of his failure was that he went further and further in excluding OKW from anything to do with the Eastern Front and, for instance, expressly forbade the officers of the Army Operations Section to give OKW any information whatsoever. In spite of repeated representations by me, Jodl accepted this and further decided that it was unnecessary to do more than reproduce the daily situation report from OKH which was then elaborated verbally by Zeitzler at the briefing conference. As a result both he and the Staff of OKW very soon found themselves excluded both from discussion and decisions on matters concerning the Eastern Front, even though they were inevitably of considerable importance both for the other theatres of war and the overall situation.[29]

Heusinger, though admittedly referring to a somewhat later period, states that:[30] 'OKW did all it could to keep us (OKH) away from its own theatres of war'. This is incorrect; the facts are as follows: contrary to Zeitzler's practice neither Jodl nor I ever even by implication gave an order that any information regarding the OKW theatres of war should or even could be withheld from OKH. At any rate up to September 1944 the Army Operations Section always had one officer dealing with these theatres. The Intelligence Section – Foreign Armies West, which was the office responsible for producing appreciations of the enemy situation in all the OKW theatres of war, remained part of the Army Staff in spite of all attempts by OKW to take it over. Commanders-in-Chief in OKW theatres of war, even when they were Luftwaffe officers as in the case of Löhr in the South-east and later Kesselring in Italy, were nominated Commanders-in-Chief of Army Groups and as such were in continuous touch with OKH. Their daily situation reports went regularly to OKH and were word for word the same as those rendered to OKW. Even therefore if OKW had put a similar stop on information regarding 'its' theatres of war as did Zeitzler on that from the East, OKH would have been able to keep itself continuously informed by other channels regarding the situation in the OKW theatres of war.

Zeitzler had started with sound, clear ideas, but the result of his efforts, combined with the spineless attitude of Jodl was that for its most important field of activity, that of the war on land, the Wehrmacht command organization at the highest level was finally split into two parallel staffs. This meant that co-ordinated advice to the

Diagram 3

HIGHER ORGANIZATION OF THE WEHRMACHT SITUATION AUTUMN 1942

Hitler in sole command

The Führer, Supreme Commander of the Wehrmacht and Commander-in-Chief of the Army

OKW Operations Staff Chief: Jodl. Deputy Chief: Warlimont (from November 1944: Winter)	General Staff of the Army Chief: Zeitzler (from July 1944: Guderian, then Krebs)	Naval Staff as Diagram 1. C.-in-C. from 30 January 1943 Dönitz. Chief of Staff from February 1943: Meisel	Luftwaffe as Diagram 1. Chief of Staff from September 1943: Korten (from August 1944: Kreipe, then Koller)
All theatres of war except the East; work on overall strategy much reduced as a result.	Eastern theatre of war.		

NOTES:

1. The OKW Operations Staff remained subordinate to the Chief of OKW (Keitel) and therefore was part of Hitler's Headquarters.

2. The Naval and Air Staffs remained each as a unit under their own Commanders-in-Chief.

3. As the basic organization progressively disintegrated new Army organizational designations appeared, as for instance:

    Artillery Division – a division with no infantry.
    Army Detachment – a weak Army.
    Combat Group or Group – formation of all arms of varying strength from a number of divisions down to one battalion.

4. Other organizations produced towards the end of the war are not given, as being of no importance.

Supreme Commander and therefore the real task of the OKW Operations Staff became impossible. The only 'victor' who emerged from this wreckage of a higher military organization was Hitler, who as a result became, in the literal sense of the words, the only man fully informed regarding all theatres of war.

General Scherff once asked Hitler about this division of the staffs and staff work at the top. Hitler is reported to have said that he was no partisan of this division but that it was unavoidable because he knew of no general capable of undertaking all that had to be done. He considered Zeitzler to be his tactical adviser with experience of the East and Jodl his adviser for the more wide-ranging questions, such as the coastal defence of 'Fortress Europe'. This reasoning overlooked the real fact; what was really behind it was Hitler's well-tried principle of *divide et impera*.

These therefore were further and final steps towards the disintegration of the higher command organization of the Wehrmacht. They ran directly counter to the principles which both Jodl and Zeitzler had so energetically preached in peace-time. This also must be reckoned among the storm signals of that time. During the days of Stalingrad which were soon to follow (to anticipate for a moment) Jodl was therefore little more than a spectator while Zeitzler fought a lonely battle with Hitler. This dichotomy was to be the hall-mark of German strategy throughout the subsequent phases of the war both in the East and elsewhere. Naturally in the broadest sense OKW still retained some responsibility for the eastern theatre but it has been, and still is, common practice to lay upon 'OKW' primary responsibility for this or that which occurred on the Eastern Front. This is both historically incorrect and contrary to the facts, for in practice that responsibility was removed from OKW at this period.[31]

During the first few weeks after taking over as Chief of Staff everything was in General Zeitzler's favour and he was without doubt the most influential personality among Hitler's military advisers. He soon found ways and means of quietly getting round the obstacle presented by the OKW theatres of war, at any rate in so far as what mattered to him was concerned. Hitler's plans provided for the exchange of worn-out divisions from the East with fresh divisions from the West and Zeitzler merely used this process to keep the East up to strength. In course of time this frequently resulted in divisions being moved to the Eastern Front which were neither equipped, trained nor in any way ready for employment in that theatre; the OKW Staff would only hear of the move through the Wehrmacht Director of Movements when units were on the way to loading points. Similarly repeated orders by Hitler were frequently disobeyed when it was a question of moving formations from the East to the West, even if only for rest and recuperation. Admittedly the situation in the East was serious and in the autumn of 1942 the forces in the West were unnecessarily large, but this procedure meant that our limited reserves were dissipated and long-term planning wrecked.

At about this time the OKW Operations Staff made efforts to put new life into the dwindling forces of the Army in the East by the simplest and most obvious procedure, that of drawing upon the excessive manpower available to the other two Services, particularly the Luftwaffe. We got no support from OKH. In the first instance, indeed, we did go hand in hand and after much urging got Keitel to screw up his courage to submit the draft of an OKW Order to Hitler, laying down that the Navy should make over 10,000 or 20,000 men and the Luftwaffe 50,000 men to the Army (our original proposal had been for figures twice this size but Keitel had reduced them). The order had hardly been issued, however, when at the next briefing conference in the Headquarters the Chief of Staff of the Luftwaffe came up to me and asked me agitatedly whether I was the originator of this instruction. When I said 'yes', Jeschonnek replied with a chuckle: 'then you'd better get ready for something!' Shortly thereafter Göring appeared, vouchsafed me not a word, but turned straight to Hitler himself with every sign of indignation. Hitler made as though he knew nothing about it, Keitel was obviously ready at once to sing small and raise no objection, so Göring in a voice of brass thundered out his well-known slogan that he was not going to let his good young National-Socialists be dressed up in the grey (meaning the reactionary) uniform of the Army. Instead he was quite prepared to raise Luftwaffe divisions, on condition however that from the Divisional Commander down to the last man they must consist solely of Luftwaffe personnel.

So the bells rang for the birth of the unfortunate 'Luftwaffe Divisions'! Hitler agreed at once, although he did not withdraw his order; he demanded twice the number of men from Göring and thereby got out of having to ask the Navy for anybody. This was the end of the matter as far as Keitel was concerned; Jodl acted as if the whole thing was nothing to do with him and although I protested I was not even supported by OKH.

Ten, and then a further ten, Luftwaffe Divisions were raised with astounding rapidity but this did not help the Army anything like as much as if the high-class recruits at the disposal of the Luftwaffe had been used to fill the yawning gaps in seasoned Army formations. The Luftwaffe divisions were full of fight but from the outset they suffered from their innate deficiencies, inexperienced leadership, insufficient formation training and to some extent unsuitable equipment. It did not help them that Hitler was particularly sensitive on the subject and tended at his briefing conferences to reject as untrustworthy reports that these units had failed in heavy fighting. In the autumn of 1943 OKW finally succeeded in getting them incorporated into the Army but this did not mean that their fighting efficiency was necessarily raised to that of the average Army division – no more did the title 'assault division' which Hitler gave them, thereby showing his partiality for them.

The small-scale reinforcements which from October onwards arrived partly from the West and partly in the form of the first Luftwaffe divisions, did no more than allow the southern flank of the Eastern Front to score some local successes. The numerous makeshift tactical arrangements which, to Hitler's joy, Zeitzler tirelessly thought up, did no better.[32] Meanwhile at the end of October Supreme Headquarters prepared to return to East Prussia. The objectives for the offensive remained unchanged – those in the Caucasus, those on the Terek, and above all at Stalingrad where for weeks now fighting had been going on for crossroads, individual factories and housing estates. The danger points on numerous other sectors of the front were unchanged too, particularly on the lower Don, which had meanwhile been taken over from the Italians by the Rumanian Third Army. A new menace now appeared in North Africa where a heavy British attack on Rommel's Army started on 23 October. The only bright spot in this dark picture of the overall German situation was the U-boat war, which was now at the height of its success both against convoys and in long-range operations. As before however OKW had no part in this nor could it influence the steady deterioration of the Luftwaffe which also had its effect on the U-boat war.[33,34]

Greater Crisis on the Horizon

THE REAL TURN OF THE TIDE

The moment at which the strategic initiative really passed out of Hitler's hands was not that of the defeat at Stalingrad nor that at Tunis three months later; it was November 1942, the month of doom in modern German history, when the enemy struck both in East and West. At the nerve centre of German strategy people had shrugged off the effects of the September shocks and there was not the smallest recognition, least of all on the part of Hitler himself, that the war had now definitely turned against Germany, although this was clear to all the world.

Between 2 and 21 November 1942 three portentous events occurred in the Mediterranean Theatre and on the Eastern Front but German Supreme Headquarters was taken completely by surprise by all of them. The tension which during the previous weeks had been almost tangible in the headquarters had not been sufficient warning for Hitler; similarly a 'survey of the overall situation in Autumn 1942' which the OKW Operations Staff now had to prepare was totally without effect. I myself put this memorandum in final form during the two-day rail journey from the Ukraine to East Prussia on 31 October–1 November. The following is a summary of its main points: the Eastern Theatre was of course now treated with some circumspection but the conclusions were clear enough: that the utmost limits of the capacity of the Wehrmacht and its allies had now been reached. There was then a detailed examination of the most likely area for the attack by the Western powers which was now clearly imminent; the conclusion was that French North Africa offered them the best jumping-off point for further attacks against 'Fortress Europe'. This was a view which had been put forward many times before and had for a time been shared both by Commander-in-Chief Navy and Hitler himself; in the autumn of 1942 however, there was no particular support for it other than general politico-military and strategic considerations. No adequate information could be provided either by our own intelligence service or that of the Italian High Command, though it later became known that the latter had reached the same conclusion based on more detailed information. In any case neither we nor the Italians had any conception that the landing was so imminent – the armada was in fact already at sea. Among the proposals with which the OKW appreciation ended appeared once more the urgent recommendation that military discussions with the French should be resumed. It is known that this 'survey' never got further than Jodl and Keitel. It was revised again in December and this, as far as I know, was the last occasion on which an appreciation of the overall situation contained any mention of the Eastern Theatre.[35]

The first thunderclap struck the headquarters the day after its return to Wolfschanze; Rommel reported that after an eight-day battle at El Alamein, he was in imminent danger of defeat. By the evening of 2 November Rommel could see no alternative to the total annihilation of his army other than to begin a withdrawal on his own initiative and contrary to all orders from Rome and Rastenburg. Hitler could do nothing other than issue messages of 'iron determination'; that same evening his well-known radio message sped across the ether; it said:

> I and the German people have been following with the utmost confidence the exploits of your leadership and the courage of the German and Italian troops under your command during your heroic defensive battle in Egypt. In your present situation you can have no thought other than to hold on, not to give way an inch and to throw every man and every weapon into the battle. In spite of his superiority the enemy must now be at the end of his tether. This will not be the first time in history that the stronger will must triumph over the big battalions. You must show your troops that they have no alternative other than to triumph or to die.[36]

This appeal by Hitler caused Rommel temporarily to countermand the withdrawal which had already begun and the result led to most serious subsequent losses. In HQ Area 2 it had a peculiar sequel. At about 0300 hours on 3 November the Operations Staff Duty Officer received Rommel's message that his withdrawal had been begun approximately five hours earlier. In HQ Area 2 we did not know of Hitler's message; it was therefore hardly surprising that the Duty Officer did not realize that Rommel's message produced anything very new and did not therefore immediately warn one of the senior officers in accordance with the standing instructions for all important information. The Duty Officer was a major on the reserve, about fifty years old and a most worthy chap both in the service and in civil life. About twelve hours later he was to be seen emerging ashen grey from Hitler's hut. He had been trying to convince Hitler that contrary to his suspicions no undercover game was in progress between HQ Area 2 and Rommel; only by the skin of his teeth had the major escaped being shot 'within ten minutes'. Instead he was demoted to the ranks and posted to a 'detention' battalion. In accordance with normal military practice I had done all I could to take the responsibility upon myself; I had even followed the unfortunate fellow to the steps of Hitler's hut but had there been stopped by Keitel. Without even being given a hearing by Hitler I was 'relieved of my post' as a punishment. Keitel told me how sorry he was that I must go in this way after I had so often and in vain asked for another appointment. Jodl was quite unmoved; I had now been his principal staff officer for several years, yet all he said was: 'for us the Führer's will is the supreme law of the land'. Schmundt however, when he heard of it, made considerable efforts to get the major's punishment reduced or at least curtailed, though he could not reverse his dismissal. I left on 4 November but the next day I had a telephone call from Schmundt to say that Hitler had recognized that I had been 'unjustly treated' and begging me urgently to return to my job; there was a similar message from Keitel the same afternoon. In both cases I replied that after the treatment I had received I would like a little time to think it over.[37] It appears that after I had left, the officers of my staff were so incensed over Hitler's arbitrary behaviour that they showed Schmundt an office instruction which I had issued a few weeks before laying down that important messages must be dealt with with the greatest care and rapidity. It was apparently this which caused Schmundt to intervene.

Rommel now hurriedly despatched his personal assistant, who in civil life was a senior Party official in the Propaganda Ministry, to explain the situation and during the next few days Hitler came more or less to accept Rommel's decision. This affair however remained in the forefront of his mind right into 1944; he went over it again and again and eventually contrived to make himself believe that Rommel should have 'stayed put up front', that that was 'the only hope of saving the whole thing' and that only 'an unfortunate chain of events' had prevented him (Hitler) intervening in time. He was not in the least worried over the wording of his appeal, although since 'triumph' was obviously impossible, only the other alternative 'die' was left. More important however, he refused to recognize that the battle in the North African desert was now governed by the availability of equipment and that with American aid on one side and the catastrophic sea transport situation on the other, the Axis powers had not the smallest possibility of keeping level. The last despairing efforts of Hitler's 'leadership' were to move a few heavy tanks to Italian harbours and then make the most frequent use of the words 'forthwith' and 'super-urgent movement'; but this could not affect the situation. On the other side Montgomery was not exaggerating when he said in his 'personal message' to the troops of the British Eighth Army that this battle would go down as one of the decisive battles of history and 'will be a turning point in the war'.[38]

The second major blow came a few days later with the landing in French North Africa. For the first time a large American army had now appeared on the confines of the European theatre of war; the enemy was now established in an area of the greatest political and strategic importance; there had been no preparations to meet the attack and there were no forces or resources of any importance available. All this faced German Supreme Headquarters with an entirely new situation and one of quite exceptional significance.

Many may ask themselves the question whether it was not the *Staff* of OKW which was more responsible for this situation than Hitler himself; after all it thought that it had foreseen what was likely to happen and had pointed it out only a week before. Could not and ought not the staff therefore to have done something on its own initiative even though its superiors refused to act? In answer to such questions I can only point out that as a senior representative of the staff I had, ever since discussions on collaboration with the French started, put the defence of French North Africa at the head of the list. Hitler had however invariably brought all my efforts to nought. The last occasion had been at the briefing conference on 15 October 1942. On the basis of somewhat vague reports Jodl had then resurrected our original proposal that the French should be allowed 'to reinforce their forces in North Africa from metropolitan territory'. In defence of the staff it should further be pointed out that in the first days of November Hitler – and this time Jodl with him – had thought that there were many other possible objectives for a landing in the Mediterranean apart from French North Africa; from all points of view it was the most obvious target but Hitler's eyes were elsewhere, although there was a major concentration of shipping in Gibraltar, although he had recently received warnings from Mussolini referring to French North Africa and finally although by 7 November it was known that the armada was on the move. It was therefore completely outside the competence of the OKW Operations Staff to take any independent action (ie action not authorized by Hitler) against an Allied landing in French North Africa; the political and military set-up was such that it would have got nowhere.

So, this event showed up all the faults of German leadership at the top to which this book has so often referred – Hitler's rigid attitude in political matters, his preconceived notions on strategy which even in this case made him blind to anything but the threat to the West and Norway, inadequate co-operation with our allies, the stultification of his own military staff; all these contributed to prevent any sensible preparations being made to counter the enemy's most obvious move.

What actually happened was in many ways typical of the jungle of crossed wires within Supreme Headquarters. On the evening of 6 November Göring, without getting in touch in any way with OKW, took it upon himself to put across Hitler's ideas to Kesselring in Rome. In spite of Kesselring's protests he wrote off French North Africa as a possible objective for a landing without further consideration. Disregarding the facts that the German air formations had for long been overworked, that the Italian fleet was hardly capable of putting to sea and that enemy escorts numbered over 190 ships, Göring demanded that the convoys should be 'attacked and destroyed by continuous action both by day and by night'. On 7 November Hitler, pursuing his own ideas, twice ordered General von Rintelen to make representations in Rome that 'all defensive preparations should be made in Tripoli and Benghazi, including the erection of road blocks'. Even at this decisive moment he once more ordered reinforcements to Crete at the other end of the Mediterranean.

As tension reached its height Hitler left the midday briefing conference and with the entire population of HQ Area 1 got into his train to travel right across Germany to Munich to a meeting of the Party 'old comrades', there to present a completely false picture of the overall war situation. The news of the beginning of the landings in French North Africa reached the train early on the following morning at an out-of-the-way station in Thuringia. All Hitler could

do was to remind the French, to whom he had administered one re-
buff after another, of an assurance they had once given that they
would defend their overseas possessions against any attack. The landings extended from Casablanca to the Algerian-Tunisian frontier, but
on the German side nothing was available to meet them except a
few U-boats and air squadrons. From the staff remaining behind in
East Prussia came the cry, voiced by General Freiherr von Buttlar,
that North Africa, which was now threatened by superior forces on
two sides, could not in the long run be held. But this passed unnoticed in the general jumble of vague political and strategic ideas
based primarily on considerations of prestige.[39]

I heard the news on the wireless early on 8 November at my
home. This was followed shortly afterwards by a telephone call from
East Prussia to say that I had been selected as the representative of
OKW to go to Vichy to organize the defence of North-west Africa
in collaboration with the French High Command. That evening I
was ordered to proceed the following morning 'with my baggage' to
Munich where the 'Führer Special' was located. I hunted round the
train which was standing on one of the tracks of the main station in
the midst of the normal traffic and was apparently completely empty.
I finally came across Jodl, only to be told that circumstances had now
changed and that Hitler would no longer count upon the French.
This made it all the more urgent, Jodl went on, that I should go back
to work in my old job; no one was present except the aides and my
knowledge and experience were indispensable; the staff had meanwhile been summoned from East Prussia but could not arrive for
another forty-eight hours. In a crisis like this I could do no other than
conform, although emphasizing that I would wish to be given another
appointment as soon as possible.

At this point the situation in German Supreme Headquarters was
a reflection of the hithering and thithering that was going on
outside. Hitler was in the 'Führer's Quarters' in the Arcis Strasse
negotiating with Ciano and Laval and never appeared in the train.
Keitel and Jodl were rushing backwards and forwards between the
Arcis Strasse and the main station. I installed myself in a small
sleeping compartment, collected the information which came
tumbling in and worked out the initial orders for the formation of a
'bridgehead' in Tunis and the occupation of unoccupied France.
The original intention had been to go back to East Prussia but the
fact that the staff had been summoned thence made it clear that

Hitler now wished to think over the new situation in the solitude of the Berghof.[40]

In a speech in a Munich beer cellar Hitler had just congratulated himself on being master of Stalingrad. Now, when he was separated by about six hundred miles from OKH and nearly thirteen hundred miles from the scene of action, the third great blow of these weeks hit him between 19 and 21 November – the city which had been fought for for so long was encircled by the Russians. This might have been anticipated when the enemy broke through on the lower Don – but all eyes were then on Rostov; it might have been averted had we not clung to our original objectives in spite of increasingly inadequate resources. Now, just as in North Africa, the situation had to be retrieved when the moment had passed and with resources whose inadequacy was even greater. All that was available to stem the Russian flood was a solitary tired German armoured division in Army reserve which had long since been frittered away in the maelstrom of events and some 'emergency units' dreamt up by Zeitzler composed of scrapings from the rearward services – clerks, cooks and drivers.

All this hit the headquarters when it was dispersed as was usual when Hitler was resident in Berchtesgaden. He himself was in the Berghof, the only military personnel with him being the aides. Keitel, Jodl and the other military members of HQ Area 1 were lodged by Lammers in the 'Little Reich Chancellery' on the edge of the town. The Operations Staff was in its special train in Salzburg station. OKH, which was primarily responsible for advice and action, remained in the woods of Masuria near Angerburg; OKL was in that area too, though obviously without its Commander-in-Chief who was for the most part busy elsewhere. On 21 November under the pressure of events Jodl moved the staff nearer to Berchtesgaden into the Infantry Barracks at Strub. This was still far enough in all conscience from the Little Reich Chancellery but it was to serve as the location for the staff whenever Hitler was subsequently in the Berghof. The next day the entire Headquarters trekked back once more to Wolfschanze in East Prussia.

On return to East Prussia the daily briefing conferences were resumed; the record of the first of these in the Operations Staff War Diary reads: 'the Führer is confident regarding Sixth Army's situation at Stalingrad'. Meanwhile 'unoccupied France' had been occupied smoothly and weak German-Italian forces had formed a bridgehead around the town of Tunis without opposition. So by the end of November there was once more a deceptive atmosphere of confidence in German Supreme Headquarters. There was no realization that this time the tide of the war had really turned and we went back to the dance of tactical expedients with Hitler as master of ceremonies.[41]

PART V

SETTING SUN

November 1942 – Summer 1944

CHAPTER 1

Signs of the Times

IT IS A FACT, characteristic of the overall direction of the German war effort, that from the end of 1942 planning was confined strictly to minor details. Our war potential was still high enough and the area we occupied large enough to permit pursuit of a sound, intelligent strategy, which might have led to a satisfactory end to the war. Hitler's policy is, however, best described in the words of a letter he wrote to Mussolini on 20 November. In it he said: 'I am one of those men who in adversity simply becomes more determined,' adding that he had 'only one thought in his mind – to fight on'.[1] This was an untutored policy of striking out in all directions; it stood out in sharp contrast to the proposal made by Mussolini then and many times later that 'the war against Russia having become purposeless, this chapter must now somehow be closed' in order to concentrate all our forces against 'England who is still our enemy Number One' and against the serious threat of Anglo-Saxon air superiority. Hitler considered this to be merely 'squaring the circle' and, although it was now becoming ever clearer that the war could not be won, did not think it worthwhile taking up the time either of the political authorities or the OKW Operations Staff with any more detailed examination of the idea.[2]

Hitler's policy in major as in minor matters ran directly counter to all laws of the art of war. His every thought and action became increasingly centred on holding what had been won, winning back what had been lost and never giving up anything anywhere. This being his attitude of mind, any thought of being forced on to the strategic defensive never entered his head. But this is what happened, though no word of it ever appeared in the string of OKW directives which we prepared with such urgency. The more we were forced on to the defensive, the more important did an appreciation of the enemy and his potential become; yet in spite of the series of unpleasant surprises we had had, sufficient importance was never attached to this. The more difficult the situation became the more frequently would Hitler say that the enemy would soon be 'at the end of his tether'. No thought was ever given to relinquishing or even taking a risk in any area, however worthless or non-essential it might be; still less was the evacuation of whole theatres considered. Yet only thus could reserves have been made available which would have enabled us to regain some form of freedom of initiative and to use mobility instead of remaining rigidly bound to pieces of terrain. No! We must hold on because otherwise we should 'lose heavy equipment'; we must stand where we were because this was the most effective form of defence; we must tie the enemy down because otherwise he would turn up somewhere else, even though the result was to tie ourselves down until it was too late. It was on these 'principles' that the 'decisions' were based; they were made only day by day; they came late and emerged as a result of interminable monologues; they were unhappily expressed as orders couched in peremptory terms; they led to the loss of one area after another and to an increasing surrender of the initiative to the enemy.[3]

This book has already described the more disastrous weaknesses of Hitler's leadership; there was no question however of him suddenly becoming less active, as is often thought to have been the case after the events of November. It is true that a month later the Operations Staff War Diary notes with striking frankness: 'as before no decisions were taken; it looks as if the Führer is no longer capable of making them'.[4] But this was really nothing new. His physical condition was not the deciding factor in the further decline of German leadership from the turn of the year 1942–43. Similarly (it is hardly necessary to add) commanders in the field remained loyal to him. My own conclusion – and its correctness has frequently been proved – is that the explanation lies rather in the fact that Hitler still pictured the worn-out German Wehrmacht as capable of any exertion and as the shining weapon of war which it had once been; moreover his closest advisers did nothing to shake his obstinacy.

For a long time Jodl laboured under the effects of the September quarrel and, although he boiled over occasionally, was obviously determined to do nothing to shake the Dictator's self-confidence again. General Zeitzler initially had no alternative but to resign himself to the role of assistant – which was what his job was. In any case, having seen many generals at work over a period of years, I have no hesitation in saying that I know of none who, in their position, could have done as well, let alone better. Occasional attempts were made to get Hitler to give up military command which, as before, was primarily concerned with Army business, but so long as he refused to do so any stronger personality in Zeitzler's position would have been worn out even more quickly than Zeitler was.

On the question of personalities certain comments from various quarters at this time are of interest. Mihai Antonescu, the Rumanian Minister of Commerce and a relative of the Marshal, is said to have told the Italian Foreign Minister after one of his frequent visits to German Headquarters in December 1942: 'Jodl seems to me to have become more fossilized during the last year. The new Chief of Staff, Zeitzler, is not in the old Prussian tradition.'[5] Goebbels says in his diary of 20 December 1942: 'the appointment of Zeitzler has done a lot of good. Zeitzler has introduced a new method of work at headquarters clearing away everything except essentials. This has relieved the Führer of a lot of detail, and everything doesn't depend upon his decision.' On 2 March he says:

> Göring judges the Führer's Headquarters very harshly. He is especially antagonistic towards Jodl, who, he tells me, has even begun to tell jokes about the Führer. That certainly won't do. . . . Göring considers the working methods of the headquarters quite wrong, especially the fact that stenographers are always present during the staff conferences and take down every word. In the long run this will of course put the Führer at a disadvantage. For the Führer never makes any bones about his opinions, while the generals – Zeitzler, of course, excluded – always talk for the written record. . . . Göring considers General Schmundt as the only honest and trustworthy personality in the Führer's Headquarters.

On 9 March 1943 Goebbels says: 'the Führer continues to be very well satisfied with Zeitzler, who is at present his most effective assistant in the conduct of the eastern campaign. Keitel plays only a very subordinate role.' Bodenschatz is characterized as 'a cold cynic'. 'Of the Luftwaffe he now thinks well only of Jeschonnek. Jeschonnek was an absolute fanatic for truth, he said; he saw the situation clearly and had no illusions.' Zeitzler is considered the only one 'equal to the job' of Commander-in-Chief of the Replacement Army but 'he needs Zeitzler as Chief of the General Staff of the Army'.

Once more the evil effects of the faults in the higher organization must be emphasized. Zeitzler still kept a veil drawn over the Eastern Front and this, together with Hitler's attitude to his allies made it ever more impossible for the OKW Operations Staff to take an overall view of the war situation; in any case the staff became increasingly occupied with jobs connected with the command of the OKW theatres of war. The Section 'Senior Officer – Army' had long since been turned into a second Army operations section and Hitler made the Q Section of the OKW Operations Staff increasingly responsible for supply questions. Neither section however had any troops or resources at its disposal and was entirely dependent upon allotments and co-operation from the High Commands of the Services, primarily OKH. In view of Hitler's underestimation of the enemy, it was particularly unfortunate that, as a result of stubborn resistance by Zeitzler, we never succeeded in getting the Intelligence Section – Foreign Armies West transferred from OKH to the OKW Operations Staff in spite of the fact that it was almost exclusively concerned with the OKW theatres of war. The section remained in Berlin; the head of it was restricted to a once- or twice-monthly visit to the OKW Operations Staff in East Prussia. He was never allowed to see Hitler. There was a similar situation as regards military government in the rear areas of the OKW theatres of war; although the operations and communications zones began to overlap more and more, Zeitzler would never allow the OKW Operations Staff to have anything to do with the working of military government.

As far as the Army was concerned, the division of command responsibility meant that the OKW Operations Staff could do little more than collect the daily situation reports; the same was the case with the Luftwaffe and the Navy though for a different reason – their command system was solid under their respective Commanders-in-Chief who had a direct personal relationship with Hitler. This rule even applied to naval and air forces employed or (primarily in the case of the Navy) merely accommodated in the OKW theatres of war. The fighting capacity of the Luftwaffe was all the time deteriorating menacingly but we had no real insight into what was happening. In the war at sea, where Grand Admiral Dönitz, the outstanding U Boat Commander, had taken over as Commander-in-

Chief in spring 1943, and the only field in which we had hitherto been on the offensive, defeat was staring us in the face; yet OKW was no more than a spectator at the briefing conferences. The effects of the submarine offensive were of the highest strategic significance but we were in no position to judge or to estimate their effect upon the situation as a whole; nor were we in a position to calculate the value of the results achieved for use in a long-term appreciation of the overall situation. Thus in the shapeless confusion which Hitler spread around him, he allowed his own working staff to wither away and go to seed.

Once we had lost the initiative work in Supreme Headquarters was characterized by long periods of circumscribed, monotonous activity. For the remainder of this period therefore, I shall restrict myself more than hitherto to a description of particular events. In many cases extracts from the shorthand records of individual briefing conferences will give a better idea of the work and atmosphere in the headquarters than any words of mine.

CHAPTER 2

Stalingrad to Tunis

THE HEAVY DEFEATS of Stalingrad and Tunis stand like two memorial pillars at the gate of this period of the war. Their origin, the course of events and the ultimate outcome must all be laid primarily at the door of the man in supreme command – Hitler himself.

The two scenes of catastrophe were only once brought together in a single strategic picture; on 29 November 1942, when the situation both in the South and in the East had altered so decisively, General Jodl asked his staff to produce 'on three pages' a new 'overall appreciation of the situation'. The results of this he immediately anticipated by his own 'thesis' which was as follows:

North Africa is the glacis of Europe and must therefore be held under all circumstances. If it is lost we must expect an Anglo-Saxon attack against south-eastern Europe via the Dodecanese, Crete and the Peloponnese; we must therefore pacify and secure the Balkans.

In the West and North, he continued, it was unlikely that the enemy would undertake major operations in the immediate future. On the other hand: 'we must finally establish a firm front in the East so that next spring we can take the offensive at least in one area'.[1]

As far as North Africa was concerned Jodl's instructions echoed Hitler's views rather than those of the General Staff when he used the words 'must be held under all circumstances', coupling them immediately thereafter with the words 'if it is lost'; note moreover that this was an OKW theatre of war shared with the Italians, yet Rome was not even consulted. A new feature, attributable most probably to Hitler's own 'intuition', was the fact that the Balkans now figured suddenly as the main target of Anglo-Saxon strategy; yet the idea of a move into Italy seemed much more likely and had been set out clearly in the 'survey' which the staff had prepared at the beginning of November. Once again the Italian High Command had not even been consulted. The moment was one for strict limitation of our commitments but now an enormous area which, unruly though it was, we had hitherto only had to occupy, was raised to the status of a theatre of war and accordingly started to swallow up forces.[2]

Jodl's instructions were in many respects indicative; it will be noted that the East appears only at the end without the name Stalingrad even being mentioned. When Jodl spoke of 'a firm front' he probably reckoned that he had said all that, in Zeitzler's view, OKW was entitled to say about the eastern theatre. In spite of many post-war indications to the contrary, by 'a firm front' Jodl almost certainly meant that there should be a withdrawal to a shorter line; it probably never entered his head that the front might be on the Volga and therefore include Stalingrad. This shows clearly that it was not OKW which was pressing for Stalingrad to be held – there were others who were doing that!

It was characteristic of Jodl's dictatorial methods that he never discussed the 'three pages' either with his staff or with me. The paper was in fact in no sense a true appreciation of the situation. It consisted primarily of proposals for a different distribution of forces and for the mobilization of new resources. We on the staff did not feel that this was enough and did all we could to get agreement to forces being moved to the East from West and North in spite of the fact that this was to some extent contrary to Hitler's policy.[3] This fact shows also that there are no grounds for the reproaches commonly made against OKW that it hoarded unnecessarily large forces in 'its own' theatres of war and therefore just like the 'fleet in being' of the first World War, kept an equally useless 'army in being'.

Jodl's 'directions' for the appreciation had contained no mention of Stalingrad and as far as I remember neither he nor his staff had anything to do with subsequent developments in that area. This does not mean that he did not on various occasions support Hitler's demands. His statements, however, were based only upon his own views and these in turn only upon impressions which he must have got from listening to discussions between Hitler and Zeitzler. He was not in a position to make any examination of the situation independent of OKH since Zeitzler refused to give either him or his staff any information. It is remarkable that the OKW Operations Staff War Diary carries very few entries regarding events at Stalingrad; for instance on 21 December 1942 all it says is: 'at the briefing conference there was a long discussion between the Führer and the Chiefs of Staff of the Army and Air Force regarding the situation in the southern sector of the Eastern Front'.

It may be that Jodl was not present on this occasion or that he kept in the background and said nothing – both most unlikely contingencies; but in either case this entry makes it crystal clear that he, and therefore OKW, had remarkably little influence over Hitler's decisions on which hung the fate of Stalingrad. This is also clear from the shorthand records of the briefing conferences, the first 'fragments' of which are from this period; extracts of those held on 1 and 12 December 1942 and 1 February 1943, the day following the end at Stalingrad, are given below.

These fragments also show no trace of any heated arguments or disagreements between Hitler and his principal adviser for the Eastern Front; admittedly this judgment is based on records for only three days out of seventy but it checks with my own memory. It is true of course that during these days and weeks Zeitzler discussed his worries and his plans about Stalingrad in private with Hitler more frequently than was usual in normal times and that no records of these discussions were made. I also remember quite clearly that Zeitzler was obviously very depressed over the steady deterioration of the situation at Stalingrad and, for instance, for days at a time put himself and his immediate staff on to the 'restricted rations' allowed to the defenders of Stalingrad (by the middle of January according to the OKW Diary the daily ration was $2\frac{1}{2}$ oz. bread, $6\frac{1}{2}$ oz. horsemeat, $\frac{1}{2}$ oz. fat, $\frac{1}{2}$ oz. sugar and one cigarette); Zeitzler's object was undoubtedly to prove the more convincingly how totally inadequate this ration was. Against this however, in the OKW War Diary of 25 November the proposal that Sixth Army should 'now move westwards', ie should evacuate Stalingrad and break through the ring, is attributed only to the Air Force General, Freiherr von Richthofen. Two days later, dealing with Field Marshal von Manstein's assumption of command of 'Army Group Don', the War Diary once more records talk of 'reasonably favourable' prospects – the impression I had gained from the conference concerned. On 2 December the War Diary speaks of great 'confidence' in the plans for the relief of Stalingrad by means of a counter-attack by 'Hoth's armoured group' from the area of Kotelnikovo – completely overlooking the fact that nothing like the number of supply sorties promised by Göring had been carried out.[4]

On 12 December, the day of the start of this counter-attack, Hitler treated himself and his audience to a repetition of his thesis that: 'we must under no circumstances give it (Stalingrad) up. We should never get it back again.' He then returned to the argument of the loss of 'heavy equipment' and Zeitzler agreed with him saying: 'we have a vast amount of army artillery there'. Hitler immediately re-emphasized his determination, using even stronger words: 'we can never replace what we have there. If we give it (Stalingrad) up, we in fact give up the whole object of this campaign.'[5]

There is a further point regarding the shorthand records. It will be remembered that in Jodl's instructions of 29 November the name Stalingrad never appeared – it almost seems as if people were shy to use the word; in the records it will be noted that the situation at Stalingrad, the focal point of the whole war at the time, was never dealt with at the beginning of the discussions but that every other conceivable subject, some extremely trivial, was considered first, taking up hours of the discussions and pages of the records.

On 18 December the Italian Eighth Army collapsed, a decisive factor in the fate of Stalingrad; less than a month later, on 15 January, the Hungarian Second Army disintegrated and on the same day the German ring round Leningrad was broken; all this led to the greatest anxiety in the headquarters not only concerning each event itself but for the general effect they might have on our allies. Many of us asked ourselves then (and many may ask themselves today) whether this did not imply that, in the light of the rapidly changing situation, the fate of Stalingrad and the hundred thousand men there should not have been considered afresh every day and before everything else. On 15 January 1943 when our own front had already been driven far back and the Russian stranglehold round the city was growing tighter, Hitler instructed the State Secretary in the Aviation Ministry, Field Marshal Milch, to 'employ all his resources to supply the Sixth Army'; it was no more than an empty gesture.

Many have tried to justify the catastrophe by stating that only because considerable Russian forces were tied down in Stalingrad was it possible to withdraw the southern flank of the Eastern Front.

This may have been so – the uncertainties of war are such that no one can be certain. But this cannot in any way compensate for or erase the serious mistakes of leadership made by Hitler during the previous weeks and months. Nor can it justify the fact that, rigid and obstinate as always, he refused the commanders whom he appointed at the last moment the resources and powers essential to enable them to cope with the situation, in particular power of command over the considerable forces in the nearby area of the Northern Caucasus and over the Sixth Army itself. On the evening of 22 January, urged on by Manstein, 'General Zeitzler put the question whether Sixth Army should now be authorized to capitulate'; Hitler refused and once more demanded that 'the army should fight to the last man'. On 28 January, disregarding alike those who were alive and fighting and those who had died, he took the first steps towards 'the reconstitution of Sixth Army'.[6] Yet this was the man who, when the end came on 31 January, exploded with indignation and heaped abuse on the heads of the commanders. Though he had himself long since given up, in his view no one else was entitled to do so! His comprehension of military matters was no better than his understanding of morale; at the briefing conference on 1 February he demanded: 'we must let the commander in the northern pocket have something (meaning a radio message) telling him that he is to hold the pocket under all circumstances. The pocket must be held to the last man.'[7] This could not stop the end coming there also the next day.

The discussion of 1 February (see pp. 300 and 535), a discussion which I shall never forget, is in many ways of particular interest. It is a good example of Hitler's attitude, which was subsequently to be repeated over and over again. On 1 February he was insisting that the Donetz Basin must 'under all circumstances be held', this time basing himself on economic arguments. He even went so far as to state that unless the resources of this area were available 'he could not carry on the war'.[8] So it went on again and again until the end came in the heart of Berlin.

Fragment no. 29[9]

    Evening session, 1 December 1942 in Wolfschanze

ZEITZLER: Nothing special to report from Manstein's group at Kotelnikovo.

    There was a sharp attack today on the Chir front; it extended from Chir station, Colonel Tschuecke's front, across Abraham's and Schmidt's to Fiebig's. The attack was repulsed all along Colonel Tschuecke's front and 100 prisoners were taken.

There was a small break-in yesterday on the next sector. There was to be a counter-attack today but this has not made much progress because of continued enemy pressure. There were one or two tanks shot up here. We propose to put in parts of 336 Division tomorrow to throw the enemy out.

There was an attack on the next sector. Three tanks were shot up. All positions held. Also an attack on the next sector, that of Colonel-General Schmidt; six tanks shot up. All positions held.

In Fiebig's sector there is a small village called Kirjev; this was penetrated by enemy cavalry, about a thousand strong. There's an interesting point here. Prisoners were taken from 40 Guards Division and 321 Division. Both these divisions have hitherto been opposite the north-west front of Sixth Army. The prisoners stated that they moved up by forced march three nights running. This makes it look as if the enemy is thinning out his front opposite Sixth Army in order to reinforce his break-in near Chir. The fact that Sixth Army has not been heavily attacked today supports this. About a hundred tons were flown in to Sixth Army today.[10]

Going further north; 22 Armoured Division and the Hollidt Group have not been attacked. On the other hand, this afternoon Group Hollidt's communications and headquarters were heavily bombed. This is the enemy's normal preparation for subsequent attacks.

Nothing to report on the Italian front. The Pasubio Division was attacked by strong fighting patrols (two to three companies). Some prisoners were taken who stated that the enemy would attack the Pasubio Division tomorrow and iron out the whole salient; one to two divisions and two hundred tanks were said to be in position. I have told the Army Group to do something about it whatever happens. Similar small-scale attacks were started on the front of the Rumanians. The Army Group has brought up an armoured infantry company from 298 Division on to the front of Pasubio Division and has incorporated into the division a pioneer battalion from 298. The whole regiment (the map shows '1/3 298') has been alerted and brought up behind the left flank of Pasubio Division. The Luftwaffe has made one anti-aircraft battery available which has also been posted in rear of Pasubio Division. That is all that we can do for the moment.

Five days ago I sent the Italians an anti-aircraft specialist. He discovered a new depot containing 9,000 hollow charge rounds. He got them across to the Italians together with the German Pioneer Training Detachment, so that they can now produce some small German assault detachments armed with both normal ammunition and explosives.

...

JODL: The military commander in France reports: yesterday was comparatively quiet. No apparent change in the attitude of the population. No incidents with demobilized French troops.

There was a burglary at a town hall in the department of Seine-et-Loire. The French police managed to arrest six armed criminals, all members of a terrorist group.

HITLER: Good! The police are good. We should make use of them and work with the police only. Himmler knows his police. He may use somewhat questionable methods but gradually he gets the people under control. That way we form firm links with the police!

JODL: They give a very good impression.

HITLER: The police are more unpopular than anybody else in the country and so look for support to some more powerful authority than their own State; that means us. The police are certain to go on urging us not to leave the country.

JODL: The number of French workers engaged to work in Germany passed the two hundred thousand mark a few days ago.

HITLER: That's increasing then. To begin with these people have got nothing and then they say to themselves that at least they'll be out of danger. They don't want war. Why should they? They all feel: whatever may happen the whole war has been a lot of nonsense.

JODL: May I now refer to the command set-up in Africa. This is of course a question of organization. The Italian attitude is 'leave well alone'; but before long they'll be saying 'of course we must command in this theatre'. So far they've done nothing about this.

HITLER: In the first place we're the only people who are doing anything there at the moment; secondly if there's any question of attacking, you can be sure there won't be any Italians around.

JODL: That's why they don't refer to the fact that we have quietly taken over command in that theatre. They haven't said a word about it.

HITLER: They can't do, what's more. We shall have four motorized divisions down there, and if you count in the paratroopers, etc., they come to about a division. That means five divisions. Count in the two infantry divisions and that makes seven. With seven divisions we are more or less carrying on the war by ourselves. They're not fighting. From the equipment point of view we've got to go it alone there. The Italians are of course doing the sea transport. But we can make some shipping available now that we've laid hands on the French. If we hadn't beaten the French we wouldn't have had any shipping. Once the situation up there's been cleared up. . . .

KRANCKE: Then we can give them Tunis and we can take Algiers.

HITLER: They can be responsible for the administration of the whole thing.

BODENSCHATZ: We must be responsible for the anti-aircraft defence though.

KEITEL: And supply too!

I would like to refer to the anti-guerilla war too. Only yesterday we got an order ready about that.

HITLER: I think we must have a preamble here. The essential thing about anti-guerilla warfare – one must hammer this home to everybody – is that whatever succeeds is right. Here's the most important point: if someone does something which is not according to instructions but which leads to success or if he is faced with an emergency with which he can only deal by using brutal methods, then any method is right which leads to success. The object must be to exterminate the guerillas and re-establish order. Otherwise we shall get to the same position which we had at home with the so-called emergency defence programme. As a result of that instruction we finally got to the position in Germany where no policeman and no soldier dared to use his weapons. It was such an elastic instruction that the individual said to himself: 'if unfortunately I kill this chap, then I am for it! If he kills me, I am for it too. But how can I judge it so that I put him out of action without hurting him and at the same time don't get put out of action myself?' That was the famous elastic paragraph in the emergency defence law and the result was that in fact anybody who had a weapon was for it whether he was a policeman or a soldier – odd, wasn't it. The most ridiculous example was the incident at Zabern. But the police had lots of incidents. On the one hand was the order 'do that', on the other hand if they did, they were going to break the emergency defence laws.

So I think we want a paragraph here; 'notwithstanding all the above, the annihilation of the guerillas is an overriding duty. Therefore anything which assists in the annihilation of the guerillas will be considered right and conversely anything which does not contribute to the annihilation of the guerillas will be considered wrong.' Then everybody will be free to act. Anyway in a lot of cases what's the chap to do! What are they to do when the bastards push women and children in front of them? I saw this myself in Chemnitz; those Red bastards held children in front of them and then spat at us. We could not retaliate. God help us if we'd done anything to the children!

It's the same thing with the anti-guerilla war. If they push women and children in front of them the officer or NCO must be authorized, if necessary, to shoot them down ruthlessly. The only thing that matters is that he should make a job of it and wipe out the gang. We must give absolute support to the man who's carrying the gun. It's all very well to give him general instructions; but then you must support him absolutely so that the poor devil doesn't have to say: 'I shall be held responsible for this later.'

What do you propose to do: let's say the bastards go into a house and barricade themselves in it and there are women and children in the house. Is the chap to set the house alight or not? If he sets it alight he will burn innocent people as well. No question about it! He must set it alight. It is no good saying: 'the ordinary soldier mustn't do this, it must be an officer'. No! When the poor devil's there with six or seven men what's he to do? That was the tragic position the police were in, that only an officer could act. Have you ever heard of an officer being present when the police wanted him! The wretched constable was just there as naked as the day he was born.

That's why the French police cling to our German police because for the first time in their lives they feel authority is behind them. The French police have never had such a thing before! Previously if there were riots in Paris and the police fired, they used to get it in the neck. They were hauled up in front of the Cadi. They were told to protect the parliament and act against the demonstrators. How were they supposed to protect parliament when the demonstrators were coming on? If the demonstrators had come on and the police hadn't protected parliament then they would have been punished for doing nothing. And so they shot and got punished for shooting.

You have to be frightfully careful in matters like this not to put the ordinary fellow into an impossible position. You have to try and imagine all the time what the soldier is thinking. It's all very well to sit round the table here and say that it's a matter of commonsense. 'How can you be so stupid? – can't you think man? – haven't you thought about this?' The poor devil can't think; he's fighting for his life, for his existence! So the wretched soldier or NCO cuts the cackle and shoots and kills so-and-so many women because he thinks that otherwise he'll never get through the place.

JODL: There's no question of that here. In battle they can do what they like. They can hang them, hang them upside down, draw and quarter them – there's nothing about that here. The only limitation here is after-action reprisals in those areas in which guerillas have been living and that is something which the Reichsführer himself is very cautious about. He says: 'I must be careful I don't spread guerilla activity and drive off the entire male population. The word goes round from village to village and then 2,000 men will go rushing off to the guerilla areas.' Apart from this there's not a word about what people may or may not do. This only gives certain results of reconnaissance and operations.

HITLER: But still I think we ought to write it down that if the chap thinks that to do his duty he must use the severest methods, then he's absolutely right and will be backed up under all circumstances.

JODL: This instruction is more for the commanders. The SS have more experience in anti-guerilla action.

HITLER: I know they've got more experience. But do you know

what people say about the SS because they've got this experience? People are always saying they're brutal.

JODL: That's not true. They work very well. They use the stick
and carrot method like everybody else!

HITLER: People will forgive them the carrot but not the stick.

KEITEL: There's not much talk about it in the guerilla area. I'm
happy to say there's very good co-operation. Everybody's working well together and under one command. In those anti-guerilla
actions laid on by Bach-Zelewski he was in sole command both
of the police and of the troops from the divisions in the area.

HITLER: That Bach-Zelewski is a clever chap. When he was in the
Party I always used him for the most difficult jobs. When we
had a job breaking down Communist resistance somewhere I
would bring him along and he would put it across them!

Fragment no. 8
  Midday conference 12 December 1942 in Wolfschanze
Beginning 12.45

HITLER: Has there been some disaster?

ZEITZLER: No, my Führer. Manstein reached the obstacle and
captured a bridge. The only attacks were on the Italian front.
One regiment here was alerted during the night and reached
its battle position at 10 am. That was good because the Italians
had already put in all their reserves.

HITLER: I've had more sleepless nights over this business in the
south than over anything else. One doesn't know what's going
on.

BUHLE: They're not reliable.

ZEITZLER: We must do something like we did last night as
soon as possible. If the Russians had seized their opportunity,
there'd have been a disaster during the night. The Army
Group only wanted to bring the regiment up early in the
morning. But we actually got it into position by 10 am.

Nothing much has happened in Seventeenth Army. There
are more agents' reports about a landing in the Crimea; they're
waiting for really bad weather, snow showers, etc.

HITLER: That seems improbable. Can our navy lay on the
weather like that!

JODL: If it's like that they can't land.

HITLER: The Russians will get through somehow. We wouldn't

be able to land in a snow shower or anything like that. I admit that. But that doesn't go for the Russians.

KRANCKE: That is if it's not too bad. If it's freezing and everything is iced up it is bad. But when it's merely snow showers and just about freezing point, then it can be done.

HITLER: They will land just the same. Just like in fog – they land in fog.

I wanted to say something about this Georgian battalion or company. I must say, I don't know – the Georgians are not Mohammedan. That means they are not a Turkoman battalion. The Georgians do not come from the Turkish race. The Georgians are a Caucasian tribe who have nothing to do with the Turkish people. I think only the Mohammedans are reliable. I don't think any of the others are reliable. That can happen to us anywhere because one has to be frightfully careful. I think raising battalions from these Caucasian peoples is very risky; on the other hand I see no danger in raising purely Mohammedan units. They're always ready to fight.

ZEITZLER: I have sent down a list of questions in order to get something to go on. Baltiz questioned a Russian general about the Georgians and he was very forthcoming. He replied that we should find the Georgians neither good nor bad; they found the same.

HITLER: That's right. All they worry about is being independent from everybody. As far as I can hear they are very unreliable from everybody's point of view. Since Stalin is a Georgian himself, I can quite well imagine that many of them are flirting with Communism. They have had a form of self-government. The Turkoman peoples are Mohammedan. The Georgians are not a Turkish race they are a Turkish-Caucasian tribe probably with some northern blood too. Then I don't trust the Armenians either in spite of what people say, either Rosenberg or the military staff. I think the Armenian units are just as unreliable and dangerous. The only people I think are reliable are the real Mohammedans, ie the real Turkoman peoples. What their fighting capacity is however is another matter; I can't judge that.

(*The Wehrmacht report is produced.*)

HITLER: Tell me now: where are those tanks the rats were supposed to have got at?

ZEITZLER: They were with 22 Armoured Division. Can I now give the order for these preparations to proceed?

HITLER: The most important thing is that we should get this road.

ZEITZLER: Blocking that road doesn't make much difference because there's a side road here. If we merely block the main road the enemy can use the side road. But we shall have to extend out to Shikola if we are to be quite sure.

HITLER: We must remain in this area in order to have the road. That's unfortunate.

ZEITZLER: We can't do that. We must keep our only reserve available. I've had it looked into and the Mountain Regiment can't get here before the 20th.

HITLER: I wonder whether they'll get here even by the 20th. If they don't dig in they'll have to withdraw here.

ZEITZLER: I think that's a pretty naturally strong position however.

HITLER: When we withdraw I am always afraid of equipment being left behind. That means you've got men but no equipment. Can't start anything – quite apart from the morale aspect.

ZEITZLER: If we withdraw according to programme we shall get it back; there's a position here and very little in it. 16 Motorized Division carried out a very successful attack taking 150 prisoners and coming back with them.

HITLER: They're not fighting a war of movement down there; they left the tanks behind and did nothing about it – trench warfare.

ZEITZLER: They should have pushed their flanks much further out. Comparatively little on this front. I've cleared up the business about the order to withdraw; it will be toned down a bit. He wanted to give an order to withdraw.

Now the situation in this area: Field Marshal Manstein called me early this morning. He has captured the bridge at this place. There is a little pressure now starting against 23 Armoured Division. Those are probably the forces they brought up. Resistance here was not very great. Very heavy fighting flared up here during the course of the day. The enemy captured Ritchev. That's most unfortunate because of the bridge. That was the line of communication we wished to use to bring forces up. The attack spread as far as this point, whereas here it's more or less died away. We intercepted a radio message from VIII Cavalry Corps saying that they were taking up a defensive position. It is still not clear what the enemy is doing up here. It may be merely a reaction to our radio traffic. Before we moved this was very high. It may be, however, that he is preparing something. The main attack on Sixth Army was in this area. Field Marshal Manstein called about keeping this attack going;* he put his views on paper and here it is. (*Produces it.*)

HITLER: He has got a front of fifty miles as the crow flies.

ZEITZLER: He has put his views on paper. You might like to read it. There's no question of moving 16 Division. If we withdraw 16 Division the whole Rumanian front will collapse, and we shall never be able to re-establish it. Seeing there's a gap here he wonders whether some armoured forces can't be pushed up. At least that's the only explanation I can make of his proposals.

HITLER: We must see what forces he's got here first. He's still got two strong divisions. One has got 95 and the other 138 tanks.

ZEITZLER: Of course there's always some risk in withdrawing two divisions.

HITLER: I agree entirely but he's got some Luftwaffe formations too, and something can be done with them. When does the next infantry division arrive?

ZEITZLER: That's a long time; it will be eight days before we get it here. We had hoped to put 11 Armoured Division in here. That would have been more or less all right. If we can't do that, the two armoured divisions will have to stay put. 23 Division will be attacked from the flank and will have to operate so. That leaves only 6 Division. So if there are counter-attacks and we must maintain this line of communication, that's a difficult situation. If we move 17 Division down from here there's a risk there too. But this attack by two armoured divisions may get stuck and then it may be that two days later we shall be forced to bring 17 Division down, and that means we shall have lost a day.

HITLER: Did he want to put 17 Division in here?

ZEITZLER: He wanted to bring it up here and bring this one across here.

* From Kotelnikovo towards Stalingrad

HITLER: 17 Division's not worth much.

ZEITZLER: What about 11 Division then?

HITLER: That's only got 45 tanks.

ZEITZLER: It's had 49 up till now. There are some unserviceable. It had to leave one battalion up here; as an emergency measure we could put in a regiment of 306 Division.

HITLER: When did 11 Division lose all these tanks? Up there it had 70 or 80.

ZEITZLER: As far as I know it arrived with 49 tanks.

HITLER: And now there are more unserviceable.

ZEITZLER: Of course there are always some temporarily unserviceable. The figure always goes up the day following bad weather.

HEUSINGER: At one time 11 Armoured Division had 57.

HITLER: It moved from up there with 73 or 75.

ZEITZLER: I'll look into it again. I haven't got the figures in my head. In my experience one must always reckon with ten to twenty tanks unserviceable owing to the weather.

HITLER: I'd like to hear the whole situation first and we will come back to this business at the end.

The discussion continues on these lines dealing with tactical detail on the Russian front. This part of the record will be found in Appendix A p. 521

HITLER: I've received another report that he* is withdrawing here. (Africa.)

JODL: Yes, he is. There is no doubt that the enemy has started his first major attack here and he will probably continue it on the 13th. Air reconnaissance confirms that his air force is ready and that he has moved his bases up. He has got his main fighter force with 130 single-engine and 120 twin-engine aircraft in the area north of Agedabia, and then there are 100 single-engine and 40 twin-engine aircraft in the area between Sollum and Marina. Radio interception indicates that he is poised as he was before our offensive against El Alamein and is ready to attack here. The Air Commander Africa also considers that in the immediate future we shall be faced with an English offensive aiming at Tripoli. In comparison our own forces are weak as long as the main body remains in Sicily and the majority of them are in rear of the final position.

* Field Marshal Rommel.

HITLER: Who says that is the final position?

JODL: The Duce has given that order.

HITLER: The conversation the Reichsmarschall had wasn't as clear as that.

JODL: Rommel says the same in his telegram.

HITLER: What does he say?

JODL: He says: 'Troops remaining in the area ... are being withdrawn to the final position.' There you have the word 'final'. In view of the overall situation that's what he reckons it is.

To continue. He beat off yesterday's attacks, including those from the south but says that the attacks will undoubtedly be continued in this sector today and that he cannot afford to put in all his forces in case the enemy should also attack from the south even if only with small forces. As a result of the fuel situation he is in no position to conduct offensive or mobile operations but was just able to withdraw to this position. He must remain here until the 15th by which time he will be mobile again. Therefore he can't commit himself to anything. Considering his fuel situation that's understandable. If he were fully mobile he could go around this way, which is what he wants to do, and so slip out of any enveloping movements.

HITLER: I must say he has got an enormous army and it seems to have had enough fuel to get back here from the Alamein position. They didn't do that on water. The whole time they've apparently practically had no fuel. If they'd brought the fuel up instead of going back themselves they could have operated up front. No doubt about that. It would have been simpler to operate up front merely with a couple of divisions. After all, all that's necessary are the tanks and a little artillery. They've gone back a thousand miles taking with them household stuff and everything else they could lay their hands on. Of the men we've lost I'll bet that 50 per cent were lost during the retreat. Which means that the real losses up front were probably extraordinarily low.

There is no doubt that we were wrong to be over-influenced by the sinking of that 4000-ton steamer, and not to push our initial offensive through. That's Kesselring's impression and Ramcke's too; the latter says: 'we can't understand why we didn't go on; the English were completely routed; all we had to do was to push on and attack from some flank.' But really I think one shouldn't leave a man too long in a position of such heavy responsibility. Gradually he loses his nerve. It's different if one's in the rear. There of course one keeps one's head. These people can't stand the strain on their nerves. It should really be a principle not to leave a man in a theatre of war too long. There's no point in it. It's better to relieve him. Then someone new comes in who wants to earn his laurels and is relatively fresher. I am therefore determined that as soon as the first rush is over we will relieve a number of generals who in themselves are perfectly all right – even field marshals; we'll simply order them to take so-and-so many months' leave so that they can return to the front completely recovered. Think what it's like. He has to go on shadow boxing out there with a few wretched units. So it's not surprising if after two years or so he gradually loses his nerve and gets into a situation where he says: 'I'll hold on ...' then things which to us in the rear don't appear so terrible, seem frightful to him. Last year we had cases of people up front simply losing their nerve as a result of the frightful weather conditions saying to themselves: 'it's easy for them in the rear to talk; they don't have to stay out in this weather'. That's right too. We must also arrange so that people are not constantly exposed to the same sort of pressure. If I put a high level staff under mortar fire for three weeks I can't be surprised if they lose their nerve. That's the reason for the Feldherrnhügel.*

Except in the last resort, where the general must be the standard-bearer because it's a matter of life and death, he must be back behind. In the long run you can't command in the midst of the roar of battle.

One thing's certain: in this small area one man can keep his eye on almost the whole battlefield. It's not a question of communications; instinct comes into it. When you do that for two years eventually your nerves go. That's Göring's impression too. He says that Rommel has completely lost his nerve.

Then there's the tragic business with the Italians. The eternal uncertainty. We get that too. I couldn't get to sleep last night – it's the feeling of uncertainty. If it was an all-German theatre, it's possible that we could do something and one would feel

* From a well-known comedy by Rhoda-Rhoda, lampooning generals who 'lead their regiments from behind,) (cf. W. S. Gilbert).

that we could plug the holes somehow. At least you wouldn't have a whole army disintegrating in a day. The Russians have announced that they've captured 9,400 prisoners – Axis forces; they hardly captured any Germans, just Rumanians. The first air reconnaissance report says that huge grey columns were on the move over there – apparently all prisoners – and others are moving in the opposite direction so that you can't tell whether they are Russians or Rumanians. Once a unit has started to run, the ties of training and organization quickly go unless there is iron discipline. It's miles easier to go crashing forward with an army and win victories than to bring one back in good order after a setback or a defeat. Perhaps the greatest feat of 1914 was that they managed to get the German army back after making fools of themselves on the Marne and to get it to stand and reorganize on a definite line. That was perhaps one of the greatest feats. You can only do that with very high-class disciplined troops.

JODL: We managed to do that here too with the German troops.

HITLER: We managed it with the Germans but not with the Italians; we never shall with them. So if the enemy breaks through anywhere there'll be a catastrophe. If a man lives continually under this pressure, gradually he'll go to pieces.

JODL: We only had the Italian Eighth Army on a small sector of the front; but his front is primarily Italian.

HITLER: Perhaps it would have been better to have recalled him straight away, and sent down some other chap with strict orders to hold on.

JODL: I don't think you can argue much about what he's done. He's like someone who's been living on a diet of milk and bread and is then asked to take part in the Olympic Games. He hasn't had any supplies for weeks. In the East they scream if they're two trains short.

His intention is to go back step by step in order to gain time for the construction of this position here; in view of the fuel situation he can't do anything else. There were still parts of XXI Corps here who have now been ordered to move up here. He will wait here until the English have built themselves up again. They've got to build up again and bring up their artillery. That will take a few days.

HITLER: It's to be hoped so.

JODL: Of course the English know that a considerable proportion of our forces are being moved back. That may have been the reason why they attacked somewhat earlier here.

HITLER: How much can he comb out of this enormous German supply train for the defence of this position? Is it all on the move to Tripoli?

JODL: No, on the contrary; six or seven days ago he reported that he had combed out all the rearward services as far as he could and brought the men up into the line.

HITLER: Because in a position like that 10–20,000 Germans pushed in between the Italians might hold things for a bit. It can't be done with Italians alone.

JODL: He also reports that he has laid on all sorts of mining operations, particularly on the Via Balbo and will continue with it.

HITLER: Mining is very difficult because one can only do it to the rear and if you are withdrawing you haven't got the time and so the enemy can see every mine along the roads.

JODL: No, they are doing it in front of the position too. All he wants is an improvement in the fuel situation because he's not fully mobile. If the enemy succeeds in going right round by the south he'll be in a very difficult situation but the lighter traffic from the base at Sfax is going quicker than before. They are no longer reporting single lighters.

HITLER: Up to now it hasn't worked at all.

JODL: It was used by single lighters. Anyway Kesselring felt very relieved this morning; he claimed that since yesterday a great weight had been lifted from his mind with regard to the whole supply problem.

HITLER: There you have the two opposite ends of the scale. Rommel has become the greatest pessimist and Kesselring a complete optimist. That's no end of a step forward.

Fragment no. 47

Midday Conference, 1 February 1943

The conference starts with a discussion of tactical detail on the Russian front. This part is to be found in Appendix A p. 535. It is then concerned with the Russian report that Field Marshal Paulus and a number of other generals including Generals von Seydlitz and Schmidt had been taken prisoner in the southern Stalingrad pocket.

HITLER: They have finally and formally surrendered there. Otherwise they'd have concentrated, formed square and shot it out using their last bullet on themselves. When you think that a woman's got sufficient pride just because someone's made a few insulting remarks to go and lock herself in and shoot herself right off, then I've no respect for a soldier who's afraid to do that but would rather be taken prisoner. All I can say is: I can understand it in a case like that of General Giraud – we arrive, he gets out of his car and is collared. But …

ZEITZLER: I can't understand it either. I still wonder whether it's true. Whether perhaps he isn't lying there badly wounded.

HITLER: No it's true. They'll be taken straight to Moscow and put into the hands of the GPU and they'll blurt out orders for the northern pocket to surrender too. That Schmidt will sign anything. A man who hasn't got the courage at a time like this to take the road that every man has to take one day won't have the strength to stand up to that. He'll suffer mental torture. We put too much emphasis on education and too little on character training.

ZEITZLER: It's impossible to understand that type of man.

HITLER: Don't say that! I have seen a letter … Below got it. I can show it to you. He (an officer from Stalingrad) said: 'I have come to the following conclusion about these people' and then it said: 'Paulus: ?; Seydlitz: should be shot; Schmidt: should be shot'.

ZEITZLER: I too have heard bad reports about Seydlitz.

HITLER: And among them there is 'Hube, *the* man!' Of course one might say it would have been better to let Hube stay there and get the others out. But since the value of men is not immaterial and since one wants men for everything in war, I definitely think it was right to get Hube out.

In peace-time in Germany about 18,000 or 20,000 people a year choose to commit suicide although none of them are in a situation like this, and here's a man who sees 45,000 to 60,000 of his soldiers die defending themselves bravely to the end – how can he give himself up to the Bolshevists? God that is …

ZEITZLER: It is something quite incomprehensible.

HITLER: But I had my doubts before. It was at the moment when I heard he was asking what he should do. How could he even ask such a thing? Does it mean that in future whenever a fortress is besieged and the commander is called upon to surrender he is going to ask: 'what shall I do now?'

He did it easily enough! (These words probably referred to Udet who committed suicide after he had broken down as Air Officer in charge of Equipment.) Or Becker: he got the equipment shop into a muddle; he ... did it and then shot himself dead. How easy it is to do that! A revolver – makes it easy. What cowardice to be afraid of that! Ha! Better be buried alive! And in a situation like this where he knows well enough that his death would set the example for behaviour in the pocket next door. If he sets an example like this, one can hardly expect people to go on fighting.

ZEITZLER: There is no excuse; when his nerves look like breaking down he must shoot himself first.

HITLER: When one's nerves break down there is nothing to do but say 'I can't go on' and shoot oneself. In fact you could say that the man ought to shoot himself. Just as in the old days commanders who saw that all was lost used to fall on their swords. That goes without saying. Even Varus told his slave: 'now kill me!'

ZEITZLER: I still think that they may have done that and that the Russians are merely claiming to have captured them all.

HITLER: No!

ENGEL: The odd thing, if I may say so, is that they have not announced whether Paulus was badly wounded when he was taken prisoner. They may well say tomorrow that he died of his wounds.

HITLER: Have we got any precise information about him being wounded?

...

The tragedy has happened. Now it may be a warning.

ENGEL: They can hardly have got the names of all the generals right.

HITLER: There will be no more field marshals in this war. We'll only promote them after the end of the war. I won't go on counting my chickens before they're hatched.

ZEITZLER: We were so completely sure how it would end that we thought we'd give him what he longed for most. . . .

HITLER: One had to assume that there would be a heroic ending.

ZEITZLER: One couldn't imagine anything else.

HITLER: How can you do anything else when dealing with men? I must say that every soldier who risks his life over and over again must be a fool. If the little private soldier is overcome by it all, I can understand that.

ZEITZLER: It's much easier for a unit commander; everyone looks to him. It's easy for him to shoot himself. It's difficult for the ordinary fellow.

HITLER: If a wretched little chap is hit by all this and says – – – – and lets himself get taken prisoner, I can understand that. But then I must say: how heroically they ... there's no arguing about that. Of course many fought like Germans! ... and yet we can't manage it, although our commanders are so intelligent and our soldiers so well trained and finally our equipment is so superior to that of the Russians. Yet apart from Stalingrad we were always superior.

As soon as I heard it last night I asked Puttkamer to check whether the news was out. If it hadn't already been given out on the wireless I'd have stopped it straight away.

What hurts me so much is that the heroism of so many soldiers is cancelled out by one single characterless weakling – and I'll tell you what the man will do now. Think of it! He arrives in Moscow and think of the rat trap he's in! He'll sign anything. He'll make confessions, issue proclamations. You'll see. They'll now plumb the depths of lack of character. It's true to say: one bad deed always leads to another.

ENGEL: One thing: tomorrow Major von Zitzewitz is due to speak to the home and foreign press about Stalingrad. Should that be stopped?

HITLER: No.

ENGEL: I merely ask because of course there will be questions; among other things the question.... The best would be to keep it all very general.

HITLER: One doesn't know for sure if a man knows anything: you can't get that out of him direct. But character is the first essential with soldiers and if we can't teach that, if all we can do is to bring up intellectual and mental acrobats and athletes, then we shall never get a race capable of standing up to the heavy blows of fortune. That's decisive.

ZEITZLER: Yes, in the general staff too. For the first time I have given general staff insignia to a liaison officer who had not had general staff training because he had done wonderful staff work in arranging the withdrawal of his division. It doesn't matter whether or not he'd done the eight-weeks training course. I took immediate action. I just sent down an order: 'You are a general staff officer as of today.'

HITLER: Yes, one must select brave, daring people, who are willing to sacrifice their lives, like every soldier. What is 'life'? ... the nation; the individual must die any way. It is the nation which lives on after the individual.

But how can anyone be afraid of this moment which sets him free from this vale of misery, unless the call of duty keeps him in this vale of tears! Well now ...! They announce they've captured Paulus. I want a distinction made between prisoners and missing. When the enemy breaks through and gets there without fighting, one knows they have been taken prisoner. The others must be posted as missing.

I don't know how we should proceed in the case of Paulus. We must let the commander in the northern pocket have something that he is to hold the pocket under all circumstances. The pocket must be held to the last man....

ZEITZLER: So you agree that I should send a message in this sense?

HITLER: Yes! I keep on thinking of this: the Rumanian General Lascar was killed with his men. I am glad I gave him the Oak Leaves Cross. Queer how these things happen! When I heard it about 10.30 last night – I'd gone to bed early – I got hold of Puttkamer straight away to see whether the radio message had already gone out. Then the Russians announced: Marshal Paulus captured with his entire staff. The entire staff surrendered. Now the Russians will ....

ZEITZLER: Just what I feared! I thought: they'll play some disgusting game with Paulus' body, and now it's even worse.

HITLER: Any minute he'll be speaking on the radio – you'll see. Seydlitz and Schmidt will speak on the radio. They'll shut them in that rat trap and two days later they'll have got them so conditioned that they'll speak straight away. And there's this beautiful woman, a really very beautiful woman, who is insulted by some words. Straightaway she says – it was only a triviality – : 'so I can go; I'm not wanted'. Her husband answers: 'get out then!' So the woman goes off, writes a letter of farewell and shoots herself....

Did the report that they were wounded come before Jänecke left or after?

ZEITZLER: I will check. I will call Jänecke. He must have known about it, if it was before he left.

HITLER: We must get that clear. Then we must make out that the staffs fought to the last man and that they were only taken prisoner when they were wounded, overwhelmed and faced by superior forces.

ZEITZLER: That is undoubtedly what most of the staffs did.

HITLER: We must say that this was no surrender but that they were overwhelmed.

ZEITZLER: We can put that in the report. The Russians will give another picture of it. Let us get our story into the world press first.

HITLER: Say that they've been without rations for months and that the Russians were able to overwhelm many of them.

ZEITZLER: I think this is the better line to take. . . .
As regards the Russian communiqué we must check to see whether there are any errors in it. For a single mistake – for instance a general who couldn't have been there – would prove that everything they have published was taken from some list they have captured somewhere.

HITLER: They say they have captured Paulus as well as Schmidt and Seydlitz.

JODL: I don't know about Seydlitz. It's not quite clear whether he was not in the northern pocket. We'll find out by radio. Who are the generals in the northern pocket anyway?

HITLER: He was definitely with Paulus. I'll tell you one thing: I can't understand how a man like Paulus wouldn't rather die. The heroism of so many tens of thousands of men, officers and generals is cancelled out by a man like this who hasn't got the character when the moment comes, to do what a weakling of a woman can do.

JODL: But I'm not yet certain that that is correct.

HITLER: There were a man and wife living together. Later the man died a painful death. Then I got a letter from the wife; she asked me to look after the children. She said she couldn't go on living, in spite of her children. Then she shot herself. That's what a woman can do; she's got the strength and soldiers haven't! You'll see; within a week Seydlitz and Schmidt and Paulus too will all be speaking on the radio.

JODL: I am sure of it.

HITLER: They'll be taken to the Ljubljanka, and there the rats will get at them. How can they be such cowards? I don't understand it.

JODL: I am still not sure.

HITLER: Unfortunately I am. You know, I don't believe this story of Paulus being wounded any more. It doesn't seem to fit. They must think that they.... What are we to do?

What hurts me the most personally is that I went on and promoted him field marshal. I wanted to give him his heart's desire. That's the last field marshal I promote in this war. One must not count one's chickens before they are hatched.

I just don't understand it. When a man sees so many men die – I must really say: how easy it is for our ... he can't have thought of that. It's ridiculous, a thing like this. So many men have to die and then a man like this comes along and at the last moment besmirches the heroism of so many others. He could have got out of this vale of tears and into eternity and been immortalized by the nation and he'd rather go to Moscow. How can he even think of that as an alternative. It's crazy.

JODL: That's why I am still not sure.

HITLER: It's just as if I were to say today that I would hand over a fortress to General Förster; then I'd know straightaway that he'd be the first to haul down his flag. There are others who wouldn't do it. It's tragic that in a moment like this so much bravery should be besmirched.

JESCHONNEK: I think it's possible that the Russians have reported this on purpose. They are such clever devils.

HITLER: In a week they'll be on the radio.

JESCHONNEK: The Russians might even arrange for someone else to do the talking.

HITLER: No, they'll talk on the radio themselves. You'll hear it soon enough. They'll all speak personally on the radio! First they'll call upon the people in the pocket to give themselves up and then they'll say the meanest things about the German Army. You have to realize that they'll be taken to Moscow, put into the Ljubljanka and there 'worked over'. When someone's not got the courage at a time like this....

I've already told Zeitzler he must send a message to Heitz that they must hold on in the northern pocket.

KEITEL: Heitz was in the southern pocket and he's not mentioned in the Russian report.

JODL: Yes and that's why we must now put the question and get it quite clear who actually is in the northern pocket at the moment. If the report includes names of people who are in the northern pocket, it is a list which they have found somewhere and then published. One thing is clear – they have not mentioned somebody who was in the southern pocket and has definitely been killed – Hartmann.

KEITEL: He was killed four days ago.

JODL: Yes.

HITLER: If Heitz was in the southern pocket and is not mentioned ... I am convinced that the staff as a whole acquitted themselves bravely and honourably.

The discussions about North Africa recorded in these fragments do not bring out the fact that Hitler was at the time toying with the idea of the complete evacuation of the whole of North Africa. There was in fact an indication of this in Jodl's instructions to his staff mentioned at the beginning of this chapter; shortly afterwards on Hitler's instructions a series of questions on the sea transport situation were put to Commander-in-Chief South, Field Marshal Kesselring. This document included the following pretty clear indication: 'depending on your answer, the Supreme Command may well take very far-reaching decisions'.[11] Nevertheless no precautionary action was taken in North Africa to avert the impending disaster.

Any questioning of the possibility of holding North Africa in the long run after the events of early November was initially totally rejected by those on high; it can in fact be traced back to Rommel. On 29 November he unexpectedly appeared in Wolfschanze direct from the desert of Syrtes. His object was to bring the High Command, while there was still time, face to face with the decision totally to evacuate North Africa. Contrary to his previous friendly welcome he was most coldly received by Hitler who forthwith cut the ground from under his feet by quoting a remark of Göring's that it was only 'a short hop' to Tunis and stating that supply across the Mediterranean was now assured for the future and could meet all requirements.[12] (The real truth and the insincerity of Hitler's statements are highlighted in the Operations Staff War Diary of 7 December 1942 which says: 'just now the Führer considers it a positive advantage that for the moment Rommel's Army has insufficient fuel to enable it to withdraw further'.) That same evening Jodl noted: 'North Africa will be lost all the same'. A few days later however, while briefing the newly appointed Commander-in-Chief in Tunis, Colonel-General von Arnim, Hitler laid stress once more on the plans he had formed during the period immediately following the Allied landings. Arnim's Fifth Panzer Army at this time consisted of little more than a number of hastily-collected units, the equivalent of one or two German divisions with very little transport or heavy weapons; Hitler's idea however was that, after driving the enemy from port to port as far as Casablanca, it should finally throw him out altogether.[13] In contrast to these ambitious plans, when Count Ciano and Count Cavallero arrived in East Prussia representing Mussolini and made the most urgent request for reinforcement of the Luftwaffe to protect the traffic to Tunis, Hitler had to refuse because of lack of resources. In spite of this both sides confirmed once more the decision 'to hold North Africa', and so Hitler paid all the less attention to the Italian request. The views of Commander-in-Chief South, Field Marshal Kesselring, had a considerable influence on Hitler's attitude. He was optimistic about future developments both in Tunis and as regards the sea supply situation. Kesselring expressed the same opinion when he made a verbal presentation in Wolfschanze on 12 January 1943.[14]

This being the atmosphere and climate of opinion at the top it is hardly to be wondered at that Supreme Headquarters scarcely noticed, let alone made use of, the fact that an opportunity now existed to avert almost certain catastrophe in North Africa by timely withdrawal. There was a further opportunity when the final collapse at Stalingrad took place; Rommel purposely made use of the moment to hurry on his withdrawal, crossed into Tunisia undisturbed by the enemy and joined up with Arnim. The Fifth Panzer Army in the Tunis 'bridgehead' was still superior to the enemy and the sea transport situation was such that it would in all probability have been possible at this moment to get away the bulk of the troops.[15] North Africa would have been given up but a large number of very high-class formations would probably also have been saved.

Hitler however thought quite otherwise! For him the arrival of

Rommel's Army in Tunisia heralded the moment for the start of his offensive plans.[16] There were undoubtedly considerable political and strategic advantages in holding Tunis – the least that could be done – and these completely blinded him to the tactical necessities, primarily the fact that land, sea and air reinforcements would be necessary and were unobtainable. It had so far not even proved possible to clarify the command set up in Tunisia; authority ran from Hitler and Mussolini, through the two high-level Defence Staffs, to Kesselring and thence to the German Army Commanders, of whom there were now two, side by side. In spite of all his fine words and in spite of all possible pressure from OKW, Hitler always put Mussolini's susceptibilities ahead of the military requirements. When finally the command organization was settled, Commander-in-Chief South reaped one minor advantage from it in that from now on the Operations Section of his newly formed inter-service staff was integrated into the Comando Supremo in Rome. It seemed therefore that, after having fought side by side for almost three years, there was at last to be some close co-operation between the allies, at least on this level; it soon became clear however that this arrangement was not to last nor did it lead to mutual confidence.[17]

This chaotic situation led me to ask Jodl if I could go to Tunis to get a picture of the situation on the spot, and after many fruitless attempts to persuade him at the end of January and early February, I finally got him to agree. I had to pass via Rome and this gave me the opportunity of getting in touch for the first time with Colonel-General Ambrosio, who had replaced Cavallero as Chief of the Comando Supremo after the loss of Tripolitania. My trip lasted in all ten days during the first half of February, and included not only the Comando Supremo and Commander-in-Chief South in Rome but both German Commanders-in-Chief in Tunis and last but not least the troops in all parts of that country. Everything I saw and heard led me to the conclusion, already reached by Field Marshal Rommel, that there could be no question of attack but that evacuation of North Africa should be the order of the day. On the way back I broke off my journey in Rome and had an interview alone with Kesselring in his small office in a simple house in Frascati, high above Rome. There I told him quite frankly that this was the main conclusion that I had reached as a result of my trip. The words were barely out of my mouth when Kesselring stopped me with the warning which I can still hear: 'walls have ears'. There is of course no doubt that Kesselring was far better qualified to judge than I was; my opinions were based merely upon the impressions of a few days' trip. Disregarding for the moment his natural optimism, he could invoke the experience and personal impressions gathered during innumerable trips to the front. He did not however succeed in convincing me.

During my final flight back I thought all this over carefully and decided that I would report to Hitler in the same sense as I had to Commander-in-Chief South. This intention however came to an abrupt end when, as we assembled next day for the midday conference in the headquarters in East Prussia, to my great astonishment I saw Field Marshal Kesselring. He was enthusiastically greeted by Hitler and given the floor straight away so that he might describe the latest developments in the Tunis-Mediterranean theatre as he saw them. This produced another example of Kesselring's natural inclination to look upon the most serious weaknesses and difficulties of any situation as having been partially overcome, the moment the slightest sign of an improvement appeared and to start talking of victories when they were still no more than plans and intentions. Hitler then unexpectedly turned to me with the phrase which he always used to lower grade staff officers 'and what about you?' I had hardly got out my first sentence, however, giving an indication of a point of view opposite to that of Kesselring, when Hitler, who realized at once what I meant, brusquely brought the discussion to an end with the other phrase which he normally used in such cases: 'have we anything else?' I immediately left the map room, not however without having received a rebuke from Göring to the effect that this time I had tried to argue with a Field Marshal of *his* Luftwaffe and to 'disturb' Hitler. To my surprise, when I got outside I was followed by Schmundt, who stopped me with the words: 'you obviously wanted to report something quite different to Kesselring; the Führer must hear it. I will get you a special date today; you can rely on that.' This idea came to nothing – primarily because the next morning Hitler, with a restricted following, including Jodl and Schmundt, moved to the forward headquarters in the Ukraine where they remained for about four weeks. I took the opportunity to press Keitel once more for the change of employment he had promised me. The Chief of OKW renewed his promise but stated that he could not at the moment contemplate a change, since

Jodl was away and on return was to take a long leave, the only one by the way which he took throughout the war.

The only course now open was to submit a written report to Jodl. In this I expressed a view completely opposed to the offensive plans which were still floating round and pointed out that the two Allied armies from east and west would shortly effect a junction and thereby cut off Tunis totally by land. I continued that by the middle of March we must expect a converging attack by superior forces which our weak covering forces could not possibly withstand and that the whole edifice would therefore collapse 'like a house of cards'. There was no way of materially altering this situation because of the transport position; so far we had been able to get only the most essential motor vehicles across; according to the calculations of the Comando Supremo we would subsequently be able to meet only 50 per cent of the requirement (60,000 tons a month); there was therefore no advantage either in staying where we were or in attacking or even withdrawing to a very restricted 'bridgehead' immediately around the towns and harbours of Bizerta and Tunis, as Rommel had meanwhile proposed. I avoided using the word 'evacuation' in this initial assault upon the general attitude of negation and my final and decisive sentence read: 'only by preparatory planning of our future course can we avoid serious repercussions which may have political implications, and only thus will it be possible at the same time to make preparations for the defence of Southern Italy'.[18]

The report was then despatched to the forward headquarters where nobody took any notice of it. Keitel, and the rest of the staff with myself at its head, remained behind in Wolfschanze; for once therefore he was free of the deadening presence of Hitler All agreed with my forebodings[19] and Keitel together with his staff worked energetically to try and overcome the sea transport difficulties by every conceivable means.

On 23 February the attack in western Tunisia failed in its over-ambitious objective of 'demolishing'[20] the Allied front and got bogged down; the small forces available for the attack were withdrawn to their starting points and reorganized for the next blow against the British Eighth Army on the south-eastern front. This brought the usual forceful phrases from Hitler's camp. 'The withdrawal of the two Armies to a restricted bridgehead would be the beginning of the end'; the only tactics holding out any prospect of success were said to be 'limited but concentrated attacks'; the

'reserve line' (in the Gabes Area) was to be fortified 'most strongly
and at once'; the Luftwaffe was to 'gain time by increased offensive
activity'; and above all sea transport must be 'at least doubled and
later trebled'. These were mere empty words, bearing no relation to
the forces or time available. On 6–7 March the attack against the
British Eighth Army was brought to a halt as soon as it had begun.
This brought from Hitler the final word, this time also supported by
the Italians, that 'Tunis was a strategic position of the first order'
and 'of decisive importance for the outcome of the war' and 'all
available resources' must be used to hold it.[21]

This excess of confidence may well have been influenced by the
fact that on 13 March Hitler returned to East Prussia from the
Ukraine (Vinnitsa) with the air of a victorious war-lord, clearly
considering himself and *his* leadership primarily responsible for the
favourable turn of events in the East which had temporarily ended
the withdrawal after Stalingrad. Goebbels' diary of 20 March 1943
says: 'the Führer is very happy that he has succeeded in completely
closing the front again'. The real organizer of this 'lost victory'
was Field Marshal von Manstein but Goebbels' only mention of
him in his diary at this period is to express anger that Hitler should
have visited him, saying that the Führer 'does not seem to know
how infamously Manstein behaved towards him', (entry for 11
March). The following remarkable panegyrics from Goebbels' diary
of this period are also of interest: 'Sepp Dietrich is one of our best
troop commanders; he is, so to speak, the Blücher of the National-
Socialist movement.' Entry for 9 March: 'the Führer was excep-
tionally happy about the way the Leibstandarte was led by Sepp
Dietrich. This man has personally performed real deeds of heroism
and has proved himself a great strategist in conducting his operations. The Führer awarded him the Swords for his Knight's Cross.'
Entries for 15 March and 8 May: 'the SS formations in the East are
going from victory to victory ... in the opinion of the Führer the
SS formations did so magnificently because of their unified National-
Socialist indoctrination. Had we brought up the entire German
Wehrmacht as we did the SS formations, the struggle in the East
would undoubtedly have taken a different course.'

To return to North Africa – in Tunisia events moved rapidly to
the final catastrophe of 10–13 May. Rommel who had long since
reached the limit of exhaustion was relieved;[22] shortly after the middle
of March the Allied offensive opened from both west and south

and forced us to withdraw to the restricted bridgehead in northern Tunisia; Arnim, Rommel's successor sent Jodl a letter asking for 'instructions should the struggle end in defeat' and got no answer;[23] Hitler and Mussolini met in Berchtesgaden where the only one to look facts in the face was Ambrosio – to Hitler's fury;[24] last but not least Kesselring continued to give forth optimistic forecasts and make proposals for the movement of reinforcements.[25]

Between 10 and 13 May the catastrophe occurred. Two German-Italian armies went into captivity; they totalled about 300,000 men – the same number as the defenders of Stalingrad during the final battle for the city. Some form of a belated evacuation movement had been begun in the middle of April but had only succeeded in getting rid of the 'useless mouths' ('*mangiatori*'). The air formations and a few of the fighting troops were also able to escape at the last moment.

This time there were no open recriminations by Hitler against the generals in command. But when, as was my duty seeing that I was representing Jodl who was on leave, I started to report at the briefing conference on the latest events and the losses sustained, I got a signal from Keitel to stop; the Supreme Commander of the Wehrmacht had apparently to be spared even a sober military report of the results of his leadership. For the same reason presumably there was not a word of the loss of Tunis in the report Grand Admiral Dönitz made to Hitler on 14 May on his return from another visit to Rome.[26] The following extracts from Goebbels' diary, obviously reporting conversations with Hitler at the headquarters, are also relevant:

9 May: The North African ... hymn of heroism ... has retarded developments for half a year, thereby enabling us to complete the construction of the Atlantic Wall and to prepare ourselves all over Europe so that invasion is out of the question.
10 May: Nothing will make him (Hitler) happier than to exchange his grey uniform for the brown, to visit theatres and cinemas again ... and be a human being again among humans. He is absolutely sick of the generals. He can't imagine anything better than having nothing to do with them. His opinion of all the generals is devastating. . . . All generals lie, he says; all generals are disloyal; all generals are opposed to National-Socialism; all generals are reactionaries. . . .

I am glad the Führer has such a high opinion of Rommel.

11 May: We discussed the situation in Tunis in detail. The Führer now regards it as hopeless.[27]

Shortly thereafter, at the beginning of July 1943, Hitler himself made the following statement to senior officers on the Eastern Front:

Naturally I have tried to reckon whether the undertaking in Tunis, which eventually led to the loss of both men and equipment, was justified. I have come to the following conclusion: by the occupation of Tunisia we have succeeded in postponing the invasion of Europe by six months. More important still, Italy is as a result still a member of the Axis.

If we had not done this, Italy would almost certainly have defected from the Axis. The Allies would at some stage have been able to land in Italy unopposed and push forward to the Brenner and as a result of the Russian breakthrough at Stalingrad, Germany would not have had a single man available to put in there. That would inevitably have led rapidly to the loss of the war.[28]

None of these statements corresponded with the facts as we knew them at the time and in the light of subsequent events and the plans of the Allies as we know them today, none of them were correct. Moreover, just as in the case of Stalingrad, there is not a single word of the possibility that a timely withdrawal might have averted the catastrophe in Tunis.

The end in North Africa put an exceptional strain on relations with Italy which had for some time been clouded by events in the Balkans. Both Axis partners had been intriguing for political leadership in south-eastern Europe and the disagreements now began to affect military co-operation particularly in the struggle against Mihailovich and his Chetnik partisans whom the Italians in many ways favoured. This led Hitler to despatch Ribbentrop to Rome at the end of February to make representations to Mussolini and the Comando Supremo and I was ordered to go there to support him.

During the journey in Ribbentrop's special train I found myself in an unwonted 'civilian' atmosphere and this impression was heightened by the formal reception at the 'main station' in Rome – a peacetime scene with large numbers of young men around in black diplomatic uniforms. During the next few days at the Palazzo Venezia my primary job was to present the situation and the wishes of OKW to Mussolini. It soon became clear that the Chief of the Comando Supremo was much less inclined than was Mussolini to range himself behind Hitler's views and requirements; moreover the subsequent negotiations which I conducted with Ambrosio left me with the clear impression that Mussolini now had little authority in military circles. Agreement was finally reached, generally on the lines we required, but only after Mussolini had had to intervene and after a lively exchange of Italian counter-proposals and drafts of orders which went on into the evening of the second day. Ribbentrop was apparently more or less satisfied and took off the next day with his usual followers for a breath of spring air in the Campagna; he was very vexed with me that I did not attend the official farewell ceremony and went back by air. However it soon became clear that neither the Italian authorities in Rome nor those in the area of the revolt had any intention of abiding by the agreements.[29]

On 8 to 10 April 1943 Hitler and Mussolini met in Salzburg but this was only one of a number of 'state visits' which took place at this time in and around Berchtesgaden. As far as I remember a whole string of senior representatives of the allied powers appeared for a one- or two-day visit to be briefed on the situation and discuss future war prospects. Discussions with the allies were rare occurrences and so, as any good staff would, the OKW Operations Staff prepared comprehensive briefs dealing with all fields of common military interest – command organization, distribution of forces, delivery of equipment, administration and economics; for the most part they came back without even having been seen by Hitler or at least obviously without having made any impact. In general not even Keitel was present at these discussions; Hitler conducted them in his own way, which meant that their purpose was primarily propaganda; he gave his military staff neither the authority nor the opportunity to discuss essential military questions with the staffs of the visitors.

The meetings were generally held in the Castle of Klessheim near Salzburg, a beautiful baroque building built by Fischer von Erlachs. This was used as a 'government guest-house' and the visitors were accommodated there in a series of suites. As always, the military briefing conference took place at midday but on such occasions was turned into a 'show' for the visitors, all good news being emphasized and bad news as far as possible suppressed. Everybody

then went to lunch, usually an unpretentious affair without ceremonial, speeches or toasts. For the rest of the day the senior officers
on both sides were condemned to wait around in the passages and
salons for Hitler to end his discussions.

This reminds me of a particular incident between myself and
the late King Boris of Bulgaria. Hitler had a high opinion of him,
did not put on a 'show' for him and generally received him in the
Berghof. One evening about this time (the King had actually not
much longer to live) Hitler could not be present and King Boris
was fobbed off with a 'marshal's reception' in Klessheim with
Ribbentrop as host. I was ordered to attend instead of Keitel and
Jodl neither of whom could be there. The King got up shortly after
the end of the meal and also brought the subsequent 'get-together'
in the great entrance hall rapidly to an end. He knew me from
previous meetings and while saying goodbye all round, to Ribbentrop's astonishment and discomfort, he took me by the arm and led
me off to his sitting-room next door. With the King's piercing eye
upon me I suddenly found myself faced by a series of penetrating
questions about the real war situation and future prospects. It was a
difficult moment; I had to steer a middle course between the truth
and the limits imposed by my authority and duty. Remarkably
enough no one ever asked me subsequently about this conversation.
However, fate was kind to the King and spared him having to witness
the collapse of his country and the total bankruptcy of the German
leadership to which he had committed himself.[30]

During this same period came the decision of the Allies at the
Casablanca conference to demand 'unconditional surrender' from
the Axis powers but as far as I remember hardly any notice was
taken of it in German Supreme Headquarters. In any case there was
no examination by the OKW Operations Staff of its military consequences. In view of the censorship applicable to all but the
innermost circle of the headquarters, it seems more than likely that
the OKW Operations Staff did not at the time even hear of the
Allied demand.

CHAPTER 3

East-South Tug-of-War up to the Collapse of Italy

A FRESH BASIS AND FRESH DISSENSIONS

Whatever the propaganda line may have been, the full import of the loss of North Africa was immediately recognized by the German Supreme Command. Now that the Tunisian bridgehead had gone, the theatre of war was no longer a comparatively restricted area of the North African coastline but the entire sweep of the Mediterranean. Major Allied forces had become available for employment elsewhere. The opening of the main and feeder lines of communication through the Mediterranean, which had been closed for so long, was calculated to be tantamount to a gain to the enemy of about two million tons of shipping for the movement of troops and supplies. But of all the dangers which now threatened, it was clearer than ever before that, coming on top of our previous disasters, these latest events, and still more probable future developments in the Mediterranean area, threatened the very core of the Axis alliance.

Immediately after the fall of Tunis, therefore, the OKW Operations Staff prepared a 'survey of the situation should Italy withdraw from the war'; its mere title shows that it could not have appeared except on instructions from Hitler. Its starting point was the view still generally held in the headquarters that the Balkans were the most likely target for Western strategy in the Mediterranean; the coasts were barely defended, the population was in revolt, the area contained valuable raw materials and last but not least, it offered the possibility of breaking into Fortress Europe from the south-east with all the strategic and political consequences that implied. The most probable initial enemy objectives, the argument continued, were the large Italian islands which, together with southern and perhaps central Italy, would provide a bridge and a springboard for a further Allied advance across the Adriatic. On the Axis side the relative strengths on land, on sea and in the air meant that anything other than a defensive strategy was out of the question. Even for this, however, if the war was to be kept as far as possible from the heart of Europe and so from the frontiers of Germany, at least some temporary reinforcements for Italy and the Balkans were essential and this would inevitably involve drawing on the Eastern Front. Reserve formations were already being built up, primarily from the 'Tunis pot', in Sicily and to a lesser extent in Sardinia and Corsica, but as an immediate measure it was also necessary to reduce to the minimum the forces available in the Western theatre, where clearly no major landing operations were likely to take place so long as the main Allied forces were in the Mediterranean. A proposal was put forward by Mussolini, Kesselring and OKM to relieve the situation in the Mediterranean by an offensive through Spain to Gibraltar but this was (quite rightly) turned down by Hitler on the grounds that 'we are not in a position to carry out such an operation'.[1]

Initially Hitler agreed with our appreciation and the proposals emerging from it. He disagreed however with his staff and with Mussolini, both of whom considered Sicily the most likely objective for a landing; he considered that it would be Sardinia. He was reinforced in this opinion by the well-known trick played by the English secret services whereby papers fell into his hands apparently from an aircraft shot down over the Spanish coast, mentioning among other things the code name 'Sardine'. He also considered that these papers confirmed his view that the Peloponnese and the Dodecanese were the most likely Allied targets in the Balkans area – precisely the purpose of the British documents.[2] When he came to consider the lines which must be held even without Italy, he gave proof in the first instance of unwonted caution; on 19 May he said that an attack on the Balkans was 'almost more dangerous than the problem of Italy which, if the worst comes to the worst, we can always seal off somewhere' (sic!).[3] As the catastrophe in Tunis receded into the background and his confidence therefore revived, his horizon widened in its usual way and he now demanded that, even should Italy collapse, Fortress Europe should be defended everywhere on the perimeter. This now being his objective he appeared quite prepared to subordinate the interests of all other theatres of war, including the East, to the requirements of the Mediterranean whenever and for as long as necessary. There still being no superior co-ordinating staff, he himself gave verbal orders to OKH at the beginning of May to be prepared at any time for the rapid movement of six armoured divisions from the East to the South; these were to include three named SS Panzer Grenadier Divisions, whose appearance he considered would have a considerable effect upon the Fascist elements in the Italian armed forces and population. For similar reasons he instructed Field Marshal Rommel, who had now recovered, to make all preparations in collaboration with OKW to take over as Commander-in-Chief in Italy in place of Kesselring the moment an Italian collapse, in whatever form, took place. He himself briefed Rommel personally, as he did the Commander-in-Chief in the Balkans, Colonel-General Löhr. On the other hand, anxious to keep matters secret from our allies, he forbade any written instruction, merely taking from the OKW draft the code names 'Alarich' for German protective measures in Italy and 'Konstantin' for the Balkans.[4]

A more detailed account of these events and at the same time a striking picture of the atmosphere in German Supreme Headquarters at the time is provided by the following extracts from the shorthand record of certain briefing conferences.

Fragment no. 5
Discussion with Sonderführer* von Neurath concerning Italy on 20 May 1943

Present: The Führer Ambassador Hewel
       Field Marshal Keitel Major General Schmundt
       Field Marshal Rommel Colonel Scherff
       Colonel-General Löhr Lt-Col. Langemann
       Lt-General Breuer Sonderführer von Neurath
       Lt-General Warlimont Hauptsturmführer Günsche
Conference opened 13.19 hours.

HITLER: You've been in Sicily?
VON NEURATH: Yes, my Führer. I've been down there and I spoke to Roatta whom I have known since the days when he was head of the Attaché Section in Rome. Among other things he told me that he hadn't much confidence in the possibility of defending Sicily. He claimed that he was too weak and that his troops were

---

* Sonderführer was a title used for certain civilian experts who were given temporary military status. There is no English equivalent.

not properly equipped. Most important, he has only one motorized division; the rest are static troops. Every day the English are busy shooting up the engines on the railways so that movement and supply of locomotive spare parts is almost if not quite impossible. Crossing from Giovanni to Messina my impression was that traffic on this short crossing is almost at a standstill. I think there are six ferries in all but only one appeared to be there. This one was, as they put it, 'wrapped in cotton wool'; they are apparently being saved for more important purposes.

HITLER: What are these 'more important purposes'?

VON NEURATH: Well my Führer at one moment the Italians say 'when the war is over' – that's a very frequent expression; at another moment they say: 'you never know what's going to happen'. In any case this single ferry is not working. It may be there's just something wrong with it. But the German people I spoke to down there didn't think so. The German troops in Sicily have undoubtedly become pretty unpopular. It's easy to see why; the Sicilians consider that we have brought the war to their country and that we've snapped up more or less everything they have. We're now going to be the reason for the arrival of the English which however – and I must emphasize this – the Sicilian peasant would be quite pleased about; he thinks that would mean the end of his tribulations. This is quite understandable for the simple peasant; he can't look beyond the end of his nose and his object is always what will make life most comfortable quickest; once the English arrive, that's the end of the war. That's the general opinion in Southern Italy – that once the English come the thing will be over quicker than if the Germans are still there making life unpleasant.

HITLER: What are Italian official circles doing about this?

VON NEURATH: My Führer, as far as I know the Prefect and other officials who are still around are not doing much about it; they see it and they hear it but they always say the same thing. I've pointed it out to them on many different occasions, and have said: 'when a German soldier is openly cursed in the street as an enemy or something like that, which one hears of pretty often particularly in Sicily, what do you do about it? You can't let that sort of thing go on permanently.' Then they always say: 'what are we to do? That's public opinion! That's the way the people feel and you haven't made yourselves popular. You've requisitioned here and eaten up all their chickens there.' I reply: 'we're not here for fun but because there's a war on!' But they always seem to make some sort of an excuse; they merely say: 'We can't do anything about it; German soldiers curse Italian soldiers too'. In my view some more severe action ought to be taken, particularly by the authorities; they ought somehow to make more of an example of the more flagrant cases than they have done up to now.

HITLER: They won't do anything.

VON NEURATH: It's very difficult. In the north they do take action. But the Sicilian is quite different from, say, the northern Italian. Looked at overall it's most unpleasant that they should have let things get into this state.

The air threat or air superiority over Sicily is extremely serious. There's no doubt about it. I don't suppose that's news to you. Palermo has been pretty well flattened – large areas of the town including many beautiful old buildings, but it's primarily the harbour. It looks as if what many people have told me is now true, that the harbour's in such a state that the English won't be able to use it themselves. Apparently it's quite different with the results of the English attacks on Cagliari in Sardinia; it's striking that there the town and the warehouses adjoining the town have been practically rubbed out but the harbour installations and the moles are still more or less intact.

HITLER: That's the report....

WARLIMONT: That's what Admiral Ruge reported.

VON NEURATH: And then, my Führer, the Italian Crown Prince is down there as Commander-in-Chief of the Italian troops. I'm not quite clear if he is Commander-in-Chief of the Italian troops in Sardinia or Sicily or in Sicily and Southern Italy or only in Southern Italy.

It's significant that he holds a lot of inspections down there and that General Roatta is very busy with him; what's more on General Roatta's staff there are a large number of officers – Italian staff officers – who are known to be pretty pro-English. Some of them have English wives, others have English connections of some sort.

HITLER: What have I been saying all along!

VON NEURATH: Personally in so far as I know him (Roatta) I wouldn't trust him further than I could kick him.

HITLER: No!

VON NEURATH: I've always thought him very foxy.

HITLER: Foxy? He is the Fouché of the Fascist revolution, a completely spineless spy. He is actually a spy.

VON NEURATH: He is a born secret service man, a typical example of one. In any case I am convinced personally that he is up to some game. The Germans down there confirmed that it was noticeable that he was increasingly trying to build up some sort of a position for himself so that he would be all right if the English attacked Sicily. I don't know how far he'll be able to do this; I am not well up on that; I don't know. But I think that I can warn you now that he's definitely up to some dangerous game.

HITLER: My view exactly!

VON NEURATH: He is the absolute ruler of Sicily; there's no doubt about that; that he has achieved. His headquarters is in Enna. Everybody dances to his tune; that's confirmed on all hands and everybody says: 'without General Roatta's approval and authority nothing happens'.

HITLER: Have you talked to Kesselring about this?

VON NEURATH: I told General von Rintelen about it, my Führer.

HITLER: We must be very careful. Kesselring is no end of an optimist and we must be careful that in his optimism he doesn't fail to see the moment when optimism must be a thing of the past and severity must take its place.

VON NEURATH: The Luftwaffe in Sicily is for the moment having a very hard time. The attacks are so heavy that I assume our losses on the ground must be correspondingly high. In some cases they can hardly get off the ground.

WARLIMONT: It was somewhat different yesterday. 27 aircraft attacked, 7 were shot down and we lost none.

HITLER: There aren't enough airfields anyway.

KEITEL: They are too concentrated.

VON NEURATH: They are concentrated.

Morale in Rome goes up and down, my Führer. It is very unpleasant. We know about the plutocratic crowd; they of course think along English lines. The Duce is pushing new measures through with great energy and the people think that they will result in a more equitable distribution of the burden of the war. But I think this has all come a bit late. Black marketing and racketeering have become habits which have taken root and spread and it's going to be frightfully difficult to stop that in one fell swoop. What he is doing is certainly not making him popular just now.

HITLER: How can you get rid of this in a country where the leaders of the armed forces and of the State, etc. – where the whole country is nothing but a mass of corruption? Have you been in Northern Italy too?

VON NEURATH: No, my Führer, I only passed through.

HITLER: How long were you in Rome?

VON NEURATH: I was there seven days this time.

HITLER: Seven days. What is the attitude of the people in Rome to Germans?

VON NEURATH: It's such that the German soldiers have disappeared from the streets. Germans are only in uniform in the headquarters and at the railway station. All these agreements which I don't know in detail have resulted in the headquarters being moved out of the town so that the military impression ...

WARLIMONT: That comes from the time ...

VON NEURATH: No, that's nothing new. I believe it was urged by the Vatican. For the rest Rome looks just as before.

HITLER: Like in peace-time?

VON NEURATH: Yes, like in peace-time. No doubt about it. People were always astounded when they came from Africa and found the streets presenting a picture as if nothing had happened in the last two years. But you're always told: 'we are a poor people; we've not got the uniforms or the boots to give our soldiers, so it's much better that we just let them stroll in the streets'.

HITLER: They could at least have let us have them as a labour force; then they could have worked.

ROMMEL: That wouldn't suit the plutocrats. They'd have been 'spoilt' by us.

VON NEURATH: Naturally, in the Italian view people would have been completely 'spoilt' by our advanced social system.

HITLER: How many workers have we in Germany at the moment anyway? Do you know that, Hewel?

323

HEWEL: We had 230,000; they were to be gradually released from June onwards.

HITLER: From June?

HEWEL: I'm not completely in the picture, I can find out.

HITLER: You can do that afterwards.

KEITEL: Call Sauckel; he'll know exactly.

HITLER: And what about Roatta himself? I am quite clear in my mind: a certain section in that country has consistently sabotaged this war from the beginning. From the beginning! It was sabotaged first in 1939. By their sabotage these people succeeded at that time in stopping Italy's entry into the war. Or rather she didn't actually have to enter the war; if Italy had only declared at the time that she stood with Germany as she was obligated to do by the treaties, then the war wouldn't have broken out; the English wouldn't have started nor would the French. It was this way with the English: two hours after the decision had been taken that Italy would not enter the war – it was immediately transmitted to London – England hurriedly signed her Treaty of Assistance with the Poles. It hadn't been signed up till then. Two hours after the end of the meeting the treaty was signed. We've seen the same thing happen later. Every memorandum I sent to the Duce was immediately transmitted to England. So I only put in things which I wished definitely should get to England. That was the best way to get something through to England quickly.

VON NEURATH: This sort of trafficking with England is still going on. The night before last on the train the submarine commanders from Spezia told me that they had absolute proof that the battleship *Ventroy* (?) is in communication with Malta every morning from eight to ten. When a German security officer arrived to look into it and found out the truth, he was immediately arrested by the Italian Authorities on suspicion of espionage because they realized that he had found out the truth. That's a dead sure story.

HITLER: Is there anyone here from the Navy? It doesn't matter. We must watch out now that the submarines in the Aegean ...

KEITEL: I've already made a note of it. We'll include all that. There are new thoughts and ideas coming in all the time. [For the order dealing with the defection of Italy.]

HITLER: The ships and everything but especially the submarines.

KEITEL: All the Fleet auxiliaries are included in our notes.

WARLIMONT: On the French coast....

HITLER: If they're on the south coast of France they can stay there but not in Italian harbours – Spezia, etc. Günsche, measure on the map how far it is from England to Munich and the distance by air from Corsica to Munich. This Roatta is a spy though!

VON NEURATH: It's the same thing with the Göring Division. The worry is that we shan't be able to get it out of Sicily if the gentlemen there won't co-operate.

HITLER: As I've said, we must think whether we want to bring the Göring Division out. In my view perhaps we shouldn't.

KEITEL: I've always felt we should hold it in Southern Italy.

ROMMEL: It won't be able to get back. I don't believe what Field Marshal Kesselring has said – that it would be able to get back across the Straits under enemy pressure. A few individuals might get back but none of the equipment nor the bulk of the troops. It will all go down the drain.

KEITEL: Yes, it'll go down the drain. My suggestion was that we should quietly pull back parts of the Hermann Göring Division to Southern Italy so that we should still have the division available as such, but not do more than that. Can we get this ferry going again?

VON NEURATH: That ought to be possible straight away, Field Marshal.

HITLER: Well then!

VON NEURATH: We can get along even without this ferry.

HITLER: That's so. The ferry is not the decisive factor, determination's the decisive factor!.

VON NEURATH: It's certainly the most important!

HITLER: If you're determined you'll find a ferry. After all, when there were twenty or thirty lighters which we or the Italians had, ours were always 60 per cent serviceable and the Italians 10 per cent. There was always something wrong with them. And it was probably the same with the tanks. I've always been struck with the speed with which the Italian tanks melted away each time they were used; there was hardly an Italian tank available for two or three days afterwards; they were all in workshops. It's just a question of determination.

SCHMUNDT: England to Munich is 675 miles. And Corsica to Munich 470 miles.

HITLER: Another point – write this down: the ammunition supply for the anti-aircraft we have down there must be so worked that it can be stopped at any time and that they haven't got too big stocks. Keep them short!

WARLIMONT: Yes, the anti-aircraft we've transferred to the Italians.

HITLER: All the anti-aircraft.

ROMMEL: Would it be possible, my Führer, for the Italians to send more troops to Sicily and hold it instead of us?

HITLER: Anything's possible of course, the question is whether they *want* to defend it. If they really want to defend it then anything could be done. What worries me is not that it *can't* be defended – for with real determination it can be defended, there's no doubt about that; we could send over troops straight away – but what worries me is that these people have no will to defend it; you can see they've no will. The Duce may have the best intentions, but he will be sabotaged. I've read Bastianini's speech. It's a stinking speech of course; no doubt about that. This speech is – I don't know if you've read it....

KEITEL: No, I've not read it; I simply saw a short note this morning that he'd spoken.

HITLER: There was a telegram. I've got it over there. The general lines of the speech were: Italy and Germany are fighting for the right, etc. and the others for the wrong and unconditional surrender would be intolerable for the Italians – that sort of thing – and Italy will rally round her King and defend her army and her King. At the word 'King' there was ostentatious applause in the Senate from certain people. There now!

All in all a rotten speech, a very rotten speech and it merely reinforces my feeling that at any moment there may be a crisis there on the lines that we've been discussing. Löhr, you will have to think about your objectives and your problems from this point of view, and ...

KEITEL: My Führer, we have discussed with him thoroughly the points you made to him yesterday and also the written instructions you gave him yesterday; he knows the ideas.

LÖHR: Yes.

HITLER: And you?

BREUER: Yes.

HITLER: One has to be on the watch like a spider in its web.

Thank God I've always had a pretty good nose for everything so that I can generally smell things out before they happen. So far whenever the situation looks difficult it has always turned out for the best.

KEITEL: I'm not worried, but we must help him, particularly over Crete, Rhodes and the supply to the South.

HITLER: It is really of decisive importance that we hold the Balkans: copper, bauxite, chrome and most important of all to ensure that if the Italian affair happens, we don't have what I would call a complete crash there.

LÖHR: The situation is difficult until 117 Division is operational. It's arrived but is not yet ready.

HITLER: Meanwhile we may be able to get 1 Division down there.

LÖHR: If only we had a little armour.

HITLER: 1 Division will move so that ...

KEITEL: The fighting troops! We've laid this on exactly as we did on the Eastern Front. And then Colonel-General Löhr should also be warned that apart from detailed instructions which don't give anything away, only those who have to know should be let into the secret. No one else needs to know.

HITLER: No one needs to know why and all instructions you give you can give out of your own knowledge. No one needs to know more that is necessary for his job. For instance, if someone wants to know because of something to do with appointments, that is nothing to do with him. Every measure must be examined from this point of view: the principle must always be that we must be careful and in case there is a collapse, with which we must always reckon, we can intervene in order to help. That's the main theme isn't it?

LÖHR: Yes.

HITLER: It may of course happen quite differently – have you got anything else?

KEITEL: The Duce had an audience of the King this morning and has summoned Rintelen for later.

HITLER: What time was Rintelen's appointment?

WARLIMONT: He was to report straight away, my Führer, when he had an appointment. The last time I spoke to him was 11.15.

HITLER: How late is it now?

WARLIMONT: Two o'clock.

HITLER: When's Zeitzler coming?

WARLIMONT: He's coming at 3.30.

HEWEL: (*Producing a paper.*) These are just a few thoughts of mine.

HITLER: There's nothing new about these two worlds. They were always there. Even at the time of his Abyssinian war. If I'd stood out against Italy then, it would have collapsed straight away. I told him then that he should not have.... I told him at the time: 'I'll chalk that up against you'; we'll chalk this up against him too. I felt that quite clearly at the reception in Rome – I remember it quite well; these two worlds stood out quite clearly; on the one side was the obvious warmth of the Fascist reception, and so on, and on the other side the absolutely glacial atmosphere of the military and the Court. People who were more or less nobodies or otherwise cowards. In my view everybody who has more than £10,000 a year is in general a coward, because they want to go on living so that they can sit upon their £10,000. They lose all courage. If a man has £50,000 or £100,000 he is quite happy. Those people don't make a revolution or anything else. So they're against any war; so they don't mind if they see their people starving. They've got a hide like a rhinoceros. If there was just distribution in a land like that, if everybody got at least what he was entitled to, even the people in England would begin to wonder about the possibility of extending the Empire. But that's not the way it is. Those people have a damned good time; they deny themselves nothing, they've got everything and the poor devils down under are the only people who have a bad time. I saw in Rome how Fascism was placed all right. It couldn't do anything against the Court circles. A reception at court is something revolting to our ideas – I wouldn't even speak of it otherwise. But it was the same even at one given by the Duce, and why? Because the whole court circle pushed its way in. It's the same with Ciano. I was supposed to take Countess Edda Ciano in to dinner. Suddenly Philip turns up with his Mafalda and the whole programme has suddenly to be turned upside down. Great excitement. Then I had to take this Mafalda in to dinner. What does she mean to me? As far as I am concerned she's nothing but the wife of a German company director. Period! Nothing more! Then her mental equipment was not so great that I would say she would cast a spell over anybody. I'm not talking about whether she was good looking or not, but just about what she had up top. But that showed what it was like: completely penetrated and undermined by this gang in the Quirinal although all the Fascists and the Life Guards were there too; the split showed up quite clearly. The court officials said they were ...

The great question for me is what's the Duce's state of health? That's the decisive factor with a man who has to take such important decisions. What does he reckon the odds are, if for instance, the Fascist revolution goes under? There are the two problems. For either the nation is Fascist and sends the monarchy packing – what chance does he think the people have got – or what does he think will happen if the King takes over power. Difficult to say. He said something when we were dining together at Klessheim; he suddenly said: 'Führer, I don't know, I have no successor in the Fascist revolution; one can always find a successor as Head of State, but there's no successor in the revolution.' That's of course very tragic. His troubles began in 1941 while we were in the second headquarters down there on the railway – the Russian campaign had started.

KEITEL: Yes, down there in Galicia where the big tunnel was.

HITLER: In the evening we talked about the Russian commissars; that there couldn't be two authorities, etc. He was thinking hard and I was sitting there with him in the train. Then suddenly he said to me: 'You are right, Führer; there can't be two authorities in an army; but what do you think, Führer; what is one to do when one has officers who are against the government, who have second thoughts about the constitution? They say that because they are officers they can have mental reservations; when someone comes along with a constitution or a government they say: 'we are monarchists, we are servants of the King'. That's the difference; that was already the problem in 1941.

It was even worse in 1940. On 28 October when I came back – that was 1940 – he suddenly said: 'you see, I have no confidence in my soldiers; I've no confidence in my generals; I can't trust any of them.' That's what the man said to me on the very day that the offensive against Greece – or was it Albania – started.

Of course the question is – if the Duce was fifteen years younger today, there would probably be no problem; but he's sixty and that makes it more difficult – the question is how fit does he feel. But in my view these two worlds have always existed. They've never got rid of one of the two worlds and it sits there weaving its web – that shows up with everybody who comes from down there. This evening probably – what's his name?

KEITEL: Djurisic.

HITLER: He'll probably be with the King. You'll probably find this robber baron is related to the royal family. Oh yes, in ordinary life it's of course very difficult to marry off a daughter if her father's a sheep stealer and has been locked up umpteen times; but in Court circles there's no shame about that, it's rather an honour; all the titled gentry compete for the princesses, although the good Nikita is really nothing but a tramp who came from Austria, carried out one extortion after another and played the two off against each other – Italy and Austria. He's the chap who used the World Postal Union as part of the fraud and who swindled the Austrian State out of one-and-three-quarter million kroner. The Emperor had to pay for that out of his private purse. No end of a scandal! But that doesn't matter with 'well-bred people'.

KEITEL: My Führer, we've now got the general lines – nothing firm yet – for the instruction dealing with the possible employment of Rommel's army, also that for Löhr which I showed you yesterday. Löhr has been briefed on the general lines and he knows it all but he can't take any paper with him.

HITLER: We must be frightfully careful about papers just now.

KEITEL: I know that's what you want. New points arise every day, for instance this submarine question (*produces a paper*). There's a general introduction which says nothing and gives away as little as possible. But the main point is what comes later – command organization, forces, supply, all of these must be thought of and something new appears every day. Today for instance the U-boat question and the AA artillery question, etc. We would like to fill this out now. Rommel's already read it. He knows the general lines.

ROMMEL: Yes, I've been shown it.

KEITEL: He would like to add certain things. So far it's all theory. Then there are the orders which set things in motion – transport of forces and the like. But we must get the details clear.

Someone must go over to C.-in-C. West and discuss with him how he can, if necessary, get forces across to take over that part of the Mediterranean coast occupied by the Italians. These details only occur to one gradually; they only occur to one when you're writing it all down. That's why we've put it on paper.

HITLER: So you think, Rommel, it's better we should keep the two parachute divisions back?

ROMMEL: Yes, definitely.

HITLER: Both divisions will be available to you for your own operations.

KEITEL: We could move them into northern Italy.

ROMMEL: I am very worried, my Führer, that the Italians may suddenly collapse and close the frontier, particularly the Brenner. Those chaps have worked at it for five years. Gambara and also Navarini have let fall chance remarks to the effect that they might possibly turn and act against us. I don't trust these guys; it seems to me that if they change sides they might possibly make the English a present and say: 'we'll close the frontier and let no Germans either in or out'. So I think it's best if these divisions are initially outside. . . .

HITLER: I'd like to think that over quietly.

KEITEL: Yes, it's not so firm yet that we ought not to have another good look at it. But fairly soon we'd like to get the general lines clear. It must be put on paper or something will get forgotten. We can always change the introduction if you like, but the main lines. ...

HITLER: I'll read that through quietly.

WARLIMONT: The section on the South-east is attached.

KEITEL: That would be the basis for Rommel's job.

WARLIMONT: Do you want the maps as well?

HITLER: No, I don't need those.

WARLIMONT: They are very good maps; perhaps I could send them across to you, my Führer.

HITLER: Well, if you like.

(Conference ended 1530 hours)

For all those involved this was the start of planning for the defence of the Mediterranean without Italy. Until our Axis partner finally collapsed in September 1943 the principle was that nothing must be done that could not equally well serve for a *common* defence and that anything must be avoided which could give the Italians any excuse for renouncing the alliance. There were therefore definite limitations on any German action which concerned Italian territory, whether or not it was intended to ensure our own security in the event of Italy going out of the war.[5]

The true German intentions cast a shadow over relations with Italy which as the months went by led to increasingly serious disagreements. We were trying, as a precaution, to get the largest number of German formations into Italy as quickly as possible; although this was completely justified by the existing situation, it encountered increasing Italian mistrust which conversely increased Hitler's suspicions. On our own side the proposal to transfer a number of armoured formations from the eastern theatre to the Mediterranean revived the smouldering rivalry between OKH and OKW. Both these problems showed up clearly the faulty organization of the Supreme Command and the lack of a superior co-ordinating staff.

At the beginning of May, Kesselring announced to Mussolini that three new divisions would be formed from the not inconsiderable remnants of German formations which had not got across to Tunis. This met with the most unforthcoming reply that three divisions would make no difference to the situation: what he wanted was tanks and aircraft. A few days later, on 12 May, after an acrid discussion between Ambrosio and Kesselring about the command of German troops on Italian territory, Mussolini flatly refused to allow two additional German divisions into Italy; instead he sent a letter to Hitler the same day demanding immediate delivery of 300 tanks, 50 anti-aircraft batteries, and aircraft for 50 fighter squadrons, a figure which the chief of the Comando Supremo raised on 21 June 1943 to 2,000 aircraft and equipment for 17 tank battalions, 33 self-propelled artillery battalions, 18 anti-tank or assault gun battalions and 37 mixed anti-aircraft battalions.[6] These demands could only be met in so far as German war material was available over and above our own requirements and could be delivered immediately; it would not have been right to do more. Meanwhile whatever their reasons, a number of Italian generals succeeded by the end of June in wearing down Mussolini's objections so that, in addition to the three newly-formed divisions, two German armoured divisions and two Panzer Grenadier Divisions from the West were moved into Italy. All however were lacking in equipment and training which could not be made good before August. German reinforcements for the Balkans were even smaller – and here there were no Italian objections. In general all that could be done was to move the few formations we had, most of which were not fit for battle, nearer the coasts which were everywhere occupied by Italian troops. Hitler did manage to get one solitary armoured division, also from the West, into the Peloponnese, disregarding the fact that there was no possibility of using it as a formation anywhere in that mountainous country.[7]

There was no intention of withdrawing forces from the East other than in an exceptional emergency, but it was important for OKW that the divisions selected should not be otherwise committed or even employed until further orders. The usual difficulties were encountered, for Zeitzler refused to give OKW any detailed information regarding the location of units or plans for their movement. Since in many other respects OKH was necessarily involved in plans for the South, Zeitzler seized the opportunity to make a new attempt to get the command of army forces in Italy and the Balkans once more under OKH. Our disagreements were bedevilled by the fact that the army formations held in readiness for the Mediterranean theatre were at the same time the core of the attacking forces for the only major offensive operation of 1943 in the East. The operation had been planned since March and was intended to iron out the Kursk salient; it was known as 'Citadel'. The date for this attack was put off again and again and it therefore became more and more probable that it would overlap with the anticipated start of the Allied offensive in the Mediterranean. On 18 June therefore the OKW Operations Staff submitted an appreciation to Hitler leading up to the proposal that, until the situation had been clarified, Citadel should be cancelled and that a strong operational reserve at the disposal of the Supreme Command should be constituted both in the East and in Germany, the latter by the formation of new units. The same day Hitler decided that 'although he appreciated the point of view of OKW', Operation Citadel should definitely be carried out, and he laid down the date of the attack as initially 3 and subsequently 5 July. The result was that this unhappy operation, which in Hitler's words 'should be a beacon to the world', opened just five days before the Allied landing in Sicily began; the forces employed in the attack, which were at the same time the most important reserves in the hands of the Supreme Command, were in most cases reduced to remnants. [8]

Jodl had returned from leave towards the end of June and he also raised emphatic objection to the premature commitment of the central reserves in the East; he pointed out both verbally and in writing that a local success was all that could be hoped for from Operation Citadel and that it could have no strategic significance for the overall situation. Hitler was clearly shaken but was eventually influenced by others and stuck to his decision. As a by-product he apparently found it necessary to take up several days of his own and his staff's time dealing with a complaint by Zeitzler that Jodl's representations constituted interference with the responsibilities of the Army. [9] There have been many accounts to the effect that, after it had been so often postponed, Zeitzler himself no longer wanted to carry out Operation Citadel. With a minor transposition, a remark of Hindenburg's is relevant here; he was often asked who should really get the credit for the victory of Tannenberg, himself or General Ludendorff; the old man is said to have given the apt reply: 'what do you think? Who would have had to carry the responsibility if the battle had been lost?' Operation Citadel was more than a battle lost; it handed the Russians the initiative and we never recovered it again right up to the end of the war.

THE FALL OF MUSSOLINI

Hitler's faith in Italy had from the outset been based almost exclusively on Mussolini personally. When therefore on 14 May Hitler asked Grand Admiral Dönitz, who had just returned from Rome, whether he thought 'that the Duce was determined to go all the way with Germany right to the end', all those who heard it realized that the whole basis of the military alliance was in question. Commander-in-Chief Navy's report had given Hitler no particular grounds for this unprecedented suspicion but a few days later he repeated it before a wider audience. His own observations and pre-occupations were probably at the bottom of it, rather than Italy's unfavourable military situation and the unhappy consequences these seemed likely to produce. It had started with his preoccupation over Mussolini's poor state of health, only too obvious at the meeting in April; his suspicion grew as a result of the dissensions over the Balkans which had lately led to an unwontedly sharp exchange of letters; finally there was Mussolini's aversion to the despatch of further German troops to Italy. He had even been unwilling to receive the Waffen-SS training teams accompanying the equipment for an armoured division which Hitler had 'given' him. A possible explanation for his attitude was that as Head of the Italian Government he wanted Italy to be defended only by Italians; but this was belied by the news, confirmed from many quarters, that in the late spring of 1943 work had been resumed on the fortifications on the Italian side of the Alps frontier, and these for the most part could only be directed against Germany. Remarkably enough however, Hitler tried to pass over in silence both this fact and its unmistakable far-reaching implications. On the other hand he appeared most uneasy when Mussolini refused, except on conditions, to accept an invitation to a further meeting in the second half of May. All preparations were made – the headquarters had just returned to East Prussia and was now hurriedly transferred back to Berchtesgaden; the meeting did not take place however, ostensibly because Mussolini would only meet on Italian soil which Hitler refused to do on grounds of personal security. Meanwhile large and completely impossible demands for delivery of German war material continued to arrive; they began to look more like a pretext to get out of the war than evidence of a determination to make a new start.[10]

During the following weeks the Allies did no more than capture, almost without a fight, the small, heavily fortified Italian island of Pantelleria, the 'Italian Gibraltar'. Hitler began gradually, though somewhat hesitantly, to recover his confidence in his Italian ally. He would frequently say that the ordinary Italian soldier and the young officer reared in the school of Fascism, when called upon to defend their Motherland, would perhaps give proof of soldierly qualities surprising both to friend and foe. This idealistic estimate based on airy-fairy ideas soon began to obscure the military realities, the most important of which was that there was a fatal gap between the level of equipment of Italian forces and those of the Allies. Even Kesselring pleaded for a sober factual estimate; but none was made.[11]

The blanket of self-deception and wishful thinking was rent to pieces by the enemy landing in Sicily on 10 July 1943. On the third day of the attack Commander-in-Chief South had to admit, not only that the Italian coastal defence, including that of the recently fortified base of Augusta, had failed totally but that the island 'could not be held with German forces alone'.[12]

This estimate was Kesselring's way of showing his disappointment, not only with the Italians whom he now reproached bitterly, but also with Hitler for having refused to release for the defence of Sicily the additional German formations which had meanwhile been assembled in Southern Italy. Preoccupation over the possible collapse of Italy had been a good enough reason for Hitler's hesitation but this was not recognized in Rome, still less when the success of the landing led to a sudden snap decision to release them. In addition to the two divisions and numerous anti-aircraft units already in action on the island, two further German divisions together with other units were now to be hurriedly flown or otherwise transported to Sicily. Mussolini's principle demand was for air support and major Luftwaffe reinforcements were now ordered up from the West, South-east and North. In the enthusiasm created by this belated activity both Dictators rapidly reverted to unrealistic ideas; Hitler thought that the enemy could be thrown back into the sea and Mussolini telegraphed that: 'both the moral and material effects on the enemy of a defeat at his first attempt to enter Europe would be incalculable'.[13]

These alluring prospects soon disappeared, and on 13 July Hitler issued an order taking over command in Sicily himself. Kesselring was still wanting to fight for time but Hitler laid down that the objective should be: 'to halt the enemy forward of Etna'. It fell to General Hube, commanding XIV Armoured Corps, to do the best he could with this instruction and an OKW officer was despatched to tell him verbally 'unobtrusively to assume overall command of the Sicily bridgehead himself, cutting out all Italian Headquarters'.[14] In addition a 'German Commandant of the Straits of Messina' was appointed and authorized, if necessary, to use his own men to man the remaining Italian coastal batteries. Thus the German Supreme Command – working from East Prussia! – took a direct hand in matters which were the responsibility of subordinate Italian Headquarters in the island. Mussolini and the Comando Supremo made no more than a passing protest. Hitler must have felt that he was justified when, via Kesselring, he learnt that Mussolini had issued an urgent appeal pointing out the 'serious consequences for the morale of both the Italian and German peoples' which the loss of Sicily would entail.[15]

Thus a small bridgehead around Etna had become a vital point, decisive for the fate of the Mediterranean theatre, the future of the Axis and perhaps much more besides. In this situation Jodl on 15 July personally produced one of his rare written appreciations.[16] His object was clearly to get the main strategic picture back into the foreground; he went even further than Kesselring and stated flatly that 'as far as can be foreseen Sicily cannot be held'; it was not clear, he continued, whether Sardinia or Corsica, the Italian mainland or Greece would be the enemy's next objective but in any event the main object of our strategy must be to safeguard Southern Italy as the glacis for the defence of the Balkan peninsula. He then reverted to the conclusion which his staff had reached on purely military grounds on 19 June, the day after the unfortunate decision regarding Citadel,[17] and stated that unless the political situation was completely cleared up, it would 'be irresponsible' to keep German troops south of the Apennines, ie south of the mountain range running east and west north of the Arno. The first pre-requisite was 'to clean up the Italian military command organization and to take the most energetic measures against any sign of disintegration in the Italian armed forces'. Echoing many of Hitler's statements of this period he accused 'wide circles within the Italian officer corps of masked treachery' and attributed to the Comando Supremo the intention of using the German formations on Italian soil 'in such a manner as to ensure their annihilation'. Following Hitler's example Jodl liked using high-sounding phrases and in his peroration called for 'a general clean-up in Italy as the second phase of the Fascist revolution' which must end in the 'elimination of the present Comando Supremo and the arrest of all persons hostile to us'. German generals were to take over command at all important points in the Mediterranean and their head should be Field Marshal Rommel 'as being the only commander under whom many officers and soldiers in Italy would gladly serve'. There were then detailed proposals for 'unity of command', which in Italy should nominally be held by Mussolini but in the Balkans be transferred to Germans. Finally there was a 'demand to Italy' that reinforcements for Italian troops in exposed areas, as for example in southern Italy, should invariably be provided on the same scale and at the same rate as the German. This demand remained on the agenda right up to the break-up of the Axis; it was never met.

*

In its politico-military sections this dissertation did little more than repeat views which had been expressed often enough recently in the inner circle but it gave the most open expression yet to the discords which history shows are the invariable forerunner of the collapse of a military alliance. Hitler recoiled before Jodl's conclusions primarily out of consideration for Mussolini's prestige. Instead he tried, as a first step, to obtain a more reassuring picture of affairs in Italy, and ordered to the headquarters certain military leaders and political personalities in whom he had confidence. But during the resulting discussions both Grand Admiral Dönitz and Field Marshal Rommel expressed views similar to those of Jodl; Rommel even went so far as to say that there was not a single general in the Italian Army on whom he would rely to co-operate unreservedly with Germany. Hitler could see the whole basis of his Axis policy crumbling and gave evidence of unwonted self-criticism by merely saying: 'there must nevertheless be some worthwhile people in Italy; they can't all have become bad all of a sudden'. He seemed however sufficiently impressed to conclude that Germany was now alone in the Mediterranean and could not do more than defend Northern Italy. As before he considered the best solution to be to keep our ally within the Axis, provided always that we could be sure that she would remain loyal. Discussions followed with the German Ambassador who had been summoned from Rome and with Prince Philip of Hesse, the confidential liaison officer to the Italian Court. From these emerged the decision to seek final clarification by reviving the meeting with Mussolini which had been postponed since Tunis. Agreement was hurriedly reached on a meeting in Northern Italy. That same day, 18 July, we set off for Berchtesgaden. Hitler now set aside even his worry over his personal security. Before leaving, however, he was persuaded to postpone the announcement of Rommel as the commander selected to defend the Apennine peninsula – this on representations from Göring and the German Ambassador in Rome, both of whom considered that they knew the frame of mind of Mussolini and the Italian public better than did Hitler and Jodl.[18]

The meeting in Northern Italy was known as the Feltre meeting, after the town where was the country house in which it took place; it was the first of three which preceded the break-up of the Axis. It was also the last in the long series at which both Hitler and

Mussolini apparently both wielded their old power. But the day at Feltre opened under unhappy auguries. It started with Hitler's decision to call off Operation Citadel in the East as offering no prospect of success – a decision in which the situation in the Mediterranean and the requirements of the other theatres of war played no part; it ended with a sharpening of the disagreements between the two allies. With hindsight it is clear that Mussolini, and still more his advisers, had come to Feltre determined to take Italy out of the war with or without the agreement of Germany. On his side Hitler's primary object was to bolster up his friend and ally and make sure of his continued support.

A night was spent in Berchtesgaden and very early in the morning (because of the danger from enemy aircraft) we landed at an airfield near Treviso. We were received by Mussolini who was in his usual dark-grey militia uniform; there was then a journey of at least two hours by car, rail and then car again, offering little opportunity for a preliminary *prise de contact*. On arrival at the country house we assembled informally in a summerhouse, but merely to listen to an interminable speech from Hitler. He dealt principally with the raw material situation, the comparative level of armaments, manpower and losses on each side both past and future – all set out in propagandist and didactic terms. The evening before I had submitted a memorandum to Hitler based on that of Jodl, though without its political overtones, giving the most urgent military points under the heading 'Unity of Command', not a word on the subject appeared. He became a little clearer on the question of Sicily and to the utter astonishment of his staff stated among other things that a number of additional German formations would be sent to the island which 'would enable us ultimately to take the offensive'. At this point however he made formal demands that the supply of Sicily should be assured and the fighting capacity of the Italian forces raised. If the worst came to the worst, he concluded, the fight must be continued on the mainland and in the Balkans, where the interior must be completely pacified in order to free all available forces for coastal defence.

Hitler was the only one to speak. An Italian duty officer appeared with a message, which Mussolini handed on to Hitler, that the first Allied air attack on Rome had taken place that very morning; Hitler took no notice of this news and after a pause of only a second or two his flow of words continued.

Highly embarrassed by the course of the 'discussions', we then

339

went to lunch, which Mussolini and Hitler took apart from their staffs. Immediately thereafter we started the journey home. I was so concerned to get the urgent question of command organization cleared up that, when we transferred from the cars to the train, I got Keitel to go across the rails to Hitler to remind him of it. Keitel returned merely with the answer that 'the conditions for the fulfilment of our requirements do not exist'. During the rail journey there was some discussion between the senior representatives of the two Supreme Commands but these were perforce limited to further examination of some of the questions already raised by Hitler.[19]

Subsequent accounts have shown that immediately on returning from Feltre, Mussolini accepted the views of his advisers and as early as 20 July informed the King that he hoped by the middle of September 1943 to have dissolved the alliance with Germany.[20] Hitler on the other hand returned from the meeting convinced that he had once more brought his friend and ally back on the rails.[21] The Comando Supremo was pressing for the despatch of further German troops to Italy and Hitler became all the more ready to meet their requirements when a series of assurances arrived from Rome during the next few days that Sicily would be held 'with all our resources' and 'to the last man'. Italy further declared that she was in agreement with the new command organization for the Balkans which OKW had been urging for so long. Field Marshal Rommel had been designated as the only German commander capable of dealing with the situation should things in Italy go wrong, but Jodl was now so far influenced by this new-found confidence in the loyalty and determination of our ally that he proposed to Hitler that Rommel should be given the command in Greece, in spite of the fact that for weeks now he had been preparing himself for his job in Italy. Jodl also instructed his staff to cancel the orders for plans Alarich and Konstantin.[22]

Only a few days later reports from the German Military Liaison Officer in Rome began to present quite a different picture. People were most disappointed there, so ran General von Rintelen's report, at the small scale of German assistance recently announced; it was far below expectations. The prospects for a successful defence of Sicily were rated 'very small'. In addition 'all influential military and political quarters' were expressing grave doubts whether Germany was capable of furnishing effective assistance 'in the defence against invasion'. It was also indicative that at the same time the

Italian military authorities began to press with increased insistence for all German formations in Italy to be placed under their command. The situation seemed even more remarkable when a number of reports arrived that the Italian fortifications on the Alpine frontier were being supplied with ammunition and the frontier garrisons alerted, while German rail transport was being stopped at the Brenner for no apparent reason.[23]

Finally on 24 July Hitler's special attention was aroused by the politically important news that the Fascist Grand Council had been summoned to meet in Rome. This was followed by a report that 'there is talk of the Duce having been persuaded to give up personal command of the three Services'.[24] All this led to unmistakable uneasiness in German Supreme Headquarters and the briefing conference on the following day became more or less designedly a 'demonstration of determination'. First the situation in the Etna bridgehead was discussed and the opinion expressed that it could be held indefinitely, then the good progress in defensive preparations in Sardinia. At this point Jodl produced a *Proposal for Overall Distribution of Forces up to the Autumn*. In this OKW made one more attempt to substitute some long-term strategy for snap decisions by Hitler, to get a policy more in keeping with Germany's defensive posture and to get strong, concentrated 'operational groups' formed both in Italy and the Balkans as reserves. This was a wide-ranging document and therefore necessarily dealt with the Eastern Front, particularly in view of its drain on our resources and of the fact that, since the failure at Kursk, the best that could be hoped for there was to stabilize the situation. Hitler was invariably influenced by graphic statistics and so agreed with our picture of the situation at once. As regards the Eastern theatre he said: 'it must give up forces. That is quite clear. Here, (meaning the Mediterranean) is where the decisive events will take place. If the worst comes to the worst we must milk the East even more. That must be done.' To show how his thoughts regarding Italy were running he then added: 'we ought surely to be able quickly to form ten to twelve or thirteen divisions out of the wreckage of the Italian Army'.[25]

The OKW's great plan was destined never to be carried out. The Eastern theatre continued to suck in more forces, the proposal to form a reserve in the Balkans proved unnecessary and in Italy the plan was rapidly overtaken by events. Hitler's uneasiness was such that during this same conference he interrupted Jodl's presentation and turned abruptly to the representative of the Foreign Ministry to ask what was the state of affairs in Rome. The arguments and counter-arguments as given in the following extract from the record produce a striking picture of the last hours preceding the fall of Mussolini.

Fragment no. 13
   Midday Briefing Conference, 25 July 1943

HITLER: Any news Hewel?

HEWEL: Nothing definite yet. Mackensen has merely sent a telegram suggesting that we might say that the Reichsmarschall's trip* is now doubtful because of the latest events. We shall get more details. So far he has found out that Farinacci has finally persuaded the Duce to call a meeting of the Fascist Grand Council. That was scheduled for yesterday; it was postponed to 10 pm because agreement could not be reached on the agenda. He has heard from various quarters that it was a par-ticularly stormy meeting. Since the members are sworn to secrecy he hasn't got anything authentic yet – merely rumour. One of the most persistent rumours is that they are trying to persuade the Duce to install a Head of Government, a Prime Minister, who in fact would be a politician, Orlando, who is eighty-three and played quite a part during the First World War. The Duce would be President of the Grand Fascist Empire. These are all just rumours; we must wait.

   It's also said that at ten o'clock this morning the Duce and a number of generals went to see the King and are still there. The King has received a whole series of personalities. Among others Buffarini is there.

HITLER: Who's he?

HEWEL: Buffarini is a Fascist. Another report I have on ... is that this crisis in the Party is becoming a crisis of the State. It is said that the Duce is still much influenced by the meeting in northern Italy and is determined to continue the fight. That's all that's come through so far.

HITLER: That fellow Farinacci is lucky that he was in Italy and not here when he pulled his trick. If he had been here I would

* For Mussolini's birthday 29 July.

have had him carted off straight away by Himmler. That's what happens here on these occasions. What's going to come out of it anyway?

HEWEL: But as I've said Mackensen stresses that these are only rumours. It's clear there's a real crisis there, and Mackensen thinks that we should do nothing and be very careful in this crisis; the Duce has repeatedly told him that he doesn't want his birthday mentioned. Mackensen is going to find out what people think about it. To let the Reichsmarschall appear down there just now would of course be.... But I'll get more details.

HITLER: That's the state of affairs. Göring has been through many crises with me and in a crisis he's ice cold. You can't have a better adviser in a crisis than Göring. In a crisis he's forceful and ice cold. I've always noticed that when it's a case of break or bend he's ruthless and as hard as iron. You can't have a better man; a better man can't be found. He's been through all the crises with me, the worst crises, and that's when he's ice cold. Every time things got really bad he became ice cold. Well, we'll see.

Throughout the evening, the night and the morning of the next day news came tumbling in from Rome about the 'resignation' of Mussolini and the formation of a new government under Marshal Badoglio. In German Supreme Headquarters this was taken to mean that Italy was preparing to lay down her arms. During the three briefing conferences which took place during this period those present saw Hitler give a shocking and shattering exhibition of confusion and lack of balance. Of course there were difficult decisions to be taken, particularly since Rommel had just been despatched to Salonika and plans Alarich and Konstantin, which contrary to Jodl's orders had not yet been cancelled, could not be put into operation because of continued assurances from Rome that the war would be continued on the side of Germany. By one of the accidents of history Hitler's behaviour in all its details can be seen from the records of three successive conferences all of which have been preserved;[26] basically he was simply yelling for revenge and retribution. It was only with the greatest difficulty that Jodl was able to get any orderly military thinking done and turn Hitler's mind on to the urgent necessities of the situation.

343

Fragment no. 14
  Briefing Conference, 25 July 1943, 2130 hours

HITLER: You know about the developments in Italy?

KEITEL: I merely heard the last few words.

HITLER: The Duce has resigned. It is not confirmed yet. Badoglio has taken over the government. The Duce has resigned.

KEITEL: On his own initiative, my Führer?

HITLER: Probably at the request of the King under pressure from the Court. I told you yesterday where the King stood.

JODL: Badoglio has taken over the government.

HITLER: Badoglio has taken over the government and he is our bitterest enemy. We must see straight away whether we can find a method of getting our people back on to the main land [*from Sicily*].

JODL: The decisive point is are the Italians going to fight or not?

HITLER: They say they'll fight but that's treachery! We must be quite clear: it's pure treachery! I am still simply waiting for news of what the Duce says. What's-his-name is now trying to speak to the Duce. I hope he'll get hold of him. I'd like to get the Duce here straight away if he can be got hold of, so that we can straight away get him back to Germany.

JODL: There's only one thing to do if there's any doubt.

HITLER: I've been thinking about ordering 3 Panzer Grenadier Division to occupy Rome forthwith and lay hands on the whole government.

JODL: These troops here can remain until those are withdrawn.

HITLER: All we can do is to try and get the men back in German ships, abandoning the equipment – equipment here, equipment there – doesn't matter. The men are more important. I'll be getting news from Mackensen any minute, then we'll see what comes next. But anyway the troops here [*Sicily*] must be off straight away!

JODL: Yes.

HITLER: The most important thing now is to secure the Alpine passes; we must be ready to gain contact with the Italian Fourth Army and we must lay hands straight away on the French passes. That's the most important thing. To do this we must get formations down straight away, if necessary 24 Armoured Division.

KEITEL: That's the worst thing that could happen, that we should not get the passes.

HITLER: Has Rommel left yet?

JODL: Yes, Rommel's left.

HITLER: Where is he now? Is he still in Wiener Neustadt?

KEITEL: We can check that.

HITLER: Check straight away where Rommel is. We must ensure that we now.... Anyway one armoured division is ready that's 24. The most important thing is to get 24 Armoured Division into this area straight away so that it can then be pushed through here on one of the railways and then concentrated here. Then the Feldherrnhalle Division, which must be about here, must at least lay hands on the passes. That leaves us only one division near Rome. Is the whole of 3 Panzer Grenadier Division here in the area of Rome?

JODL: It's there but not fully mobile, only partially mobile.

HITLER: What equipment and assault guns has it?

BUHLE: 3 Panzer Grenadier Division has 42 assault guns.

HITLER: Then, thank God, we've still got the Parachute Division here. Under all circumstances we must rescue the people here [*Sicily*]; they're no good here; they must cross, particularly the paratroops and the Göring Division. The equipment doesn't matter a damn, they must blow it up or destroy it. But we must get the men back. There are 70,000 men there now. If they're flown out they'll be back quickly. They must put out a screen here and then withdraw the lot. Only personal equipment, leave everything else behind, they don't want more. We can deal with the Italians with small arms. No point in holding here. If you want to hold on to something all you can do is to hold here, but not here. Here we shan't get away with it. Subsequently we shall have to withdraw to somewhere about here, that's obvious. The most important thing is to get the formations across quickly and get the Leibstandarte away and on the move.

ZEITZLER: Yes, I'll give the order straight away.

KEITEL: Destination as before.

ZEITZLER: We have to prepare first. I must first get the rolling-stock up. I could work on thirty-six trains a day – thirty-six trains that means two to three days before I've got the rolling-stock. I'll start right away.

(*General Zeitzler leaves*)

345

JODL: We should really wait for precise reports of what's going on.

HITLER: Of course but on our side we must start thinking. There's no doubt about one thing: being traitors of course they'll say that they'll stick to us, that's clear. But that's treachery and they won't stick to us.

KEITEL: Has anyone talked to this fellow Badoglio, yet?

HITLER: We've got the following report meanwhile: Yesterday the Duce appeared at the Grand Council. At the Grand Council were Grandi whom I've always thought a swine, Bottai and above all that fellow Ciano. They all spoke against Germany in the Grand Council saying there was no point in carrying on the war further and they must try and get Italy out of it somehow. A few were against it. Farinacci etc. spoke up but they weren't as effective as those on the other side. Then this evening the Duce told Mackensen that under all circumstances he was going to go on fighting and would not surrender. Then suddenly I heard that Badoglio wanted to speak to Mackensen. Mackensen said he had nothing to talk to him about. Thereupon Badoglio became more insistent and eventually sent a man....

HEWEL: In fact Mackensen sent one of his people to Badoglio.

HITLER: He told him that the King had just charged him with forming a government, now that the Duce had laid down his office. What does he mean by 'laid down'? Probably this bum.... I've said that that statement of Philip's ... we've gathered that already.

KEITEL: Absolutely the attitude of the Royal House! For the moment the Duce has got nothing to act with – nothing, no troops.

HITLER: Nothing! I always told him that; he's got nothing! It's true he's got nothing. Those people took good care to ensure he had nothing to act with.

The Minister has now instructed Mackensen to call at the Foreign Ministry. He'll probably get the official announcement there. I assume that's what it'll be. Then the Minister asked if I agreed that Mackensen should go and see the Duce straightaway. I told him he should go and see him and if possible try and persuade him to come to Germany at once. I should like to think he wants to talk to me. If the Duce comes that'll be good – if he comes – I don't know. If the Duce comes to

346

Germany and talks to me that's good. If he doesn't come or if he can't or if he resigns because he doesn't feel fit – which wouldn't surprise me with such a pack of traitors – then one doesn't know. Anyway what's-his-name said straightaway that the war would be continued but that doesn't mean a thing. They have to do that because that's treachery. But we can play the same game; we'll get everything ready to lay hands on the whole boiling, the whole crew. I'll send a man down tomorrow to the Commander of 3 Panzer Grenadier Division with an order to drive into Rome with a special detachment and arrest the whole government, the King – all that scum but primarily the Crown Prince – to get hold of this rabble, principally Badoglio and the whole gang. And then you watch them creep and crawl and in two or three days there'll be another *coup*.

KEITEL: The only unit from plan Alarich still on the move is 715 Division.

HITLER: Has it anyway got the assault guns, all 42 of them?

BUHLE: It must have the 42 assault guns. They all arrived.

JODL: Here is the layout (*produces a paper*).

HITLER: How far are they from Rome?

JODL: About sixty miles.

HITLER: Sixty? Forty miles! It can't be more than that. If he gets going with motorized troops he can get in and arrest all that scum.

KEITEL: Two hours.

JODL: Thirty-five to forty miles.

HITLER: That's no distance.

WAIZENEGGER: Forty-two assault guns in the division.

HITLER: Are they there with the division?

WAIZENEGGER: Yes.

HITLER: Jodl, work that out straight away.

JODL: Six battalions.

KEITEL: Ready for action, five only partially ready.

HITLER: Jodl work out straight away an order we can send to 3 Panzer Grenadier Division, an order telling them to tell no one but to drive into Rome with their assault guns and arrest the Government, the King and the whole crew. Most important of all I want the Crown Prince.

KEITEL: He's more important than the old man.

BODENSCHATZ: We must arrange to pack them into an aircraft and fly them off straight away.

HITLER: Into the aircraft and straight off, straight off!

BODENSCHATZ: Provided we don't lose the baby on the airfield!

HITLER: There'll be another crew in a week you see.... Then I'd like to speak to Göring.

BODENSCHATZ: I'll tell him straight away.

HITLER: Of course the decisive moment will come when we've got enough strength to move in there and disarm the whole gang. The story must be that a *coup* against Fascism was carried out led by treacherous generals and Ciano – who isn't popular anyway.

(Telephone conversation between Hitler and Göring – the stenographer could not hear Göring's questions or answers.)

Hello Göring. I don't know. Have you had any news – well there's no direct confirmation yet but there's hardly any doubt that the Duce has resigned and that Badoglio has taken his place. It's not a question of possibilities in Rome, it's a question of fact. – That's the truth, Göring, no doubt about it – what? – I don't know; we're trying to find out – of course that's nonsense; he'll keep going but don't ask me how. Now they will see how we keep going. That's all I wanted to say to you. Under these circumstances I think it would be a good idea for you to come here straight away. What? – I don't know. I'll tell you about that then. But you'd better assume that it's true.

(End of telephone conversation)

We've had a mess like this once before: that was when the government fell here.*

(KEITEL: 10.0 am in the main conference room.)

HITLER: That was a bit different. I trust they haven't arrested the Duce. But if they have it's even more important that we go in there.

JODL: That would of course be different. Then we should have to go in. The most important thing is to get the trains across which are now stuck here. The order was given yesterday that everything should if possible move into northern Italy even if they can't get further forward than this, so that at least

---

* Belgrade, at the end of March 1941.

we can get some forces across into northern Italy here. Then in that case....

BUHLE: These people here are also available.

HITLER: Use them straight away! Straight away – if necessary of course.

KEITEL: That's why we withdrew them as far as this.

HITLER: We can do that straight away, that's clear.

KEITEL: The next infantry division.

HITLER: Splendid! Wave them on. If they're not used here they will probably ... of course treachery alters everything.... We must be clear this bastard Badoglio has been working against us all the time, here, in North Africa and here, everywhere. Has Rommel gone?

DARGES: We'll check at once, my Führer.

HITLER: If he's gone we must of course get him back straight away.

KEITEL: It's possible that he'll still be in Wiener Neustadt. He went to get his baggage.

HITLER: Then get him to come up here first thing tomorrow morning in a Condor and I'll give him his orders. If the thing has developed, then of course everything will be under the command of Field Marshal Rommel and everybody will take orders from him only. Is Himmler here?

DARGES: No he's on the road; he's due back tomorrow.

HITLER: Check that. (Darges: Yes.) We must draw up a list straight away. It must obviously include Ciano and then Badoglio and many others, primarily of course the whole gang but obviously Badoglio dead or alive. (Hewel: Yes.) The first measures to be taken are: 1, to get the formations straight away on the move towards the frontier so that we can get across whatever we can, so that these formations can ...

JODL: These formations down here must be told straight away what their job is, but under all circumstances they must lay hands on all the passes.

KEITEL: That was in the secret instructions to the battalion in Innsbruck.

HITLER: Is it still there?

KEITEL: It's still there but the Mountain Warfare School has been disbanded. 715 has instructions and also 3 Panzer Grenadier Division and either the HQ or one regiment of Feldherrnhalle.

3 Panzer Grenadier have their instructions. They had a secret instruction from C.-in-C. West for Plan Alarich. They were forbidden to give any information or make any extracts so as not to attract attention to these things. 3 Panzer Grenadier can do it. We hope they can collaborate with ...

HITLER: Aren't they there?

KEITEL: No, they're not there.

VON PUTTKAMER: We must warn the Navy about what's happened. They're scattered about everywhere all among the Italians in the harbours.

HITLER: Of course, but as far as possible we must get people across here.

GÜNSCHE: Field Marshal Rommel left this morning for Salonika and has now arrived there.

HITLER: Then he can fly back again tomorrow morning. He's presumably still got his aircraft.

CHRISTIAN: It's his old crate of a Heinkel 111.

HITLER: How long will it take him from Salonika?

CHRISTIAN: He might get here by 3.0 or 4.0 pm. He'll have to land once to refuel.

HITLER: In six to seven hours time then.

BUHLE: Six hours.

JODL: We once got here in two and a half hours from Salonika in a Heinkel.

SPEER: At least he hasn't got my 'lame duck'. That's something different.

HITLER: You and your 'lame duck'! If the good Mackensen hadn't had it recently he wouldn't have been able to land. I heard that our good Hewel called Frau von Mackensen and said Mackensen's aircraft was overdue. That's very 'diplomatic'; that's why you get made an ambassador.

Everything else will be all right – well now, Jodl, I'll repeat: First, an order to 3 Panzer Grenadier Division and if necessary to the formations here to support the action in Rome; similar orders to the Luftwaffe round Rome and if it's still there to the anti-aircraft etc., so that they know what's happening. That's one set of things. Then get along the other formations straight away. The two things must of course go together. Third is to prepare to evacuate all German forces from this entire area. These here must be got back, naturally keeping a screen in front of them. All rearward services must be moved back at once, crossing here. Doesn't matter. Take with them small arms and machine guns but nothing else; let everything else go. That's 70,000 men we've got down there and some of the best possible men among them. We must arrange that the last of them are motorized and get straight on board. We've got enough German ships here; there's a lot of German shipping there.

JODL: It's almost entirely German.

HITLER: The anti-aircraft must remain here and keep in action all the time. The anti-aircraft over there is the last to be withdrawn. They should blow up everything and get across last.

CHRISTIAN: Are no Italians to cross with the German troops?

HITLER: We must do it so quickly that if possible it's all over in a night. If we're only getting across the men with no equipment – nothing – it should be completed in two days, one day.

BUHLE: Today or tomorrow, my Führer, we must give an order to the General Staff that as far as vehicles are concerned this area must have priority, ie everything which is on the assembly line or on the way to the East. Otherwise these formations will never get there.

HITLER: We can leave that till tomorrow. I must do a bit of thinking about something else; we must be careful about the business with Hungary.

JODL: Then C.-in-C. South must have a guard.

HITLER: Yes.

JODL: 3 Panzer Grenadier Division must put a strong guard round the whole headquarters.

HITLER: Yes.

JODL: Otherwise they'll get the headquarters.

HITLER: Yes, but we can play that game too, I'll get their headquarters, they won't know what's hit them.

JODL: We must have half an hour to think all this over quietly.

BODENSCHATZ: What about the Italian workers?

HITLER: They're not there any more.

SPEER: We want the labour.

JODL: Don't let any more Italians across the frontier apart from those already there – those in Germany.

SPEER: They work very well; we can make good use of them in the Todt organization.

HITLER: The moment this thing breaks I needn't worry any more about the King of the Belgians. I can cart the King off straight away and lock up his whole family.

JODL: Agents have reported a secret meeting in the headquarters in Cairo on 20 June between the King of England and General Wilson, Commander-in-Chief of Twelfth Army which has been detailed for Greece.

HITLER: They're in touch with these people here, with the traitors.

JODL: Then there's this message which may be connected with it. It comes from a somewhat controversial personality in Switzerland who has often provided extremely good information: 'once the Allies have stabilized the situation in Sicily an attack on the mainland is planned towards Rome using fresh troops from North Africa. Occupation of Rome is looked upon as psychologically most important. A provisional national government will be installed in Rome at once. The Fascist Party will be dissolved and Italy and Albania will be freed from Fascist dictatorship. Considerable numbers of troops and quantities of equipment have arrived in Africa from America and Canada.'

HITLER: That certainly all adds up. Ought we not to get 2 Parachute Division ready and alerted at once?

JODL: That might possibly be necessary to reinforce Rome.

HITLER: Yes, so that we could rush it into Rome straight away.

JODL: That's all we can tell him (*Kesselring*) for the moment.

HITLER: No there's nothing more. He should have a strong guard ready. He mustn't go anywhere himself, not to any meeting and he must receive people only in his headquarters. The best would be to say that he's sick, or we could say that we've called him back here to report.

JODL: He must stay down there.

KEITEL: I'd let him stay down there. He can command and we can give him orders. He's got the machinery available. He mustn't leave his headquarters – absolutely not, and anyone who comes to see him should have a military escort; he shouldn't receive anyone and of course he should not leave his headquarters or go to any meeting. We'll lay that down precisely.

HITLER: Well then, Jodl, you'll get it all ready.

JODL: These orders, yes.

HITLER: We must of course play the game from now on as if we thought that it was going to succeed.

JODL: Yes we must do that.

(Meeting ended 22.13 hours)

Fragment no. 15

Briefing Conference, midnight, 25–26 July 1943

JODL: Then there are a number of other questions, my Führer. C.-in-C. South-east has been instructed to report at once whether he can carry out plan Konstantin with the forces he has at the moment; the same for C.-in-C. West in the case of plan Alarich. Now it's all changed. But all the same they must now themselves make proposals as to how they will carry out their job in the changed circumstances – they've each lost a number of divisions. Their report should come in tonight by teleprinter. They had had the news. We said nothing else. How do matters stand with coal trains for Italy? So far we've let them go.

HITLER: We must do everything which makes it look as if …

JODL: Then there is the question: should all travel and private communications to Italy be stopped?

HITLER: I wouldn't do that yet.

KEITEL: No, not yet.

HITLER: All persons of any importance must call off their visits and no further authorizations will be given.

JODL: I have spoken to Kesselring. He has heard the proclamation but we've now no touch with him. In fact there's now a new Commander-in-Chief and a new Head of Government. Kesselring now wants to get in touch with the King and with Badoglio, which in fact he must do.

HITLER: Must he? Yes, I suppose he must.

JODL: He'll do that first thing tomorrow, to sound out the situation.

HITLER: And the good Hube says: 'everything's all right here!'

KEITEL: Hube knows nothing, he's merely repeated what the …

HITLER: You see how dangerous it is having 'non-political generals' in such a political atmosphere.

JODL: We've issued the order to alert 2 Parachute Division at once and hold all available transport aircraft ready.

CHRISTIAN: I shall have the report of what is available shortly. But there's now another question, my Führer: Field Marshal von Richthofen in 2 Air Fleet has up to now been using 100 JU 52 transport aircraft for the supply of 1 Parachute Division in Sicily; ten were shot down today. He wanted to withdraw them. C.-in-C. South wanted to take over these aircraft and in view of the latest developments use them to bring troops from northern to central Italy. 2 Air Fleet asked for instructions from C.-in-C. Air. I have told C.-in-C. Air that there must be no more telephone conversations on the subject and everything must now go via C.-in-C. South.

HITLER: C.-in-C. South must run all this and concentrate everything under his own hand. I have already told Göring that there must be no more telephoning.

CHRISTIAN: That came up from below, my Führer; C.-in-C. Air did not start it; it came from 2 Air Fleet. The question now is: should 2 Parachute Division have these aircraft?

HITLER: 2 Parachute Division takes priority; that is the most important; that's quite clear.

KEITEL: The order reads: 'if necessary abandoning heavy equipment, which must be destroyed if unavoidable; no further issue of orders by telephone, even in camouflaged form'.

HITLER: No, I would put: 'all heavy equipment'.

KEITEL: Then it reads: 'if necessary abandoning all heavy equipment, which must be destroyed if unavoidable'. Then 'no further issue of orders even in camouflaged form; instructions only via liaison officer'.

HITLER: By liaison officer whose instructions must also be in cipher.

HEWEL: My Führer, the question arises whether we should cut telephone communications through the postal authorities. The Post Office has put the question. Journalists' reports are still going. That's probably what they're getting at; whether we shouldn't cut everything except the military lines.

HITLER: We could say that all lines were required for military purposes and official communications.

HEWEL: It's primarily the journalists who of course are now very—

HITLER: Only for official communications.

HEWEL: Only for ministries?

HITLER: Only for ministerial and military communications.

KEITEL: '... whose written instructions must be encoded.' So that there's nothing in what they've got on them.

CHRISTIAN: What about teleprinter and radio?

HITLER: Teleprinter scrambled and radio enciphered. But can't things be deciphered?

KEITEL: No, that's the procedure the Navy use.

HITLER: Teleprinter scrambled and radio enciphered.

KEITEL: '... or encoded radio messages.'

HITLER: All right.

JODL: Then reconnaissance this afternoon established that movement was taking place along the north coast of Sicily eastwards from Palermo. There were approximately fifty vessels including eight large ones; the rest were small, probably landing craft; direction not quite clear but probably east. It looks therefore as if there's going to be an attempt at a landing in rear of our right flank.

HITLER: Is the Luftwaffe all ready for it?

JODL: The Luftwaffe has been warned.

CHRISTIAN: Yes, we have that from C.-in-C. South.

HITLER: All the same I think we ought to send an officer down there straight away.

JODL: The aircraft is ready, it will only have to wait for first light.

HITLER: We must send an officer to tell Hube how to act. First get the rearward services back and across, while the front line holds and then gets back itself in a single night. They must get away in a single night – men only. The rearguard must go on shooting and put up a show.

JODL: Another thing which must be transmitted verbally is the plan for Rome.

HITLER: That must happen under all circumstances; that's quite clear. We can't deal with it here; we must strike back and we must make sure we get the whole Government. The Parachute Division must have plans to jump in the Rome area. Rome must be occupied. Nobody is to leave Rome and then 3 Panzer Grenadier Division moves in.

JODL: What about the units on the move – those from 26 Division.

HITLER: That's not quite clear in the order as written; 'which are unloaded', it should say that they are to be unloaded there.

KEITEL: It means 'the units to be unloaded', ie in addition to those which have been unloaded. I read it through twice. I also thought it would perhaps be better to put 'the elements of 26 Armoured Division to be unloaded.'

JODL: They were partially unloaded because they couldn't get further forward and had to go on by road.

HITLER: Then you must add 'units which have been unloaded and are still to be unloaded'. Here: 'in addition to the units already unloaded, the remainder of 26 Armoured Division is to be unloaded and placed under command of 3 Panzer Grenadier Division'.

HEWEL: Ought we not to tell them to occupy the exits to the Vatican?

HITLER: That doesn't matter; I'll get into the Vatican any time! Do you think I worry about the Vatican? We can seize that straight away. The whole diplomatic corps will be in there. I don't care a damn but if the whole crew's there, we'll get the whole lot of swine out. That is ... then we'll say we're sorry afterwards; we can easily do that. We've got a war on.

BODENSCHATZ: There'll be most of the ... do you think that's safe.

HEWEL: We'll lay hands on a lot of documents there.

HITLER: There? Yes, we'll get some documents there. We'll get some evidence of treachery! How long will the Foreign Minister take to get the instruction out to Mackensen – pity he isn't here.

HEWEL: It's probably gone out already.

HITLER: All right then.

HEWEL: I'll check at once.

HITLER: Is this some journalistic effort covering twelve pages? I'm always afraid of you chaps; two or three lines is all that's wanted.

I've thought of something else, Jodl – if they attack tomorrow or the day after I don't know whether the formations are concentrated yet – I would get them to attack once more in the East. Then the Leibstandarte could take part once more; because until the equipment arrives ...

KEITEL: The rolling-stock.

JODL: It can of course do that; it would of course be better if we could firm up the position there before it leaves.

HITLER: That would of course be a good thing. Then we can just move the one division, the Leibstandarte. It must be the first to get on the move and can leave its equipment there. It can leave a lot of equipment there; no need to take its tanks with it. It can leave them there and be supplied from here. It can get them here. Well then the tanks stay there. And the division gets tanks here; there are plenty of stocks. That's simple. As soon as the division arrives, tanks will be available for it.

HEWEL: I wanted to ask about the Prince of Hesse; he is standing around here all the time. Shall I tell him we don't want him?

HITLER: I'll see him and have a word with him.

HEWEL: Naturally he's asking questions of everybody; he wants to know everything.

HITLER: On the contrary that's a good piece of camouflage; it's like a prison wall. That's definitely a good thing. When we've been planning something we've often had people around who knew nothing and then everybody else thought: 'if they are there, everything's all right'. I am a bit worried that Göring isn't keeping to his job.

BODENSCHATZ: I've already told him that quite clearly.

HITLER: You must be fearfully polite. I'll give him all the proclamations we've got here – they're more or less public. Philip can read those through at his leisure; there's no danger in that. But take care you don't give him the wrong things. I don't know where they are. Look and see you don't give him the wrong ones! Now the movements. When can the first begin? Best it should be concentrated!

JODL: We'll know that soon. This is 305 Division which is ready.

HITLER: And what about 44?

JODL: That's ready; it depends on the rolling-stock. 44 Division will not be released until tomorrow. But I think it can start to move during the course of tomorrow.

HITLER: Is 44 Division motorized? (JODL: No.) Is it a three-regiment division?

KEITEL: It's a fully battle-worthy three-regiment division. We wanted to get it down here a month ago; Rommel was very keen to have it because it was ready. But at that time you refused. So we brought down the Brandenburg division as being less noticeable.

HITLER: The Brandenburg isn't there either.

KEITEL: It's gone too. It was in Innsbruck but things have altered a bit.

357

HITLER: These two formations may have to deal with a pillbox or two; oughtn't we to give them something, either a Tiger or something like that, in case they run into difficulties; a Tiger would knock down a couple of pillboxes straight away if it hit the slits. (KEITEL: Of course.) Perhaps you could check straight away with Buhle what Tigers there are in the training schools etc.

JODL: Anything we lay hands on we must get to Innsbruck.

HITLER: We only need one or two, just to shoot up a couple of pillboxes and then move on to Krain. They'll soon deal with one or two pillboxes. If a couple of Tigers come along and shoot them up, that'll soon be the end of them. They'll go straight through the concrete they've got. If necessary we could use Panthers. Perhaps we could see whether we couldn't get one or two out of the schools – assault tanks too.

KEITEL: I'll talk to Buhle.

HITLER: I want to see Guderian too.

(*Meeting closed 00.45 hours*)

Fragment no. 16

Midday Conference, 26 July 1943

HITLER: Any fresh news, Jodl?

JODL: No. A meeting has been arranged with Badoglio for 6 pm; up to now he's been too busy to have time.... Some are yelling: 'peace, peace!', others are hunting down Fascists.

HITLER: That's good.

JODL: So far it's nothing but baby games like on Ash Wednesday.

HITLER: That might however be like the Ash Wednesday we once had.

JODL: We've spoken to the headquarters and they have assured us that, should there be any danger, they have one airfield completely in German hands.

HITLER: Another question: have you any information when this parachute division will be ready to jump?

JODL: It's been alerted but there's no news yet when it will get the additional troops.

HITLER: Jeschonnek ought to know that.

JODL: They ought to be arriving about now.

HITLER: Has movement started here [*Sicily*] – would it be possible at least to get the tanks across?

358

JODL: Of course while we still can't get any men across we must try and get across the most valuable equipment.

HITLER: With priority to the tanks! According to yesterday's report there are 160 tanks there.

And what can we do here [*Sardinia*]? How can we get them away from there, primarily the men?

JODL: I should like to propose that we take them to Corsica if that's possible and concentrate them there.

GÖRING: That's my view too – make Corsica as strong as possible.

HITLER: They'd have to leave all their equipment if they went to Corsica. We must discuss today how we can get them over to Corsica.

Where is 10 SS Division? Is it here?

HIMMLER: It's here; it arrived recently.

JODL: It's not quite ready but nearly.

HITLER: I've had a very good report about the Göring Division – just what you'd expect; it's an average picture of our young men.

JODL: I read it.

HITLER: These young men are fighting like fanatics because they come from the Hitler Youth. They're young German kids, mostly sixteen-year-olds. These Hitler Youth chaps generally fight more fanatically than the older people. So if these two divisions fight as well as the SS divisions ...

HIMMLER: They're now good divisions, my Führer.

HITLER: ... if they fight like the Hitlerjugend Division, in fact like all our young people. They've been brought up on the right lines. The others will be amazed. They're only young chaps but they've now been training for a long time.

HIMMLER: Both divisions trained from 15 February to 15 August. They're now in good shape. They were inspected by Dollman, Blaskowitz, Rundstedt and the rest and they all said they were completely satisfied.

HITLER: What's the average strength of each division and what's the average age?

HIMMLER: On an average they have 400 officers and about 3–4,000 senior NCOs. They're older – about twenty to thirty. The average age in the two divisions is eighteen-and-a-half, reckoning from the Divisional Commander down to the private soldier.

HITLER: So you could more or less say eighteen?

HIMMLER: Yes, eighteen.

GÖRING: Not long ago it was being said that it was the people between twenty-six and thirty who fought best.

HIMMLER: On an average, yes, but only from the point of view of physical strength.

HITLER: If they'd been trained as long as that.... Before that they taught young people God knows what.... They're all youngsters who joined up at seventeen, some of them even earlier in order to get in ... they've fought marvellously – unparalleled bravery ... the others were wretchedly trained – two months training ... some before April, some after April, some during April and during the other months we had about fourteen days ... those were some exercises, exercises in the Oberwiesenfeld training area ... these are definitely better.

HIMMLER: Actually they are well trained.

HITLER: So these first five divisions are there; has 24 Armoured Division got there yet?

JODL: 24 Armoured Division's got there.

HITLER: It must be put in here, that's obvious. We must ensure that we can get a division from the East down here quickly in support.

JODL: Then, my Führer, Field Marshal von Rundstedt is arriving at Italian Fourth Army today [*on the eastern sector of the French Mediterranean coast*].

GÖRING: On a visit.

JODL: One of a current series of visits. Up to now relations have been good. I think this is very good....

GÖRING: Excellent!

HITLER: But he mustn't stay there long; he must move off as quickly as possible. He must get through with it quickly. We must ensure that as quickly as possible ... he must get a detailed picture of the situation today ... Göring....

GÖRING: What Italian forces are there in Rome?

HIMMLER: My Führer, we could try to get this division out of the Duce. We gave it twelve assault guns, twelve Mark IV tanks, twelve Mark III tanks; that makes 36.

HITLER: He must ensure that we get the whole division – that it comes over to us.

GÖRING: The guns at any rate.

HIMMLER: Then the training teams are there too.

JODL: When can I give this order?

GÖRING: Are we actually issuing an order?

HITLER: They're transmitted on scrambled teleprinter.

JODL: That's quite safe.

HITLER: Scrambled teleprinter, what more do you want? Otherwise we can't give him any orders at all. Otherwise he won't know what we want.

GÖRING: I thought perhaps in this case it ought to go by special liaison officer.

HITLER: Liaison officers are more dangerous still, if they've got papers. They have to be in cipher.

GÖRING: Why not keep it in his head?

HITLER: But you can't keep too many things in your head.

HIMMLER: I can still use radio to my division in Rome.

HITLER: In cipher?

HIMMLER: Yes, in cipher.

HITLER: And that's quite safe?

HIMMLER: Quite safe. We've just made up a new code. Finished making it yesterday. I can give them the order to ...

GÖRING: That must be safe.

JODL: The order must go to Kesselring, otherwise he won't know what future intentions are. The information he then gets ... again quite a different situation....

HITLER: So move them down here, Jodl, so that they can get in here or alternatively get across the Brenner.

JODL: There's no difficulty in getting across the Brenner; trains are running.

HITLER: Yes, but if they suddenly occupy it?

JODL: Then there's the other point....

HIMMLER: And South Tyrol rises!

HITLER: There are no south Tyrolese there; they've all been withdrawn.

HIMMLER: There are one or two still there. The Italians are ... if you seize it ... they would go into their pill boxes, I am convinced of that.

HITLER: ... Innsbruck Garrison ... and makes his Tigers available ... have you talked to Thomale about this business? (JODL: Yes.) About this?

SCHERFF: Thomale was here just now.

JODL: I've spoken to him already. At least we've got something over there in the east, near Tarvisio, that's the next regiment.

HIMMLER: I was just about to say what about this regiment....
I can anyway get that here ... this Mountain Regiment. Can we get it up straight away?

HITLER: What's this police regiment here?

HIMMLER: That's the police regiment in Marseille. My Führer, we could, with the one in Laibach and Trieste.... I very much want to keep the one in Laibach.

HITLER: But we could get that one along.

HIMMLER: I can do that straight away.

HITLER: Should we do that straight away?

JODL: I assume they are acting this way because they've been ordered to take increased precautions – we shall hear about that today.

HITLER: Anyway when the tanks arrive the whole rabble will run like nothing on earth.

HIMMLER: Will our tank detachments get as far as this?

HITLER: Down to here, but we must see. The Leibstandarte is leaving its tanks behind and drawing up others here.

GÖRING: I'm not worried. There's no question of these good-for-nothings stopping us on the Brenner.

HITLER: If our tanks arrive....

GÖRING: I think it's a very good idea to let the paratroopers jump. Himmler's people can do that better than mine. Do it at once! ...

GÖRING: Can I ask again about the parachute division, my Führer. Where do you mean it to land?

JODL: The object of the parachute division is to prevent anybody getting out of Rome.

HITLER: Everything must be occupied – all the exit roads. You only want quite small detachments; they can dig themselves in and then nothing can get by.

GÖRING: Not all at the same time then ... what is being concentrated at the airfields....

HITLER: Everything else we shall need in the city can be landed at an airfield. I don't know which for the moment. But we must be sure to get away from the airfield quickly, because we must reckon on the Allies attacking straight away. We must get away from the airfield in a flash.

GÖRING: And blow up whatever we can.

JESCHONNEK: Could we not send a liaison officer down to Southern France today or early tomorrow to General Student or to 2 Parachute Division and tell them where to go.

GÖRING: The detail of where they've got to jump.

JESCHONNEK: We can't say exactly what the situation will be this afternoon or early tomorrow.

HITLER: The situation will be just the same. Rome will still be Rome. The exit roads must be occupied. That can be done anyway.

GÖRING: Who had best cordon off the Vatican City from the capital?

HITLER: That's the job of the formations which go in, primarily 3 Panzer Grenadier Division. The units which land come after. Now here are three so-called active Italian divisions. I don't think they'll do much, though, if we make a show of force against them.

JODL: 12 Division is in Rome; the others are further away....

KEITEL: I don't believe they had any military units down there and they wanted to get hold of some quickly.

HEWEL: They'd apparently prepared everything very well; the newspapers ... notices had all been prepared that the Chairman of Stefani had shot himself etc.

HITLER: Who?

HEWEL: The Chairman of the Stefani News Agency shot himself. At least that's the story.

HIMMLER: My Führer, people have been arrested too – Germans who didn't belong to the Embassy and were under some suspicion that they'd been giving information or something – women too.

HITLER: The Foreign Ministry must get that – tell our Ambassador at once: all Germans must be released forthwith or we shall take the most energetic measures. Of course we must act quickly – that's the most important thing. In this case speed is the most important thing.

Now Rommel, here's the problem: first to get our forces back because we can't hold Sicily any longer, that's out of the question; it's questionable whether you can hold the toe of Italy but that doesn't matter. The most important thing is to remain concentrated so that at least you can fight.

JODL: May I refer to the command organization; Field Marshal

Rommel will command down there ... alternatively we must have a division of responsibility – that Field Marshal Rommel acts here ... and that Field Marshal Kesselring gets additional forces from the south up here. As soon as they arrive they come under command of Field Marshal Rommel; otherwise it won't work; from Munich it is....

HITLER: I agree to all that, but I still think overall command should go to Rommel. Field Marshal Kesselring hasn't got the reputation. We'll publish that the moment we move in – Field Marshal Rommel! Secondly all Fascist divisions will come over to us ... we must get the Fascists back straight away, that must be our object ... battered formations and regular divisions ... and volunteers.... Himmler's had a very good idea: any man who wants to can go home; we'll get Farinacci to announce that – we'll get him into this today – any Italian soldier can go home ... we shan't get those who go home; they're no use anyway.

HIMMLER: We could perhaps take them to Germany later as a labour force.

HITLER: Of course, but they're not much use – the next thing is to try and get the men away from here. That's the main job here, apart from the precautionary measures here. The third thing is the occupation of Rome for which the paratroopers jump and 3 Panzer Grenadier Division moves in.

GÖRING: But the orders must be given on the spot. You can't command that from Munich.

HITLER: The orders will be given and the commanders will be responsible for carrying them out and then at the same time German divisions will move in ... if any unit looks as if it's going to offer resistance, fire must be opened on it ruthlessly; that's the only way. This thing's got to succeed ... that means that with the Hermann Göring Division we've got six – and two good ones among them.

GÖRING: The Opposition will of course call on the Allies for help and beg to be protected. So where will the enemy land?

HITLER: But it will be some time before he is in a position to land.

GÖRING: Of course he can always put down parachute troops the same as we can.

HITLER: Of course he can, but ...

GORING: I only thought I'd raise the point.

HITLER: To begin with, as always happens in such cases, they'll be caught on the wrong foot.

GÖRING: If Rome surrenders there'll be no call for assistance to the Allies.

HITLER: They've done that already. Some have taken to their heels because the Italians are ... Italy's divided, they're hunting down Fascists – who shot himself, the Chairman of Stefani?

HEWEL: Yes, the Chairman of Stefani shot himself.

HITLER: We must ensure that all this is co-ordinated, that people wait for a signal and that then it all starts. We must ... for instance 'Fascist Freedom Army' ... we must set up a provisional Fascist Government straight away which can install itself there and give orders ... all Fascist soldiers and officers must have a National-Socialist ... we must be sure that the National-Socialist ... we must ensure that these Fascist soldiers and officers join National-Socialist formations. This old man of seventy-three ...

HIMMLER: Can I give the order to my commander down there straight away? ... Urgent that those who are trained arrive.

HITLER: He won't be able to do it.

HIMMLER: That's another division. These are really only militia.

HITLER: But there are so many others in between!

GÖRING: At least use the tanks and assault guns; they are German manned.

HITLER: Our people are the only ones who will do anything. There's time. They'll give the order. If this has got to happen, they'll give the order. They'll hear the proclamations and one hopes they won't stop up their ears. No need for secrecy any more ... it will be out on the radio. If the Stefani radio obviously ...

GÖRING: Where is parachute division headquarters?

JODL: We could use it for this business; it's the only available headquarters.

HITLER: Who is it.

JODL: Student.

HITLER: Splendid! He is the man for this sort of thing. Just right. ... (*Hewel produces record of a conversation between Mackensen and Badoglio.*) What a pack of lies! Listen to this! (*Reads*), 'fundamental co-operation'! What impertinence!

HEWEL: He is trying hard.

HITLER: If only I could lay hands on the bastard!

GÖRING: What a nerve with this letter!

HITLER: He's an old hard-boiled enemy of ours. It was he who was primarily responsible for stopping Italy coming into the war on 25 August 1939, and it was primarily that which led to England and France coming into the war and signing the Polish Treaty.

GÖRING: But to write a letter like this! It's a piece of play acting! A Punch and Judy show! ...

DÖNITZ: That's too much. I can't do anything to stop ... that there should be U-boats in Spezia and Toulon and that five or six should lie off Spezia. If we can't work it by propaganda, the best would be to seize the ships as soon as possible.

HITLER: They will be in Toulon....

DÖNITZ: Yes, perhaps we could seize them beforehand. I have only got U-boat crews in Spezia and they've got nothing but rifles and revolvers. They're not equipped for anything else. So if we want to seize the ships we must have adequately equipped troops. But anyway I think the Italians will give themselves up.

HITLER: Have you any idea ...

GÖRING: We've got people there.

DÖNITZ: But they're not mobile and they are only 300 men. We've got two U-boats there. You can't do much propaganda with 300 men. And of course they're not trained, they're just sailors. I think, my Führer, that we must try and stop the people getting away.

HITLER: I've already said that a special army formation should be got ready for this purpose.

DÖNITZ: Better wait a bit; we don't know.

GÖRING: But haven't you got U-boats lying off?

DÖNITZ: I've got U-boats lying off in case they run for it. One must wait to see how things develop. It's also possible that there may be a split in the fleet and that the younger officers will arrest the older.

JODL: In my view the most urgent thing is to transfer Student's staff to Kesselring. Then to send a liaison officer to Kesselring who can discuss the Rome operation verbally with Kesselring and Student. He knows nothing about it and then he can tell us forthwith what forces he can concentrate and how long he wants so that we can more or less set a date.

HITLER: The date must be laid down by *us*, otherwise we shall never get to the end of it and there'll be endless delays and that's no good. We've always laid down the date. Even in the Serbian operation we decided on the date and laid it down. You can't leave that to subordinate headquarters.

JODL: But for the moment it's only the subordinate headquarters which can tell me what's available apart from 3 Panzer Grenadier Division.

HITLER: The other thing's our affair. We can tell the paratroopers....

GÖRING: There are nine battalions.

JESCHONNEK: We must get nine infantry battalions going quickly. They'll have to be flown in three waves. I'd like to propose that as far as possible we agree details about the second wave with Field Marshal Kesselring – he must decide where it's to land.... In addition, 1 Parachute Regiment can be brought up ... Naples.

HITLER: You can't land the first wave without ... no good. The first thing to do is to block the exit roads in a flash. Special detachments must be detailed.

JESCHONNEK: ... the first wave without the Italians noticing ... as soon as it's clear we mean to cut off Rome.

JODL: We must definitely do that. We could only drop them into the blue if we could bring the whole division in in one wave and let it come down any old how.

HITLER: But who can guarantee that he won't smell a rat straight away? Every airfield is swarming with Italians and when a lot of parachute troops come down – what then?

JODL: I think we can do it if we give out that the paratroops are on the way to Sicily. If the Italians seem hostile to the paratroops while they're landing ...

HITLER: They won't do that.

JODL: I don't think so. But the moment they jump that's something different.

HITLER: Then some of them will scram and the thing's gone wrong. We must be clear about that.

GÖRING: There's one parachute division in Sicily.

JODL: Yes, there are parachute troops everywhere.

GÖRING: Perhaps we could arrange to deal direct with the Italians about transport aircraft ... say that we're merely flying to Rome and landing there ... primarily to get air space ... we'll have to have them to back up the first wave.

HITLER: I wouldn't say that the parachute troops ...

GÖRING: No, the first!

JESCHONNEK: I Parachute Division.

GÖRING: Save supplies for them. We can say officially that we don't ... but we require trains to bring them to Italy. That would be the first wave. Then they fly back and we say officially: we can only get as far as Rome; airfields forward of that are destroyed; we can't fly further because of yesterday's losses. They'll lap up all that. We have had losses flying to Sicily. In my view we're risking too many crews flying there, so we can't go further than Rome. We'll tell the Comando Supremo officially that we want trains to Reggio for the parachute troops so that they can cross to the division they belong to. And then the second wave arrives.

JESCHONNEK: Another point is that if they're all to jump, not all the aircraft arriving are fitted.

JODL: We should perhaps reinforce this area and that over there. The supply situation in Sicily is all right for the immediate future. (*Produces the Wehrmacht report.*) May I ask for a decision. In my view this is what must happen: a liaison officer must fly to Rome to tell Kesselring verbally about the Rome operation and Student must get there at the same time so that he can also be put in the picture.

HITLER: We don't need two. Student should come here first and take the liaison officer with him.

GÖRING: Get Student here straight away.

JESCHONNEK: That'll take longer if I may say so. General Student is in Southern France.

HITLER: All the same the thing's not going to happen first thing tomorrow morning. How long will it take him to get here from Southern France?

JESCHONNEK: General Student can get here today. Then he can leave early tomorrow.

HITLER: I think it's right to get General Student here, then he can take the thing over.

KEITEL: He can also deal with the Government.

HITLER: We haven't got as far as that yet. After all the first echelon of the ...

JODL: That's got nothing to do with the Rome operation. Parachute troops arrive, other troops arrive, one train leaves after another. But if they jump the alarm will be given in Rome.

HITLER: They'd cotton on straight away.

GÖRING: Kesselring merely says that because of the threat here the parachute troops ...

HITLER: Because of the losses here?

GÖRING: No, because of the threat here they must land in the Rome area and go on to Reggio by rail. We could say that they must await the arrival of the second wave so that they can go on together.

HITLER: Yes.

WARLIMONT: Nothing important to report from the South-east or the eastern Mediterranean. Our own movements went according to plan. Early today Colonel-General Löhr paid the visit to the commander of the Italian XI Army which Field-Marshal Rommel had planned. The upshot is that this Army has received no order from Rome. He said he considered the arrangements satisfactory but could not conform until the order had arrived. It was agreed with Rome yesterday that the takeover of command should take place. It now remains to make enquiries in Rome and press that the order should be given. In addition, my Führer, C.-in-C. South-east has reported the new distribution of forces which he considers necessary in this new situation. (*Produces a paper*). The situation in Rhodes and Crete is unchanged.

HITLER: What's happening here?

WARLIMONT: ... reinforced Regiment 92 because he considers it urgently necessary to get some German troops into the area between Montenegro and the northern Greek frontier where there is at present nobody.

HITLER: This regiment is more or less here. There is no need to worry that ...

KEITEL: The initial movements always take the longest. Subsequent movements always go quicker than ...

WARLIMONT: He had detailed 100 Jäger Division for this area. It was originally intended for the Peloponnese but has been making slow progress because of the block on the railway. This one also is intended to move up to defend the coast of Albania, if necessary.

HITLER: It can't do that.

WARLIMONT: The important points, my Führer, are these two bases, Valona and Durazzo. The whole Konstantin plan is based on the assumption that no further forces will be available from the East. It must be emphasized that these two bases should be occupied so that at least we have the main ports in German hands.

HITLER: But they're unprotected.

WARLIMONT: They're not strong bases.

HITLER: When does Weichs get here?

KEITEL: He should be here tomorrow. He leaves Nuremberg today and should be here early tomorrow.

ROMMEL: Is Weichs probably coming here?

HITLER: Does that worry you?

ROMMEL: No.

HITLER: I don't know how Weichs' health is; he's a very calm chap.

KEITEL: I've spoken to him and he's ready for anything.

HITLER: He must be a really outstanding officer.

KEITEL: Weichs was originally with mountain troops.

WARLIMONT: C.-in-C. South-east's other proposals deal with ... to get the available divisions nearer the coast with the proviso here that 1 Armoured Division should be in reserve at the Isthmus of Corinth so that it can be employed towards the north as well. Apart from 1 Armoured Division there's only one single division and that must stay up front. And the four fortress battalions.

HITLER: Apart from this division there's only one there?

WARLIMONT: He wants to push up 117 Division nearer the western and southern coasts. 104 Division and 1 Mountain Division have similar orders. Then in here can come a further battalion from the Brandenburg Regiment which is at the moment employed on an anti-guerilla operation. One division is already here in the area west of Belgrade, and the other will follow shortly.

HITLER: When does the police regiment arrive?

WARLIMONT: The one from Finland? That was due to leave

Danzig on 1 August. It will take at least fourteen days to get down here.

HIMMLER: It could come down this way.

WARLIMONT: 18 Police Regiment is due in this area.

HITLER: And the Prinz Eugen?

WARLIMONT: It was supposed to move here but it must stay here until he gets reinforcements because it may be necessary to occupy the coastal fortifications. The same applies to 114 Jäger Division. That leaves 297 Division in the Belgrade area. It's not yet ready.

HITLER: We must quickly ...

WARLIMONT: If you agree then, my Führer, 100 Jäger Division will not be moved down here to Crete, so that we can at least occupy these two main bases.

HITLER: What do you think, Rommel?

ROMMEL: Well, these two divisions are not in a particularly good position. Yesterday the southern division had been cut off by the road being blocked and it was being supplied by water; there's water both to right and left of it. It can't get to the coast; it must just protect the road. The Bavarian Division is in a bad situation too. It's got water both to right and left and has not yet got up to the coast. There's nothing to be done with the Italians.

HITLER: We can more or less count them out.

GÖRING: As I've said, my Führer, perhaps we ought to give them instructions that they should try and disarm the Italian divisions down there because otherwise they'll sell their weapons.

HIMMLER: I got that across the Italians yesterday.

WARLIMONT: C.-in-C. South-east has given general instructions that all weapons are to be removed from Italian troops the moment they show signs of wavering.

HITLER: They'll sell them!

GÖRING: They'll sell the buttons off their pants for English pounds.

WARLIMONT: He then asks about reinforcement by Bulgarian forces; this would make additional divisions available in the event of an attack. He has discussed this with the King but the question is whether the latter will stick to it in the present situation.

HITLER: That we shall have to see.

WARLIMONT: Finally he asks whether the area Fiume-Trieste will come under his command if Italy collapses.

HITLER: Löhr does? What an idea! That area will be under Rommel, it's part of Italy.

WARLIMONT: Yes, part of Italy.

HITLER: He couldn't deal with it with the forces he has available.

WARLIMONT: Can we now get on with this instruction regarding 92 Regiment?

HITLER: He can get the other one across first. I think we want a strong armoured force here which can drive down either here or down there.

WARLIMONT: That ought to be held in Salonika ready to move.

HITLER: Anyway, we've already used armoured divisions here.

GÖRING: Yes, but the result was ...

KEITEL: We went right down as far as the Peloponnese.

GÖRING: ... that's against infantry divisions....

KEITEL: Sepp Dietrich roared right through them with his division.

GÖRING: As soon as a firm decision is made. One can't avoid taking one here. We must have a firm stop line here so that these people can't come on and that those people there are secured in the rear.

WARLIMONT: In the interior there was a discussion on 23 July with leading representatives of Mihailovic. The most important results were: all sabotage plans to be put into operation forthwith ... cessation of hostilities against Tito and co-operation with him as ordered by the King of Yugoslavia.... Roosevelt and Churchill are supposed to have given a guarantee to re-establish the State. Stalin is said to have shown no interest. Preparations for landing 20,000 parachute troops – that's of course Balkan exaggeration. We must push through the Serbian home guard, Serbian frontier guard and Serbian volunteer corps. No action is to be taken for the moment against these forces. Then there are some additional instructions.

These records show that once the initial confusion had been overcome the aims of the German High Command, reduced to their essentials, were as follows: in Italy to put plan Alarich into operation as far as possible, including securing the Alpine passes, but not to give Rome any excuse finally to renounce the German alliance – as a result Field Marshal Rommel was still held back in readiness in Munich;[27] to prepare to evacuate all German troops from the larger islands; to limit the defence of Italy to the northern

Apennines and therefore not to send newly-arrived German formations south of this obstacle; on the French Mediterranean coast and
throughout the Balkans to take over all sectors held by Italian troops
as laid down in plan Konstantin.

These were the jobs of OKW and they resulted in one of the
busiest periods of its existence.[28] Meanwhile Hitler pursued his
plans for a coup in Rome, the re-establishment of the Fascist regime
and the liberation of Mussolini. OKW had no part in these special
plans and in any case it was hard to see what these foolhardy ideas
had to do with any possible future German-Italian strategy. During
this period, once the military presentations were over, the map
room was generally cleared of all but an extremely restricted circle;
only the initiated remained behind; they included Jodl who however made no secret of his opposition to the raid on the Government
in Rome; the same applied to Field Marshal Kesselring, though
both had initially agreed to it.[29] By 5 August Hitler had realized
that in the form so far envisaged this part of his plan was impracticable if the move of additional German formations into Italy was
to be carried out peacefully. Initially nobody knew where Mussolini
was but much planning for his liberation continued, resulting in an
odd form of activity, aptly described by a member of the headquarters as 'a game of cops and robbers'.[30]

THE BREAK-UP OF THE AXIS

During the few weeks between the end of July and the final collapse
of Italy on 8 September 1943, the disastrous aberrations caused by
the headquarters' state of schizophrenia stood out with particular
clarity. Two wars were being conducted so to speak side by side, one
in the East, the other in the South. Each kept the high-level staffs
concerned so busy that neither really realized the pressures to which
the other was being subjected. Jodl, for instance, in his paper on
distribution of forces in the autumn, had made light of the existing
situation in the East, although the main event there had been an
attack by overwhelmingly superior Russian forces against the Orel
salient. Similarly in spite of the extremely serious situation in the
South, Zeitzler refused to make available more than one Panzer
Grenadier division, the SS-Leibstandarte. In both cases there were
no previous discussions between the two staffs; Hitler alone decided.[31]

In the Mediterranean action against the enemy was for several weeks confined to the small Etna bridgehead. OKW was far more occupied in imposing Hitler's will on our own ally and countering the measures taken by Rome. (After the war the then Chief of the Comando Supremo stated that in his orders of the end of July 1943 precautions against German action took precedence over defensive measures against any possible Anglo-American landing.) We were therefore under double pressure both from within and from without, and our pre-occupations regarding future developments on both fronts formed a tangled web; tension became all the greater when opinions within the headquarters began to differ regarding the ultimate aims of the Italians. Only Hitler and Göring remained unshaken in their belief that 'treachery' was at work; in spite of this even Hitler felt that it was better to try to keep Italy on our side, hoping for a new turn of events as a result of the liberation of Mussolini. Grand Admiral Dönitz, who spent much time at the headquarters, now became one of his most intimate advisers, in addition to Jodl; on purely military grounds both were inclined to keep the alliance in being, even with a non-Fascist Italy. They were supported by Kesselring and Rintelen in Rome, who for their part would hear of no questioning of the sincerity of the new regime; though with less emphasis, Field Marshals Rommel and von Rundstedt were of the same mind. All however were pressing for the twilight period to be brought to an end and some clear relationship established as soon as possible; in this they were at variance with Hitler who, for instance, continued to postpone the evacuation of Sicily in order that this should not be an excuse for the Italians to renounce the alliance, and in this Dönitz agreed with him for reasons of maritime strategy.[32]

The first task of OKW in this situation was to adapt plans Alarich and Konstantin to the new developments. By the end of July they had been brought up to date, combined so that a single plan was applicable to Italy, the Balkans and the West and issued in writing under the code name 'Axis'. For the first time Field Marshal Rommel was now provided with a full Army Group staff; he was given certain reserve formations in the Innsbruck area with which to secure the Alpine passes, in particular the Brenner, but as before was not allowed to appear in person.[33]

We were now trying to filter as many additional formations into northern Italy as possible. From the end of July this, together with Rommel's instructions, led to repeated conflicts with the authorities in Rome and in some cases also with local Italian headquarters. The procedure was almost invariably the same; Hitler would go off into wild threats and imprecations; OKW would then try to get the essential military points accepted via General von Rintelen in Rome, who as a result had a most difficult and uncomfortable job; the result generally was that the Italians at least gained a little time, which in their difficult situation was undoubtedly of considerable value to them. By these methods we finally succeeded in completing our precautionary move forward to the northern Apennines – the most important aspect of the preparatory measures for plan Axis; on the other hand we had no clear concept of how further operations should be conducted should Italy collapse. Hitler was still trying to put off the evil day when long-term decisions would have to be taken and in this case could hide behind the excuse that orders could not be kept secret from the Italians. Grand Admiral Dönitz has recorded a phrase actually used in connection with the continued defence of Sicily but applicable to innumerable other similar situations: 'the Führer considers that there is much to be said for both points of view and has not therefore finally decided'.[34]

The highlights of the period following the fall of Mussolini were the two German-Italian meetings in Tarvisio and Bologna. I was present at the first which took place on 6 August, little more than two weeks after that at Feltre; only Jodl and Rommel went to the second and last on 15 August. It is more or less certain that at the Tarvisio meeting the Italians had already made up their minds to find some way of escape both from the alliance and the war – though at that time they possibly still hoped to do so in agreement with their Axis partner. Hitler still refused to consider any outcome other than victory. The meeting in Bologna took place five days after the Italians had made their (secret) request to the Allies for an armistice. Under these circumstances there was little likelihood of any result from either of the two meetings.

The Tarvisio meeting was between the two Foreign Ministers and the Chiefs of the Comando Supremo and OKW, Ambrosio and Keitel; Hitler had brusquely refused an invitation from Badoglio to a personal meeting on the grounds that he was a Head of State. The German object in the discussions was to clarify relations with Italy; OKW had therefore prepared a programme for the military part of the discussions practically identical with that for Feltre. It included: prevent the enemy setting foot on the Italian mainland or in the Balkans: an equal number of German and Italian formations to be employed in southern Italy with a stronger German backup in central and northern Italy: agreement on strategy at all higher staff levels. Hitler's instructions were that there should be no more than a general politico-military *tour d'horizon*. It would be enough he said to listen and 'put on an act of good faith'; there must be no reference to a possible evacuation of Sicily. His instructions on security were even more detailed: we were only to appear as a body; we were to undertake no individual negotiations and under no circumstances were we to eat or drink anything which had not previously been tasted by our hosts. As the German special train arrived at Tarvisio station, where the Italian train was already waiting, between each pair of windows along the corridors of the two coaches stood an SS man with sub-machine gun at the ready!

The morning conference was attended only by the heads of the political and military delegations. Ambrosio evaded all questions regarding his appreciation of the situation and future Italian intentions. On the other hand he protested against the manner and rapidity of recent German troop movements into Italy, culminating with the statement that in Rome they had the impression that they were no longer 'master in their own house' and that OKW seemed to regard Italian territory merely as 'a glacis for the defence of Germany'. Keitel rejected these accusations but, being bound by Hitler's instructions, could not give any details of his own views. Both sides then went to lunch in the restaurant car of the Italian train, where Hitler's warnings were completely disregarded. Thereafter a military discussion took place in which each side manifested complete agreement with the wishes of the other as regards disposition of forces, but once more no mention was made of command organization. The meeting ended with a plenary session at which Ribbentrop declared that Germany would carry on the war together with Italy until victory was won and Ambrosio gave an explicit assurance that, within the limits of her capabilities, Italy would continue to fight on the side of her ally. Plans for the combined defence of the Apennines were to be discussed later at a time to be mutually agreed.[35]

In spite of this significant postponement, we on the German side were inclined to agree that Ambrosio's assurances and his agreement to German requirements represented an advance in the Italian position. Ribbentrop and his suite went back to the Wörther See for a one- or two-day visit to the Schloss Hotel, from which it was said all visitors had been cleared; Keitel and his staff spent the night in the train and on the next morning flew back from Klagenfurt to Wolfschanze.

We had no sooner got back to the headquarters than fresh news that very day threw doubt upon Keitel's report. Two Alpini divisions had arrived in the area of the Brenner and, contrary to recent agreements for combined protection of the roads over the passes, the Italians were now demanding withdrawal of the German posts. This produced severe new disagreements; on the other hand light Italian naval forces were at this time acting vigorously as far even as Gibraltar; from Southern France and even from the Balkans came reports of satisfactory contacts between the allies.

In view of these contradictory reports we, in the headquarters, once more urged that the situation should be cleared up, on which occasion Jodl was to be heard muttering that the negotiations should be conducted quite differently and that he would have no difficulty in succeeding where we had failed at Tarvisio. Taking up the proposal made at Tarvisio, it was proposed that at a further meeting the Italians could be forced to show their hand if we produced our own appreciation of the situation and a plan for the distribution of German forces based on data to be provided by Rommel and Kesselring. A new memorandum was therefore drawn up, the most noteworthy points of which were that for the first time the possibility of Allied landings in the Bay of Salerno were mentioned, and the northern Apennines were again given as the final and principal line of defence. Kesselring went further and repeated his proposals for the reinforcement of German troops in Sardinia and southern Italy but this was flatly rejected by Hitler. The latter still refused to proceed further with the evacuation of Sicily, though unobtrusively this had already gone quite a long way.

The new meeting we wanted was in fact triggered off by the Italians themselves. On 11 August they made known their decision to withdraw to Italy their Fourth Army from southern France and some of their divisions from the Balkans. In reply OKW demanded discussion of these questions, emphasizing at the same time that it expected 'on this occasion fully to clarify the overall strategy and command organization for the defence of Italy and of the southern bastion of Fortress Europe'. Rome agreed to the meeting and designated the Army Chief of Staff, General Roatta, as its representative. On the German side Hitler hoped for great things from the appearance on this occasion, in addition to Jodl, of Field Marshal Rommel as Commander-in-Chief German troops in Italy.[36]

The results of these discussions were no better than might have been expected in the circumstances. Looking back it is clear that whatever methods we employed could matter little, since, unknown to their former ally, the Italians had already been in touch with the Allies for some days. The opening scene of the meeting on the German side was the appearance of a complete motorized Waffen-SS battalion to escort the German generals from the airfield to the meeting place. On arrival the battalion threw a cordon round the place including in it the Italian security detachment. Outside the open door of the conference room SS men goose-stepped up and down past the Italian ceremonial guard, over whom they towered head and shoulders. The German representatives were armed when they finally took their places at the table. Jodl took the floor and, abandoning all pretence at courtesy, coupled the German agreement to the withdrawal of Italian troops from southern France with the question 'whether these were for use against the English in southern Italy or against the Germans on the Brenner'. Roatta remained quite calm, produced a number of sound objections to the German concept, which was unmistakably based on Plan Axis, and so far demolished the German position that Jodl was eventually reduced to suggesting that final agreement on the questions under discussion had best be left to the two Supreme Headquarters. His great expectations thus came to nought and early in the afternoon he telegraphed to the Chief of OKW that: 'Italian intentions are no clearer than before', adding that 'our reasons for suspicion are still as valid as ever'.[37]

This uncertainty was to last for several weeks longer and meanwhile both allies did all they could to prepare for the change which was obviously coming. The Italians – or at any rate many in important positions – increasingly gave us the impression that they were trying to paralyse all Wehrmacht movements which might affect the conclusion of their agreements with the Western powers; this went so far that Hitler came to think that they were trying to confine German troops in southern and northern Italy, now numbering about 100,000, to defined areas in which they could, at the appointed time, hand them over as a birthday present to the Allies. Meanwhile the German Supreme Command pushed on with its preparations to defend Italy without the Italians or even against their opposition;

the preparatory measures covered ever wider areas and came ever closer to involving the use of force.[38]

The first action was to allow Field Marshal Rommel and his staff to cross the frontier on 16 August. His area of command was for the moment limited to northern Italy with the result that we now had in Italy two German senior headquarters, one behind the other, while alongside them and loosely connected to them, was the whole Italian command organization. At the same time, in view of Hitler's continued indecision, Jodl and Kesselring took it upon themselves to order the last German troops in Sicily to make a fighting withdrawal to the mainland on 17 August. There had been no previous agreement between OKW and the Comando Supremo before this final decision was taken. Remarkably enough even Hitler accepted this strategically significant event in silence and, contrary to all previous practice, bowed to the inevitable. Kesselring still had his eye on Apulia and the air bases there, so it was left to OKW once more to draw his attention, by a directive dated 18 August, to the imminent threat to the coastal area of 'Naples-Salerno' and to give him a direct order to move the bulk of his armoured formations to that area. One of the Army's senior and most experienced commanders, Colonel-General von Vietinghoff was made available to command them in the nick of time and his Tenth Army Headquarters was formed on the spot.[39]

OKW was still without any reliable information on what was going on between Rome and the Allies; we therefore continued to negotiate with the Comando Supremo and General Roatta, thereby leaving open to the Italians the possibility of remaining on the side of Germany. So the Axis powers remained unhappy bedfellows in an alliance which had lost all form and meaning; one side was dependent upon the Allies who were slow to move; the other continued in its determination not to be the one to take the first step leading to the final break. Even on 4 September, the day after the British landing on the Italian mainland at Reggio di Calabria, we received renewed assurances from the highest military authorities in Rome – and yet, as subsequently emerged, the surrender agreement had been signed the day before. On the same day, on top of all the uncertainties and threats in the Mediterranean, came an urgent call for more forces – yet another – from the East, where after continued heavy defensive fighting the situation was becoming serious. This led German Supreme Headquarters to review its previous policy. Jodl himself prepared an appreciation on 6 September and came to the conclusion that we were no longer justified in holding unused reserves indefinitely in the South. He proposed that 'we should take the initiative in cutting the cords entangling us in Italy' and the next day Hitler gave his agreement. An ultimatum to this end was prepared but before it was completed Italy's unconditional surrender was announced on the afternoon of 8 September and the Rome-Berlin 'Axis' thus finally disintegrated.[40]

On a more personal level one or two sidelights of this period are worth mentioning. On 31 August General von Rintelen, who had given outstanding service, was dismissed in a manner which was now to become the normal – his successor appeared at his door, unannounced, carrying a letter from Keitel. Rintelen made every effort to be given an appointment at the front but was retired before the end of the war on express instructions from Hitler.

I had had to leave the headquarters on 5 September to have an operation. I reckoned I would be away three months and therefore made urgent representations that during this period a successor for me should be found, as had so often been promised. This time it really looked as if I would succeed but while I was still in hospital, Hitler issued the order to which I have already referred, laying down that some twenty named officers in senior headquarters were to be kept in their posts for the duration of the war; they included Jodl, Zeitzler, Heusinger and myself.

Prince Philip of Hesse had been kept hanging about in HQ Area 1. The day after the collapse of Italy he emerged from Hitler's hut to find the SD waiting for him and was arrested. On 10 September Goebbels noted in his diary: 'the Führer has drawn the right conclusions as regards the royal family; the Prince was transferred to Gestapo Headquarters at Könisgberg.'

CHAPTER 4

Facing War on Two or More Fronts

After all the previous upheavals the third great crisis of 1943, the surrender of Italy, was taken calmly in German Supreme Head-quarters; yet it heralded the breakdown of Hitler's European policy. On the evening of 8 September OKW issued the codeword 'Axis' bringing into force 'the orders which had been prepared for months and which had been brought up to date on 29 August in the light of the existing situation'; they covered the whole area of the Medi-terranean from the Gulf of Lions to Crete and Rhodes, and placed all responsibility and all defensive measures entirely in German hands. The next day it became clear that the great take-over from the Italians was going smoothly, thanks not merely to the work of the OKW Operations Staff but to able and intelligent handling by local German commanders – last but not least thanks to the Allies, who ruined the Badoglio Government's plan by premature an-nouncement of the surrender, by failing to carry out the plan for dropping American parachute troops in the Rome area and by restricting their landing operations to the mainland of southern Italy. The only major failure in the 'Axis' programme was that the Navy and Air Force proved unable to prevent the Italian Fleet going over to the enemy; it went to Malta and hauled down its flag there. Hitler's hope that a large number of young men, supposedly fired by the Fascist spirit, would volunteer to fight in the German Wehrmacht, also proved false. Much propaganda was made of the liberation of Mussolini but this also turned out to be a disappoint-ment; when he visited the headquarters shortly thereafter he was clearly a broken man, incapable of further effective influence on the Italian people. Even Hitler thereupon treated him as a fallen giant, had him closely guarded and only let him appear when he thought it would be useful. Mussolini for instance proposed that a new army of about 500,000 men should be raised, but Hitler cut him down to a total of four divisions and some minor naval and air force units.[1]

Initially there was no firm view in German Supreme Headquarters as to what the next move by the Allies was likely to be. On the evening of 8 September when the great convoys moving towards the west coast of Italy had been detected some hours before, it was thought that 'an enemy landing in the Rome area was more probable than in the area of Naples'. Our own intentions however remained unchanged and were clearly expressed by Jodl who noted: 'the most urgent problem is to get Tenth Army and the Luftwaffe out of southern Italy'.[2] This comment is important for two reasons: first it gives the lie in so many words to the common accusation that OKW left Commander-in-Chief South and his troops in the lurch or was even prepared to sacrifice them; secondly it proved that it was still the intention to conduct the defence of Italy on a line considerably further north. OKW is also accused of having refused a request from Commander-in-Chief South to move down forthwith the two armoured divisions in northern Italy to counter-attack the enemy who had landed early on 9 September in the Bay of Salerno; had it done so it would have been entirely right. The distances were vast (about 450 miles) and there were other important considerations which made such a movement impossible; moreover all second World War experience, both in Europe and the Far East, proves that most probably, even with these reinforcements, it would not have been possible to stop the enemy gaining a foothold. In any case when Commander-in-Chief South stated on 12 September that he intended to 'throw the enemy back into the sea', it hardly looked as if he was short of forces. Although it went beyond his instructions this would undoubtedly have been the best solution; it gave an indication of what future tactics in Italy were to be. Hitler immediately decreed that 'Commander-in-Chief South will defeat the enemy who have landed at Salerno', but OKW, adhering to the current plan, managed to add: 'even if this can be completely or partially achieved, the bulk of our forces will then be concentrated in the Rome area' (preparatory to further withdrawal).[3] Goebbels' diary of 10 September says: 'naturally we shall not be able to hold southern Italy. We must withdraw northward beyond Rome. We shall now establish ourselves on the defence line that the Führer has always envisaged, namely the line of the Apennine Mountains. ...

The aim of our military operations must be to free a number of divisions for the Balkans. Without a doubt the spearhead of the Anglo-American invasion will be pointed in that direction in the immediate future.'

This order also disproves another widely held misconception – that the temporary successes achieved by Kesselring at Salerno and immediately thereafter led to a reversal of previously approved plans for further strategy in Italy. In fact on 9, 13 and 17 September OKW issued a whole series of instructions of greater or lesser importance but all showing clearly that the basic intention was to hold 'the shortest possible front on the Apennines'. For instance, all units destined for southern Italy were halted north of the Apennines and Army Group B (Rommel) was instructed forthwith to reconnoitre and construct 'the most favourable defensive line in the Apennines'. In these orders it was still the intention that as soon as the concentration in the northern Apennines began, the staff of Commander-in-Chief South should be disbanded and Rommel should take over command of all German troops in Italy – a slight change from the previous proposal. On 25 September OKW, with Hitler's approval and certain minor additions, agreed to Rommel's proposals for the lay-out of the position in the northern Apennines and promised him for its defence twenty-one German divisions, to which were added later four neo-Italian divisions.[4]

All our plans were however changed by the situation in the Balkans. In spite of all our fears, the precautionary measures laid down in Plan Axis were in general carried out successfully; but it soon became ever clearer both to Commander-in-Chief South-east and to the Supreme Command that the forces available were totally inadequate for the defence both of the coasts and of the interior of this enormous area. This situation was aggravated by the fact that the main attack by the Western powers was expected there and that Hitler not only clung to his determination to defend the outer coastal perimeter but now wanted to include the island outpost chain: Cythera, Crete, Rhodes. He continually reverted to his preoccupation over the Rumanian oil area and now produced numerous additional political and military arguments such as the prevention of the establishment of an Allied line of communication to Russia through the Aegean and Dardanelles, and the necessity of countering enemy pressure on Turkey and her entry into the war. In his usual

way he returned to this theme almost daily, stating that 'the operations of the Russians and the unrest stirred up by England in the
Balkans must be looked at as part of the same picture'. He did not
however mean that there was any co-ordinated enemy strategy or
that the Red Army was likely to get as far as the Balkans; on the
contrary he tried to assume that there must be a conflict of interests
between the British and the Russians in south-eastern Europe which
he was sure would have decisive consequences on the course of the
war. His train of thought led him to the conclusion that for this very
reason 'there could be no question of withdrawal, since we could
then look on as *tertius gaudens*, quite apart from the fact that the
Balkans were necessary for their oil, bauxite, copper and other
metals'.[5]

Faced with this high-flown argument, composed as usual of a
hotchpotch of political, economic and military ideas, OKW was
once more in a difficult position when, in agreement with Commander-in-Chief South-east, it tried to insist that the defence of the
Albanian-Montenegrin-Dalmatian coastline must be the basis for
all plans for the area. Our argument ran that the enemy's 'prospects for a thrust into the heart of Europe were equally good' from
this coastal area as 'from the Channel coast'. The danger was all
the greater since the guerillas had been considerably reinforced by
numerous Italian deserters. There were also a number of most disturbing reports that Hungary and Rumania might 'shortly follow
the Italian example'.[6]

In order to ensure that a sensible policy based upon this reasoning
was adopted in the Balkans, OKW once more reverted to the procedure it had used so often, that of inviting the responsible Commander-in-Chief to discuss the question personally in the Headquarters. Field Marshal Freiherr von Weichs* appeared on 24
September and emphasized most strongly his opinion that, in view
of the shortage of resources of all types, the scope of his task of
defending the Balkans and the surrounding island area must be
considerably reduced. Going into detail he stated that it was of
course important to hold an outer ring as long as possible. If however the expected landing occurred, the greater part of the Greek

---

* In August 1943 he had taken over the newly formed Headquarters Commander-
in-Chief South-east in Belgrade. Colonel-General Löhr (Army Group E) thereafter
commanded in Greece and General Rendulic (II Armoured Corps) in the northern
Balkans.[7]

land and sea area 'must be regarded merely as an outpost'. The only defensive position was a line east and west through Salonika which would then provide the necessary flank protection for the main front in the northern Adriatic. Only by such a reduction of commitments would it be possible successfully to bar the enemy's advance into the heart of Europe. A formidable ally of Commander-in-Chief Southeast and OKW in this struggle to get a commonsense strategy adopted proved to be Commander-in-Chief Navy who told Hitler flatly that the outermost islands in the eastern Mediterranean were valueless in the present situation. In view of the enemy's clear superiority on land, on sea and in the air 'he could bypass them and force them to surrender merely by cutting off their supplies. Forces and equipment which could not be replaced' would thus once more be lost 'without any compensating strategic advantage'.

On occasions Hitler would admit that these arguments were militarily sound but he was entirely unshaken and clung to his political point that the whole Balkan area, including the islands, must be defended. When it came to finding ways and means to do this Grand Admiral Dönitz's ideas produced a new and unexpected solution: the evacuation of Sicily, he stated – to which he had been opposed – had now opened the way for the enemy in southern Italy but he could still be prevented from using it as a springboard for an attack across the Adriatic if we held on to Apulia and in particular the great airfield area of Foggia.[8] This was enough for Hitler! He disregarded the fact that Dönitz, Weichs and OKW were all opposed to defending the outer Balkan ring; a few days later, when Foggia had already fallen, he similarly disregarded an OKW memorandum entitled *Possibilities for Future Strategy in Italy and the Southeastern Area* and now became determined not merely to hold 'the entire south-eastern area' but to continue to oppose the enemy in southern Italy. There was a further discussion in the headquarters on 30 September; Kesselring had just opted for 'a mobile strategy to economize our forces' but Hitler now more or less talked him round to his ideas, whereas Rommel who did not know the situation in southern Italy in detail, said nothing. Both of course realized that this fundamental alteration in the strategy in Italy would not be without its effect upon the change in command organization which had still not been put into force.[9]

The future in the Mediterranean was finally settled by a series of orders; the first issued on 1 October laid down that the defence of

385

Italy should now be conducted much further south, on the line Gaeta-Ortona instead of that in the northern Apennines which had been planned and prepared for months. These orders culminated at the end of October when, contrary to all previous plans, Field Marshal Kesselring was given command of the whole of Italy and Rommel was withdrawn for other tasks. In his orders for the South-east Hitler rode over renewed attempts by Jodl to get approval for at least preparatory measures for the construction of rear covering positions and not only insisted on holding the entire Balkans but now demanded that a large number of islands should be occupied which had previously been held by the Italians. In addition to the Southern Sporades the following were now to be defended 'as a minimum': in the Ionian Sea – Corfu, Cephalonia and Zante; in the Aegean – Scarpanto, Milos, Cos, Leros, Samos, Chios, Mytilene and Lemnos. At his conferences he would dismiss any allusion to the lack of resources by a remark like: 'we must be strong in the north (ie the northern Balkans) but not too weak in Greece'; similarly he refused to give authority for the construction of positions in the rear because of 'the unfavourable psychological effect which this might have.'[10]

As a result of these instructions bloody battles took place in the Aegean to wrest isolated islands back from the English; in the remainder of the Balkans the situation degenerated into one of continuously spreading internal unrest, while the considerable forces and resources employed on coastal defence never came in contact with the enemy.[11] In Italy Hitler's new orders initiated a period of almost six months static warfare in the area south of Rome, best known by the name of the Cassino Monastery which became the focal point of the battle. The battle is primarily remembered for the bravery of the troops on both sides but from the strategic point of view it was a period of the war which, at the latest by the middle of November when the supposed danger in the Balkans had become less imminent, had lost all object. The struggle in northern Italy was an exhausting one and no doubt it held up the enemy for a considerable period but from the German point of view in the fifth year of the war it was totally unjustified, particularly since the long exposed coast of Italy offered the Allies opportunities for landings which could at any time have brought upon us a new catastrophe. Furthermore, both the Eastern and Western theatres were deprived of forces which could have been made available in considerable numbers if a timely withdrawal to the northern Apennines had been made.

The situation in the South and South-east threw an ever greater workload upon OKW, particularly since both Hitler and Jodl became more and more insistent on laying down every detail 'from above'. The move of every division, by number, was plotted on the map in Wolfschanze; any splitting up of formations, as often happened when things went wrong in the Italian theatre, had to be approved by Hitler. In the Balkans the Supreme Command directed the employment of forces against the insurgents and the routing of transports in the Aegean; in the Abruzzi it laid down the trace of every position and the fall of every barrage; from 15 December Commander-in-Chief South-west* had daily to report progress in construction of the Cassino line.[12] The Q Section of OKW became responsible for the administration of the rear areas. On Hitler's instructions Mussolini was given authority only over the Po Valley but even here his 'Republican-Fascist Government' had to accept considerable limitations to its sovereignty. 'High Commissioners' in the form of German 'Gauleiter' were charged with the administration of the frontier areas in northern Italy from Istria to Tyrol, for Hitler proposed to incorporate these in the 'Great German Reich' since they had previously been Austrian territory. Particularly severe restrictions were placed on former Italian soldiers who for the most part were shipped off to Germany as 'military internees'.[13]

Hitler's Mediterranean strategy threw a far greater strain upon the German war potential than the military situation justified and no long-term compensating economies were made in other theatres. One elementary principle governed everything but there was no great lofty idea behind it and no thought of concentrating upon essentials; instead the Supreme Command had only one object, to defend the occupied areas everywhere on their outermost perimeter and on other fronts to plug such holes as appeared as quickly as possible. This was the principle in Scandinavia, where even in Denmark a resistance movement now appeared, necessitating an increase in security forces; it applied to the West too which had to furnish the main reinforcements for Italy. Our position there became so weak that in the late summer of 1943 Commander-in-Chief West

* From 21 November 1943 Field Marshal Kesselring and his staff were designated C.-in-C. South-west.

had seriously to consider the possibility that the Allies might forthwith establish a bridgehead across the Channel as a preliminary to a subsequent invasion.[14]

The dichotomy within the Supreme Command meant that OKW normally had little to do with the Eastern theatre, but now the extremely serious situation there forced OKW to pay some attention to it in addition to its cares for 'its own' theatres of war. Hitler's large-scale demands for the Mediterranean meant that all possibilities of further reinforcement had been exhausted and the plans for the construction of an 'East Wall', which Zeitzler had at last managed to get through after much effort, were overtaken by the increasingly rapid advance of the Red Army.[15] In this situation the senior Army staff officer in the Operations Staff, Major General Freiherr von Buttlar, in my absence made it his priority job to convince Jodl and via him if possible Hitler, of the necessity of constructing a firm defensive position on the great river barrier of the Dnieper. Buttlar went so far as to propose emergency measures on the lines of those which a year later were adopted in the West; his idea was that training schools and other mobilizable units of the Replacement Army, together with an increasing number of the superfluous young men in the Air Force and Navy, should be formed into improvised formations and man the river obstacle in order to give the worn-out divisions, as they withdrew from the East, at least the possibility of pausing and reorganizing. Jodl however rejected it all. He was not prepared to attribute any particular importance to the obstacle of the Dnieper and, based upon Zeitzler's daily situation reports, he was not prepared to concede that the army in the East was incapable of defending the obstacle with its own forces. In any case, he said, it was not the job of OKW, which had no detailed knowledge of the situation in the East, to anticipate the requirements of the headquarters responsible. Buttlar's final plea that stabilization of the situation in the East must have a considerable effect upon defence against the forthcoming invasion in the West did not move Jodl to act.[16]

In early autumn the Russians reached and crossed the Dnieper, but the resulting widespread criticism of the attitude of OKW did not discourage General von Buttlar and his staff. It was primarily due to their tireless efforts to find every sort of expedient that in addition to all the previous reductions in the OKW theatres of war during the period between October and December 1943, four infantry divisions, $7\frac{1}{2}$ armoured and Panzer Grenadier divisions and one parachute formation were made available for the East from the West, South and South-east. An Army Order issued by Hitler on 28 October 1943 begins with the words: 'I have transferred to the East divisions from the South and West in order that, by a counter-attack, the enemy forces which have crossed the Dnieper may be annihilated. This attack will result in a decisive reversal of the situation on the entire southern flank of the front.'[17] These reinforcements however became available not as a body but in driblets, generally too late, and in insufficient numbers to affect the crisis which had meanwhile worsened; this was primarily the fault of Hitler and his refusal to take decisions in good time. About this time even Bormann became 'much concerned over the war situation' and confided to his 'party comrade' Goebbels: 'it is so hard to get the Führer to make any decision'.[18] Goebbels further comments in his diary on the situation in the East as follows:

10 September 1943: The depressing thing is that we haven't the faintest idea what Stalin has left in the way of reserves.

8 November 1943: Himmler was especially opposed to Manstein, whom he regards as a first-class defeatist. The crisis in the southern sector of the Eastern Front would not have had to become so serious had a man of real calibre been in Manstein's place.... The Führer received Manstein in the HQ. Contrary to expectations, the interview is said to have passed off well, and it is assumed that Manstein is to return to his post. I (Goebbels) regard this as a grave disaster.

(*On 16 December 1943 Jodl notes in his diary:* 'the Führer expressed himself most forcibly to Speer and myself on the defeatist attitude in Manstein's staff as reported to him by Gauleiter Koch.)

15 November 1943: The situation in the East is causing us great anxiety. What is it to lead to? The Soviets have reserves at their disposal of which we hadn't the faintest idea.

The following extracts from the shorthand records of the briefing conferences held on 27 and 28 December 1943 give a shatteringly graphic picture of Hitler's lack of decision in this difficult situation.

Fragment no. 7
Discussion with Colonel-General Zeitzler, 27 December 1943

ZEITZLER: My Führer, I believe that this is the winter offensive.

HITLER: Quite right, but all the same what completely new armies has the enemy got? He's just got the same old forces.

ZEITZLER: He's got nine armoured corps completely rested. They've done nothing for weeks.

HITLER: That's right, but they're still the same old forces. He's got no new ones. One thing I don't understand. In these armoured corps, the tanks alone are no good to him. They always say they lose a lot of men in the tanks; some are burnt and some shot up.

ZEITZLER: He's in the same boat as we are. We've no worries about tank personnel. We've always had replacement crews.

HITLER: I'll think over all that again this evening.

ZEITZLER: All right, but I would like a decision. Every day is valuable.

HITLER: Well the decision stands.

ZEITZLER: Can I give the order? That at least would help.

HITLER: Yes, you can give it. He's got one division available. But to give up this* – it's all very well, Zeitzler to talk in a solemn voice and say it's gone. But when we get to the position where it really has been lost, then friend Manstein won't take any responsibility for it.

ZEITZLER: That's obvious.

HITLER: We're going to have a difficult time; there's going to be a major crisis here** and that will have an immediate effect on Turkey. They want to force Turkey into the war by 15 February. If there is a crisis in the Crimea then they'll make propaganda out of it. Then friend Manstein will refuse to take responsibility and will say that's a political affair.

ZEITZLER: Yes, and it will be very serious because we shan't be able to save much.

HITLER: We shan't be able to save anything. The consequences will be catastrophic. They'll be catastrophic in Rumania. This is a major position here. As long as we can remain here and here and as long as we have the bridgeheads, construction of airfields here will be a risky business.

ZEITZLER: Yes; this will only happen if we do nothing up here and let things develop and then there's the whole question of the future in First Army area.

HITLER: Watch out now; we've had one or two cases like this

* The Southern bend of the Dnieper.　　　　** The Crimea.

where everybody said that all was lost. Later it suddenly turned out that we could stabilize the position.

ZEITZLER: It's just that this is such a vital area for us; it's so close.

HITLER: I agree entirely. I didn't release 4 Mountain Division for nothing. But there is nothing to show the enemy's got an entirely new army; it's merely forces which have been rested. When you say this is the beginning of the winter battle – it's merely the continuation of the same battle; they're not different.

ZEITZLER: That's why I haven't yet called it the winter battle.

HITLER: The enemy wants to ensure that we have no time to recuperate and so goes on fighting. That's all. But you've already seen here that somewhere he comes to the end of his resources. Here he's fought himself out. Gradually it all came to nothing.

ZEITZLER: It's just a question whether he didn't do that intentionally so as to start again up there.

HITLER: No, I don't think so.

ZEITZLER: All the same he doesn't seem to be in any difficulty. He just didn't push on here.

HITLER: That's because he can't do any more. You mustn't think he's like one of the old giants who simply becomes stronger when he's laid out.

ZEITZLER: But he's kept going for so many months in a row.

HITLER: He must get out of breath one day. I've read this report. In my view the decisive thing is that in fact the morale of the troops isn't good. That's the decisive point.

ZEITZLER: That's why I always pass on these reports. I have to take account of things like that.

HITLER: When all's said and done, I'm the one who's always pointing this out. I talked about it here with the armoured corps people. They say the infantry's just not fighting. That's not always the case. Some divisions fight well and nothing goes wrong on their front. When someone says to me: there's no point trying to work on the morale of the infantry – I'll tell you one thing, Zeitzler, I'm a man who has personally built up and led perhaps the greatest organization on earth and I'm still leading it. I've had cases where the news has come through from certain areas: we shall never beat the Social Democrats here, or: we shall never get the better of Communism here; it's quite impossible we shall never get rid of it. It was always clear that it all depended on the local leaders. If this is the general view that it's all quite right and there's no point in trying to raise the morale of the infantry, all I can say is: I once heard a major talking and I said to myself it's useless talking to the troops, I've listened to it umpteen times and it's useless. Of course if an officer says to me there's no point in talking to the ordinary soldier all I can say is: that proves that you've no influence. Next door there's another chap in charge and he's got his people in the palm of his hand. You've got no influence and you must get out.

ZEITZLER: Yes, the troops mirror their commander.

HITLER: Yes, invariably.

ZEITZLER: And I'm quite clear, if the troops are bad the commander is either dead or he's a bad commander.

HITLER: When commanders get killed a bad one comes along. That's clear.

If he runs out of breath here and we can do it with the forces we have available, then later we'd be tearing our hair out. This won't be the end of the matter but if we can twist the thing round here – Manstein is just washing his hands of these forces. He knews well enough they'll attack here. He says they won't make a frontal attack because then they'll wear themselves out. He's not going to go on; he's just washing his hands of it in order to make himself feel happy. Unfortunately I can't do that; I can see the time coming when this affair's going to work up into a crisis. I can see all the consequences it will have. That means decision. People go on saying: we'll fight on to victory – all that fighting on to victory means to me today is to stabilize the thing somehow.

ZEITZLER: That's quite clear. If we can stabilize, from our point of view that's victory. But we can't beat him.

HITLER: We can't expect anything more at the moment. But we mustn't forget that last winter we were in a frightful position. Nevertheless by May we had so far recovered that we almost thought we ourselves could attack and in July we did actually attack.

ZEITZLER: It's just that we're so very stretched. The moment one gets things organized, something new happens and we're under pressure all over again.

HITLER: The happy moment will be when they can dig themselves

in and build a defensive position. We must weed out the commanders in the really bad divisions as soon as we can. That
we must do. I've studied this report and all that I can say is
that it's quite clear that there are divisions here which are
absolutely wretched. But when a commander says there's no
point in trying to influence the men all I can say is: there's no
point in your influence. You've not got the force of character
to influence anybody. What he says is the absolute truth. The
only thing is he's looking at it merely from his point of view.
He's completely lost his influence. I know that. During the
First War I knew regimental commanders whose influence
was rock-bottom because they didn't take anybody seriously.
Then we had other regimental commanders who could get
things organized in a flash even in the worst situations and
had the troops as steady as a rock. It just depends on the man.
In those formations I've had something to do with* I know
precisely if a formation has a good commander or not. You
can see from looking at the formation, just like in a mirror.

Then I think back to my local organization. At each
election I had districts where I knew for sure on the evening of
the election that we would win. Why? I can hardly say: it
might be Franconia or Cologne – Cologne was as red as could
be – or East Prussia. What of East Prussia! It was completely
reactionary and against us. Or Mecklenburg or Thuringia.
Thuringia was scarlet but in one place I had Koch, in another
Sauckel and in another Ley. They were the chaps. In other
places unfortunately I had no really good man and there it
was difficult. I knew exactly! The good districts were those
where there was a good leader.

It's just the same today. Things went wrong in Kassel not
long ago. No harm in talking about it. The man was sacked of
course. He wasn't up to his job. No good saying; 'yes it was
easy in Berlin and Hamburg'. On the contrary it was more
difficult in Hamburg. There we had a chap who was as tough
as steel, who couldn't be broken by anything, while the chap
in Kassel simply broke down. He wasn't up to it. In fact the
commander is a reflection of the state of his troops and the state
of the troops is a reflection of the character of the commander.

Often it can be disastrous. For instance a good commander

* The Waffen-SS.

arrives, gets killed, another arrives and gets killed too. Naturally every case of that sort has its effect on the troops. If the troops are particularly fond of their commander, if a good commander goes, the effect is always worse than if a bad one goes. We have all experienced that. That's also possible. But one thing's certain: if the morale of the troops is bad, it's always something to do with their commander.

It's easy to say these things. We've been through it, Zeitzler. We've withdrawn to a shorter line and found we couldn't hold that either. Alternatively we would certainly have been able to hold it if we had been more mobile and units had had more spirit of self-sacrifice. Then we'd have been able to save a lot.

We've had a classic instance. The whole Nevel catastrophe was caused by the small-minded selfishness of the two Army Group commanders who acted like little egoists and wouldn't help each other. Now we've got to hold a longer line; that's all right; it must be all right. I can see the consequences here; they're very far reaching.

ZEITZLER: Both for the troops and for this position.

HITLER: For the troops it's catastrophic. We've simply got to defend this second Stalingrad* if at all possible. We can't just cold bloodedly turn our backs on it because it's got nothing to do with Field Marshal von Manstein's Army. We can't do that; we must remember there will be men lost here.

Next point: you may say – more important purposes. But perhaps we can achieve the more important purposes without that. Something else may happen. It may happen that Turkey enters the war. In Rumania it all depends on the Head of State. If he loses his army here – you must read the letters he's been writing to me.

ZEITZLER: No. My only thought is that the disaster might be even greater. That's my only reason.

HITLER: Yes, we must see. I've been wondering whether we can take the risk of putting 16 Division in down there.

ZEITZLER: I thought that over and over yesterday. I said to myself last night: we must think whether to bring down 16 Division.

HITLER: Zeitzler, I must say one thing: this is not as difficult a decision as that about the Crimea. If we withdraw here, the

* This means the Crimea, which had been cut off by land.

Crimea is lost. We must think very hard whether in these circumstances we should take 16 Division. We should then be bringing up 44 Division and one division here and 16. That's three formations if the worst comes to the worst until the other becomes mobile.

ZEITZLER: We can spare them for the moment. But looking into the future it's going to be difficult up there. In the long run we can only get things organized if we withdraw from this salient. In my view it's been just as bad at Petersburg.

HITLER: It's not so bad. If we withdraw there ... take out a couple of divisions. It's not so bad as it is here. It's here that it's the worst; so it will have the worst effects. We might be forced to withdraw a bit here in order to save a division.

ZEITZLER: No. That wouldn't be so bad but if you think of the big issue.

HITLER: Of course it would be unfortunate because of the Finns but it wouldn't be so bad as it is down there. I think the loss of the Crimea is the worst thing that could happen. It would have the worst possible effect on Turkey. The Finns can't give up; in the last analysis they've got to defend themselves.

[There follows here Fragment no. 10, the record of a long and detailed discussion, primarily between Hitler, Jodl and Zeitzler, of tactical detail on the Eastern Front. The record is to be found in Appendix p. 536.]

Fragment no. 11
Meeting with Colonel-General Zeitzler, 28 December 1943

HITLER: Let's look at this now. I thought all this over. I thought it over this way and that last night. We can't clear up the situation here without a considerable increase in forces. The worst that can happen in the North is that there might be trouble with the Finns. That may suit us quite well. They've got to go on fighting anyway. Then down here if the worst comes to the worst we may lose the Crimea, the iron-ore area of Krivoirog and Nikopol. So if we don't clear up this affair! Now from the economic and supply point of view the loss of these areas down there is much more serious for us than the loss of those up there, so that I've decided to bring up the necessary reinforcements.

I can't take anything of any size from the West. We can only get the necessary forces by taking them out up there. This is what I thought. If the worst comes to the worst we must make do with the formation which is here in the Oranienbaum what's-its-name. That should be more or less enough to cover the business at Narva. We must hold this along here for as long as possible so that he can't get in there. That means that these formations here are more or less available. With what is here we can more or less pack up and occupy this line. I think that even now we could get twelve divisions out of Army Group North.

ZEITZLER: Yes. Then it fits very well that Küchler is to come tomorrow. I'll work all this out today and submit it to you. The railway business is going very well. Then we've got the two groups, 16 Armoured and 1 Armoured; they've got some offensive capacity and we must concentrate them. Down here we can pull out 4 Mountain Division and 17 Armoured Division and as second echelon we bring along 101 Division and 16 Panzer Grenadier by rail. They can get on the move straight away with the two others between 6th and 8th or possibly 12th. Then we have one further echelon. Can I get things going on these lines?

HITLER: Yes.

ZEITZLER: Now there's this question: Manstein is complaining that the Fourth Panzer Army has got rather too large a front. He's right. Now I wanted to suggest that down there we take over Sixth Army (Sixth Army has only one corps) and place the corps direct under the Army Group and then I would be for the idea – I can talk to Manstein again – that we should bring Sixth Army up here instead of Hollidt and put Hube in there. I have more confidence in Hube than in Hollidt. There are mobile formations up there and Hollidt has no experience with mobile formations.

HITLER: Here we stay on the defensive.

ZEITZLER: Yes. Hollidt should do more there, and Schörner is there too. It's not so bad there. If you agree I will get that going.

HITLER: Yes.

ZEITZLER: Now the tanks. Since 7 December the following have arrived: for First Panzer Army 294, for Fourth Panzer Army 94, for Eighth Panzer Army 154, total 542. They are mostly still on rail and haven't yet got to units.

HITLER: But tell me one thing: how many tanks have we given Army Group South including those of the five divisions which we brought up here. So far as I can calculate it's had well over a thousand assault guns and tanks.

ZEITZLER: It's had everything which came up. Last month I gave them 100 and this month a further 80.

HITLER: He carries on as if he was being treated like a Cinderella. In fact he's the only one who's had anything.

ZEITZLER: He snaps up more or less everything. We started giving Army Group Centre something for the first time two or three weeks ago. Apart from that Army Group Centre's been badly treated.

So may I now get this going straight away, my Führer? The first division can start moving this evening.

(Conference ended)

Many lessons emerge from these wearisome dialogues – wearisome I have no doubt for the reader too. The longest and most important is that which took place between 11 pm and 1 am (fragment no. 10; see p. 536) in that it showed once again the dire consequences of the Supreme Command's schizophrenia[19]. Hitler had recently issued an instruction that all questions concerning both the East and the other theatres of war should be submitted to him only in the presence of both Chiefs of Staff, Jodl and Zeitzler;[20] but this made little difference. The advice given to him could in the nature of things only be one-sided and he kept to himself alone the prerogative of weighing the pros and cons and giving orders accordingly. There were continuous arguments about the distribution of forces but there were other serious conflicts of interest, an example of which is the following incident:

OKH had for some time been pressing for Army Group North to be withdrawn behind Lake Peipus and Narva. As always, Hitler was opposed to any loss of territory; moreover in the north with his eye on the Finns, he was even less inclined to approve a withdrawal, though it would have shortened the front considerably and though he was frequently urged to do so as the conference records show. In order to avoid having to face up to the tactical necessities urged on him by the Army he turned to Jodl and got him to list the strategic disadvantages which the loss of the head of the Gulf of

Finland would entail. OKW had no detailed information on the situation on the Eastern Front and was therefore in no position to weigh the opposing points of view. In this way Hitler played off his military 'working staffs' one against the other and so, even in a case of this importance, was able to take whatever decision happened to please him, quoting in support of it whichever point of view suited him best.[21]

After the surrender of Italy the Western powers had begun to exert increased pressure on Finland and, well ahead of time, OKW had taken the first steps to ensure that it would not be caught unawares should the Finns also fall out of the war. On 28 September OKW *Directive no. 50* was issued, based upon detailed proposals by Colonel-General Dietl, Commander-in-Chief of Twentieth Mountain Army and entitled *Preparations for the Withdrawal to Northern Finland*. Oddly enough, although the proposal was the exact opposite of the policy adopted in Italy and the Balkans, Hitler agreed without further argument; he realized that there was no possibility of remaining in the country without the co-operation of the Finns, still less if they were hostile. The only area which it was proposed to retain was the nickel-ore area of Kolosjoki – Petsamo in the far north, to which communications could be kept open via Norway. Preparations were therefore made in good time and resulted in the completely successful withdrawal of German troops during the autumn and winter of 1944. This was a true example of 'forward planning'. In October 1943 Jodl visited Mannerheim and came back with an optimistic impression; at times Hitler's estimate of the political situation would lead him to say that 'the military considerations were no longer urgent'; but all the time OKW kept the plans up to date.[22]

During the autumn of 1943 a variety of reports from Hungary and Rumania led Supreme Headquarters to prepare protective measures for the event of the defection of these allies also. It seemed more than likely that this would occur in the forseeable future; they had suffered severe losses in the East and now all land communications with the numerous Rumanian divisions in the Crimea had been cut. Both countries were, however, so situated geographically that there could be no question of any arrangement which did not meet the requirements of German strategy. In contrast to Italy and Finland, moreover, Hitler reckoned on making increased use of their war potential, working through new governments which he proposed to install. When, however, at the end of September 1943, OKW examined the details of a military occupation of both countries, we soon reached the conclusion that for the foreseeable future the forces of the Wehrmacht would be insufficient to deal even with Hungary alone, unless the Rumanians could be persuaded to take part in the action against their neighbour and co-ally! This led to the conclusion that military action against both countries simultaneously would obviously not be possible, and the recommendation therefore was that 'the political authorities must ensure either that this situation does not arise or that the internal conditions in both countries are such that there will be no co-ordinated military resistance'. The plan for the occupation of Hungary underwent many alterations as the situation changed, and was eventually suddenly announced and put into action in March 1944. As regards Rumania, Hitler's views altered after repeated conversations with Marshal Antonescu; preparations were therefore no longer considered necessary and were pigeon-holed.[23]

Bulgaria's obligations to Germany were political only, and even after the death of the King there was no sign of her loyalty wavering. On the German side, however, it became ever more difficult to meet the obligations undertaken when German troops first appeared on Bulgarian territory; these provided for a rapid combined attack on Turkey in Europe should that country enter the war – Operation 'Gertrude'. When the Turks and the Western powers seemed to be drawing closer together at the beginning of December 1943, OKW prepared what were patently no more than emergency measures; the plans previously prepared looked both inadequate and unlikely of fulfilment. In particular a rapid combined attack on Turkey in Europe hardly seemed possible now. I visited Sofia in the middle of January in answer to a request by the Bulgarian Chief of Staff for a detailed briefing on German views of the war situation and was received by the 'Regency Council'. From the beginning of 1944 the Bulgarian 'shadow front' against Turkey was placed entirely on the defensive.[24]

The Spaniards requested the return of the Blue Division, to which OKW had to agree.[25] As before we had only occasional contact with Japan via the liaison organizations on both sides. The war situation in the Pacific was such that there could clearly be no question of any early or effective assistance to the German Eastern Front from that quarter.[26]

*

All these plans and all these events were the outward and visible sign of a leadership determined not to admit that its sun was setting, and determined to paper over any cracks which might give signs of weakness. Yet on 3 November 1943, in the first preparatory directive for defence against invasion in the West, the German Supreme Command rose to the level of real strategy once more. The opening sentences of the instruction read:

> The hard and costly struggle against Bolshevism during the last two and a half years, which has involved the bulk of our military strength in the East, has demanded extreme exertions. The greatness of the danger and the general situation demanded it. But the situation has since changed. The danger in the East remains but a greater danger appears in the West: an Anglo-Saxon landing! In the East the vast extent of the territory makes it possible for us to lose ground,´ even on a large scale, without a fatal blow being dealt to the nervous system of Germany.
>
> It is very different in the West! Should the enemy succeed in breaching our defences on a wide front here, the immediate consequences would be unpredictable. Everything indicates that the enemy will launch an offensive against the Western front of Europe, at the latest in the spring, perhaps even earlier.

The orders which followed made it abundantly clear that reinforcement of the defensive capacity of the West was to be initiated without delay with the object of preventing any penetration of the coastal defences. The directive continued:

> Should the enemy ... succeed in landing ... the problem will be by the rapid concentration of adequate forces and material, and by intensive training, to form the large units available to us into an offensive reserve of high fighting quality, attacking power and mobility, whose counter-attack will prevent the enemy from exploiting the landing, and throw him back into the sea.[27]

This directive (No. 51) was the starting point and framework on which the German Wehrmacht prepared for its great task of defence against the forthcoming attack on Western Europe (in which Denmark was included); operationally it laid down the principles upon which the battle at the start of the invasion was conducted. A few days earlier a separate order had been issued to Commander-in-

Chief West instructing him, as a precaution, 'to reconnoitre a defensive position on the general line Somme–Marne – Marne-Saône Canal – Swiss frontier', in other words a reserve line through Central France. Although he reported on this in the middle of December, the proposal was never followed up.[28]

In his book *The Struggle for Europe*[29] Chester Wilmot, who is as a rule particularly well informed on the German side, states that Hitler had been designedly misled over the number of divisions available in England, but this was not in fact the reason which led him in the autumn of 1943 to order the precautionary measures against invasion given in *Directive no. 51*. In the later stages of the war he became increasingly prone to question at least 'dialectically' even the most obvious dangers, and this tendency began to appear at this period; the clearer the information became on the state and progress of the enemy's preparations, the more often did he express doubts on the seriousness of Allied intentions.[30] Significantly enough the first words in Jodl's diary for 1 January 1944 are: 'enemy intentions for 1944 – the Atlantic Wall or the Balkans' – written certainly to some extent under the influence of some remark to this effect by Hitler the day before but giving proof also of his own longstanding obsession with the supposed attraction of the Balkans. From time to time therefore opinions wavered and other possible targets for a landing were considered, such as southern France, Portugal or Norway, but this did not noticeably deter OKW from pursuing its task of reinforcing the West.[31] In December. in fact, a form of tabulation was made of 'forces to be furnished in the event of a major landing' from all the OKW theatres of war.[32] Changes were so continuous however that it soon became clear that it was useless, and even Hitler himself eventually came to the conclusion that only the Atlantic coast from Holland to Normandy was worth consideration; at his briefing conference on 20 December 1943 he stated: 'there is no doubt that the attack in the West will come in the spring; that is entirely beyond question', and again: 'there is no doubt that they have made their decision. The attack in the West will take place any time from the middle of February or early March.'[33]

In spite of all this, contrary to his own convictions and his own orders, Hitler continued, literally up to the day before the invasion, to prejudice the defensive preparations in the West in favour of the East or even of Italy. In the same briefing conference on 20 December, for instance, General Buhle protested to him:

If by January we can in fact get the ... tank battalions for the west ... then nothing untoward can happen there; but (*he continued after an interjection by Hitler*): if we take everything away from the West we can only hope! No sooner have I got something together (*meaning in home depots*) than it's gone.

Who are you saying that to? thereupon stormed Hitler. I'm not going to have you reproaching me for always taking formations away. You must speak to Zeitzler(!) .

But he then went on to reveal the real situation when he said: 'but it is very difficult for me. I look at the situation in the East every day; it's horrible. Another five or six divisions (!) might be decisive and lead to a great victory.'[34]

Nevertheless withdrawal of both personnel and equipment from the West quietly went on until, on 28 December, urged on by OKW, Hitler issued an explicit instruction that no more withdrawals were to take place without his authority.[35] Even so the extracts from the conferences of this period quoted above prove that he had not the determination to stick to his own principles either as regards the West or the East; he would neither economize on the one nor build up the other.

Detailed study of the facts will show that the intentions expressed in *Directive no. 51* were honoured more on paper than in reality. This stands out clearly if the somewhat sketchy instructions in that directive are compared with the conclusions of a 'general examination' of the situation made by Commander-in-Chief West at the end of October. This ended with the words: 'if the Supreme Command considers that a major attack is coming then ... reserves must be provided. In rear there must be a centrally placed and fully mobile reserve Army'.[36]

Instead what the German Supreme Command proposed, and indeed all it could propose, was little better than a series of expedients. As time went on it became ever clearer that the defence against the invasion would have to be undertaken primarily by the forces already available in the West; it equally became clear that these forces had neither the numbers nor the fighting capacity to stand up to a large-scale battle of attrition.[37] Furthermore even at the lower levels there was no unity of command – witness the fact that at the end of *Directive no. 51* were listed no fewer than seven independent headquarters, Commander-in-Chief West being merely number five, which were ordered to report on their plans and dispositions to Hitler himself – not to OKW.[38]

On 20 December 1943 Hitler stated for the first time:[39] 'if they attack in the West that attack will decide the war' – and he meant: 'if this attack is not repulsed the war is lost!' This of course implied that there was an alternative – that should the invasion be successfully defeated there might be a more favourable outcome to the war. If this was the way things looked and had there been a real Supreme Commander of the Wehrmacht, he might have felt impelled to point out to his political masters the unlikelihood of a successful defence, however great might have been the conflict between his inclinations and his responsibilities thereby entailed; but in Germany there had been no Supreme Commander since 1938. It was far beyond either the capabilities or the prerogatives of the Chief of the OKW Operations Staff, who was in any case in a position to survey only part of the overall strategy.

By the turn of the year 1943–44 therefore both Hitler's policy and his strategy had run into a cul-de-sac. The only loophole was offered by the German long-range rockets, the so called V-weapons, which were expected to be available shortly. On Hitler's orders they were to be aimed exclusively at London and he anticipated that as a result of this 'long-range battle', if the invasion were not actually prevented, it would at least be considerably delayed and its progress seriously affected. OKW was only let into the secret of the V-weapons in the autumn of 1943, and was then made responsible for all organizational and tactical questions preparatory to their employment in the field. We soon reached the conclusion that 'the quantity of high explosive which can be delivered daily is less than that which could be dropped in a major air attack'. The staff did not, however, have a chance to follow this up, for in February 1944 it became known that the V-weapons and in particular the larger A4 rocket (the 'V2'), would, contrary to expectations, not be available until a later date.[40]

Directive no. 51 was the last of the series of consecutively numbered directives whereby, starting on 31 August 1939, the Supreme Command had made known its decisions on strategy and tactics. This does not imply that the headquarters subsequently became less active in issuing orders. But as the command organization dissolved into splinter groups and as the content of its instructions became more and more an expression of the impressions or dictates of the moment – in other words as the quality of the leadership deteriorated, so did the form in which its instructions were issued. The disappearance of these directives, which constituted the Supreme Command's well established instrument of co-ordination, was hardly noticed by those directly involved; certainly none of them raised any objection.

I got back to the headquarters at the end of November. As might be expected from this short description of the main events during my absence, I expected to find a whole row of new, and in some cases entirely unexpected, jobs awaiting me. Before I had had time to come to grips with them, however, I was given the special task of speaking on the war situation to a meeting of leading German editors called by the Head of the Reich Information Service, in Weimar. As a basis Jodl gave me the notes he had used a few weeks before for his talk to the Reichsleiter and Gauleiter.[41] I discarded Jodl's top dressing of political and party slogans and reduced my talk to a bald sober military presentation, coloured at the last moment by my journey by road from Berlin to Thuringia through the ruined, and in some cases still smoking, German countryside.

Up to August 1943, German Supreme Headquarters had treated the air offensive more or less as a routine matter but since the attack on Hamburg at the beginning of that month more attention was paid to it. When the first news of this attack arrived, Hitler unexpectedly appeared during the night in Jodl's hut and, obviously more shaken than he had been since the time of the Norwegian campaign, gave vent to bitter reproaches. Jodl and his staff however had always been designedly excluded from the strategy of the war in the air, and did not even know the background of the steady deterioration of the Luftwaffe; they were therefore hardly the correct target for Hitler's complaints. Subsequently the air attacks became far more devastating and Hitler – not without reason – began to direct his criticism at Göring; the staff were only spectators, but on occasions the atmosphere in the map room became such that they felt it best to leave quietly. Hitler himself now began gradually to take over the tactical, technical and organizational command of the Luftwaffe, particularly in so far as the new weapons, the 'jet fighters', were concerned. Serious illusions and mistakes, similar to those the Army had had to put up with for several years, soon began to be visible.[42]

Facing War on Two or More Fronts

Up to the beginning of 1944, the year of the invasion, the continued discrepancy between what German Supreme Headquarters intended and what it actually did had resulted in the forces available in the West, measured in battle-worthy army formations, being actually smaller than in the previous autumn. If the situation maps of 7 October 1943 and 11 January 1944 are compared, they show a loss of four divisions against an increase of seven untrained 'battle groups' of about regimental strength. In a survey of the situation about the turn of the year Jodl had told Hitler: 'the reinforcement of the West is in full swing, as is the training of new formations. In all there are 1·3 million soldiers in the West.'[43] These figures meant little as regards battle-worthiness, and neither Hitler nor Jodl had any illusions as to what this calculation really meant. The word 'reinforcement' was only too likely to raise false hopes; all that was happening was the arrival of a few regimental groups which had recently been mobilized by the Replacement Army, shifts of individual divisions within the western theatre and supply of equipment for newly formed units, particularly armoured units, which were still totally unready for battle. There was not a single divisional-strength formation in this remarkable 'reinforcement'.

OKW was eventually able to form into divisions individual battle groups, cadres and recruit units, but thanks only to the additional time accorded us by the enemy. The vast majority of Army formations in the West consisted of so-called 'static' divisions; only a few of them, and these only partially, could be made mobile by horse transport and other local expedients and so in some way be equipped as 'mobile reserves', the task for which they were intended. Apart from occasional disconnected remarks by Hitler, no thought was given to reinforcement from the bulk of the Army in the East. Once the situation in Italy had calmed down, OKW hoped to get two motorized formations from that theatre, and one infantry division from Scandinavia. Naval and air reinforcements were just as scanty; air and anti-aircraft units could not be spared from the defence of Germany, and were only made available after the beginning of the invasion.[44]

The sheer numbers of the measures taken tended to conceal their ineffectiveness but over and above all these preparations, in the forefront of Hitler's thoughts was always the Atlantic Wall. Propaganda on the subject had been carried on so long that he now seemed to be deceived by it himself; he had never even seen the Wall, and his picture of it was based principally upon the tonnage of concrete and numbers of workers employed and on comparisons with the fortifications of the Siegfried and Maginot Lines. He took far more notice of the pictures brought back by non-military photographers specially despatched for the purpose than of the sober reports of the Wehrmacht headquarters responsible or of the members of his own military staff. Construction continued in 1944 but the requirements and proposals of the Army were subordinated to the construction of colossal coastal and even field artillery positions, of U-boat shelters and, in the later stages, of emplacements for the V-weapons – all ordered by Hitler personally down to the last detail.

At the turn of the year came a crumb of comfort for Supreme Headquarters; after a rapid check of the defences in Denmark, Field Marshal Rommel took over command of the northern coastal sector in the West down as far as Brittany. By his tireless activity, by his originality of thought, both on tactical and technical questions, and by the inspiring influence of his ubiquitous personality, he did all that was humanly possible to compensate for the weaknesses of the defence. When I visited him, however, in his first headquarters at Fontainebleau, he confided to me that he had no real confidence in success.[45]

In the first half of January, Jodl set forth on one of his very rare trips to visit the area between the mouths of the Scheldt and Seine; this was generally considered the most likely area for a landing and Jodl wished to get a personal impression of the state of the defences. His diary entries between 6 and 13 January 1944 give a fairly complete picture of his tour. Even more than in the office he seems to have become submerged in a mass of detail and gained no real understanding of the situation. Only occasionally do the serious gaps in the whole basis for the defence emerge, as for instance when he writes:

9 January: Withdrawals to the East have been on a vast scale. 319 Division in the Channel Islands has only 30 per cent of its original establishment.

7 January: The best people have been removed. The officers are good and the men are good but they cannot act. Re-equipment is producing chaos. The Corps has twenty-one different types of battery.

11 January: Transfer of officers to the East must cease. The regimental commanders are new and so are several battalion commanders.

711 Division has only six battalions including one Caucasian[46] ... it has no modern anti-tank equipment.

12 January: 10 SS Armoured Division (newly formed) is asking to be relieved of construction duties. It has carried out no major exercises. Its armoured group is only semi-mobile.

13 January: There is chaos in Cherbourg with the three Services alongside each other ... situation in Brest bad.

9 January: How *is* the air defence against the invasion to be carried out? Major action against the enemy air forces is not possible. Fighters can carry out minor attacks against shipping and targets at sea. We must not accept battle with the enemy air force.

This trip therefore led to no new concept and no better realization of the limitations of the defence. There was however one good result; shortly after Jodl's return the most important harbours on the Channel and Atlantic coasts were declared fortresses on the lines of the 'strong points' in the East and provided with concrete fortifications on the landward side. This had been Hitler's idea and the great importance he attached to it was obvious when a little later he assembled the commandants of the 'fortresses' at the headquarters and himself briefed them on their duties. In the wider framework he had not been prepared, even under the threat of invasion, to invest Commander-in-Chief West with the plenary powers of a true Commander-in-Chief of all three Services, either in his own sphere or in the hinterland with its jumble of civilian authorities; so now, in spite of all representations by OKW, he could not bring himself to invest the fortress commandants with full powers of command even in their small areas. In spite of the persistent 'chaos' (to use Jodl's word) in the command organization and in so far as they could be held, these 'fortresses' did, as is well known, later form a thorn in the flesh of the enemy's supply organization for months after the invasion, and had a considerable effect upon the operational situation.[47]

Jodl's notes on his trip gave the first indications of the disagreements between Rundstedt and Rommel over tactics for the defence; they were to occupy the time of the headquarters well after the start of the invasion. Briefly they were as follows: Rommel, influenced primarily by his experience in Africa of the enemy's devastating air superiority, wanted to concentrate the defence and therefore the forces, including the armoured formations, in the immediate area of the coastline. Rundstedt, working on more classical lines, wanted to keep as high a proportion as possible of his meagre reserves deep back in the theatre, in order to launch a concentrated counter-attack against the enemy once he had landed and once it was there-fore clear what the area and objective of the landing were. Supreme Headquarters initially tried to strike a happy mean between these differing opinions – seemingly all it could do in view of the increasing uncertainty regarding the probable landing area. Since the reserves were however far too small anyway, this did not greatly improve the prospects of a successful defence.[48]

For a long time Supreme Headquarters, Rundstedt's headquarters in St Germain, and Rommel's in Fontainebleau were convinced that the most likely area for a landing was the Straits of Dover. Hitler of course continually talked round and round the subject and reckoned on other possibilities which from time to time led to addi-tional OKW instructions. The OKW Operations Staff however, soon began to realize that it must stick to the predetermined line, for on 6 April 1944 Hitler went so far during his briefing conference as to express doubt whether 'the whole thing' – ie Anglo-American preparations for invasion – was not 'a bare-faced piece of play-acting' and whether it was not a 'completely bare-faced bluff'.[49] Finally, in spite of all his wavering, Hitler himself decided that the defence should be concentrated between the Scheldt and Seine – a decision proved by the concentration of forces on the ground, the number of fortifications, the number and type of coastal batteries and mobile reserves, and all other criteria by which defensive capa-city can be judged. His conclusion, and that of most others, was based upon the fact that in this sector the enemy's naval and air forces could be employed with maximum effect in view of the short dis-tances involved, that there were long stretches of coast suitable for a landing and several worthwhile ports, that it was the shortest way to the Ruhr, the heart of the German arms industry, and that the majority of the launching sites for the V-weapons threatening the enemy were located there.

In April 1944 Hitler suddenly, and without apparent reason, included Normandy in his category of probable landing areas, ranking it almost on a level with the Straits; but this produced no change in the main lines of the plan for the defence. It will be remembered that the Normandy peninsula, and Brittany also, had been placed high in the order of probable danger areas in a number of previous OKW orders. Similar hints had been thrown out in an examination by the Operations Staff and in the OKW instructions to Field Marshal Rommel of November 1943 for 'study of the counter-attack against an enemy who succeeded in landing', also in certain remarks by Hitler in February and March 1944.[50] This time however things were different, for Hitler now demanded that the northern coast of Normandy be reinforced with the utmost speed. Since, however, he laid down that there must be no weakening in the Straits sector, resources which could be made available were extremely slim.[51] Nevertheless one of the newly-formed infantry divisions which was moved to Normandy at this time was never identified by the enemy intelligence until they met it in battle on the coast.

Hitler never gave any reason for his change of view other than that information in gradually increasing detail regarding dispositions in southern England made it appear likely that there would be a landing in Normandy, where was the great port of Cherbourg and where the Cotentin Peninsula could easily be cut off. Moreover the area could be reached by enemy fighters, though we in Germany were still unaware of their greatly increased range. There is however still no completely satisfactory explanation of the reason which led Hitler suddenly to attach such greatly increased importance to Normandy. It may be that this was an instance of his oft-quoted 'intuition'. It is more likely, however, that he had certain intelligence reports on the subject which may well have been known to him alone, since from the beginning of 1944 the secret service ('Abwehr') had been taken out of the hands of Canaris and transferred to the so-called 'Reich Central Security Office' (*Reichssicherheitshauptamt*) of the SS. It is also remarkable that Hitler did not pat himself on the back particularly when, a bare two months later, his opinion proved correct, though the explanation of this may be that, in company with all other important commanders and advisers, he continued for some time to anticipate the *main* landing in the Straits area.[52]

*

Hand in hand with the increasing uncertainty over the area of the invasion went an even greater uncertainty over its timing. At the beginning of 1944 Supreme Headquarters had been convinced that it would come early but as the months went by the basis of this conviction vanished. Moreover the tension springing from this uncertainty increased, not merely as a result of the uncertainty itself but because the other far-off fronts, all of which were fighting furiously, were crying out for the forces concentrated for the defence against the invasion or ear-marked for it.

Hitler and his advisers were not strong enough to resist the pressure, although it was fully realized that the success of the invasion would be decisive for the outcome of the war. German Supreme Headquarters could not bring itself to make planned economies in the other theatres of war and no less than four times between January and June 1944 upset the whole layout of the defence in the West by withdrawals of greater or smaller forces. The prospects of a successful defence were small in the first place but they were further seriously reduced by the antics of the Supreme Command.

The Allied landing at Anzio–Nettuno on 22 January was the first occasion for a withdrawal of forces. Although almost 250 ships were employed, it came as a complete surprise to Commander-in-Chief South-west and was only detected when the enemy was already on shore. In his previous appreciations and in his conversation with Jodl when the latter visited the battle headquarters on Mount Soracte north of Rome on 4–5 January 1944, Kesselring had stated that an early landing in rear of his front was improbable. On 6 January the OKW Operations Staff had called intelligence representatives to a special meeting to discuss increased reconnaissance and surveillance of the southern theatre; the only result was that the OKW Intelligence Section's report on 20 January had stated: 'there are no indications that any major undertaking in the Mediterranean area is imminent'.[53]

Maintenance of a defensive position south of Rome was now of no further strategic importance and in view of the overall German situation one would have thought that this attack deep in its rear could lead to no other conclusion than that now was the moment, before a new catastrophe developed, to withdraw rapidly to the northern Apennines. But instead Jodl stated flatly that here was clearly a first attempt on the part of the Allies to weaken and disperse the German reserves by minor attacks on the periphery of occupied Europe preparatory to the main attack across the Channel. Our only answer, he stated, must be to smash this enemy initiative at the outset and teach him such a lesson as might perhaps even stop the major invasion in the West.[54] This was grist to Hitler's mill! He outdid Jodl with the words: 'if we succeed in dealing with this business down there, there will be no further landing anywhere'.[55] Supported by Jodl he then proceeded, by a series of precipitate decisions, to do exactly that at which the enemy was supposed to be aiming. Two motorized divisions, for whose movement to the West orders had already been issued, were now retained in Italy. A corps headquarters was hurried up from Germany together with cadres and recruiting units amounting to considerably more than a division, with a liberal allocation of tanks; finally one infantry division and one tank battalion were summoned from the West. All this to 'throw the enemy back into the sea'. I had all I could do to stop a further proposal to withdraw two additional divisions from the West.[56]

A fruitless struggle developed round the bridgehead, during the course of which the following significant incidents occurred: Hitler himself laid down the tactics for the counter-attack and clung to them, although it was to be carried out by totally inexperienced troops and in face of protests by the commander responsible, Colonel-General von Mackensen. On 28 January he issued his order for the 'Battle of Rome'[57] which sounded like the call of a revolutionary fanatic. He employed every turn of his peculiar method of expression to present this action as one far surpassing in importance anything which could possibly take place in a 'subsidiary theatre of war' such as Italy; for the first time his language gave so clear an indication of his lack of confidence in the leaders of his own Wehrmacht that it could not but shake any military system to its foundations. 'The battle must be hard and merciless' he stated, continuing with the berserk phrase 'not only against the enemy but against all officers and units who fail in this decisive hour'. By the beginning of March the first and then the second counter-attack had bogged down in blood and mud; the entirely impractical plans to bring the main Allied front 'crashing down'[58] had come to nought. Hitler thereupon adopted the most extraordinary procedure; he summoned from the battle at Anzio-Nettuno to the headquarters, then at Berchtesgaden, fifteen comparatively junior officers and for two whole days, in the presence only of Keitel and Jodl, interrogated them himself about the course of the battle.[59] Deep in the flank of the Army in Italy the

Anzio-Nettuno salient threatened both its front and its rear communications; it continued to immobilize reserves earmarked for the West; yet no thought was given as to whether the situation did not necessitate some less hazardous and expensive solution in the Italian theatre.[60] Instead the activity of the OKW Operations Staff was limited to the issue of a stream of orders and demands for reports on the construction of static positions, combined with research into the lessons of the trench warfare of the First World War. One of the OKW liaison officers, Major von Harbou, was killed in one of the resulting 'fox holes'.

The stubborn German defence did have some effect upon Allied plans. Churchill's plan for the capture of Rhodes and a move into the Aegean[61] had to be given up and the landing in southern France postponed. But from the German point of view this was of minor importance. Nothing was in fact achieved, except to ensure that in its hour of danger, the West had available three to four divisions fewer than before.

The West was bled a second time for the occupation of Hungary. Quiet had reigned there for months; yet on 28 February 1944 suddenly, and as far as HQ Area 2 was concerned without apparent reason, the plans were taken from the pigeon holes and transformed into orders. A concentric move up to the Hungarian frontiers had to be hastily organized by the OKW Operations Staff. The forces originally earmarked had for the most part already been sucked in by the Eastern Front, but such was Hitler's rage and thirst for revenge against the Hungarian Regent, Admiral Horthy, that he committed the error of raiding the western theatre once more, though the task was of secondary importance and the season now far advanced. A corps headquarters, certain army troops and the newly formed 'Armoured Training Division' (Panzer Lehr Division), a particularly valuable formation, was snatched from the forces preparing for defence against invasion and moved into Hungary on 19 March. Parts of another armoured division from the West (21 Armoured Division) were already on rail when Hitler was persuaded to cancel the move since the occupation was proceeding so smoothly. As for Anzio, so now for Hungary, the Replacement Army was made to furnish a number of regimental strength combat groups which had just been mobilized for the West, although they would have been of particular value there since they were motorized. Just as in Italy, these forces remained in Hungary and then, with other formations furnished by the South-east, were drawn into the insatiable maw of the eastern theatre. Only with great difficulty, and then only a few weeks before the invasion, did OKW manage to get the formations withdrawn from the West, including the Panzer Lehr Division, returned to their proper station.

Other incidents in connection with the occupation of Hungary were in many respects more like 'a game of cops and robbers'; the Wehrmacht in any case had only a subsidiary role to play. It was, however, an unhappy experience to have to stand around once more in the ante-rooms of Klessheim Castle and try to entertain our Hungarian colleagues, while in the next room Horthy was being forced back by Hitler on to the straight and narrow path of loyalty to his alliance and armed assistance to his ally. By a series of machinations the Regent's return was delayed long enough to ensure that when he arrived at the Burg in Budapest the honours were done by a German guard. The occupation was under the command of Commander-in-Chief South-east, Field Marshal Freiherr von Weichs and in passing it should be noted that, to his credit and with the energetic support of OKW, he contrived to stop the Hungarian armed forces being disarmed – one of the main points in Hitler's programme. When their country was occupied, the vast majority of the Hungarians continued to treat the Germans as allies, as indeed they did when, immediately thereafter, they had to defend their own frontiers against the Red Army which had pushed forward as far as the Carpathians.[62]

During these months the most serious and most continuous drain on the forces preparing for defence against the invasion was constituted by withdrawals to the Eastern Front. Little more than a month after the tap had been turned off at the end of 1943, forces and resources destined for the West began to drift off again in the opposite direction via the Replacement Army and depots in Germany. On 21 January Jodl notes in his diary Hitler's decision – not the only one of its kind: 'equipment now available in depots for Panzer Jäger Battalions of divisions in the West to go to the East'.

The following month the same thing happened to the last three mobile regimental groups of the Replacement Army, before they had even been formed into a division, and towards the end of February one infantry division (214 Division) followed from Norway.

In March Hitler was so shaken by the catastrophic developments in the southern sector of the Eastern Front, developments for which he himself was responsible by clinging to lines which had long since become untenable, that he threw overboard all the principles laid down regarding the relative importance of East and West. Away went three newly formed divisions from Poland, one from Denmark and two from the South-eastern area, all of which were immediate or potential candidates for the West.[63] On the night of 24 March he began raiding the resources of the West in earnest. Jodl notes in his diary: 'Assault Gun Battalions of 326, 346, 348 and 19 Luftwaffe Divisions to go to the East', and then 'Commander-in-Chief West gives up 349 Infantry Division' and the next day the last and most serious blow: 'II SS Corps to be moved with the utmost urgency'. The Panzer Lehr Division having been withdrawn to Hungary, the West was now left without a single battle-worthy fully operational armoured division at a moment when the invasion might come any day.

It is true that Hitler only reached this decision after deliberating on it for some days; it is also probably true that, without this assistance, the First Panzer Army in the East, which was now in a pocket in the northern foothills of the Carpathians, could not have escaped encirclement.[64] This does not alter the fact however that, in view of the threat hanging over the West, the German Supreme Command ought never to have let things get to such a pass. Contrary to his normal practice, Hitler in this case took a risk which can only be characterized as a gamble. Had there been an Army Chief of Staff responsible for all theatres of war, such a situation would never have been allowed to develop. Some of the responsibility must be laid at the door of Jodl. Admittedly he had long since given up all pretensions of dealing with the situation in the East in detail, and had thereby renounced one of the essential elements of his job. Nevertheless he could have produced sound reasons to stop this destruction of the framework of the defence in the West, so laboriously built up and yet still inadequate.

Even in this case it never entered Jodl's head either to consult his staff or to give them time or opportunity to put forward any other point of view. He did no more than pass on Hitler's order shortly after midnight to General von Buttlar, Senior Officer Army in the Operations Staff. The views of Commander-in-Chief West were never asked for.

He, like the OKW Operations Staff, was simply told in telegraphic form what reinforcements he could expect in the West. On 24 March Jodl notes: 'C.-in-C. West will get 331 Inf. Div. (Wahn) complete by 15 April' and on 25 March: 'SS Adolf Hitler and if possible also 3 Mountain Div. to return (from the Eastern Front). Weapons, MT and tanks to be moved to the West.' These were but vague instructions, all the less likely to be carried out since OKH under Zeitzler, as Jodl knew only too well, invariably found ways and means of evading orders to withdraw worn-out divisions from the Eastern Front.[65]

There was therefore from the outset little likelihood that, once it had done its job, II SS Corps with its two fully equipped armoured divisions would return to the West. It even looks as if Jodl played some part in Hitler's decision to retain these two divisions for an indefinite period in order to use them as the core of a counter-attack on the southern sector of the Eastern Front. It was not until 12 June, almost a week after the beginning of the invasion, that Hitler was persuaded, most unwillingly, to give up the plan for this counter-attack and order the corps to be moved back to the West. These were the facts; yet on 31 August 1944 he stated to two generals: 'if I had had 9 and 10 SS Armoured Divisions in the West this affair (the success of the invasion) would probably have never occurred. I had not got them because of a criminal, and I must repeat criminal, attempt here to carry out a coup.' (Meaning the 20 July coup.)

The first sentence of this statement is to say the least questionable; the remainder was either the product of a completely confused memory or a gross and intentional falsification of the truth. Keitel, the only person present who really knew what had gone on, kept his mouth shut.[66]

Shortly thereafter the Crimea had to be evacuated with heavy loss, and this once more cost the OKW theatres of war one or two battalions.[67] On 12 May came the fourth and last instance of the German Supreme Command breaking all its principles and raiding the meagre forces available for defence against invasion. On that date the Allies resumed their offensive in Southern Italy. So far there had been none of those further attacks on the perimeter of Fortress Europe which Jodl's strategic theories had prophesied after the landing at Anzio – though this had not prevented the meagre German reserves being scattered to the four winds. Now there seemed little doubt that the strategy behind the Allied offensive was to prevent any move of German forces from Italy to the West. Hitler's continued determination to cling 'to every inch of territory' and his alarm at the loss of prestige which the imminent fall of Rome would entail, meant that he conformed to the enemy's plan even more exactly than might have been expected. Any idea of withdrawing forces from Italy had long since been forgotten; on the contrary within a week of the beginning of the offensive he threw into the South formations from Hungary and Denmark amounting to three divisions and when, on 25 May, the enemy succeeded in effecting a junction south of Rome between the main front and the Anzio salient, he followed them with a fourth untrained division from the South-east. This strategy of dancing to the enemy's tune culminated on 2 June in his order to move to Italy 19 Luftwaffe Division which had for long been guarding one of the most threatened sectors of the Western Front; simultaneously he withdrew a number of heavy tank units.[68]

These measures by Supreme Headquarters by no means met Kesselring's demands; with complete disregard for the overall situation, he had demanded, in addition to complete replacement of losses, no less than five fully operational divisions together with air reinforcements. Jodl too played some part in these decisions; he thought reinforcements necessary in order 'somewhat to reduce the immense risk of simply leaving the Ligurian Coast uncovered'. He did not seem to perceive that the long-overdue withdrawal of the Army in Italy to the northern Apennines would have achieved the same object with smaller forces. All that his staff could achieve was the issue of an order on 1 June for 'a major effort for the rapid fortification of the Apennines position'.[69]

The additional forces could do nothing to prevent the loss of Rome which occurred on 4 June. They could fulfil no other purpose and were merely sucked into the vortex of defeat in which ever greater losses were caused by Hitler's repeated orders to 'give up as little territory as possible' and 'to reconstitute the front north of Rome as far to the south as possible'.[70] In the West invasion was on the doorstep, yet it was once more deprived of one division, a number of armoured units and any prospect of reinforcement from the other OKW theatres.

In the Balkans and in the Aegean the defence of the coasts and islands had meanwhile relapsed into a state of total inactivity. In the spring however, it was only with the greatest difficulty that Hitler was dissuaded from occupying the island of Lissa (now called Vis) on the Dalmatian coast, which the Allies were using as a base for communication with Tito.[71] I was regarded as the Balkans 'expert' and, contrary to normal practice, therefore took an active part in the repeated discussions of this question at the briefing conferences. I pointed out that, even should the operation succeed, the enemy would have no difficulty in establishing himself on one of the numerous other islands, to which I received the ill-humoured and unconvincing reply: 'you might just as well say: what's the good of eating today because I shall be hungry again tomorrow'. Meanwhile a continuous struggle went on in the Balkan hinterland, but German Supreme Headquarters either could not or would not realize the deadly threat posed to the thousands of miles of defended coastline in south-eastern Europe by the possible junction of Tito's forces with the Red Army in the Danube Plain. The 'partisan war' smouldered on, highlights being Operation Rosselsprung in May 1944, when Tito only escaped by the skin of his teeth from a parachute attack by a Waffen-SS unit, and the high price which was publicly placed on his head.

In the western Mediterreanean it became clear early in the year that the Allies were preparing a landing operation and the coast was accordingly fortified from the Gulf of Lions to the Gulf of Genoa. All that the Supreme Command could do to meet the requirement here, however, was to produce one or two formations from the Replacement Army and ensure that individual divisions were reorganized and rested in this area. A command organization was set up ready to receive further reinforcements; an Army Headquarters directly under Commander-in-Chief West was formed in south-west France at the end of April 1944; this later became Army Group G under Colonel-General Blaskowitz, commanding First Army on the Biscay Coast and Nineteenth Army on the French Mediterranean Coast; the latter was in touch on the east with the Ligurian Army under the Italian Marshal Graziani, formed in the late spring of 1944 – but that was under Commander-in-Chief South-west.

Denmark had originally been considered as a likely landing area almost in the same category as the West; it was now hardly referred to. Norway on the other hand, even in this period, was still one of Hitler's major preoccupations and whenever possible additional forces and resources were allocated to it. In the North the OKW Operations Staff got a new job of considerable complexity when Hitler conceived the idea of occupying the Aaland Islands should Finland go out of the war; his object was to use them, and also the island of Suusari in the Gulf of Finland, as bases from which to maintain the blockade of the Baltic against the Russians. Hitler was now inclined to put all possible pressure upon the Finns, including the stoppage of German arms and grain deliveries; this was resisted by Jodl and Dietl, who pointed out that, whatever might happen, it was from the military point of view most undesirable for Germany needlessly to affect the 'comradeship in arms'. On 25 June Dietl was killed in an aeroplane accident. Hitler continued to waver.[72]

In all these tasks both the interests and the forces of the Navy were frequently intimately involved but this led to no closer contact or co-operation between OKW and OKM. All naval questions, including even those of minor importance, were generally dealt with personally and alone between Hitler and Commander-in-Chief Navy, Grand Admiral Dönitz, who spent much time at the headquarters. As a result of enormous exertions the outlook for the U-boat war was now becoming more favourable again and there were many occasions when the requirements of reconnaissance or coastal defence would have made desirable a unified command other than through the person of Hitler; yet in all these matters OKW remained restricted to its routine job of being a report-collecting centre.[73]

By the middle of May preparations for 'long range warfare' against England had reached a stage at which the middle of June could be laid down as the starting date for the firing of V-1 rockets from ground and air; they were to be supported by air attacks and long range artillery. The target was still London. Detailed instructions laid down by Hitler himself were issued to Commander-in-Chief West regarding the tempo of the attack;[74] in fact firing could not begin before 15 June, ie ten days after the start of the invasion, and the larger, faster and much more effective V-2 rockets only became operational at the beginning of September 1944, when to all intents and purposes everything was over.

The steady deterioration of the strategic situation was not without its effect upon relationships within the headquarters. There were a number of differing straws in the wind. For instance in the midst of all the preoccupations of this period, on 30 January 1944 the 'Day of the Rise of National-Socialism', Jodl and Zeitzler were both promoted Colonel-General and invested with the 'Golden Party Badge'. Jodl apparently felt himself even more closely bound to Hitler personally, as his extremely odd attitude to me in an incident shortly to be related showed.[75] Zeitzler's 'discipleship' on the other hand gave increasing signs of weakening, as a result of Hitler's continued senseless 'leadership' in the East and the continual defeats resulting therefrom. Field Marshal von Kluge had been the victim of a serious accident; on 30 March 1944 Colonel-General Hoth and Field Marshal von Küchler were dismissed and Hitler next proceeded to dismiss Manstein and Kleist, the last of the long established senior commanders on the Eastern Front, saying that 'the time for major operations' was past and that the new 'policy' of 'rigid static defence' required new men. This led to a sharp disagreement with Zeitzler, after which he did not remain long. General Heusinger was temporarily appointed as his substitute.[76] It was significant that when Field Marshal von Kleist was dismissed, Jodl commented to me: 'to think that a man like that could ever have been a Field Marshal! The man couldn't even express his thoughts clearly' – a good example of the attitude of mind and language which now began to become characteristic of Hitler's entourage.

The incident between Jodl and myself referred to above was this: at about this time I received from a relative, a leading industrialist and therefore connected with Göring's war economy organization, a warning couched in most cautious terms (it was buried among other matters in three letters) that Göring had been heard to state privately that Manstein and I were the leaders of a 'Catholic Freemasonry' working against National-Socialism. (Field Marshal von Manstein, be it noted in passing, is not a Catholic.) For some time Göring had ceased to reply when I said good morning to him. I therefore went to Jodl, told him the whole story and asked him to put things right. All Jodl said was: 'if it is true (meaning the "Freemasonry") your place is in a concentration camp, not in the Führer's Headquarters.' Disgusted I made for the door, merely remarking that it was hardly the answer I expected from someone with whom I had worked for so long. Jodl thereupon unbent somewhat, but only to the extent of saying: 'you'd better talk about it to Bodenschatz' (Göring's Liaison Officer). The latter straight away to work to try and clear matters up, but I used the opportunity to ask Keitel once more to be relieved. Keitel however refused on the grounds of Hitler's order.

There was now a new personnel policy, enthusiastically supported by Jodl and implemented with increasing vigour. In the wings of this the 'National-Socialist Leadership Organization' (NSFO), founded by Hitler at the end of 1943 came much to the fore. It was staffed by selected 'National-Socialist Leadership Officers' and Hitler's intention was that it should inspire the Wehrmacht with National-Socialist 'ideology' and so raise to new heights the determination to resist. Hitler himself took part, in that he normally made the closing address at the regular 'National-Socialist Courses of Instruction'.

At the end of January 1944 one of these closing scenes took place, contrary to custom, in Wolfschanze and a number of the headquarters officers were present. Hitler stated that he expected the most senior officers of the Wehrmacht to close their ranks ever tighter around him and his leadership, the more difficult the situation became. Manstein interjected: 'and so they will', which Hitler quite rightly took to imply a protest at the mistrust clearly implicit in his words of the attitude of the senior officers of the Wehrmacht, although for good or ill they had now obeyed him for more than four years. As a result of Manstein's interruption Hitler lost the thread of his speech, and a revolting witch hunt against the Field Marshal on the part of the Supreme Commander and certain generals of his 'immediate entourage' followed.[77] This incident showed clearly the fundamental cleavage which ran through the senior officers of the Army.

In HQ Area 2 we contrived to avoid being subjected to this Party supervisory system in military clothing which, significantly enough, did not work through 'the normal channels'. When the NSFO Headquarters asked us to accept an NSFO Officer, the Staff Adjutant, who was a war-disabled colonel replied: 'we've got no time here for such nonsense'. When I heard of this comment I got it put in somewhat more acceptable form but retained the sense of it.

Signs of disintegration were now beginning to appear, and a number of additional tasks of considerable magnitude came the way of OKW. Thus, we had to take over the Brandenburg Division, a special formation previously under Admiral Canaris and somewhat comparable to the British Commandos; henceforth it was OKW which had to allot it by regiment or battalion to the higher headquarters, according to the situation and their requirements.[78] We had to take over from Admiral Canaris' office a Field Intelligence Section which was henceforth incorporated in and directed by the Operations Staff. We had to organize and issue orders for the employment of a Field Security Service to maintain discipline in rear of sectors of the front which were threatened or had collapsed.[79] We resumed our efforts to concentrate under OKW as a unified service those military organizations, such as hospitals and MT, which were used equally by all three Services. We became increasingly involved in problems of supply and administration in the OKW theatres of war.

CHAPTER 5

Invasion

On 5 June 1944, the day before the invasion, German Supreme Headquarters had not the slightest idea that the decisive event of the war was upon them. For twenty-four hours more than five thousand ships had been on the move across the Channel towards the coast of Normandy but there had been no reconnaissance to spot them. Equally neither Rommel, nor von Rundstedt, nor OKW, had made any appreciation pointing out that, in view of the weather and tides, a landing in the immediate future was even probable. In fact, of course, because of bad weather the Allied Supreme Commander, General Eisenhower, cancelled his initial order for the start of the armada early on 4 June, when some convoys were already at sea, but gave the final go-ahead the same evening. Although he was still worried about the bad weather, the decisive factor was that, had it been further postponed, tides would have precluded launching the operation before 19 June or possibly even early July.[1]

The German command organization at all levels was in fact working in the dark because of the complete inferiority of the Luftwaffe; this makes it all the more incomprehensible that, in so far as I am aware, no notice was taken of the warning signs emanating from the Intelligence Service. In HQ Area 2, for instance, we did not even know that for some days now there had been wireless silence in the concentration area in southern England – the normal indication of an imminent attack, though admittedly frequently used for deception purposes. Equally we did not know that as early as January 1944 Admiral Canaris had discovered the text of a radio message to be transmitted from England shortly before the start of the invasion as a standby signal to the French Resistance. The message consisted of two completely innocent sounding lines of poetry from Verlaine's

Chanson d'Automne; the first, 'Les sanglots longs des violons de l'automne', formed the warning order to be given on the 1st or 15th of the invasion month; the second, 'Blessent mon coeur d'une longueur monotone', the more immediate warning to be given forty-eight hours before the start of the invasion. On the afternoon of 5 June the Intelligence Service informed Jodl that during the night of 4 June the second of these two sentences had been heard by the Security Section of Fifteenth Army. But no action was taken.

The actual sequence of events with all its implications only became known to the staff as the result of a subsequent inquiry which must have been ordered by Hitler. As far as I remember it emerged that as soon as they got the message, Fifteenth Army forwarded it by teleprinter to Army Group B (Rommel), Commander-in-Chief West and the Chief of the OKW Operations Staff; Commander-in-Chief Fifteenth Army, Colonel-General von Salmuth, was the only one to act, ordering standby on the evening of 5 June; even he only did so, however, after numerous reports of major sea and air movements had been received from the intercept service shortly before midnight. This inquiry into the reasons for the inaction of all those involved from the most junior headquarters right up to Jodl must have been abandoned under the pressure of events. It must therefore be presumed that none of those involved, including Jodl, attached much importance to the information; it may have been that, unlike Admiral Canaris, who had meanwhile fallen into disfavour and been dismissed, they did not realize its import; alternatively they may have been waiting for some more definite confirmation.[2]

All the headquarters concerned were fully aware that this phase of the war was of decisive importance, and they had been tireless in their efforts to get the defence to as high a pitch of efficiency as was possible in view of the serious gaps in our forces produced by five years of war; but Hitler's repeated raids on the West for forces for other theatres had upset the balance. The first and most important task of the defence was still 'by the concentrated fire of all weapons to *stop* the enemy landing either from the sea or from the air and to destroy him *on the sea, on the beach* or in the air landing zone'.[3] All that was available to do this, however, were 'static' divisions, totally untried, mostly composed of the older classes of conscript and completely inadequately equipped. The motorized and armoured divisions were held as 'mobile reserves'; they were intended, should the defence on the coasts and beaches fail, to counter-attack any enemy who might have landed and defeat him; but the majority even of these divisions had no battle experience. Only ten such divisions were available in all, and on 5 June four of them were not yet operational because OKH had, as usual, been dilatory in moving such remnants of them as remained from the Eastern Front.

The air situation was even worse. The original plan was still in force laying down that the meagre reinforcements available should only be flown in when the invasion started. Accordingly, prior to 5 June, the enemy had made good use of his absolute air superiority and had seen to it that: all bridges over the lower Seine and Loire were destroyed, thus cutting all reinforcement routes to the probable battle area: no reconnaissance had penetrated for a considerable period and as a result not a single bomb had fallen on the concentration areas, ports and shipping assembly areas in and around the British Isles.

Even had the approaching armada been detected, there was therefore little likelihood that it would suffer more than 'pin-pricks' from the Luftwaffe or the inadequate naval forces available. Supreme Headquarters and the higher headquarters in the West remained convinced that, in spite of all this, they would be successful in repelling the attack. Looking back it seems that the only grounds for this optimism must have been undiminished confidence in the superiority of the individual German soldier.

First developments were unpromising. Supreme Headquarters was in Berchtesgaden in its usual scattered accommodation. The first news arrived about 3 am on 6 June when Commander-in-Chief West reported major air landings in Normandy. All Operations Staff offices in the Strub Barracks were immediately fully manned. The staff officers in the 'Western Group' were kept busy passing the most important information by telephone to Jodl's aides in the 'Little Chancellery' at the other end of the town. At about 6 am General Blumentritt, Chief of Staff to Commander-in-Chief West, gave me the first indication that in all probability this was the invasion and that Normandy was apparently the area. He urged on behalf of his Commander-in-Chief, Field Marshal von Rundstedt, that the so-called 'OKW reserves', consisting of four motorized or armoured divisions, should be released so that they could move from their assembly areas to positions nearer the front.

This was the first and most important decision which Supreme

Headquarters had to take and I therefore immediately got on to Jodl by telephone. It was soon clear that Jodl was fully up to date with all the information, but in the light of the latest reports was not yet fully convinced that here and now the real invasion had begun. He did not therefore consider that the moment had arrived to let go our last reserves and felt that Commander-in-Chief West must first try to clear up the situation with the forces of Army Group B. This would give time, he considered, to get a clearer picture whether the operation in Normandy was not a diversionary attack prior to the main operation across the Straits of Dover.

General Jodl took this decision on his own responsibility, in other words without asking Hitler; forever after it was the cause of the most bitter accusations against OKW. The German defeat in Normandy with all its fatal consequences was, people said, primarily due to this failure to release the OKW reserves.

In my own view these accusations are unjustified and to some extent aimed at the wrong person. Assuming that the four divisions concerned were the Supreme Headquarters reserve in the full sense of the word, no one could have considered releasing them at a time when even the forward headquarters still had no clear picture of the situation and before the first enemy landing craft had touched the beach.[4] It was not for instance until 10.30 am that Headquarters Army Group B considered the situation sufficiently definite to inform their Commander-in-Chief, Field Marshal Rommel, who had been in southern Germany since 4 June. The Chief of Staff of Army Group B in his book published later states flatly that it was 'out of the question' and adds that 'one must have the nerve to wait'.[5] OKW could therefore hardly be expected to issue 'Operational Instructions during the first few hours'.

The errors of the Supreme Command in fact went far deeper than this. The four divisions were really no more than Commander-in-Chief West's reserves, for on 6 June no other forces existed which could be made available. The fact that the divisions were labelled OKW reserves was merely another instance of Hitler's interference in the command of operations – starting as always from the supposition that he and no one else was capable of reaching the one correct decision. Commander-in-Chief West had accepted this limitation of his authority, and he could therefore hardly expect that his request, made in the very first hours of the invasion, would be accepted. In view of Hitler's well known indecision it must therefore have come as a pleasant surprise to Rundstedt when, at 2.30 pm on the same day, after one or two preliminary 'partial' decisions, he was given full authority over at least two of these divisions; moreover they were the two best armoured divisions.

There is a further point of considerable importance in trying to form an opinion on this subject. Even on the first day it was clear that the enemy's undisputed air superiority made impossible any daylight movement of motorized formations even far in rear of the battle area.[6] It would therefore have been far better if the main reserves had been moved nearer the threatened coastal sector *the night before* but this would obviously only have been ordered had our reconnaissance been better and had all those concerned taken more notice of the intelligence services's reports. The interval between the early morning and the early afternoon of 6 June was therefore of little importance. The truth was that as soon as the invasion began, the fundamental reason for the unhappy developments of that first day and all those that followed was abundantly clear – the inferiority of our forces was such that it could not be compensated for either by the ability of the commanders or the bravery of the troops.

The second accusation frequently made against OKW is that the Luftwaffe reinforcements bore no relation whatsoever to those laid down. This also should be cleared up. The OKW Operations Staff had been allowed to know little of the conduct of the war in the air; we were therefore unpleasantly surprised to find that the 'Gruppen', the standard unit used by us to order and by OKL to report air reinforcements, when they actually appeared on 6–7 June were at only a third of their planned strength, in other words consisted only of ten instead of thirty serviceable aircraft. In addition, during transfer to the West, the air formations were split up as a result of enemy action and bad weather, resulting in further numerous losses. The first few 'jet fighters', 'miracle weapons' like the rockets upon which Hitler had counted so much, made little difference[7]; the enemy's air superiority was even greater than had been expected and from the first day of the invasion the Luftwaffe's inferiority was so great that it became the prime factor in making any command action or movement well nigh impossible.

In Berchtesgaden the various portions of Supreme Headquarters, each of which was dependent upon the other if it was to do its job, remained in touch throughout the morning by telephone only. Jodl with his aides was in the little Reich Chancellery, his staff was in the Strub Barracks and later Hitler was in the Berghof. As news continued to flow in, making it look as if this was no diversionary attack, discussions regarding the release of the reserves went on, for the most part direct between Jodl and the Chief of Staff to Commander-in-Chief West. About midday the usual assemblage collected for the briefing conference, but on this particular day there was a Hungarian State visit in honour of which the conference took place in Klessheim Castle, at least an hour by road from the offices of those involved. As usual when visitors were present it was a 'show piece', but in view of events in the West a preliminary conference took place in a room next to the entrance hall. I and many of the others were keyed up as a result of the portentous events which were taking place and as we stood about in front of the maps and charts we awaited with some excitement Hitler's arrival and the decisions he would take. Any great expectations were destined to be bitterly disappointed. As often happened, Hitler decided to put on an act. As he came up to the maps he chuckled in a carefree manner and behaved as if this was the opportunity he had been awaiting so long to settle accounts with his enemy. In unusually broad Austrian he merely said: 'so, we're off'. After short reports on the latest moves by ourselves and the enemy we went up to the next floor where the 'show piece' was laid on for the Hungarians, who were led by their new Prime Minister, General Sztójay, previously for many years Military Attaché in Berlin. The usual overestimates of German forces and confidence in 'ultimate victory' were more than normally repellent. The low point of this highly unsatisfactory day in so far as Supreme Headquarters was concerned is the entry in Jodl's diary: all it says for 6 June 1944 is: 'Ops. Staff (ie his own staff). Why have orders not been issued to put in 189 Reserve Div. and bring 2 SS Armoured Div. up? 277 Div. to be relieved by 34 Inf. Div. from 12 June', – just the usual details in fact, blotting out the big picture.

The same day a junior staff officer from the Operations Staff was despatched as liaison officer to the battle area in Normandy. Meanwhile, the day before, I had asked to go to Italy in order to get a personal picture of the progress of construction of the 'Apennine position' and thereby obtain a better background for orders on future strategy in this theatre. In the light of the new situation the question now arose whether I should still go. Jodl was inclined to think that, contrary to Hitler's original instructions, the withdrawal after the fall of Rome should be carried right through to the

Apennine position and that only on arrival there should we go back
on to the defensive. After enquiring from Hitler, therefore, he confirmed that my journey should proceed. So, in spite of the pressing
situation in the West, early on the morning of 7 June I set forth; I
did not get back to Berchtesgaden until the 12th.

Search the pages of Jodl's diary of this period as you will, no
mention will be found of any strategic thoughts or decisions on the
situation in the West. There are pages recording a report by the
Commandant of Crete, in which Hitler's comments are echoed
and a critical examination is made of the number and positioning
of individual anti-tank guns and coastal batteries and finally even
of the state of training of individual infantry companies on this distant island. There are other passages which have little to do with the
situation in the West; there is a summary of General Student's report
on progress in the formation of a 'Parachute Army', and on 12 June
there are other details including an adverse report upon a staff officer
who Hitler had discovered was Halder's son-in-law. There is no
mention even of the decision to bring back from the east II SS
Armoured Corps consisting of 9 and 10 SS Armoured Divisions.[8]
Neither Jodl nor the Operations Staff War Diary makes it clear that
at latest by 9 June, from the point of view of Supreme Headquarters,
the first phase of the battle against the invasion was over, and the
intention to defeat the enemy on the coast and on the beaches before
he could develop his superior strength had failed. Neither, moreover,
make it clear that the problem was now no longer that of moving up
additional reinforcements, but that the moment was one for a re-
examination of the whole basis of our future strategy. The problems
of strategy and reinforcements were of course interconnected; both
were decisively influenced by the fact that Supreme Headquarters,
as also indeed Commander-in-Chief West and Field Marshal
Rommel, were convinced – and remained so for a long time – that,
although the landing in Normandy could no longer be regarded
merely as a diversionary manoeuvre, a second attack across the
Channel would follow shortly.[9] Hitler himself was preoccupied both
with Brittany, generally thought to be a likely area, and also with
the French Mediterranean coast.

Rommel and the OKW Operations staff, with the significant
exception of Jodl, independently reached the conclusion that every
risk must be taken and all available forces concentrated for a rapid

counter-attack against the enemy who had just landed – as indeed *Directive no. 51* laid down; no one else reached this conclusion. The most important step was to move from the Straits to Normandy the bulk of Fifteenth Army, then to collect all forces which could be made available rapidly from other parts of France, and so be in a position to launch a decisive counter-attack.[10]

This was too bold a decision for Hitler. He would allow no reduction in the strength of Fifteenth Army. Any other possible reinforcements however could not arrive for days or even weeks. The result was that, though the Supreme Command clung to its decision to recover the entire length of the Normandy coastline, the only forces available to do so were those already on the spot, and they had been proved inadequate. Just as at Anzio, it did little good to issue orders that the enemy bridgehead, which meanwhile had been extended considerably, was to be broken down by concentrated local counter-attacks and then 'demolished in detail'. With this object orders were now issued that the armoured formations which, along with all other available forces, had meanwhile been drawn into the defensive battle, should be relieved and used as a concentrated force. Hitler decided that the main area for this offensive-defensive should be the eastern flank of the bridgehead near Caen; Rundstedt and Rommel were, however, already becoming worried about the western flank and the protection of Cherbourg.[11]

These operations were set in motion with every display of confidence, but we in the Strub barracks were anything but convinced. As usual Jodl refused to discuss in detail. Although I was then his immediate subordinate, it was not until long after the war that, to my great astonishment, I learned from other sources that at this period Jodl and even Keitel were talking on very different lines. Grand Admiral Dönitz has recorded a conversation with both of them on 12 June 1944 as follows:

Keitel and Jodl consider the situation very serious, although they still see a chance that with luck we can keep the bridgehead confined. The best hope would lie in an unsuccessful enemy landing attempt at another point. It is doubtful whether the enemy will make such an attempt. The most likely spot for it would be the coast between Dieppe and Boulogne or between Calais and the Scheldt River. It is hoped that the long-range bombardment of London will on the one hand divert enemy aircraft and on the other induce the enemy to attempt a second landing in northern France. If the enemy succeeds in fighting his way out of the present bridgehead and gains freedom of action for mobile warfare in France, then all of France is lost. Our next line of defence would be the Maginot Line or the old Siegfried Line. Field Marshal Keitel believes that even then there is still a chance to defend Germany. General Jodl does not commit himself in this respect, since everything depends on how the situation develops and on how many troops we can save.[12]

Throughout the battle in the West Jodl never spoke to Hitler in this vein, any more than he did to his own staff.

On my return from Italy the reception I got from my superiors both had its long-term implications and was typical of relationships within the headquarters. Even before I left I had been convinced that in the existing situation it was more necessary than ever to turn the naturally strong Apennines position into the main defensive line in the Italian theatre, and that only an eventual withdrawal to this prepared position would allow us to free forces from Italy for the West. My opinion had been reinforced by the urgent representations made to me by the Chief of Staff of Kesselring's Army Group regarding the state cf the troops, and also by a three-day road journey through the northern Apennines. But when, speaking from northern Italy on the evening of 10 June, I gave Jodl a preliminary report of my impressions, his reply made it clear that once more premature decisions had been taken, based entirely on Hitler's will – and this in spite of the fact that I had been specially despatched to report on the situation and he had not even heard my views. 'I can only advise you most emphatically', said Jodl on the telephone, 'to be most careful when you get back here and make your report.'

The date for my report was then postponed several times. Hitler was clearly unwilling even to hear me and at one of the briefing conferences of this period Keitel whispered to me to 'pack it up' and make no report at all. I refused indignantly, not merely because I knew more about the situation than anyone else but because I felt that I must represent the interests of the forces in Italy, which were still fighting a heavy rearguard action. When finally, later that day, the time for my report arrived I got out hardly more than a few sentences. I had brought a number of documents containing figures and technical data to support my point of view, but since they ran counter to his preconceived notions Hitler dismissed them with a flood of objections and misgivings and, when I refused to budge, signalled to his aide to take away the maps and tables without looking at them.

No one supported me. Summing up, Hitler declared that 'it was obvious' that it would be 'seven months' before the Apennines position was ready. Kesselring's order to withdraw to this position within three weeks was cancelled and Hitler now demanded that the front 'should be stabilized at least on the latitude of Lake Trasimene'. At the same time the 'Gothic Line', as it had hitherto been called, was demoted to 'Green Line'. Field Marshal Kesselring was in disfavour for several weeks. When he arrived at the Berghof at the beginning of July to make a verbal report he got no further than I had. Hitler's verdict was: 'the only area which offers protection against the enemy's superiority and restricts his freedom of movement is the lower gut of Italy'. Jodl was careful to note this down adding the following sybilline sentence: 'graphic description of the situation by the Führer and insistence on the necessity (sic) of fighting for every square mile of ground and every week of time'. In defence of this physiologically-expressed strategy and to justify his aversion to the Green Line, Hitler insisted on quoting for the hundredth time the figures for men and material used in construction of the Siegfried Line. Jodl records: 'it was 450 miles long, and at times 700,000 men were employed. 350 trains arrived daily and an equivalent amount arrived by IWT. It took 18 months using German labour only. There were 4,000 concrete mixers.'

The end result of these decisions, in which politics and prestige were the dominant factors, may be summarized thus: two months later, at the end of August, our forces, which were practically at the mercy of the enemy's air superiority, had to withdraw to the Apennines position just the same; they were by this time completely exhausted and the position was therefore immediately overrun by the enemy at its weakest point, the Adriatic flank. It was only then, when it was much too late, that the first forces were released from Italy to reinforce the West.[13]

In German Supreme Headquarters all strategy for defence against the invasion was becoming increasingly lost in a morass of indecision on major matters and interminable discussions of detail. Surprisingly enough however, ten days after the beginning of the invasion, Hitler

decided to discuss the situation personally with Field Marshals von
Rundstedt and Rommel at Margival near Soissons, where was to be
found Battle Headquarters W2, prepared in 1943 by the Todt
organization for Supreme Headquarters in the event of invasion.
Commander-in-Chief West had asked that either Jodl or I should be
despatched to the West 'to discuss future strategy', and this was the
reason for the journey. In view of the situation as it was in the middle
of June 1944, there was no intention that Hitler should remain in
Margival for any length of time. This was the last time he went to
France; it was also the only occasion on which the large headquarters
installation was used for its true purpose though, as they withdrew
later, German troops made temporary use of it as a strong point.

War books have produced many dramatic reports of this meeting,
ranging from a demonstratively hostile attitude on the part of
Rommel to a headlong flight because of the fall of a V-1 rocket
which had gone off course. None of these appear in Jodl's notes;
he was the only member of the OKW Operations Staff to take part
and the whole journey only lasted a day. The only point of interest
in Jodl's notes is that 'statement on enemy air superiority' figures as
number one. Neither in the briefing conferences which followed[14]
nor in Jodl's remarks to me, which as always were few and far between, was there the smallest indication of anything particular
having happened. The official records of the meeting are as unin-
formative as many other Supreme Headquarters documents of this
period.

The two commanders in the West naturally came to Margival
expecting to get some indication of the future intentions of Supreme
Headquarters; they were also undoubtedly determined to make
clear to Hitler that the resources so far allotted or promised would
not be adequate to defeat the invasion. All my experience however,
leads me to suppose that Hitler cut both Field Marshals short the
moment he felt so inclined. If he needed any urging to do this the
the situation would have given him an opening, for just at this
moment the burning question was how to avert the imminent
threat that the Cotentin peninsula and therefore Cherbourg would
be cut off from the rest of Normandy. Hitler had to accommodate
himself as best he could to the probability that this would occur and
that with it would go all his illusions about the 'destruction in detail'
of the bridgehead at this particularly important point. The responsible Army Headquarters (Seventh Army) wished to withdraw as

many forces as possible southwards but Hitler merely re-emphasized his demands that the largest possible forces should be thrown into the 'fortress' of Cherbourg. The only result was that, when the Americans captured Cherbourg, ten days later, they captured several thousand additional prisoners, whose loss was sorely felt at the fighting front. Meanwhile OKW was instructed by Hitler to make a detailed inquiry to see whether his order had been carried out down to the last available man.

There is some indication of what the remainder of the discussion in Margival was like from the entry in Jodl's diary for 17 June which reads: 'the Führer approved a minor adjustment of the front of 1 SS Corps in accordance with the situation'! There is no indication that the main plan was discussed, although that very afternoon an OKW order on the subject was issued providing for the 'concentration of four SS armoured divisions in the area west of Caen-Falaise, decision on their use in a counter-attack role being reserved to the Führer in accordance with the situation'. These four SS divisions (1, 2, 9, 10) were either still in reserve or on the move forward, and up to the end of June Supreme Headquarters was continuously occupied over the use to which Hitler intended to put them and with the issue of orders for the purpose. The first phase of the defence against the invasion, the prevention of the landing, had failed; the second, that of 'local counter-attacks', had hardly been possible anywhere; now we entered the third phase, that of the concentrated counter-attack. The direction of the attack was to be Balleroy, a small village on the coast approximately in the centre of the bridgehead; the immediate object was to drive a wedge between the British and American sectors.

In the next few days however the increasing superiority of the enemy together with Hitler's wavering leadership resulted in these plans too coming to nought almost before they had been formed. On 24–25 June the Operations Staff sent Jodl a memorandum dealing with Commander-in-Chief West's immediate intentions, and urging that every risk should be taken in the other coastal sectors, that the forces available for the attack should be considerably increased and that 5 July should be laid down as the date for the concentrated counter-attack. On the same day however Hitler gave orders that those formations which had arrived should not wait to concentrate their full strength but should be prepared at any moment to counter an enemy break-through by offensive action. This put an end to the last hope of regaining the initiative and meant the end of any possibility of doing other than dance to the enemy's tune. The indecision at the top was further underlined when Hitler at the same time began to toy with the idea of using the newly-arrived armoured formations to relieve Cherbourg and therefore of moving them to the west coast of the Cotentin peninsula. Commander-in-Chief West, assailed on one side by the enemy and on the other by his own Supreme Headquarters, considered this move at right-angles to the direction of the enemy's main effort and in face of the full weight of his air power, to be impossible, but the more he argued the more obstinately Hitler clung to this new idea – even when on 26 June Cherbourg had fallen.

Until almost the end of June the Supreme Command darted hither and thither like a will o' the wisp with its plans for elimination of the bridgehead by counter-attack, but before the end of the month they had all come to nothing, for the last recently-arrived armoured divisions had to be used on purely defensive tasks as part of the ring, now stretched almost to breaking point, which still held the enemy in Normandy. There was no more talk now of attack or of 'destruction'. The invasion had succeeded. The 'second front' – or rather the third – was established. Hitler might now have thought back to his statement that an Allied success in the West would decide the war and have drawn the necessary conclusions from it; but instead he was to be seen in front of the assembled company at a briefing conference, using ruler and compass to work out the small number of square miles occupied by the enemy in Normandy and compare them to the great area of France still in German hands.[15] One's thoughts went back to those early days of the Polish war. Was this really all he was capable of as a military leader? Or did he think that this elementary method would have some propaganda effect on his audience? It was a sight I shall not readily forget.

PASSIVE DEFENCE – UP TO THE END OF JULY

The next phase of the battle in Normandy covered the whole of the month of July; it was one of purely passive defence.

Its beginning was marked by a second conference between Hitler and the two Commanders-in-Chief in the West who, without thought for the urgency of the situation at the front, were summoned to Berchtesgaden on 29 June. After their departure there was a conference in the evening with a wider circle. Jodl's notes of it are as usual confined to details and it is Dönitz' account which shows most clearly that it was now recognized for the first time that all thought of major offensive operations in Normandy must be abandoned. In the background of the discussions, though never referred to, stood ominously the catastrophic developments on the Eastern Front. On 22 June, the third anniversary of the opening of the Russian campaign, the entire centre of the Eastern Front had been split wide open and Army Group North was facing a threat of encirclement. In Italy Hitler's order was forcing Kesselring's army to expend their failing strength in a useless attempt to stand up to a superior enemy in the open and they were therefore under continuous heavy pressure. In Finland the Russians had forced their way across the Karelian Isthmus and there were signs that the bonds of the alliance were loosening; the same was true even of the Bulgarians. Out at Berchtesgaden the effects of the continuous air attacks on Munich, the 'capital of National-Socialism', were becoming visible. More and more frequently enemy aircraft appeared even over the Berghof. A few days previously Colonel-General Dietl had been killed in an accident and not far away preparations for a State funeral were in progress; it took place two days later with sombre pomp; to many of those taking part it looked like the funeral of the Third Reich.

The OKW Operations Staff had nothing to do with the preparation for these conferences other than the normal assembly of the daily situation reports, to which in those days we frequently attached comments and suggestions addressed to Jodl. The staff in the Strub barracks does not seem even to have been told that the conferences were to take place and no member of it was present; we therefore had no opportunity of expressing our views either on the situation in Normandy, with its now clearly visible threat to the occupied areas in the West, let alone on the general situation. The staff had an overall picture; it had well-documented forecasts ready; it had detailed knowledge of the capabilities of both sides – and all this was available to Hitler as the basis for his decisions. But he preferred to give the assembled commanders-in-chief, as usual in the form of a long speech, the results of his own unaided reflections. Jodl was present at these discussions but the notes he made subsequently in his diary give no indication that he ever expressed an opinion; the entries are in dialogue form leaving the impression that his position resembled rather that of secretary.

The accounts by Commander-in-Chief Navy deal more with substance; from them it may be deduced that the conclusions of the two conferences on the situation in the West added up to the following: the possibilities of major offensive operations were limited by the enemy's air superiority and in coastal areas by the overwhelming fire power of his navy; no date for any attack could be laid down since, as a result of the air situation, no reliable forecast could be made of the times at which formations would arrive or be assembled or when supplies would come up; we must under all circumstances prevent a war of movement developing, since the enemy would then be able to develop his crushing superiority both in the air and in transport resources; it was therefore of vital importance to build up a firm front, confine the enemy to his bridgehead, wear him down by maintaining an uninterrupted war of attrition and then finally throw him back into the sea.

These were little more than instructions for continued self-deception; as the protests at the conference showed, they demanded both from the navy and the air force far more than could be done, but the following day, complete with numerous details, they were issued as an order drafted by the OKW Operations Staff, and were supplemented by a second order on 7 July.

These orders stated in so many words that it was now no longer possible to carry out the plan for an attack towards Cherbourg nor that for a major armoured offensive to divide the British and American forces. Hitler was particularly uneasy over the flank of the British zone east of the Orne because of its threat to Paris; initially therefore he insisted that, as soon as reinforcements arrived, this salient should be eliminated. But the idea soon silently faded away. He still refused to release for Normandy the forces of Fifteenth and Nineteenth Armies, though the latter included three armoured divisions which had meanwhile become operational. OKW made repeated and urgent representations on the subject but even beyond the middle of July had still not overcome Hitler's hesitation, primarily because, as a result of reports from Commander-in-Chief West, he was still worried about further landings in the Straits and the Mediterranean. In the OKW orders therefore a 'reduction in strength' of the other coastal sectors was merely 'considered as a possibility', although no forces or resources of any significance were made available for Normandy from any other source. Our repeated demands that the armoured divisions should be pulled out of the front to reconstitute a reserve were similarly without effect.[16]

While we in the headquarters were busy with the follow-up to the conferences just concluded Commander-in-Chief West, apparently influenced by the unsatisfactory course of events, decided to revive his own original concept of a mobile defence. He had hardly got back to France when, on the basis of an appreciation by General Freiherr Geyr von Schweppenburg, Commander of 'Armoured Group West', he proposed exactly those tactics which Hitler had just laid down as being 'under no circumstances' permissible. Rundstedt forwarded the original of Geyr's appreciation; it stated that only by adopting 'elastic tactics' could we 'at least temporarily seize the initiative', whereas continuation of the policy of 'plugging holes, an inevitable concomitant of static defence', would leave the initiative permanently in the enemy's hands. It was a clear attack on Hitler's principles and was supported by Field Marshal Rommel.

In the headquarters the proposal produced considerable uneasiness and a permanent state of agitation, though from very different motives. In accordance with the 'usual channels' the teleprinter message was first received by the staff in the Strub barracks; there we thought that this might at last offer an opportunity of diverting the attention of 'those on high' from the tactical imbroglio to the bigger picture. On Hitler's staff it was necessary to express oneself carefully if one wished to have any prospect of one's words being either read or listened to; in passing on the message to Jodl we therefore added that, if Commander-in-Chief West's proposal to abandon the idea of 'fighting the decisive battle in Normandy through to the bitter end' were 'considered dispassionately', it implied the evacuation of France and the rapid occupation of the shortest and strongest defensive position, the Siegfried line.

It would undoubtedly have been better had the two commanders in the West taken the opportunity of their visit to Berchtesgaden to put these proposals forward verbally, but even had they done so Hitler would almost certainly have rejected them just as completely and uncompromisingly as he did now. He must have felt it an affront to his leadership but he could also base his refusal on the facts that: mobile operations in the West would expose the troops even further to the enemy's absolute air superiority; the bulk of the infantry divisions were not really capable of carrying out major movements on foot; the further we were driven from the coast the smaller became the prospects of effective employment of ground-fired rockets against England.

The severity with which the proposal was turned down was shown by the fact that its author, General von Geyr, was relieved of his command. Even Field Marshal von Rundstedt had to be told by Keitel that when he appeared in Berchtesgaden, he had given the impression of being much in need of rest and had therefore better take a long leave. On 7 July Field Marshal von Kluge, who had recovered from a serious car accident, took over; he had for some time been present regularly at the briefing conferences in the headquarters and was therefore well up in the current ideas. When the new Commander-in-Chief was nominated no one could have foretold that, barely six weeks later, he was to choose suicide rather than execution by Hitler.

It must be presumed that Jodl did not even mention to Hitler his staff's comments on Commander-in-Chief West's proposal, although they were completely in line with the views which he himself had expressed a few weeks earlier in discussion with Dönitz. Similarly no notice was taken of the alternative to which the staff had once more referred, that a last attempt to save the situation in Normandy should be made 'by using all available forces and accepting the consequential risks'. We were caught in a situation in which, from the military point of view, there were clearly no prospects of success and we continued, by using half-measures and inadequate resources, to accept heavy losses and continually to give ground in order to maintain the fiction of a defence which was in fact on the point of breaking down.[17]

On 9 July, after months in Berchtesgaden, the headquarters returned to Wolfschanze earlier than expected. Hundreds of labourers were working in shifts turning the previous flimsy pillboxes of HQ Area 1 into mammoth concrete forts. There was a hubbub of noise and movement putting an end to the peace and security we had guarded so jealously. Hitler had however insisted on moving at this moment because the collapse of Army Group Centre with its limitless consequences for the adjacent fronts, made him feel that he must be close by so as to be able continuously to exert his personal influence on the commanders in the East.[18] This made it all the more remarkable that during the months we had been in Berchtesgaden he had done no more than repeatedly summon Army Group commanders to make the long journey there, and occasionally to see individual senior officers of OKH, his staff for the eastern theatre; the Army staff as a whole had remained, as always, in Angerburg; in addition its chief, Colonel-General Zeitzler, had for some time been sick and was no longer at his post.[19]

The return to the field headquarters in East Prussia meant that we were for once – just as at the same period of 1941 – unwontedly close to the front. Three years before, however, as the army streamed eastward this impression had soon disappeared; now the problem was to collect on the frontiers of East Prussia and put some order into the remnants of defeated divisions and endless columns of refugees as they came flowing back. As never before in the war the work of the OKW Operations Staff began to revolve primarily around the defence of the frontiers of the Reich. The most urgent task was to issue the basic orders for the construction of an 'East Prussia position'. In general terms only the resources of East Prussia were available, together with men unfit for military service. New agreements on division of responsibilities had to be reached with the Party and State authorities against the moment when operations would be taking place on the territory of the Reich. The Replacement Army together with the comparable organizations of the Navy, the Air Force and the SS had to get ready for a crash mobilization of all units, schools and other establishments capable of providing any form of fighting troops. All these instructions were initiated as a result of the imminent threat to East Prussia, but their principles were soon applied to the other frontier regions and even to those neighbouring areas beyond the frontiers, such as South Tyrol and Friulia, which Hitler still intended to incorporate in 'the Great German Reich'. For the construction of defensive positions the Gauleiter were everywhere nominated as the 'foremen' since, in accordance with Party doctrine, they were responsible for 'leading the people' and therefore responsible for the levy of all sections of the population. The local Wehrmacht headquarters had no function other than to act as expert advisers.[20] There were many protests against these insulting instructions by Hitler which contravened all military requirements, but they were unheeded. The period had begun in which the Party and its Gauleiter, who had for long been acting as 'Reich Defence Commissars', began to arrogate to themselves increasing responsibility for the defence of the Reich.

On 17 July the news reached the headquarters that Field Marshal

Rommel had been badly wounded in Normandy while trying to avoid the fire of an enemy ground-attack aircraft.[21] He disappeared from the scene in the West and no successor was nominated. Field Marshal von Kluge took over command of Army Group B in addition to his responsibilities as Commander-in-Chief West; leaving the staff of Commander-in-Chief West in St Germain, he moved to Rommel's previous headquarters in the Chateau of La Roche-Guyon on the lower Seine. As a result Lt General Speidel, Chief of Staff of Army Group B, became his senior staff officer for the Normandy battle.

On 20 July the bomb exploded at the briefing conference. To me it seemed almost like just retribution for all the reverses and horrors which both the troops and the commanders of the Wehrmacht had suffered since the beginning of the invasion. In a flash the map room became a scene of stampede and destruction. At one moment was to be seen a set of men and things which together formed a focal point of world events; at the next there was nothing but wounded men groaning, the acrid smell of burning, and charred fragments of maps and papers fluttering in the wind. I staggered up and jumped through the window. As my mind cleared my thoughts turned straight to my colleagues. The most urgently in need of help was Colonel Brandt, a staff officer highly thought of by everybody and once a world-famous show rider; he had a leg shattered and was vainly trying to heave himself up to a window to get away from the scene of horror. Most of us collected outside in front of the hut, pale and shaken; those who were apparently unwounded supported their comrades until the ambulances arrived. Long before that, however, the man who was the real target of the attack had regained his own hut, supported by Keitel and apparently undamaged, apart from the fact that the dark trousers below the field grey coat were torn to ribbons from top to bottom.[22]

In order to try and save valuable documents I went back once more into the map room, this time with the suspicious eye of the SS guards upon me and followed by their warning that there might be further explosions. As I reached it my head swam, there was a loud buzzing in my ears and I fainted. My driver and batman who, even in this headquarters, had not lost the loyalty characteristic of the German soldier,[23] were already on the spot and they got me out of the 'area' through road blocks, double guards, pass checks and suspicious interrogations.

Because of the reconstruction of the headquarters I was temporarily accommodated in the Görlitz inn nearby; on reaching the peace of my room, half-asleep and half-awake, I began to try to probe what had happened. The first question was 'why?' How often as a daily spectator at the source of the misery which Hitler's military 'leadership' was bringing upon the Wehrmacht, the nation and the country, had my indignation been such that I had myself been tempted; but it had never been more than a 'pale thought'. But who was it – where had he come from? Perhaps General Fellgiebel was on the right track when he called out to me as we left HQ Area 1: 'that's what happens when you put the headquarters so near the front'. Had an enemy agent managed to slip in among the workmen? The idea never even entered my head that the culprit might be ˉone of us, even when, thinking back, I realized that Colonel Graf Stauffenberg was not amongst those I had seen after the attack. I thought back to the scene which is still unforgettable today; just before the beginning of the conference Stauffenberg had arrived, frightfully crippled, the very pattern of a warrior, evoking feelings both of horror and respect; Keitel had introduced him and Hitler had received him without a word, merely with his usual searching glance. Stauffenberg must have left the map room before the explosion, unnoticed in the general coming and going – that was as far as my thoughts went.[24]

When I got back to my office at about 6 pm I heard from my staff rumours about the background and the deeper implications; I felt I must go over to HQ Area 1 to get further news. The first person I found was Field Marshal Keitel who, in a great state of excitement, told me all that was so far known and ordered me forthwith to inform commanders-in-chief in all OKW theatres of war by telephone of what had in fact happened; OKH was similarly to inform commanders on the Eastern Front. While I was carrying out this order and speaking to Major General Stieff, head of the Army Organization Section from an extension in Jodl's hut, Jodl suddenly appeared, his head bandaged, and rapped out ill-humouredly: 'who are you talking to there?' It was all I could do to stop him snatching the receiver out of my hand. Jodl clearly suspected that his own deputy was involved in the conspiracy against Hitler; as was shortly to become obvious, his suspicions were in no way removed by the furious argument which followed.

The same evening Jodl came over to HQ Area 2 and made a speech to the officers of the staff, amounting to a renewed solemn affirmation of devotion to the Supreme Commander of the Wehrmacht. As is the habit of military men we listened to him in silence. In so far as one could tell while still so close to events, there were few of those present who approved of all he said but there were probably even fewer who rejected it out of hand. The majority however were hoping in their hearts that now at last the leadership of the Wehrmacht would change and that the war could be ended before Germany went down in chaos. This thought led involuntarily to another: would not the final disaster possibly be hastened were the ultimate factor in our strength, the unity between people and armed forces now outwardly personified by Hitler, to disappear and would not therefore the enemy be the main gainer? Not a word of these or of the many other thoughts which crowded upon us was spoken at the time. Everyone kept his mouth shut both to his superiors and to his subordinates, except when those few who were indubitably of the same mind were together. It therefore came as a complete surprise when shortly afterwards we heard that one of the conspirators was Colonel Meichssner, Chief of the Organization Section in the OKW Operation Staff and an outstanding staff officer. There was nothing anybody could do to save him from death by hanging.

There was a macabre sequel of a different type. At the briefing conference held on the next or the following day in Hitler's gloomy hut Göring, as 'senior officer', together with Keitel presented to Hitler 'the desire and the demand of all the Services' that 'the Hitler salute' should be made obligatory for all members of the Services. Göring characterized this as a special 'indication of unshakable loyalty to the Führer and of the close bonds of comradeship between Wehrmacht and Party'. Hitler accepted the request without comment. A pin could have been heard to drop among the other participants.[25]

Another result was that from now on I was one of those officers whose briefcase was searched by the SS guards before entering the map room. The following day I appeared with my maps and papers open in my hand but even so, until Hitler arrived, my every movement was watched.

Notwithstanding the events and excitements of 20 July, the war, the front and the soldiers fighting soon reclaimed all the energies of the staff. Knowledge of the non-military reasons for the coup, realization of the political significance of the revolt against tyranny and its crimes, disgust at the refinements of the revenge exacted by the Dictator – all that came later.

During the days following 20 July, the menace of Normandy to the entire German position in the West became ever clearer. The resulting pressure, combined with that of Commander-in-Chief West and OKW who were now in agreement that 'the further the enemy in Normandy advances southwards the less likely does a second landing become', eventually persuaded Hitler to release for Normandy a part of the reserves which, six weeks after the landing, were still standing idle in rear of other sectors of the coast. Two armoured and four infantry divisions were accordingly moved in from the Straits and the Biscay coast. Hitler refused however further to reduce the forces of Nineteenth Army on the Mediterranean.[26]

Meanwhile Jodl was becoming more preoccupied with the overall strength of the army including the Eastern Front and including the newly-formed units which Colonel General Fromm, Commander-in-Chief of the Replacement Army, had announced during a recent visit to the headquarters. (Fromm was a controversial figure and was replaced by Himmler on 20 July.) By 23 July the pressure of events was such that it was possible to discuss even with Hitler the construction of a fall-back position in the West. It was however only to be a precautionary measure and to consist of an entirely new 'main defensive line' in central France using the Somme, Marne and Vosges on the lines reconnoitred by Commander-in-Chief West in the late autumn of 1943. All that resulted therefore from the proposal by the staff of OKW to Jodl at the beginning of July, that a timely large-scale withdrawal should be made to the strong defensive zone of the Siegfried line, was merely an order for additional construction. Strategy in Normandy was to remain unaltered. Hitler appointed as his special representative for the construction of this position the Air Force General Kitzinger in whom he had particular confidence; he was at the same time nominated Military Governor France in succession to the unfortunate General Heinrich von Stülpnagel.[27]

In Jodl's staff however we went on pressing. We were convinced that any decisions which could in the end be expected from Hitler would, as so often and on so many other occasions, be 'too little' and 'too late'.

When therefore the Americans attacked on the western flank of the Normandy bridgehead on 28 July, we saw in this a new opportunity to push the point of view we had put forward early in the month. Even to make a dent in Hitler's obstinacy was however still incredibly difficult as shown by the fact that the new memorandum bore the cautious title *Thoughts on Strategy in the Event of a Breakthrough*. In fact we were in close accord with Commander-in-Chief West, Field Marshal von Kluge, who at this period made it a habit – probably because we had had so much to do with each other in peace-time – of ringing me up early each morning and giving me a detailed picture of the situation. By this method he could at least be sure of support for his views and proposals but he was hardly likely to get any rapid decisions since, even in this pressing period, Hitler and Jodl could not be seen before 11 am, any decisions had then to go through the process of endless discussion at a briefing conference and were therefore unlikely to be reached before early afternoon. This merely underlined further the ponderous working of a Supreme Command which insisted on laying down itself every detail in every theatre of war.[28]

At about 9 pm on 30 July the headquarters heard that a battle was in progress for the Avranches defile, the last barrier to an American break-out into the open spaces of France. This was the moment chosen by Jodl to give Hitler a draft of an order 'for possible withdrawal from the coastal sector' (a cautious method of describing the evacuation of France) which had emerged from the staff's 'thoughts'. As was usually the case in matters of such importance, Hitler just took the paper without really reading it through. It was not until the briefing conference at midday the next day, 31 July, that Jodl could note in his diary:

> The Führer is not averse to the order for a possible withdrawal in France. He states however that he does not consider such an order necessary *at this moment*.
> 1615 hours. Called Blumentritt (Chief of Staff Commander-in-Chief West) and told him in guarded terms that such an order *might be expected* and that he should start *now* with preparations and studies within his headquarters. A small operational staff must study the problem.[29]

There had therefore been a delay of about 48 hours between the issue of this 'warning order' and the submission by the staff of the draft order to Jodl. Meanwhile the American breakthrough at Avranches had happened. The reports arriving in the headquarters did not make it entirely clear that the defile had finally been opened; I was however due to leave the next day on a visit to the front in Normandy and I therefore felt it necessary to be personally briefed on the Supreme Commander's future plans. Up to now OKW had only sent liaison officers to the front from time to time. I had repeatedly asked Jodl to allow me to go and see the situation in the West for myself but he had so far refused on the grounds, first that Hitler had twice discussed it with the two former commanders-in-chief and then that Field Marshal von Kluge was fully *au fait* with the Supreme Commander's intentions. These arguments were soon overtaken by the continuous deterioration in the situation but then the events of 20 July entailed further postponement of my plans; the doctors would not allow me to fly because of the effects of the explosion on my brain and ears. Eventually this obstacle too was overcome on condition, however, that I did not go above 3,000 feet.

When I took leave of Jodl late in the afternoon of 31 July I got no clear answer to my questions. This trip however, more than any other, put me in mind of Hantsch's fateful mission at the battle of the Marne in 1914 and I therefore insisted that, as the representative of OKW, I must be able to discuss matters with Commander-in-Chief West and answer all his questions. As a result, during the night 31 July–1 August I was verbally briefed by Hitler – something which had never happened in all the five years of war. As always Hitler immediately took the floor and started with a broad appreciation of the situation on all fronts; this told me nothing I did not know already and was of use only as general background for my meetings in the West. When he came to Normandy Hitler showed that, undeterred by the fact that the situation was on the point of exploding, he was still clinging to the instructions which for a month now had been proved to be impracticable; they were summed up in the words: 'The object remains to keep the enemy confined to his bridgehead and there to inflict serious losses upon him in order to wear him down and finally destroy him.' OKW alone was to be responsible for any precautionary measures in rear of the operations zone in the West.

There was no point in putting any further questions. Even the meagre instructions which Jodl had given General Blumentritt during the afternoon had now clearly been overtaken. As the discussion went on during the night it emerged that the 'small operational staff' was to be formed, not under Commander-in-Chief

445

West but within OKW – in other words yet once more a staff within a staff; it further became clear that its job was to be the same as that of Commander-in-Chief West, with the added requirement that the Siegfried Line was to be put in order and in addition extended as far as Holland to cover the Ruhr area.[30] In passing it should be noted as a historical curiosity that when this order was issued it gave rise to a general search for the keys of the Siegfried Line forts. No-one knew where they were. I do not remember where or how they were eventually found.

The report from Commander-in-Chief West next morning, 1 August, to an unbiased reader could mean nothing other than that the enemy was well on the way to breaking out into the wide open spaces of France. I was present at the midday conference but, in spite of this supreme crisis, when Jodl raised the question whether Hitler had any further instructions for me, all I got, ground out with every indication of ill-humour, was: 'You tell Field Marshal von Kluge to keep on looking to his front, to keep his eyes on the enemy and not to look over his shoulder.' Field Marshal von Kluge had reported that his sole object was to stop the breakthrough 'by ruthlessly denuding other sectors'. This was no doubt the primary reason for the absence of further instructions but it was also unfortunately only too well calculated to reinforce Supreme Headquarters', and primarily Hitler's, conviction that the battle in Normandy could be continued for an indefinite period on the same lines as hitherto.

Early in the afternoon I set off from East Prussia by air accompanied only by my ADC, Captain Graf Heinrich von Perponcher, an officer who both personally and militarily was exactly suited to his job. A few hours later Jodl noted in his diary:

> 1700 hours. The Führer allowed me to read Kaltenbrunner's report on Lt Col Hofacker's statement regarding conversations with K(luge) and R(ommel) – (ie on their complicity in 20 July).
>
> The Führer is looking for a new C.-in-C. West. He intends to interrogate R(ommel) once he is fit and then dismiss him without further ado.
>
> The Führer asked me my opinion about W(arlimont?)
>
> The Führer is in two minds whether to send Warl(imont) to the West. I offered to go myself. The Führer doesn't want that. I pointed out that to call W(arlimont) back would be somewhat

obvious, so he agreed to let his trip proceed. I spoke to him in the evening at Tegernsee where he had landed to refuel.'[31]

I knew nothing of all this and was therefore considerably surprised when, as soon as I landed at an airfield near Munich, I was called to the telephone to speak to Jodl. The instruction I received was that when I met senior officers in the West I should 'keep my ears open about 20 July'. This seemed to me both incomprehensible and hardly in keeping with my position or my job. It was not until May 1945 when we were both in prison that Jodl told me with a chuckle, though still with a note of menace in his voice, that that afternoon Hitler had demanded that I should be ordered back forthwith, giving as his reason that: 'he's off to the West to arrange with Kluge for a fresh attempt on my life'. He (Jodl) had then apparently stated that, although I had previously been in close contact with the General Staff of the Army (considered to be one of the main sources of the 'conspiracy'), he saw no reason for such suspicion. He undertook however to keep an eye on my journey as far as possible. So, nine months after it all happened, I eventually got the explanation why, contrary to all custom, I was continually being called on the telephone by Jodl during my stay in the West – culminating in an order to return forthwith.

FROM THE BREAK-THROUGH AT AVRANCHES TO THE END IN NORMANDY

As it so happened my trip to Normandy occurred precisely at the moment of greatest crisis; it also produced a coincidence of a more personal sort; early on 2 August I arrived at Strasbourg and in accordance with current instructions changed there from aircraft to car; as I did so I realized that exactly 30 years before on the same day and in the same place, which had been my first station, I had left for the First World War as a nineteen-year-old gunner subaltern.

During the afternoon I met the Chief of Staff to Commander-in-Chief West in St Germain and in the evening Kluge and his staff in La Roche-Guyon; there were no important changes either in the situation or our intentions. On the morning of 3 August however at about 7 am the Field Marshal asked me to go and see him and the interview turned out to be of far-reaching importance. An order had just arrived from Supreme Headquarters to mount a strong counter-attack from the area east of Avranches in order to re-establish positions on the coast and so once more close the ring in southern Normandy.

As far as I was concerned I had no new instructions; I could therefore only state that before I left there had not even been a hint of such plans and that in so far as they were not occupied with day-to-day developments, the staff had been working primarily upon future strategy much further back in the western theatre. As the Field Marshal knew from his visit to Berchtesgaden it had been recognized by the end of June that there were no further possibilities of conducting an offensive defence. There could be no doubt that once more Hitler had taken a snap decision without any preliminary study or other form of preparation by his staff; it looked as if this must have been taken the previous night; there was no need for me to point this out. There had clearly been no one in Wolfschanze prepared to try to stop this order, so it was now up to me to see what the prospects of this counter-attack were – could it at least temporarily seal off the breakthrough and therefore make a more or less orderly withdrawal possible? Kluge said that this was so obvious an idea that he had of course considered it. If however by his order Hitler was now prepared to take responsibility for the withdrawal of considerable armour and artillery from the other flank at Caen, which was equally hard-pressed, that of course produced a new situation. He was afraid that even these forces would be inadequate, but in any case – and on this we were in complete agreement – very rapid action was necessary if the ground was not to be cut from under the feet of the operation by the continuous progress of the breakthrough. While I was still in his office Commander-in-Chief West started the first telephone calls to subordinate headquarters to get more precise information on which to base his orders.

I spent all day at the front getting back to La Roche-Guyon in the evening by which time Army Group B's initial orders for the counter-attack had gone out. People seemed more confident that the counter-attack would succeed; I heard of no serious doubts or objections.[32]

The next day I visited the front again and had many opportunities of confirming that every headquarters concerned was doing its utmost to ensure the success of the counter-attack; I then attended a discussion in Paris between Kluge and the Navy and Air Force commanders to ensure that they would throw everything they had into the support of the operation; I subsequently visited 3 Air Fleet and the Military Governor France, ending by visiting Rommel in hospital in a Paris suburb. During the afternoon of 6 August I was summoned back by Jodl. The counter-attack from which so much was expected, began early on 7 August in the area of Mortain.

When I got back to the headquarters I found that people already knew that, after making some initial progress, the attack had been smothered by mass Allied air attack. Only then did I find out that there had been considerable disagreement between Hitler and Commander-in-Chief West the evening before the attack regarding its timing and that Kluge had stuck to his point of view and his intention.

This was the background therefore when early in the afternoon of 8 August with only Jodl present I found myself facing Hitler in the gloomy room in his bunker to make my report to him. Hitler said nothing as I entered and equally nothing as I described the enormous difficulties of combat and movement in Normandy, the overwhelming superiority of the enemy and the efforts made on all hands to ensure the success of the counter-attack. He did not even interrupt when in fulfilment of my special instructions – though in a sense quite different from that which he supposed – I gave a summary of what I had heard in connection with 20 July. I stated that many senior officers were indignant at Reichsleiter Ley's speech and the accusation it contained that officers, particularly those with an aristocratic background, were 'collectively guilty' of the attempt on his life. I concluded by commenting that the failure of the counter-attack was certainly not due to any lack of preparation. This drew from Hitler his only comment; with a harsh edge to his voice he said: 'the attack failed because Field Marshal von Kluge wanted it to fail'. I was thereupon dismissed. Jodl said nothing, merely commenting in his diary: '1630 hours. Report by Warlimont. Large number of duty trips'.

It was not until I got back that I discovered that on the afternoon of 6 August I had been bypassed and a new representative of the headquarters had been despatched to Kluge in the person of General Buhle, the Chief of the Army staff attached to the Chief of OKW, whose job had nothing to do with operations. His mission was even at this late hour to press for the attack to be postponed. I then heard that on the afternoon of 7 August, obviously struck by the initial success at Mortain, Hitler had issued a further order laying down – no less – that once the coast had been reached at Avranches a beginning should be made with rolling up the entire Allied position in Normandy!

This was a completely unrealistic object but the Supreme Commander clung to it, issuing a bewildering series of orders following each other with ever-increasing rapidity, and with equal rapidity being overtaken by the even faster-moving course of events. An end was finally put to this method of command when the encirclement of the army in Normandy in the Falaise pocket on 19 August brought another disastrous defeat. The Operations Staff War Diary indeed records that 'a good half' of the troops thus encircled fought their way out, characterizing this as 'one of the great feats of arms of this campaign'. But this is no excuse for the Supreme Command; by clinging rigidly to impracticable plans it had once more sent a great army to death or imprisonment without having any major strategic object to justify the sacrifice. Shortly before this Hitler had taken two further decisions; on the one side – too late! – he had ordered up a further six-and-a-half divisions from the Straits area to Normandy; on the other side – too soon! – he had ordered up for immediate employment in the West four groups of the jet fighters which were gradually becoming available in increasing numbers; the Luftwaffe wanted to wait another week when three times that number could have been used in a large-scale surprise operation. Neither of these two decisions however could now alter the outcome.[33]

Field Marshal von Kluge was dismissed on 17 August. Hitler suspected him not only of complicity in the 20 July *coup* but also of trying to make contact with the enemy in order to surrender. On 15 August, when for some time it was impossible to get in touch with Kluge from the headquarters, he unexpectedly gave vent to his suspicions in front of the entire audience at the briefing conference. Shortly thereafter in Wolfschanze he himself briefed for their new command positions in the West the two junior generals to whom reference has already been made in another connection. Only Keitel was present. Hitler then expressed the following opinions about Kluge and in the same breath about Rommel and the consequences of 20 July:

Fragment no. 46
Discussion between the Fuhrer, Lt General Westphal and Lt General Krebs on 31 August 1944 in Wolfschanze

HITLER: You know that Field Marshal Kluge has committed

suicide. He was anyway under serious suspicion and if he hadn't committed suicide would have been arrested straight away. He sent his staff officer away. But it didn't come off. English and American patrols pushed forward but apparently they didn't get in touch with him. He sent his own son into the pocket. The English have announced that they are in touch with a German general and the officer who was probably the contact man has been arrested. He was a prisoner of the English and the story is that they let him go; anyway this was the tale he told. But there were other reasons for arresting him. This was the man who was supposed to be the intermediary, who according to the idea of all these people was predestined to change the course of fate so that we should surrender to the English and then march with the English against Russia – an idiotic idea. And then what a criminal idea – giving up all that German territory in the east. They seem to have been ready to give up everything back to the Vistula ... possibly to the Oder ... might as well say the Elbe. 15 August was the worst day of my life. It was only by accident that this plan didn't come off. It's the only way you can explain everything the Army Group did; otherwise it would all be completely incomprehensible.

The staff of Seventh Army (*meaning Army Group B*) – I must say this to you – is not in good shape. You would be wise, General Krebs, to take with you people from here whom you can trust, of whom you are sure and whom you can charge with a complete clean-out of this staff. The fact unfortunately is that, when successful, Field Marshal Rommel is a great and spirited commander but when the slightest difficulties occur he turns into a complete pessimist.

He (Rommel) has done the worst thing a soldier can possibly do in cases like this; he's been looking for some way out other than the military way. In Italy he prophesied imminent collapse. That hasn't happened so far. Events have proved him completely wrong and I have been justified in my decision to leave Field Marshal Kesselring down there; I reckoned that politically he was an incredible idealist but that militarily he was an optimist and I don't believe you can be a military commander unless you're an optimist. Within certain limits I think Rommel is an extraordinarily brave and able commander.

I don't regard him as a stayer, and that's what everybody thinks.

KEITEL: Yes, it's looked more and more like that.

HITLER: I've just said: the time's not ripe for a political decision. I think during my life I've given adequate proof that I can win political victories. I don't need to tell anybody that I wouldn't miss an opportunity to do so. But of course it's childish and naive to hope that at a time of severe military defeats a favourable political moment will arrive when one could do something. Moments like that arrive when you've had victory. I've proved that I've done everything to come to terms with England. In 1940 after the French campaign I offered an olive branch and was ready to give things up. I wanted nothing from them. On 1 September 1939 I made a proposal to the English or rather I repeated the proposal which Ribbentrop made to them in 1936: I proposed an alliance in which Germany would guarantee the British Empire. It was primarily Churchill and the anti-German crowd around Vansittart who were against the proposal; they wanted war and today they can't go back on it. They are reeling to their ruin. The moment will arrive when disagreements between the Allies will be so great that the break will come. Coalitions have always failed right throughout history; you just have to wait for the moment, however difficult that may be. It's been my particular job ever since 1941 never to lose my nerve and whenever something collapses always to find ways and means of patching it up somehow. I must say: no greater crisis than the one we've had this year in the East could be imagined. When Field Marshal Model arrived Army Group Centre was nothing but a yawning gap. It was more of a gap than a front and finally it became more of a front than a gap ... and then to go and say that these divisions in the West had been totally im- mobilized, that they had no German equipment, that they had God knows what for rifles, that we had sent all the trained divisions to the East, that there were only training divisions in the West, that we only used the armoured divisions in the West for reinforcements and sent them off to the East as soon as they were trained! If I'd had 9 and 10 SS Armoured Divisions in the West the whole thing would probably never have hap- pened. No one told me about it and then people make a criminal attempt at a *coup* here* and think that they can side with the English against the Russians or – the next idea, that of Schulenburg – with the Russians against the English or – the third and damned silliest – play off one against the other. Too naive altogether!

... Carry on the fight until there's a prospect of a peace that is reasonable, of a peace tolerable for Germany which will safeguard the existence of this and future generations. Then I'll shoot him. I think it's pretty obvious that this war is no fun for me. I've been cut off from the world for five years. I've not been to a theatre, a concert or a film. I have only one job in life, to carry on this fight because I know that if there's not an iron will behind it, the battle cannot be won. I accuse the General Staff of failing to give the impression of iron determination, and so of affecting the morale of officers who've come here from the front and when general staff officers go up front I accuse them of spreading pessimism.

It's tragic to see young officers being courtmartialled and telling the court ...

... A section of the General Staff, the head of which is completely right, that is Gehrcke and so far we've not found a single man who had anything to do with this business. But there are other sections, Quartermaster, Organization, Foreign Armies, etc. who've been led into this deplorable business by their Chiefs.

I was the target for what happened here. If it had succeeded it would have been a catastrophe for Germany. It did not succeed and so now we've got a chance finally to lance this boil. But we can't discount the damage done to us externally; what do the Rumanians, the Bulgarians, the Turks, the Finns and the other neutrals, etc. think? What damage has it done to the German people – of course now the ... has got under way and things are coming to light which make your hair stand on end. The German people's kept its mouth shut so far but now everybody's talking ... frightful things are going to come out in the East; they're only just becoming clear; the scandal that German officers exist who make overtures, that there are German officers and generals who surrender; but that's all similar to what's just happened in the West. That's the most

* See Comment on this, page 415 above.

shocking thing that's happened yet. I believe that you, Westphal, are going to a staff (Commander-in-Chief West) which has hardly been infected at all. In the first place Field Marshal Rundstedt is completely straight and above suspicion. Blumentritt is also completely all right and personally above suspicion. I merely think that he's not got the training to run a staff like that and that he's overburdened by the whole thing. There's nothing against him at all.

KEITEL: The only one in the staff was a Q officer, Colonel Fink, who was posted there a few weeks before. He was one of Wagner's creatures.

HITLER: I myself twice promoted him (Field Marshal von Kluge). I gave him the highest decorations. I gave him a big gratuity so that he should have no worries and I gave him a big supplement to his pay as Field Marshal. So for me this is the bitterest and most disappointing thing which could happen. The way he got into it may well have been a tragedy. Perhaps he just drifted into it – I don't know – and perhaps he couldn't see any way out. He saw that quite a number of officers had been arrested and was afraid of what they would say. The most heavily implicated is his nephew and he said so to the court, whereupon the President, Freisler – and he was right – brought the sitting to an end straight away so that he could check the evidence and interrogate the Field Marshal. He was already dead. So naturally Freisler said to himself: this must stop somewhere or everyone will lose confidence in the Wehrmacht commanders.

It's like a western thriller.

When you look at all these people, Stieff and all that crowd – they are a shattering lot. Way back I dismissed a man like Colonel-General Hoeppner not merely because he disobeyed an order but because he'd turned into a miserable little character. Kluge himself was convinced that he must go. Now I've been proved right. During the trial it was obvious to everybody present what little men they were. The public said: how could these people ever have become officers?! Yes, how could they? I had to take what was available and I've tried to get the best ones up to the top.

The staff you'll be taking over, Krebs, is undoubtedly a rotten one; you must be clear on that. I can only say to you: make sure you clean the shop up as quickly as possible; that you get Field Marshal Model ...

We'll fight on the Rhine if necessary. That's quite all right. Whatever happens we'll go on with the battle until, as Frederick the Great said: one of our damned enemies is too tired to fight any more and then we'll get a peace which will secure the life of the German nation for the next fifty or one hundred years and which, above all, will not besmirch our honour for a second time, as happened in 1918. This time I'm not going to keep my mouth shut. Then no one said anything.

Things could have turned out differently ... a split-second and you're rid of it all. You can rest and have peace forever. But I'm grateful to fate for letting me live on. For I think ...

I don't want to broadcast this. I don't want to put the German Wehrmacht to the shame of going on talking about it. If it became known that Field Marshal Kluge was planning to lead the entire army in the West to surrender and himself wanted to go over to the enemy, that might perhaps not lead to a breakdown of morale of the German people but it would at least make them despise their Army. So now I'd rather keep my mouth shut about it. We have merely told the generals that he committed suicide. He did commit suicide. The information given out previously was false. That was ... people were saying that he had already ... and had had a stroke. Actually he was waiting for the English patrol which ... they missed each other. He lost his ... when the ground-attack aircraft came in. He stayed where he was, couldn't go further and drove back again. ...

As far as I know it is still uncertain whether there is any truth in the vague accusations that Field Marshal von Kluge was trying to arrange for a surrender in the West.[34] Had he done so however he would, when all said and done, merely have been drawing the logical conclusion from Hitler's view that if the invasion succeeded the war was lost. Shortly before he committed suicide he had sent a letter to Hitler begging him to bring the war to an end; for anyone who was as close to the Field Marshal as I was, this was no more than a proof of the clarity of his vision and the integrity of his character.

Kluge's successor as Commander-in-Chief West and at the same time Commander-in-Chief Army Group B was Field Marshal Model; he was hurriedly briefed in the headquarters and then despatched westwards to make the impossible possible once more. In fact this change meant that at the moment of greatest danger the western theatre was leaderless. Hitler was much more interested however in getting hold of Kluge's body as quickly as possible and wreaking his vengeance upon it.

On 15 August the Allies landed on the Mediterranean coast and southern France went up in flames. This was a move which clearly threatened to dislocate the entire German position in the West and seeing it coming even while I was away at the beginning of August, General Freiherr von Buttlar had been pressing continuously for some clear strategic direction should the coasts of central and southern France have to be given up as well as Normandy. Jodl however would go no further than to agree to the issue of the written instructions for the fortification of the rear position already planned. Nevertheless on 7 August the staff produced a draft order following up their previous proposals, confirmed this time by the conclusions of the initial studies of the special staff under Lt Colonel Kleyser which had just been formed by Hitler. The draft proposed that withdrawal should be begun forthwith from Brittany to the Maritime Alps, but Jodl turned it down on various pretexts and instructed that it should be pigeonholed for use only in extreme emergency. A second draft was prepared by the staff on 9 August but it was not until the evening of 13 August, when definite information on both the place and time of the Mediterranean landing arrived, that Jodl could be persuaded to take it along and urge for a decision. As Jodl had anticipated, however, even now Hitler turned it down and refused to give 'operational instructions for the western theatre including Nineteenth Army, beyond those necessary for the tasks immediately ahead'. Commander-in-Chief West who had been pressing somewhat half-heartedly in the same direction as OKW, had therefore to do the best he could with the 'general mission' of destroying the enemy in the Alençon (Normandy) area and 'defending with all available resources' the south coast of France against the new landing now imminent.

As soon as news began to arrive on 15 August, it became clear that the somewhat loosely organized German defence on the Mediterranean coast was in a position of hopeless inferiority – there had for instance been no air forces in the area for a very long time. Even then Hitler merely made a series of disconnected remarks about what Nineteenth Army should do if things went badly. It was not until the afternoon of the next day that he could be persuaded to agree to the withdrawal of 'non-operational headquarters and units west of the line Orleans–Clermont-Ferrand–Montpellier'. Only a few hours later however on the same evening he was forced to extend his order and instruct 'Army Group G to disengage, apart from the forces remaining in Toulon and Marseille' and to take up a position in the area of Dijon on the southern flank of the planned defensive line.

As far as I remember Hitler seemed extremely downcast that four years after the brilliant victory of 1940 he should be forced to evacuate France. Although the enemy invasion had now succeeded and there was practically no prospect of further resistance in the West, he made no reference to the opinion he had expressed only a few months earlier that this would be decisive for the outcome of the war. Nor did he refer to the fact that this meant the end of the vaguely expressed general strategy for 1944 – to recover the initiative in the East once the invasion had been defeated. None of those who might have done so reminded him of it. Yet on 19 August, the day of Falaise, Hitler's attitude was similar to that following Stalingrad; in other circumstances it might have done credit to a defeated commander and statesman, but in his case, that of a man who seemed to have lost all qualities of leadership, it showed up the falsity of his views and dragged his people and his country further into the abyss. Jodl's diary shows what his attitude was:

19 August. The Führer discussed the equipment and manpower position in the West with Chief of OKW, Chief Army Staff (General Buhle), and Speer. Prepare to *take the offensive in November* when the enemy air forces can't operate. Main point: some *25 divisions must* be moved to the West in the next one to two months.[35]

The concept of the 'Ardennes offensive' had been born.

PART VI

THE DEATH THROES

Summer 1944 – May 1945

CHAPTER 1

To the End of 1944

THE HEADQUARTERS UNDER THE SHADOW OF 20 JULY

The account of the last phase of the war is based only to a very
limited extent upon my personal experience in the headquarters.
Immediately after landing from my trip to Normandy I began to
get severe attacks of giddiness; there were other things which showed
that there was something wrong with my nervous system and it
began to be difficult both to move about and to do my work. The
staff doctor and Dr. Morell, Hitler's 'personal physician', both
reported on me but their reports were evidently considered inadequate by the authorities. It was not until the neurologist attached to
an Army headquarters nearby had given an opinion ending with an
urgent recommendation, that my superiors became convinced that
I was in fact suffering from shock resulting from the bomb explosion
on 20 July. Even then Jodl kept me in the Headquarters for a further
week since he himself went off to Berlin for a few days at the end of
August – beginning of September. Finally early in September I was
given sick leave and was never fit for duty again. When I took leave
of Hitler, though I had been on his staff for five years, all he said
was: 'go and lie down for a bit'; they were the last words he ever
spoke to me. Later I received the special badge awarded to those
who had been wounded on 20 July. Initially General Freiherr von
Buttlar took over my job. From 8 November 1944 General August
Winter succeeded me as Deputy Chief of the OKW Operations
Staff.

It was probably more than the shock of the bomb which had
affected my health; the depression of the last few weeks had something to do with it. Not only within Headquarters but at the front
and among our allies everything which the German war machine
had so far held together and driven forward seemed to be tumbling
about our ears.

461

Hitler himself was now quite obviously a sick man. His actual injuries on 20 July had been minor but it seemed as if the shock had brought into the open all the evil of his nature, both physical and psychological. He came into the map room bent and shuffling. His glassy eyes gave a sign of recognition only to those who stood closest to him. His chair would be pushed forward for him and he would slump down into it, bent almost double with his head sunk between his shoulders. As he pointed to something on the map his hand would tremble. On the slightest occasion he would demand shrilly that 'the guilty' be hunted down.

Hardly a day passed without new outbursts of rage against the perpetrators and accomplices of 20 July. New names were forever coming up; they were mostly those of men who had devoted their whole lives to the military profession or who had been noticed as young enthusiastic officers on the staff. As each name was mentioned, in the background stood the spectre of the gallows. The briefing conference produced horrifying accounts of the way these early victims were brought to death and ignominy but I do not propose to torture either myself or the reader with them. Hitler seemed to feel that even among those who stood round him there were some who had perhaps not been unmasked. Lest anyone should misunderstand him, as the fronts began to collapse in all directions he would say over and over again to those around him, irrespective of whether they had anything to do with the plot or not: 'anyone who speaks to me of peace without victory will lose his head, no matter who he is or what his position'. While this manhunt proceeded he rode on, completely disregarding the fact that he himself had said the war was lost – he had used almost exactly these words once again at the end of August while discussing the possible loss of the Rumanian oil area with General Gerstenberg, the German commandant of the region. He was presumptuous enough to consider that it was 'providence' which had preserved him on 20 July and now expected that other 'miracles' would give the war a new turn, although in earlier days he had heaped scorn upon the heads of any enemy leaders who had used this sort of language.

On the military side Hitler's physical disabilities and his passionate preoccupation with the persecution of his political opponents affected neither his determination nor his resolution; more even than before these were decisive for everything. As far as he was concerned his mistrust of 'the generals' was greater than ever; moreover the attitude of his responsible advisers gave the immediate observer the disturbing impression that they were now guided, not by sober military considerations but by a discipleship complex, if possible more unquestioning than before. As an example, Hitler succeeded during this period in setting the seal on his disastrous method of command by proclaiming as an order the principle that the sole responsibility of all commanders, even the most senior, was to carry out his orders unconditionally and to the letter. In face of the enemy an NCO or private soldier had no right to question the soundness or likelihood of success of an attack ordered by his company commander; similarly the Supreme Commander of the Wehrmacht was not prepared to share responsibility for his decisions with Commanders-in-Chief of Army Groups or Armies. They were not allowed to ask to be relieved if they did not agree with his instructions. Weight was given to this unprecedented order by the menacing terms in which it was couched; its consequences were of equal significance both for the command mechanism and the spirit in which command was exercised.[1]

As Chief of OKW Field Marshal Keitel would look around him with a martial air, and he outdid himself with words and gestures indicating agreement with every word which fell from Hitler's mouth; in fact he was more than ever labouring under the strain of his position and the unhappy responsibilities it carried with it. He was the senior member of the 'court of honour' whose task it was to root out of the Wehrmacht those suspected of complicity in 20 July. He was quite prepared, though in this case not entirely without hesitation, to hand over military government in Belgium and Northern France at the moment of greatest danger to a civil administration under a Gauleiter – the only reason was that Hitler wished to get General Freiherr von Falkenhausen, whom he loathed, out of Brussels because he was suspected of having too close relations with the Belgian royal family. Keitel did indeed seem somewhat shaken when early in September, standing as always close to Hitler's left-hand side at the map table, the latter handed him a memorandum from Speer, the Armaments Minister, stating flatly that the war must shortly be brought to an end because of the destruction of irreplaceable powder and explosives factories. Being unfit I had a chair near Keitel. He said nothing, put on an air of half righteous indignation, half secret agreement, and handed me the letter to read. As Chief of OKW he had here an opportunity to say exactly the same and to go on saying it; he had innumerable grounds to do so; but he rejected it indignantly with the phrase he always used on such occasions: 'General Warlimont'.

Even more was it the duty of Jodl to speak the fateful words of ultimate defeat which was now staring us in the face. As Chief of the OKW Operations Staff he had both the knowledge and the authority, and he could at least have acted and advised in this sense. Instead he cast himself in the role of poet laureate of Germania; in Hitler's presence and in terms no less menacing than his own, he declaimed at the briefing conference: 'fortunately the Allied demand for unconditional surrender has blocked the way for all those "cowards", who are trying to find a political way of escape'.[2] Little did he think that one day he himself would have to sign the surrender document. When the new Army Chief of Staff asked that he should be solely responsible for supervising Army general staff officers, Jodl refused with the words: 'the General Staff Corps ought actually to be disbanded'.[3] This was simply another way of confirming the attitude he had always adopted to his own staff.

From 21 July the Chief of Staff of the Army was Colonel-General Guderian who had thus reached the summit of his ambitions. He was however in official terminology only 'acting', since General Buhle, whom Hitler had wished to designate as successor to Zeitzler, had been wounded by the bomb and was unlikely to be available for an indefinite period. Via Keitel I learned that there had been considerable hesitation over the nomination of Guderian; it may be that Hitler remembered his earlier efforts to get the 'higher organization' of the Wehrmacht changed or possibly he was aware of Guderian's conversation with Jodl in November 1943 when he had tried to prepare the ground for Hitler to renounce the post of Supreme Commander and had failed in front of Jodl's 'boot face' and laconic refusal.[4]

Guderian had, however, been no friend of OKW long before that. A full year before, after a 'long conversation' with him, Goebbels had noted in his diary: 'he (*Guderian*) complained about the inactivity of OKW, which does not contain a single real leader'.[5] The new Army Chief of Staff made it abundantly clear that he thoroughly disapproved of Hitler's conduct in refusing to let senior officers in the high-level staffs go to employment with troops. Shortly after 20 July Heusinger was dragged out of hospital in Rastenburg and arrested by the Gestapo[6]; as his successor Guderian nominated

General Wenck, who had a great reputation both on the staff and with armoured formations; as his immediate subordinate he gave him Colonel von Bonin.

As Army Chief of Staff Guderian's duties were still restricted to advising Hitler on the eastern theatre although both in East and West the fronts were now coterminous with the frontiers of the Reich. When he took over, the situation was at its most difficult but he went about his new job with his characteristic energy; he did not however, as Zeitzler had done, waste any effort trying to get the other theatres of war back under OKH. Nevertheless he did, as was natural to his job, regard all other theatres and their interests as secondary to the East. In his impetuous and vivacious manner he would often use strong language even at the briefing conferences. From his general outlook and the consequential personal animosities it soon became clear that, even under the extreme pressure of the situation, the change in Army Chief of Staff was unlikely to bring any change in the unhappy relationship between the two top level staffs of the Wehrmacht. Although we were franker in our dealings with each other, it did not enter the head of any of the senior army officers concerned with the overall direction of the war to make common cause with OKW or co-operate in opposition to the continuance of a war already lost.

In all operational questions the Navy and Air Force continued to go their own way. There were brilliant individual exploits and great efforts were made to make the new U-boats and fighters operational but neither of these two Services could now have any decisive influence upon the course of the war; even in this hour of need no attempt was made to achieve real unity of the Wehrmacht even on comparatively unimportant matters. For instance on 29 June at the height of the battle of Normandy Hitler had stated that: 'every modern vehicle (*meaning lorry*) from the Navy, Air Force and civil life must be collected for the (*Army*) transport service'. Yet on the very next day Commander-in-Chief Navy contrived to put spokes in the wheel of the follow-up instructions from OKW.[7] Two months later Guderian made efforts to get vehicles out of the Air Force to bolster up the armoured forces and even went personally to Hitler about it. The result was the following discussion at the briefing conference on 1 September 1944 which, coming at this stage of the war, gives a bizarre impression of empty pomposity on the part of Hitler and Keitel entirely out of keeping with the subject under discussion.

GUDERIAN: All that's necessary is for the Reichsmarschall to give his agreement.

HITLER: I am giving the agreement now. We have got a Defence Staff. We have got an organization the envy of every country in the world, OKW. No one else has such a thing. It hasn't been much talked about merely because the Army Staff didn't like it.

KEITEL: (*as usual using stronger words to express the same idea*)*: Has in fact fought hard against it!

HITLER: (*taking up Keitel's expression*): Has in fact fought hard against it! After we had fought for years to get this organization.

GUDERIAN: 3 Air Fleet has such a large number of lorries.

THOMALE: (*MT Inspectorate*): We must flush them out.

KREIPE: (*Chief of Staff Luftwaffe*): We've already lost so many using them on Army jobs (*refuses*).

HITLER: All the same I am convinced that taking into account their job, the Luftwaffe is better off for lorries than the Army. No doubt about it. But this is not the point – we don't want to quarrel about trifles but ... (*takes no decision*).

In the spring of 1944 further efforts were made to set up certain special unified Wehrmacht organizations, but these made no better progress. Basically Hitler was opposed to any form of unification and he now shied away from giving orders to the Navy and Air Force to which their Commanders-in-Chief were likely to be opposed. Keitel merely seized upon Hitler's attitude as an opportunity to avoid the obligations which his own better judgment and the pressure of his staff might have brought upon him.[8]

COLLAPSE OF THE FRONTS AND ALLIANCES

In these circumstances I was profoundly thankful to escape from a headquarters in which all thought was governed and all initiative stifled by injury and sickness, by silence and denials, by mistrust of everybody and above all by Hitler's personal thirst for revenge. Yet I long remained depressed that I should have had to leave just at this moment when events at the front, as the following account will show, demanded a last despairing effort to ward off the catastrophe that was upon us.

* All words in italics are the author's.

Of Japan no word had been heard for a long time. At the beginning of August Turkey had broken off diplomatic relations with the Reich. On 20 August, while the battle of the Falaise pocket was still raging, two German and two Rumanian armies of Army Group South Ukraine disintegrated almost totally between the Black Sea and the Carpathians in face of an attack by superior Russian forces. Rumania now lay open to a Russian attack and on 25 August her people, infuriated by Hitler's counter-measures, deposed Marshal Antonescu, renounced the alliance with Germany and declared war upon the Reich. This meant the loss of the oil area of Ploesti while at the same time, refinery by refinery, the German oil industry was being reduced to rubble by the Allied air forces. This event was immediately preceded by the defection of Bulgaria, which began negotiations for an armistice on 24 August, and demanded the withdrawal of the German military mission and all German troops. Only Hungary remained, under pressure, at our side. A serious insurrection broke out in Slovakia. At the beginning of September Finland declared that its 'comradeship-in-arms' was at an end and sought an armistice with the Soviet Union.

In Italy the left flank of the Apennines position, which had been occupied far too late, was overrun and the whole position in danger of being rolled up. In the West, in the face of deep armoured thrusts by the enemy, withdrawal proceeded, in some places verging on rout; only Nineteenth Army fought steadily back from the Mediterranean coast. Hitler issued repeated orders – to stand forward of the Seine, to defend, and then to recapture, Paris,[9] to occupy the line in central France which had been planned so late; all were overtaken by the rush of events or simply disregarded by Model who, being sure of Hitler's confidence, felt he could exercise some freedom of initiative. On 25 August the Allies moved into Paris; on 4 September the city and port of Antwerp fell undamaged into the hands of the English, although the entry to the mouth of the Scheldt still remained blocked. At sea losses of U-boats were heavy and results meagre. An ever-increasing number of German cities were reduced to rubble and ashes by terror attacks from the air. Production of war equipment which had remained at a high level up to the end of 1944, ceased; traffic came practically to a standstill.

The threads of control had to a large extent slipped from the hands of the Supreme Command. The OKW Operations Staff hoped as a result of the patent pressure of events at last to get some long-term decision but Hitler apparently felt that his repertoire of tactical expedients was not yet exhausted and all could still be saved that way. His flow of speech was incessant. He refused all sensible measures; he demanded the impossible. He clung undeterred to his principle of static defence and could not be persuaded voluntarily to give up anything or even to consider any long-term plans, however obviously necessary they might be. One or two highlights from individual theatres of war best illustrate the situation.

As regards south-east Europe when Hitler briefed me for my trip to Normandy during the night 31 July–1 August he delivered himself of the following:

Naturally the Balkans are the major worry. I am entirely convinced of one thing: if the Turks, just like the Finns, were today to be convinced that we could stick it out, they would not lift a finger. All these people are worried only about one thing: that perhaps they might fall between two stools. That is their worry. If therefore we could contrive to fight a really decisive defensive battle somewhere or to win some victory somewhere – if we could contrive to re-establish these people's confidence that we shall stick it out and that we are withdrawing merely to shorten our front – then I am convinced that we shall be able to get Turkey to adopt at least a wait-and-see policy. It is no joy to the Turks to see the strongest European anti-Bolshevist and anti-Russian power eliminated and replaced by a completely unstable counterweight of questionable value and reliability in the form of the Anglo-Saxon powers. That doesn't please the Turks.

Then naturally in Bulgaria they are beginning to think: now what happens if Germany collapses? Small powers like us can't get away with it. If a great power can't get away with it, we can't.

So in my view there is something else which is dependent upon stabilizing the Eastern Front. In the last analysis the attitude of all the small Balkan states is dependent upon it – the Rumanians – the Bulgarians – the Hungarians – and also the Turks.

Nevertheless we must take certain precautions. The most essential initial precaution for us is and remains to secure the Hungarian area (... vital importance ...).

The second and equally important is of course the attitude of Bulgaria. Without Bulgaria it would in fact be impossible for us to secure the Balkan area and so continue to get iron ore from Greece.

Any English landing in the Balkans or in Istria or on the Dalmatian islands would be a matter of the utmost danger.

An English landing could produce catastrophic results. In my view we cannot stop a landing on the islands, etc., in the long run, if the enemy employ major forces. There is only one question here. In the last analysis I believe the question is whether the Allies are really in agreement about this area.

I can hardly believe that the Russians would hand over the Balkans to the English. It may well be that something will happen as a result of tension between the Russian Bolshevists and the Allies: that the English will try to lay hands at least on the Aegean islands for themselves. Theoretically at least that is conceivable. They will certainly not act in concert.[10]

Yet when, on 22 August, the German commander in the South-east was summoned to the Headquarters by the Operations Staff, Hitler's attitude was quite different. Tito had broken into southern Serbia and our object now was to obtain Hitler's agreement to proposals for co-operation with the nationalist leaders Nedic and Mihailovic in a common effort against Communism in the interior. Instead of giving a decision Hitler went off into a long historical survey of the 'danger of a greater Serbia', saying that they were 'the only real people in the Balkans'. Although the Russians were on the point of crossing the Dniester and Pruth, breaking into the Danube plain and so driving deep into the rear of the entire coastal front in the south-east, Hitler would hear of nothing other than that Germany must 'determinedly resist all plans for a greater Serbia'. Jodl summarized his point of view as follows: 'a Serbian army must not be allowed to exist. It is better to have some danger from Communism.' It seems almost incredible that in these discussions there is not a word about the possibility of a change in the attitude of Rumania. It took place only twenty-four hours later; yet the German political authorities had no inkling of the true state of affairs; they simply thought that the threatening approach of the Red Army would lead the Rumanians to defend themselves to the end. This was an instance in which the dichotomy between the two military staffs within the Supreme Command was particularly disastrous, for there was no clear dividing line between the areas for which OKH and OKW were responsible. The commanders in the South-east could do nothing to improve this situation since, as in all other theatres, they were bound by Hitler's security instructions forbidding direct communication with neighbouring theatres; the only information they received on the overall situation was that given them in broad terms by OKW once a week in the so-called *News sheets*.

The other ally in Commander-in-Chief South-east's area, the Bulgarians, were equally ready to desert. Yet at the meeting on 22 August there was no mention of them either, other than to say that they might perhaps withdraw their occupation forces from Serbia. Although our forces were stretched to the limit, Hitler thereupon demanded that the Bulgarians should be replaced by German formations, including the cadets from a military academy. Four days later, however, on 26 August, the German representative in Sofia reported, leaving no doubt that, as Jodl put it in his diary: 'there was nothing more to be got either by politics or diplomacy' out of the Bulgarian government. Only then could Hitler be persuaded to agree that 'preparations should be made for the withdrawal of all troops south of the line Corfu–Yannina–Kalabaka–Mt Olympus'. At the same time he ordered that, as a precaution against a Bulgarian defection, a new front 'must be formed along the old Bulgarian-Jugoslav frontier'. This at least had the advantage that we were able rapidly to withdraw two divisions from Greece and one battalion from Crete.[11]

All these measures may have been inadequate but at least they had some basis of military reasoning. The further plans and orders however with which Hitler proposed to counter the defection of the allies were little short of fantastic – just as in Italy. In the midst of this raging crisis which engulfed practically every theatre of war and threw up political problems of the widest significance, the Supreme Commander of the German Wehrmacht was obsessed with hatred and thirst for revenge and spent his time trying to despatch the few aircraft which could be 'scratched together' in the Balkans to attack defenceless Bucharest. Their target was to be the young king's palace for he, Hitler thought, was his principal opponent. The oil area of Ploesti he proposed to secure against the mounting flood of the Red Army by using a solitary SS Parachute battalion which was employed somewhere in Jugoslavia on anti-partisan operations – it was probably cut to pieces as it flew in; in any case it was never heard of again. On 26 August an OKW order was issued declaring the Rumanian forces disbanded apart from any which might wish to be incorporated in the Wehrmacht; the remainder were considered to have agreed to the 'perfidy of their government' and thereby to have become prisoners of war[12] – an illustration of how unrealistic the views in the Headquarters were; though probably not known at the time, the Rumanians had in fact declared war the day before. In Bulgaria there was to be a *coup-de-main* employing both subterfuge and force to recover the tanks which Germany had delivered during the war. Hours of repetitive discussion were spent on its preparation.[13]

On 8 September the Bulgarian government declared war on its former ally, thereby producing 'a deadly threat to the communications' of German troops in Greece. It was not until six days later that, with obvious relief, Jodl noted in his diary: 'the Führer orders that everything which can be got out of the Aegean islands should be withdrawn'. He adds however: 'from the political point of view it is hoped that wherever we withdraw we can kindle and fan strife between Communist and nationalist forces' – showing that even at this late period Hitler was still hoping to extract some political advantages from a military evacuation. For some time he had believed, not without justification, that as a result of their political disagreements with the Russians, the English would be prepared quietly to allow German troops to remain in Greece but now his object was to stir up strife all-against-all in the areas we had hitherto occupied. On the other hand he still thought that in the midst of this general confusion we could go on using the chrome ore mines in northern Greece and gave orders that 5,000 Luftwaffe personnel should be left there to protect them. It was not until 3 October that the 'order for withdrawal from Greece, Southern Albania and Southern Macedonia' was given – and not until 2 November that the movement was completed. After all this tergiversation 16,000 men were left on Crete and about 6,000 on Rhodes and Leros because of lack of transport. At the same time Hitler was forced to agree to our urgings that the Dalmatian islands and the east coast of the Adriatic should be evacuated.[14]

Surprisingly the Western Allies allowed all these movements in the coastal area to proceed practically undisturbed. The main threat to the Supreme Command's belated precautionary measures came from the Russian advance in the Danube plain, where the wavering attitude of Hungary, under the leadership of the Regent, once more presented a danger. Their attempts to escape from the German clutches by making overtures to the Allies failed, and a military delegation appeared in German Headquarters; at a conference during the night 12–13 September Hitler gave them to understand that 'there would shortly be a great German offensive to recover Rumania'. The Hungarian Chief of Staff transmitted 'an assurance of loyalty from the Regent and Hungarian nation'. Ten days later, when the Russians had already reached Temesvar and Arad, came another twist in this game of deception; Hitler ordered 'three to four parachute battalions' to stand by 'in order to lay hands on the Regent' and all preparations to be made for the 'Arrow Cross' under ex-Major Ferenc Szalati to take over the government. In the end Hungary's national frontiers became of little account and the area was one in which some of the fiercest battles of the eastern theatre took place; as a result it ceased to be the responsibility of OKW.[15]

In the far north the withdrawal from Finland, apart from one or two critical moments, went better than anyone had expected. The preparations laid down in OKW *Directive no. 50* of the autumn of 1943 had been kept up to date in spite of continual political wavering; so when Field Marshal Mannerheim, who had just been made President, announced the end of the 'comradeship in arms' in a personal letter to Hitler couched in most chivalrous terms, movement proceeded as planned. In this case each side respected the other, so there was no question of Hitler-type special measures. He also agreed with unexpected rapidity to give up his plan for occupation of the Aaland islands, both because of its possible effect upon Sweden and also because forces were not available. Commander-in-Chief Navy, who was concerned for the defence of the Baltic, urged that the attempt to capture the Finnish island of Suusari should proceed; it failed on 15 September with temporary adverse effects upon the 'standstill agreement' with the Finns, which had been concealed from the Russians, and with other highly unfortunate consequences on the evacuation movement from the country. Hitler's original plans had provided for German troops to remain in the northern nickel ore area. This seemed highly unwise unless the Finns were in agreement and OKW's resistance to the plan was in this case supported by Speer who stated that German industry had adequate nickel reserves. At the end of September 1944 the OKW Operations Staff produced an appreciation of the situation covering the whole of Scandinavia and Finland; it dealt with the sea supply situation and the essential increased protection for bases in Norway for the new U-boats coming into service, weighing up the pros and cons and the repercussions thereof on the West; it was therefore one of the rare truly inter-service strategic documents produced. Hitler gave his agreement, though he later tried to disavow it, but as a result, in spite of Russian action and arctic weather, the withdrawal along the coasts of the Arctic ocean to the frontier of Norway was successfully completed by the end of January 1945 – an outstanding achievement on the part of the Commander-in-Chief, Colonel-General Rendulic, and his high-class troops[16].

Although there was now no longer any need to consider the Finns, and in spite of urgent representations by the Chief of Staff of the Army, Hitler clung doggedly to his tactics of holding on at all costs in the northern sector of the eastern front. The immediate result was that early in October Army Group North, consisting of twenty-six divisions, was cut off in Courland.[17] This opened the way for the Red Army into north and east Prussia; for several weeks both the enemy and German Supreme Headquarters were in the same province.

In Italy, as has already been shown, Hitler's rigid strategy produced a situation in which no real long-term use was made of the strong defences of the Green Line in the Apennines nor were forces made available for other fronts. Neo-Italian forces now appeared on both sides; though hardly anyone noticed it, there could have been no clearer sign of the breakdown of that policy which had once set out to unite the whole European continent around the Rome-Berlin Axis.

In Supreme Headquarters the tendency was to lay all blame for the fact that the Green Line had not come up to expectations on the local commanders. The Operations Staff War Diary of 15 December 1944 records Jodl as saying to the Chief of Staff to Commander-in-Chief South-west: 'one of the worst and most momentous errors was to allow the left flank of the Apennines position to be pushed back as soon as the position was occupied'. General Röttiger to whom this criticism was addressed was in agreement with Jodl as regards the facts, but in his post-war study of the problem rightly objected that 'this was one of the strategic errors forced upon the Army Group by OKW...its results were felt right up to the end of the Italian campaign'. Charges of this sort were hardly justified; in September, after a detailed examination, it had come down against any withdrawal' to the line of the Po or to the so-called 'forward Alps position'; reasons given were that the ground was unfavourable for defence, northern Italy would be lost, Allied air bases would be brought closer to the Reich and the Vienna basin would be threatened. The only advantage anticipated from this withdrawal was that a larger number of formations would become available; as the battle went against us, however, losses became so great that even this proved illusory; yet when Kesselring pressed for withdrawal to the Alps to be begun forthwith, Hitler finally decided on 5 October that 'the Apennines front should be held, not merely until late autumn but permanently and northern Italy thereby be retained'. Every single German soldier must be convinced of this purpose, he said. In fact quite apart from the political and economic reasons, from the military point of view (eg in the light of the Balkans situation) hardly any other choice was open – *always provided that the war was to continue.*[18]

There was no tendency in German Supreme Headquarters to minimize the seriousness either of the situation or of the effect of the subsequent relentless, almost uninterrupted, advance of the enemy. For instance at the briefing conference on 6 November 1944 Jodl stated that the Allied air forces were using this theatre as a bombing training area since there was no anti-aircraft defence. Commander-in-Chief South-west begged to be allotted at least temporarily 'a couple of hundred fighters' but Hitler refused. Jodl added: 'we can give absolutely nothing more to Italy' and a few days later Keitel hastened to reprimand Colonel-General von Vietinghoff (he had taken over from Field Marshal Kesselring, who had been injured in a road accident) for the continued loss of territory in the Adriatic sector. Keitel was here for once taking a hand in operations and he used his habitual phrase in such cases, that he had passed on 'with all severity' Hitler's order 'that a stop must be put forthwith to the withdrawal tactics which had become normal in the Po Valley'.

Jodl's influence on events was limited to telling General Röttiger in the middle of December that the 'guiding tactical principle' for the Italian theatre must be to fight 'doggedly' for every square yard. It was a 'dangerous principle', he went on, to try to stop a breakthrough by defence in depth. Voluntary withdrawals weakened our own forces rather than the enemy. That way one might save a couple of divisions but endanger a couple of Armies. There was an unmistakable tendency on the part of local commanders to give way on the left flank; this was merely playing into the hands of the enemy whose intention was to drive the German forces away from their communications via Carinthia and Tyrol and up against the Swiss frontier. These were the ideas which the Führer, on the basis of similar experiences the previous year on the eastern front, was putting forward almost daily, and in Jodl's view they must clearly form the guidelines for future action in Italy. The war diary continues:

> The Chief of the OKW Operations Staff therefore requires that in future no thought should be given and no proposals made for voluntary withdrawals on the left flank of Tenth Army and that attention should be directed to methods and expedients designed to prevent another inch being given up between the Via Emilia and the Adriatic.

So with this background and to the accompaniment of continuous interference by the Supreme Command down to divisional level, the heavy, costly battle of attrition on the Apennines position went on.[19]

THE ARDENNES OFFENSIVE

It is more than likely that the strong language used by Jodl to Commander-in-Chief South-west was influenced by the view held in German Supreme Headquarters of the prospects for the Ardennes offensive, set for the next day 16 December 1944.

This was the Wehrmacht's last major offensive operation but, as before, there had been no preliminary examination of the overall situation by the OKW Operations Staff. Hitler's plan to go over once more to the offensive in the West at the earliest opportunity had been in the forefront of his mind ever since the final phase of the battle in Normandy, and so from the outset consideration of any other strategy, whether in East or West, was out of the question. The first general directions for an 'offensive rebound' were issued by OKW on 20 August; a more ambitious plan emerged on 3 September while withdrawal in the West was still in progress; in neither case did the Ardennes figure. The original plan visualized an attack by such forces as could be quickly concentrated against the right flank of the Allied thrust under General Patton which – on the German model – was charging forward southwards from the area of Dijon (Plateau de Langres) without regard for its flanks. The object was to re-establish a line on the obstacle of the Marne but this was rapidly overtaken by events. Hitler was quite undeterred and his ideas became daily more ambitious. His next plan was to assemble a strong offensive grouping in the area still untouched by the battle, west of the Vosges; this was to consist of parts of Nineteenth Army which was still moving up the Rhône, such remnants of the armoured formations from the West as were still operational, two Panzer Grenadier divisions ordered up from Italy and some newly-formed units from Germany – all under command of Fifth Panzer Army. The initial task of these forces was to form a new front forward of the Vosges but its 'subsequent and principal task' was to advance against the flank and rear of the Allies at a time still to be decided and thus bring about a fundamental change in the situation in the West. In order to free for this offensive forces from the right flank and centre of the front these sectors were authorized, contrary to all custom though still with strict limitations, to conduct a fighting withdrawal.[20]

These ambitious plans were another example of Hitler's disregard of the rules of time and space; moreover he took no account of the fact that the forces at his disposal were extremely weak; the plans accordingly came to nothing as soon as they were born. Under the pressure of fresh severe reverses, of which the rapid loss of Antwerp came as a particularly unpleasant surprise, Jodl managed on 6 September to get Hitler back to the view he had held on 19 August that 'a major decisive attack in the West is not possible before 1 November'. He could not however get Hitler to lift his order that Fifth Panzer Army was to make local counter-attacks, though this was now accompanied by an uninspiring order from Supreme Headquarters recorded as follows in Jodl's diary of 11 September: 'the Führer requires an order issued that Fifth Panzer Army should under all circumstances attack the enemy in the rear. The Führer forbids any frontal attack against the main enemy forces.'

The intention and the plan to reverse the situation in the West by a major offensive at some period remained unchanged. The same day actual preparations were started with the order: 'Sixth Panzer Army to be formed under Obergruppenführer Dietrich, who is to be charged with the reconstitution of that Army'.[21]

While the situation became more and more serious the OKW Operations Staff, as the responsible headquarters, had to get busy with the numerous other measures designed to reconstitute the Army in the

West. Meanwhile Hitler himself put pressure on the Luftwaffe to get their new fighters into service for the forthcoming offensive. Progress was however considerably hindered by his additional technical requirements regarding performance of the aircraft. On the very afternoon before my departure this question had led to sharp disagreements with Göring.[22]

As a further preparation for the forthcoming offensive Hitler summoned Field Marshal von Rundstedt to the headquarters in East Prussia at the beginning of September, intending to appoint him once more Commander-in-Chief West. He had always regarded Rundstedt as a wise old head in matters of major strategy and at the briefing conferences of the next few days he treated 'his' most senior Field Marshal with unwonted diffidence and respect. Rundstedt sat there motionless and monosyllabic, but a few days later, on 5 September, took over command. Model's command was thereby reduced to that of Army Group B – the northern and central sectors of the Western Front. Colonel-General Blaskowitz, the commander in the south, was dismissed shortly thereafter; at the briefing conference on 1 September Hitler said of him: 'If he contrives to do that (*ie join up Nineteenth Army rapidly with the main body*) then I will make him a solemn apology for everything' (*referring to the disfavour in which he had been since his opposition to the occupation policy in Poland in 1939*).[23]

During the weeks and months which followed the enemy attacked almost uninterruptedly, but the guiding principle of Hitler's strategy remained to safeguard the basis for the forthcoming offensive. The room for manœuvre was becoming visibly smaller and the forces available for the defence continuously weaker, yet Hitler persisted in the opposition, which had now become part of his nature, to any form of strategy involving the relinquishment of less important areas in order to make possible a major strategic offensive; the prospects of success therefore became smaller and smaller. After the fall of Antwerp, Hitler ordered the right flank, which was only gradually getting back into some sort of order, to form a bridgehead at the mouth of the Scheldt, then to stand on the Albert Canal (roughly on the line of the Belgian-Dutch frontier) and to defend it stubbornly – an order which was only made possible because in the nick of time the Luftwaffe was able to make available the First Parachute Army, formed from its superfluous manpower. This and the fact that there were still considerable German forces in the 'fortresses' of Dunkirk,

Calais and Boulogne, forced the enemy to make his first pause of any length and had a considerable effect upon the whole subsequent course of operations. By 10 September the fortresses were occupying approximately one-third of the forces of Montgomery's Army Group,[24] and in spite of their superiority the Allies did not succeed in breaking the blockade at the mouth of the Scheldt until 3 November; the first convoy only entered the harbour of Antwerp on 28 November.[25] Hitler's decisions were also considerably influenced by determination to retain the last available bases for the V-weapons within short range of England, particularly since the V-2 rockets, which were much more effective, were due to become operational about this time.[26] On the other hand wrongly, uselessly and entirely for prestige purposes, he left a complete infantry division on the Channel Islands; its withdrawal was now out of the question.

For a time it seemed that a strategy of concentrating at the decisive point might be adopted but this was pushed completely into the background by the battle around Aachen. Not only was the town threatened but the first fort of the Siegfried Line was lost and shortly after the enemy broke through the second line of frontier fortifications. On 14 September Jodl records in his diary Hitler's *diktat* that: 'in the Siegfried line every foot of ground, not merely the fortifications, is to be treated as a fortress'.

On 16 September there followed an order signed by Jodl which both in spirit and language seemed to be modelled on Stalin's proclamation of 1941:

> In numerous sectors in the West the battle is now taking place on German territory. German towns and villages are being fought for. This fact must inspire us to fight with fanatical determination; in the combat zone every able-bodied man must give of his utmost. Every bunker, every dugout, every town, every village must become a fortress against which the enemy will beat his head in vain or in which the German garrison goes under in hand-to-hand combat.

It looked as if even the plan for the offensive had been temporarily forgotten for the order continued: 'there can no longer be any large-scale operations on our part. All that we can do is to hold our positions or die.'[27]

On 30 September, two weeks later, there followed an order signed by Keitel; this enlarged on Hitler's instructions and attempted to set

478

out some form of organization, though at the same time the Chief of
OKW showed himself nervously anxious not to meddle in the job
of the 'Gauleiter and Reich Defence Commissars'.[28] A few days
before, on 25 September, Hitler's 'decree concerning formation of a
German home-guard' (Volkssturm) had been issued; it was counter-
signed first by Bormann and secondly by Keitel, and it charged the
Party with the formation and leadership of this 'last levy'. Two
months later came the moment for the issue of a further order by
Hitler, this time signed by Jodl:

> If, as a result of negligence or lack of energy on the part of com-
> manders or troops, the enemy succeeds in breaking in to the
> fortified zone (of the Siegfried Line) that constitutes a *crime* of
> incalculable consequence. The Führer is determined in such
> cases to bring those responsible to justice immediately.[29]

The British parachute operations at Arnhem led to no particular
action on the part of Supreme Headquarters. On the afternoon of
the first day, 17 September, the news occupied the greater part of the
briefing conference in Wolfschanze but Hitler remained unusually
calm, for at the same time it was reported that the German reserves
in the area had been thrown into the battle.[30] Montgomery's operation failed in its major objective, the capture of the bridges over the
Maas, Waal and Rhine, but Supreme Headquarters played little
part in this result. The attitude of mind regarding the bitter battle
being fought is shown clearly enough by the entry in Jodl's diary for
21 September when, undoubtedly quoting Hitler, he says: 'the
Führer uses strong language about the folly of allowing bridges to
fall intact into the hands of the enemy'.

The OKW Operations Staff was now caught up in a series of
greater or smaller crises; it was busy with innumerable detailed
problems arising in many neighbouring areas as a result of the completely changed situation in the west (such as the reinforcement of
the defences on the German North Sea coast and stronger guards on
the Rhine bridges);[31] it was permanently involved in a time-wasting
contest with the demands of the East for the dwindling manpower
and equipment reserves. This was the situation when, at the beginning of the sixth year of the war, the staff was called upon for the
first time to lay on a major offensive operation and to make all
preparations for it, something which had hitherto been the responsibility solely of OKH and its Operations Section. The situation

already presented enough apparently totally insurmountable difficulties but now, at this late stage of the war, the whole futility of the
higher organization of the Wehrmacht stood out starkly. All that
the Chief of the OKW Operations Staff had available for his job as a
second Army Chief of Staff were the brains and energies of the few
selected Army staff officers of his own staff. For all other forces and
resources required for the operation, starting with the forces to be
used and information about the enemy and ending with supply, he
was perforce dependent upon the Army, upon Army personnel and
Army installations – and yet he was not one of them; he did not
belong to them; he did not really know them and he did not live
with them. For years now he had been at Hitler's side or in his
immediate presence; he more than anyone was therefore inevitably
under the influence of the unrealistic determination of the Supreme
Commander, and he was less likely than anyone to be able to stand
up to it. There is nothing to show that this is how Jodl looked at
things; on the contrary many of his subsequent remarks while in
prison lead to the supposition that he thought his great moment had
come. It is difficult however to escape the thought that, had it not
been condemned to labour under this disadvantage, this ill-starred
military undertaking might perhaps never have begun.

By end September–early October 1944 OKW's preliminary
studies had produced the conclusion that the area Monschau-
Echternach offered the best prospects for the offensive. Hitler's
instructions were that from this area 'the main thrust should be
directed north-west in the direction of Antwerp'. The forces available consisted primarily of two Panzer Armies and the date was set
for the end of November.[32]

With this as a basis the Operations Staff developed detailed plans;
security instructions were so strict that the staff was not allowed to
follow normal procedure, so Commander-in-Chief West and the
other senior commanders destined to carry out the attack were not
informed. The operation was initially known by the code name
'Wacht am Rhein' (Watch on the Rhine) and the plans were
submitted to Hitler by Jodl on 9 October.[33] Comparatively little is
known about this stage of the procedure, but it is clear that even
on this occasion Hitler made it his business to alter the objectives
in many respects, and as always to widen them. Jodl notes in his
diary: 'the Führer orders: 1. Left flank to be extended to include
Bastogne and Namur; 2. A second attack from north of Aachen

southwards along the Meuse; 3. There must be a flank guard. The flank guard is to act offensively.'

It seems more than likely that it was on this day and no later that the objective of the operation was finally laid down; it was to drive in one sweep through the Eifel and Ardennes across the Ourthe and Meuse and right through Belgium to the Channel coast at Antwerp. Hitler was clearly trying to resurrect in miniature the basic concept of the offensive in the West of May 1940, though the miniature was far too large for the existing circumstances. Three days later on 12 October when 'the plan had emerged from the phase of consideration into that of elaboration', OKW issued a first warning order. This was merely intended, however, to camouflage the real objectives from our own troops and their commanders.[34] In passing it should be noted that this was the moment at which Hitler despatched his henchmen, including his new senior aide, to force Field Marshal Rommel to commit suicide.

On 3 November, barely three weeks before the date set for the attack, Colonel-General Jodl appeared at Army Group B Headquarters to brief the assembled senior commanders in the West on the plans for the offensive.[35] He stated that the enemy situation and the terrain in the Eifel area offered a certainty of a successful breakthrough. The armoured formations which would follow up immediately would, within two days, cut the communications of the American First Army and Montgomery's Army Group and thereby set the stage for the subsequent destruction of twenty-five to thirty enemy divisions. Vast quantities of material of all types which the enemy had assembled in this area for his attack across the Rhine, would be captured or destroyed. Speaking in Hitler's name, Jodl even gave detailed instructions on the tactics for the attack. He justified the date selected by the advantages of operating in the new moon period. At the decisive point of the attack a total of sixteen divisions, including eight armoured divisions, would be available, divided between Sixth SS Panzer Army under Sepp Dietrich and Fifth Panzer Army under General von Manteuffel. Seventh Army was to be responsible for protection of the southern flank; in the north a minor holding attack was to be made.

From the outset Jodl left no doubt that these directions came from Hitler and were therefore unalterable. Nevertheless, as one man, the assembled commanders protested, primarily against the distance of the objective – over one hundred and twenty-five miles away. The forces proposed, they said, even if they could be concentrated and more or less adequately equipped in time, which recent experience showed was improbable, were nothing like adequate, particularly under winter conditions. During the discussion a counter-proposal was made for a 'limited solution'. It consisted merely of eliminating the enemy break-through at Aachen, which had meanwhile fallen, and as a result recovering the neighbouring forts of the Siegfried Line. In the most favourable situation it might then be possible to advance to the Meuse. Only if, contrary to all expectation, the subsequent situation allowed, would it be possible to consider a rapid regrouping of forces and an advance to a more distant objective.

Jodl remained totally unyielding in face of these and all other objections. He replied that he knew the way Hitler's mind ran and that the 'limited solution' would 'merely postpone the day of reckoning and would not make the Western powers ready to negotiate', thereby revealing that the Supreme Command's real objective was political. For the same reasons and for military reasons as well, he replied to the proposal to postpone the attack to 10 December with 'never, no never'. Nevertheless on the day after this meeting the commanders concerned transmitted to the Headquarters in writing their proposal for the 'limited solution'. As they had in face of Jodl, so they now sought to circumvent Hitler's obstinacy by pointing out that if all went well the 'major solution' might well develop from the limited one. Their primary object, however, was to give the Supreme Command a truer picture of the general state, the training and lack of mobility of the troops, which Jodl's dissertation had led them to believe was not realized.

Such contemporary accounts as there are leave no doubt that the representations of the commanders in the West, among whom Model and Manteuffel were prominent, kept the Headquarters urgently busy during the following period. Completely disregarding them however, Hitler on 10 November signed the order prepared by OKW entitled *Order for Assembly and Concentration for the Attack (Ardennes Offensive)*. The objective for the operation was now put on a politico-strategic plane, and was given as 'to destroy enemy forces north of the line Antwerp–Brussels–Luxemburg and thereby change the course of the campaign in the West and perhaps of the entire war'. The fact that there was no question of changing the objectives was underlined by Hitler's words introducing this order – that he was determined 'to accept the maximum risk in order to proceed with this operation and was prepared to abandon both territory and positions should the anticipated enemy attack on either side of Metz and subsequent advance into the Ruhr area materialize'. The date for 'conclusion of the concentration' was now given as 27 November.[36]

The commanders continued to protest by all means available to them. On 25 November OKW had to give Commander-in-Chief West 'a final answer' telling him that 'the Führer ... is unalterably decided on the objective and scope of the attack ... he is totally opposed ... to the idea of a "limited solution"'. Two days later Jodl was despatched to the West once more. He notes in his diary: 'returned from the West and reported to the Führer; 1. Major solution stands'. Then he adds: '2. Formations still required must be obtained. Proposal follows.'

At the time therefore at which the offensive was due to begin, it was still short of a number of complete formations; meanwhile there had been 'delays in the resting and reconstitution of the Army' as a result of continuous severe defensive fighting. There were therefore 'continual' postponements and the date for the attack was finally set at 10 December.

In preparation for the attack the Supreme Commander dealt with a mass of detail, most of which had to be issued by OKW as 'tactical instructions' – the senior commanders in the West had their hands held down to the smallest details. A few extracts from Jodl's diary will show what went on:

3 November: the Führer does not wish to give Tigers to the mobile formations but to allot them in small units to the infantry ... The King Tigers (*Tiger Mark II*) are too heavy and are having chassis trouble.

10 November: ... Three thousand tons (? fuel ? transport capacity) ... at the moment not guaranteed from Italy or Army Group North (the East) ... Shelters for tanks, ice on roads ... The Home Guard to collect captured equipment in the forward areas.'

17 November: Everything must be dug in the night before.

1. First built-up areas and headquarters – then one minute artillery concentration.

2. Then over to the artillery.

3. Flat trajectory fire not to be concentrated on railway stations where it does no good.

18 November: All attacks to begin simultaneously or the enemy will get warning. Night attack only if the troops are fit for it. Armoured sanding machines (*sic*). All Alsatians must be got out of front-line divisions.

28 November: Three blankets per man for the attacking troops in the West. Can they be transported? Boots. Get units to report.

6 December: Navy frogmen to be attached to Sixth Panzer Army (Meuse canal).

Some of these entries are obviously taken from the 1918 Army regulations 'for position warfare attacks'; others are based on Hitler's personal experiences as an infantryman at that time. There were no comparable instructions for the Luftwaffe.

On 20 November 1944, when the concrete of the great towers of Wolfschanze were still hardly dry, Hitler was ready to leave. The offensive in the West was imminent, but an equally compelling reason to move was the fact that the Red Army was now knocking at the door of East Prussia. An intermediate stop was made in Berlin, where as always happened there and was also the rule in Berchtesgaden, the different parts of Supreme Headquarters were scattered far and wide – even within sections the offices and living accommodation covered a wide area. Hitler and some of the aides lived in the concrete shelters of the Reich Chancellery which had been heavily damaged by bombing. Keitel and Jodl occupied the old alternative accommodation for OKW in Dahlem. The staff under General Winter was initially accommodated in a Luftwaffe building nearby, moving later to Zossen alongside OKH. The senior officers of OKW and of the three Services in general met only at the briefing conferences in the Reich Chancellery which as usual took up hours and hours.[37]

On 18 December Hitler moved from Berlin to the headquarters known as 'Adlerhorst' (Eagle's Eyrie) – the camp of Ziegenberg at Nauheim in Hesse which had been prepared as far back as 1939 for the campaign in the West.[38] In the spring of 1940 the Todt organization had made ready the Ziegenberg country house solely (and fruitlessly) for an 'immediate entourage' supposed to be in high spirits and on the way to an easy victory. Now HQ Area 1 was in deep underground shelters beneath a wooded hillside. The staff and HQ Area 2 were accommodated far off in Friedberg. OKH was back in its accommodation of the early war period at Zossen near Berlin.

In spite of all their previous rebuffs on 2 December Generals Model and von Manteuffel made a last attempt to get Hitler to change his plans for the attack; Sepp Dietrich and the Chief of Staff to Commander-in-Chief West, General Westphal were also present. The discussion went on for hours and Field Marshal Model, as spokesman for the generals, was frank and insistent; but all in vain. Hitler refused even to discuss the 'limited solution', which he characterized as a 'partial solution'. All he would agree to were certain measures to improve the still seriously inadequate equipment of the troops.[39] The sort of problems still outstanding emerged from Jodl's diary which records:

8 December: 7,150 cubic metres fuel available; a further 6,000 on the way together with 2,400 from the East. The remainder must come from production and must be moved up urgently. ... Ammunition: out of 64 trains 55 have arrived, 3 have left and 4 have been loaded.

12 December: Seventh Army is still short of two bridging columns, a pioneer battalion from the East and above all of rubber boats.

On 7 December the attack was postponed to 14th. On 12th it was finally postponed to 16th – again reminiscent of the western campaign of 1940.

Such were the shortages, and there were many others; the commanders responsible had repeatedly shown that they were opposed to the operation. With hindsight therefore the 'Ardennes offensive' can be regarded only as a desperate undertaking, doomed to failure before it had even started. Although Supreme Headquarters had already thought up excuses in case the operation should fail, the outlook there at the time was very different. On 15 December, the day before the attack, Jodl despatched the following to Field Marshal Model: 'the final decisions have been made; ... everything points to victory. The magnitude and scope of which ... depends entirely on the handling of the operation; ... if ... these basic principles for the conduct of operations are adhered to ... a major victory is assured.'

As always before any great campaign Hitler assembled all the senior officers taking part in the offensive down to divisional commander in the headquarters at Adlerhorst on 11 and 12 December

1944 (half of them on each day). As he had done ten days before in Berlin to General von Manteuffel, he now made a long speech, explaining in addition to the main military reasons, the political motives which had led him to his decision.[40]

War is of course a test of endurance for those involved. The longer the war goes on the more severe this test of endurance. This test of endurance must under all circumstances continue as long as there is the slightest hope of victory. The moment all hope of victory disappears people's determination becomes insufficient to withstand the test of endurance, in the same way as a fortress will go on fighting as long as there is hope of relief. It is therefore vital from time to time to destroy the enemy's confidence in victory by making clear to him by means of offensive action that his plans cannot succeed. A successful defensive can never achieve this as effectively as a successful offensive. In the long run the principle that the defensive is stronger than the offensive does not hold. We must not forget that the total manpower available on our side is still just as great as that of the enemy. We must not forget that a considerable proportion of our enemy's strength is tied down in east Asia facing Japan, facing a power which, even without China, comprises well over one hundred million men and, from the technical equipment point of view is a major factor.

Nevertheless we must be clear that, although a prolonged, stubbornly conducted defensive may wear down the enemy, it must in all cases be followed by a successful offensive. From the outset of the war therefore I have striven to act offensively whenever possible, to conduct a war of movement and not to allow myself to be manoeuvred into a position comparable to that of the first World War. If this has nevertheless occurred, it has resulted primarily from the defection of our allies, which naturally had its effect on operations. Wars are, however, finally decided when one side or the other realizes that the war as such can no longer be won. Our most important task therefore is to force the enemy to realize this. He will realize this most quickly when his forces have been annihilated and his territory occupied. If we ourselves are forced onto the defensive, then it must straight away be our task from time to time to make it clear once more to the enemy by means of ruthless offensives that he has nevertheless not won the war but that it will be continued without flinching. The psychological effect upon the enemy must be increased by missing no opportunity to make it clear to him that, whatever he may do, he can never reckon upon us surrendering. Never, never. That is the decisive point. The slightest sign of an inclination to surrender means that the enemy's hopes of ultimate victory will rise once more, that his population, which has lost all hope, will recover its hope and be prepared once more to accept all afflictions and privations. This is the danger of publishing defeatist memoranda as was done in 1917, or of publishing official documents, as was done in that year, which had been known to the enemy years before and which attempted to keep up morale by stating that some miracle would happen, and that this miracle would transform the situation at a stroke. The enemy must be made to realize that under no circumstances can he succeed. Once he comes to realize that – from the attitude of the nation, of the armed forces and finally as a result of the severe reverses he suffers – then one day his nervous energy will collapse. That will happen which happened to Frederick the Great in the seventh year of his war and which can be accounted his greatest success. People may say: yes, but then the situation was different. It was not different, gentlemen; at that time all his generals, including his own brother, were near to despairing of success. His Prime Minister and deputations of Ministers from Berlin appeared and begged him to put an end to the war since it could no longer be won. The steadfastness of one man made it possible for that battle to be carried through, and the miracle of a change in the situation eventually to arrive. The counter-argument that this would never have happened had there not been a change of Sovereign in Russia is totally irrelevant. For if he had surrendered in the fifth year of the war a change of sovereign in the seventh year – in other words two years later – would have meant nothing. One must await the moment.

The following must also be considered, gentlemen. In all history there has never been a coalition composed of such heterogeneous partners with such totally divergent objectives as that of our enemies. The states which are now our enemies are the greatest opposites which exist on earth: ultra-capitalist states on one side and ultra-Marxist states on the other; on one side a dying empire – Britain; on the other side a colony, the United States waiting to claim its inheritance. These are states whose objectives diverge daily. And anyone who, if I may use the phrase, sits like a spider in his web and follows these developments can see how hour by hour these antitheses are increasing. If we can deal it a couple of heavy blows, this artificially constructed common front may collapse with a mighty thunderclap at any moment. Each of the partners in this coalition has entered it in the hope of achieving thereby his political objectives ... either to cheat the others out of something or to get something out of it: the United States' object is to be England's heir, Russia's object is to capture the Balkans, to capture the Straits, to capture Persian oil, to capture Iran, to capture the Persian Gulf; England's object is to maintain her position, to strengthen her position in the Mediterranean. In other words one day – it can happen any moment, for on the other side history is being made merely by mortal men – this coalition may dissolve, always on the assumption that under no circumstances does this battle lead to a moment of weakness in Germany.

We have of course had our points of weakness from the beginning of the war, weakness consisting primarily in our allies. It was a major source of weakness for us that we had no strong states as allies, only weak states. But all the same for a time they did their duty by us. We must not complain and we must not wail about it. We must merely realize with thankfulness that for a time at any rate these states fulfilled their purpose. We were enabled for years to make war far from the borders of the Reich. Even now we have only been driven back to our frontiers in places. In many areas we are still far from the old Reich frontiers. In any case, as before, we are now carrying on the war from a situation which gives us every possibility of holding out and sticking it through, particularly if we can eliminate the danger here in the West.

Gentlemen, on other fronts I have accepted sacrifices – sacrifices which could perhaps have been avoided – in order to make it possible to act offensively again. When at this moment I speak of an offensive, the man who is exposed to the rigours of the battle, particularly those who are suffering from the enemy's complete air superiority, may perhaps be worried and may say: 'can one even think of such a thing? It wasn't like this in 1939 and 1940; then more or less everyone was convinced that the war could be won by an offensive in the West.' On the contrary gentle-men! I did not write memoranda in order to knock at open doors. I wrote memoranda in order to break down closed doors. I would not have had to hold innumerable repetitive conferences in order to get across my conviction that we had to act offensively in the West. ...

The official view was that we should conduct a defensive war and that was what I had to combat in those years. People accepted the fact that we must act offensively against Poland. But to act offensively against France and against England, that people thought was lunacy, a crime, a Utopia, a hopeless undertaking. The course of events proved the opposite. We cannot today even imagine where we should have got, had we not then dealt with France. The objection may be made that there is a major differ-ence between 1940 and the present situation: at that time the enemy's army had no battle experience, and now we are facing an enemy we have learned to know in war. That is true, gentle-men. But as regards relative strength there is little difference, apart from the Luftwaffe – that is of course a most important factor to which I will come in a moment. As regards relative strength: in 1940 we carried out our offensive in the West with a total of about 100 divisions, say 110, and of those about 86 were used in the offensive. They were not all first-class divisions, some of them were improvized formations formed only a few months before and some could not be really regarded as first-class. The formations available for this offensive are not all first-class. But on the enemy's side his formations are not all first-class either. Some of our units are tired but the enemy has tired units too and has suffered heavy losses. We have just had the first official announcement from the Americans that in three short weeks they have lost more than 240,000 men. Those are simply colossal figures – far greater than we ourselves believed they had lost. So he is fought-out too. From the technical point of view the two sides are about equal. As regards armoured forces, the enemy may have more tanks available but with our new Marks we have the better tanks.'

A speech like this, made to unprejudiced soldiers, must have had some effect, however aware they may have been of shortages and inadequacies. General von Manteuffel wrote: 'on the credit side the commanders took away from this conference a picture of the enemy's overall situation. They had been given an appreciation of the situation from the one source in a position to see the full military picture and it seemed to give an assurance of favourable conditions.'

As is well known Operation 'Herbstnebel' (Autumn Mist) – the new code name – began at 05.30 hours on 16 December. The enemy was taken completely by surprise and considerable initial successes were achieved in the area of the northern Eifel which was not strongly defended. Forward elements of Manteuffel's Army later got within a few miles of the Meuse at Dinant, though they were considerably behind the planned schedule and their sister army on the right was hanging far back. Supreme Headquarters was carried away by these partial successes and was completely the prisoner of its own wishful thinking; it therefore entirely failed to realize that with every day which the enemy was allowed for the movement of his considerable reserves, the prospects of a major victory, getting anywhere near the planned objectives, were becoming more improbable. Jodl's diary of 18 December gives a good idea of the attitude of mind: 'the Führer commands that the remaining enemy pockets must be broken up from the rear. They must be cut off from the rear so that they cannot be supplied; they will then surrender'. Shortly thereafter, however, the focal point of Bastogne, instead of surrendering, began to absorb an ever greater proportion of the attacking forces; the weather cleared and in spite of all the efforts of the Luftwaffe the Allied air superiority began to make itself felt. There were many individual acts of heroism but gradually the roles became reversed and the attacker was forced on to the defensive. On Christmas Day, Commander-in-Chief West asked that the attack should be halted since not even the 'limited solution' was now possible. In spite of all this Hitler not merely clung to the major plan but began to toy with even more ambitious ideas.

As the enemy brought up his large-scale reserves against the German break-through in the Eifel the picture changed; Supreme Headquarters thereupon revived an idea which had already been considered on 17 and 25 November, at which time the enemy had broken through into Alsace.[41] There had then been discussion whether to abandon the plan for the Ardennes offensive at the last moment in favour of an 'operation for the recovery of Alsace and

Lorraine'. The OKW Operations Staff had made a preliminary study of the operation in October and produced a draft before the end of November; this was now resurrected preparatory to a new second offensive.[42] They managed to convince themselves in Adlerhorst that this operation would not only produce further partial successes but in view of the movements which it would force upon the enemy, would allow the front, which had meanwhile bogged down in the Ardennes, to get going again, cross the Meuse and reach its original objective. This concept was based on no true strategic appreciation and the resources required were even less likely to be available than they had been for the Ardennes offensive. Yet on 28 December 1944 Hitler propounded it in glowing terms to the commanders concerned as the following extract from *Fragment no. 27* shows.

In general the plan for the operation is clear. I am fully in agreement with the measures which have been taken. In particular I hope that we can push the right flank* forward rapidly so as to open up the approaches to Zabern and then push straight on into the Rhine plain and liquidate the American divisions. Our objective must be the destruction of these American divisions. I hope that by then the fuel situation will allow us to concentrate fresh forces, to regroup** and to strike a further blow as a result of which I am completely confident that, as our forces increase, we shall be able to destroy additional American divisions. For by that time our forces should have become somewhat stronger. I hope that I can support this next attack with ... additional divisions, one of them a first-class one from Finland. Unless this operation is cursed with bad luck from the outset it should in my opinion succeed.

I do not need to explain to you again how much depends upon it. It will to a large extent be decisive for the success of the first operation.*** If we can carry out these two operations A and B, and if we succeed, the threat to our left flank*** will automatically vanish. We shall then start the third battle straight away and smash the Americans there completely. I am entirely convinced that we shall then be able to turn left.

Our first object must be to clean up the situation in the West by

* From the area Zweibrücken-Bitsch.
** In Upper Alsace.   *** In the Ardennes.

offensive action. This object must be fanatically pursued. There may be some who in secret will object saying: 'yes but will it come off?' Gentlemen, the same objection was raised to me in 1939. I was told both verbally and in writing that the thing could not be done; that it was impossible. Even in the winter of 1940 I was told: that cannot be done. Why don't we hold on in the Siegfried Line?; we've built the Siegfried Line so why don't we let the enemy bang his head against it and then possibly attack him afterwards? Let him come on first; we may be able to advance later. We've got these wonderful positions; why run unnecessary risks?' What would have happened to us if we had not attacked then? It's exactly the same today. Our relative strength is no less than it was in 1939 or 1940. On the contrary if in these two attacks we succeed in destroying both these American groupings* then the balance will swing clearly and finally in our favour. In the last analysis I am counting on the fact that the German soldier knows what he is fighting for.

The only thing which is not in our favour this time is the air situation. That is why we are now forced to take advantage of the bad winter weather. The air situation forces us to do so. I cannot wait till the weather gets better. I would be happier if we could somehow hold on till the spring. I would then perhaps be able to make available an additional 10, 15, 20 divisions and we could attack in the spring. But in the first place the enemy also would have got 14 to 20 new divisions across. Secondly I do not know whether the air situation will be any better in the spring than it is now. If it is not, the weather in the spring will give the enemy a decisive advantage, whereas now there are at least some weeks before there can be carpet-bombing of troop concentrations. That means a lot.

You will realize from the following how important it is to bring this thing off: the enemy now knows all about the flying bombs. He has of course completely rebuilt some of them. We know that. He is already producing them. There is no doubt that, just as we are harassing England's industrial areas all the time with these flying bombs, they will be able practically to demolish the Ruhr area by massive use of them. There is no protection against them. We should not even be able to use fighters against them. I would rather not talk about the heavy rockets. There's absolutely no

* In Alsace.

defence against them. Everything therefore indicates that we must clear up this situation before the enemy gets super-weapons of this sort into service.

The German people have breathed more freely in the last few days. We must make sure that this relief is not followed by lethargy – lethargy is the wrong word, I mean gloom. They have breathed again. The mere idea that we were on the offensive again has had a cheering effect on the German people. And if this offensive can continue, as soon as we get our first really great victories – and we shall have them for our situation is no different from that of the Russians in 1941 and 1942 when everything was against him, when he had an enormous front but when we went over to the defensive and he was able to push us slowly back by limited offensives – if the German people see this happening, you may be sure they will make every sacrifice which is humanly possible. They will answer every call. They will be afraid of nothing – whether I order a new levy on clothing or a new levy on something else, or whether I call for men – the young men will come forward with enthusiasm. The German people will react. I must say that the nation acts as well as anybody could expect. There are no better people than our Germans. Individual bad examples are merely the exceptions which prove the rule.

Finally I wish to appeal to you to go into this operation with all your verve, with all your zest, with all your energy. This is a decisive operation. Your success will automatically bring about the success of the second operation. The success of the second operation will automatically bring about the collapse of the threat to the left flank* of our offensive. We shall then actually have knocked out half the enemy forces on the Western Front. Then we will see what happens. Then there will be 45 additional German divisions and I do not believe that in the long run he can stand up to those. We will yet be masters of our fate.

Now that the date has been fixed for New Year's Eve I wish to say that I am particularly grateful to all those headquarters which have done the gigantic work of preparation and which have taken upon themselves the great risk of being responsible for it. I consider it a particularly good omen that this has been possible. Throughout German history New Year's Night has always been a night of good omen for our arms. For the enemy this New

* In the Ardennes.

493

Year's Night will be an unpleasant surprise. He does not cele-
brate Christmas: he celebrates New Year. There could be no
better start to the New Year than dealing him a blow like this.
And when on New Year's Day the news spreads through Germany
that we are on the offensive again in a new area and are succeeding,
the German people will say to itself that, although the end of the
old year was miserable, the new one has begun well. That is a
good omen for the future. Gentlemen, I should like to wish each
of you personally good luck.

Gentlemen, there is one thing more: secrecy is a pre-requisite
for the success of this operation. Anyone who has not got to know
about this operation should not know about it. Anyone who must
know something of it, should know only what he needs to know.
Anyone who must know something of it should not be told earlier
than is necessary. That is imperative. And no one should be
allowed to go up to the front who is in the know and who might
possibly be captured. That is also imperative.

Before the operations in Alsace (code name 'Nordwind' (North
Wind)) could have any effect upon the area of the main attack in
the north Hitler was forced, at the beginning of January 1945, to
the conclusion that 'continuation of the Ardennes operation now
offers no prospects of success, since Army Group B is now faced with
fifty per cent of the enemy forces'. All movement in Alsace also
soon came to a halt but it was several days before Hitler's advisers
could persuade him that this meant the definite end of his ambitious
plans in the West. It was not until 14 January, the day before the
headquarters returned to Berlin that the Operations Staff War
Diary finally admitted that 'the initiative in the area of the offensive
has passed to the enemy'.

Marked by vast sacrifices in blood and treasure the story of the
war in the West was nearing its end.

CHAPTER 2

Disintegration to Capitulation

A fitting introduction to the last phase of the war is a talk between
Hitler and General Thomale, Chief of the Inspectorate General of
Armoured Forces; it took place in Adlerhorst during the night 29–30
December 1944. Hitler was at his best in conjuring up day dreams
both for himself and other people. He said (*Fragment no. 30*):

Not long ago I was reading a volume of Frederick the Great's
letters. In one of these letters he wrote (it was in the fifth year of
the Seven Years War): 'I started this war with the most wonderful
army in Europe; today I've got a muck heap. I have no leaders
any more, my generals are incompetent, the officers are no commanders, the troops are wretched.' It was a devastating estimate.
But nevertheless that man got through the war. What's more if
you read the estimates about the Russian troops, they're wretched.
But they carry on just the same. So the important things are the
eternal human qualities, the qualities which are really basic to
the military profession. Military qualities don't show themselves
in an exercise on a sand model. In the last analysis they show
themselves in the capacity to hold on, in perseverance and
determination. That's the decisive factor in any victory. Genius
is a will-o'-the wisp unless it is founded on perseverance and
fanatical determination. That's the most important thing in
human existence. People who have brainwaves, ideas, etc., will
get nowhere in the end unless they also possess strength of character, perseverance and determination. Otherwise they merely
ride their luck. If all goes well they are up in the air; if things go
badly they're down in the depths and give up everything straight
away. One can't make world history that way. World history can
only be made if, in addition to high intelligence, in addition to
thorough knowledge, in addition to continual alertness, a man has
fanatical determination and the courage of his convictions which

495

will make him master of himself. That's what matters to the soldier in the last analysis, that at the moment of crisis he feels that those who command him have these qualities. Some don't like it, those are the bad ones. But the good ones feel that they are playing some part; they say: 'why have we had to make all these sacrifices? But we shall only have to go on doing so as long as the war lasts'. That's certain. No one can last for ever. We can't, the other side can't. It's merely a question who can stand it longer. The one who must hold out the longer is the one who's got everything at stake. We've got everything at stake. If the other side says one day: 'we've had enough of it', nothing happens to him. If America says: 'we're off. Period. We've got no more men for Europe', nothing happens; New York would still be New York, Chicago would still be Chicago, Detroit would still be Detroit, San Francisco would be still San Francisco. It doesn't change a thing. But if we were to say today 'we've had enough', we should cease to exist. Germany would cease to exist'.

This is no bad description by Hitler of the general politico-strategic concept on which German Supreme Headquarters was working at the close of the war. It was most simply expressed in the slogan that we must not lay down our arms 'at five minutes to twelve', as National-Socialist theory maintained had happened in November 1918. But for the man who was at the helm of German destiny the moment at which the decisions for war and victory would present themselves lay hidden in the mists of his political and military wishful thinking. In the forefront was his conviction that the enemy coalition would collapse, and he was continually thinking that he had discovered new indications of it. Secondly his 'faith' was based upon our 'miracle weapons'; they were a remarkable achievement of German engineers and craftsmen but there was no reason to think that they would have a 'lightning' or even early and decisive effect comparable to that later achieved by the first atom bomb.[1] Meanwhile both the people and the Wehrmacht were left largely in the dark over the real situation; their last energies were whipped up by a propaganda presentation of the Allied demand for unconditional surrender[2] and – though with more caution – of the news of the horrors perpetrated by the Russian rabble when the Red Army first entered East Prussia.

Such reasoning might do some good politically, but no military war plan could be constructed on such shifting ground, as at one time even Hitler in his more sensible moments had recognized. So in this final phase of the war German Supreme Headquarters and its strategy was torn in all directions – between East and West – between attempts at ambitious operations for which neither forces nor resources were available and the pitiless march of events which continuously overtook their planning; between the grizly heroism of a determination not to recognize the approach of catastrophe and day-to-day activity in a dreamworld of armies, divisions and regiments capable of fighting.[3] The determination of one man possessed of the devil governed everything; the machinery of command churned out orders in normal form[4] though there might be no one to receive them. Yet the German soldier and, as he became more directly involved in operations of war, the German civilian followed this lead with self-sacrifice and energy.

Hitler's leadership was therefore now without object or objective but the last crazy orders continued to issue forth stamped with his own faults and his own phraseology. He proposed to withdraw from the Geneva Convention as a protest against the bombing of civilians and as a stimulus to last-minute resistance, but was talked out of it.[5] At the beginning of March 1945 from the gloomy shelters of the Reich Chancellery thundered the empty threat to the soldiers of the Wehrmacht that their relatives at home would have to answer for it if they were taken prisoner unwounded. On 19 March there followed the order that before a further yard of German territory was relinquished to the enemy all industrial establishments and supply depots were to be destroyed – without regard even for the bare necessities of life of the population.[6] Finally – on 15 April 1945, only fourteen days before cheating fate by suicide, he issued this call to the soldiers on the Eastern Front: 'anyone ordering you to retreat will, unless you know him well personally, be immediately arrested and if necessary killed on the spot, no matter what rank he may hold' – a scurvy reward for the discipline and loyalty of the Wehrmacht which had borne the burden of the war for five and a half years.

Keitel was the only senior officer to follow these developments in all their details. All he said in his evidence was: 'after all our efforts (referring to March 1945) had failed, Germany's defeat was absolutely clear. It was only the sense of military duty, rooted in the oath we had sworn, which compelled me and all of us to fight on.'[8]

In the middle of January, even before the enemy had brought

our offensive in the West to a halt, the Supreme Command was forced unwillingly to turn its attention to the East. The first warning camewhen the Ardennes battle was at its height. On 24 December Guderian appeared in Adlerhorst. The Red Army had driven deep into north-west Hungary and Budapest was cut off. He did not feel therefore that it was sufficient for Hitler and his headquarters to get merely secondhand information on the situation in the East. Jodl's notes on this meeting (he is wrong about its date) give the impression that Hungary only was discussed and that some emergency reinforcements were provided from the OKW theatres of war. In his own account, however, Guderian states that the object of his journey was to transfer the centre of gravity of such German war potential as remained to the eastern front, in view of the Russian superiority both in numbers and offensive equipment almost all along the front. He states that he forecast 12 January as the date for the probable opening of the Red Army's attack. Guderian's book is eloquent of his horror at the threatened abandonment of the eastern German provinces, of his repeated arguments with Jodl who was 'even more dangerous than Hitler in his determination not to relinquish the initiative which he thought he had recovered in the West', and of his memory of 'the grim and tragic Christmas Eve in the most unchristian atmosphere' of the headquarters. All this makes Guderian's account ring truer than Jodl's.

Subsequent events however prove that Guderian's representations did not move Supreme Headquarters to make a plan to counter the forthcoming Russian attack across Hungary, should it reach dangerous proportions. Hitler simply refused to take the situation seriously; Guderian had with him data on the strength and intentions of the Red Army worked out by the Intelligence Section Foreign Armies East under the direction of its experienced Chief, General Gehlen. Hitler rejected it all as 'pure bluff' and 'rubbish'. In spite of all reverses and disappointments Jodl was still determined to maintain the offensive in the West, though it may be that he thought thereby to shake the enemy off so effectively that a breathing space would be gained which could then be used to allot more forces to the East. Guderian reported verbally again on New Year's Eve, and yet again on 9 January 1945. At the briefing conferences in Adlerhorst the Operations Staff reporting officers emphasized on many occasions the dangers building up from the enemy bridgehead over the Vistula at Baranov. All this made no difference to Hitler. Nor was any thought given, as the battle area shrank, to placing all Army forces once more under their own General Staff. On the contrary Jodl held on to 'his' divisions in the West and even reinforced them as far as possible by formations released from Finland and Norway; Guderian returned to Zossen with, in his own words: 'a harsh order from Hitler that the Eastern Front must help itself and make do with what it's got'.[9]

The great Russian 'Baranov offensive' reached Upper Silesia and the middle Oder in one sweep. As early as the fourth day the appreciation of the situation in Supreme Headquarters began to change. Yet on 15 January, the evening before the headquarters moved from Adlerhorst, Jodl's diary merely carries the sentence: '19.20 hours. Guderian calls and begs urgently for everything to be thrown into the East'.

The next day however the diary shows signs of panic snap decisions soon to be proved impractical; it says: 'the Führer demands crash action to move two Armoured and two Infantry Divisions rapidly from Libau (Courland)'.

The same day Hitler ordered that Sixth SS Panzer Army, the first formation he had allowed to be withdrawn from the Ardennes for rest, should 'be thrown into Hungary to protect the vital oil area'. A few weeks before Hitler had given a direct order behind Guderian's back for the immediate move of an SS Panzer Corps from the centre of the Eastern Front to Hungary. Guderian now lost his temper. On the first morning after the Headquarters had returned to the Reich Chancellery in Berlin[10] he appeared and stormed at Jodl; all he got in answer was a shrug of the shoulders. There is nothing to show that Jodl had had any hand in the decision; its result was to disperse the few reserves available from the West and, instead of using them for the primary task of protecting the German eastern frontier, send the majority of them off on a move to Hungary which was bound to last a matter of weeks. In any case Guderian got no support from Jodl when he protested against this order, and he therefore got nowhere. In his evidence after the war Keitel lifted the veil from these events, admitting that Hitler 'considered the protection of Vienna and Austria as of vital importance' and that he would 'rather see Berlin fall than lose the Hungarian oil area and Austria'.[11]

On 17 January Warsaw was evacuated by the last four weak battalions defending it. This was done without Hitler's knowledge and without an express order from him. When he heard of it he went into a paroxysm of rage, proving, according to Guderian's account, that he at last realized that he himself was responsible for the rapid collapse of the Eastern Front. 'He completely lost any comprehension of or interest in the frightful general situation,' says Guderian, 'he could think of nothing but the misfortune of losing Warsaw. ... The next few days he devoted to studying the loss of Warsaw and to punishing the General Staff for what he regarded as its failure.' Guderian repeats Hitler's words: 'its not you I am after, but the General Staff. It is intolerable to me that a group of intellectuals should presume to press their views on their superiors. But such is the general staff system and that system I intend to smash.' In spite of all Guderian's protests Colonel von Bonin, the Chief of the Army Operations Section and two of the lieutenant-colonels on his staff were arrested and, with Guderian himself, subjected to days of interrogation by the notorious Chiefs of the SD, Kaltenbrunner and Müller. Bonin finally landed in a concentration camp in which he remained to the end of the war.[12] Meanwhile the battle for eastern Germany, to which all energies should have been devoted, went on.

The OKW Operations Staff may not have been directly involved in these affairs but there can be little doubt of the effect produced upon its officers. This merely became deeper and more lasting when they found that they were responsible for drafting the following order, issued on 21 January 1945 as a result of the Warsaw incident:

'I (*Hitler*) order as follows:

1. Commanders-in-Chief, Corps Commanders and Divisional Commanders are personally responsible to me for reporting in good time:

(a) Every decision to carry out an operational movement.
(b) Every attack planned in divisional strength or upwards which does not conform with the general directives laid down by the High Command.
(c) Every offensive action in quiet sectors of the front, over and above normal shock-troop activities which is calculated to draw the enemy's attention to the sector.
(d) Every plan for disengaging or withdrawing forces.
(e) Every plan for surrendering a position, a local strong-point or a fortress.

They must ensure that I have time to intervene in this decision if I think fit and that my counter-orders can reach the front-line troops in time.

2. Commanders-in-Chief, Corps Commanders and Divisional Commanders, the Chiefs of the General Staffs and each individual officer of the General Staff or officers employed on General Staffs are responsible to me that every report made to me, either directly or through the normal channels, should contain nothing but the unvarnished truth. In future I shall impose draconian punishment on any attempt at concealment, whether deliberate or arising from carelessness or oversight.

3. I must point out that the maintenance of signals communications, particularly in heavy fighting and critical situations, is a prerequisite for the conduct of the battle. All officers commanding troops are responsible to me for ensuring that these communications, both to higher headquarters and to subordinate commanders, are not broken and for seeing that, by exhausting *every* means and engaging themselves personally, permanent communications in every case are ensured with the commanders above and below.'[13]

Hitler's intention in issuing this order must have been to achieve his long-sought end, completely to muzzle the Wehrmacht – or rather the Army. By the contemptuous terms in which it was couched he was clearly giving full expression to his hatred of General Staff officers and their traditional intellectual independence. Subsequent orders, which were to a large extent impracticable, gave him the opportunity, as the whim moved him, to carry out his despicable threats of punishment.

On the day this order was issued Hitler took further action intended to stem the Russian flood in the East; it proved totally illusory. Guderian had proposed that a new Army headquarters, 'Army Group Vistula', should be formed to 'close the gap opened by the Russian offensive, stop the breakthrough ... towards Danzig ... and the encirclement of East Prussia and to assemble the reinforcements moving up for the purpose'. Hitler now nominated Himmler as Commander-in-Chief of this Army Group! It was a vital and difficult job for which Guderian had proposed Field Marshal Freiherr von Weichs who had been Commander-in-Chief Southeast and was now unemployed. He thought he had Jodl's agreement.

When however he submitted the agreed nomination to Hitler, he suffered, as he says, 'a great disappointment'; Jodl unfortunately let fall a chance remark regarding the Field Marshal's deep religious convictions; this resulted in Hitler turning the proposal down flat and nominating Himmler instead. Guderian was 'appalled' at this 'preposterous suggestion' but could do nothing; eventually even Hitler was forced to recognize that Himmler was totally incapable of dealing with the problems of command of military forces.[14]

Fighting in 'the East' was now taking place almost exclusively on German territory – soon even in central Germany; both the defence and a number of fruitless counter-attacks were overwhelmed by superior Russian forces. All this resulted in ever sharper disagreements between Hitler and Guderian[15] from which Jodl was careful to keep aloof. This was now a war on two fronts in the truest sense of the word and it was taking place within the frontiers of Germany, but there is not a sign that Jodl ever attempted to exert a real influence or to take matters really in hand; all he did was to shuffle forces hither and thither and allocate the dwindling reserves of ammunition and fuel.[16] The only occasion on which the OKW Operations Staff took a certain hand in the direction of operations was in the attack in southern Hungary, for which forces from the OKW South-eastern theatre were brought across the Drava, now the dividing line between that theatre and 'the East'.[17] The fact that this reinforcement was possible at all was thanks only to the outstanding achievement of Field Marshal Freiherr von Weichs and Colonel-General Löhr; although there had been much initial hesitation over withdrawal from the Balkans, they succeeded in getting the forces of the South-east back successfully from the whole enemy-dominated area – an operation in which Supreme Headquarters had no hand.

On another occasion Jodl does seem to have tried to calm Hitler down. The day after the issue of Hitler's 'muzzling order' General Hossbach (before the war he had been Senior Wehrmacht Aide, had been debarred from general staff employment by Hitler and had meanwhile risen from Regimental Commander to Commander-in-Chief of an Army) on his own initiative withdrew from the bend of the Narev and fought back westwards to the Vistula with his Army. Guderian records that Hitler went off into wild threats on this occasion also; Hossbach and the Commander-in-Chief of the Army

Group to which he belonged, Colonel-General Reinhardt, were dismissed but no further action was taken against them.[18] This was the time at which the Allies were re-drawing the map of Europe at Yalta. Oddly enough it was also the moment chosen by German Supreme Headquarters to realize that there were considerable potentialities, at least of a propaganda nature, for the conduct of the war against Soviet Russia in the Russian General Vlassov, who had been captured in the summer of 1942. The Press and Propaganda Section of the Operations Staff under General von Wedel had long been trying to get support for Vlassov's idea of forming a 'liberation army' to fight Bolshevism. As in all other political matters however, Hitler was unwilling to undertake obligations which might later tie his hands in setting up 'the new order' in Europe. In November 1943 Jodl had stated in his speech to the Gauleiter that 'the inclusion of foreigners in the forces must be approached with caution and scepticism'. In September 1944 (much too late) Himmler, who was responsible for all foreign troops in German service, was authorized to conclude an agreement with Vlassov, in theory designed rapidly to produce one to two divisions. What Hitler and Göring thought of this reinforcement is shown by the discussion at the briefing conference on 27 January 1945 given in the following extract from *Fragment 24/25*:

GUDERIAN: Vlassov wanted to make some statement.

HITLER: Vlassov doesn't mean a thing.

GÖRING: And the idea is they should go around in German uniform. One sees these young chaps everywhere. That only annoys people. If you want to lay hands on them you find they're Vlassov's people.

HITLER: I was always against putting them into our uniform. But who was for it? It was our beloved Army which always has its own ideas.

GÖRING: They're going around that way at the moment.

HITLER: I can't put them into anything else because we haven't any uniform. At the time I wanted to put the foreigners ... we'll do anything; Mr von Seeckt sold German tin hats to the Chinese. People have got no pride. They'll put any old good-for-nothing into German uniform. I was always against it. I was always against putting the Cossacks into German uniform. They ought to have been given Cossack uniform and Cossack badges of rank to show that they were fighting for us. Much more romantic. It never occurs to the Englishmen to dress up an Indian as an Englishman. We're the only people who've got no shame because we've got no character. Otherwise one wouldn't go peddling German tin hats to other people. The English let the Indians go around as natives.

GÖRING: Vlassov's people have got themselves so involved over there that they'd be punished if they were caught.

HITLER: Don't say that! They'll desert just the same.

GÖRING: That's all they can do – desert; they can't do anything else.

GUDERIAN: Are we to get the division forming at Münsingen operational as soon as we can?

HITLER: Yes, get it operational.

FEGELEIN: The Reichsführer hoped that he would be given command of both divisions.

HITLER: Vlassov would desert.

GÖRING: Deserting's all they can do. At least they won't be eating.

This was probably why Jodl's diary of 12 February says no more than: 'propaganda announcement about the employment of Vlassov troops. A warning for the Soviets'.[19]

It will now be clear that in the closing years of the war German Supreme Headquarters and its military staff put no real drive behind the formation of a co-ordinated war plan or as the phrase then was 'overall strategy'. Similarly the part played by the Headquarters in the strategy of the OKW theatres of war was limited almost entirely to matters of detail, to interference and to criticism. In the far North once the withdrawal from Finland and the construction of a defensive position on the Lyngen Fjord had been completed, all that remained to be done was to co-operate with the Navy, which in this case carried the main responsibility, in getting the largest possible number of formations back across the Skagerrack onto the mainland. Hitler however was still preoccupied with the possibilities of landings in Norway, and so in January 1945 there was some movement in the opposite direction, one ski brigade being sent north. Jodl meanwhile got his staff to examine whether, in view of the overall situation, the entire sweep of the coasts and frontiers of Norway could or should be defended.[20] For political and economic reasons Hitler vetoed the evacuation even of the most northerly part of the country. No operations had taken place in the area for years, but troops were maintained there right up until the end of hostilities.

In the South-east the great withdrawal had been successfully completed, but Hitler now demanded that certain forward positions should be retained far longer than was justified, resulting in further serious losses in battle with Jugoslav formations. Tens of thousands of German officers and men, together with their chivalrous Commander-in-Chief, Colonel-General Löhr, either fell into the hands of a vengeful enemy in the neighbouring areas of upper Italy or were handed over to him subsequently by the Allies; they later met their death as prisoners of the partisans.

In Italy the orders to Commander-in-Chief South-west remained unchanged in spite of all the upheavals both in East and West, and although further formations were withdrawn from him by Supreme Headquarters. Field Marshal Kesselring, who had been reinstated as Commander-in-Chief, was in agreement with Supreme Headquarters' repeated instructions on these lines; on 22 February 1945 he stated that: 'the Führer ... will never give agreement ... to a withdrawal, since under present circumstances this would ruin the morale and determination of the troops'. Colonel General von Vietinghoff however, who succeeded him from the beginning of March, protested; his protest was turned down and he had to get along with his instructions as best he could. The result of adherence to this principle was that when, on 9 April 1945, the Allies loosed their last great attack, reached Bologna on 21 April and so laid open the whole plain of the Po, the entire Army Group, which by then had no fuel and was practically immobile, disintegrated. OKW thereupon issued orders for withdrawal to the southern foothills of the Alps, but these were too late. Supreme Headquarters had then split and on 26 to 29 April (the moment at which Mussolini was killed while fleeing to Switzerland) 'headquarters South' issued appeals for 'fanatical determination to fight' and 'fanatical resistance' – but there was no one to hear them. There were encouraging exhortations to concentrate in the 'bulwark of the Alps Keep' but they bore no relation whatsoever to reality.[21] On 2 May the Commander-in-Chief on his own initiative brought the unequal struggle to an end by an armistice agreement for which preparations had long since been made.

OKW was still primarily preoccupied with the West. In February, a few weeks after our own offensive had been broken off, the enemy resumed his attack and broke into Germany on a co-ordinated plan and in increasing strength. Hitler's orders remained as rigid as ever; for instance: 'no soldier, no vehicle and no weapon was to cross the Rhine eastwards without the authority of an Army headquarters'; in another area the troops were bidden to remain in the forts of the Siegfried Line, though they might be encircled by the enemy and though their numbers were inadequate to occupy the line fully. So in spite of its courage and self-sacrifice the remnants of the German Army were to a great extent expended forward of the Rhine.[22] On 7 March a surprise American attack captured intact the bridge at Remagen; Hitler took a series of counter-measures – he tried in vain to recapture the bridgehead bringing up all available forces from Army Group B; there were courts martial and sentences of death on those held responsible; yet another Commander-in-Chief West was appointed. The only result was that when, on 22–23 March, the Allies began to cross the Rhine at many points, they found their task much easier than they had anticipated.

Hitler had selected Field Marshal Kesselring to succeed Rundstedt. He was comprehensively and personally briefed in the bunker beneath the Reich Chancellery in Berlin on 10 March, and then appointed Commander-in-Chief West. Hitler's views on this occasion were summarized in his statement that 'in the present phase of the war the sole and only task is to bridge the gap until Twelfth Army (a newly-constituted formation under General Wenck), the new fighters and more of the new-type weapons are ready for use'. Kesselring deduced from this that his task in the West was 'to hold on' and clean up the Remagen bridgehead.[23] He thereupon made a detailed inspection of his staff at Ziegenberg and of his subordinate armies and reappeared in Berlin on 15 March; he had much to say on the actual state of affairs at the front and on the unsatisfactory supply position, but the attitude to his proposals was unforthcoming – not surprising since at one of the briefing conferences of this period the cry still was that it was hoped to hold the Channel Islands for a further year.[24] Jodl's notes on this conference contain the first mention of the Western Front in his diary for two months; he says: 'Kesselring wants a free hand to withdraw 416 Div. The Führer does not give it him but says that if 416

Div. is in danger of being cut off from the north it must pack up.'

That a note such as this could come from the Chief of an overall Operations Staff in a situation in which everything was at stake may appear extraordinary. No less extraordinary was the effect which the presence of Hitler was still capable of exerting; Kesselring's report on the meeting runs:

> As I drove back from the Führer's Headquarters in the night 15–16 March I had the impression that Hitler stubbornly believed that we could defeat the Russians in the East and that what was happening in the West neither surprised him nor particularly worried him. He took it for granted that once the Russian front had been consolidated, he would be able with the forces so released and his newly-created divisions to clean up in the West. He was equally convinced that his orders to increase supplies would be carried out to the letter.[25]

The most graphic picture of the activity and atmosphere of the headquarters at this period is given by Jodl's diary and fragments of the record of a briefing conference both dated 23 March 1945 – ie shortly after the beginning of the Allies' Rhine crossing. Even at this late date Jodl's diary merely contains the usual details: '559 (Division) has 14 tanks; 190 Division has 4 battalions and 3 artillery battalions; 14 ammunition trains and 18 petrol trains are on the move.'

There follow one or two unpleasant remarks on non-military matters; obviously echoing Hitler he says: 'there are one and a quarter million workers in the Ruhr area. They are lying around eating their heads off and doing nothing – they must work on the railway.' This was all the thanks the workers in the Ruhr got for all they had done for the war industry, and for their tenacity under years of bombing.

The picture is completed by the record of the briefing conference at which the only senior officer present was General Burgdorf, the Chief Military Aide.

HITLER: The greatest danger really seems to be the second bridge-head, the bridgehead at Oppenheim.

BURGDORF: Because the enemy managed to bring up his bridging equipment so quickly.

HITLER: A pontoon bridge!

HEWEL: The Rhine isn't all that wide there.

HITLER: It's a good two hundred and fifty yards! It's only necessary for one man to go to sleep on a river obstacle and a frightful catastrophe can occur. The existence of the upper bridgehead has probably saved some of the formations down below. If it hadn't existed and if the enemy had used all his forces to push southwards up the Rhine, no one would have got away. The moment one lets oneself be pushed out of the fortified zone that's the end of it. The commanders have handled this wretchedly. From the top down they've drummed into the troops that it's better to fight in open country than in here.

BURGDORF: Minister Goebbels is asking for authority to turn the east-west avenue in Berlin into a runway. It would be necessary to remove the lamp standards and clear the Tiergarten for twenty yards either side. He thinks it would be a good idea because the east-west avenue could then be widened later.

HITLER: Yes, he can do that. But I don't think all that's necessary. Fifty yards is wide enough.

ZANDER: I've got here the last three radio messages from Hanke* (*produces them*).

HITLER: I'd like to see all the last radio messages.

ZANDER: They're in the protected accommodation in the Party Chancellery; I'll get them along.

HITLER: Get them along straight away! A telegram arrived in which he said that the enemy is now using very heavy artillery and that he's nothing to counter it with. He asked for heavy infantry howitzers. But as usual people have been messing around with the infantry howitzers. The Army Group was supposed to supply them. But I've ordered them to be supplied from the main depot and I've had it checked straight away whether heavy infantry howitzers are available there. Buhle registered astonishment. In fact they had to be furnished by the Replacement Army. The Army Group had no infantry howitzers. It took an unconscionable time. Then they said they wouldn't fit into the aircraft – then that they would go in if stripped – then that they couldn't land. Actually they're just afraid to land. Now they say that if they get the howitzers in they can't put in any ammunition. All we're talking about are

* Gauleiter of Lower Silesia trapped in Breslau.

six aircraft and six cargo gliders. Something else can be used for ammunition. But Hanke is a tank man – he doesn't understand. If they really want something to shoot the enemy out of blocks of houses there are better weapons; but we can't get them in. There are no better weapons which can be got there than the heavy infantry howitzers. But if you merely put in eighteen rounds a gun, that's a mess. With eighteen rounds a gun you can't do anything – although of course an infantry howitzer can level a house down to the cellar with one shot.

BURGDORF: Can I give Minister Goebbels the go-ahead?

HITLER: Yes. But I don't see why it's got to be made wider. We aren't going to land a *Goliath* and that's only one hundred and sixty feet wide.

VON BELOW: If JU52s are going to land in the dark the street lamps will cause trouble.

HITLER: All right for the street lamps; but to level twenty to thirty yards of the Tiergarten either side ...

VON BELOW: That's hardly necessary.

HITLER: There's no need for more than fifty yards' width. It's no use either because it couldn't be reinforced either side. That's completely useless.

JOHANNMEYER: It's merely a question of the pavement and the bank.

VON BELOW: I don't believe levelling for twenty yards is necessary but we must get rid of the street lamps.

HITLER: He can remove the street lamps.

BURGDORF: Then I can pass that on.

HITLER: It's just occurred to me: ME162s and ME262s could take off from the east-west avenue.

VON BELOW: Yes, it's long enough.

HEWEL: But not with the Victory Column in the middle.

BURGDORF: That would have to be demolished.

HITLER: It's almost two miles to the Victory Column. That's long enough ...

BURGDORF: Then there's another question: what's to be done about Guderian's leave at this moment?

HITLER: I'd like to get a final medical report about Wenck and one the doctor will stick to. One moment he swears he's fit and another that he isn't – finish – period. All they do is talk and say that on such and such a day he can come out of hospital.

Now they apparently don't even know whether he's got to have an operation.

BURGDORF: The doctor told us he thought it essential that Wenck should stay in hospital until 15 April, though he is agitating to get out earlier.

VON BELOW: May we stop the smokescreen, my Führer, when you are not at the Obersalzberg? The smoke screen is put up every time we go there and we're running short of acid.

HITLER: Yes, but that's the end of everything, we must be clear about that. That's the last protection we have. The bunker will be alright and I don't mind about my house but the complete set-up will go. If Zossen gets shot up one day where shall we go then? One heavy attack on Zossen and that's the end of it. Probably a good part of it's gone already.*

BURGDORF: It's quite all right to work in. The buildings are still all there, and there are enough huts. If the huts are destroyed then it can't be used.

HITLER: I saw that picture. It showed a three foot concrete wall. That's army concrete they used there. It oughtn't to have been demolished by one bomb once it had been built.

BURGDORF: I would like to refer to the layout at Air Fleet Reich, which I once visited. If I'd had any idea that a thing like that existed in the neighbourhood of Berlin I'd have said it's lunacy. It could take OKW, OKH and your own staff, my Führer. Then at Wannsee – that's the old anti-aircraft school – they've got a vast bunker; five feet of concrete on top and four floors one below ground and three above. I saw that by chance.

HITLER: No one's ever told me about this.

BRUDERMÜLLER: The first two battalions of the 6,000 parachute troops left the combat area** today and are to be loaded in the Bolzano area. But the Brenner stretch is still out of action as the result of air attack. So we are reckoning on three days before they get to Bolzano. Convoys returning empty will be used as far as possible – but there are not very many of them because little ammunition's being used. The main body will have to get to the Bolzano area on foot.

HITLER: Then they won't get to Bolzano in three days. From there

---

* There was a heavy air attack on the camp of Zossen on 15 March.
** In the Apennines.

(*the combat area*) to Bolzano is a good 3 weeks on foot – 20 days, 14 days, at least 10 days.

BURGDORF: Even from Trento to Bolzano is a day's march.

BRUDERMÜLLER: It's very difficult to calculate time at the moment. There are only a few convoys returning empty; there are comparatively few going forward because there isn't much shooting and therefore they don't need much re-supply.

BURGDORF: Can't they go at least partially by rail? They could always unload and load again. Getting on and off rail is nothing, since it's only men with small-arms.

HITLER: The point is to get ready the 7,000 men to whom these 6,000 are to be attached. The 6,000 must be incorporated straight away the moment they arrive. The 6,000 must be briefed in transit on what's happening, so that they can form a fresh division at once. Then they will be fit for defensive operations at least. Then we'll have to see where we'll put them. No need to decide that now.

That's two formations which can get here. The other two formations – I don't know yet, they must be units from the interior. We must improvise something ...

Now we must see exactly what foreign units we still have. For instance the Vlassov division is either fit for something or it isn't. If it's fit for something it must be regarded as a full-scale division. If it's fit for nothing ... it's lunacy equipping a division of 10,000 or 11,000 men while I can't raise German divisions because I can't equip them. I'd rather raise one German division and equip it fully.

BURGDORF: The Indian Legion.

HITLER: The Indian Legion is a joke. There are Indians who can't kill a louse, who'd rather get eaten themselves. They won't kill an Englishman either. It's nonsense purposely to put them up against the English. Why should the Indians fight more bravely for us than they did in India under Bose? They used Indian formations under Bose in Burma to liberate India from the British. They dispersed like a flock of sheep. Why should they be any braver with us? I think that if you could use the Indians to turn prayer wheels or something like that they would be the most indefatigable soldiers in the world. But to use them for real serious fighting that's ridiculous. How strong are the Indians? Anyway, it's nonsense. If you have weapons to spare you can afford a joke like that for propaganda purposes. But if you've got no weapons to spare, these propaganda jokes are just irresponsible ...

BORGMANN: General Thomale and General Buhle report that at the moment there's no formation available which can be sent to Oppenheim. There are merely 5 Tiger Mark VIs at Sennelager which will be ready today or tomorrow and could be put in in the next few days. In the next few days there will be a further 2 so that the unit could be raised to a strength of 7. Everything else is already committed, and for the moment nothing else is ready.

HITLER: They are at Sennelager?

BORGMANN: Yes.

HITLER: Actually they were meant to go to the upper bridgehead.

BORGMANN: Yes, to Remagen, to 512 Battalion.

HITLER: When can they move?

BORGMANN: They will be ready today or tomorrow. They could probably move tomorrow night.

HITLER: Then we'll take that up again tomorrow. If we only knew which of the 16 or 17 Tigers they got back could be repaired and when! That would be the most important thing.

In the West the enemy had now crossed the Rhine, and in the East our counter-attack had failed almost before it had begun. A general enemy advance into the heart of Germany was now therefore imminent but German Supreme Headquarters clung on in its 'ivory tower'. Hitler now began to say that the true lesson of the war was that the German people would go under because it had proved to be the weaker in a life and death struggle.[26] That being his attitude of mind the sacrifice of our youth, the loss of our country, the flood of refugees, the misery and terror of the bombing meant nothing to him. Guderian made desperate attempts to bring the horror to an end, but he was the only one. On 28 March he showed for the second time exemplary 'moral courage' in protecting his subordinates but on that very day he had to go and, as I had been before him, was thankful to escape from this atmosphere in which he had been confined – though only for a few months and for a few hours at a time.[27] Even at this stage Jodl could not pluck up courage to bring finally to an end the division and the dichotomy between the OKW and OKH operations staffs. General Krebs, who had only just recovered from wounds received during the bombing of Zossen, was nominated the new Chief of Staff of the Army, and charged with advising Hitler on 'the Eastern Front'. It was only when enemy forces from East and West met at Torgau on 25 April that this unhappy 'organization' received its death blow. Krebs was killed in the final confusion around Berlin; he had been a friend of mine for years and I can only hope that his firmness of character and sense of humour carried him through those difficult weeks of proximity to Hitler.

Meanwhile Supreme Headquarters ground on outwardly unchanged. The briefing conferences still took place twice daily, the midday conference drifting further into the afternoon and the evening conference nearer towards midnight. By the beginning of April, the type of question being discussed was whether it was better to defend the Weser or to rest the flank on Holland, Emden and Wilhelmshaven. The next day arrived a report that 'the front at Minden and Nienburg had been pierced' and the enemy had formed four bridgeheads across the Weser.[28] On 9 April Königsberg was lost and its defenders, though they had fought to the death, were condemned as usual. On 13 April Vienna was captured and the old propaganda line raised its head once more as Hitler said: 'Berlin will remain German and Vienna will become German again'. The death of Roosevelt had been announced the day before, raising great politico-strategic hopes; Hitler and many of his entourage foresaw the collapse of the enemy coalition, just as at the end of the Seven Years War the coalition had collapsed on the death of the Empress Elizabeth of Russia. An order of the day from Hitler dated 15 April 1945 ends with the words: 'now that fate has removed from the earth the greatest war criminal of all time (meaning Roosevelt), the turning point of this war will be decided'.[29]

The final change in the organization of German Supreme Headquarters took place in mid-April when the Russians advanced against Berlin and threatened to encircle the capital. As a precaution orders had already been issued on 11 April for 'the formation of dispersed headquarters (one in the north and one in the south) because of the increasing difficulty of centralized direction'. The next day Grand Admiral Dönitz obtained Hitler's agreement to move the Naval Staff to the coast if necessary; on 15 April OKW issued more detailed instructions should the enemy from east and west meet and so cut land communications in central Germany.

So the dividing line between East and West which had existed ever since 1942, found itself suddenly changed ninety degrees. A northern headquarters under Dönitz was given full command of the northern sectors of both the Eastern and Western Fronts, of Denmark, Norway and Air Fleet Reich; the southern headquarters under Kesselring was in charge of the southern sectors of the Eastern and Western Fronts, the South-east, Italy and Air Fleet 6. This new command organization was however only to come into force for that sector where Hitler himself was not, was to be implemented only on his express instructions and only in so far and for as long as communications prevented him continuing to exercise supreme command in both areas.[30]

The new organization was never more than partially implemented. 20 April was Hitler's birthday, of which no particular notice had been taken in the headquarters since 1941 when it had coincided with the rapid victory in the Balkan campaign. This time however the usual circle gathered in the Reich Chancellery. 'One after another ... according to seniority Göring, Dönitz, Keitel and Jodl ... were summoned ... to the little sitting-room next the map room so that each might individually present his birthday wishes.' Two days later, as the Russians pressed on into the suburbs of Berlin, Hitler suddenly declared that he would never leave the city. Keitel has recorded in his memoirs what Hitler is supposed to have said but if comparison is made with the well-known macabre events of 'the last days' his account has the ring of the discipleship complex which still dominated him rather than of the truth. He attributes to Hitler the Napoleonic phrase: 'I will fight before Berlin, in Berlin or behind Berlin,' and the next day, 'I shall defend the city to the end. Either I survive this battle for the capital ... or I go down in Berlin with my men.'[31]

Hitler still clung to the belief, for which there were no military grounds of any sort, that somehow the fortunes of war would turn. Even Keitel apparently shared it, for on the evening of 22 April he started to organize an operation to relieve Berlin, primarily based upon Wenck's Army. The next day he and Jodl were present at the briefing conference in the Reich Chancellery; for both of them it was destined to be the last time they were to see Hitler after more than two thousand days of war. When they got back that evening to their temporary headquarters in the barracks at Krampnitz near Potsdam they found the staff detailed for the northern area already preparing to move in face of the advancing Russians. Hitler had given repeated and explicit instructions that under no circumstances were they to be caught in Berlin, instructions against which Keitel had protested in vain as he had about Hitler's decision to remain; so that night 'OKW North' consisting of parts of the OKW Operations Staff and parts of OKH moved to a camp in a wooded area between Rheinsberg and Fürstenberg. Dönitz with the naval staff had meanwhile moved to Plön, so on a fresh instruction from Hitler, Keitel, assisted by Jodl, took over command of the northern area – the first command he had held throughout the war. In their new position of authority they were undeterred and they went on striving, although commanders in the field were to a large extent unwilling to obey them; they issued orders, they organized, they dismissed commanders, they appointed new ones; Keitel was always on the move, Jodl formed the fixed point at headquarters. Not only did they appear to believe that they could relieve Berlin (Hitler with whom they were from time to time in touch by telephone or radio thought the same) but they apparently thought they could continue to conduct the overall defence of the Reich.[32]

During this period Jodl had a personal, though belated, triumph for which he had striven for almost ten years. On 25 April he could note in his diary: 'night 24–25. The Führer signs the order for the command organization and the centralization of the staffs.' There follows this manuscript diagram.

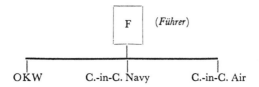

– a milestone showing that the greatest of the three Services and the one on which by far the greatest burden of the war had fallen, OKH, had now ceased to exist. It had been absorbed by OKW. The last 'official' Army Chief of Staff, who had now no means of exercising command, was trapped in Berlin with Hitler.[33]

The southern echelon of OKW, equally consisting of parts of the OKW Operations Staff and parts of OKH, left Zossen on the evening of 22 April under Lt. General Winter, Deputy Chief of the Operations Staff. According to the latest instructions this part of the staff was to move to Berchtesgaden and 'get in touch with the Reichsmarschall' who had meanwhile pushed himself in as Commander-in-Chief of the southern area in place of Kesselring.[34] Göring had little joy, however, from this last extension of his authority, for the next day he was dismissed from all his offices and only just escaped being arrested and shot on Hitler's instructions. He had sent a telegram saying that he proposed, presumably on an order from Hitler, to initiate negotiations with the Western powers. When this arrived in the bunker in Berlin it was seized upon by Bormann, the 'Chief of the Party Chancellery', as an opportunity to accuse Hitler's designated successor of treachery and so eliminate a rival.

The southern echelon of OKW also apparently clung to the end to the belief that repeated calls for 'fanatical resistance' could somehow give a turn for the better to the war situation or the final result; calls were issued 'to stand firm to the end like a soldier'[35] – one hardly likes to criticize.

Early in the afternoon of 29 April, Keitel had to move his headquarters further north from the camp in the woods near Fürstenberg, and arrived that evening on the Dobbin estate in Mecklenburg. There at 11 pm he received the last radio message from Berlin of any military import:

> To Chief OKW Operations Staff, Colonel-General Jodl
> 1. Where is Wenck's advance guard?
> 2. When will he arrive?
> 3. Where is Ninth Army?
> 4. Where is Holste's Group?
> 5. When will he arrive?
>
> Signed: Adolf Hitler[36]

In spite of its laconic terms the message reveals that in the bunkers of the Reich Chancellery they were still, even at this stage, hoping that the capital would be relieved and they themselves liberated. There was no reply to the message.

Eighteen hours later Hitler was dead and his body had been burnt. The manner of his end was one last proof that to the depths of his being he was no soldier.

On 3 May a new headquarters collected itself around Grand Admiral Dönitz at Mürwik near Flensburg. His Order of the Day issued on 1 May in his capacity as Head of the Government and of the Wehrmacht interpreted the outcome of the war in a sense still applicable today; he said:

> I assume command of all Services of the armed forces with the firm intention of continuing the fight against the Bolsheviks until our troops and the hundreds of thousands of German families in our eastern provinces have been saved from slavery or destruction. Against the English and the Americans I must continue to fight for as long as they persist in hindering the accomplishment of my primary mission.[37]

The last action of historic importance which the senior generals of German Supreme Headquarters were called upon to carry out was to sign the act of unconditional surrender – Colonel-General Jodl at 2.41 am on 7 May in Rheims, Field Marshal Keitel about midnight the next day in Berlin-Karlshorst.

On 23 May 1945 the entire government of the Reich was arrested; Keitel had been made prisoner of war some ten days before.[38] The remnants of German Supreme Headquarters of the second World War then dispersed for ever.

APPENDICES

APPENDIX A

Additional Fragments of Hitler's Conferences

FRAGMENT NO. 8, 12 DECEMBER 1942. *See p. 296*

ZEITZLER: In general nothing to report here. On the Italian front the enemy got as far as here yesterday and punched a hole twelve hundred yards wide. Then our reserves made a night march here when they arrived at 10 am and so were available if anything happened. It looks as if the situation is more or less all right. If there were to be a counter-attack here this morning it would be advisable to keep the regiment here.

The enemy then attacked again, he felt his way forward – here yesterday and here early today. He made a small penetration here. The Army Group thereupon acted quickly on their own initiative. They put in one regiment of 385 Div. and ordered the remainder of the division into this small sector, so that the Cosseria Division is now available. I think that was right.

There there were only small-scale attacks. The enemy attacked west of Svoboda, penetrated a short way and withdrew again. It looks for the moment as if he's not quite ready. It may be that it was only a holding attack. But with the Italians you never know what's going to happen. The enemy may make a small-scale tactical attack and score a considerable success.

HITLER: They were driven back everywhere here?

ZEITZLER: Only at this point. A regiment of 385 Div. was put in there and the division has taken over command of the sector.

HITLER: But isn't there an escarpment here?

ZEITZLER: Yes, it is in fact tank-proof. There is no report of enemy tanks.

HITLER: If only we'd had another two weeks available these formations would have been here. I wanted to give the Italians these tanks. It's just that we've lost 14 days. On the other hand you know, if we'd had three more German divisions there the supply situation would have been difficult, unless the railway was working better.

ZEITZLER: The supply situation is beginning to be somewhat worrying. It was fairly difficult before and now we've got the troops trains. We have to do a jig-saw puzzle every evening with the QMG to get the trains pushed through.

HITLER: Is this feeder line ready?

ZEITZLER: The line's ready.

HITLER: Completely ready?

ZEITZLER: Yes.

HITLER: All the way to here?

ZEITZLER: Yes, it's already in use. It has one or two minor defects, it's not yet been completely ballasted but we're getting everything out of it we can. I've often had to fit supply trains in with troop trains. One can do both at the same time.

HITLER: If you look at the areas of danger this front is still the main danger-point. The Italians are our weakest allies, and there is practically nothing behind them. Schulte's coming up and then there's the Guard battalion. We must tack Schulte's brigade on to them somehow, so that at least we can hold there; that should bolster them up a bit. But when you think that they were attacked only by infantry without tanks, that the ground was in their favour and that they were enormously superior in artillery and yet they withdraw – then it looks black to me. What's the present state of the Cosseria division?

ZEITZLER: Six battalions as far as I know.

JODL: A normal division; it only arrived today. It has not yet been engaged.

HITLER: And what about the Cuneense division? That's an Alpini division.

HEUSINGER: There are three Alpini divisions.

HITLER: They will be better. And what about the Celere division?

JODL: The original ones were Celere, Torino and Pasubio. The Third of March Division is a Fascist formation.

ZEITZLER: There is a Third of January Division and a Third of March Division.

JODL: They are Fascist divisions.

HITLER: Have they been pulled out or are they up in the front?

JODL: They form the reserve, and the reserve battalions have been put in here.

ZEITZLER: 27 Armoured Div. is also not very strong. Not much happened on its front. It looks better on the map than it is in reality.

HITLER: One thing occurs to me. There's nothing at all here. If he attacks here, there's nothing against him.

ZEITZLER: The most we can do would be to push in one regiment of 306 Div. That's the only way out. The Army Group propose to bring down one regimental group as far as this. But then if anything happens up here tomorrow we'd have to use that regiment here.

HITLER: How many tanks has 17 Armoured Div. got?

ZEITZLER: Not very many; 58 – all short gun.

HITLER: That's no good, particularly here. All they can do would be to shoot hollow charge.

ZEITZLER: 11 Armoured Div. has 30 long gun.

HITLER: They can only be used against infantry, and with hollow charges perhaps against T34s. How many shorts have they got?

ZEITZLER: In all the Div. has 19 Mark IV short and 29 Mark III short.

HITLER: They can of course use hollow charge but 11 Armoured Div. is the only one worth having for this attack.

ZEITZLER: Agreed. And he thinks he can make it available. I was pleased to hear that 11 Div. was more or less free. We can bring it up across the bridge.

HITLER: But he can't bring it up at all now; if the village has gone we've lost the bridge too.

ZEITZLER: One can't say how things will go today. That's two to three miles. Those are tanks of 14 Armoured Div. That is a detachment from 14 Armoured Div., and that is this group here.

HITLER: When will Schulte's arrive anyway?

HEUSINGER: It's in process of arriving; the first train arrives today.

HITLER: Where's it going?

HEUSINGER: It will be pushed forward to Millerovo and brought on up from here.

HITLER: Where is my guard battalion going?

ZEITZLER: That will go to 17 Armoured Div. – all in the same movement.

HEUSINGER: If the movement goes according to plan it will be completed by the 18th.

HITLER: Then of course we've nothing to put in here, unless if necessary we group this brigade and this battalion together?

JODL: And attach them to 11 or 17 Armoured Div.

HITLER: In order to get a mobile reserve here. We must think about this. At least this battalion's got modern equipment. It might perhaps be possible to attach it to 17 Div. to make it a bit stronger; 17 Div. can't do much at present. Or I was thinking that perhaps we might leave 17 Div. here or bring it across here temporarily and put this newly organized brigade into this area here. It's got 21 tanks. At least it's more or less mobile, and could intervene here.

ZEITZLER: For the moment it looks as if there's no danger here and that will come later.

HITLER: The enemy will attack like lightning. He will suddenly move up and we've got nothing here. What we have there is nothing but a bluff. Of course you can say that we will bring up a regiment from 306 Div. That we must do – it's the minimum. But we can't bolster up the front with any certainty with that alone. So suppose we put 17 Div. in here in order to make 11 Div. available. What is the state of 11 Armoured Div. anyway?

ZEITZLER: 11 Div. is good; it has fought very well and knocked out a lot of tanks. It has 5 battalions in all, 1 of full strength, 4 of moderate strength. 29 medium anti-tank guns, 6 light batteries, 3 heavy batteries. 100 per cent mobility. It has about $3\frac{1}{2}$ days' supply. As for tanks 7 Mark III, 30 Mark III long, 5 Mark IV long, 42 tanks in all. Fighting efficiency rated 2.

HITLER: There's something else we must do. It's just occurred to me as a result of what we've been saying. We must make a distinction between two things when estimating fighting efficiency, ie the battle-worthiness of a unit or formation as such, and the strength of that formation. Strength and fighting efficiency are two entirely different things.

SCHMUNDT: Last time we reckoned on strengths.

HITLER: Otherwise it can well happen that a very brave division bleeds itself to death and is then labelled a second-class division merely because it has fought bravely, whereas another division which has just stayed put will be labelled high-class merely because it's at full strength. A differentiation must be made between strength and classification.

ZEITZLER: That is more or less what Küchler says. I asked him what was the basis of his classification of the police divisions. Here's his answer (*produces it*).

HITLER: Fighting efficiency rated 4. The classification must be based on an overall appreciation of the morale of the troops and the quality of the commanders; that gives one more or less of a picture. The quality of the commanders and the morale of the troops is the real test of quality; then you must take strength into account so as to get a complete picture. One thing by the way: I would rather have a unit which temporarily may be at low strength but is at the height of its morale and led with determination than a unit which may be at full strength but has poor morale. Look here: these people are at full strength; they've not yet fought. I tell you rather than these people here I'd damn sight sooner have one of our own high-quality divisions, even if it was fought out and only 30 per cent the strength of the other. That's the most important point; that's what we must aim at.

One of them is good. We must always ensure that there is something here. Anyway here are three divisions, 297, 29 and 3. We must also think of these three divisions for this business.

ZEITZLER: My real worry over the next few days is to hold on if the enemy really gets as far as this. He meets resistance and then two to three days later something happens here.

HITLER: Then of course it will fold up. If we get away with it, it will fold up. But it's quite clear that this has got the makings of a crisis. Of course the enemy will have difficulties too because he'll be getting himself a long way from any railway.

ZEITZLER: He's now using this railway as far as this point. He has always been able to get engines up as far as this bend. I've been surprised he got it going so quickly.

HITLER: The Luftwaffe really must destroy these two bridges. Christian, this railway must under all circumstances be hammered so that the enemy can't go on using it.

Looking at the big picture I've thought of one thing, Zeitzler; under no circumstances must we give it* up we should never

* Stalingrad.

get it back again. We know what that means. I can't lay on any surprise operations. Unfortunately it's too late now. It would all have gone quicker if we hadn't hung about at Voronezh. Then we'd have got through in the first rush, but it's ridiculous to imagine that we can do it a second time after having withdrawn and abandoned our equipment. We couldn't take everything with us. The horses are worn out. They can't pull anything any more. I can't feed a horse off another horse. If it was Russians I'd say that one Russian could eat another. But you can't get a nag to eat another nag. That's no good so they're a write-off. And a horse can't say: it'll be better in a day or two – give me a feed of oats. It won't be better in a day or two. Anything which can't be brought out by MT will have to be abandoned. There are a lot of heavy howitzers there and they'll all be lost.

ZEITZLER: We've a vast amount of army artillery there.

HITLER: We can never replace what we have there. If we give it up we in fact give up the whole object of this campaign. It's ridiculous to think that I could get there a second time. This winter we could construct a covering position with the forces we have. The enemy can bring up additional forces on the railway. When the ice breaks up he can use the Volga for transport. He knows what hangs on it. So we shall never get this far again. Anyway we've shed too much blood getting there. I think that's obvious, so I would say we should only be able to clean up the centre of the city when the floods come in the spring, for they'll flood this area. There'll be a period, and it will last several weeks, during which this whole area will be completely flooded. The river will be fifteen to twenty miles wide and down there still wider, with a few isolated islands. If you look, there are no built-up areas round the city; it's just an island. The rest is just scrub, and in spring it'll be under water.

KRANCKE: Particularly when the ice gives out.

HITLER: Then we shan't be able to clean the situation up. The artillery will be driven miles away and the enemy won't have anything to worry about.

But the important thing is to hold on to this place. Obviously we've got to clean the business up under all circumstances. Once we've got that, I look at this salient and it reminds me of

Kharkov. Here's a salient building up. The Kharkov salient stretched almost as far as Krasnodar.

HEUSINGER: That went down as far as here and then across to here and then up to here.

HITLER: It was perhaps a bit bigger but anyway it's a somewhat similar situation. The only advantage the enemy has got over us is that he has got the railway. Moreover this railway which is being built up towards the Italian front is still only under construction. So that's got nothing to do with it.

ZEITZLER: No that one hasn't. I'd like to bring a railway expert and the QMG along with me tomorrow to discuss this question.

HITLER: The way the whole thing looks it seems clear that initially we never thought he could surround the place. I'd like to constitute a German group with the object of breaking out here so as to finish the business. That will really be the next decisive move. But we must wait and see whether we can do it. It may be that it can't be done because the enemy will probably be expecting it; that leaves nothing but to use our main forces for the old attack, stay put here and wait to see what he does in the pocket. He is probably expecting us to try a pincer movement from both flanks. The question is whether we can do that. We can get formations up to this point provided that we can get the railway going so that we can supply them. We could organize a couple of armoured groups here. I think the first thing is that we must deal with this affair and then do the old attack. If we can get further in this direction, then he will have to withdraw from the salient. Then we could see whether we could get as far as here. We'll hardly be able to do more.

Of course he will be expecting two things. To begin with he will be expecting us to drive forward here. So I think that initially it would be right to attack from south to north in order to break up the whole thing and deal with it in detail, and only then to carry out an attack eastwards. But of course all this is castles in the air. The first thing is to try and make forces available for it.

Of course it's most important to see how the Italians get on today. One thing I don't see and that is how I can possibly get away from here today, Jodl.* I can of course cancel everything.

* To Berchtesgaden.

JODL: There will be a lot of other problems left in the air too.

HITLER: I agree. We can make up our minds at the last moment. What are the train connections?

JODL: In general there's a connection every two hours. It's very seldom necessary to go as much as three hours without a connection; as a rule it's every two hours, sometimes more often.

BODENSCHATZ: If the radio is functioning we can keep in touch that way.

HITLER: Can we get anything like a proper picture by radio? Is that possible and how long will it take? Everything has to be encoded. How long will it take to deal even with a minor question?

JODL: That's no good.

HEWEL: One can telephone from the station.

HITLER: From every station?

JODL: It's a bit more difficult from temporary stations than from the permanent ones. But you will get through in any case.

HITLER: If I do go, I'll cut out Berlin. We'll see today and tomorrow.

ZEITZLER: We're going to have some very important days with very important developments.

HITLER: It seems to me this point is very dangerous, because there's nothing there. If only there was something here – good, I see there's a regiment coming up. And here he's moved down another regiment. But that means he is then here now. If we now go and take away 17 Armoured Div. there's nothing here at all. The question is whether at the end of it all we shall think it isn't perhaps so crazy and whether we couldn't get by with the forces of 27 Armoured Div. and the equipment coming up with it; then perhaps we could move in here and combine my guard battalion with Schulte's brigade. Those would be comparatively strong formations. If we could get them up by rail, 17 Armoured Div. could be released. Alternatively perhaps we could leave 17 Armoured Div. here, because the main attack probably won't reach this point, and bring up this brigade which with its 21 new tanks is stronger than 17 Armoured Div. with its old equipment. Anyway, what's the state of 17 Armoured Div.?

ZEITZLER: It's got five strong battalions. That's what Manstein wants.

HITLER: That's quite clear.

ZEITZLER: Schulte's brigade hasn't been used offensively yet. It's all right for defence. It's pretty strong in anti-tank guns; it's got 50.

HITLER: With the men now arriving it will be up to strength. We could give up 17 Armoured Div., and if necessary put Schulte's brigade into this area, if that is possible or if there's a crisis. It's only just arriving in the Millerovo area. So nothing's been lost. If necessary we can bring it up into this area.

JODL: Was a new formation organized for this attack then?

ZEITZLER: There's no report of that today.

HITLER: Jodl, you know how it looks. It'll be something like this in three days' time. That bastard'll bring it off. For two months now he's been bringing up equipment and now at the last moment he'll bring up the troops. Suddenly he'll appear with so-and-so many brigades. There'll be nothing behind these brigades and that's ridiculous, but a pack of hounds will kill a fox. If I attack with three or four divisions, I'll guarantee to get as far as that, if there's nothing there. If nothing happens, that means no one's there. What's the last moment for deciding to pull out 17 Armoured Div.?

ZEITZLER: The decision must really be taken today. We're taking a calculated risk in one place or another. Somewhere we've got to take a risk.

HITLER: Can he get it across anyway?

ZEITZLER: Early this morning 23 Div. was pinned down fairly quickly by a flank attack; so it looks as if today 23 Div. will have to stay where it is and 6 Div. will push on. So it would be good if we had something to follow up with.

HITLER: What's happening with the Luftwaffe formations which are being brought up behind?

ZEITZLER: He'll want those to put out a screen here, because this movement's going fairly far.

HITLER: What's happening with the formations which will be released here?

ZEITZLER: There are very few of them. Initially he'll move them up here.

HITLER: Well now, he'll get two formations here and an additional three formations here. Of the latter three, only 29 Div. is at reasonable strength. 3 Motorized Div. I believe is almost worn out, and 297 Div....

ZEITZLER: It's fairly good, it's still all right.

HITLER: I mean just for a screen.

ZEITZLER: Everybody's very pleased with 297 Div. just now; it's first-class. There was a lot about it in the report. But I don't think the enemy will attack here yet; he has moved everything away. The whole attack depends on whether we can punch a hole through here.

HITLER: Yes. 306 Div. is coming up but has one regiment detached. It has three regiments.

JODL: It's 100 per cent complete right up to the last man. Nine battalions.

HITLER: But one regiment's detached. It has nine 7·5 cm self-propelled, or hasn't it?

JODL: No, towed.

HITLER: It's got 6 and 22 Div. has 18.

ZEITZLER: Yes. It's been reinforced.

HITLER: That one's pretty weak: one 7·5 cm and two 7·6 cm and he's bringing down one regiment from 294 Div. That means there's no reserve up here.

ZEITZLER: I think that's better from the operational point of view.

HITLER: What does that mean here?

ZEITZLER: Movement and armour, the latter dug in.

HITLER: He always digs his armour in, and then comes out again.

ZEITZLER: He always comes out again – it may be an anti-frost precaution.

HEUSINGER: The intelligence picture is that between here and here the enemy has 16 rifle divisions, 2 armoured brigades and 4 cavalry divisions.

ZEITZLER: That can of course alter suddenly. We don't know what he's got back behind.

JODL: But he can't put in a major attack all along the front both against the Italians and here.

ZEITZLER: That's what I say. He'll do something here and something there. But it depends what you think.

HITLER: When has the decision got to be taken?

ZEITZLER: The sooner the better.

HITLER: Is it good enough if we take the decision during the course of the day, so that at least we can wait and see how the attacks get on? If they go well and if the front holds, then I would say that we don't need to use Schulte's brigade up here but we may well be able to hold it in readiness down there. Then I would be prepared to take a chance and use it. When does it arrive?

HEUSINGER: The first train should arrive today and the movement be completed by 18th.

HITLER: Is Schulte's brigade completely motorized?

BODENSCHATZ: Yes, two battalions completely motorized.

HITLER: If necessary they can push on from Millerovo.

BUHLE: It's a first-class defensive formation.

BODENSCHATZ: It has three companies each with twelve 40 mm anti-tank guns.

HITLER: I agree, but if I attach my guard battalion to it – that's been trained for the offensive. The twenty-one tanks it has are not for defensive jobs; they have been used in many places for counter-attacks.

BODENSCHATZ: Then there's a mixed anti-aircraft regiment with three heavy batteries. It's got enormous defensive capacity.

JODL: 36 heavy anti-tank guns and 3 batteries of 8·8 cm.

HITLER: If we'd got it here, then I'd be happy. Then we could withdraw everything. Then we could push 17 Armoured Div. in here. But today we must wait. With the forces he has available the most important thing is to reorganize. Otherwise if he loses the bridge he can never bring up reinforcements.

ZEITZLER: He will have to go round this way. There is no report about the bridge. The last report was from the Italians that individual soldiers could get across.

HITLER: It's ridiculous having a whole division which has never fought. Has it ever been in battle?

JODL: No, not yet; it's a completely new division.

HITLER: The chaps will put us to shame. The Italians won't mind if we take it away from them.

JODL: He won't make out with one division.

ZEITZLER: He won't get there, and I am afraid that if we wait a whole day it will be more difficult later; he's got himself pinned down. But if we attack straight away it would go through.

HITLER: I think it will go like this: let us assume that 23 Armoured Div. gets stopped here but that 6 Div. gets through. Then we can bring up this new division behind 6 Div. 6 Div. will still be in the lead. In my view the greatest danger is that 23 Div. might not get as far as this. With its 95 tanks I think it must be able

531

to, but I am convinced that in any case 23 Div. can reach this obstacle. It ought to be able to get the better of what it's up against. According to the latest reports the enemy has 85 tanks in all and 23 Div. alone has 95. How many tanks has 23 Armoured Div. got?

ZEITZLER: 26 Mark IV long, 26 Mark III long; that's good. I am afraid too that it will get stuck here.

HITLER: It may well get stuck there. But then 6 Div. will still go on and the other can follow after. I think in that case the other can merely form a screen. The breakthrough must be made by 6 Div. and on this sector 3 Motorized Div., 29 Div. and 297 Div. must hold. 3 Motorized Div. must try and roll the enemy up behind the obstacle, and 297 Div. too.

ZEITZLER: That means that we shall have a salient there and another there, and for the moment only one side of this salient will be secure.

HITLER: 11 Armoured Div. could look after that.

ZEITZLER: If that is included we might be able to join the salients up. But if it's not in the attack it will get stuck in the salient. We must have infantry for the defence. 11 Armoured Div. has a comparatively small sector. It has a comparatively large proportion of infantry but few tanks. But one wants a good proportion of infantry for the defence.

HITLER: It will be all right if 17 Armoured Div. arrives with all its infantry – it has fewer tanks than 11 Armoured Div. and is less battle-worthy.

ZEITZLER: Manstein is already collecting together what he can. If he can free 17 Armoured Div. he'll be able to do everything. What secretly worries him is that they both might get stopped. That's understandable.

HITLER: How many tanks have they both together?

HEUSINGER: All in he has about 130 tanks.

HITLER: That's not much. He'd better leave the tanks here. We've enough tanks. He should use them for the initial assault and then withdraw them at once. Of course it's always possible that the other fellow will make off in a hurry in order to throw everything in here.

ZEITZLER: So as to attack with one group on this side and another group on that side.

HITLER: The armoured division must deal with that.

JODL: It will deal with it all right. The trouble is the enormous area and the few formations we have. The enemy can always infiltrate round behind again.

HITLER: That's right. But if you fold up this bit, up as far as here we're holding but if nearly half the front gives way then the enemy's got the lot. It can't be worse than it is now. So if they've been able to hold here, they can hold there; the only difference is that previously their supply situation was sound. What he has here is less effective because his supply situation is so difficult.

ZEITZLER: We are going to put an armoured corps in here to conduct a mobile defence, because there's no solid front around here.

HITLER: As soon as the junction has been made, 23 and 6 Armoured Divs. can stop here. Then we can operate in either direction as necessary. It's quite clear that this is not the best imaginable situation. But it must be an absolute principle that we do not withdraw from here* We mustn't let this attack get bogged down. Time is pressing.

JODL: If you think we've got to hold here I would attack there also. Letting anything stay put in this situation is a questionable idea.

HITLER: What's happened there?

ZEITZLER: Nothing in particular. There was a counter-attack by the local reserves in progress.

HITLER: They've got nothing there. Poor devils. There's absolutely nothing behind. They're labelled 'Guards' units and they are nothing but labour battalions.

ZEITZLER: They're Luftwaffe units there.

HITLER: I take it all back – what's that?

ZEITZLER: Those are the groups.

HITLER: That's pretty thin.

HEUSINGER: It is thin, but then there is a division up here.

ZEITZLER: That one up here is the only one which can really be regarded as battle-worthy.

JODL: But to halt 17 Armoured Div. here because the enemy might possibly attack, and then he won't attack – I don't know.

HITLER What do you hear of 6 Armoured Div.?

ZEITZLER: The second echelon of 6 Armoured Div. is still short of two train-loads.

* Stalingrad.

HITLER: Do they include the tanks?

ZEITZLER: No, they are unimportant baggage trains.

HITLER: If it's as good as it's said to be, 23 Armoured Div. will hammer all this back into shape and then the idea is that it should move into this area. The main thing is that we should then go all out to re-establish this front. If the division can get across here then we ought to be able to re-establish touch*. Once we've re-established touch then we can quickly widen the corridor, and that will help morale, for the word will go round that touch has been re-established. The moment the first columns get through, however lousy they may be, the world will look different.

ZEITZLER: They are getting very restive and asking to be relieved. But that would all change in a flash.

HITLER: The moment they know they have got themselves free everything will change. Everyone's had experience of that. I'd like to wait until 2 o'clock to see if we get news of how things are going. Or perhaps we could now have a look and see what the Italian front is like. And Hungarian too. And I would like to say that once the Group has started to get to Millerovo ... and then one could use it in any direction.

ZEITZLER: Then we could use it as a mobile group. There doesn't seem to be any danger here at the moment. But the fronts are very wide.

HITLER: Anyway there are much better formations here; what's the anti-tank defence like?

ZEITZLER: Here it's bad and here it's better again.

HITLER: But here it ought to be quite good. You see the bastard's got across here. Anything further north?

ZEITZLER: No, nothing special further north.

HITLER: One thing is certain; under no circumstances can we take 16 Motorized Div. away. If we do everything will break down in the rear.

ZEITZLER: There's no question of that. It's not my understanding that he has any intention of doing that.

HITLER: Anyway it can't go as quick as all that. The division has to be concentrated first. It would take days before it really arrived. When does 7 Armoured Div. arrive? Doesn't it get here from 28th onwards, or something like that?

* With Stalingrad.

ZEITZLER: 26th is the earliest possible date. At present it's a day behind.

HITLER: 27th then?

ZEITZLER: It could be 27th.

HITLER: That's still fourteen days away. And it takes how long?

ZEITZLER: The fighting troops could arrive in six days.

FRAGMENT NO. 47, 1 FEBRUARY, 1943 *(See p. 300)*

HITLER: I'll think about this again. I can tell you one thing: in that case* there is no hope of a satisfactory end to the war in the East. We must be clear about that. (ZEITZLER: Yes.) I can't do it without equipment. I can't do it just with men. I've got the men all right but in that case I'd have no equipment. The question is what do we want. We are now on fronts of three miles *(ie average battalion sectors)*, but at least I can give the fellows guns and ammunition. If we do this we may well be on fronts of two miles, but I would have no guns and no ammunition. If you think you can fight better on a front of two miles without ammunition than on a front of three miles with ammunition, then of course you're right.

ZEITZLER: Yes, that's a question. At the moment it doesn't enter into it, but it may do later.

HITLER: No, later and now! At this very moment the whole armaments programme is going to the devil. Our entire tank programme would come to a stop – it is dependent on electro-steel. The same with the gun programmes. Instead of turning out 600 a month we would only be able to do 150. The great ammunition programme would come to an end. It's falling behind schedule already. It's now slowing down gradually but it will do so more rapidly. That way I'll never get anywhere. If I withdraw I would lose ... there would be the most god-awful confusion and the enemy would pursue. We know well enough what withdrawals mean.

ZEITZLER: That's quite clear but if we hadn't carried out these withdrawals the situation would be even worse. They must withdraw there and down here – here in the Panzer Army's sector.

HITLER: I've said from the start: I am quite clear that if we can't

* ie if the Donetz Basin were given up.

get away with it here, that leaves only the two bridgeheads. That's obvious. If we had done what the good Manstein wanted, there would have been no withdrawal, but everything would have gone to hell. If I had given way to Manstein they would not have withdrawn. There would have been no Panzer Army any more and he wouldn't have got Seventeenth Army back; everything would have collapsed. I've always been worried that he stopped here too long.

ZEITZLER: Now I thought that we could push 337 Div. from France straight away in here behind 4 Armoured Div., and next to it part of 78 Div., and so start building up a bit of a force. And then we must see what happens with the attack by the SS formations. If we move the Reich Division up here, that will of course re-establish the situation. But that'll take time. I rather think that we've simply got to use it down there.

HITLER: We'll see. Everything depends on how quickly 4 Armoured Div. comes up. If 4 Armoured Div. gets half way ...

ZEITZLER: There are fifteen trains on the way. Movement is slow because everything is being destroyed by bombing. Seven trains should arrive today.

HITLER: Once 4 Armoured Div. arrives we've got a force. After that comes 337 Div. There's another force. Then we might lay hold of 78 Div. With those we've got a force with which we might be able to get control of the thing. We must wait and see. If we could get a grip that way it is ...

FRAGMENT NO. 10   (*See p. 395*)

Discussion between Hitler, Jodl and Zeitzler (first on telephone, later in person) 27–28 December, 1943.
Also present: Field Marshal Keitel, Lt. General Schmundt, Major Borgmann, Sturmbannführer Darges. Conference begins 23.19 hours.

HITLER: Read this, Jodl (*produces a paper*).* No one's reported that. I don't know what he means. *Two* bridgeheads here? I thought it was a question whether we held one or the other. That's not to say that we may not be able to cut off the head of his salient. We've done that once. We cut off two divisions not long ago

---

* Proposal by Field Marshal von Manstein for clearing up the situation in the southern elbow of the Dnieper.

and threw back the whole attack. What does he mean by 'not cut off'? That presupposes that he attributes strength to the enemy which he hasn't got anyway – here are the conclusions he draws from this: if he can really make a success of it here, he hopes to make five divisions available. It's quite clear that some of the forces must move straight down here; he assumes that he can release forces from the elbow of the Dnieper and he says; 'they will not be able to get them into the area of Berdichev as quickly as that' (he doesn't need to bring them up here – that's not necessary). 'In case the decisive moment of the winter campaign should arrive in the next few weeks in the southern sector, and we should therefore try and gain a decision. It is hoped' (what does he mean by 'it is hoped') 'to break through westwards to the lower Dnieper via Kirovograd or Krivoirog and that as a result the enemy forces will be finally exhausted'. How can he imagine that the enemy will be exhausted with a concentration like that? He might as well say that he will be 'finally exhausted' here too. That's just juggling with ideas.

Now, the first result of course is ... I have given permission for a withdrawal here, that they should bring up 4 Div. here and then 16 Div. can be brought down here.

JODL: He means the Kamenka position.

HITLER: That goes further south.

JODL: He means this position, which runs west of Kamenka.

HITLER: This position means giving up the bridgehead here. That's why I've been thinking once more whether we couldn't hold a smaller bridgehead here – there is a smaller bridgehead here – in order to force the enemy to maintain forces here. Now I think the position should not go up here but should come along here but it means that we could no longer hold that. That means losing Nikopol and Krivoirog. He himself estimates that he will want 5 to 6 divisions to 'achieve an operational result'. He's so far got 3 divisions.

JODL: It all depends what your appreciation of the danger here is. He is optimistic because at the moment the enemy is not pressing very hard here. He obviously takes a very favourable view, and there he is very worried.

HITLER: This is Vinnitsa here. That is quite clear.

JODL: It all depends on that.

HITLER: But he can't get away with it that way. Just read this

537

telegram through. It means he's keeping three divisions in line which he could have taken out. 4 Div. is better than any of the divisions he's taking out. 16 Div. which he's taking out from up there is better and he himself is bringing up 17 Div. Remember his earlier forecasts when he said that to clean the thing up properly he would have to have 5 armoured divisions and 3 infantry divisions. He got them.

BORGMANN: My Führer, General Zeitzler wishes to talk to you.

(Telephone conversation with General Zeitzler.)

ZEITZLER: My Führer, I've had to call you. Manstein has just called to ask what we can do about his telegram.

HITLER: I am just discussing it with General Jodl. The results he pictures of course are nothing but castles in the air. I'd like first to discuss it with General Jodl. Perhaps I'll call you back later. Or can you get over here?

ZEITZLER: Yes, my Führer, I can come over.

HITLER: Then I think you'd better come along. (ZEITZLER: yes.) Thank you.

(End of telephone conversation.)

Perhaps Scherff could come too if he's there.

BORGMANN: He's sick but I'll ask again.

HITLER: Then leave him where he is; we don't want to wake him up.

JODL: He reports the enemy has 47 rifle divisions and 9 armoured corps here. That reinforces the idea that the main attack will be here. That I agree. The fact that he's no longer attacking in the Crimea is proof that he's waiting for an easier moment.

HITLER: It'll be easier for him as soon as we've gone from here. Then he can do it. He'd have to use a couple of divisions here. If there's no more danger here, what does he want with forces here? If we evacuate here, then he is superior to us here. Here it's all quite simple if, as Manstein thinks, he doesn't intend to cut that off completely. The problem is this: in the operational sense he can't get any decision from this battle. He can't do it; he can't seal it off anywhere. All he can do is bring it to a halt somewhere. He can't do more for the moment.

JODL: I don't think so either because the forces we can make available from here ...

HITLER: He can't use those.

JODL: ... no better off than they were last winter.

HITLER: That's ridiculous.

JODL: They've all had an extremely bad time.

HITLER: There's just one division here, the armoured division, and perhaps 3 Mountain Division. The rest's all imagination.

JODL: There's hardly anything to be done with the rest.

HITLER: 4 Mountain Division is worth more than three divisions from here because in the first place it's a good division and in the second place it's up to strength, whereas these are not up to strength.

JODL: It's clear he's had to put something in up here. 4 Mountain has already been ordered up.

HITLER: The first trains with 4 Mountain are on the move today.

JODL: And he's moving 16 Div. up too.

HITLER: The Artillery Division is here too. 'It is rather to be hoped' (that's no way to put it) 'that the enemy will try to break through between Cherkassy and Kirovograd and thereby finally exhaust himself'. What does he mean by 'finally exhaust himself? There's no point in his breaking through here. He can break through here just as well as up there. That's no proof. There's this one bridge down here, across here. It's important that if possible we hold the lower bridgehead. As long as we've got a crossing the enemy won't be so sure that he can attack here. If the last bridgehead has gone then ... Let me talk to Zeitzler again – it's quite clear he's worried about Vinnitsa. His headquarters is here.

JODL: That's the main railway. That's the last main line.

HITLER: The one via Shmerinka.

JODL: Shmerinka is the main junction.

HITLER: 'Operation' ... I loathe these pompous expressions. That's not an operation; it's nothing but a pompous expression.

JODL: The short point is that he doesn't think he can hold here with the forces he has, that he wants fresh forces and that he doesn't know where to get them from. So he wants to get them from down there by shortening his line.

HITLER: Now that way he gets three divisions, one from here, one from here, one from the centre, and then he takes out another one from here – 17 Div. That makes four divisions. In his last telegram he asked for five, though at that time he had no idea that he could get this division or 16 Div. This is worth more than the others.

JODL: That doesn't really make much difference. He's already had four divisions. The danger to the entire flank is still there. It makes no difference whether you cut off that bit and draw in the bridgehead. He is echeloned so far forward anyway that if the enemy pushes through here he'll cut the l. of c. He would have to move up from Odessa if he ... but that can't be the reason. The question is making forces available. It's agreed that he wants more than he's got now.

HITLER: There's no question of clearing up the position by attacking; he can't do that because he can't work with what he's got. That's ridiculous. He's merely using words there to cover himself. Zeitzler should be bringing the map with the positions marked on it. He can do practically nothing with that. The most he could do would be to use one or other of the armoured divisions. He could pull out one here himself. In fact he'll get the forces he's asked for, the difference being that they'll be better than those he'd have been able to get out from here.

JODL: The question remains whether we should meanwhile get one or other of the Rumanian divisions into position.

HITLER: ... so that it would be here? I've always wanted to reinforce here. The Crimea can hold on so long as we have at least one bridgehead here. These I suppose are worth nothing?

JODL: Neither worth anything. They are the ones which he* is forming back at home.

HITLER: He won't let go of those he's got at home. He's always got his eye on Hungary. It's madness but ... They're too close up here. They'll lose their nerve. It would be better if he put his headquarters further back here.

JODL: But he's got to hold this rail junction, otherwise it'll be bad.

HITLER: Now there's 4 Div. which we can put into line first, and then 16 Div. here, and then he must attack here with 16 Div., the Leibstandarte and 1 Armoured Div. But to try and pretend that the enemy has got 47 completely fresh divisions and that we can't stop them ... they can be stopped here. At one moment he says they're bad formations and at another that they're completely fresh. That's a report cooked up for the purpose. He's thinking of his own front only and has brought

* Marshal Antonescu.

everything down here. He removed 16 Armoured Div. which ought to have been here, but as a result the whole thing collapsed, otherwise today the front would be here. He can't do anything with these divisions. It's nonsense to try and attack with these divisions; he can't lay on anything. He says he hopes the enemy will attack with these forces here too because then he'll wear himself out, but that's nothing but a lot of words – 'similarly further reinforcements from the West will be unavoidable'.

JODL: Something could be made available from here too.

HITLER: If that can be done something will be available.

JODL: The second concentration is just here. It was only here that he went flat-out, hoping as a result to draw off forces.

HITLER: He's quite happy about this. He even hopes to draw off forces in this direction because then the enemy will 'wear himself out with frontal attacks'. He won't attack frontally but I'm worried that with what he's got left he will drive through here. One can't really tell where the artillery division is.

BORGMANN: It was shown in the Kasatin area.

JODL: It was attacked from the rear. An attack went in behind it this way today.

HITLER: We must wait and see whether the attack's as serious as all that. He's simply driving round with his armour where there's no opposition.

Pity – there's only a sixteen-ton bridge here. But of course it will have to be packed up. 25 Armoured Div. has been a complete failure from the word go. Yet it was very well equipped with the best equipment

JODL: Initially its men were good too.

HITLER: Dietrich told me that the division had of course been issued with MT. He said: 'if only we had it! We've only got broken-down old lorries, and all theirs were like a new pin, straight from the factory.' But the one at fault here is undoubtedly the Divisional Commander who hadn't got it in him to make anything of the division. So we can't take anything from here. On the contrary they want it up there because there's a similar crisis there. 147 Reserve Div. is I suppose a training unit from the Replacement Army, isn't it? And what about 454?

JODL: That's on the usual internal security organization – two training divisions have been incorporated, 143 and ... three training regiments.

HITLER: Where are they approximately?

JODL: As far as I know they are furnishing replacements for these divisions here.

HITLER: Could we get hold of them in a crisis?

JODL: We can of course take the cadres. Then there are a further two divisions forming in Poland.

HITLER: What are they like?

JODL: I don't know. That's not my business. Zeitzler's forming them.

HITLER: If we could be sure that nothing would happen in the West for six to eight weeks I would say that we could send them to the West and bring over two divisions from there.

JODL: There's nothing left there except the youngsters; 9 and 10 SS.

HITLER: I can't let those go; they are armoured formations which he is forming up in rear.

JODL: There simply are no other divisions there except those of Class 22 which will not be ready till February. They haven't yet got their equipment. As far as personnel are concerned, they're about the 11,000 mark.

HITLER: And from the Balkans, could we get two from there?

JODL: Of course we could – as usual!

HITLER: Then they must send these two across to Rome.

JODL: They must send these two to Italy so that we can get out 90 Div. and the Hermann Göring.

HITLER: Couldn't we bring this to a halt? So that we move across these two here, the training or reserve divisions?

JODL: One must give up one or the other. We must take 371 Div. That is a normal newly-formed Stalingrad division which, since it was reorganized, has only been used for anti-partisan operations. Otherwise it's at full strength.

BORGMANN: 147 Reserve Div. is partially employed on railway protection; parts are being used to form new units. As far as the others are concerned we are checking to see what has occurred. I shall have the details straight away.

HITLER: We can't take them off railway protection either. So all this adds up to nothing and he won't get a single additional formation. This one won't get there a day earlier. It just means that the other fellow will have additional forces available. Then Manstein will say he can't get them round as quick as that. But he hasn't got to get them round; all that's necessary is to bring them up here. He can thin out divisions here, transfer them to this area and then drive in this direction. But that's a risk and to me it's worse than the whole business down here.

The first point is: I am sure he must move his headquarters from here – if people are under pressure like that they'll never make sensible decisions – unless the attack of 1 Armoured Div. gets through.

JODL: The trouble with these strong-point tactics is that the enemy will move into this gap.

HITLER: Where is the Luftwaffe anyway? We never hear a word of it.

JODL: The parachute troops?

HITLER: Yes, the parachute troops.

JODL: 2 Parachute Div. is in this area. 9 Div. is also fairly good, as well as 4 Mountain Div.

HITLER: 9 Div.? No, it's no good. And this here is 3 Div.?

JODL: 97 Jäger Division.

HITLER: I believe it's all right; it always was. 3 Mountain Div. and 97 Jäger Div. are also good. I believe 9 Div. is bad. So really all he can pull out of here is 3 Mountain Div. which is no better than 4 Div. and considerably weaker. Well now, recently he asked for 5 to 6 divisions. He's got one division here as a result of the business we've just approved – that's one out of this 5 or 6 – one division here and another there – that makes three and then up above ... he can pull out 17 Div. so that in fact he's now got 4. Not so long ago he asked for 8 divisions. He got 3 infantry divisions and 5 armoured divisions. But then he can say that he had to give up the infantry. But instead he got an additional infantry division – the Parachute Jäger Division. So in fact he did get 8 divisions. It's a bottomless pit. Then of course he was very much influenced by the jinx of Hoth at Kiev. We're only just beginning to realize what a disastrous effect that man had. He was the worst type of defeatist. There are incredible stories which only come to light gradually. People are only just plucking up the courage to report them.

His headquarters is badly placed in this situation; he's

sitting here right on top of the focal point of the battle. His headquarters will be better somewhere else; of course it would then be further away but it would be better. Vinnitsa is of course a bad headquarters for him.

But the move up of the infantry divisions from here isn't going any quicker either. Always the same story; it always takes the same time. He can more or less release whatever he can get from here. He refers to 'counter-manœuvre'. He shouldn't talk of 'counter-manœuvre' but call a spade a spade – running away. Then this affair won't be any good and he'll come back as far as this. (JODL: probably.) Anyway he shouldn't talk of 'counter-manœuvre'.

JODL: He'll merely man the obstacle because as time goes on ...

HITLER: Here he'll get bogged down frontally. What does that mean 'get bogged down frontally'? It doesn't matter now. In any case I'm definitely keeping these forces here. In any other case I'm not so sure I would keep them. When he says he can't get them round as quick as the other fellow, that's the question. He can get all the forces he's got back there round quickly, if nothing's going on here. It's nothing but scheming and fibbing, that's all I think it is.

JODL: The worst problem was the question of holding this small area. Now we've got this and that.

HITLER: And that too. That's a typical example; we should have been able to hold this if at the time he hadn't taken out 16 Panzer Grenadier Div., trailed it round here, so that here everything was pulled out and the whole thing folded up. They were one division short here. No need for that. 13 Armoured Div. could have been relieved earlier. Then it would all have been all right. It was untrue that the line ... we came up against the line which in theory had been fortified. We would have been able to secure this and would have been able ... to ... obstacle which is the last available and which must be held under all circumstances. If we go back from there, that will be a catastrophe. Here we've always got the possibility of going back to there.

Just the same here. They occupy the obstacle which is the one to be held under all circumstances and then if they go on rushing back further, there's nothing you can do. Then everything collapses. He had five armoured divisions at that time;

1, 24, 25 and the Leibstandarte and – which was the fifth?
Once more: 1, 14, 25, 24 and the SS – 14 Div. was up here.

JODL: That's 16 – here is 14.

HITLER: 14 got here all the same?

BORGMANN: I'm not absolutely sure, my Führer.

HITLER: It did though.

JODL: 14 Div. came from the West.

HITLER: Yes, from the West. As far as fresh troops are concerned
he got 1 Armoured Div. from the Balkans, 14 from the West,
25 from the West, 24 from Italy and the SS; that makes 5
armoured divisions and in addition there were 3 infantry
divisions plus a parachute division. In fact he got more than
he asked for. He asked for 8 divisions. With them he was supposed to be able to do the whole thing. He got 9 divisions, and
all battle-worthy divisions, better than any others on the whole
front. Now he wants 5 to 6 divisions. Of this number he could
pull out one here straight away; he gets one from here – that
is 4 Mountain Div., he gets 16 Armoured Div. from up there,
he takes 17 Div. from here; these two must count as at least two
divisions. And he behaves as if he hadn't got anything. His
strength relative to that of the enemy is better than anywhere
else on the entire front. The fact that the morale of some of his
troops is bad results from the general attitude up above.

Here it's catastrophic. Look: they couldn't hold this line
simply because they didn't make the necessary lateral move. A
line like this must be held. These numerous salients of course
work both ways; the enemy has them too. If the enemy goes
round here and then across here he'll have to give up forces
straight away. Then this can't be held any more. When that's
pulled in, that can't be held either.

BORGMANN: 14 Div. came from the West and 24 Div. from Italy
at the end of July.

HITLER: They had at least 700 tanks. The Leibstandarte had
250, 25 Armoured Div. had 200, 24 ...

BORGMANN: About 150. It was in Upper Italy, about the area in
which we were.

HITLER: 1 Armoured Div.?

JODL: It had fewer.

HITLER: Something over 100. And 14?

JODL: That had about the same.

HITLER: It had more than 150. The others were all more or less up to strength.

BORGMANN: That's about 850 in all.

HITLER: And then he's had many times that as replacements – at least 400–500 tanks.

BORGMANN: About 100 a month, so that's three to four months' worth.

HITLER: He got many more than that. You must count in assault guns too. He's had a large number of assault gun battalions. The Tiger Battalion was brought up too. He's had well over 1,500 tanks in this period.

BORGMANN: This arrived at 23.10 hours today.

HITLER: That's probably a day later?

BORGMANN: No, just now.

HITLER: There he is sitting in Vinnitsa and he's quite happy. He must move his headquarters straight away. No good – he can't be here unfortunately. The best place would really be Czernowitz; otherwise Lemberg might be better unless the attack of 1 Armoured Div. goes through here. We must see about that.

(*General Zeitzler arrives*)

I'd like to get two things square, Zeitzler. Field Marshal von Manstein has put in two requirements. One was a few weeks ago – that came to 5 armoured divisions and 3 infantry divisions, ie a total of 8 divisions. That was what he asked for then.

ZEITZLER: I'll check the exact figures.

HITLER: 5 armoured divisions and 3 infantry divisions. He got 5 armoured divisions, and they were the best we had anywhere, most of them straight from rest and training; then he got 3 infantry divisions and a parachute division in addition! So he got 9 divisions. No other sector of the front has been reinforced in the way Field Marshal von Manstein has, although he is no weaker relative to the enemy than anyone else. It simply depends on the morale, and that results from the fact that nothing positive ever comes out of that headquarters. It's a purely negative attitude; it's particularly negative in this area where we've just sacked Hoth. He was particularly futile here. Anyway here he got what he asked for. The day before yesterday we approved the withdrawal here in order that, as he said, he could make 5 to 6 divisions available. He himself didn't reckon he'd get more. He's got these people here and of these formations, apart from 3 Mountain Div., there's nothing as good as 4 Mountain Div. He was given 4 Mountain Div. He gets 16 Armoured Div. from up there. He's got no armoured division as good as that here. He can himself make a division available here and he can take out whatever's best. That means three, including two first-class formations which he wouldn't otherwise be getting.

He'd never have got them merely by withdrawing here. Three first-class formations – he can take one from here – in addition he can pull out 17 Armoured Div. and here 5 Armoured Div., which means he's got two more than he had any right to expect. But he goes on as if nobody had ever allowed him anything. Actually he's had everything he's asked for. The idea that he could quickly bring up these formations here or bring down those here is a pipe dream. Everything in this telegram is a pipe dream. It is just a dream world; there can be no planned operations here any more. I'm happy if we can stabilize the situation; I don't expect more apart from that. This is nothing but words. I don't expect a decisive development or a 'suc-counter-manœuvre which I have proposed ...'

He says here: 'I consider that 4 Panzer Army will not be able, with the present planned reinforcements, to prevent the rail communications, particularly at Shmerinka, being cut. I consider therefore that an immediate decision regarding the counter-manœuvre which I have proposed ...

That's no 'counter-manœuvre'. Why don't they call a spade a spade and say 'withdrawal'. I hate these expressions. Why doesn't he say: ' ... is necessary regarding the withdrawal', for that's what it is, all the more so since it will be a remarkably difficult operation. 'Therefore the move of further forces from the West is unavoidable.' He's no idea what's going on in the West, or whether something is happening there, and anyway, it's none of his business. He must leave it to us where they come from. You've spoken to him again. What does he say now?

ZEITZLER: He considers it absolutely essential that the withdrawal should succeed. As a result forces will be released here.

HITLER: They won't be released. Look here, it's always the same thing. He's always sung the same tune. Of course the forces have become available, but they're then whistled round here and now he's got them in here. It's always the same game: forces become available on both sides, not only on ours. He's got to admit that. But then he says this: (*reads*). What are these consequences he's talking about? Oh, I see!

ZEITZLER: The loss of Shmerinka ... from the area north of Cherkassy ... being moved towards the Crimea.

HITLER: Have you got information about this?

ZEITZLER: It seems to fit. We have an agent's report that 33 trains were on the move down there. That could be a mechanized corps. But of course it's only an agent's report.

HITLER: He talks here about 5 to 6 divisions becoming available – what does this mean: 'as a result 5 to 6 divisions could be released for the left flank of the Army Group'. So in fact he gets these 5 to 6 divisions somehow.

The next bit is pure daydreaming: 'of course enemy forces will also be released in the bend of the Dnieper; he will not however be able to get them into the Berdichev area as quickly as we can'. Where does he get that from? There's no need for the enemy to move his forces up. If we are here, there's nothing threatening him. So he can then withdraw his formations, his reserve formations, and bring them up extremely quickly; if necessary he can withdraw them from the front. The formations on the front are not in fact first-class; I get reports on this every day. I saw today that there's not a single formation even half-trained. There's nothing else ready for battle. What does he want to do? He's got one division here; that must be 3 or 4 Div. That's the only formation that's worth anything. Have you the classifications there, Zeitzler?

ZEITZLER: Yes, I've got them.

HITLER: 'He will not be able to get them into the Berdichev area as quickly as we can. It is to be hoped that the enemy ...' You know, when people say 'we hope that' it means 'that's what suits us and we think the enemy will do what we want'! That's no military way of putting things: 'it is to be hoped that the enemy will use the forces he has available in the bend of Dnieper or on the Nogai Steppe to try to break through westwards via Cherkassy and Kirovograd, via Kirovograd or the lower Dnieper, and as a result finally exhaust his forces in frontal attacks'. What does he mean 'finally exhaust his forces'? If the enemy can make forces available he will break through again! Why doesn't he use the same argument here when he says they must wear themselves out! Here there are just as many forces as we have – how many divisions has the enemy got in this area anyway? Have you the order of battle? Have you got it marked on the map?

ZEITZLER: No, it's not made up yet.

HITLER: Perhaps you could get somebody over with the order of battle. Well, now, there's a strongpoint here and here, and here is the Cherkassy strongpoint and a strongpoint here! The enemy won't do what we hope, he'll do what hurts us most. He'll do two things: either he'll go across here with the forces which have been released and attack here from the bridgehead and so dislocate our position. He can get across here at any time – we can't stop it, or if he doesn't do that he'll go round here pulling in that from here. Manstein expects that he'll bring up the forces from Cherkassy straight away. He says it isn't possible to do it from Kremenchug, so he won't take them from there. According to his reasoning we can get up here quicker from this point than he can from Kremenchug, but there's no support for that idea. If we clear out here, he can get here quicker with his forces than we can get up from here. What's the rail transport position? How are they going to move these forces anyway?

ZEITZLER: Rail transport is slow here; here you can use this stretch. I've marked it here, here is the main line and from Krivoirog the line goes from Saporoshe along here for a bit. Then it goes here from the area where you see 17 Armoured marked ...

HITLER: These must go by MT but those must go on foot?

ZEITZLER: They'll have to get these people around this way.

HITLER: Here is 14 Mountain Div. on the move already.

ZEITZLER: It's on the move.

HITLER: For the moment then it's out of the whole business?

ZEITZLER: It'll be a day or two of course before it gets to the railway.

HITLER: Right, but now there seems to be another division coming along. That's the second that's got to get up here. And what about 17 Armoured Div.?

ZEITZLER: That will be moved from here. If he can release some infantry divisions here, then he'll pull out the motorized formations, move them a certain distance by MT and then do this on foot.

HITLER: It's not certain they can move by MT. The railway's going to be at full stretch with this for the next few days. I don't know whether he's putting an infantry division in up here or what?

ZEITZLER: Yes. As soon as these arrive it'll become available.

HITLER: But first these must be brought up from here?

ZEITZLER: This is the railway here; it goes along here and right through.

HITLER: But he must bring them up this way below here. We can't do more for the moment. Is that today's information marked?

ZEITZLER: I marked this up last night; that's Kasatin.

HITLER: One thing I think is essential: that he should get out of Vinnitsa straight away so that he doesn't lose his nerve. He'll lose his nerve and there's no sense in that.

ZEITZLER: From the technical signals point of view we have made the preparations; Balti, that's about in the centre. That's possible from the signals point of view.

HITLER: Lemberg!

ZEITZLER: Yes, Lemberg's a bit far off. I'll look and see if we can find something, perhaps Tarnopol. He reported last night from Balti that they were preparing that.

HITLER: He must get out of Vinnitsa; there's no sense in that. There must be a special detachment at Vinnitsa to burn the whole headquarters down and blow it up. It is most important there should be no furniture left, otherwise the Russians will send it to Moscow and put it on display. Burn the lot.

JODL: Balti is no good, that's in Transnistria; that's Rumania.

HITLER: Is it in Transnistria?

JODL: No, Balti is Rumanian, it's in Bessarabia.

ZEITZLER: What they mean is Balta.

HITLER: Where is Vinnitsa? I don't think this is right.

ZEITZLER: The communications there are bad. That's the main worry unless we can use the railway through Rumania. The Rumanians have not let us use the railway. I've tried everything.

HITLER: I think it's right that he goes to Tarnopol.

ZEITZLER: Yes, I'll get that made ready.

HITLER: Have you any news of the attack of 1 Armoured Division?

ZEITZLER: No, my Führer, no result yet, although I've already spoken to him about it.

HITLER: I am convinced they'll get through.

ZEITZLER: It's difficult to say. There are 300 lorries following them, and that makes it look like a mechanized corps.

HITLER: How many men does a lorry carry? Twenty men?

ZEITZLER: The Russians take many more – perhaps twenty though.

HITLER: That makes 6,000 men.

ZEITZLER: It's not necessarily only personnel on these lorries; it may be something else. The number of lorries is about what a mechanized corps would have with it on the move.

HITLER: Then it might be three to four thousand men?

ZEITZLER: My Führer, what I am worried about is that one can only begin to have some effect upon the enemy here from 30th onwards. I am convinced that in three or four days there will be a battle for Vinnitsa.

HITLER: That makes no difference.

ZEITZLER: It makes this difference, my Führer: things may so develop that this area here is surrounded. That's what I'm worried about.

HITLER: There's nothing can stop that. We can't do more than what's already in train – we can't stop that!

ZEITZLER: We could go back to the Kamenka position.

HITLER: If he goes back he must hold there. It doesn't matter whether he holds there or there.

ZEITZLER: Then we should have gained six days, in case we should have to fall back further.

HITLER: The important point is this: when he speaks of operations was he imagining that he could move in here?

ZEITZLER: If you think of the situation developing this way he can get through to here. And then we'd be in a very unhappy situation. Then we'd only have ...

HITLER: It wouldn't make any difference that way. It would be a little better should we have to break our way out here later, for if we cut loose from the l. of c. here we shall have to fight our way through. I think it would be better, Zeitzler, to get the individual formations put in here as quickly as possible and block that. That's the most important point.

ZEITZLER: Yes, my Führer. Five days ago I wanted to leave things as they were and move the three armoured divisions up there straight away. Then we'd have had three formations available, and wouldn't have got our backs against the wall. But in my view this is all less important than the question of taking something away from here.

HITLER: He could at least pull one division out quick.

ZEITZLER: The affair ought to have worked out on its own. Then we should only have had a short move forward with these three formations and been able to attack through here. But now everything's arriving in driblets and I'm afraid it'll be the same with the Leibstandarte and 1 Armoured Div., and I'm worried that the formations down here too together with ...

HITLER: Whatever units he can get up here must be put under command of 1 Armoured Div. or the Leibstandarte. He can't work it any other way. He must more or less incorporate them into 1 Armoured Div. or the Leibstandarte. Are they arriving on the line Novograd–Voltchinsk–Zhitomir?

ZEITZLER: They're coming along the main line. If we lose that later we shall have to go over to this line.

HITLER: The important point is that they should be put under command of the Leibstandarte or 1 Armoured Div.

ZEITZLER: In that case we can put them in here.

HITLER: There's nothing else to be done, Zeitzler, but bring up forces to stabilize the position. If the operation here doesn't come off, this operation can't take place; that doesn't alter the overall result. If you hold here or here today, it will be only a question of one day. There they have had to withdraw in a hurry again. This doesn't alter the final result.

ZEITZLER: Formations will become available, that's clear.

HITLER: They won't be able to get the formations which do become available up here any earlier. There's no point in it.

ZEITZLER: Perhaps we could take a big risk here and bolster up the front with the formations released by that.

HITLER: How are we going to get them up there? On paper! If a motorized formation moves up there from here, it'll be played out!

ZEITZLER: We've carried out some large-scale movements.

HITLER: With tanks?

ZEITZLER: The tracked vehicles can move by road like that.

HITLER: They must go by rail.

ZEITZLER: We can't get enough rolling stock up here.

HITLER: Naturally, that's clear, but you won't get them here. They'll make one division available. You'll get one here and one can come out here. One's already on the move to ... If only we had this business here and we had a division here, then we could drive in here and follow up here. But the moment we do that the enemy will straight away move in here.

ZEITZLER: He could also move in this way.

HITLER: I admit that but he'll no longer be tied down here. You see the strongpoint is here. If we withdraw, the strongpoint can be moved across here straight away. He can scram from here straight away. It's not as Manstein says that he can bring the forces up here quicker. But apart from that, what do we look like? Let's take this list of the formations. First, 335.

ZEITZLER: High morale. Makes a good impression. Four battalions moderate strength, three battalions average strength.

HITLER: 97 Jäger Division?

ZEITZLER: 97 Jäger Division; good, particularly high morale.

HITLER: 9 Division?

ZEITZLER: High morale, good – 17 Div. is good, particularly high morale – 211 Div. is good, also high morale. 67 Div. was bad a couple of days ago. I asked about it a day or two ago. The ones down there were good. 9 Div. was always good.

HITLER: What's the state of 24 Armoured Div.?

ZEITZLER: No classification has been made. It's up to strength, battleworthiness rated 1.

HITLER: And what's 258 like?

ZEITZLER: Not high morale.

HITLER: But 3 Mountain Div. is good?

ZEITZLER: Particularly high morale. 3 battalions moderate strength, 1 average strength, 9 batteries – 302 Div. not high morale, battleworthiness rated 4, 5 battalions average strength, 2 battalions weak. 294 Div. not high morale, 1 battalion up to strength, 2 battalions moderate to average strength, 3 battalions weak.

HITLER: It's no good for anything then. And 123 Div.?

ZEITZLER: Not high morale, although lately it's fought well. 25 Div. not high morale either, it's gone down lately. 304 Div. has gone down too.

HITLER: Those are the formations he will bring out here first. What's the state of 257 Div.?

ZEITZLER: More or less all right.

HITLER: Now he must put something in here. He can only take one formation out here and that will be 257 Div. But here he's got nothing but low-morale formations. One formation must come out here. Where's this line? Does it go along here?

ZEITZLER: That's the Kamenka line.

HITLER: Where is the bridge? Is it here?

ZEITZLER: The bridge is here.

HITLER: The Nikopol bridge. The lower bridge?

ZEITZLER: The lower bridge is here. Here is one bridge and here are the ferries.

HITLER: The ferries stop in winter. And the bridges?

ZEITZLER: The pontoon bridges have been taken down.

HITLER: They're not there either, then. That means there's only one bridge.

ZEITZLER: There's the seventy-ton bridge, and then the weather may change.

HITLER: Why change? What do you mean?

ZEITZLER: That for the moment they can be used.

HITLER: That won't last, it'll all freeze up. And then they can come up from below. That's the great danger, that he blows it up once it's frozen and when the business is over it's back where it was. This is of course merely a question. Before this everybody said, if that is blown, then the greater part of this will go under water. So it can't really be as thick as all that.

ZEITZLER: There is about seven inches head of water to come down.

HITLER: Seven inches is not so frightful.

ZEITZLER: But these bridges will be carried away.

HITLER: Another question, Zeitzler: what do these two divisions look like which you've got there back behind? Wait a minute, we'll have a quick look at these two divisions. 46 Div.?

ZEITZLER: Good, particularly high morale.

HITLER: But weak – and 387 Div.?

ZEITZLER: Not good morale – 306 Div. not good either, and comparatively weak.

HITLER: What does 16 Panzer Grenadier Div. look like now?

ZEITZLER: Good. 1 strong battalion, 3 moderate strength, 1

average strength. 17 batteries, 25 heavy anti-tank guns, commanded by Schwerin.

HITLER: He wants to bring it out?

ZEITZLER: No, not yet; that was merely an idea; *if* he should bring it out.

HITLER: Supposing he could make a formation available here? (ZEITZLER: yes.) Grossdeutschland is pretty weak?

ZEITZLER: Grossdeutschland? Yes, high morale but very weak – 9 Armoured Div. has 6 high morale battalions, 3 moderate strength, 4 weak, 11 batteries – 15 Div. particularly high morale, 3 average strength battalions, 2 weak – 62 Div. high morale, 4 average strength battalions, 1 weak.

HITLER: And what happens if we shorten this bridgehead?

ZEITZLER: He couldn't do that now. He says shortening it would be no good. My own view was that we could shorten it. But of course it wouldn't do much good.

HITLER: He says: two small bridgeheads.

ZEITZLER: I don't know either how he's thought that up. I told him clearly: reduce in depth. He initially wanted to shorten in length. There's no question of that; that doesn't save us much.

JODL: He meant two small bridgeheads.

ZEITZLER: That's probably what he meant, but we must hold just one permanently.

HITLER: Of course I think it's important that we evacuate here as late as possible and if possible that we don't evacuate at all. The enemy won't be able to concentrate forces. That means the forces will be about equal. He'll get across here straight away. But quite apart from that he won't get anything else from the Crimea. That's nothing to do with Manstein. He'll say 'that's Army Group A's job, nothing to do with me'. Just look at the formations he's got here. How many formations are there here? My guess is that there are at least 30 to 35.

ZEITZLER: That's about it.

HITLER: We could put them in here but then the whole thing will be blown sky high from the rear. If he wants to abandon the line in here altogether, he'll have to have those people who are here. He must abandon the line, but that won't save us anything.

ZEITZLER: It will make about ten formations available, three to four down there and five up here.

HITLER: Five? One's gone already, it's here now. One's gone from here and must be replaced. You must count them in too. Three to four down here? That way he won't get ... the line must be manned, it's not manned now.

Now look, if you look at the thing overall: we couldn't hold here; but now we've got to hold the same size bridgehead; we've got to – and still take formations away!

That was the cry then: back! It was a typical retreat, everybody lost their nerve. Kleist included – everybody back! Nobody can say that this was more difficult than that or than the entire front which we now have. Then we wouldn't have had all these difficulties in the Crimea and needn't have had any forces here. We could have had that here. We mustn't try and make out that we couldn't have held that. It was just that the word went round: everybody back! Sometimes it becomes a real mania. If only we could now have some success somewhere! I have seen two retreats during which I said: we can risk it. During one we bulldozed our way along. So I said: that won't lose us much. So I agreed to that.

The second one I proposed myself. That was from this pocket at Orel. If the attack succeeded we had to get out. That was sensible. But this here has been an idiotic retreat, I must say.

BORGMANN: There are 27 rifle divisions and 4 armoured corps in the area. Here at this point there are 17 rifle divisions. Then north-west of Krivoirog there are 16 rifle divisions and 1 armoured corps. At Kirovograd there are 24 rifle divisions and 5 armoured corps.

HITLER: Is that here? That comes into it too.

BORGMANN: In the area of the break-in here there are 13 rifle divisions and 1 armoured corps, at Cherkassy 4 rifle divisions, 1 armoured brigade. In the area of this break-in, 42 rifle divisions, 9 armoured corps, 1 cavalry corps in the first wave and 2 armoured corps in there; 3 armoured corps not yet identified.

HITLER: How many identified armoured corps has he in this area?

ZEITZLER: He's got nine. The others may possibly come along if they come up by rail.

HITLER: I wonder whether we ought to take something out of the bridgehead, although of course the bridgehead is tying down the main body of the enemy. Oh yes, I wanted to ask you something else, Zeitzler: haven't we got two reserve divisions in Poland?

ZEITZLER: Yes, recruits. One division is up in the Korosten area employed on railway guard duty; that's where the big loop is.

BORGMANN: That was 147 Div. It's got 7 battalions of which 3 are at Korosten; 4 battalions are recruits; 1 pioneer battalion, 1 artillery battalion.

143 Div. has 10 battalions of which 7 are recruits and 3 are employed with Second Army on anti-partisan operations.

HITLER: I thought there was something further back?

JODL: There are two newly-formed divisions in Poland. Isn't that Class 22 or 21?

ZEITZLER: That must be Class 21. If it's Class 21 they should be well on with their organization.

HITLER: I was asking for another reason – whether we couldn't perhaps put one or both of these divisions over to the West in the hope that nothing happens there for a bit and we could get a couple of other formations from there. But Jodl says there's nothing available in the West, that they can't give up any more armoured formations.

JODL: There are no infantry divisions in the West which are in any way suitable for employment in the East. There's only one we can take, and that's destined for Italy.

HITLER: Could we get that along? What sort of a division is it?

JODL: It's 371 Div.

HITLER: Where is it exactly?

JODL: It's at the moment taking part in this operation.

HITLER: In this operation.

JODL: In a harvesting operation east of Zagreb. It will have started in the next few days.

ZEITZLER: It's in the south-east – 371?

JODL: It's under C.-in-C. South-west, as it was before.

HITLER: Battleworthiness rating 2?

ZEITZLER: 371 Div. Two battalions generally good; there are four in all; the first is the best.

HITLER: How soon could it get up here if we replaced it with one of these divisions in Poland?

JODL: That's no good; it wouldn't help at all; it would merely mean an unnecessary delay in its formation. The result would merely be that only one division would go to the West instead of two. Then Kesselring would only get 71 Div. and would have to give up the Hermann Göring, ... and 90 Panzer Grenadier Div. would have to stay there.

HITLER: How long would it take to get here by rail?

ZEITZLER: Where is it?

JODL: South-west of Zagreb.

ZEITZLER: It will be quite some time before we get it here, because rail communications are bad and trains are small.

HITLER: How long once it's got on the railway?

ZEITZLER: Not too long, it should get here in six or seven days.

HITLER: If only I could have put in something here instead of 24 Armoured Div.! But if we take that away, then we can't hold here.

ZEITZLER: Yes, we'd be taking a risk. If we were lucky it might be all right. But so far we've not been able to do it. We've always had to use it to re-establish the situation.

JODL: And what are these Rumanian battalions doing there, 5 and 14?

ZEITZLER: We can't use those.

JODL: Not even on security jobs?

HITLER: We must take something from here. What good divisions are there here?

ZEITZLER: There's nothing very wonderful there; 101 Div., 307 Div. Luftwaffe Div. – and they've got enormous sectors. 101 Div. is all right; it's good but it's got a very wide sector. 307 Div. morale's not good.

HITLER: How many battalions has 101 Div. got?

ZEITZLER: Eight strong battalions and one weak.

HITLER: I've had another idea; that we take this division from the Balkans, hoping that we can hold there for a bit. The question is whether we can; then we can take out another formation immediately after 4 Mountain Div.

ZEITZLER: I'll have to get the rail details worked out.

JODL: The relief of formations takes a fairly long time.

ZEITZLER: The Führer's not thinking of relief; he means take the division out first and take a risk there for a day or two.

HITLER: Until the other one arrives.

ZEITZLER: Rail movement round this way takes a long time because we have to go through Rumania.

HITLER: That's no good; all formations you take out from here must come up this way.

ZEITZLER: You saw how long it took with 4 Mountain Div.

HITLER: Then we must go round this way. You can't get round there. We can't take all the armoured formations away from here or there will be a crisis. They can't make out with infantry divisions alone. We must have a certain number of armoured formations in here. Then following 44 Div. we could get one other good infantry division.

ZEITZLER: Yes, let's say 101 Div.

HITLER: Of course it couldn't take its artillery with it; that must stay here. No – when the other arrives it will have artillery with it, and I'd naturally much rather put the division in here.

ZEITZLER: Yes, so that it gets into the battle straight away.

HITLER: That's my idea too with Langemark.*

ZEITZLER: I've had a long talk with the Reichsführer today about this – about the possibility of using either 'Reich' or Leibstandarte. In the case of 'Reich' the advantage is that it can accept them quite easily, the disadvantage that it may have to go into battle straight away and even straight from the train.

The second possibility is to attach them to 'Wiking'; technically this is difficult because it must go right round before it can arrive. The Reichsführer doesn't want to use 'Wiking' under any circumstances, because that will bring Flemings and Walloons together. Down here they would be on a quiet sector but would have no formation on either side of them.... The Reichsführer is in favour of using 'Reich'. He says it will be best to attach them to 'Reich'. He says the German personnel have battle experience. Therefore he wouldn't be so worried.

HITLER: I got someone to give me the organization of the new Nederland Legion today. What's its strength overall? 6–7,000 men?

DARGES: About 7,000 men.

HITLER: It's got colossal firepower. Have you got it there? You should look at it! It's worth thinking about this sort of organization. It's got more firepower than any other division and has 6,500 or 7,000 men. But it's weak in artillery. It's only got two battalions. But the third battalion wouldn't make much odds. The others have mostly got only nine batteries.

* Title of a newly formed Waffen SS division not ready for action.

ZEITZLER: Mostly nine batteries.

HITLER: Now that would be a risk which we might perhaps have to take. Would you talk to Kleist and see whether he's prepared to take it on?

ZEITZLER: Yes. They were very worried about 4 Mountain Div.

HITLER: These formations arrived instead of 4 Mountain.

ZEITZLER: The battalions?

HITLER: He'll be getting an additional division here which is of the same strength. Of course we don't know how it'll make out but as far as strength is concerned it is equivalent.

Perhaps not from the artillery point of view because it won't be able to take all the artillery with it. But don't let's deceive ourselves, Zeitzler, he can't lay on any major operations with these formations. If he can't hold there, there will be a pot mess until this arrives here or there.

But that doesn't matter a damn. More to the point is that we must absolutely insist they hold here. For the moment we can do nothing other than take up a covering position with these formations. We can't carry out any form of attack. The infantry divisions are out of the question for any form of attack. They can't do it these days. We saw how 5 Jäger Division achieved nothing. Now that's a good formation but its power of penetration is zero. If they try and attack up there with 12 Div. it'll be exactly the same thing. These infantry divisions have no power of penetration; they can't attack in winter; they just can't do it. Last year we only used armoured formations and Panzer Grenadier divisions in attack. The infantry just can't do it; they're completely useless. The infantry gets stuck in the snow and shot down. They can't take cover properly. There's nothing to do except try and plug the hole. A couple of armoured formations. He must get around that way. If it's possible for him to get 16 Panzer Grenadier Div. out, that's good, but for the moment that's all that can be done.

If he started to get the idea of going back with his army in order to get freedom of manœuvre – if he goes back in this direction – and then one doesn't know what the army will look like. I read all the reports about these retreats. I could kick myself today that I gave permission for them. It wouldn't have been any worse up forward – on the contrary. But it's just as I said; it's all happened under pressure; the formations got back in the hell of a mess. The retreat was worse than any defensive battle. But I'm astounded when you look at these formations how they've managed to recover!

ZEITZLER: My Führer, when they're static for a time, gradually things get better. They get replacements and get their wounded back.

HITLER: I'm astounded how quickly they've improved. As regards this affair, we should have been able to hold that and then there wouldn't have been a crisis here. So that we wouldn't have been cut off. They were afraid that they would be forced back that way, and so packed up straight away! It's becoming a mania, a real disease. After all, this isn't a trifle. It's 220 miles, half the width of the entire Western Front. We talk about the battle of the Marne, but we're doing it all the time. There's a break-through and we give up a colossal front of 220 miles. 220 miles was the entire right wing of the army in 1914.

JODL: But, my Führer, we don't want the sort of crisis where one day we have to say: 'here's another army cut off. We must avoid that, otherwise the whole thing will break down. So we must call up the last division which can be moved from the West in order to save a whole army, otherwise the entire Eastern Front will collapse.' Then we should lose the war because nothing's happening in the West. There can be no question of risking a crisis on the Stalingrad model.

ZEITZLER: That's my view. I've reached the same conclusion as Manstein, but for other reasons. My reasons are these: the enemy's been moving forward at about ten miles a day so that on 29th and 30th he gets as far as this. That means that probably at the end of the year or on 1 January there will be a battle for Vinnitsa. Then the new formations will arrive – 16 Armoured Div. at about twelve trains per day, the Jäger Div. from down there at about three to six trains a day. Of course that wouldn't be a completely satisfactory position because the defence line would be longer. But I don't see any danger from Korosten southwards.

HITLER: You've come to the conclusion, Zeitzler, that we must withdraw the whole front here?

ZEITZLER: My immediate conclusion is that we must start this operation – then we make some formations available.

HITLER: We won't get them up there in time, Zeitzler, for the enemy will be able to make fresh formations available on his side too.

ZEITZLER: My Führer, the question is this: either we can more or less stabilize the situation so that the front holds here; in that case it's all right and we should be able to get through with this business. This salient here will soon be a source of danger. We are so stretched here that he can always get through at the angle here. That will remain the main danger. Therefore we want to try to get back here. Second point: things do not go right and he gets over here as far as Transnistria. Then we can do nothing except let these people fight their way back. That'll be difficult because we've only got one bridge.

HITLER: If he pushes in here with his divisions couldn't that be even worse than if we followed....

ZEITZLER: Voluntarily?

HITLER: We've come back this far on our own accord! That's demoralized the troops. They fought all right, Zeitzler. I spoke to innumerable people. They say they just don't understand it when they have to abandon a position where they've spent all their energies digging themselves in. Just think how many rifles we've produced in Germany in the last six months, and how many we've got now; that's the way to calculate.

ZEITZLER: I've shown you the lists every month in which that is given.

HITLER: It just doesn't fit. Each month we've produced more than 200,000 rifles. Of course you may say that the newly formed units get them. No! how many have we got? A total of 6·1 m. has gone down to 5·1 m. It's gone down! That means there's been a loss of 1·5 m. rifles. That happened here in the East. Where else could we have lost rifles like that? Only here! Now that's hopeless. That's the best proof – the number of rifles we've lost. Taking the overall total we've fewer than we had. It's no good saying there have been newly formed units. The total is smaller and they've been lost here in the East as a result of these 'successful withdrawals' during which the men chuck their rifles away.

This is the way it is: the men fight bravely, they repulse the enemy, they are brave and courageous, they fortify all their positions but then the word goes round: back! You can't have a front of 250–300 miles where everything is all right. There's a break-through up there, and as a result back you go 250 miles. You can't explain that to the troops.

ZEITZLER: I see no hope, my Führer, if he's got here already.

HITLER: Now this is the way it is; you may say: Stalingrad was something different; that happened over there. But here it's ridiculous. There are good communications here in all directions.

ZEITZLER: The communications are very bad here.

HITLER: They are bad, but nothing on the Stalingrad model. The business here, that's the most difficult! Well then, you will talk to Kleist to see if they can take the risk.

ZEITZLER: Yes, one thing – concerning 371 Div.; I'll talk to Jodl to see how we can get it out of there.

HITLER: If the worst comes to the worst we can do one thing – move in here and push forward a few battalions as quick as we can, so that at least there's something there.

JODL: We must first find out how long their movement will take before they arrive.

HITLER: How long will it take to get back here?

ZEITZLER: It's simply a question of rail calculations. It will be a couple of days before 101 Div. reaches the railway because 4 Div. is more or less along the railway.

HITLER: You can't do more than that. If you could get one division back ...

ZEITZLER: If the worst comes to the worst we can pull that one back.

HITLER: If you bring it back you get the whole of the front into a mess, and you don't know whether the enemy won't follow up hard. We just don't know. We've seen what the results of these withdrawals are.

ZEITZLER: Up here he thought he could hold on a bit longer. There's nothing to worry about there; the worry is down here.

HITLER: He's got a blob here and he's got blobs there. If we withdraw he may attack again straight away here.

ZEITZLER: It may lead to that. But of course he can still attack this way, even if we don't go back.

HITLER: That's not right either; he's been attacking all the time. I've got another report today about the other fellow's supply situation. This is the most miserable and precarious supply system there's ever been – nothing very wonderful.

When could we get news how this attack is going? This may indicate a few tanks; one can't really tell.

ZEITZLER: It didn't look that way today. We shan't hear that till this evening. Because we're only in touch by radio.

HITLER: Well try and get the news through straight away. Get in touch with the Army Group; see when you think you can do it. It's a complete division of seven battalions. Artillery you've got.

ZEITZLER: Nine batteries.

HITLER: Assault guns and anti-tank guns? Heavy or light?

ZEITZLER: Heavy anti-tank guns.

HITLER: Only heavy?

ZEITZLER: One pioneer battalion, one reinforcement battalion.

HITLER: Do you want to take that along?

ZEITZLER: There'll be recruits among them. It means really there are only eight battalions.

HITLER: And this division here has nine?

ZEITZLER: 101 Div. has 1 weak battalion and 8 strong. But two battalions which have been in the East have just been added; we should perhaps leave them here in the first place.

HITLER: Yes, we can leave them here initially.

ZEITZLER: We can leave some artillery there too.

(Conference ended 0109 hours)

APPENDIX B

Three Pieces of Evidence

1 Extract from Jodl's 'confidential report' on me dated 1 March 1944. This figures as Nr Rep 502/VI–W24 in the 'Personality Files' now held in the State Archives in Nuremberg.

'As my Deputy in charge of the entire staff he is of incomparable value to me.

He is now frozen in his present appointment by order of the Führer.'

Signed
Jodl

2 Extract from a Report (S 70) in the same Personality File.

P ... , Major, OKH   Berlin 31 August 1944
Army Liaison Staff
Personnel Office.

On 30 August 1944 Colonel (on the Reserve) Freiherr von B ... appeared in this office. He told me that he had had an appointment in the OKW Operations Staff and had left the Führer's Headquarters on 16 July. He was glad he had not been in the HQ on 20 July. In his view the 'worst of the lot' was General Warlimont but he was slippery as an eel and so would get away with it. I thereupon remarked to Colonel von B ... that I assumed that he had reported what he had just told me to the proper quarter. Colonel von B ... replied that he had on several occasions made known his point of view both verbally and on paper to the proper quarters.

Signed
P ...

To Major General Maisel,
Chief AG 2.

3 Statement dated October 1946 sworn by Colonel-General
Jodl before the US prosecuting authorities in Nuremberg
(extracts):

Warlimont's primary job was to allot work throughout the
staff and indicate the general lines on which it was to proceed.
He supervised everything. He would get instructions from me,
discuss them with the staff officers concerned, check the drafts,
sign them and send them on to me.

He had a special additional duty in that he dealt direct with
Field Marshal Keitel on all questions which I did not handle or
which were of no interest to me. I dealt almost entirely with
operational questions. Without any participation by me Warlimont dealt with all problems of administration in occupied
areas, all economic questions, in short everything non-operational ...

On operational matters he directed the preliminary work and
put up the results to me. On other matters he worked to Keitel
without passing through me. In every case where a document
carries the heading *WF Stab Qu*, that means as a rule – I
repeat, as a rule, not invariably – that it was concerned with
matters dealt with by Warlimont direct with Field Marshal
Keitel. I would see individual documents from time to time,
but in general I did not. He had much more to do with these
matters than I.... On all questions labelled *Q Section* therefore
Warlimont was far more involved than I.

Signed

Jodl

Several further pages of the statement then deal with my supposed
independent action, particularly in connection with Hitler's *Commando* order of October 1942.

This statement, made by an officer for whom I had worked for
years, I found extremely disturbing. I was dumbfounded to find it
included in the evidence for the prosecution in the so-called OKW
Trial (1947–8).

When it was produced in evidence by the prosecution my counsel
for the defence, the late Dr Paul Leverkuehn of Hamburg, immediately lodged an objection in that, in the first place, the contents of
the statement ran counter to the verdict of the International Military
Tribunal on Jodl, which had condemned him on numerous counts

connected with the Q Section of the Staff, including in particular the *Commando* order; the statement was also contradicted by clear documentary evidence, again particularly that concerning the *Commando* order; secondly, the maker of the statement, having been executed meanwhile, could not be cross-examined by the defence.

The court nevertheless accepted Jodl's statement, though with the cautionary remark by the President: 'for what it is worth'.

During the later stages of the trial several witnesses stated both verbally and in writing that Jodl's statement was incorrect in so far as the matters of interest to the prosecution were concerned. Nevertheless the Court's verdict on me was based principally upon this statement and in fact quoted considerable portions of it textually in the grounds for the verdict.

I have only gone into the detail of this affair because it forms part of the history of 'the Headquarters'. I have long been convinced that the opinion of my late friend and counsel for the defence was correct – that, having been made *in extremis mortis*, the statement should, from the *personal* point of view, be considered as of no lasting importance.

APPENDIX C

Chronology

1933
30 January   President von Hindenburg appoints General von Blomberg Defence Minister in Hitler's Government and nominates him (though not publicly) Supreme Commander of the Wehrmacht.

1934
2 August   Death of Hindenburg; Hitler becomes Führer and Chancellor of the Reich – and as such *de jure* Supreme Commander of the Wehrmacht.

1935
16 March   Announcement that Germany had 'regained her liberty of action in defence matters'; universal military service, open pursuit of rearmament; Blomberg publicly appointed Reich War Minister and Supreme Commander of the Wehrmacht.

1938
4 February   Hitler's seizure of military power; dismisses Field Marshal von Blomberg without appointing a successor; takes over *de facto* Supreme Command of the Wehrmacht; nominates General Keitel, in his capacity as Chief of his military staff, Chief of Oberkommando der Wehrmacht (OKW); Commander-in-Chief of the Army changed (Colonel-General von Brauchitsch replaces Colonel-General Freiherr von Fritsch).

12 March   Invasion of Austria – the Anschluss.

29 September   The Sudeten crisis ended by the Munich agreement; the Wehrmacht moves into the Sudetenland.

1939

15–16 March	Military occupation of the 'remainder of Czecho-Slovakia'. The Protectorate of Bohemia and Moravia set up.
22 May	The *Pact of Steel* between the Reich and Italy.
23 August	German-Soviet Treaty of Non-Aggression, including a secret supplementary agreement concerning Poland and the Baltic States.
25 August	Cancellation of the initial order for attack on Poland.
31 August	Renewed order for attack on Poland on 1 September.
3 September	England and France declare war on the Reich.
17 September	The Red Army moves into Eastern Poland.
27 September	Hitler announces his decision to act offensively in the West.
6 October	Hitler's offer of peace made before the Reichstag; rejected by England on 12 October.
26 October	Military Government in Poland replaced by the 'Government General'; Eastern Poland incorporated in the USSR.
7 November	Offer of mediation to the belligerents by the Belgian and Netherlands Sovereigns – rejected by England and France on 12 November and as a result considered null and void by Hitler.
30 November	Beginning of the Russo-Finnish 'Winter War'.
12 December	First German consideration of occupation of Norway.

1940

16 January	Start of Allied preparations for military action in Scandinavia.
16 February	The German supply ship *Altmark* captured by British destroyers in Norwegian territorial waters.
12 March	End of the Russo-Finnish Winter War.
28 March	Decision by Supreme Allied War Council to mine Norwegian waters on 5 April and occupy bases in Norway.
7 April	Allied Expeditionary force embarks.
9 April	Start of German occupation of Denmark and Norway.

10 May	Start of German attack in the West.
15 May	Dutch forces capitulate.
	British aircraft attack the Ruhr area.
28 May	Belgian forces capitulate.
10 June	Last Norwegian forces capitulate.
22 June	Franco-German armistice agreement.
19 July	Hitler's peace speech in the Reichstag. Rejected by England on 22 July.
31 July	Hitler's order for preparations for attack on Russia.
13 August	Beginning of air battle (the Blitz) over England.
27 September	Three-Power Pact – Germany, Italy, Japan.
23 October	Meeting between Hitler and General Franco in Hendaye.
24 October	Meeting between Hitler and Marshal Pétain in Montoire.
28 October	Italian attack on Greece.
11–12 November	Italian fleet suffers heavy loss from British carrier attack on Taranto.
12–13 November	Molotov, Soviet Foreign Minister, in Berlin.
7 December	General Franco refuses to agree to a German attack on Gibraltar.
9 December	Severe defeat of the Italians in North Africa, withdrawal to Tripoli (Wavell's offensive).
18 December	Issue of *Barbarossa* Directive for attack on Russia.

1941

12 February	General Rommel arrives in Tripoli as Commander of a German 'back-up formation'.
27 March	Military putsch in Belgrade. Hitler decides to extend to Jugoslavia the Balkan campaign already planned (for the support of Italy).
5 April	Jugoslav-Soviet Non-Aggression Pact.
6 April	Start of German campaign in the Balkans.
13 April	Russo-Japanese Treaty of Friendship and Non-Aggression.
17 April	Jugoslav forces capitulate.
21–23 April	German–Italian armistice agreement with Greece.
28 April	Rommel on the Libyan–Egyptian frontier.
2 May	Start of British military measures to suppress the rising in Iraq (which had broken out 3 April).

10 May	Clandestine flight to England of the 'Führer's Deputy', Rudolf Hess.
20 May	Start of German attack on Crete.
24 May	Start of operations in the Atlantic by German surface forces; destruction of the *Hood* (24 May), sinking of the *Bismarck* (27 May).
8 June	British and Free French forces march into Syria.
22 June	Opening of attack on Soviet Russia.
25 August	Occupation of Iran by Soviet and British forces.
24 September	End of the Kiev series of battles.
2 October	Resumption of the offensive towards Moscow.
18 November	British offensive in North Africa.
29 November	First major withdrawal in the east by Army Group South, including evacuation of Rostov.
Early December	Start of Soviet counter-offensive.
7 December	Japanese surprise attack on Pearl Harbour.
8 December	USA declares war on Japan.
11 December	Hitler declares war on USA.
19 December	Hitler takes over as Commander-in-Chief of the Army.

1942

21 January	Renewed offensive by Rommel in North Africa.
12–13 February	Passage of *Scharnhorst*, *Gneisenau* and *Prinz Eugen* through the Channel.
April–May	Air offensive against Malta.
7 June–4 July	Occupation of the whole of the Crimea and capture of Sebastopol.
20–21 June	Capture of the fortress of Tobruk, breakthrough into Egypt.
28 June	Start of second summer offensive in the East.
7–8 August	Beginning of the change in the war situation in the Pacific with American landing on Guadalcanal.
19 August	British-Canadian raid on Dieppe repulsed.
30 August–2 September	German–Italian front immobilized at El Alamein after failure of an attempt to advance further.
August–September	Battles of the approaches to Stalingrad, penetration into the Caucasus.
23 October	Opening of British offensive at El Alamein.

2–3 November	Start of Rommel's withdrawal from El Alamein.
7–8 November	Anglo-American landings in French North Africa.
19–21 November	Soviet counter-offensive at Stalingrad leading to the encirclement of the city and of the German Sixth Army.

1943

14–25 January	Casablanca Conference; demand for 'unconditional surrender' of the Axis Powers.
31 January	Grand Admiral Dönitz succeeds Raeder as Commander-in-Chief Navy.
31 January–1 February	Surrender of Stalingrad.
16–20 March	The greatest convoy battle of the war; 42 German U-boats sink 21 ships of a total of nearly 142,000 GRT losing only one U-boat.
13 May	Collapse in Tunis; end of the war in North Africa.
24 May	German U-boat offensive against convoys in the North Atlantic called off as a result of heavy losses.
5 July	Last German offensive in the east (*Citadel*) – called off on 15 July after achieving nothing.
9–10 July	Allied landing in Sicily.
24–25 July	Revolution in Italy; Mussolini made prisoner.
8 September	Surrender of Italy.
9 September	Allied landing at Salerno.
12 September	Mussolini liberated by German troops in the Gran Sasso.
13 October	Italy declares war on Germany.
23 October	Red Army breakthrough on the lower Dnieper; as a result the Crimea cut off (1 November).
3 November	Preparatory directive from OKW against invasion in the West.

1944

22 January	Allied landing at Anzio–Nettuno in rear of the German front in Central Italy.
19 March	German occupation of Hungary.
4 June	Defeat of Kesselring's Army Group in Central Italy culminates in the evacuation of Rome.
6 June	Start of invasion in Normandy.

22 June	Collapse of Army Group Centre on the Eastern Front.
13 July	Soviet offensive against Army Groups North and Northern Ukraine.
20 July	Bomb attack on Hitler in the headquarters.
31 July	Allied breakthrough at Avranches.
2 August	Turkey breaks off relations with Germany.
15 August	Allied landing on the French Mediterranean coast.
19 August	Encirclement of considerable portions of the German forces in Normandy at Falaise.
20 August	Start of Soviet breakthrough on the front of Army Group South Ukraine.
23 August	Revolution in Rumania; declares war on Germany on 25 August; loss of the Rumanian oil area.
25 August	Defection of Bulgaria; declares war on Germany on 8 September. Allies march into Paris.
4 September	Finland gives up the struggle against the Soviet Union.
11 September	The Americans reach the German frontier north of Trier.
25 September	Hitler's decree setting up the *Volkssturm* (Home Guard).
3 October	Order for evacuation of Greece.
5 October	Soviet breakthrough to the Baltic south of Riga; encirclement of Army Group North (later called Army Group Courland).
11 October	First breakthrough by the Red Army into East Prussia.
2 November	Completion of the evacuation of Greece.
16 December	Opening of the Ardennes offensive.
24 December	Encirclement of Budapest.

1945

12 January	Opening of general Soviet offensive against Germany from the bridgehead across the Vistula at Baranov.
17 January	Evacuation of Warsaw.
4–12 February	Yalta Conference.
1 April	Encirclement of the Ruhr area complete.

12 April	Death of Roosevelt.
14 April	Fall of Vienna.
21 April	Collapse of the German front in Italy.
25 April	Junction of American and Soviet forces at Torgau on the Elbe.
30 April	Suicide of Hitler.
7–8 May	Signature of the unconditional surrender of the Wehrmacht on instructions from the newly-formed Government of Dönitz.
23 May	Dönitz's Government arrested and taken into captivity by the Allies.

APPENDIX D

Sources

I · DOCUMENTS

These include: 'Directives', 'Operation Orders', 'Special Instructions', 'Orders of the Day' and such other directions by Hitler to the Wehrmacht as were drafted and distributed by the OKW Operations Staff; orders by the Commander-in-Chief of the Army and the Commander-in-Chief of the Navy – some in the form of regular orders, some as teleprinter messages or records of telephone conversations; military correspondence between Hitler and higher Wehrmacht HQ's, in particular 'Memoranda', 'Appreciations of the Situation', reports, information to allies; War Diaries; contemporary records (personal diaries) kept by officers in senior posts and by others; shorthand records of Hitler's briefing conferences – the majority from photostat copies.

The directives and other operation orders are the only ones which cover the entire war period almost without a break. All other documents cover limited periods only; in some cases parts of the records have not been found and have presumably been lost; in others the authors concerned left their posts prematurely; in yet others the records were either not continuous or began only at a later period. At some periods all these causes were at work to cause gaps in our basic information.

The following is a more detailed picture of the main sources employed:

1937–38

(*Up to 29 September 1938*) The personal diary of Colonel (as he then was) Alfred Jodl (referred to as Jodl's Diary). At the time he was Chief of the National Defence Section (Section L) of OKW; from spring 1938 he was Chief of the OKW Operations Office. The diary has not yet been published.

1939

14 August–31 December	The personal diary of General (as he then was) Franz Halder (referred to as Halder's Diary). He was at the time Chief of Staff of the Army. The diary is in process of publication.
22–25 August 13 Oct.–30 Dec.	Jodl's Diary[1] – from 13 October this has been published (with numerous editorial errors) in *Die Welt als Geschichte* 1952/4 and 1953/1.
September– December	Commander-in-Chief Navy's records of his conferences with Hitler. These have been published in Brassey's Naval Annual, London–New York, under the heading *Führer Conferences on Naval Affairs, 1939–1945* (this applies also to subsequent periods). Referred to as 'Naval Affairs'.

1940

1 January–26 May	Jodl's Diary. State of publication as for 1939.
1 January–24 December	Halder's Diary.
1 August–31 December	War Diary (*Kriegstagebuch*) of Section L[2] of the OKW Operations Office (later Staff). References: OKW/WF Amt (Stab)/Abt L and KTB OKW/WF Stab/Abt L (WF Stab/L).
8 August–21 December	Notes on Section L Conferences[2]. These, the War Diary and all other OKW Operations Staff War Diaries are in process of publication.
January– December	Naval Affairs.

1941

3 January–24 March	War Diary of Section L of the OKW Operations Staff.
7 January–25 June	Notes on Section L Conferences.
16 January–31 December	Halder's Diary.
January– December	Naval Affairs.

Appendix D

1942

1 January–24 September	Halder's Diary.
1 April–30 June	War Diary of the Historical Section of the OKW Operations Staff.
12 August–31 December	War Diary of Section L of the OKW Operations Staff.
January– December	Naval Affairs.
December	Fragments of the shorthand records of Hitler's briefing conferences[3] (referred to as 'Fragments') – annotated and edited by H. Heiber, Deutsche Verlags Anstalt, Stuttgart 1962.

1943

1 January–17 March	OKW Operations Staff War Diary ('Reports' – *Aufzeichungen*).
1 January–31 March	War Diary of Section L of the OKW Operations Staff (official text).
1 July–31 December	OKW Operations Staff War Diary.
13 December–31 December	Jodl's Diary (not published – applies also to those parts dealing with 1944 and 1945).
January– December	Naval Affairs.
February– December	Fragments.

1944

1 January–31 December	OKW Operations Staff War Diary[4].
1 January–31 December	Jodl's Diary.
January– December	Naval Affairs.
January– December	Fragments.

1945

1 January–7 May	OKW Operations Staff War Diary.

577

Appendices

1 January–21 May	Jodl's Diary.
January–end April	Naval Affairs.
January–end March	Fragments.

II · BIBLIOGRAPHY [5,6]

Akten zur Deutschen Auswärtigen Politik, 1918–1945, Series D. Imprimerie Nationale, Baden-Baden, 1950

Ansel, W.: *Hitler confronts England*. Duke University Press, Durham, North Carolina, 1960

Armstrong, A.: *Unconditional Surrender*. Rutgers University Press, New Brunswick, New Jersey, 1961

Beck, L.: *Studien*, edited by H. Speidel. Koehler Verlag, Stuttgart, 1955

von Blomberg, W.: Memoirs and manuscript notes – not published.

Bor, P.: *Gespräche mit Halder*. Limes Verlag, Wiesbaden, 1950

Bradley, O.: *A Soldier's Story*. Holt, New York, 1951

Bryant, A.: *Triumph in the West* (The Alanbrooke Diaries). Collins, London, 1959

Cavallero, Count Ugo: *Comando Supremo, Diario*. Capelli Editore, Bologna, 1948

Churchill, W. S.: *The Second World War*. Cassell, London, 1948

Ciano, Count Galeazzo: *Diario*. Rizzoli, Rome, 1946. *Diary*, edited by Hugh Gibson. Doubleday & Co Inc, Garden City, New York, 1946

Ciano, Count Galeazzo: *L'Europa verso la Catastrofe*. Arnoldo Mondadori, Milan, Genoa, 1948

Demeter, K.: *Das Deutsche Offizierkorps in Gesellschaft und Staat*, Bernard & Graefe, Frankfurt/Main, 1962. Translated by Angus Malcolm, to be published by Weidenfeld and Nicolson, London, 1965

Dönitz, K.: *Zehn Jahre und Zwanzig Tage*. Athenäum Verlag, Bonn, 1958. *Memoirs, Ten Years and Twenty Days*, translated by R. H. Stevens. Weidenfeld & Nicolson, London, 1959

Ellis, L. F.: *War in France and Flanders*. HMSO, London, 1959

Appendix D

Erfurth, W.: *Geschichte des Deutschen Generalstabs.* Musterschmidt Verlag, Göttingen, 1957

Goebbels, J.: *Tagebücher, 1942–43.* L. P. Lochner, Zürich, 1948. *The Goebbels Diaries*, translated and edited by Louis P. Lochner. Hamish Hamilton, London, 1948

Görlitz, W.: *Keitel.* Musterschmidt Verlag, Göttingen, 1961

Görlitz, W. and Quint H.: *Adolf Hitler.* Musterschmidt Verlag, Göttingen, 1960

Görlitz, W.: *Der Zweite Weltkrieg.* Steingrüben Verlag, Stuttgart, 1951

Greiner, H.: *Die Oberste Wehrmachtführung, 1939–1945.* Limes Verlag, Wiesbaden, 1951

Greiner, H.: *Aufzeichnungen zum KTB WF/Stab* (The OKW Operations Staff War Diary).

Guderian, H.: *Erinnerungen eines Soldaten*, 4th Edition. Kurt Vowinckel, Heidelberg, 1951. *Panzer Leader*, translated by Constantine Fitzgibbon. Michael Joseph, London, 1952

Halder, F. *Tagebuch*, edited by H. Jacobsen. W. Kohlhammer Verlag, Stuttgart, 1962. *Diaries.* Infantry Journal Inc, U.S.A.

Heusinger, A.: *Befehl im Widerstreit.* Rainer Wunderlich Verlag Hermann Leins, Tübingen & Stuttgart, 1950

Hillgruber, A.: *Das deutsch-ungarische Verhältnis im letzten Kriegsjahr. Wehrwissenschaftliche Rundschau*, 2/1960

Hitler, A.: *Tischgespräche im Führerhauptquartier, 1941–1942*, Athenäum Verlag, Bonn, 1951. *Hitler's Table Talk*, translated by E. Fitzgerald & R. H. Stevens, with an introductory essay by H. R. Trevor-Roper. Weidenfeld & Nicolson, London, 1953

Hubatsch, W.: *Die deutsche Besetzung von Dänemark und Norwegen, 1940.* Musterschmidt Verlag, Göttingen, 1952

Hubatsch, W.: *Grosses Hauptquartier, 1914–1918.* Jahrbuch des Ostdeutschen Kulturrates vol. 5, 1958

Hubatsch, W.: *Hitlers Weisungen für die Kriegführung, 1939–1945.* Bernard & Graefe Verlag für Wehrwesen, Frankfurt/Main, 1962. *Hitler's War Directives*, edited and with an Introduction and Connecting Narrative by H. R. Trevor-Roper. Sidgwick & Jackson, London, 1964[7]

International Military Tribunal: *The Nuremberg Trial*, 1949. English version, 1947–1949

Jacobsen, H. A.: *Fall Gelb, Der Kampf um den deutschen Operationsplan der Westoffensive 1940.* Franz Steiner Gmbh, Wiesbaden, 1957

Jacobsen, H. A.: *Dokumente zur Vorgeschichte des Westfeldzuges 1939–1940*. Musterschmidt Verlag, Göttingen, 1956

Jacobsen, H. A.: *Der Zweite Weltkrieg in Chronik und Dokumenten*. 5th edition, Wehr und Wissen Verlagsgesellschaft, Darmstadt, 1961

Jacobsen, H. A. and Rohwer, J.: *Entscheidungsschlachten des Zweiten Weltkriegs*. Bernard & Graefe Verlag für Wehrwesen, Frankfurt/Main, 1960

Kesselring, A.: *Soldat bis zum Letzten Tag*. Athenäum Verlag, Bonn, 1953. *Memoirs*, translated by Lynton Hudson. William Kimber, London, 1953

Klee, K.: *Das Unternehmen Seelöwe*, Musterschmidt Verlag, Göttingen, 1958

Klee, K.: *Quellenkritische Untersuchung über die OKW-Weisung Nr 32* (printed in manuscript form)

Langer, W. L. & Gleason S. E.: *The World Crisis and American Foreign Policy. The Undeclared War 1940–1941*. Oxford University Press, New York, 1953

von Lossberg, B.: *Im Wehrmachtführungsstabe*. Nölke, Hamburg, 1949

von Manstein, E.: *Verlorene Siege*, Athenäum Verlag, Bonn, 1955. *Lost Victories*, translated by A. G. Powell, Methuen, London, 1958

de Mendelssohn, P.: *The Nuremberg Documents. Some Aspects of German War Policy 1939–45*. Allen & Unwin, London, 1946. *Die Nürnberger Dokumente*, Wolfgang Krüger Verlag, Hamburg, 1947

Müller-Hillebrand, B.: *Das Heer 1933–1945*. E. S. Mittler & Sohn Gmbh, Frankfurt/Main, 1956

Playfair, I. S. O.: *British Official History of the Second World War. The Mediterreanean and the Middle East*. HMSO, London, 1954–60

Raeder, E.: *Mein Leben*, vol. 2. Verlag Fritz Schlichtenmayer, Tübingen-Neckar, 1957. *Struggle for the Sea*, translated by E. Fitzgerald. William Kimber, 1959

von Rintelen, E.: *Mussolini als Bundesgenosse*. Rainer Wunderlich Verlag Hermann Leins, Tübingen & Stuttgart, 1951

Ritter, G.: *Staatskunst und Kriegshandwerk*. Verlag Oldenburg, Munich, 1954

Rommel, E.: *Krieg ohne Hass*. Verlag Heidenheimer Zeitung, Heidenheim, 1950

Rommel, E.: *The Rommel Papers*, edited by Captain B. H. Liddell Hart, translated by Paul Findlay. Collins, London, 1953.

Roskill, S. W.: *British Official History of the Second World War. The War at Sea*. vol. 1. HMSO, London, 1954

Appendix D

Ryan, C.: *The Longest Day*, Gollancz, London, 1960

Schramm, P. E.: *Kriegstagebuch des Oberkommandos der Wehrmacht* (OKW War Diary). Bernard & Graefe, Frankfurt/Main, 1961

von Senger und Etterlin, F.: *Krieg in Europa*. Kiepenhauer & Witsch, Cologne & Berlin, 1960

Shirer, W. L.: *The Rise and Fall of the Third Reich*. Secker & Warburg, New York, 1961

Speidel, H.: *Invasion 1944*, Rainer, Wunderlich Verlag Hermann Leins, Tübingen, 1949. *We Defended Normandy*, translated by Ian Colvin. Herbert Jenkins, London, 1951

Supreme Command – U.S. Official History. The European Theater of Operations. Washington, 1954

von Tippelskirch, K.: *Geschichte des Zweiten Weltkriegs*. 3rd edition, Athenäum Verlag, Bonn, 1959

Ufficio Storico (Italian Official History). Stato Maggiore Esercito, Rome

von Vormann, N. (Army Liaison Officer to the Führer and Supreme Commander): Manuscript in the Institut für Zeitgeschichte, Munich

Wehrwissenschaftliche Rundschau, 1959–1961

Weygand, L. M.: *Mémoires, Rappelé au Service*. Flammarion, Paris, 1951

Wiskemann, Elizabeth L.: *The Rome-Berlin Axis*. Oxford University Press, 1949

Wilmot, C.: *The Struggle for Europe*, Collins, London, 1952.

Ziemke, E. F.: *The German Northern Theater of Operations, 1940–45* Department of the Army, Pamphlet 20–271, Washington, 1959

APPENDIX E

The Author's Career

February 1913	Graduated from High School at 18 and accepted as cadet in 10 Foot Artillery Regiment of Lower Saxony, at Strasburg in Alsace.
August 1913– *May 1914*	Military Academy, Danzig.
June 1914	2nd Lieutenant.
First World War	Battery officer, Adjutant (Battalion, Regiment, Brigade) and Battery Commander in the West and in Italy.
1918	Lieutenant in Märcker's 'Free Corps'.
1922	Transferred to the Reichswehr in 6 Artillery Regiment at Minden, Westphalia; seconded for training as 'staff assistant' (General Staff).
1926	Three months' language leave in England; appointed Captain on the General Staff in the autumn. First appointment – 2nd assistant to Chief of Staff (General Staff); then in Economics Section of the Defence Ministry and (temporarily) in the Foreign Armies Intelligence Section.
May 1929	Attached to US Army for a year to study industrial mobilization.
Autumn 1930– *Spring 1933*	Battery Commander in 1 Artillery Regt at Allenstein; then Major on the staff in the Industrial Mobilization Section of the Defence Ministry; Chief of the Section from 1935.
Summer 1936	Military Plenipotentiary of the Reich War Minister with Gen. Franco in Spain (Lt.-Col.).
1937–1938	Commander 2nd Bn., 34 Artillery Regt. Trier,

	then Commander 26 Artillery Regt., Düsseldorf (Colonel).
September 1938	Chief of the National Defence Section (General Staff) in OKW. From November 1938 also responsible for the duties of Chief of the Operations Staff.
September 1939– September 1944	Deputy Chief of the Operations Staff. Promoted successively Major General, Lieutenant General, General.
September 1944	Transferred to OKH Command Pool, and not further employed.

NOTES

Notes

FOREWORD

1. From Arnold Toynbee's *Study of History*. See also Gerhard Ritter's *Staatskunst und Kriegshandwerk*, vol. 1 pp. 70 *et seq.* Based on the character and work of General von Clausewitz, Ritter draws a striking picture, still valid at the beginning of the Second World War, of the spiritual heritage of the profession of arms in Prussia and Germany. Its culminating sentences are: 'heroic determination in battle is the common attribute of all these patriots (of Clausewitz's day). It attempts the apparently impossible because it relies on victory through moral superiority. This is in the best tradition of the soldier. It has given the Prussian-German army many a victory and much more besides. But when turned into a political code of conduct, as at the end of the First World War and during the Hitler period, it leads to irretrievable disaster. For that which in the soldier is the height of courage, in the statesman is likely to be irresponsible temerity.'

PART I · INTRODUCTION

1. Reproduced in Hubatsch, *Hitlers War Directives* 1939-45 p. 3 (hereafter referred to as 'Hubatsch, *Directives*' or Hubatsch, *Weisungen* – see Bibliography, Note 7).

2. Jodl returned on 23 August 1939 (see his diary entry of that date); from that date I was responsible only for Section L (see also pp. 45-46 of this book).

3. It is a remarkable historical fact that in the list of mobilization appointments no less a person than the then Major-General Rommel was designated as 'Commandant' of the Führer's Headquarters. As such he was responsible for security and interior economy. He actually took up his appointment before a proper headquarters had been organized.

PART I · CHAPTER I

1. There is documentary proof of this, including that of the so-called *Keitel-Memorandum* of April 1938 published by Görlitz in *Keitel*, pp. 154 *et seq.* (see particularly Section c).

2. The term 'total war' is used here in the military sense, ie the harnessing of all the human and material resources of a State to the object of winning the war. (cf. Beck, *Studien* and *Die Lehre vom Totalen Kriege*.)

3. In cases where the Reich Minister for War and C.-in-C. of the Wehrmacht had no section within his own staff (OKW) capable of dealing with these matters, he gave directions through other ministries and organizations in his capacity as Permanent Dep-

uty to the Head of State, under the Law for the Defence of the Reich of 21 May 1935. After Blomberg's departure, Göring took over this function. His responsibilities were redefined in the Second Defence Law of 4 September 1938. Neither law has been published so far but they are included in the Nuremberg *Documents*.

4. Beck, *Studien*, p. 138.

5. From February 1934 this office was designated 'Wehrmachtamt' (Defence Office). In cases where the Defence Office had to take Governmental action in the name of the C.-in-C. of the Wehrmacht it used the title Oberkommando der Wehrmacht (OKW – Supreme Command of the Armed Forces). cf *Akten zur Deutschen Auswärtigen Politik* vol. III, document 138; in this Keitel is writing on 2 December 1936 to the Foreign Ministry and uses the title 'Oberkommando der Wehrmacht' in a way which shows that it was then already a generally recognized designation. The view often put forward in military documents that the title OKW was only introduced in February 1938 is wrong. In fact it was the title Chief of OKW (instead of Chief of the Defence Office) which was introduced at that time.

6. See Beck, *Studien*, 'Der Anführer im Kriege' pp. 24 – 25. Also W. Hubatsch, *Grosses Hauptquartier, 1914–1918*.

7. Extract from Beck (see note 6) pp. 33–36.

8. Note the following entries in Jodl's diary about this time, regarding Blomberg's resignation in January 1938:

JODL to KEITEL: The man may go but his achievements will remain.

HITLER to KEITEL: I regard decisive and unified leadership of the Wehrmacht as something sacred and inviolable.

KEITEL to JODL: The unity of the Wehrmacht has been preserved.

JODL: Any murky aspect of this business is outshone by the certainty that the achievement of the first Field-Marshal of the Third Reich, the unification of the Wehrmacht and of its leadership, lives on. If fortune is with us, this can never again be disturbed.

9. From his diary of 10 April 1937.

10. Published in Jacobsen's *Der Zweite Weltkrieg in Chronik und Documenten* (hereafter referred to as 'Jacobsen, *Chronik*'), pp. 97 *et seq*.

11. See Jodl's diary of this date. I am particularly interested in this because I reached a similar conclusion in the summer of 1939 in connection with the preparations against Poland (see p. 24 of this book).

12. I can vouch for this personally. I had just returned from several months as Military Plenipotentiary to General Franco and was invited to this conference between Hitler and his C's-in-C.

13. I can vouch for this personally. See also Jodl's diary of 2 February 1938, which contains the following extract from the record of an argument between Hitler and Keitel over the replacement of Colonel-General Freiherr von Fritsch: 'Personnel appointments are *conditio sine qua non*. The Führer has always wished it to be so and promised Blomberg to speak to Fritsch but nothing has occurred.' Subsequently, on

8 November 1939 Keitel talked to me in the same vein saying that Blomberg must be held primarily responsible for the fact that the 1901–1914 classes of conscripts, the so-called 'white block', were never called up and that as a result there was a serious shortage of trained reserves at the beginning of the war.

14. See Jodl's diary 26 January 1938: 'the Führer has no intention of making Göring Reich Minister for War'.

15. Jodl's diary 28 January, 4 and 8 March 1938.

16. Jodl's diary 27 and 28 January 1938.

17. Jodl's diary 13 June, also 31 January, 2 and 18 February 1938.

18. From Bor, *Gespräche mit Halder* (hereafter referred to as '*Gespräche*') pp. 75 and 78.

19. Jodl's diary 27 January 1938.

20. Use is made here of information from Halder in *Gespräche* (Bor, pp. 115 and 117); see also Keitel's own admission in Görlitz: *Keitel* p. 169.

21. Jodl's diary of this date.

22. From Görlitz, p. 179; see also Jodl's diary 10 and 11 March and his statement before the International Military Tribunal (hereafter referred to as *IMT*) vol. XV, p. 355 and vol. XXIV pp. 335–7 Document 102–C; see also Heusinger, *Befehl im Widerstreit* (hereafter referred to as 'Heusinger') pp. 26 and 27.

23. Jodl's diary 10, 12, 13 September 1938 (punctuation as in original); see also Keitel's description in Görlitz pp. 182–4 and 188 *et seq.*

24. From Beck's memorandum to Brauchitsch early August 1938.

25. The extent to which this authority was unquestioningly recognized is shown by the fact that in an extract from a note by Keitel quoted in Jodl's diary of 22 September 1938 appears the expression 'order from the Supreme Authority'.

26. See also Jodl's extraordinary letter dated 28 July 1938 reproduced in Görlitz, p. 215, note 142, in which he refers to the Army General Staff as 'the enemy'!

27. The addendum is reproduced in Hubatsch, *Weisungen*, pp. 17 *et seq.* under the heading 'Directive Case White'. Sub-paragraphs 1, 2 and probably 3 of paragraph I are the parts drafted by Hitler in person. The short paragraph 4a is the agreed draft proposed by the OKW Operations Staff and the Army General Staff for the '*object para*' for the Army's operations; this formed the basis for the annexes dealing with the other two Services. The end-date ('possible at any time from 1 September 1939') does not appear in the text of the Directive.

It should be explained that: (*a*) paragraph I in Hubatsch's reproduction probably belongs to the heading (see also Greiner p. 31, *Die Oberste Wehrmachtführung*, hereafter referred to as 'Greiner'); (*b*) the expression 'directive' was used during the war for the more important orders from Supreme Headquarters. (See p. 30 of this book.)

28. Jodl's diary 21 and 22 September.

29. As recorded in *Aktenpublikationen* vol. II, document 623.

30. See W. Görlitz and H. Quint, *Adolf Hitler*, pp. 357 and 358.

31. Quoted from the minutes drafted by Lt. Colonel Schmundt published in Jacobsen, *Chronik* pp. 109 *et seq.* The list of those present, which precedes the minutes, was presumably drawn up before the conference and not corrected afterwards. It is wrong in that I was not present and did not even know about it. This did not prevent the Nuremberg tribunal bringing up against me the fact that I was supposed to have been present.

32. Hitler had in his mind allotted this task to the Italians in the event of war with the West, although there was no time set for it. (See also p. 55 of this book.)

33. Cf Lossberg's description in his *Im Wehrmachtführungsstabe.* This differs on matters of detail.

34. Greiner (above) p. 34 says 'further Wehrmacht preparations proceeded in accordance with the timetable'. This is misleading since the timetable laid down no measures or instructions other than those already approved by Hitler based on the plans and intentions of the Service C's-in-C. as presented to him.

    General Halder's comment in his *Gespräche* (Bor, p. 124) that the timetable gave Hitler an indication of the situation and movements of individual divisions and therefore cut across measures for which the Army Staff was responsible, is incorrect.

35. When the timetable was presented I was on leave out of the country.

36. For the contents of this speech see Greiner pp. 38 *et seq.* This passage was drafted on the basis of my memory of it which I passed on to him that evening.

37. See para. 4 of *Directive no. 2 for the Conduct of the War* in Hubatsch, *Directives*, pp. 5 *et seq.* The rest is in the preceding directive (p. 3).

38. In his *Studien* (p. 37) General Beck supports the theory that basically the Supreme Commander should remain in the capital but that the Operational Commander with a small staff should direct operations on land from the decisive area.

39. The composition of the 'Führer Special' was an AA truck at head and tail, a number of carriages for signals and press representatives, an office carriage and a sleeping and living-room carriage for Hitler, several normal type sleeping-cars and a restaurant car.

PART I · CHAPTER 2

1. A distinction should be drawn between the 'directives for the conduct of the War' and 'operation orders'. The latter was a term used by the Army and signified orders issued by the Army General Staff for the movement of large formations (Army Group or Army) at the outset of a campaign or of an important fresh phase of operations. The examples given here and later show clearly the distinction between these two types of order and also the gradual change in the character of the directives issued by OKW.

2. It is worth remembering that before the First World War the 'Great General Staff' had been carrying out operational studies over a period of ten years or

more. Up to 1942 the OKW Operations Staff did not even have an Intelligence Section. Even after that date the Intelligence Section was capable only of collecting information, not of making intelligence appreciations.

3. Further details of what happened in the 'Führer Special' in so far as they do not appear elsewhere have been taken from the account which Vormann wrote after the war. In this he says that in his instructions from Brauchitsch and Halder his most important task as 'Army Liaison Officer to the Führer and Supreme Commander' was to prevent Hitler and his staff (Keitel and Jodl) interfering in any way with the command of the Army. See also Halder's diary for 24 August 1939, the day before Jodl's return to OKW, which contains what must have been a note for a talk with the Chief of OKW: 'Keitel, no interference with operations (Jodl)'.

4. See Hubatsch, *Directives*, pp. 7 and 8.

5. Halder's strictures (*Gespräche*, Bor, p. 142) regarding the failure of OKW at this juncture are consequently not altogether justified.

6. See *Secret Supplementary Protocol* of 23 August 1939 published in Jacobsen, *Chronik*, p. 119 and elsewhere.

7. See Müller-Hillebrand, *Das Heer*, vol. II p. 33 and Görlitz, *Keitel* p. 222.

8. See Halder's diary for 25 September 1939. This says unequivocally: 'Stülpnagel: Report from Warlimont on the Führer's intention to attack in the West.'

See also Vormann - quoted above.

PART II · CHAPTER I

1. See Jodl's diary 24 Oct. and 15 Nov 1939,. 8 Jan., 14, 22, 24, 26, 29 Feb. 1940; also Halder's diary 25 Feb, 1940.

PART II · CHAPTER 2

1. Beck, *Studien*, p. 36.

2. Even in these cases Jodl insisted on making any report himself. See for instance his diary for 18 December 1940 which reads: 'Chief of L Section reports on his trip'. This is all that he says of my report on my conversations with General von Manstein, Chief of Staff of Army Group A, in his Headquarters in Coblence which contained the germ of the *Manstein Plan*. (See Manstein, *Lost Victories*, p. 112.) The next day Jodl reported to Hitler the most important points raised by Manstein; his diary for 19 December says: 'the main Army effort to be in a different area (Army Group A or B)'.

3. Jodl's diary, 13 October 1939. See also Bor, pp. 80 and 88.

4. See: (a) Heusinger, p. 165, where he records Hitler as saying to Schmundt: 'I intend to make it quite clear that the Commander alone carries the responsibility and has the power of decision. The staff are his specially trained experts – no more!'; (b) Guderian, *Panzer Leader* (hereafter referred to as 'Guderian'), p. 465: 'Jodl withdrew completely into his work most of which he did with his own hands'; (c) Jodl's evidence before the International Military Tribunal

frequently shows traces of lapse of memory but vol XV p. 296 states: 'I worked in this way: when my report (at Hitler's daily briefing) was finished, I went into an adjoining room. There I immediately drew up the teletype messages and orders for the next few days.... Warlimont then took them along to my staff where they were sent off'; (d) Jacobsen: *Entscheidungsschlachten des Zweiten Weltkriegs*, p. 290: 'the National-Socialist General Staff officer is no more than an "assistant" to the commander'.

5. This procedure was frequently employed by Jodl. It is of some importance to remember this when dealing with documents headed *OKW Operations Staff, Section L*. This heading does not necessarily indicate that the section as a whole or its chief or its officers had had any hand in drafting the contents or even knew what they were. Jodl frequently merely asked Section L registry for a 'reference number' and then drafted the document himself or got his aides to do so.

6. See Görlitz, *Der Zweite Weltkrieg*, vol. I, p. 80, and *Keitel* p. 430. As against this see Jodl's diary 29 January, 'our advance in Poland', and 3 Feb. 1940, 'photographs of drum-head services – would the Führer approve?' (for publication in the *Wehrmacht Illustrated News*). As far as Poland is concerned, note that OKW Directive no. 5 of 30 Sept. 1939 (Hubatsch, *Directives*, pp. 10 *et seq.*) gave general directions that military government in Polish occupied territory should be under the authority

of the C.-in-C. of the Army. Two weeks later Hitler cancelled this, in spite of desperate resistance by Keitel, and substituted the notorious system of civil government under Frank.

7. See Heusinger, p. 210.

8. e.g. 7 and 12 February, 17–18 and 24–25 March 1940.

9. *IMT*, vol. XV p. 371.

10. Published in Jacobsen, *Dokumente zur Vorgeschichte des Westfeldzugs*, (hereafter referred to as *Dokumente*) p. 4 *et seq.*

11. *IMT*, vol. XV p. 376. An excellent description of the reasons leading the C.-in-C. of the Army to adopt a defensive attitude is to be found in Tippelskirch, *Geschichte des Zweiten Weltkriegs*, p. 30. See also the following which differ somewhat from the C.-in-C.'s. description: (a) that of the Chief of Staff of the Army who describes the concept of the operation as something of an afterthought (see Bor above p. 149); (b) that of Field Marshal von Manstein (above) p. 83 *et seq.*

12. See Hubatsch, *Directives*, p. 13.

13. *IMT*, vol. XV, p. 371. The only exception to this was the 'special arrangements' for Denmark and Norway (see Part II, Chapter 3 of this book) but here again certain reservations must be made.

14. See Jodl's diary, 21 October 1939. The initial operation order appears in Jacobsen, *Dokumente*, pp. 41 *et seq.*

15. See Jodl's diary, 22 October 1939.

16. See Jacobsen, *Dokumente*, pp. 46 *et seq.* and Hubatsch, *Directives*, pp. 16 *et seq.* The proposals of the Services formed the basis for *Directive no. 7* (Hubatsch, *Direc-*

Notes

tives p. 14) issued by OKW on
18 October 1939. This laid down
the broad lines of the strategy
for the start of our offensive, or
in the event of attack by the
enemy ('Sofortfall' – Surprise
Attack). It was completed by an
addendum dated 15 November
under reference *OKW/WF Stab
20/39 g. Kdos* (Hubatsch, *Weisungen*, p. 36).

17. See Jacobsen, *Dokumente*, pp. 59
and 64 *et seq.*, also comments in
Hubatsch, *Directives*, p. 21.

18. See Note 2 and Jodl's diary 1
February 1940 (recording
Schmundt's return from the
West but with no mention of
his conversation with Manstein);
13 Feb. 1940 ('I draw attention
to the fact that the thrust via
Sedan is a deep dark path on
which the God of War may lie in
wait for us') 17 Feb, 1940: otherwise unimportant notes on Manstein's presentation to Hitler on
that day. See also p. 62 below.

19. See the general account in
Jacobsen, *Fall Gelb*, p. 141.

20. See Hitler's order of 17 January
1940 which has not been published. Also Jodl's diary 30
March 1940: 'the Führer is
busying himself with the constitution of new formations. L II
(Section L, Organization Working Group) has been ordered to
carry out a survey of resources,
personnel and equipment, to
see whether and when new units
can be formed'.

21. Extracts from OKW's 'Special
Instructions' for this eventuality
are given in Hubatsch, *Die
deutsche Besetzung von Dänemark
und Norwegen* (hereafter referred
to as Hubatsch, *Norwegen*) pp. 443
et seq.

22. See *Directive no. 9 – Instructions for
warfare against the Economy of the
enemy*, dated 29 November 1939,
reproduced in Hubatsch, *Directives*, pp. 18 *et seq.* and its addendum dated 26 May 1940 (*Weisungen*, p. 44).

23. This emerges clearly from
Arthur Bryant, *Triumph in the
West*.

24. See Jodl's diary 22 November
1939 where the last few lines
refer to a conversation between
Jodl and the Naval C.-in-C.s.
staff officers, while the C.-in-C.
was alone with Hitler; the subject was the shipping requirement for a landing. Also on 1
December 1939: 'Army Staff
Study arrives ... landing in England'. See also Greiner (above)
p. 111; this shows that Jodl
attended only Raeder's June
presentation, not that of May
1940.

25. See Halder's diary 27 March
1940. Hitler reckoned that, if
asked to get themselves ready
at the time the German offensive
opened, the Italians would require six weeks before they
could attack on the Upper
Rhine, always provided that a
large-scale German victory was
in prospect.

26. Also Jodl's diary 20 May 1940.
Apparently it was only on this
date that the Army Staff was
told by Hitler 'not to pursue the
original idea further'. See also
Halder's diary of 21 May.

27. This is the only possible explanation of Hitler's observations
noted in Halder's diary of 24
April 1940, which in any case
may have been no more than
passing remarks: 'the Dardanelles and Bosphorus should be

closed by the Luftwaffe working from a base at Brindisi'. The same is true for a parallel remark: 'he is thinking about surprise attacks on Crete and also on English ships in Gibraltar'.

28. See Jodl's *Gauleiter* speech of 7 November 1943, already referred to (see also Jacobsen, *Chronik*, p. 436). He told his audience that 'Hitler has always kept an eye on this threat; even while the campaign in the west was still in progress, he told me that as soon as the military situation allowed he was determined to put an end to this danger'. I was only put in the picture by Jodl on 29 July 1940, when Hitler's mind was already made up.

29. From Manstein (above) p. 73.

30. See Görlitz, *Keitel*, p. 149.

31. See pp. 51–52 of this book and Jodl's diary of 11 November 1939 concerning the employment of Guderian's Corps. See also Halder's diary 1 January 1940: 'conversation with Keitel of OKW. (1) Reasons for tensions. Discontent over praise of Fritsch (*by the C.-in-C.*). Lack of confidence at the top in everything including the Navy and the Four-Year Plan. (*This must have been a comment of Keitel's while he was trying to argue his way out of his difficulties with the Army.*) (2) Pointed out difficulties of conducting a battle. Interference with the Commander very dangerous. (*This certainly from Halder who called a spade a spade.*) Assurance from Keitel that there was no intention of interfering.' (Comments in brackets by the author.)

32. Jodl's diary 15 October 1939.

33. See the account in Greiner (above) pp. 66–68. This is based partly on what Keitel told me, partly on what I heard myself. See also Heusinger, pp. 72 *et seq.* and Jacobsen, *Fall Gelb*, pp. 44 *et seq.*

34. See Jacobsen's detailed report based on eyewitness accounts in *Fall Gelb*, pp. 44 *et seq.*

35. See Erfurth, *Geschichte des deutschen Generalstabs*, pp. 282–3 and 298–9.

36. See Jodl's diary 28 January–3 February 1938.

37. I was present on both occasions, once after Hitler's speech in the Berghof on 22 August 1939, the second time at a briefing in the Reich Chancellery towards the end of October 1939.

38. I heard this myself.

39. See Jodl's diary for these dates.

40. *Führer Conferences on Naval Affairs* (hereafter referred to as '*Naval Affairs*').

41. See Jodl's diary 31 October 1939: 'C.-in-C. Air is worried lest there should be no occupation of Holland. Sent Jeschonnek to see the Führer evening 30 October'. Further, on 5 January 1940: 'present ideas differ radically from the decisions given by the Führer to C.-in-C. Navy on 30 December'.

42. See Jodl's diary 4 December 1939.

43. Halder's diary of 23 November 1939 records Hitler as expressing displeasure at the reluctance of the Army, and particularly the General Staff, to trust him and follow his lead.

44. See Jodl's diary 26 October 1939, 17 January and 13 February 1940, and Halder's diary 9 November 1939.

45. See Jodl's diary 15 October 1939 and 3 January 1940, Halder's diary 1 January 1940.
46. See Jodl's diary 9, 10 and 11 November 1939.
47. See Jodl's diary 17 February 1940.
48. See Jodl's diary 4 March: 'if it is true that Colonel-General Rundstedt is sick, he should be replaced by List'.
49. See Jodl's diary 26 October 1939. This shows that in spite of considerable pressure, the Luftwaffe steadfastly refused to give OKW information on the numbers of transport aircraft available.
50. See *Naval Affairs*, 26 January, and Halder's diary 20 January 1940.
51. See Jodl's diary 19 March 1940. To judge from his comments he was entirely in accord with Hitler's change of mind.
52. See Jodl's diary 15 March 1940.
53. See the comments on this period in the book by Count Ciano, the Italian Foreign Minister, *L'Europa verso la Catastrofe* (hereafter referred to as '*Catastrofe*').
54. See Jodl's diary 22 March 1940; for the operation across the Rhine see p. 55 of this book. As far as is known the Italian General Staff never took these plans of Hitler's very seriously.
55. Both memoranda are reproduced in the Italian Official History, *In Africa Settentrionale, La Preparazione al Conflitto*.
56. See Greiner, *Aufzeichnungen zum Kriegstagebuch OKW/WF Stab Abt L.* 28 January 1941 (hereafter referred to as Section L *War Diary*).
57. See his book *Mussolini als Bundesgenosse*.

PART II · CHAPTER 3

1. This is also the title of the comprehensive and very well documented book on the subject by Professor Hubatsch already referred to.
2. See *Naval Affairs* and Jodl's diary both of this date; also *Naval Affairs* of 10 October and 8 December 1939 which show that Raeder had previously alluded to this question but that Hitler had taken no notice; also Raeder *Struggle for the Sea*, pp. 157–72.
3. This memorandum and its annexes are given *in extenso* in Hubatsch, *Norwegen*, p. 15.
4. Jodl's diary of 12 December 1939. (Punctuation not in the original has been added by the author to make the passage intelligible.)
5. Churchill, *Second World War*, vol. I p. 432.
6. Diary of 10 and 12 March 1940, the date on which peace was concluded. The assumption that the Allies were equally embarrassed is entirely correct (see Hubatsch, *Norwegen*, pp. 177 *et seq.*).
7. As far as I have been able to discover, this appreciation has not been preserved.
8. See Jodl's diary 13 and 14 March 1940. This also contains the significant remark: 'misleading reports in the American press'. The explanations given by Jodl to the International Military Tribunal are in vol. XV pp. 377–8.
9. From Rosenberg's private diary of 9 April 1940 – see Hubatsch, *Norwegen*, p. 454.
10. See *Hitler's Table Talk*, p. 438–9. Hitler's comments in April 1942 greatly overestimate the im-

portance of Norway compared to bases on the Atlantic and Channel coasts.

11. See: (a) Hubatsch, *Norwegen*, pp. 40 and 41. After exhaustive research he says: 'the Naval Staff hung on to the last moment before agreeing that nothing other than force was possible. Many studies and conferences had reached different conclusions but they remained convinced that maintenance of Norwegian neutrality was in the best interests of Germany'. (b) *Naval Affairs*, 23 February 1940; also Raeder's remark to Hitler after the *Altmark* incident on 16 February: 'maintenance of Norwegian neutrality is the best solution both for continuance of the iron-ore traffic (from Narvik) and from the overall point of view'. (c) Jodl's diary 14 March 1940: 'C.-in-C., Navy is still doubtful whether this is the moment to play the card of preventive action in Norway'. To complete the picture however, it should be added that on 26 March 1940 Raeder again urged that the operation be carried out saying that it would have to be done sooner or later. (*Naval Affairs*, 26 March.)

12. Jodl's diary 21 and 28 March 1940.

13. Jodl's diary 13, 18 and 19 December 1939. Note that there is no further mention of calling in Quisling as Hitler had originally intended; this never in fact occurred. There is also no allusion to a possible Norwegian appeal for assistance as grounds for German intervention.

14. See: (a) Halder's diary 1 January 1940: 'OKW Memorandum.

Führer has held up Jodl's memo. Dep. C of S(I), get hold of it'. (b) Halder's diary 10 January: 'memo on Norway. Working Staff in OKW'. (c) OKM *War Diary* 13 January 1940 reproduced in Hubatsch, *Norwegen*, pp. 404 *et seq.* (d) Jodl's diary 23 January 1940: 'to be worked up entirely within OKW'.

15. OKW/Ops. Staff Order of 25 January 1940. See also Jodl's diary of 26 January on 'Presentation by Göring and General Jeschonnek', as usual giving no further details. The explanation probably is that the original order was not issued till 27 January although dated 25 January. (Photostat copy shows that the date was altered subsequently.)

16. Jodl's diary 5 February 1940 (he actually says 'still isn't there').

17. Jodl's diary 19 February 1940.

18. Halder's diary 20 February 1940.

19. Jodl's diary 20 and 21 February; Halder's diary 21 February 1940.

20. Halder's diary 21 February 1940.

21. See US Official History *Supreme Command* pp. 53–55.

22. Jodl's diary 29 February 1940; for the original wording of the directive see Hubatsch, *Weisungen*, p. 49.

23. According to Jodl's diary of this date Halder was apparently satisfied with information he had got from some source or other (? the aides); he notes in his diary: 2 April: 'the Army will shortly be taking over Exercise Weser' ... *3 April*: 'C.-in-C. Army is to take over Denmark on D plus 3 (three days after occupation)'. This did in fact happen – on 12 April.

24. One of the most grotesque consequences is shown by the comment in Halder's diary of 19 April 1940 quoted here merely as an example: 'Falkenhorst has not a single aircraft of his own. He has been referred to Fassberg, Lüneburger Heide'.

25. Halder's diary 5 March 1940

26. See Jodl's diary 28 March 1940: 'The Führer comes into the map room in the evening to protest vigorously that he will not have the Navy sugaring off (*sic*) straight away from the Norwegian ports. Narvik, Trondheim and Oslo must continue to be occupied by naval forces or a bad impression will be made on the Army ... *29 March*: The Führer has a conversation with him (*Raeder*) alone about maintaining ships in the ports. The Grand Admiral refuses to do so in Narvik. He will see whether Trondheim can be organized as a base forthwith ... *2 April*: Objections from C.-in-C. Air that the Navy is putting to sea again. The Führer doesn't like it either but is unwilling to interfere too much in what are purely naval matters.'

27. The C.-in-C. of the Fleet had been ordered not to engage British naval forces in the area during his withdrawal from the North Sea.

28. The Chief of Staff of the Army evidently pocketed his pride on this occasion in the hope of getting a reasonable strategy adopted.

29. This appreciation was initiated by the senior Army officer in Section L, Lt.-Colonel von Lossberg, and he drafted most of it.

30. Jodl's appeal for support to the C.-in-C. of the Army shows that he was not convinced that Hitler would necessarily abide by the order he had already issued; in any case it left many aspects of the problem still undecided. Regarding Hitler's behaviour during this period see the graphic description in Ansel, *Hitler confronts England* (hereafter referred to as 'Ansel'), pp. 60–61.

31. Once these land communications were secured the occupation forces in Southern and Central Norway were mutually supporting.

32. Gerhard Ritter, *Staatskunst und Kriegshandwerk*, vol. I, p. 245.

PART III · CHAPTER I

1. From Jodl's diary 2 May 1940.

2. See Jodl's diary 28 February and 3 March 1940.

3. See Jodl's diary 7–9 May 1940.

4. *IMT*, vol. XV, pp. 295 and 300.

5. From Görlitz, *Keitel*, pp. 233 and 234. See also Hubatsch, *Weisungen* p. 53 which quotes from the War Diary of Army Group A some of the 'Führer's desires'; these were given to Army Group A in a manuscript note from Keitel – obviously by-passing OKH.

6. For an example see p. 95 of this book.

7. See Jodl's diary 24 May: 'new crisis of confidence (between Hitler and the Army); the Reichsmarschall reported that OKH had issued an order to Army Group B which was not in line' (with Hitler's requirements). (Words in brackets added by the author.)

8. See Halder's diary 11 and 12 June 1940.

PART III · CHAPTER 2

1. From Ellis, *The War in France and Flanders*, p. 63, HMSO, 1953.
2. See Jodl's diary 18 May. This 'supplementary order' was a sequel to *Directive no. 22* which was given to the Army leaders at this meeting but apparently is not to be found (see also Hubatsch, *Directives*, p. 26).
3. See Halder's diary 18 May 1940. Even on this occasion Hitler did not gnaw the carpet for the very good reason that there was no carpet.
4. Halder's diary 19 May, Jodl's diary 20 and 21 May 1940. The entry in Jodl's diary of 20 May closes with the words: 'there is a special note in the file by the Chief of OKW about Hitler's excitement when told over the telephone by the C.-in-C. of the Army that Abbeville had been captured' (this note has so far not been found).
5. Halder's diary 25 and 26 May 1940.
6. This account is from Ansel pp. 73 *et seq.* and is the result of exhaustive conversations and correspondence with former senior officers of the Luftwaffe.
7. See also Lossberg's account of this interview.
8. This is the substance of a letter I had in the spring of 1949 from the late Field Marshal von Rundstedt as soon as the story appeared that it was he and not Hitler who gave the order to halt before Dunkirk. Churchill and others are supposed to have got this from the Army Group A War Diary. Since historical research has produced differing conclusions, it should be noted

that Heusinger's account (pp. 89–93) is similar. See also p. 189 of this book.
9. See p. 55 of this book. Halder's diary of 21 May 1940 notes at this point the following significant remark by Keitel: 'we'll let them come to us'. See also Görlitz, *Keitel*, p. 235.
10. From Ciano's diary 2 June, and his *Catastrofe*.
11. Halder's diary of 1 June. Author's italics.
12. Badoglio also wrote to Mussolini on 1 June suggesting that war should not be declared before the end of June at the earliest. (*Preparazione*, pp. 80 and 190/191.) See also Halder's diary 13 June: 'Visit from Italian MA. He seemed pretty unconcerned.'
13. Halder's diary 5 and 6 June 1940. Author's italics.
14. Manstein (referred to above) p. 276.
15. Manstein p. 134.
16. The armistice agreement was actually signed on 22 June.

PART III · CHAPTER 3

1. OKW Order dated 14 June 1940 based on statements by Hitler on 7 June 'concerning future manpower and equipment plans'.
2. See Section L Conference Records 14 August and 11 October 1940; Section L War Diary 8 October 1940.
3. See Klee, *Das Unternehmen Seelöwe*, (hereafter referred to as 'Klee') pp. 60 and 61. This gives an indication of the dates concerned, stating that on 25 June the senior Air Force Staff officer of Section L wrote to the Chief of Staff of the Luftwaffe to inform him that Section L proposed

shortly to submit to Hitler an outline plan 'for a crossing of the Channel'. Ansel pp. 115 and 116 cites a number of witnesses to this.

4. See p. 55 of this book. Greiner (p. 111) bases his statement on information provided after the war by the Chief of the Naval Historical Section. He makes it clear that he, and therefore also his immediate superior (myself), knew nothing of these events at the time. See also Klee, pp. 57 and 58 and Ansel, pp. 81 and 103. According to Klee (p. 61 and Note 182) OKL was aware of Hitler's refusal.

5. Ciano's diary 18–19 June 1940 p. 267.

6. See Klee, p. 60, Ansel p. 105.

7. Document 1776–PS *IMT* vol. XXVIII pp. 301–3. Regarding Russia see also Part II, Chap. 2, Note 28.

8. These orders are reproduced in Jacobsen, *Chronik*, pp. 149, 151 and 163; see also Hubatsch, *Directives*, pp. 34 and 37.

9. From Ciano, *Catastrofe*.

10. An expression used by Ansel to describe the officers of Section L. For a foreign observer it shows a remarkably clear understanding of relations within German Supreme Headquarters.

11. There is detailed proof of this in the descriptions of the subsequent course of events in Section L War Diary, Klee and Ansel.

12. There are numerous notes in the records of Section L Conferences of this period regarding last minute postponements due to the bad weather which continued for some time.

13. See Section L War Diary 23 and 25 September 1940, also Ansel,

pp. 190 and 191, and Klee, p. 159; the latter gives the date of the first order from C.-in-C. Air on Operation Sea Lion as 27 August 1940.

14. From Klee, p. 39–43 (quotations from p. 43 – author's italics).

15. Section L War Diary 9 August and Halder's diary 30 and 31 July 1940.

16. Reference of this document is OKW/WF Stab/Abt L(I) g. Kdos Chefs dated 12 August 1940. (Author's italics.) See also the relevant comment in Records of Section L Conferences 24 September 1940: 'our strategy seems lately to have become dominated by consideration for the susceptibilities of the Reichsmarschall and the Italians'.

17. Reference of this document Chef WF Stab g Kdos. Chefs of 13 August 1940; plans for the capture of Gibraltar were initiated in July 1940.

18. Section L War Diary 5 September, 29 October, 1 and 4 November, also Section L Conferences 29 October and 15 November 1940.

19. A few days later, on 1 August 1940, I was in fact given accelerated promotion to Major General, together with a number of officers of my own seniority.

20. Besides myself there were Lt.-Colonel von Lossberg, Captain Junge (Navy) and Major Freiherr von Falkenstein (Air Force).

21. At the beginning of my imprisonment in May 1945 I had given these facts to certain American authorities as presumably of historical interest. It never crossed my mind that they could be made the basis of an accusation of a 'crime

against peace'. I would like to register here my regret at having thus contributed to the evidence for the prosecution against my superior officers. To complete the picture – in April 1962 the competent UN authorities were unable to agree upon a definition of 'aggression'. The USA, in spite of all her previous efforts, refused to take part in the debate saying that it was 'a useless and expensive waste of time'. The Soviet representative unilaterally cited as examples 'Suez, Bizerta, Cuba and the Congo'.

22. Ansel, pp. 175–6. See also pp. 55–56 of this book.

23. According to Halder's diary this discussion between Hitler and Brauchitsch went into details such as the time required for the move forward, strength of forces required, estimate of Russian strength, etc. (See also Klee, pp. 191–3.)

24. According to Jodl's statement to us Hitler had already made his decision to attack Russia before the date of this entry.

25. Raeder had left the Berghof on 31 July just before the new plans had been announced; see Halder's diary 31 July 1940: 'Raeder leaves'.

26. See also Ansel, pp. 180–1.

27. See Hubatsch, *Directives*, pp. 39 *et seq.* Also Section L War Diary extracts 4, 5 and 6 November. Also Records of Section L Conferences 13 November 940: 'Head of Section L is unhappy about the changes to Directive no. 18 ordered by the Chief of the Operations Staff regarding Operation Sea Lion'. See Klee, pp. 216 and 217 and Hitler's remarks on 9 January 1941 to the heads of the three Services: 'a landing in England would only be possible if complete air superiority had been achieved and England was therefore partially paralysed. Otherwise it would be a crime'.

28. See Section L War Diary 9 and 20 January 1941.

29. Section L War Diary 6 December 1940. See also Note 30 below.

30. See Section L War Diary 7, 9 and 14 August: 'Chief of Operations Staff reports that as a result of the staff study of operations against Gibraltar submitted by Section L on 8 August the Führer has decided on the major operation (Capture of Gibraltar)'. Note also further pressure exerted by Chief of Section L recorded in Section L Conference 14 November 1940, para. 2 of the addendum to *Directive no. 18* of 27 November 1940 and the draft of *Directive no. 19* ('Felix') in Hubatsch, *Weisungen*, pp. 72 and 74.

31. See Section L War Diary 7, 9, 21, 30 August, 5, 11, 20 September and 2 November, also Section L Conference Records 2 November.

32. See *Naval Affairs* 26 September and 27 December and Section L War Diary 2 September 1940.

33. See Section L War Diary 1 November 1940. A few days later, on 12 November, the Italian battle fleet suffered a crippling blow, losing three capital ships by aerial torpedo attack in Taranto harbour.

34. See Halder's diary 23 and 26 September and Section L War Diary 25 September 1940.

35. See Section L War Diary 1

October (author's italics) and
Section L conferences 30 September and 29 October 1940.
36. This phrase appears in Halder's
diary as early as 27 September.
37. See Ciano, *Catastrofe*, and Section L War Diary 1 and 4
November 1940; Ribbentrop
told Ciano that he 'would
probably shortly be meeting
Laval and proposed to bring
him right down to earth'.
38. Section L War Diary 28 October.
39. Section L Conference 2 November 1940.
40. Section L War Diary 1, 4 and 6
November (the quotation is from
the latter date) also Section L
Conferences 4 and 27 November
1940.
41. See Section L War Diary 1–4, 6,
7, 8, 11, 12, 20 December. Section L Conferences 2 and 4 December and Halder's diary of 8
December 1940. The latter shows
that the Army Chief of Staff proposed that immediate preparations should be made for occupation of the whole of France and
that he was primarily influenced
by Franco's refusal to co-operate
in an attack on Gibraltar. The
relevant *Directive no. 19—Operation Attila* is reproduced in
Hubatsch, *Directives*, pp. 44 *et seq.*
See also General Weygand's
memoirs which give an obviously secondhand, and in places
very inaccurate, account of the
Franco-German meetings in
Paris.
42. Weygand, *Rappelé au Service*, vol.
3, pp. 464 and 477–8.
43. Regarding my own efforts see
Section L Conference 10 January 1941: 'The view of the
Head of Section L is that the
Italian reverses should lead to

increased military co-operation
with France. The Berghof however seems to want to pigeon-
hole any further consideration
of policy towards France.'
44. See Section L Conferences 19
and 29 May; as regards the contents of the treaties see Halder's
diary 27 May 1941 under the
heading *Negotiations with Darlan.*
45. From Weygand's *Memoirs*, pp.
428–37, also 423–7. See also p.
122 of this book.
46. See Section L War Diary 6, 8
and 10 December; also Hubatsch,
Weisungen, p. 78 and Section L
Conference 10 January 1941;
this shows that Section L had no
part in these comings and goings
and that the Chief of Section L
and C.-in-C. Navy expressed
the view that the plan should be
pursued.
47. Section L War Diary 13 November 1940.
48. *Naval Affairs*, 27 December 1940.
49. The OKW order of 10 December 1940 initially visualized only
units 'approximately equivalent to a group' but in the
same month they were followed
by the complete corps at a
strength of about 180 fighter and
ground attack aircraft. (See also
Section L Conference 27 Nov.
1940.)
50. For the final phases of these
negotiations see relevant entries
in Section L War Diary 5 December 1940, 9 January and 3
February 1941, Halder's diary
5 December 1940, 16 January
and 3 February 1941, *Directive
no. 22* dated 11 January 1941
(Hubatsch, *Directives*, p. 53) and
the Annexes which followed a
few weeks later (Hubatsch, *Weisungen*, pp. 95–100.)

51. See OKW *Directive no. 18* dated 12 November 1940 and Section L War Diary of 10 February 1941 which gives a detailed description of the military negotiations conducted by me with representatives of the Bulgarian General Staff. See also OKW *Directive no. 26* dated 3 April 1941 (Hubatsch, *Directives* p. 63) in which Hitler's principles for dealing with allies are put very clearly. Those quoted in the text appear in Section L War Diary of 4 March 1941.

52. A good example occurred on 27 March 1941 when Hitler, without the slightest warning, insisted that Yugo-Slavia be included in the plan for the Balkans (see Jacobsen, *Chronik*, p. 226). OKH immediately produced detailed proposals (see Heusinger's account p. 112 *et seq.*). The usual procedure was then followed by the OKW Operations Staff and a directive (no. 25) was issued the same day giving Hitler's orders. (see Hubatsch, *Directives*, p. 61 and Section L Conference 27 March 1941).

53. See British Official Naval History by Roskill *The War at Sea*, vol. I, p. 515 and Langer & Gleason, *The Undeclared War*, p. 415.

54. See OKW *Directive no. 27* dated 13 April (Hubatsch, *Directives*, p. 65).

55. See also: Section L War Diary 3 February 1941 where Hitler comments upon the close connection between 'our victories in North Africa and events in the Balkans'. Halder's diary 17 March 1941: '*Hitler*: the Balkan operation must carry on until

we have gained a firm base for air superiority in the eastern Mediterranean'. Halder's diary of 24 January 1941 shows that there were similar thoughts current in OKH: 'proposal to the Führer that early action in the Balkans would relieve the situation in North Africa,' and on 24 April 1941: 'early capture of Crete would be of the greatest assistance to Rommel'.

OKM still laid great stress on gaining superiority in the Mediterranean but was not prepared to allocate forces for this purpose owing to the necessity of keeping their submarines concentrated.

56. For further details see pp. 131–132 of this book.

57. For details see Section L Conferences 21–23 April, Halder's indignant comments in his diary of 21 and 23 April and Heusinger pp. 116 *et seq.*

58. See OKW *Directive no. 28—Operation Mercury* dated 25 April 1941 and reproduced in Hubatsch, *Directives*, p. 68.

59. According to Section L War Diary the 'reduction' of Malta was initially proposed as the most urgent task for X Air Corps by the Chief of Staff of the Luftwaffe during a conference with Hitler on 3 February 1941. Section L thereupon examined the possibilities of capturing the island (Section L War Diary 6 and 8 February 1941) and concluded that prospects were good. They were vigorously supported by the Navy. The proposal came to nothing because Göring was against it. (Most of this can be proved but parts are from my own memory which is quite clear.)

60. See OKW Instruction dated 7 May which was followed by a Directive on the Middle East (no. 30) reproduced in Hubatsch, *Directives*, p. 72. See also Section L Conferences 4, 7, 21, 28, 31 May and 3 June 1941. The record on 28 May notes 'of the 15 HE 111 which have arrived in Iraq only one is serviceable'.

61. See Section L Conferences 5, 9, 10, 11 and 19–23 June and 'Instructions for the Felmy Special Staff' (Hubatsch, *Weisungen*, p. 134) which show what we had learnt from these affairs.

62. The fact that this directive was in draft form is confirmed in Klee's *Quellenkritische Untersuchung* which is specially written for this purpose. The draft and the subsequent second version of it are reproduced in Hubatsch, *Weisungen*, pp. 129 *et seq*. The final version of the Directive is in Hubatsch, *Directives*, pp. 78 *et seq*.

63. See Section L War Diary 17 February 1941.

64. From an OKW Order to the 'German Afrika Korps' (Rommel) dated 3 April 1941; see also Halder's diary 14 and 15 May 1941.

65. See Ciano, *Catastrofe*.

66. See Section L Conference 4 June 1941.

67. See *Naval Affairs* 6 June 1941.

68. See British Official History (Playfair) vol. II, pp. 248 *et seq*.

69. Section L Conference 4 June 1941.

PART III · CHAPTER 4

1. This study was the work primarily of Colonel von Lossberg and was based upon preparatory work done by the Army General Staff. As far as I can remember it was only submitted to Jodl some time after the middle of November 1940. The records of Section L Conferences mention this paper as having been presented on 19 September. This seems highly improbable since at that time all the high-level staffs of the Wehrmacht were primarily occupied with Operation Sea Lion. If this is in fact an error the reason for it probably is that, as far as I remember, the War Diary officer was only told about plans for the eastern campaign considerably later and therefore probably made the entry subsequently, making a mistake in the date.

2. Published in de Mendelssohn, *The Nuremberg Documents*, pp. 254–5.

3. Section L War Diary 14 November and Section L Conference 15 November 1940.

4. It is doubtful whether this paragraph in the directive (no. 5) originated in OKW or OKH. Molotov, the Soviet Foreign Minister, arrived in Berlin the next day.

5. Field Marshal Paulus was produced by the Russians as a witness for the prosecution at Nuremberg. He had been specially detailed by the Chief of Staff of the Army in the summer of 1940 to take charge of preparations for the Russian campaign. See *IMT* vol. XV p. 518, also 370.

6. See Halder's diary and Section L War Diary both of 5 December 1940.

7. See Section L War Diary 12 and 16 December and Section L

Conference 14 December 1940; on the fuel question see Greiner, pp. 337–8; see also Section L War Diary 8 March 1941 and the internal memorandum submitted to Jodl immediately thereafter which stated: 'the extremely serious situation in this respect may well have a considerable adverse effect on operations'.

8. See OKW *Directive no. 21— Operation Barbarossa*, Section III A, paras 1–3 (Hubatsch, *Directives*, p. 50). de Mendelssohn (German edition), pp. 317–18 reproduces a 'minute' which shows that on 17 December, Hitler produced the idea of diverting considerable forces from the centre to the south also. He is also said to have stated that 'we must deal with all problems on the continent of Europe during the course of 1941, since from 1942 onwards the US will be in a position to intervene'.

9. Section L War Diary 9 January 1941.

10. The code name 'Barbarossa' (Red Beard) is said to have been selected by Hitler himself. He wished to underline the historical parallel with a 'crusade' and by the word 'Red' to indicate that it was directed against Bolshevism. See Section L War Diary 17 and 18 December 1940.

11. Halder never mentions this in his diary.

12. See Section L War Diary 9 January, 3 February and 18 March, Halder's diary 16 January, 3 February and 17 March, de Mendelssohn, pp. 269–70 and published records of the meeting of 3 February 1941.

13. In so far as Section L War Diary is based upon this source, the scarcity and inaccuracy of the information made available must be remembered before judgment is passed on the value of the War Diary.

14. Section L War Diary 18 January 1941. The rest is from my own memory which is quite clear on this subject.

15. Section L War Diary 9 January 1941.

16. See OKW *Directive no. 23* dated 6 February – *Directions for operations against the English war economy*, (Hubatsch, *Directives*, p. 56). The instructions on deception of 15 February 1941 have not so far been published.

17. See Section L War Diary 18 March and the wording of the 'Cover Note' to the Barbarossa Directive given in Greiner, pp. 366–7; also Halder's diary 17 March 1941.

18. Section L War Diary 18 March (end).

19. Halder's diary of 17 March 1941 gives an example of Hitler's self-contradictory estimates of the value of non-German forces. On 25 June he notes: 'we were told of the letter of 21 June sent by the Führer to the Duce just before the start of Barbarossa. It contains a series of disconnected ideas of which the following is a remarkable example: "justification of the attack on Russia by using the Russian situation map"'. The OKW Directive of 17 June 1941 produced a long list of 'requirements' for Sweden which the Foreign Ministry was to forward to the Swedish Government. See also: (a) Barbarossa Directive of 18 December 1940 Section II and Section

L War Diary 4 February; (b) Section L War Diary 8 and 13 March; Section L Conference 11 March and Halder's diary 4 May 1941; (c) OKW Instructions of 1 May 1941 reproduced in Hubatsch, *Weisungen*, pp. 91–92.

20. Section L Conference 28 May and Halder's diary 26 May 1941.

21. Section L War Diary 5 June 1941; Antonescu had previously been briefed on Hitler's instructions by the 'C.-in-C. German Troops in Rumania'; the written brief was prepared by Section L on 23 May 1941 but has so far not been published.

22. See references in Section L Conferences of 3 June (to Hungary) 5 June (to Finland, Sweden and Hungary) and 6 June (to Slovakia).

23. I heard this myself.

24. See Section L War Diary 29 January, 6 and 17 February, 6 March 1941; see also Greiner pp. 373–82 for a graphic and detailed description; the directive is reproduced in Hubatsch, *Directives*, p. 58.

25. See: (a) Section L War Diary 8 March and Section L Conference 16 June; (b) Hitler's instructions at the close of his 'appeal' on 30 March (see pp. 160–1 of this book) given in Greiner, pp. 371–73; (c) Section L Conference 16 June; (d) 'Points exercising the Führer' in Halder's diary 20 June 1941.

26. From Halder's diary 14 June and the instructions of 9 June 1941 from 'Hitler's Military Aides'; See also Heusinger, pp. 120–3.

The following is the list of those present:

I. Morning and afternoon.

1. Army:
   Field Marshal von Brauchitsch
   Colonel-General Halder
   Lieut-General Paulus (Deputy Chief of Staff I)
   Colonel Heusinger (Chief Operations Section)
   Lieut-Colonel von Gyldenfeldt (Aide to Commander-in-Chief)

2. Navy:
   Captain Wagner (Chief Operations Section)

3. Luftwaffe:
   Reichsmarschall Göring
   Field Marshal Milch
   General Jeschonnek (Chief of Staff)
   General Bodenschatz (Minister's Private Secretary and Liaison Officer)
   Major-General von Waldau (Chief Operations Section)

4. OKW:
   Field Marshal Keitel
   General Jodl
   Major General Warlimont
   Major Christian (Aide to Chief OKW Operations Staff)

5. Personal Office:
   Colonel Schmundt
   Captain von Puttkamer (Navy)
   Major Engel (Army)
   Major von Below (Luftwaffe)

II. Morning.

1. Silver Fox (Code name for North Finland Operation).
   Army:
   Colonel-General von Falkenhorst (Army HQ Norway)
   Luftwaffe:
   Colonel-General Stumpff (5 Air Fleet)

2. Group 'South'
   Army:
   Field Marshal von Rundstedt (Army Group South)
   Field Marshal von Reichenau (Sixth Army)
   General von Stülpnagel (Seventeenth Army)

Colonel-General von Schobert
(Eleventh Army)
Colonel-General von Kleist
(1 Armoured Group)
Luftwaffe:
Colonel-General Löhr (4 Air
Fleet)

III. Lunch for all concerned, to
which were invited in addition:
Army:
Colonel-General Fromm (C.-
in-C. Replacement Army)
Luftwaffe:
Colonel-General Udet (Chief,
Equipment Dept, Luftwaffe)

IV. Afternoon.
1. Navy:
Grand Admiral Raeder
Vice Admiral Fricke (Chief of
Staff)
Captain Schulte-Mönting
(Aide to C.-in-C.)
2. Baltic:
Admiral Karls (Maritime
Group North)
Vice Admiral Schmundt (C.-
in-C. Baltic)
3. Group 'North'
Army:
Field Marshal Ritter von Leeb
(Army Group North)
Colonel-General Busch (Six-
teenth Army)
Colonel-General von Küchler
(Eighteenth Army)
Colonel-General Hoeppner (4
Armoured Group)
Luftwaffe:
Colonel-General Keller (1 Air
Fleet)
4. Group Centre
Army:
Field Marshal von Bock (Army
Group Centre)
Field Marshal von Kluge
(Fourth Army)
Colonel-General Strauss
(Ninth Army)
Colonel-General Guderian (2
Armoured Group)
Colonel-General Hoth (3 Ar-
moured Group)

Luftwaffe:
Field Marshal Kesselring (2
Air Fleet)

27. See Section L War Diary 8
March ('rough draft in 8–10
days'), and Section L Conference 6 June 1941 (second draft
approved by Hitler). The final
version of the timetable seems to
have been retained among the
Nuremberg documents. Its contents appear partially in de
Mendelssohn (p. 279) from
which the following is quoted
with all reserve: 'From 18 June
the intention to attack need no
longer be camouflaged. 21 June
1300 hrs—latest time at which
operation can still be cancelled.
H Hour (for start of the invasion)
22 June 0330 hrs' (Halder's
diary of 14 June states that this
was brought forward to 0300).

28. See Section L Conferences 21
March and 21 June 1941.

29. From Section L Conference 19
June 1941; see also 18 June.
Some of these reports, particularly those from Admiral Canaris' services, were produced in
the same way. They have been
preserved but, so far as I know,
not published.

30. (a) Halder's diary for 1941 notes
the following:

7 April
Morning reports. Russian dispositions give food for thought. The
catch-phrase is that the Russians
want peace and will never initiate
an attack. If one forgets this one
must admit that their present dispositions would enable them to
launch a surprise attack which
would be remarkably uncomfortable from our point of view.
26 April
Russia: No change in the general

situation since 1 April. An increase of ten Divisions in the west since that date. The peace strength of the army has been raised (now about 170 Divs.) and may be regarded as equivalent to war strength. Trainloads of equipment are moving up continuously – presumably to bring the army up to war strength. (He then adds much convincing detail.)

5 May
Colonel Krebs arrives back from Moscow where he has been filling in for Köstring (German MA). He found them most forthcoming. Russia will do all she can to avoid war. Apparently long-range bombers are being concentrated near the German frontier. Trainloads of fortification equipment are moving up to the frontier. No troop concentrations observed.

22 June
The overall picture of the first day of operations is this. The enemy was taken by surprise by our attack. He was not tactically disposed for defence. Troops in the frontier zone were dispersed in billets. There were only weak outposts along the frontier.

(b) Heusinger reports (p. 130) that on 25 July the Chief of the Intelligence Section (Foreign Armies East) stated: 'I incline to the view that the strength of these forces was raised first as a precaution against us but also with an eye on the possibility of attacking westwards.'

(c) The order of battle of the Red Army on 22 June 1841 as given in Wehrwissenschaftliche Rundschau 6/1961 was as follows:
Northern Front:
Commander-in-Chief
Lieut-General M. M. Popov
Chief of Staff
Major-General Nikishev
Fourteenth Army
Lieut-General W. A. Frolov

Seventh Army
Lieut-General F. D. Gorolenko
Twenty-third Army
Lieut-General P. S. Pshennikov
North-Western Front:
Commander-in-Chief
Colonel-General Fedor I. Kuznetsov
Chief of Staff
Major-General P. S. Klenov
Eighth Army
Major-General P. P. Sobennikov
Eleventh Army
Lieut-General W. I. Morozov
Twenty-seventh Army
Major-General N. E. Bersarin
Western Front:
Commander-in-Chief
General Dimitrij G. Pavlov
Chief of Staff
Major-General W. E. Klimovskich
Third Army
Lieut-General Vassili I. Kuznetsov
VI Cavalry Corps
Major-General Nikitin
XI Mobile Corps
Major-General Mostovenko
XIII Mobile Corps
Major-General Akhlyustin
Tenth Army
Major-General K. D. Golubev
VI Mobile Corps
Major-General Khazkelevich
Fourth Army
Major-General Korobkov
XIV Mobile Corps
Major-General Oborin
South Western Front:
Commander-in-Chief
Colonel-General M. P. Kirponos
Chief of Staff
Lieut-General M. A. Purkaeev
Fifth Army
Major-General Potopov
IX Mobile Corps
Major-General K. K. Rokossovsky
Sixth Army
Lieut-General I. N. Musychenko
IV Mobile Corps
Lieut-General A. A. Vlassov

Twenty-sixth Army
   Lieut-General F. J. Kostenko
Twelfth Army
   Major-General P. G. Ponedelin
V Mobile Corps
   Major-General Alekseenkov
Southern Front
(formed on 24 June):
   Commander-in-Chief
      General I. W. Tyulenev
Ninth Army
   Lieut-General Tcherevichenko
II Cavalry Corps
II Mobile Corps

Sources:

Jeremenko: Na zapadnom naprawlennije. Moscow, 1958
Platonov: Wtoraja mirowaja voina (1939–45). Moscow, 1958
Poppelj: Wtjazkuju poru. Moscow, 1959
Shilin: Die Wichtigsten Operationen des Grossen Vaterländischen Krieges 1941–5. Berlin, 1958

31. See Section L Conference 24 June 1941: 'the Führer has instructed that proposals by any State to take part in this crusade are to be welcomed with enthusiasm'.

32. Section L's first draft seems not to have been preserved, to judge from what follows. It dealt merely with the normal, essential military instructions. Hitler's instructions as passed on by Jodl are given here in full because they are essential for a full understanding of subsequent developments. They are taken from Section L War Diary of 3 March 1941.

33. There can be no doubt that these details were laid down by Hitler, not by Jodl. (Author's italics.)

34. According to Halder's diary

OKH had had the new draft for comment by 5 March.

35. See Halder's diary 13 and 14 March. On both days this part of Halder's notes is headed 'Wagner', the name of the then Army Quartermaster General, General Eduard Wagner, who was executed after 20 July 1944 as one of the leaders of the revolt against Hitler.

36. See also Halder's diary for 17 March: '15–20.30 hrs. Conference with the Führer (Colonel Heusinger present); 1–3. ... (operational questions); 4. Exposé by General Wagner on supply; 5. Rear areas. We have to create anti-Stalin republics. Stalin's secret service must be eliminated. The machinery of government of the Russian State must be destroyed. In the area of Greater Russia the most brutal methods must be employed. The ideological cadres have not got a firm grip on the Russian people. If the officials are liquidated the whole thing will fall to pieces. (Author's note: Section L War diary of 18 March makes no mention of Jodl having told me of this passage in Hitler's statement.)

37. See Halder's diary 25 March: 'Wagner (QMG)—Points to be discussed with Heydrich regarding questions at issue in the East'; see also Bor, p. 197.

38. This description is based on Halder's diary of 30 March and Greiner. pp. 370–1, in addition to my own memory. Quotations and the resulting orders are taken from Halder and Greiner.

39. *IMT*, vol. X p. 533.

40. See also Görlitz, *Keitel*, p. 259.

41. Nuremberg Document 1,471–

PS. Note that: (a) Abbreviations have been given in full since they are not readily intelligible; (b) The cover note from C.-in-C. Army to Chief OKW only included Section L in the address group because standing orders laid down that all 'Top Secret' communications addressed to Keitel in his capacity as Chief OKW were to be so routed; (c) The date 31 March is an error and must mean 30 March. There is nowhere any account of a special instruction from Hitler to C.-in-C. Army being issued on 31 March. The entry in Halder's diary concerning the draft order refers to 'Hitler's recent address to General Officers', ie that of 30 March.

42. The underlinings are in the original. I had an interview about this manuscript note with the American General Donovan who was Assistant Chief Prosecutor at the Nuremberg trial. At the conclusion of the interview he stated that he considered this proved that I was *opposed* to the issue of the Commissar Order. In his view this cleared me and should have implied that I ought not to have been put on trial.

43. This is substantiated by Lehmann's evidence during the 'OKW case', and by a comment (of no importance) on the original of the draft in his handwriting.

44. See Hitler's similar comment given in Jodl's notes of 3 March 1941 (p. 151, para. 2).

45. This so-called 'disciplinary order' was issued by C.-in-C. Army on 24 May 1941. It ends with an appeal to every officer in the Army to ensure that 'discipline, on which our victory depends, is maintained'. The primary purpose of the order was undoubtedly to counter any opposition to which Hitler's instructions on the treatment of hostile inhabitants might have given rise. In the general opinion of senior commanders, however, it gave them an excellent handle to avoid giving effect to the Commissar Order. This opinion is not invalidated by the fact that the 'disciplinary order' was issued before the Commissar Order. When the C.-in-C. submitted his draft (6 May), he was already aware that the Commissar Order was to be issued in writing.

46. Nuremberg Document 1471–PS (italics not in original).

47. This process of falsifying the reports was described in detail at the 'OKW Trial' in Nuremberg by certain commanders and by officers detailed to carry it out. The reports themselves were kept within Army channels and not submitted to OKW.

48. *IMT* vol. XV pp. 308–9.

49. See Section I para. 3 of the order as reproduced in Jacobsen, *Chronik*, pp. 572–3.

50. Jacobsen, *Chronik*, p. 571.

51. The Nuremberg Court in its verdict on the 'OKW Case' condemned me for having participated in the production of the Commissar Order and gave as grounds therefor that there was no evidence to show that I had contributed to reducing the severity of the order. In this case, as in so many others, the court could not properly evaluate the circumstances. Even so, how-

ever, it is difficult to understand why: (a) no mention was made in the grounds for the verdict of the evidence given from the witness box by the late General Müller, the then 'General Officer Specially Employed' to the effect that he was the author of the Army draft; (b) No notice was taken of my manuscript comment on the Army draft although, as already mentioned, the American assistant prosecutor in December 1945 considered that it justified complete acquittal; (c) Instead of the introductory words in my cover note of 12 May – 'OKH has submitted a draft' only a series of dots appears in the grounds for the verdict, thus leading to my being considered as the author of the Army draft, which I clearly was not; (d) Sections II and III of my cover note were omitted altogether, still less was any weight attached to them.

52. This covers all orders issued by the POW Service and the so-called 'Night and Fog Order'.

53. There are a number of reports of correspondence about the Commissar Order within OKH and between it and commanders in the field both before the campaign opened and during the initial period. There is no need to deal with this here since it never became known either to Supreme HQ or Section L. There are, however, certain references in Halder's diary for 1941:

17 August
General Müller (specially employed): Handling of Captured

Commissars (will in general be dealt with in the POW camps).
21 September
General von Thoma: Attitude of the troops to commissars (not to be shot).

Much of Halder's diary at this period is taken up with reports by the numerous other visitors to the front or to higher headquarters in the forward area, but there is no mention of the Commissar Order.

54. Nuremberg Document NOKW 200.

55. Nuremberg Document 1807–PS. As far as I can see, when recording this instruction the late General Scherff must have made a slip in referring to 'commanders' instead of 'officials'.

56. If any actual instructions on the subject were thought necessary they must have been issued verbally by OKH. (There is no mention of this in Halder's diary).

57. One of the Nuremberg documents shows that Admiral Canaris protested against this order. It gives the date of issue as 8 September 1941 and the issuing office as the 'General Armed Forces Office' (Allg. Wehrmachtamt) OKW. The order does not seem to have been preserved.

PART III · CHAPTER 5

1. Visits to Wolfschanze by the heads of offices and sections were usually the concern of the Chief of OKW; he also made regular trips to Berlin to keep in touch with the various organizations (see Görlitz, *Keitel*, p. 266).

On these occasions the following nearly always appeared in my office in HQ Area 2: Director Lehmann, Chief of the Services Legal Section, General Thomas, Chief of the Economics and Arms Industry Office, General von Wedel, Chief of Press and Propaganda, Admiral Canaris, Head of the Secret Service. General Reinecke however, the Chief of the General Wehrmacht Services, hardly ever appeared as we had little to do with his business. Canaris was usually accompanied by the heads of his three sections and he used to come, as he frequently said, 'to pour out his heart'. We could however only discuss our respective worries in veiled terms.

2. From *IMT* vol. XV, p. 312. Even in court however, both documents and witnesses proved how much truth there was in this statement. See also Appendix B to this book, Document no. 3.

3. Halder's diary 31 July 1940 and p. 132 of this book.

4. Halder adds here some thoughts on the further conduct of the war against England 'when strategy in the East will have shifted from the phase of destruction of the enemy's armed forces to that of paralysing the enemy's economy'.

5. From de Mendelssohn, p. 274.

6. This remark is also taken from de Mendelssohn's reproduction of the Nuremberg Documents (German edition). This relies to a large extent (pp. 364 *et seq.*) on the 'Barbarossa General File' which was apparently kept up by Jodl or one of his aides but never made available for Section L War Diary at the time. All quotations and details in this section (up to p. 192) are from this source unless otherwise stated.

7. See Halder's diary 24, 25, 27 June 1941. On 3 July Halder gives vent to his increasing dislike of 'the usual noises off from Supreme Headquarters' saying: 'from the tactical point of view there is of course some sense in this worry about the flanks. But that's what the Army and Corps commanders are there for. Our commanders and staffs are our strong point, but at the top they have no confidence in them because they have no conception of the strength represented by a body of commanders all of whom have been trained and educated on the same principles'. Describing a similar occasion on 10 July, Halder's remarks give a good sidelight on the habits of the Headquarters: 'the Führer was still asleep so I couldn't get him on the telephone. I therefore called Keitel and explained our ideas to him'.

8. These orders were drafted by the Army Operations and Organization Working Groups of Section L in collaboration. The first was issued on 13 July entitled *Army re-equipment – Tank Programme*; the second was issued on 14 July entitled *Manpower and Equipment Instructions based on Directive no. 32*. After more detailed examination of the equipment and spares position an OKW instruction, agreed with OKH, was issued on 8 August 1941 reducing the number of armoured and motorized divi-

sions to 30 and 15 respectively. The instruction also visualized the disbandment of 49 out of a total of 163 infantry divisions.

9. See chapter 4 above, note 8.
10. Although the word 'war' is twice used here, it may be assumed that in fact the reference is to the Russian campaign. Curiously enough Halder makes no mention of this suggestion. Probably it was not made to the C.-in-C. of the Army, as de Mendelssohn states, but via the normal channel to Colonel Heusinger, Chief of the Army Operations Section.
11. Halder's diary 30 June and 12 July 1941.
12. (a) See de Mendelssohn (German edition) for details of the conference between Hitler, Brauchitsch and Halder on 13 July; (b) For *Directive no. 33* see Hubatsch, *Directives*, p. 85; (c) For *Directive no. 35* of 6 September see Hubatsch, *Directives*, p. 96; (d) See also Halder's diary 23 July 1941 partially reproduced in Jacobsen, *Chronik*, p. 260.
13. See the fuller extract from Halder's diary of 26 July 1941 in Jacobsen, *Chronik*, pp. 260–1.
14. Halder's diary 30 July 1941: *Directive no. 34* is reproduced in Hubatsch, *Directives*, p. 91.
15. Halder's diary 5 August 1941.
16. Jacobsen, *Chronik*, p. 262.
17. The full text of the 'Supplement to Directive no. 34' is in Hubatsch, *Directives*, p. 93.
18. Halder's diary 15 and 16 August 1941.
19. The latter is given in full in de Mendelssohn (German edition).
20. Heusinger, p. 7 and pp. 132–5.
21. See Halder's diary 21 August

1941. After the war Jodl took a somewhat more sober view. He told the International Military Tribunal in Nuremberg: 'when he (Hitler) was clear in his mind what he wanted, or when he had taken some decision on his own, no further discussion was possible'.

22. Reproduced in Jacobsen, *Chronik* pp. 265–6.
23. See Halder's diary 23 August 1941 which states that Guderian was talked round by Hitler. See also the detailed and quite different account in Guderian's own book pp. 198–200.
24. Halder's diary 30 August 1941.
25. British Official History (Playfair) vol. II pp. 260–1. (German source not available.)
26. The British Official History gives the date of the memorandum as 28 August 1941. Halder's diary shows that receipt was acknowledged on 9 September and gives the main contents on 13 September (this is the source quoted); see also Jacobsen, *Chronik*, pp. 266 *et seq.* On 25 August 1941 Southern Iran was occupied by the British and Northern Iran by the Russians on the pretext that a German 'fifth column' was at work.
27. Hubatsch, *Directives*, p. 96.
28. See Heusinger, pp. 136 *et seq.* for the atmosphere in OKH at the end of October 1941.
29. Published by the Reich Information Office, 9 October 1941.
30. Diary entry of 19 November. See also entries for 29 November and 1 December 1941.
31. From Heusinger's description pp. 144–5; see also Halder's diary for these dates and Görlitz, *Keitel*, pp. 283–4.

32. In central and southern Finland the Finnish High Command operated independently, keeping in somewhat distant touch with OKH.
33. The 'Executive Instructions' nos. 1 and 2 attached to *Directive no. 37* and dated 7 and 21 November respectively are given in Hubatsch, *Weisungen*, pp. 164–8.
34. See Hubatsch, *Directives*, p. 69 (for *Directive no. 29*) and p. 74 (for *Directive no. 31*; for 'Executive Instructions' dated 15 June and 16 September 1941, see Hubatsch, *Weisungen*, pp. 127–8; see also p. 175 for the order of 15 December 1941 which laid down that 'not more than two German divisions were to be retained in the Balkans 'to safeguard areas of importance to us'.
35. See *Naval Affairs* 25 July and 17 September 1941. The text of the orders appears so far not to have been published.
36. See the order dated 29 October and OKW *Directive no. 38* dated 2 December 1941, the latter reproduced in Hubatsch, *Directives*, pp. 105 *et seq.*
37. The order was issued under a dateline as late as 14 December but had been given verbally by Hitler two or three weeks earlier (it has apparently not been published).

PART IV · CHAPTER 2

1. Halder's diary 2 and 3 December 1941.
2. Halder's diary 3–9 December 1941.
3. Halder's diary 3 December 1941: 'Heusinger, discussion of the main points to be made to OKW regarding the general situation'. On the following days there are a number of notes of telephone conversations with Jodl.
4. See Hubatsch, *Directives*, pp. 107 *et seq.*
5. See Dönitz, *Ten Years and Twenty Days*, pp. 189, 193, 195. For the preceding period Halder's diary merely contains the following note of 26 April: 'O Qu iv: If America now comes into the war, we need only reckon on her peacetime forces, ie at a maximum 5 inf. divs., 2 armd. divs., 1 para. bn., 1–2 divs. marine corps, 30 ground attack squadrons, 10 recce sqns., 20 fighter sqns.'
6. Dönitz, pp. 195 *et seq.*
7. Jacobsen, *Chronik*, pp. 282 and 288.
8. Reproduced in Jacobsen, *Chronik*, pp. 291 *et seq.*
9. Extract from the shorthand record.
10. See War Diary (KTB) of the OKW Historical Section (hereafter referred to as 'Scherff') 29 April 1942: 'conversation between German Ambassador Tokyo and the Japanese Foreign Minister Togo. The German Ambassador urged that in the Soviet Union's difficult position a thrust towards Vladivostok and Lake Baikal would be decisive and might lead to the complete liquidation of the Soviet Union. The Japanese Foreign Minister gave no definite reply.'
11. See Halder's diary 5 and also 1 December (ie before the beginning of the crisis): 'the C.-in-C.'s health has been affected by his continuous exertions and now gives cause for anxiety'.

Also Heusinger p. 151 where he describes Brauchitsch as giving him the impression at the beginning of December of 'a completely broken man'. See also Görlitz, *Keitel*, p. 287.

12. See Goebbels' diary 24 January 1942: 'morale among the people is so-and-so. There is still a lot of talk about the dismissal of Brauchitsch'.

13. See Halder's diary 19 December 1941; also p. 196 of this book.

14. See also Hitler's *Table Talk*, pp. 397–8.

15. See p. 59 regarding Field Marshal von Reichenau and Heusinger, p. 152 where Rundstedt and Dietl are also mentioned. See also Bor, *Gespräche*, p. 214.

16. Guderian, p. 325.

17. Heusinger, pp. 154 *et seq.*

18. See also Görlitz, *Keitel*, pp. 319 *et seq.*

19. Heusinger, p. 155.

20. Halder's' diary 19 December 1941.

21. Heusinger, p. 165.

22. *IMT*, vol. XV, p. 371.

23. See Heusinger's striking description pp. 176 *et seq.* and the shorthand records of Hitler's briefing conferences which appear later in this book.

24. See Halder's diary 8 January 1942 as an example (telephone conversation with Field Marshal von Kluge).

25. See Heusinger's description p. 188.

26. Halder's diary 20 December 1941.

27. There are numerous indications in Halder's diary of this period, e.g. 'a very serious day', 'a day of desperate fighting', etc.

28. Bor, *Gespräche*, p. 81.

29. Heusinger, p. 163.

30. To complete the picture of these personnel changes: (a) A month later (on 18 January 1942) Field Marshal von Bock was recalled to do a further six months as C.-in-C. Army Group South (Halder's diary 21 December 1942).
(b) For the dismissal of Guderian see his own description pp. 264 *et seq.*, Halder's diary 25 December and Heusinger, p. 154;
(c) For Hoeppner's dismissal see Halder's diary 8 January and Heusinger, pp. 162–3 where there is a graphic description of what actually occurred, based on his own memory.

31. See Halder's diary 13 January ('meeting between Hitler and Field Marshal von Leeb – no agreement'); 21 January ('whole day with the Führer, together with Field Marshal von Kluge; got back 1.0 am).

32. Goebbels' diary 21 March.

33. On many points Jodl's memory failed him on this subject too. See his evidence at Nuremberg (*IMT*, vol. XV, p. 296) quoted in note 4(c) to chap. 2, part II In the two and a half years during which I attended the briefings I only saw this procedure in operation occasionally, if at all; in any case it ran counter to all principles of the issue of orders at the higher levels. What in fact went on is described in this book.

34 See Halder's diary 8 January 1942: 'the tug-of-war with the Führer is starting again. No decision'. There are also numerous examples in Manstein, *Lost Victories*.

PART IV · CHAPTER 3

1. Jacobsen, *Chronik*, p. 288. See also Chap. 2 above, note 7.
2. Goebbels' diary 17 March 1942.
3. Heusinger, p. 186 (italics not in original).
4. This order (no. 1/42 g. Kdos OKW/WF Stab/Org–Wi Rü Amt) does not appear to have been published to date.
5. Shortly before (in February) there had been the brilliant operation of the passage from Brest through enemy home waters of the battleships *Scharnhorst* and *Gneisenau* and the cruiser *Prinz Eugen*. To anticipate for a moment, at the 'OKM Conference' dealing with 'the situation and prospects of the submarine war' (Jacobsen, *Chronik*, pp. 341 *et seq.*) the view was expressed as late as 20 October 1942 that: 'there is a good prospect that, provided we employ all our resources and exploit technology, surprise and stratagem to the full, the Anglo-Saxon powers, who are dependent on sea communications, may not be able to escape from our stranglehold, and may be worn down by a process of attrition'.
6. None of these orders appear to have been published as yet. The reference number of the OKW order was No. 55328/42 g. Kdos Chefs WF Stab/Op, that of the Navy Order OKM 1/Skl I–275/42 g. Kdos Chefs dated 23 February 1942.
7. Halder's diary 28 March; see also entries for 8, 18 and 21 March 1942, which record his preliminary discussions with his Deputy Chief of Staff and Chief of the Operations Section.
8. Heusinger, pp. 176 *et seq.*
9. Halder's diary 29 March (supplemented by his personal recollections) and 24 June 1942. 'The unfortunate Reichel affair' mentioned several times in the diary for the days prior to 24 June, refers to the shooting down of an aircraft carrying (contrary to repeated instructions) 'most important orders regarding the attack which apparently fell into enemy hands'. (20 June).
10. On 17 May Scherff was given by Hitler the new title of 'Representative for the Compilation of the History of the War'. Simultaneously he was instructed to make himself responsible for the Army War History. He was always present at the briefing conferences though his office was in Berlin. The following comment in Goebbels' diary for 5 May 1942 is indicative of what was to happen later:

> Lt. Colonel Scherff sent me from the Field Headquarters a collection of quotations about the nature of genius by a number of the great men in German history. It is extraordinarily well done. Scherff gave it as a present to the Führer on his birthday (20 April). Looked at in the light of the present day situation these quotations are most comforting. Taken as a whole they amount almost to an apotheosis of the Führer. It is impossible to conceive of a better justification of his nature, personality or method of work.

11. On 5 April Hitler had changed the original code-name, Siegfried. After Barbarossa he was somewhat shy of coupling the

great names of German legend and history with the uncertainties of military operations. On 30 June the code-name was changed to Braunschweig, this time for fear that it might have become known to the enemy.

12. Scherff's War Diary 10 May 1942.
13. Scherff's War Diary 4 and 5 April 1942.
14. See Hubatsch, *Directives*, pp. 116 *et seq.* An OKW order signed by Keitel was issued the same day giving the strictest instructions for the maintenance of secrecy of the objectives for the offensive.
15. Görlitz, *Keitel*, pp. 299 *et seq.*
16. Scherff's War Diary 5 June 1942.
17. Scherff's War Diary 14 and 28 May. The word 'tactically' hardly seems apposite here but it is in line with Hitler's subsequent methods of command.
18. *Directive no. 40* is in Hubatsch, *Directives*, pp. 111 *et seq.*, and the supplementary order of 5 December 1942 in Hubatsch, *Weisungen*, p. 182. Although the latter order indicates that further more detailed instructions from Hitler were to follow 'shortly', on 3 October 1943 the provisions of *Directive no. 40* were made applicable to Italy as they stood and were still in force at the time of the 'invasion' in June 1944.
19. See also Scherff's War Diary 3 June 1942.
20. This order has apparently not been published. Its reference was no. 5579/42 g. Kdos Chefs WF Stab/Op. Details and quotations in this section are from Scherff's War Diary 15, 18, 21 and 30 April, 1, 4, 7, 20 and 21 May 1942. There is a detailed

description of these events in my contribution to *Entscheidungsschlachten des Zweiten Weltkriegs* entitled *Die Entscheidung im Mittelmeer 1942.*

21. Scherff's War Diary 25 April 1942. The directive is in Hubatsch, *Directives* p. 121
22. Scherff's War Diary 18 and 26 April 1942.
23. Scherff's War Diary 25 and 26 June 1942.
24. Scherff's War Diary 5 April and 2 May 1942.
25. First reproduced in Jacobsen, *Chronik*, pp. 309–333.

PART IV · CHAPTER 4

1. For a detailed description see my contribution *Mittelmeer 1942* to *Entscheidungsschlachten des Zweiten Weltkriegs*; for quotations and other details see Ciano, *Catastrofe*, and Scherff's War Diary, both for 22 June 1942, also Heusinger, p. 193.
2. Scherff's diary 25 June 1942.
3. From Goebbels' diary of 20 March; in this connection I myself heard Hitler say that one of the long-term duties of members of the SS was to settle on a distant eastern frontier as 'armed colonists'.
4. See also Halder's opinion given in Part III chap. 5, note 7.
5. See Halder's diary 13 July and compare with entry for 5 July 1942.
6. The reference number of the order dealing with the Leibstandarte (which has not been published) was OKW/WF Stab 551213/42 g. Kdos Chefs; the other instruction is contained in OKW *Directive no. 45* dated 23 July 1942 and reproduced in

Hubatsch, *Directives*, pp. 129 *et seq.* The other details given here are based on Halder's diary of 6 July and my own memory. See also Heusinger, p. 197. Halder's entry for 15 August 1942 is relevant: 'new instructions by the Führer regarding permanent fortifications on the western coasts (quite impossible)'.

7. See Halder's diary 18, 19 July and 12 August; also OKW *Directive no. 45*. For OKW *Directive no. 43* see Hubatsch, *Directives*, p. 124.

8. Cf the wording used in the introductory paragraphs to OKW *Directive no. 44* of 21 July 1942 dealing with Finland – Hubatsch, *Directives* pp. 127 *et seq.*

9. See *Directive no. 41* dated 5 April 1942 referred to in Chap. 3, note 14; note particularly *Section I – General Plan* where the breakthrough into the Caucasus is the only objective. Stalingrad is only mentioned much later, in Section II C *The Main Operation.*

10. Contrary to Jodl's statement at Nuremberg given in Chap. 2 p. 220. *Directive no. 45* was in fact drafted by OKW even though it dealt exclusively with the Eastern Front. See also the comment in Halder's diary given above. These facts prove that OKH was even more closely controlled than before because Jodl now advised and influenced Hitler in his capacity not only as Supreme Commander but also as C.-in-C. of the Army.

11. At about this time I visited the higher headquarters in eastern Caucasus (Piatigorsk) which were then busy with preparations for a move into Trans-caucasia. See also Halder's diary for 9 August 1942: 'Heusinger – possibilities of operations via Iran into Iraq'.

12. See Halder's diary 7 and 22 August and Operations Staff War Diary 14, 16, 19 and 22 August 1942. The rest is from my own memory.

13. Quoted from Heusinger pp. 200–1; he probably made immediate note of the words used; in any case they are exactly as I remember them. See Halder's diary and OKW Operations Staff War Diary both for 24 August 1942.

14. Scherff's War Diary 31 May and 3 June 1942.

15. See Orders OKW WF Stab/Op No. 003142/42 g. Kdos of 14 September and 551743/42 g. Kdos. Chefs dated 13 October 1942 (neither published); also Operations Staff War Diary 17 and 20 September 1942 and *Mittelmeer 1942* in *Entscheidungsschlachten des Zweiten Weltkriegs.*

16. Operations Staff War Diary 3, 4 and 9 September 1942.

17. On the subject of the Murmansk railway see OKW *Directive no. 44* dated 21 July; for other details see OKW Operations Staff War Diary 23–30 August and 2–5 September 1942; see also Halder's diary 30 August and Manstein, pp. 261 *et seq.*

18. Hubatsch, *Directives*, p. 132.

19. See Operations Staff War Diary 16 and 22 August and 16 September and Halder's diary 15 and 16 September 1942.

20. From Operations Staff War Diary 16, 23, 27 and 28 August 1942; certain details added from memory.

21. See Operations Staff War Diary

7, 8, 9 and 15 September and Halder's diary 8, 9 and 12 September 1942 – both relevant to subsequent paras. also. Heusinger's account of the Hitler–Jodl quarrel is incorrect in that it gives the date as August 1942; it is also inaccurate on certain details. It is however, very close to the truth in its description of the atmosphere and the behaviour of those involved.

22. See also Heusinger, p. 187 who, referring to another occasion, says: 'he (Hitler) is like a prophet; he believes in his mission and considers he is working on a higher plane than the rest of us. This belief in himself and his calling is the source of his strength'. See also Heusinger's very striking picture of Hitler's mental outlook pp. 205 *et seq.*

23. See Erfurth, *Geschichte des Deutschen Generalstabs*, p. 281; also similar expressions recorded by Heusinger (p. 210) from his subsequent conversation with Hitler.

24. Shirer's description in his *The Rise and Fall of the Third Reich* p. 918, where he says 'little more than the Führer's office boy', is both inaccurate and unjust.

25. Halder's diary 4 January and Scherff's War Diary 29 June 1942.

26. The 'contact man' who occupied a senior post and was a former naval officer, was present. It is not necessary to identify him to prove the truth of an incident which is only quoted as typifying the relationships within Supreme HQ.

27. From Heusinger (who was present) p. 212. Zeitzler's other instructions were purely military and contained nothing new.

28. The Operations Staff War Diary for the immediately preceding period provides a number of examples of the extent to which Jodl's interference in operations in the East went down even into tactical detail. On 21 August it notes that an OKW liaison officer was despatched with instructions from General Jodl to II Mountain Corps (in the Caucasus), on 30 August 1942 that the Senior Officer – Army was despatched to the Crimea to press for the crossing of the Kertsch road to be speeded up. For the innovations introduced by Zeitzler into the briefing conference procedure see Operations Staff War Diary 10–13 October. The reason for the lack of detail for this and following days is given as Zeitzler's 'jealousy of his responsibilities' (*vis-à-vis* OKW). This remark hardly does justice to Zeitzler's real motives.

29. It was only in October 1942 when Zeitzler took over that the position described by Jodl in his evidence at Nuremberg, and which he related to the period of Hitler's assumption of command of the Army, actually became fact (see chap. 2, p. 220).

30. Heusinger, p. 255.

31. The most convincing proof is that the OKW War Diaries for 1943 contain simply extracts from the daily Army Situation reports. Further, from 1944 on the War Diaries were divided into volumes according to the various theatres of war but there is no volume labelled 'Eastern Front'.

32. See Operations Staff War Diary 25 October which mentions the use of small naval units to support the attack on the north-west coast of the Black Sea. On 2 November 1942 it speaks of the concentration of all the Pioneer Battalions from neighbouring divisions for the street fighting in Stalingrad. There are also a number of examples in the shorthand records of the briefing conferences.

33. On the U-boat war see the Naval Staff report of 20 October 1942 already mentioned in chap. 3, note 5. Regarding the Luftwaffe see Hitler's strictures in Operations Staff War Diary 25 October 1942.

34. The final months of the headquarters' stay in Vinnitsa saw the issue of the other 'criminal order' dated 18 October which became known during the Nuremberg trial as the 'Commando Order'. All that need be said here is that the procedure for its production was similar to that in the case of the 'Commissar Order'. The following were the salient points: Hitler's demand for the issue of such an order was based on certain actions on the part of the enemy which looked like reprisals but were in fact within the bounds of international law; Jodl thereupon ordered his staff to prepare a draft. The staff discussed with Admiral Canaris' office (International Law Section) and with the OKW Legal Section to ensure that the order was within the provisions of the laws of war. These efforts ended 8–10 days later as a result of pressure by Jodl, and a minute was submitted to him setting out the unsolved problems and containing merely the first outline of a draft order against 'agents and saboteurs'. This semi-complete draft was rejected by Jodl who then himself made five further drafts, all of which were rejected by Hitler. The order was drafted by Hitler himself who dictated it to one of his secretaries.

The above statements are based on documents produced during the 'OKW Case' at Nuremberg. They override Jodl's statements at Nuremberg (*IMT*, vol. XV, p. 318) and in particular his criticisms of his staff (see also part III, chap. 5, p. 177 and Appendix B, Document no. 3).

35. So far only a fragment of this *Survey* has been found; it consists of an Annexe from the Q Section of OKW which I have only partially evaluated and which carries the reference number WF Stab/Qu Nr. 551692/42 g. Kdos. Chefs. The remainder is from my memory which is quite clear. See also Operations Staff War Diary 1 December 1942.

36. The wording is identical with that given in Jacobsen, *Chronik*, p. 352. Neither the 'considerable reinforcements' announced in the message nor the transport to move them were available.

37. See Operations Staff War Diary 3 November 1942.

38. For a full description of events with supporting material see *Mittelmeer 1942* in *Entscheidungsschlachten*. The quotations are from those parts of Conference Record Fragment no. 46 of 31 August 1944 not reproduced here. There are further details

in Operations Staff War Diary 5–7 November 1942.

39. For a full description of events with supporting material see *Mittelmeer 1942* in *Entscheidungsschlachten*. There are also details in Operations Staff War Diary 4–10 November 1942.

40. The entries in the Operations Staff War Diary for 12–14 November 1942 were in places amended as a result of my report.

41. See Operations Staff War Diary 19–22 and 25 November 1942; also Heusinger, p. 217 *et seq.* (this is in error in stating that Hitler was at Rastenburg prior to 22 November).

PART V · CHAPTER 1

1. From Ciano, *Catastrofe*. That this was no mere turn of phrase is shown by the fact that Goebbels' diary for 20 March 1943 has Hitler using a similar expression: 'fight stubbornly and tenaciously until the enemy is knocked out'.

2. From Ciano, *Catastrofe*, 1 and 20 December 1942, and other unpublished Italian reports. See also Operations Staff War Diary 19 December 1942.

3. The quotes are typical of the phrases used by Hitler.

4. Operations Staff War Diary 21 December 1942.

5. Ciano, *Catastrofe*, after a meeting with Hitler 18–20 December 1942.

PART V · CHAPTER 2

1. Operations Staff War Diary 1 December 1942.

2. See Hitler's instruction recorded in Operations Staff War Diary 7 December 1942: 'as first

priority a German reserve group of Jäger and Mountain Divs. must be formed in the Balkans with all speed'; see also *Directive no. 47* on *Command and Defence measures in the South-east*' reproduced in Hubatsch, *Directives*, pp. 137 *et seq.*

3. According to Operations Staff War Diary and daily record the proposal was for: two armoured divisions (6 and 7), three Panzer Grenadier divisions (SS Adolf Hitler, Reich and Totenkopf), six infantry divisions, a number of assault guns, tanks and anti-tank guns not specified. Hitler however ordered that some of the infantry divisions should be replaced by newly-formed Luftwaffe divisions.

4. See Operations Staff War Diary 25 and 27 November and 2–10 December 1942; also Heusinger, pp. 217 *et seq.* Richthofen was Commander of 4 Air Fleet on the southern sector of the Eastern Front. Kotelnikov is 50 miles south-east of Stalingrad as the crow flies.

5. See Fragment 8 (pp. 525–26); see also p. 534: 'they are getting very restive and asking to be relieved, but that will change all in a flash'.

6. Operations Staff War Diary 23 and 28 January 1943.

7. See Fragment no. 47 p. 304.

8. Fragment no. 47 p. 535, and Operations Staff War Diary 4 February 1943.

9. This and Fragment no. 8 which follows are given almost in full in so far as they have been preserved, in order to give a lifelike picture of what went on at Hitler's briefing conferences. Exceptionally, a report on the East

by Jodl preceded that of Zeitzler on this particular evening, since Zeitzler was not available.

10. Göring had guaranteed 700 tons per day (Operations Staff War Diary 25 November 1942.)

11. Operations Staff War Diary 9 December 1942. Since at the same time a number of measures were taken to reinforce North Africa it looks as if this was intended merely as a threat to the Italians in answer to Mussolini's pressure for an end to the Russian campaign.

12. Göring's remark is given in Cavallero's diary 1 December 1942. C.-in-C. Navy also made a similar estimate of the problem of sea transport to Tunis on 19 November 1942 ('an easy job').

13. See Operations Staff War Diary 4 December and Fragment 29, p. 289. Other details are from unpublished accounts by those present.

14. See Operations Staff War Diary 18–19 December 1942 and 12 January 1943; also Fragment 8 p. 300; regarding the Italian visit see Ciano's and Cavallero's diaries of this period, I was particularly struck by Ciano's apparently completely carefree attitude, although at the time the Italian Eighth Army in the East was in process of disintegration.

15. This is primarily based on the views of the late Vice-Admiral Weichold who was at the time 'German Admiral Rome'. He judged from the number of ships leaving Italian ports in March and April 1943 for North Africa, ie in the opposite direction.

16. Operations Staff War Diary 19, 22, 27 and 31 January 1943.

17. This question dragged on for months. See Fragment no. 29 pp. 288–89, and the voluminous correspondence referred to in Hitler's order of 5 Jan. 1943 (not published – reference O K W /WF Stab no. 66020 g. Kdos Chefs); also Operations Staff War Diary 19, 22, 27, 31 January and 2, 3, 7, 10, 15, 18, 19, 23, 24 and 26 February and 4 March 1943. See also Ciano's and Cavallero's diaries of this period.

18. See Operations Staff War Diary 15 February 1943; further references to my trip are on 28 and 31 January and 7 and 9 February. 1943. The initial sentence of the entry for 16 February 1943 stating that I had reported verbally to Hitler is incorrect.

19. Operations Staff War Diary 23 February and 5 March 1943.

20. Operations Staff War Diary 19 January 1943.

21. Operations Staff War Diary 5, 8, 12 and 18 March 1943.

22. Operations Staff War Diary 8 and 12 March 1943 and Fragment 8, p. 298.

23. Operations Staff War Diary 18, 29 and 31 March 1943 and its relevant addendum.

24. 8–10 April 1943 (see p. 315 below). Details are confirmed by certain unpublished Italian accounts.

25. The Italian accounts referred to in Note 2 to chap. 1 give further details.

26. *Naval Affairs* of this date.

27. Reference should be made here to *Comments on Operations Section War Diary* up to 17 March 1943. These were written by the late Hr Greiner and are in some cases repeated in his book *Die Oberste Wehrmachtführung*. Greiner was

ordered to leave the HQ on express instructions from Hitler because the 'Kreisleiter' (Party leader) in his home town, Potsdam, had sent Bormann a complaint that his wife was not blacking out the house properly. We in HQ Area 2 were particularly attached to Greiner but when some time later he came to visit us, Jodl forbade him ever to enter the HQ again.

28. From the unpublished account of one of those present.

29. See Operations Staff War Diary 25 and 28 February, 6 March 1943.

30. He died on 28 August 1943. Hitler always maintained that he was murdered.

PART V · CHAPTER 3

1. *Naval Affairs*, 14 May 1943; see also Operations Staff War Diary 25 July 1943 and its references back to the dates 10 and 14–16 May 1943.

2. See *Naval Affairs*, 14 May 1943; contrary to the general belief, Hitler had instructed OKW as early as the beginning of 1943 to make a detailed examination of the defence both of Sardinia and of the Peloponnese (see Operations Staff War Diary 8 and 12 February, 1, 3 and 22 March 1943).

3. Fragment no. 4, 19 May 1943, pp. 8–9 (not in this book).

4. See Fragment no. 4; Hubatsch, *Weisungen*, p. 217 gives the draft of *Directive no. 48b – Instructions for the Defence of the Balkans without Italian assistance*. According to the Operations Staff War Diary of 14 July 1943 the idea of a written order based on this

draft was turned down by Hitler on 22 May, as was *Directive no. 48a. (Defence of Italy using German troops only)*.

5. See OKW orders dated 12 and 13 May 1943 issued under the reference WF Stab/Op. Nr. 661055/43 g. Kdos. Chefs (not published). Also *Directive no. 48* on *Command and Defensive Plans in the South-east* dated 26 July 1943 (Hubatsch, *Directives*, pp. 142 *et seq.*).

6. Extracts from an unpublished Italian source dated 19 April 6, 10, 13 May 1943.

7. See Operations Staff War Diary 21 July 1943 and Fragments no. 4 and 5 (p. 327 of this book). See also Rintelen, *Mussolini als Bundesgenosse*, pp. 197 *et seq.*, partially confirmed by unpublished Italian accounts dated 22 May and 11 June 1943.

8. See OKH Operation Order no. 6 dated 15 April and Field Marshal von Manstein's notes from 4 May to 1 July – both in Jacobsen, *Chronik*, pp. 394 *et seq.* Also Operations Staff War Diary 15 July 1943. I have added details from my own memory and that of a former colleague.

9. I remember this clearly. See also Keitel's account in *Wehrwissenschaftliche Rundschau* no. 11 of 1961, and Guderian, pp. 304–11. Also Heusinger, pp. 250 and 270. In the latter reference he records Colonel Scherff as repeating in August 1943 the view generally held in OKW: 'Hitler did not insist on the Kursk attack. Zeitzler talked him into it'. Heusinger's comment is: 'that is not correct. Zeitzler was in favour of the attack provided it could take place by mid-June.

After that he no longer pressed for it.'

Jodl's instructions to the Wehrmacht Propaganda Section for Operation Citadel are interesting. The operation was to be presented as a counter-attack to forestall an imminent Russian offensive; his object was to prepare the ground for news of a withdrawal. Official reports were to be so couched as to give the Western powers the impression that large German reserves were available in the hope that they might therefore delay their own Mediterranean plans, especially those for the Balkans (Operations Staff War Diary 5 July 1943).

10. See *Naval Affairs*, 13 and 14 May; Fragments nos. 4 and 5, 19 and 20 May, Operations Staff War Diary 25 July 1943, E. L. Wiskemann, *The Rome-Berlin Axis*, p. 298, Rintelen pp. 202 *et seq.* The remainder is from my own memory.

11. See also Senger-Etterlin, *Krieg in Europa*, p. 153 – 'Issue of orders by Hitler' where it is stated: 'General Warlimont spoke to me privately afterwards. He gave a clear appreciation of the situation. This appreciation and distribution of tasks put right those of Hitler.' General von Senger und Etterlin was at the time Hitler's liaison officer to the senior Italian HQ in Sicily, Sixth Army. His special job was to keep an eye on the use made of the German troops on the island and to steer the dispositions for the defence in the direction desired by Germany.

12. See Operations Staff War Diary 13 July 1943.

13. See Operations Staff War Diary 11 and 13 July 1943 (Mussolini's telegram of 12 July).

14. See Operations Staff War Diary 13 July. The order was drafted by Jodl himself and carries the ref. OKW/WF Stab/Op no. 661553/43. It has not been published.

15. Operations Staff War Diary 14–16 July 1943.

16. Operations Staff War Diary 15 July 1943.

17. Operations Staff War Diary 14 July 1943.

18. Operations Staff War Diary 17 and 18 July; *Naval Affairs*, 17 July 1943.

19. Operations Staff War Diary 19 July 1943. Details from unpublished Italian accounts and my own memory. I accompanied Keitel on this trip; Jodl remained behind at Wolfschanze.

20. From unpublished Italian accounts. See also Rintelen, p. 216 and Churchill, *The Second World War*, vol. V, pp. 47–48.

21. Goebbels' diary 7 May which in this case is referring to the mid-April meeting in Berchtesgaden.

22. Operations Staff War Diary 19–23 July and *Directive no. 48* referred to in note 5 above. The rest is from my own memory.

23. See Operations Staff War Diary 22–24 July 1943. It later became known from Italian accounts that from 20 July the Comando Supremo was planning to concentrate an Italian Motorized Corps in the Rome area and move two Alpini Divisions to the Tyrol.

24. Operations Staff War Diary 24 July 1943.

25. From Fragment no. 13. Extracts from subsequent parts of the same meeting are given below.

26. It may seem remarkable that in this case as in other important instances a series of several consecutive Fragments is available. The explanation is that the records were arranged in chronological order and therefore those which could be saved from the flames were consecutive.

27. The remark in Goebbels' diary on 27 July 1943 where he ascribes the fact that Rommel was temporarily held back to jealousy on the part of Keitel and Jodl is complete nonsense.

28. See Operations Staff War Diary 25, 26 July, etc.

29. *Naval Affairs*, 26–28 July 1943. These include extracts from the Conference Records for 26 July evening and 27 July midday and evening. They include Hitler's answer to a protest by Jodl: 'these are matters which a soldier cannot understand. Only someone with a political instinct can see the way ahead.'

30. There are numerous details in *Naval Affairs*, for the subsequent period.

31. See Fragment no. 14 (p. 345): 'General Zeitzler leaves' (in the midst of a discussion on the situation in Italy and its consequences). See also Fragment no. 17, 26 July (not in this book) – discussion between Hitler, Zeitzler and Field Marshal von Kluge during Jodl's absence. See also Operations Staff War Diary 4 August 1943.

32. See the detailed records of discussions in the Headquarters in *Naval Affairs*, 26–28 July, 1–3 and 9–11 August 1943. See also Operations Staff War Diary 31 July regarding Rommel's views and 5 August 1943 which

records a typical Hitler reason for clinging on to Sicily – the 'shock' which he anticipated the Allies would suffer from the liberation of Mussolini.

33. See Operations Staff War Diary 26–28 July 1943. From 'Preliminary Orders' issued on 28 July under the reference OKW/WF Stab. Nr 661746 and 661747 g. Kdos. Chefs it appears that the consolidated order was issued on 1 August 1943 as *Directive no. 49* (none of the above have been published). Hubatsch, *Weisungen*, p. 228 gives the *Special Instructions no. 1 for Directive no. 49* dated 31 July 1943. It is more than likely that the *Special Instructions no. 2* dated 3 August 1943 also form part of the directive. They are to be found on p. 223 of Hubatsch, *Weisungen*.

34. *Naval Affairs*, 26 July 1943.

35. See Operations Staff War Diary 5 August 1943 and Görlitz, *Keitel*, p. 327. The remainder is from unpublished Italian sources and my own memory. When Ribbentrop referred on this occasion to a 'liberation of Sicily', the expression had not even a propaganda implication at this time.

36. See Operations Staff War Diary 7–13 August and *Naval Affairs*, 11 August 1943.

37. For events outside the conference see Rintelen, pp. 241–3. For the course of the negotiations see Operations Staff War Diary 15 August 1943. Contrary to other evidence one Italian source states that General Roatta was informed of the Italian Government's intention to negotiate with the Allies 'several days before 15 August'.

38. See Operations Staff War Diary and *Naval Affairs* – second half of August, beginning of September in both cases.

39. See Operations Staff War Diary 8, 9, 18, 23, 25, 27, 29 August, the latter showing once more that the intention was that, on issue of the code word Axis, Rommel should take over command of the whole of Italy. See also *Naval Affairs*, 29 August and the order OKW/WF Stab/Op Nr. 661966 /43 g. Kdos. Chefs dated 18 August (not published).

40. Hitler throughout remained convinced that there was 'treachery', and his conviction was not far from the truth. During this period however, he made a series of contradictory remarks; on 17 August he told Colonel General von Vietinghoff and on 22 August Field Marshal Kesselring that he had positive proof (this is from unpublished accounts by those two officers); in between the two however, on 19 August he told Dönitz that there was no proof (*Naval Affairs*, 19 August 1943). For other points see Operations Staff War Diary 2–5 and 8 September 1943.

PART V · CHAPTER 4

1. For the execution of Plan Axis see Operations Staff War Diary 8–17 and 21 September 1943; the description is based on unpublished accounts by those directly involved both on the German and the Italian side. For the formation of neo-Italian forces see Operations Staff War Diary 9 and 19 October, 12 and 24 November, 5, 7 and 8

December, also *Naval Affairs*, 19 and 20 December 1943. The result of the discussions with Marshal Graziani in German Supreme HQ on these and other questions is contained in teleprinter message OKW/WF Stab Op Nr. 662474 g. Kdos. Chefs (not published).

2. Operations Staff War Diary 8 September 1943.

3. See Operations Staff War Diary 11 and 12 September 1943. This gives the date of C.-in-C. South's report as 11 September, but this is incorrect. Goebbels' notes a few days later on public relations policy in the headquarters concerning the battle of Salerno and on the sudden change in Hitler's attitude to certain of the generals in command are also of interest:

18 September:
The military news sources under General Jodl have been writing about a Dunkirk and a Gallipoli.

19 September:
At the Führer's Headquarters there were a couple of generals who couldn't wait. They distributed the skin of the bear before it had been killed. I have also written an energetic letter to Keitel and have demanded an end to the mistakes made so often during this war by his collaborators. What the army did at Salerno is an outstanding scandal. The exuberant reports of victory emanated from our supreme command for the south – almost directly from Kesselring. Serious disagreement with Dietrich and Jodl. They think they have been fearfully insulted.

23 September:
I asked the Führer how our marshals were doing now. He is quite satisfied with their attitude. He

spoke very favourably about Kluge, Küchler and even Manstein.... Kleist has made a very close approach to the Führer and to the National-Socialist movement.... The Führer spoke in great praise of Busch. His opinion of Kesselring's military abilities is higher than my own.... Even of List the Führer now has a more favourable opinion than several months ago.... Taken as a whole, our generals bear no resemblance to the Italians. Treason such as the Italian generals committed against Mussolini is impossible considering the mentality of the German and especially the Prussian generals. ...

4. See Operations Staff War Diary 8 September (quoted textually) and 9–13 September 1943. On the take-over of command by Rommel see entries for 29 and 30 August 1943. On 19 September he was ordered to deal with the unrest in Istria (OKW/WF Stab/Op (H) Nr. 662307/43 g. Kdos. Chefs – not published).

5. See Operations Staff War Diary 9, 10, 13, 20, 23 September in conjunction with *Naval Affairs*, 11 August 1943.

6. Operations Staff War Diary 17, 18, 23, 25 September 1943.

7. See Hubatsch, *Weisungen*, p. 224 *Special Instructions no. 3 for Directive no. 48* dated 7 August 1943.

8. Operations Staff War Diary and *Naval Affairs*, both for 24 September 1943.

9. Operations Staff War Diary 27, 28 September, 1, 4 October 1943.

10. See Operations Staff War Diary 1, 4, 6, 28 October and 6 November 1943. The orders referred to, in so far as they have been traced, are OKW/WF Stab/Op Nr. 662409/43 g. Kdos. Chefs of 4 October, 662411/43 g. Kdos. Chefs of 6 October and 006123 g. Kdos. of 6 November (all unpublished).

Jodl took it upon himself to order C.-in-C. South-east's Operations Staff at least to reconnoitre a rear position east and west through Salonika and later managed to get Hitler's agreement for construction to begin, but only under the heading 'road blocks'.

11. C.-in-C. South-east's estimate of this internal struggle is shown by his report quoted by the Operations Staff War Diary on 5 November 1943: 'the enemy is gaining a foothold in the Balkans.... Tito is our most dangerous enemy.... The problem is whether we are or are not prepared to tolerate a Bolshevist sphere of influence in the southeast – right on the Reich frontier'.

12. See Operations Staff War Diary 14, 17, 29 November, 11, 15 December and Jodl's diary 15, 16 December 1943. See also Goebbels' diary 4 December 1943: 'in Italy ... new assaults ... reserves ... so that people in the Führer's HQ are not worrying about future developments. The operations are being directed primarily by Jodl. But Jodl does not seem to me any too competent at evaluating a critical military situation. He has so often been wrong in his prognoses that personally I am unable to drop my worries about the southern Italian front.' On 23 September 1943 Goebbels had

given the following opinion of Jodl: 'a very good, solid worker whose excellent General Staff training is revealed time and again'.

13. See Operations Staff War Diary 9, 10, 14 October and 12, 21, 22 November 1943. Keitel's comment in Operations Staff War Diary of 12 November shows what his estimate of Mussolini's authority was: 'the problem was to prepare in Italy a territorial organization which could take over, should the Italian Government collapse'.

14. See Operations Staff War Diary 24–29 August and 16 September as regards Denmark; 24 August, 27 September 6, 8, 25, 30 October 1943 as regards the West.

15. For moves from West to East at this period see Operations Staff War Diary 22 August, 2 and 7 September; regarding the 'East Wall' see Operations Staff War Diary 12, 21 August and *Naval Affairs*, 28 August 1943.

16. From a letter to me from General (retd) Freiherr von Buttlar received in 1953.

17. The order has not been published. Its reference was Op Abt I Nr. 430684 g. Kdos. Chefs. It is proof of the efforts made by the OKW Ops Staff and also of Hitler's continued misappreciation of the situation in the east. See also Operations Staff War Diary 4, 7, 20, 23 October 8, 12, 16, 23 November, 3, 10, 29 December 1943 and the records of the 27 and 28 December Conferences given below.

18. Goebbels' diary 30 November 1943.

19. See Fragment no. 10 (pp. 542–557); also Heusinger, p. 291:

'Jodl and Zeitzler are each working for their own theatres, each for his own cabbage patch'.

20. Operations Staff War Diary 11 September 1943.

21. Operations Staff War Diary 17, 20 September 1943.

22. Operations Staff War Diary 23, 28 September, 1, 15, 25, 29 October, 1, 12, 19, 20 November, 13, 21, 31 December 1943 and Fragment no. 7 (pp. 394–95).

23. Operations Staff War Diary 29 October, 7, 12, 20 November, 1 December 1943 and Fragment no. 7 (p. 394–95); regarding the Crimea being cut off see *Naval Affairs*, 27 October 1943 and Heusinger, pp. 276–7.

24. Operations Staff War Diary 9, 15, 20 December 1943 and *OKW Theatres of War, I*, 1944. The latter appears in Schramm's edition of the War Diary for 1944–5, vol. IV of the full edition p. 93. (Schramm's version will henceforth be referred to as 'Schramm IV').

25. Operations Staff War Diary 8, 24 October and 17, 28 November 1943.

26. *Naval Affairs*, 10 December 1943 (report by German Admiral, Tokyo).

27. The directive is reproduced in Hubatsch, *Directives*, pp. 149 *et seq*. The directive was followed on 12 December 1943 by a detailed memorandum from the OKW Operations Staff drawing the lessons from the Allied landings in the Mediterranean (OKW Nr 007774 g. Kdos. WF Stab/Op – not published).

28. Operations Staff War Diary 31 October and 17 December 1943.

29. p. 188 of original English edition.

30. Operations Staff War Diary 11,

30, 31 December, *Naval Affairs*, 19–20 December 1943 and p. 408 of this book.

31. Operations Staff War Diary 28, 30 December and *OKW Theatres of War I 1944* (Schramm IV, p. 89); also Jodl's diary 15 January 1944.

32. Operations Staff War Diary 15, 20 December and Jodl's diary 19 December 1943.

33. Fragment 35 (not reproduced here).

34. Fragment 35.

35. Addendum to *Directive no. 51* reproduced in Hubatsch, *Weisungen*, p. 240. One of the remarkable occurrences which gave rise to this order is recorded in Jodl's diary of 14 December 1943. Without the knowledge of OKW, OKH withdrew the assault guns from the Luftwaffe Divisions, of which there were three in the West.

36. Operations Staff War Diary 3 November 1943.

37. So far only incomplete information is available on the manpower resources still remaining at this period. See Operations Staff War Diary 1943 for the efforts made by the OKW Operations Staff and its Organization Section. On 2 November we submitted a draft of a law for compulsory service for women between the ages of 18 and 45 together with a preliminary plan for a 'final levy'. Both were turned down by Keitel, the second on the grounds that 'the Führer will use the machinery of the Party for this if necesary' (a foretaste of the subsequent Home Guard (*Volkssturm*)), the first with the comment that 'the Führer would never sign a law

of this nature since it is contrary to his fundamental ideas'. 24, 27 November, 5, 11 December entries in the War Diary refer to renewed refusal by Hitler to release some of the hundreds of thousands of conscripts classified as in 'essential occupations'. He commented that 'the disproportion between fighting troops and services' should be eliminated, thus making 'at least a million men available for the front' from within the Wehrmacht. This was countered by the Luftwaffe by forming a 'Parachute Army'. 5 December. Keitel to the Head of the Medical Service: 'the manpower resources of the German people are almost at an end'. 6 December. The OKW began to draw on the 1927 Class (!)

38. For instance C.-in-C. Navy's report dated 13 November 1943 (1/SKL I Op 3404/43 Chefs – not published) begins with the words 'I report to the Führer ...'.

39. Fragment no. 35.

40. See Operations Staff War Diary 14, 21 October, 1, 7, 12, 23, 29 November, 1, 4 December, also Hitler's first instruction on the subject dated 1 December 1943 and issued under the reference OKW/WF Stab/Op (H) 662889 /43 g. K. Chefs (not published). See also Goebbels' diary 10 September 1943: 'the whole picture as regards England may possibly change'.

41. Reproduced in Jacobsen, *Chronik*, pp. 431–54. The speech ended with the words 'we shall win because we must win, or world history will have lost all meaning'. The speech formed part of the case against Jodl at

Nuremberg but he did not admit to the wording in detail as the proceedings show.

42. From my own experience supported by *Naval Affairs*, 2 August, 19 and 20 December, Operations Staff War Diary 23, 24, 27 November and Goebbels' diary 10 September 1943: 'he (Hitler) believes we shall regain mastery (of the air war) in two or three months'.

43. Operations Staff War Diary 31 December 1943.

44. See the OKW Order dated 27 December 1943 in Hubatsch, Weisungen, p. 238 and Operations Staff War Diary *OKW Theatres of War I/1944, Developments in the West 1 January–31 March* and *The West 1 April–16 December 1944* (hereafter referred to as Operations Staff War Diary *West*, and referred to in Schramm Vol. IV, Section 4). See also Fragment 10 (p. 542).

45. Regarding Field Marshal Rommel's new post see OKW Orders dated 6 November 1943 and 1 January 1944 issued under the references WF Stab/Op Nr 662642/43 g. K. Chefs and 663174/43 g. K. Chefs (not published). Also Jodl's diary 6 January 1944. The remainder is from my own memory as a result of the two trips I made in March and April 1944 to south-west and southern France for purposes similar to that of Jodl's trip to Belgium and northern France.

46. The majority of the static divisions in the West included one battalion of Russian 'volunteers', all ex-POW. With a few exceptions they did not stand up to the heavy fighting of the invasion.

47. See OKW Orders dated 19 January and 3 March 1944 issued under the references WF Stab/Op Nr 00606/44 g. Kdos and WF Stab/Op (H) West Nr 001524/44 g. Kdos (not published). Also Operations Staff War Diary *West 1944*. (Schramm IV, p. 374); also Jodl's Diary 11 January 1944. (Further details of the 'fortified area' idea are in Hitler's order issued via OKH dated 8 March 1944 and reproduced in Hubatsch, *Directives*, pp. 159 *et seq*.).

48. For the earlier events see Jodl's diary 13, 29 January and (particularly) 13 April 1944. See also p. 402 of this book and Guderian, pp. 330–2.

49. See Fragment no. 40 of 6 April 1944 (not reproduced here).

50. See Operations Staff War Diary 4, 6 November 1943, Operations Staff Diary *OKW Theatres of War I/1944* (Schramm IV, p. 117) and Operations Staff Diary *West* (Schramm IV, pp. 270, 280).

51. See Operations Staff Diary *West* (Schramm IV, p. 302).

52. See Operations Staff Diary *West* (Schramm IV, p. 298) and Fragment no. 40 of 6 April 1944.

53. See Operations Staff War Diary 5 December 1943; Operations Staff Diary *Nettuno* (Schramm IV, pp. 125–6) and Jodl's diary 4, 31 January 1944.

54. Operations Staff Diary *OKW Theatres of War I/1944* (Schramm IV, p. 89, 97–98).

55. Fragment no. 36 dated 29 January 1944 (not reproduced here).

56. See Operations Staff Diary *OKW Theatres of War I/1944 and Nettuno* (Schramm IV, pp. 98, 137, 145). See also Jodl's diary

31 January, 1944: 'at the moment 25 Mk IV tanks and 47 assault guns are moving towards Rome; these have been made available by cutting down deliveries to Panzer Jäger Bns in the West'; then on 5 February 1944: 'the Führer refuses to release 9 SS Div. for Italy. Instead he is sending an Infantry Training Regt and one Tiger Bn (45 tanks)'.

57. Hubatsch, *Directives*, p. 158.
58. The preparatory order was issued on 14 February 1944 under the reference WF Stab (H) Nr 77395/44 g. K. Chefs (not published).
59. See Jodl's diary early March (undated) and 9 March 1944.
60. Jodl maintained that any withdrawal in Italy would increase the requirement to 40–45 divisions. His reason was probably to counter demands by OKH and the Inspector of Armoured Forces (Guderian) for fresh forces for the East and so keep forces available for later movement to the West. As soon as the bridgehead battle ended OKW urged that at least one motorized division should be moved to the West, but this was not agreed. See Operations Staff Diary *OKW Theatres of War I/1944 and Italy* (Schramm IV, pp. 111 and 480); also Jodl's diary 27 March 1944 and Note 69 below.
61. Churchill, vol. V p. 334.
62. For a detailed description of the occupation of Hungary see Operations Staff Diary *OKW Theatres of War I/1944* but better still Operations Staff Diary *Operation Margarethe* (Schramm IV, p. 103 and 189 *et seq.*). Further details, particularly on the political side,

are in *Wehrwissenschaftliche Rundschau* 2/1960 (Hillgruber, *Das deutsch-ungarische Verhältnis im letzten Kriegsjahr*). For details see also Jodl's diary 9, 17, 18, 28 March and Fragment no. 40 of 6 April 1944. This contains a curt refusal by Hitler of my proposal for an early move of the Panzer Lehr Division to the West.
63. See Operations Staff Diary *OKW Theatres of War I/1944* (Schramm IV, pp. 107 *et seq.*).
64. Hitler's orders were accompanied by the most exaggerated prognostications. The *Army Operation Order* of 2 April 1944 (given in full in Hubatsch, *Directives*, p. 162) includes the following: 'the Russian offensive in the south of the Eastern Front has passed its climax. The Russians have exhausted and divided their forces. The time has now come to bring the Russian advance to a final standstill.'
65. See Jodl's diary 25, 27 March and 10 May which however, deals primarily only with plans and overall appreciations; see also the flagrant example in Guderian, pp. 323–4.
66. See Jodl's diary 10 May (end) and 30 May; Operations Staff Diary *West* (Schramm IV, pp. 314–15) and extracts from Fragment 46 of 31 August 1944 on pp. 450 *et seq.* It is striking that at this point Jodl's diary shows that he was dealing in detail with the plan for an operation in the East. This was probably due to the fact that at the time the headquarters had been in Berchtesgaden for months, whereas OKH had remained in East Prussia. It may also have been due to the

continuous deterioration in relations between Hitler and Zeitzler.

67. Jodl's diary 29 April 1944.
68. See Operations Staff Diary *Italy* (Schramm IV, pp. 491 *et seq.*). Hitler had just designated 20 Luftwaffe Division (one of the three divisions referred to) a 'Luftwaffe Assault Division', although it had so far been used only for occupation duties in Denmark, was without any battle experience and when pushed into this difficult situation, failed totally – so Kesselring reported.
69. See Operations Staff Diary *Italy* (Schramm IV, p. 497). C.-in-C. South-west had 25 divisions at this period. Rommel's estimate for the defence of the Apennines position (excluding the coasts) was 15 Divisions.
70. Operations Staff Diary *Italy* (Schramm IV, p. 499).
71. See *Naval Affairs*, 12–13 April 1944.
72. See Hitler's remark recorded in *Naval Affairs*, 12 June 1944: 'as long as the Finns go on fighting, they'll get supported. As soon as they begin to waver, all deliveries will cease.'
73. An example is the discussion about the capture of Lissa (Vis); see also *Naval Affairs*, 3–4 May 1944.
74. Given in Hubatsch, *Directives*, p. 164.
75. For Jodl's attitude see his diary of 23 March 1944:

Wedel (General von Wedel, Chief of Press and Propaganda Section)

1. Religious pictures in *Signal* (this refers to an illustrated periodical entitled *Signal* published by Wedel's Section; some 'religious pictures' had evidently given offence to Hitler and Jodl).
2. Blue sheets (refers to a restricted circulation news summary distributed to Gauleiter, government officials, ministries and senior officers) 'what leads us to suppose we shall win' (meaning that Wedel should publish an article on the subject).

76. See Manstein, pp. 544–6 and Heusinger, pp. 305 *et seq.*
77. See Manstein, pp. 511–12.
78. Jodl's diary 18 March 1944.
79. For the origin of this see Operations Staff War Diary 7 December 1943.

PART V · CHAPTER 5

1. See *Entscheidungsschlachten*, pp. 423–4.
2. This description is based upon my own experience which I did not record until 1951–2, on Operations Staff Diary *West* of 11 June 1944 (Schramm IV, p. 332) and for certain details on C. Ryan, *The Longest Day*, pp. 31 *et seq.*
3. From an order by C.-in-C. West dated 15 January 1944, partially reproduced in Operations Staff Diary *West* (Schramm IV, p. 276): Author's italics.
4. According to Ryan (pp. 150–1) the first landings from the sea took place at 0630 hours.
5. See Army Group B War Diary for 6 June 0600 hours and the hours thereafter; also Speidel, *We Defended Normandy* p. 93.
6. See Speidel, p. 96.
7. According to Jodl's diary of 8 August 1944 these aircraft were only then just becoming available in quantity in the West; see

also *Naval Affairs*, 9 July 1944 para. 3d where the Chief of Staff of the Luftwaffe is recorded as reporting that the first four of the new-type aircraft (ME 262) 'could be in action against the bridgehead within a week or ten days'.

8. See Jodl's diary 8, 9, 12 June 1944 and p. 414 above.

9. Regarding C.-in-C. West see Operations Staff Diary *West* of 13, 20 June and 3 July 1944 (Schramm IV, pp. 315, 318, 324); regarding Field Marshal Rommel see Chester Wilmot, pp. 318, 332, 346.

10. For Rommel's views see Speidel, pp. 97–98; the written proposals made by the Operations Staff to Jodl are mentioned in Operations Staff Diary *West* 13 and 24 June (Schramm IV, pp. 315–16, 319).

11. See Operations Staff Diary *West* 14, 16, 25, 30 June and relevant parts of the Annexe to this section of the Diary (Schramm IV, pp. 315, 331 *et seq.*).

12. *Naval Affairs*, 13 June 1944, Section IV. The remaining sections of this record are of interest merely as showing that the Hitler discussions in question dealt only with matters of minor importance.

13. See Operations Staff Diary *Italy* (Schramm IV, pp. 516 *et seq.*) and Jodl's diary 9, 12 June and 3 July (this contains the sentences quoted); the rest is from my own memory.

14. Only fragments of the record of the 18 June conference at Berchtesgaden have survived (Fragment 20 – not reproduced here). The following of interest emerges from it:

(*a*) Referring to the American attack on the Cotentin Peninsula, Hitler asked straight away: 'are they through or not?' Jodl replied: 'yes, they're through'.

(*b*) Jodl then reported that during the night 15–16 June firing of 'V.1's' had begun (as a reprisal). 206 weapons had been fired within 22 hours. Of these 37 (ie 18 per cent) were observed prematures. (Subsequently these reports had to be given in full detail daily.)

(*c*) Army Group B requested that 'a combat group should be brought over on to the mainland from the islands' (Channel Islands) but Hitler refused. Even on this subject Jodl agreed with Hitler; he notes 'C.-in-C. West rejected this at once'.

15. For this para. see Operations Staff Diary *West*, 17–28 June and relevant portions of the Annexe (Schramm IV, p. 317 and 332–3); also Jodl's diary 17 and 20 June 1944.

16. See Jodl's diary 29 June, *Naval Affairs*, 29 June–1 July and Operations Staff Diary *West* of the same dates (Schramm IV, pp. 321–2, 457); for the continued expectation of a second landing across the Channel see *Naval Affairs*, 12 July 1944 para. 5a.

17. See Operations Staff Diary *West* including Annexe 1 and 'Chronology'; this also gives extracts from the instructions and orders dated 30 June and 7 July referred to here (Schramm IV, pp. 323, 329 and 457–8).

18. The statement in *Naval Affairs* that C.-in-C. Navy's discussions with Hitler on 11–13 July took place in the Berghof must be an error.

19. For the general picture and atmosphere see Heusinger, pp. 328, 330, 342, 346. Regarding the 'receptions' of commanders from the front I remember those of Field Marshals von Manstein and von Kleist. I particularly remember that of Colonel-General Jaenecke, then C.-in-C. Seventeenth Army in the Crimea. He spent hours trying to persuade Hitler to evacuate the Crimea and was dismissed shortly after returning there. Field Marshal Model appeared several times. He was appointed C.-in-C. Army Group North early in 1944, then C.-in-C. Army Group Northern Ukraine and on 28 June C.-in-C. Army Group Centre as well. Each time he took over at a most difficult moment and had to restore a front which had collapsed.

20. See:

   (a) 'Decree of the Führer on the exercise of command in an area of operations within the Reich' dated 13 July 1944, signed by Hitler, Lammers and Keitel (in that order) and reproduced in Hubatsch, *Directives*, p. 167.

   (b) 'Decree of the Führer on co-operation between the Party and the Armed Forces in an area of operations within the Reich' dated 13 July 1944, signed by Hitler, Bormann and Keitel (in that order) and reproduced in Hubatsch, *Directives*, p. 169.

   (c) OKW order Nr 1852/44 g. Kdos WF Stab/Org II dated 15 July 1944 concerning mobilization of the services within the Reich (not published).

   (d) A special and more detailed order on the same subject applicable to the East Prussia Wehrkreis – OKW/WF Stab/Qu Nr 008145/44 g. Kdos dated 15 July 1944 (not published).

   (e) Addenda to the order above dealing with 'preparation for the defence of the Reich' dated 19 July 1944 reproduced in Hubatsch, *Directives*, p. 170.

   (f) Jodl's diary 22 July 1944.

   (g) 'Reorganization of command authority in the area of Army Group North', dated 23 July 1944 reproduced in Hubatsch, *Directives*, p. 175.

   (h) OKW Order dated 27 July regarding the 'Alpine Approaches' position, and the alterations made to it by Hitler on 29 July 1944, reproduced in Hubatsch, *Directives*, pp. 176 and 177.

   (i) Follow-up instructions to these decrees, and orders dated 3 August issued by the OKW Operations Staff and reproduced in Hubatsch, *Directives*, pp. 179 *et seq.*:

   (i) Order regarding 'construction of a German defensive position in the West', dated 24 August 1944 – Hubatsch, *Directives*, p. 182 with its amendment of 7 September (Hubatsch *Weisungen*, p. 275).

   (ii) 'Order placing the West Wall in a state of defence', dated 1 September 1944 – Hubatsch, *Directives*, p. 186.

   (iii) Order 'for the defence of the German position in the West and the West Wall', dated 1 September 1944 – Hubatsch, *Weisungen*, p. 282.

   (iv) Orders for 'Defences in the south-east', dated 12 September 1944 – Hubatsch, *Directives*, p. 195.

   (v) Addenda and alterations to these orders by superior governmental or Party authorities promulgated to the Wehrmacht by the OKW Operations Staff on 22 September 1944 – Hubatsch, *Directives*, pp. 197 *et seq.*

21. In this connection see Rommel's message to Hitler dated 15 July 1944. It has become famous in war books and is given in Schramm IV p. 1572. I did not know of this message at the time. It is not mentioned in the War Diaries or other non-official diaries. But see Fragment 46 reproduced on p. 450 below.
22. Dr Berger and the stenographer were killed on the spot. Colonel Brandt, General Korten, Chief of Staff Luftwaffe, and General Schmundt, Hitler's Military Aide for so many years, died of wounds shortly afterwards.
23. Particularly faithful followers of mine were the driver I had had for years, Sgt Karl Kasten, Cpl Meiner (HQ Area 2 mess orderly) and above all Sgt Georg Wüst (personal and office orderly), later reported missing.
24. An official account from a source outside OKW is to be found in the 'Chief of the Army Personnel Branch Activity Report' published in Jacobsen, *Chronik*, p. 475. My name does not appear. See also Heusinger, pp. 352 *et seq.*
25. See Jacobsen, *Chronik*, p. 482 for the sonorous terms in which Göring passed this on to the Chief of the Reich Chancellery. The 'demand' of the Wehrmacht is about as probable as the 'demands' made today by all sorts of organizations on all sorts of subjects in the Soviet Union.
26. See Operations Staff Diary *West* 19–27 July (Schramm IV pp. 326, 458) also Jodl's diary 19 July 1944 where an increased Allied concentration in Corsica is taken to indicate the immin-

ence of a landing in southern France (Nineteenth Army area).
27. See Jodl's diary 9, 12, 15 July, also Operations Staff Diary *West* of this period together with Annexe 1 and Chronology (Schramm IV, pp. 330–1, 347–8, 458, 462, 468 *et seq.*). The description of these events in the war diary does not altogether tally. This is due to the fact that I did not always have time to brief the War Diary officer fully nor, even more important, to check the entries subsequently.
28. See relevant Sections of Operations Staff Diary *West*. For instance on 28 July when the American breakthrough at St Lô was in full swing, C.-in-C. West had to ask the HQ in East Prussia for permission 'to move 116 Armoured Division into the area south of St Lô and make a local withdrawal on the left flank of LXXXIV Corps' (Schramm IV p. 327).
29. See Jodl's diary 30 July (evening) and 31 July. Author's italics.
30. Hitler's statements at the midnight meeting, including those quoted, are reproduced in the 'information' which I gave the War Diary officer on 12 August 1944 (see Schramm IV, pp. 462–3). The situation being what it was at the time, I toned down the wording of some of Hitler's statements when passing them on for the War Diary. The full text is in *Hitlers Lagebesprechungen*, pp. 584 *et. seq.*
31. The letters I have added in brackets to complete the names are undoubtedly correct except possibly for the first 'W'. This could refer to General Eduard Wagner, late QMG of the Army.

As recorded elsewhere he was an accomplice of the 20 July plot and committed suicide two days later.

32. No one else was present at my discussion with Field Marshal von Kluge that morning. The outcome is given in Operations Staff War Diary *West* of that day. I did not contribute to this and it is based on telephone conversations between Kluge and the HQ in East Prussia particularly where it says that he (Kluge) 'was fully in agreement with the substance of the order he had received', that he considered the situation 'extremely critical and was ready to run all risks and use all his resources to stop the breakthrough' (Schramm IV, p. 337).

33. On this point and throughout the rest of the chapter see the relevant sections of Operations Staff Diary *West* (Schramm IV, p. 337 *et seq.*). Note however that entries for this period, including information attributed to me on 18 August (Schramm IV, pp. 465), are subject to the same qualifications as in Note 27. This also applies to the extracts from Fragment 46 quoted here.

34. See Guderian, p. 338 where he states that he had received information to this effect as early as 18 July 1944.

35. Jodl was undoubtedly present when Hitler said this. Speer the Armaments Minister, was present because he was expected to make available for service some additional tens of thousands of men from the arms industry. The figure of 25 divisions was Field Marshal Model's initial requirement. Author's italics.

PART VI · CHAPTER I

1. See the evidence of Professor Schramm before the International Military Tribunal in Nuremberg during the case against Jodl (Schramm, IV, p. 1832). Schramm was War Diary officer at this period.

2. In *Unconditional Surrender* by A. Armstrong, recently published, appears a note by Jodl made in 1946 expressing thoughts very similar to the remarks recorded above: 'our enemies were not aiming merely at the overthrow of the Nazi régime; their object was the destruction of Germany. Could we have prevented this fate overtaking Germany, even if we had overthrown Hitler? That is the decisive question.'

3. See Guderian, p. 351.

4. See p. 215 above.

5. In his diary (27 July 1943) Goebbels also adds: 'Guderian again made ... an excellent impression. He is certainly an ardent and unquestioning disciple of the Führer.'

6. See Heusinger, pp. 356 *et seq.*

7. See Jodl's diary 29 June and *Naval Affairs*, 30 June 1944 (para. 3).

8. See p. 421 above and *Naval Affairs*, 13–14 October 1944 para. 5*b* and *c*. This mentions the plenary powers with which Hitler invested Himmler on 23 July following the coup (details in Jacobsen, *Chronik* p. 482). They produced no result.

9. On 20 August, according to Operations Staff Diary *West*, an OKW order was issued that 'the battle in and around Paris ... is *if necessary* to be carried on without regard for

the city'. (Schramm IV, p. 472 – author's italics). On 23 August 1944 a further order was apparently issued, the only copy of which is one reproduced in the HQ of C.-in-C. West. It concludes: 'the Seine bridges are to be prepared for demolition. Paris is not to fall into enemy hands other than as a heap of rubble' (see Jacobsen, *Chronik* p. 587). All I remember is that: via the appropriate section in OKW Hitler was in close control of all movement; he got one '38 cm assault mortar' moved from Germany, thinking it a particularly suitable weapon for the street fighting which he anticipated in Paris: C.-in-C. West reported that there was not enough explosive in the whole of his area to blow up the Seine bridges (see also Schramm IV, p. 348 and 358–60).

10. Information given by me, extracts from which are in Annexe to Operations Staff Diary *West* (Schramm IV, pp. 462–3), in this case supplemented from Hitler's *Lagebesprechungen* pp. 584 *et seq.*

11. See Jodl's diary 22 and 26 August 1944 (the discussion with the Commanders from the South-east is given erroneously as having taken place on 26 August); also Operations Staff Diary *South-East* (Schramm IV, pp. 680 and 708 *et seq.*).

12. The ref. no of the Order is OKW/WF Stab/Qu 2 (Ost) Nr 06601/44 geh (not published); other details not in Operations Staff Diary *South-East* are from my own memory.

13. According to Fragment 42 (briefing conference 17 September 1944 – not reproduced

here) there were further discussions on the subject between Hitler and Keitel the same day.

14. See Operations Staff Diary *South-East* (Schramm IV, pp. 687 *et seq.*); regarding Hitler's expectation of a Soviet-British conflict in Greece see Fragments 2 and 3 of the briefing conference of 6 November 1944 (partially reproduced here).

15. See Hillgruber *Das deutsch-ungarische Verhältnis im letzten Kriegsjahr* in *Wehrwissenschaftliche Rundschau*, 2/1960 and Jodl's diary 23 and 25 September 1944.

16. See Operations Staff Diary *Northern Theatre* (Schramm IV, pp. 894 *et seq.*) also *US Army Pamphlet no. 20–271–The German Northern Theater of Operations*.

17. Jodl's diary of 16 September 1944 does no more than refer to this.

18. In the evening briefing conference 31 July–1 August. Hitler dealt in detail with the principles and intentions of future strategy in Italy. (See p. 455 above and Note 30; also p. 468.)

19. See Operations Staff Diary *South-West* (Schramm IV, pp. 550 *et seq.*); Jodl's diary 11 September, 20, 23 November and Fragments 2 and 3 of the briefing conference of 6 November 1944 (partially reproduced here).

20. The order is dated 3 September 1944 and given in Hubatsch, *Directives*, pp. 189 *et seq.*

21. Jodl's diary 11 September 1944 (end).

22. In this connection see the following extract from the briefing conference of 6 November 1944 (Fragment no. 2/3). This gives a picture of the extent to which Hitler continued to concern himself with military detail.

(Author's comment: Hitler is talking to two Luftwaffe officers).

HITLER: I've thought about this business again – I don't know whether it has been reported to the Reichsmarschall – I've thought about it again and I've come to the following conclusion: there were 80 aircraft shot down recently.

BÜCHS: 82.

HITLER: Of these 80, 50 were shot down by fighters and 30 by anti-aircraft. The 30 must be counted out for the moment. 490 aircraft were engaged.

BÜCHS: 305.

HITLER: All right, 305 aircraft were engaged. Just now you said 490.

BÜCHS: No, 305. The whole Frankfurt Fighter Wing was engaged and from 4 Fighter Squadron ...

HITLER: All right, 305! Doesn't matter. Of these he said that one squadron of 42 aircraft was engaged. This squadron alone shot down 30.

BÜCHS: Both squadrons: there were two squadrons.

HITLER: With altogether?

BÜCHS: With altogether 63 aircraft. Of these, 61 were engaged.

HITLER: All right, 61!

BÜCHS: They shot down 30 four-engined aircraft.

HITLER: That still leaves 20. If you subtract 60 from 305 that leaves 240. 240 aircraft were engaged in all and shot down 20 and they themselves lost 30 in the attack squadron.

BÜCHS: 30 in the attack squadron.

HITLER: And the others lost 90. So they lost 90 and shot down 30 for 240 aircraft engaged.

CHRISTIAN: Now one thing. The attack group has another group covering it.

HITLER: I don't care a damn. I say: the covering group must attack too. It wasn't only bombers that were shot down but fighters too.

BÜCHS: That's clear.

HITLER: So the result is thoroughly unsatisfactory.

CHRISTIAN: The important point is that these 30 which were shot down by the attack group ...

HITLER: Haven't you got someone who works all this out on paper? Anyway, the Reichsmarschall doesn't know about it at all. When he was here just now he hadn't even an idea that our losses were so great because the whole picture was confused by these blasted 'not yet landed' reports.

CHRISTIAN: The situation is shown to him every day.

HITLER: I'd like to have the figures. It's complete proof that either the pilots or the aircraft are no good. It can't be the pilots because they get shot down. Therefore the aircraft are no good. The Luftwaffe always tells me the opposite: the aircraft are good. That's ridiculous. When you calculate it out the result is appalling.

BÜCHS: In the one engagement a total of 65 aircraft were originally reported missing and so far we've found a total of 38. 27 are still missing. All 38 aircraft were completely destroyed. Of the pilots 32 were dead and 6 either wounded or got back safe.

HITLER: How many are still missing? 28?

BÜCHS: 27 are still missing.

HITLER: That's quite clear. Those which have got back ... with such losses ...

BÜCHS: In Italy yesterday there was a heavy attack against railway installations, primarily stretches of line in the Triente area, carried out by two-engined aircraft. The Italians sent up 23 fighters and shot down 4 two-engined aircraft without losing any themselves.

HITLER: That's bad mathematics too. I was shown the figures just now. It takes a little time to see through these tricks. I was shown the figures for a whole month. But they ought to have told me how many sorties had been made. For a whole month it looks crazy. But the sortie figure is ...

BÜCHS: I'll show you the sortie figures. I haven't got them for a whole month however.

HITLER: Well now! That's microscopic.

CHRISTIAN: But these are only percentages, my Führer.

BÜCHS: My Führer, I'll now show you the complete sortie figures from the 1st onwards underlining the reports of those missing.

HITLER: There must be somebody who works out all this and draws conclusions and recommendations from it. Somebody must draw conclusions from it. It's no good just saying: that's the way it is!

CHRISTIAN: My Führer, there's a plan kept continuously up-to-date. ... Air Fleet Reich, Colonel General Stumpff, is responsible for it. The Inspector, Galland, has passed it on to units. The Reichsmarshall continuously has available ...

HITLER: I must say, nobody's ever shown me this table.

CHRISTIAN: My Führer, I've got little else but tables like this.

HITLER: But I've never had an analysis of it. That must be done.

CHRISTIAN: This was merely the first impression: that the attack group had shot down 30 four-engined bombers.

HITLER: 30? And the anti-aircraft 30. That leaves 20. This is the result of 260 sorties. That's a wretched result. I put up 260 fighters to shoot down 20. So if I put up 2,600 I shoot down 200. So I can't count in any way on these aircraft being ... and what's more come wind come weather they'll go on producing them. All they are doing is taking up labour and materials.

CHRISTIAN: The real reason, my Führer, was that the pilots hadn't flown for ten days.

HITLER: There are always good 'reasons'!

CHRISTIAN: But obviously that has an effect. Compare the squadron in the West which took off in bad weather but got back without losses because it's been flying in bad weather every day. That obviously has some effect.

HITLER: I'm not saying anything against the pilots, merely against the result of the engagement; you can't alter that. If you've got 2,600 aircraft you've got a possibility of shooting down 200. In other words there's not a hope that, even if we employ aircraft *en masse*, we can really break the enemy up. It's lunacy to go on producing these aircraft just to let the Luftwaffe juggle with figures!

23. From Fragment 43, 1 September 1944 (not in this book); for Hitler's other plans and orders up to this period see Operations Staff Diary *West* (Schramm IV, pp. 430 *et seq.*); Jodl's diary 11 September 1944; the orders dated 7 and 9 September 1944 issued by the OKW Operations Staff and given in Hubatsch *Directives*, pp. 192 and 193: General von Manteuffel's contribution to *Entscheidungsschlachten, Die Schlacht in 'den Ardennen'*, (*The Ardennes battle*) p. 528 (hereafter referred to as 'Manteuffel').

24. From Bradley, *A Soldier's Story*, p. 401.

25. See *Naval Affairs* 31 October–2 November 1944, para. 2c and 4a.

26. The first firings on London took place on 6 September 1944.

27. OKW/WF Stab/Op Nr 0011273 /44 g. Kdos. (Not published.) See also Hubatsch Directives, p. 197.

28. OKW/WF Stab/Qu (West) Nr 0011655/44 g. Kdos (not published).

29. Reproduced in Jacobsen, *Chronik*, pp. 509 and 518; for the preliminaries to the formation of the *Volkssturm* see Guderian, p. 362.

30. See Fragment 42, 17 September 1944 (not reproduced here).

31. See Operations Staff Diary *West* (Schramm IV, p. 379) on 'Fortification of the German Bight'; order dated 29 August 1944 (Hubatsch, *Directives*, pp. 184 *et seq.*) and its supplement dated 31 August (Hubatsch, *Weisungen*, p. 278) together with the note in Jodl's diary of 11 September: 'a North Sea HQ must be formed quickly; orders and instructions to be issued by the Operations Staff'; regarding the Rhine bridges see Jodl's diary 14 October 1944: 'charges must not be stored in the vicinity of the bridges; dangerous if attacked from the air' – an instruction by Hitler which probably later contributed to the loss of the bridge at Remagen.

32. These quotations, and unless otherwise stated all those which follow dealing with the Ardennes offensive and connected events, are from Operations Staff Diary *West*. From 17 December 1944 they are from Operations Staff Diary, *The German Wehrmacht in the last days of the War* (hereafter referred to as Operations Staff Diary – *End of War*), (Schramm IV, pp. 430 and 1342 *et seq.*).

33. Given in Jodl's diary as dated 14 October 1944. As can be

proved to be the case on a number of other occasions there appears here to be an error or slip of the pen as regards the date. This is clear from the subsequent quotations from Operations Staff Diary *West* and the fact that the order is there given as dated 12 October 1944.

34. As far as I can discover this order has not been preserved (see also Schramm IV, p. 434).

35. The description of this briefing and of these and subsequent events is from General von Manteuffel's account referred to above. There is nothing on the subject either in Operations Staff Diary *West* nor in Jodl's diary for 3 November 1944 which deals merely with details unconnected with the briefing.

36. As far as I can discover the order has not been preserved; there are extracts in Schramm IV, p. 439.

37. See Guderian, p. 409.

38. There are other opinions on the date at which the HQ moved to Ziegenberg.

39. From Manteuffel (see above).

40. Hitler was apparently only at Ziegenberg for two days in order to hold these conferences. The text given here is from Fragment 28.

41. See Operations Staff Diary *West* (Schramm IV, p. 443) and Jodl's diary 25 November 1944 para. 3 ('Possibility of attack in the South?').

42. See Jodl's diary for 27 December (where there is a sketch map of the concentration) and 29 December 1944.

PART VI · CHAPTER 2

1. The best hope for the early months of 1945 was considered

to be the new type of U-boats (*Naval Affairs*, 17 February and 7 April).

2. The Allied demand was put in even more severe terms in *Plans and Preparations for Occupation of Germany* which had been issued in the form of an order under the code-name *Eclipse* in January 1945 and of which we were aware.

3. The main events are given in the text but the following details are illustrative:

(a) The following extract from the record of the midday briefing conference 27 January 1945 (Fragment 24–25):

GUDERIAN: ... So far we have withdrawn only the rearward services, workshops, etc. They are back across the Oder. Everything else will be halted on the Oder. The Staff College must in any case close within the next few days. I would like authority to use it together with two companies of the Berlin Guard Regiment to form a firm fall-back position, strong in officers, in this area just west of the Oder to ensure there is no withdrawal there.

HITLER: Yes, and this is where you will bring in the cavalry.

FEGELEIN: You mean the Cavalry Holding and Training Regiment; it's about fifteen hundred strong and is to be put in rear of Colonel-General Schörner.

GUDERIAN: The men will have to be split up among units.

GÖRING: The only thing is that anything coming back here is bound to be weak in officers; these are good selected officers and they could be used....

HITLER: I agree. There are tens of thousands of men streaming back here and they must be collected and reorganized. They must have officers and the best we can get

too. Otherwise we'll never get a grip of them.

GUDERIAN: They were to start the business here, reorganize and bring them forward.

GÖRING: But they won't be a formed body I imagine.

HITLER: No, this is merely a stop line to collect them and reorganize them. Only the best officers could do that.

GÖRING: That's my view as well.

HITLER: And this is where the Cavalry comes in.

FEGELEIN: They can be in action the day after tomorrow.

HITLER: What's the unit called?

FEGELEIN: It's the Cavalry Holding and Training Regiment. Its about fifteen hundred strong.

HITLER: That must be put under command of Schörner to block the roads in the rear.

GUDERIAN: The Staff College can cover the roads from Breslau to Glogau.

HITLER: And from Breslau eastwards we can do it with the cavalry regiment. It's fifteen hundred strong? ...

(b) *Naval Affairs* for the period 1 January to 18 April 1945. This is the best source of information on Hitler's briefing conferences. Matters concerning the war at sea are naturally in the forefront but in addition they give a mass of detail on other subjects such as: the war on land, economic and transport problems, movement of refugees from the east, tricky problems of organization involving the various higher headquarters and ambitious plans for the peace time future. Of particular interest are the following:

1. On 18 January C.-in-C. Navy offered to make available 3,000 men to form a marine infantry

regiment. This was enthusiastically welcomed and supported by Hitler and Göring and during the days and weeks which followed the proposal was expanded and three marine infantry divisions were formed. Like the Luftwaffe Divisions, however, this led to the organization within the land forces of formations which were given preference over the Army.

2. On 13 March Hitler issued an order that the manufacture of ammunition for naval heavy guns should be resumed.

3. An argument which went on throughout 25 and 26 March over the number of batteries on a certain sector of the eastern front; Hitler had a special map prepared on the subject.

(c) On 5 and 6 April 1945 Jodl's diary is occupied entirely with the details of the planned formation of a solitary division. On 10 April the principal entry in the diary is a list of the number of batteries and guns which were made available on that day from a 'black' depot of the SS.

4. Jodl's diary 30 January 1945 states that for OKW, OKH and the Replacement Army alone the military signals system in Berlin had to handle daily 120,000 phone calls, 33,000 teleprinter messages and 1,200 radio messages.

5. See *Naval Affairs*, 19 and 20 February 1945, Guderian, p. 427 and Jacobsen, *Chronik* pp. 524–5.

6. Reproduced in Hubatsch, *Directives*, p. 206. The executive instructions are in Hubatsch, *Weisungen*, p. 304–5.

7. Issued by the Army General Staff on Hitler's instructions and signed by him. Reproduced in Hubatsch, *Directives*, p. 212.

8. From *Wehrwissenschaftliche Rundschau*, 11/1961.

9. This description is based on Jodl's diary 26 December 1944, Guderian, pp. 382–8 and Fragments 9 and 33 of the briefing conferences of evenings 9 and 10 January 1945 respectively (not reproduced here).

As regards the first two of the above sources: (a) It would seem that Jodl has made a further error as regards date; Guderian gives conclusive proof that his first meeting took place on 24 December 1944. There are no entries in the diary for the period 29 December 1944–15 January 1945; (b) Guderian is however mistaken in saying that reinforcements for the East (four divisions) were only made available after his second meeting and then only from the West. Jodl gives full details on 26 December 1944.

10. The intention was that when the HQ withdrew from East Prussia the campaign in the East should be directed from the HQ which had long been under construction in the area of Zobten near Breslau. The situation precluded anything other than withdrawal to Berlin, into the scattered accommodation there.

11. The text of Hitler's decision is given in Operations Staff Diary – *End of War* under date 22 January 1945 (See Schramm IV, p. 1413); other entries in the diary and in addition Jodl's diary of 16 January indicate that by the latter date preparations for the move were far advanced

and that Hitler's order 'to move I SS Corps to the Vienna area as OKW reserve starting 24 January' followed shortly afterwards. For the rest see Guderian, pp. 384 and 393; also Keitel's statements in *Wehrwissenschaftliche Rundschau* 11/1961.

12. Guderian, pp. 395–8.
13. The full text is given in Hubatsch, *Directives*, p. 203; there is a reference without comment to an instruction for preparation of an order of this nature in Jodl's diary of 18 January 1945.
14. Jodl's diary of 21 January merely refers to a 'discussion with Guderian and the Reichsführer SS'. The wording of the 'task' is from an unpublished account, the rest from Guderian, p. 403. (As is known Himmler had got in touch with the enemy on his own at the end of 1943: he made further attempts in February 1945.)
15. See Guderian, pp. 413 *et seq.* also Jodl's diary 15 March 1945.
16. See Jodl's diary 5, 10, 12 February 1945. Guderian states (p. 412) that the prerequisite for his major counter-attack against the Russians in the area between Frankfurt-on-Oder and Küstrin was 'prompt evacuation of the Balkans, Italy and Norway'. This could clearly be no basis for agreement on the OKW theatres of war and the way they should be dealt with. The position was reversed when considerable additional forces became available on the evacuation of Courland. In spite of all Guderian's urgings Hitler would not release them until it was too late to move them all. (See *Naval Affairs*, 18, 19, 20 January, 17 February, 17 March 1945.)

17. See Jodl's diary 30 January and 9 February 1945.
18. See Jodl's diary 26 January 1945, 'East Prussia (difficulties) Reinhardt–Hossbach' and Guderian, p. 400.
19. See p. 511 below. (Fragment 22/23 from briefing conference 23 November 1944.)
20. See Jodl's diary 18 January, *Naval Affairs*, 10 March 1945 and Operations Staff Diary – *End of War* (Schramm IV, p. 1335).
21. See Operations Staff Diary – *End of War* from which the quote is taken (Schramm IV, pp. 1444 *et seq.*).
22. From Tippelskirch, *Geschichte des Zweiten Weltkriegs*, pp. 556, 559.
23. From Kesselring, *Memoirs*, p. 244. Tippelskirch (p. 568) says the following regarding Wenck's Army:

> Hitler's final levy the ... Twelfth Army ... was supposed to be going to change the situation in the West. It was formed early in April from the last available reserves in central Germany. Its orders were to concentrate in the Harz, advance and liberate the Ruhr area and then attack again to pierce the enemy front. Further operations were then supposed to lead to the re-establishment of a firm front in the West. It is incredible that Hitler could harbour such fantastic ideas or that his staff could take seriously their job of turning them into orders. The cadres of seven divisions ... were formed ... from officer schools, armoured training centres, the Labour Service, and officers of all ranks and ages. ... The ranks were supposed to be filled by enthusiastic young soldiers, including a num-

ber of cadets and youngsters from the Labour Service. Instead of numbers the divisions had romantic-sounding names. The pace of events was so fast that Hitler's plans for this Army did not even look like being carried out. Nevertheless in the battles it fought it gave a glorious example of extreme devotion.

24. *Naval Affairs*, 12 March 1945.
25. Kesselring p. 245.
26. See Guderian, pp. 423–4 and in particular Speer's letter to Hitler dated 29 March 1945 reproduced in Jacobsen, *Chronik*, pp. 528 *et seq.*
27. See Guderian pp. 404–5, 421–2, 425 *et seq.*
28. *Naval Affairs*, 4 April, Jodl's diary 5 April and Operations Staff War Diary – *End of War*, 6 April (Schramm IV, p. 1227).
29. See Note 7. The order contained an extravagant call to the soldiers on the Eastern Front to resist to the end the 'deadly Jewish-Bolshevik enemy' who would meet the fate met by all the eastern invading hordes of old.
30. See Operations Staff Diary – *End of War* (Schramm IV, p. 1299) and *Naval Affairs*. 12 April 1945. The OKW order dated 15 April is in Hubatsch, *Directives*, p. 210.
31. The account and quotations are from Görlitz, *Keitel*, pp. 342 *et seq.* In the last sentence Görlitz has the word 'befehle' (order) instead of 'bestehe' (survive).
32. See Jodl's diary 23 and 25 April and Görlitz, *Keitel* pp. 348 *et seq.* As an illustration see also OKW/WF Stab/Op Nr 003768/45 g. Kdos. dated 26 April 1945

(not published). This purported to set in train a large-scale movement from northern Norway (see Schramm p. 1336).

33. See also the 28 April order which begins with the words 'at the Führer's order the Army General Staff is placed under the Chief of the OKW Operations Staff. Direction of operations in the eastern theatre is thereby transferred to OKW' (reproduced in Schramm p. 1591).
34. References as in Note 32.
35. The title of Field Marshal Kesselring's memoirs.
36. See Jodl's diary 29 April and the undated addendum covering 24, 29, 30 April and 1 May 1945.
37. See Dönitz, p. 445–6, also Jodl's diary 3–5 May 1945.
38. On 12 May Grand Admiral Dönitz himself found it necessary to ask Jodl whether in his opinion 'some change should or should not be made in view of the continuous attacks by the Army on the Chief of OKW'. Jodl replied that 'the animosity against the Chief of OKW stemmed from the earliest days of the Third Reich and was shown mostly by older officers. His final sentence (from his diary) 'Chief OKW must now remain' was his personal point of view and bore no relation to reality.

SOURCES

1. On the subject of his diaries Colonel-General Jodl stated as follows before the International Military Tribunal at Nuremberg (pp. 383–4 of vol. XV):

There is only one diary ... which is from the year 1937–1938. I kept no diary at all during the war but of course I filled up dozens of small notebooks. When one of these notebooks was full, I marked important passages in red in the margin and my secretary copied them out later as they might be important for writing the history of the war and for the official diary of the Operations Staff.

The only parts of the diaries referring to the war years up to the period February–May 1940 which I have discovered, are in the form of photostat copies of the 'notebooks', not extracts copied out subsequently.

2. The War Diary of Section L of the OKW Operations Staff does not exist for the period prior to 1939; for the period 1940–end 1942 it is in the form only of incomplete 'notes'. These and the 'Notes on Section L Conferences' on many occasions record remarks by me. These were in some cases included by the War Diary Officers on my instructions, or in important cases I dictated them myself. Up to the end of 1943 I invariably rechecked them for accuracy.

3. After the war a member of the 'Führer's HQ Stenographic Service' (formed in September 1942) stated in writing that their job was: 'to take a word-for-word shorthand record of the Führer's daily military briefing conferences, and of all other conversations dealing with war strategy, and to prepare a typed record of them. The Führer had ordered this shorthand record for two reasons. In the first place it was supposed to establish the truth and so be of value for the history of the war. For this purpose one copy was made available to General Scherff the 'officer charged by the Führer with the compilation of the history of the war'. In the second place the Führer wished to protect himself against the production of untrue or incomplete reports. The Führer emphasized these two reasons on many occasions in the course of conversation. For instance he would say that he was prepared to be responsible to posterity for everything which he ordered and therefore wished it all to be recorded in detail. For this reason the records were never subsequently edited or otherwise altered.

Early in May 1945 an SS official was ordered to burn all records of the Stenographic Service. The fragments preserved are remnants which were discovered subsequently. They consist partly of the original shorthand notes, partly of the typed records. In both cases the fragments are in various stages of disintegration or destruction. All in all only a microscopic portion – less than one per cent – of the complete material has been preserved.

4. From 1944 onwards the OKW Operations Staff War Diaries were divided according to theatres of war or other special subjects.

5. In view of my subject it may appear surprising that certain foreign sources are quoted. The explanation is that: I wished to draw comparisons with the

headquarters of our former enemies; certain German and foreign documents have so far only been published abroad; in other countries, research into the history of the Second World War, both official and private, has made large use of interrogation of those immediately involved in the events concerned. The Historical Research Section of the Bundeswehr however, in so far as it is dealing at all with the history of the Second World War, has so far asked me for no information of any kind, although I am the only surviving officer who was a member of the OKW Operations Staff continu-ously from 1938 to the autumn of 1944.

6. (Translator's note.) Where an English translation exists, both the German and English titles are given in the Bibliography but quotations and references have been transposed to the English version.

7. (Translator's note.) The English version does not include all the 'supplementary orders' and 'executive instructions'. In cases where the reference is given as 'Hubatsch, *Weisungen*' (as opposed to 'Hubatsch, *Directives*') this indicates that the material is to be found in the original German only.

Index

(Ranks of officers are those held at the end of the war)

Index

Rodert, 86

Rome: Air Attacks, 339; Allied attacks, 352, 381, 382, 410; Coup by Hitler, 34, 347, 355, 362ff., 373, 382, 411, 416; Loss of, 416, 427, 572

Rommel, Field-Marshal Erwin: Allied invasion, 406, 409, 425, 428, 429, 437; Commander-in-Chief Italy, 319, 337, 338, 340, 343, 345, 357, 364, 369, 372, 374; Fragments, 325, 326, 330–331, 370–71; Greece, 340; Hitler on, 298, 307ff., 314, 451ff.; H.Q. Commandant, 38; North Africa, 128, 129, 197, 203, 211, 227, 234, 235, 241, 246–47, 252, 266, 268, 269, 296, 297, 570, 572; Rundstedt, 408, 422; Suicide, 481; Tripoli, 570; Wounded, 440, 449

Roosevelt, Franklin D., 41, 208, 372, 513, 574

Rosenberg, Alfred, 68, 166, 167, 293

Rostov, 194, 203, 205, 222, 248, 255, 273, 571

Röttiger, General Hans, 473, 474

Ruge, Vice-Admiral Friedrich, 321

Ruhr, 408, 446, 507, 570, 573

Rumania: Coup Effects, 453; German Relations, 197, 232, 389, 468, 540, 558; Germany, War on, 467, 469, 472; Military Mission, 136, 143; Oil, 55, 131, 146, 253, 383, 462; OKW, 151; Russians, 161, 266, 267, 295, 467; Withdrawal from war, 384, 394, 398, 399, 573

Rundstedt, Field-Marshal Gerd von: Allied Invasion, 424, 426, 429; Dismissed, 195, 438; Italian Front, 360, 374; Norway, 89; Recalled, 234, 477; Rommel, 408, 422; Western Offensive, 95, 96, 99

Russia: Army, 34, 203, 228, 255; Balkans, 488; Berlin, 513, 514; Breakthrough, 469; Campaign, 132, 176ff., 241ff., 521ff., 571; East Prussia, 484, 496, 501; England, 107; Failure, 258; 264–65; Frontier Violations, 148; Hitler, 507; Invasion of Poland, 34–35, 56, 161, 569; Non-aggression treaty, 509, 570; Occupation Instructions, 150–62; Postponement of Attack, 130; Preparations for War, 55, 111–14, 120, 138ff.; Prisoners, 299; Retreat from, 284ff., 414ff.; War with Finland, 66, 68; War with Germany, 50, 126, 147

Rybinsk, 194

Rzhev, 251

St Germain, 408, 440

St Omer, 97

Salerno, 377, 382, 383, 572

Salmuth, Colonel-General Hans von, 423

Salonika, 55, 132, 247, 343, 350, 372, 385

Salzburg, 273

Samos, 386

Saporoshe, 549

Sardinia, 318, 337, 341, 359

Sauckel, Fritz, 324, 393

Scarpanto, 387

Scharnhorst, 571

Scheldt, 406, 408, 429, 467, 477, 478

Scherff, Major-General Walter, 173, 231, 232, 235, 258, 264, 361, 538

Schlieffen, Field-Marshal, Alfred Graf, von, 56

Schmerinka, 539, 547

Schmidt, Lt.-General Arthur, 300ff.

Schmidt, Colonel-General Rudolf, 287

Schmundt, General Rudolf: Army, 214, 230; Fragments, 325, 524ff.; Göring, 279; Military Aide, 23, 38, 131, 259; OKW, 226; Poland, 27; Warlimont, 269, 310

Schörner, Field-Marshal Ferdinand, 396

Schulenburg, Ambassador Friedrich Werner Graf, von der, 453

Schulte, Captain, 522, 528ff.

Schuschnigg, Kurt Edler von, 14

Sebastopol, 206, 232, 571

Seeckt, Colonel-General Hans von, 503

Seine, 406, 408, 467

Sennelager, 512

Serbia, 469

Index

3511M

3